THE PRICE OF EXPERIENCE

THE PRICE OF

Money, Power, Image, and Murder in Los Angeles

EXPERIENCE

Randall Sullivan

THE ATLANTIC MONTHLY PRESS
NEW YORK

Published simultaneously in Canada
Printed in the United States of America
FIRST EDITION

Library of Congress Cataloging-in-Publication Data
Sullivan, Randall.
    The price of experience : money, power, image, and murder in Los
Angeles / Randall Sullivan. — 1st ed.
      p.   cm.
    ISBN 0-87113-512-4
      1. Murder—California—Los Angeles—Case studies.
    2. Millionaires—California—Los Angeles—Case studies.   3. Hunt,
Joe.   4. Billionaire Boys Club.   I. Title.
    HV6534.L7S85   1996
    364.1'523'0979493—dc20   95-36562

DESIGN BY LAURA HAMMOND HOUGH

The Atlantic Monthly Press
841 Broadway
New York, NY 10003

10 9 8 7 6 5 4 3 2 1

To Krakovski

THE ROOTS OF THE FAMILY TREE HAD BEEN TORN FROM THE WESTERN SHORE OF Lake Michigan, where they extended beneath the stony splendor of Chicago, Joe's birthplace, out of that arable tundra to the north, between Green Bay and Lake Winnebago, a somber region of cement factories, subarctic winters, and cheddar cheeses.

Kathy Durby was a tall, pretty, square-jawed girl of Irish extraction, one of seven children whose father had forsaken the dawn-to-dusk rigors of life on the family farm for a softer and more secure job south on the Fox River in Harry Houdini's hometown, Appleton, Wisconsin. Kathy was the teenage protégé of her high school art teacher when she met Larry Gamsky, scion of a prominent local family—German by blood—that had built its real estate holdings out of the town's largest dry-cleaning business. An only son, Larry was orphaned while still a young boy. He grew up with his grandmother in one of Appleton's finest homes, attended by nurses and maids. Larry was a sassy, spoiled child, provided with charge accounts at various local stores from the age of nine, spending his summer vacations in locations so exotic that their very existence was little more than a rumor among classmates: Manhattan, Miami, Malibu. His inheritance, held in trust, was paid out to him in the form of the largest weekly allowance received by any boy in town. As a child, Joe heard often about his father sailing his own boat on the lake as an eighth grader or driving to school in a hot rod built from a kit when he was sixteen.

Larry was a bright student, good with numbers, a mechanical savant, some said, but slow to finish college, and had only recently graduated with a degree in business at twenty-six when he married Kathy, who was then twenty-three. The newlyweds moved to Chicago, and Larry worked as an advertising executive for a year, then hired on at a pharmaceutical concern, hawking drugs to doctors. Glib and charming, he was a natural salesman, earning twenty thousand dollars a year in the days when that was good money, buying a new Buick and renting an eight-room apartment on the North Shore.

Joe was barely a year old and his brother Greg not quite three when Larry's company transferred him to an obscure burg on the Indiana border called Calumet City. The new family home was a row house in a steel town populated by Polish and Lithuanian foundry workers, their faces chapped, their speeches accented, their thirsts unquenchable. It was there Larry began to recall California, reminiscing in the evenings about his childhood vacations on the Coast, dreaming out loud in those false colors that make fools of visitors who stay too long or leave too soon: golden sands, turquoise waves, magenta sunsets, and the new-money green of fan palms that clatter like tuneless chimes along the footpaths of Palisades Park. That reverie of the Pacific Rim, an overpowering if preposterous sense that somewhere on a beach between Palos Verdes and Point Dume was the threshold at which a man stopped heading west and began coming east again, had taken possession of Joe's father during his first winter in Calumet City, where streets were paved with gray slush and steelworkers brawled outside beer halls. Trapped and unhappy, his condition aggravated by Kathy's reminders that the father of two young sons had "obligations," Larry began to talk to himself behind locked doors, describing in detail his model home of stucco and sliding glass, with lemon trees out back by the swimming pool and the sundeck.

Larry brought his wife and sons with him when he made the move west. Joe was two years old then. The four of them lived for months in motels while Larry tried to find himself. He had come to California to operate a franchise selling stainless steel cookware, convincing Kathy to do the door-to-door of it while he recruited a sales staff. In Los Angeles, though, in 1962, the year local headlines divided public interest between JFK's movie-star management of the Cuban missile crisis and the true-life tragedy of Liz Taylor's decision to trade in Debbie's Eddie for Sybil's Richard, Larry found cookware an uninspiring field and yearned audibly, painfully, for something bigger, better, at least a little glamorous, possibly even important. By the time he found the Los Feliz apartment, Larry no longer even pretended to be at work. "It was as if he suddenly couldn't function," Kathy remembered.

For a time Mr. Gamsky attempted to find his way by watching TV. ABC and NBC now were transmitting in color, but the blue was so bright that it blurred images of John Glenn's splashdown after he became the first man to orbit the earth, and greens were streaked with red in shots of the heavily planted Hollywood house where Marilyn Monroe had died of a drug overdose. It was the year California surpassed New York as the nation's most populous state. The Beach Boys produced their first hit record that summer, "Surfin' Safari." Diet Rite and Tab came on the market. The L.A. Times reported that the United States, with 6 percent of the planet's population, held title to two-thirds of its automobiles. Valium was about to become available and Weight Watchers was being founded. That fall, the sound of Dick Nixon advising reporters in Los Angeles that they wouldn't have him to kick around anymore was not nearly so compelling as the sight of the Kennedy brothers sunning themselves on the patio at Peter Lawford's house in Malibu. Even men past forty began to believe it was possible to be lean, tan, serene, and self-confident, surrounded by yellow convertibles and blondes in French bikinis.

Larry Gamsky wondered why he was not among the lucky ones. Supporting Kathy and their sons with his shrinking inheritance, Larry bought a new car he could not afford and made reservations in expensive restaurants where no one remembered his name. At home, he sat for hours in a big chair by the window, staring out through the venetian blinds into day after day of sunshine. Drawn to L.A. by the ocean breezes that cool the city's face, he discovered the furnace blast of the desert at its back.

"Incapacitated" was the word Kathy used to describe her husband just before she took Joe and Greg back to Wisconsin. Larry stayed on alone, adrift, paralyzed by possibilities that kept him awake at night and drowsy during the day. He would spend whole afternoons within the cool, dark, mock-adobe walls of some Casa Conquistador or El Encanto, drinking margaritas amid wicker furniture and bullfight murals, then stagger outside into the dry heat and that whiteout of sunshine so intense that it flattened the foreground even as it dissolved the horizon. On the way home, he might stop at an intersection next to an Oscar winner in a Bentley or stand in line at Ralph's supermarket with pool attendants and gardeners. Envious and confused, seduced and ignored, he found himself alone in a place where people changed their names by notifying the Department of Motor Vehicles, where every other stranger you met had no history he could speak of and the other half made up what they told. Every night's rest in Los Angeles needed a new contingency, and yet by first light hope was in the air again, circling above the carcasses of those who could not get over or away.

Larry lost everything but his sense of entitlement during those months, plunged into a brooding meditation upon the absence of convictions that would find its bottom only when he was reduced to that condition of receptivity all true Angelenos recognize not as an end but as the beginning.

Part One

THE GREAT GAMSKY

What physicians say about disease is applicable here: At the beginning a disease is easy to cure but difficult to diagnose; but as time passes, not having recognized or treated at the outset, it becomes easy to diagnose but difficult to cure.

—excerpt from Machiavelli's *The Prince*, distributed by Joe Hunt to BBC members under the heading "Internal Problems"

1

THE FIRST TIME HE WAS ASKED ABOUT IT, BEFORE BEING DISCOVERED BY THE sound-bite specialists and the cameras in the courtroom, back when his name was given rather than taken, Dean would describe that initial encounter, the one where he and Ben had run into Joe Gamsky on the sidewalk in Westwood Village, as "a chance meeting." With each public appearance, though, as his audience grew from a few anxious insiders to a standing-room-only mob of spectators and his armed escort increased from one to five, Dean seemed less and less certain, as if he were beginning to suspect—or at least imagine—that Joe had been planning it all from the very beginning.

That was in May of 1980. Jimmy Carter was locked up in the White House, clinging desperately to his good intentions and facing his final disaster with that unblinking piety for which so many of his countrymen had come to despise him. Those two helicopters recently dispatched on a secret mission to rescue the hostages held captive at the U.S. embassy in Teheran for more than 180 days now had "malfunctioned" some two hundred miles short of their destination, crashing into Iran's Dasht-e-Kavīr desert, where the burned bodies of eight American fighting men lay among the wreckage. "The responsibility was fully my own," President Carter told the American people on live television. No one doubted that President Jimmy meant what he had said. Some question remained, though, about whether he knew what he said meant.

Ronald Reagan was out in his home state, California, where all the polls showed him far ahead of George Bush in the primary election that would decide the Republican party's presidential nomination. Reagan had just delivered his most concise statement of economic policy to date out in San Bernadino, where he told a crowd of cheering Jaycees, "What I want to see, above all, is that this remains a country where someone can always get rich."

Dean and Ben were all for that. They remembered when Mr. Reagan had taken time out from his last presidential campaign, back in 1976, to deliver the commencement address at their alma mater, the Harvard

School. Ron Reagan Jr. was in that year's graduating class, one ahead of Dean
and three ahead of Ben. A fey and remote boy, envied and ridiculed from
afar, Ron Jr. was a ballet dancer who created a mild sensation when he gave
his senior page in the *Sentinel* yearbook over to this print of some Maxfield
Parrish sylph, naked, yet of indeterminate gender, laid out in a tree swing
against the background of a castle in the clouds. At the Harvard School,
allowances were made for a son of the state's ex-governor.

Founded in the first year of the twentieth century, the private preparatory academy in Coldwater Canyon had been the bastion of L.A.'s network of inherited money and white Protestant power since its inception.
The Episcopal priests who ran the school for its first seventy years imagined themselves the moral and intellectual shepherds of their community's
future leaders. In those days, the all-male student body had been a "Christian brotherhood," twice a week attending chapel services in which the motif
"PREPARING FOR POWER" was a constant refrain. Even in the 1960s, attending classes only a few blocks from Van Nuys Boulevard, where braless girls
hitchhiked to Birmingham High in hip-huggers and halter-tops, Harvard
School boys continued to parade across their lush campus in tailored military uniforms, majestically remote from the hormonal pandemonium that
attended such events as the afternoon activity-card concert staged by a band
called the Doors at a gymnasium ten minutes away in Reseda.

At the entrance on Coldwater, four towering concrete arches met
at a pedestal mounted with a wooden cross. Set in the stone wall that separated the private school from the public road was Harvard's thoroughly
secular crest, a shield engraved with a winged lion bearing a crown. The
lion symbolized power, students were told, and the crown responsibility.
The wings were a reminder that this power must be administered respon-
sibly in the City of Angels.

Though the school was just over the hill from Beverly Hills, its students were drawn primarily from the more genteel—and decidedly more
gentile—neighborhood of Hancock Park. During the sixties and seventies,
the Coldwater campus had become a breeding ground for right-wing
political ambitions. The core members of Ronald Reagan's "kitchen cabinet"—industrialist Justin Dart, Northrup chairman Thomas V. Jones, and
movie producer Charles Z. Wick—all sent their sons to the Harvard School.
Richard Nixon's Teutonic chief of staff H. R. Haldeman not only had
attended the school himself (class of '44) but sent his two sons there to network with the heirs to such corporate empires as RCA, Home Savings, and
Carnation, with boys whose names resonated the region's growing wealth
and influence: Disney, Zanuck, Taper, Tunney.

During its ecclesiastical period the school followed the example of the by-invitation-only Los Angeles Country Club, discouraging the arriviste show-business types, with their assumed names and garish displays. LACC rigorously denied admission to anyone in the entertainment industry, which was, among other things, a convenient way of excluding Jews. The country club *had* admitted Randolph Scott as a member, but only after the former film star established himself as a successful oilman and married a Du Pont. Even then, Scott was required to pledge he would make a sincere effort to keep his old Westerns off late-night television. The Harvard School was slightly more progressive, allowing such stars as had ascended into the city's social and economic firmament—a Doug Fairbanks, say, or a Greg Peck— to send their sons to the Coldwater campus.

As its name suggested, the school had been founded to instill the sense of breeding and birthright purportedly passed on to boys at the best eastern boarding schools. There were crucial differences, of course, not least of which was that Harvard students lived at home and commuted by car, never really separated from either the influence or the observation of their parents. It was mainly the geography of Los Angeles that insulated them from the city's more unseemly elements, that vast motley throng residing in the sprawl south of the Santa Monica Freeway. Nearly all of the black or brown people whom Harvard School students knew by name were maids and gardeners. The school's athletic fields were the one location where a Harvard student might be directly exposed to those less fortunate, and the results were rarely inspiring. Harvard's teams had competed for years against the poor Catholic schools from East and South-Central Los Angeles in games that amounted to class wars. Led by quarterback Mark Harmon, *People* magazine's future "Sexiest Man Alive," Harvard's football team simultaneously ran up big scores and absorbed terrible physical abuse in the trenches. One of the school's most enduring legends involved the game that had been interrupted by a mother who sped onto the field in her Rolls-Royce, tearing turf and scattering players, to load her injured son into the backseat.

The school's religious affiliation tended to discourage many Jewish students even from applying for admission, and rumors circulated of a quota system that kept the number of Hebrews on campus in single digits. In truth, discrimination at Harvard was less a function of ethnicity than of eccentricity, so that in general only students who were fat or loud or obsessively studious—and Jewish—received the sort of serious hazing administered to that tubby bookworm from the class of '67 who was hung by his coat from a metal hook in an algebra class, dangling there until teachers cut him down.

The school experienced its own small revolution, however, in 1969, when Father William Chalmers retired as Harvard's headmaster and was replaced by layman Christopher Berrisford. Berrisford, an Oxford-educated Englishman with a sleek patrician head and a marvelously stentorian voice, eliminated the military uniforms and cut back on religious services, eschewing citations from the Book of Common Prayer to praise the more euphemistic virtues of secular humanism, speaking not of sin but of "self-control." A pragmatist, Berrisford removed Harvard from the church athletic league after a Chicano gang swinging bike chains chased the school's soccer team off the field to avenge a racial epithet. Berrisford did continue for some years to require the attendance of Harvard's increasingly Semitic student body at regular Friday services in the old chapel, the one hauled over Mulholland Drive in four pieces on the backs of semi-trucks during the famous floods of 1938. Even those hours of religious observation were enlivened, however, by the special guests Berrisford invited in to deliver the weekly sermons. A big favorite was Charlton Heston, whose son Fraser was in the class of '76. Rolling back in their pews as Heston's portentous tones resounded off stone walls famous for their acoustics, students cracked jokes about getting the truth straight from Moses' mouth.

Under Berrisford, Harvard's doors gradually were opened to all who could both meet the academic standards and afford the cost of admission. TV talk-show host Johnny Carson and crapshooting character actor Walter Matthau placed their sons at the school, where the boys attended classes with the heirs to the rising fortunes of Teledyne, Baskin-Robbins, and Blue Chip Stamps. As new money mixed with old, the transition was from aristocracy to meritocracy. The Berrisford administration's emphasis was less on breeding than on achievement, and a school that long had been academically superior was now preeminent, producing the highest College Board scores and by far the greatest percentage of National Merit scholars on the West Coast, sending students to Ivy League universities at a rate to rival Choate and Exeter.

By 1972, the year U.S. voters overlooked both the bombing of Cambodia and early reports of the Watergate break-in to reelect Richard Nixon by a landslide plurality, the Harvard School suggested a small college campus populated by prodigies. Boys twelve to eighteen strolled across twenty-three acres of terraced grounds on the San Fernando Valley side of Mulholland, with wide grassy playing fields rolling down from hillsides where homebuilders had planted fan palms among scrub oaks, and sunlight reflected in silver flashes off the swimming pools and picture windows of Neutra houses standing on stilts. Campus buildings were called halls and named for the school's biggest benefactors, connected by an intricate system of covered breezeways and concrete staircases. At the bottom of the hill, beyond the red cinder track, were outbuildings that would have been auto body or wood shops at any public high school, but which on the Harvard campus were labeled SCULPTURE, DRAWING, and PAINTING.

Harvard long had admitted one scholarship student each year, but under the clerics of the Cathedral Church of Saint Paul's these usually were the sons of faithful retainers. One of the school's first black students, scholarship recipient Marc Hannibal, the son of an Episcopal minister, was nicknamed "Hannibal the Cannibal" by his mates in the class of '65. When the layman Berrisford took over, however, Harvard began to reach out into the larger community for its best young prospects.

Among the first scholarship students admitted under the school's new administration was twelve-year-old Joe Gamsky, who followed his brother Greg onto Harvard's green lawns out of the hot, smoggy flats of the Valley floor, where the two boys had been prepared at the Gifted Children's Association on Ventura Boulevard. Joe, the younger and brighter of the brothers, had all but skipped the fifth and sixth grades at Kester Avenue Elementary in Van Nuys. This was "an unusual child," one of his teachers explained to the admissions director at the Harvard School, not merely the most brilliant boy she had encountered but the most mature as well, possessed of an almost preternatural calm. His only trespass was a quiet condescension he was as likely to direct at an adult thirty years his senior as at another child.

Arriving at the Harvard School as a seventh grader, though, Joe Gamsky was regarded not as reserved but rather as stiff and guarded. The only significant impression he made on anyone was in the classroom, where he was marked immediately as perhaps the brightest boy in the class of '77, and probably its most industrious, a shy and humorless student who made lots of As but few friends.

"At Harvard we were all watching each other all the time," explained classmate Steve Taglianetti. "Just getting into the school was supposed to be proof of some important intellectual attainment. And then when we got there, students were told from the first day that we were all competing with each other, intellectually, socially, athletically. It was made explicit; this was something the school was proud of. So it was like a power struggle from the start, everyone trying to find out who was on top of who." Recalled future Harvard '77 senior class president Brad Reifler: "The first thing that hit you about Joe was that he was very smart and very hardworking. But there was also this other quality, which is hard to describe except as a combination of smugness and defiance, like he was there to make sure all of us remembered his name."

By the eighth grade Joe Gamsky had a reputation as a combination intellectual snob and social casualty. He read *U.S. News & World Report* in the cafeteria, eschewing such unreliable sources as *Time* or *Newsweek*. In AP English, during a discussion of John Steinbeck's *The Pearl,* Joe made allusions to *The Red Pony,* just to let everyone know he'd read that too. He was most impressive in science courses, predicting the outcomes of experiments that had yet to take place, announcing aloud and in advance that the porous rock would expand if immersed in water or that the pithed frog would leap if you probed its sciatic nerve with a needle. And everywhere he demonstrated a passion for complicating issues, for exploring ramifications, permutations, and contradictions that led class discussions into realms of esoterica that left even teachers staring at him in outraged silence.

Outside the classroom, Gamsky was a comical figure for many students, a gangly, pale-faced boy with wet-combed black hair and a line of beauty marks that trickled from the right corner of his mouth. His shirts all were a little short in the sleeves. Most of the poor boys who accrued status at Harvard were star athletes, and Joe Gamsky was never going to be one of these. Nearly six feet tall in the eighth grade, he was ungainly afoot and near the bottom of his class in every sport but one—diving off the high board at the Harvard pool, which he went at with an abandon that startled the other students, who were amazed to see the geek Gamsky executing perfect half gainers while they were still learning to hit the water headfirst.

The Gamskys had no need to tell anyone at the Harvard School that their family was neither wealthy nor well connected, and though Joe continued to pass in silence, never growing red in the face or muttering about the day when *he* would fly to Cancún for Christmas as his older brother Greg sometimes did, classmates began to notice the smolder of ambition and a lust for conquest in those eyes so dark a shade of brown that they were almost black. Joe's feelings surfaced in the popular game of Poison they played in PE: "He would throw the ball at you with a vengeance, going for the head," recalled a classmate. "It wasn't a friendly game when you played it with Joe. He wanted to make you pay."

Some students understood, those few who were sent to the Harvard School by middle-class parents willing to make any sacrifice to see their sons gain every advantage. Recalled one of them, Eric Lund: "You'd see some sixteen-year-old kid wearing a new Rolex and you'd want to hide your Timex. Or you'd see some kid from your chemistry class driving through the front gate in a brand new BMW or Porsche Carerra and you'd understand at this very young age that whatever life is, it's not fair." Almost fifteen years later, screenwriter Mike Kaplan would recall vividly the afternoon he overheard a pair of eighth grade classmates discussing an idea for a game show, talking about setting up a meeting with an uncle who was a producer. "I was absolutely green with envy," Kaplan remembered. "I felt I was the one with talent, and yet these people could do things I couldn't just because they had connections." It was not so much envy as amazement he experienced, Kaplan recalled, when he arrived at the post-production party on opening night of the musical *Oliver*'s run at the Harvard School Theatre: "I was speechless. There were cakes in the shape of Oliver, there was punch in a crystal bowl, silver platters loaded with canapés and hors d'oeuvres, men in white coats serving us. All this for a bunch of thirteen- and fourteen-year-olds who had put on a school play."

Harvard students assumed access to the black-tie parties at the California Club or to the private beaches and designer cabanas of the Jonathan and Bel Air Bay clubs—that was merely the social norm. These were boys whose fathers had convinced the state legislature to pass what became popularly known as the "Golf amendment," granting tax-exempt status to country clubs on the grounds that private golf courses protected land from commercial development. At Harvard, greater status by far was accorded to those admitted to the exclusive Argyle Balling Club, founded by Dan Sarnoff, grandson of General David Sarnoff, the ambitious office boy who had built RCA and its subsidiary NBC into the planet's most powerful media empire during the years after World War II. The Argyle Balling Club grew its own marijuana on a remote corner of the campus and organized orgies at the homes of vacationing Harvard parents, inviting girls from a more modest Catholic school nearby—"just a bunch of peasant women from the Valley who wanted to fuck rich boys," Sarnoff described them to classmate David Talbot. The Balling Club's most famous function had been the *Deep Throat* party Sarnoff staged at his parents' Beverly Hills estate while they were away for the weekend, projecting the porn classic onto bedsheets strung between the mansion's chimneys. Dan hired a team of USC football players to protect his parents' old masters, but security had broken down when the estate was invaded, sacked, and looted by more than a thousand party crashers. Half the Beverly Hills Police Department was called out to quell the riot. Afterward, the *Deep Throat* party became the ultimate point of reference for students who attended Harvard during the 1970s, and the essential consideration was this: Either you had been there or you hadn't.

The Gamskys hadn't, and neither had their friend Eric Lund. "What knowing you're excluded does is drive you inside," Lund said.

"You're the butt of jokes, you're left out of everything that's supposed to be most desirable. What people put in that position usually did was go one of two ways, either get into serious self-destruction, probably by using harder drugs, or they got very studious and driven."

The bookworms and burnouts watched through lenses of awe, envy, and abhorrence as the class of '77's tastemakers, a clique of rich boys centered around the triumvirate of Bob Wyman, Bob Beyer, and Brad Reifler, made a campus ceremony of presenting one another with expensive birthday gifts such as cashmere sweaters and graphite tennis racquets. "You wanted to get those things but you knew you couldn't give them," recalled Peter Kleiner, another middle-class kid who had found his sanctuary in the campus theatre. "All you could do was look." "I remember once being invited up to Bob Wyman's for a screening at the theatre in their house in Bel Air," recalled Kleiner's friend Mike Kaplan. "The opulence of that scene upset me in a way that was physical. These people had so much."

On campus, the center of social life was the senior parking lot, where students in their last year could park their Porsches and BMWs, their T-tops and Firebirds, creating the occasional stir by arriving in a parent's Stutz Bearcat or Ferrari Testarossa, all in neat rows on a shaded sheet of asphalt that offered excellent views of the sunny faculty lot where the school's teachers broiled their Toyotas and Datsuns. A space in the senior parking lot was the ultimate privilege, one Harvard students began to anticipate as seventh graders, except of course such boys as Joe Gamksy, who rode his bicycle to school until the tenth grade, when he began commuting by RTD bus. The poor boys heard only vague rumors of the spectacular feats performed by such luminaries as young Greg Bautzer from the class of '78, son of one of Southern California's most successful attorneys, a senior partner with Bob Wyman's dad in the powerful firm of Wyman, Bautzer, and Kuchel: Greg began hanging out in the senior parking lot when he was only a sophomore and made himself a legend there by his practice of lighting cigarettes with hundred-dollar bills.

"The rich kids all tell you that they don't remember any discrimination on the basis of wealth or status or social connections," said Eric Lund. "That's like the duck hunter who says it isn't a violent sport—well, go ask the duck. You're not invited to their parties, you're not invited on their trips. So you put your energy into proving something to somebody somewhere. I left Harvard with forty-five units of Advanced Placement college credits because I didn't have much else to do but work and study. Joe was like that, too, only where I was kind of loud and raw about it, Joe went into himself. I at least swam and played water polo. Joe wasn't good at sports and he had this pixieish face, these very unformed features, and his nose was always in a book. He got very quiet, but with this intensity that just burned through the silence. There was this quality of grim determination. He was pretty humorless. He was going to show them all up."

Joe achieved his first real prominence on campus by defending another scholarship student, Jamie Hogan, against an English teacher named Mr. Rock. Jamie was a hyperkinetic kid with an Australian accent, very bright and a terrific soccer player but also someone who seemed unable to sit still, even in class. Jamie literally would crawl onto the furniture, burbling these little cooing noises, completely unconscious of it. One day Mr. Rock had blown up at him, making some very cutting remarks about self-control, then sending Jamie out into the hallway to wait alone until class was dismissed. Joe Gamsky had gotten very hot in the face. He sat silent for a few moments, then stood up to publicly challenge Mr. Rock, telling this grown man he had no right to speak to Jamie that way; Jamie just had more energy than he knew what to do with, and it was the job of a teacher, a real teacher, not to suppress that energy but to channel it. Mr. Rock told Joe to sit down but the boy refused, and the two of them faced off right there in the classroom, debating the responsibilities of the teaching profession for fifteen minutes. Joe just wouldn't back down. The other students watched the crescents of sweat expanding under Mr. Rock's arms as Joe kept after him, never really losing his temper but never relenting either, until finally it was Mr. Rock who subsided into silence and took his seat at the front of the room. The next morning, even upperclassmen were pointing out this Joe Gamksy kid who had shut down the teacher.

By ninth grade, a certain mystery and no small amount of speculation surrounded the younger Gamsky. He was not just remote but actually secretive. Anyone who made plans to see him on the weekend had to make a firm appointment by Friday because he would not give out his home phone number. He might call you, but always from a pay phone. The other students had yet to meet the mother, though they did see Joe's father occasionally, delivering the boy on the back of a Harley-Davidson motorcycle in the parking lot before school. The elder Gamsky was an odd lanky figure with shaggy hair and hollow eyes, a man the other boys imagined as the sort of B-movie mad scientist who emerged from his basement laboratory one morning filled with some new and terrible knowledge that would produce giant lizards or radioactive spiders. While the older brother, Greg, acted ashamed of Mr. Gamsky's appearance, Joe seemed positively proud of his father's peculiarity. His second son described the strange man as a psychologist involved in some experimental field of behavior modification and let it be known that in his home the children did not address their father as "sir" or "Dad" but simply as "Larry." "I don't think of myself as Joe's father," Mr. Gamsky would explain. "I'm his teacher."

During his freshman year at the Harvard School, Joe Gamsky found a solution to his sense of social exile: the school's enormously successful speech and debate squad. Forensics was accorded an eminence at Harvard unrivaled at any other school in Southern California. On the Coldwater campus, a star debater was regarded as at least the equal of the boys who captained athletic teams. Harvard's tennis, volleyball, and soccer squads all won, but debate *dominated*. "Berrisford would send out memos congratulating the debaters who won every Monday morning," recalled Steve Taglianetti. "He didn't do that for the football team." Harvard's debaters had been coming in waves for years, neatly groomed boys in coats and ties, disgorged by the dozens from their chartered buses, at once overwhelming and offending their plain-clothed public school opposition, winning tourney after tourney, undefeated in Southern California for as far back as anyone could remember. The school sent a large contingent to the National Forensics League tournament every summer, and Harvard teams returned each September with so many new trophies and plaques that the debate room was in a constant state of remodeling to accommodate the gleaming hardware that overflowed its glass-encased shelves.

All this was the dominion of the school's most successful coach, Ted Woods, a chubby, balding, hyperintense little Mormon bachelor whose bearing vacillated between acute anxiety and giddy delight. Woods was able to load his squad with talent by implementing a virtually infallible recruiting program: Every Harvard student was required to take public speaking as a ninth grader, and every ninth grader was informed he would receive an A in this course if he attended a minimum number of debate tournaments.

Joe Gamsky was one of those boys who needed no inducement. He got involved in debate even before his freshman eligibility, working in the school library as a research assistant for his brother and Greg's partner, Eric Lund. "I could tell right away, just watching him put together research files and outline arguments, that Joe was a lot brighter than Greg," recalled Lund. "And Greg was no slouch—he was like me, a bright kid being better than bright just by main strength and force of will. Joe was every bit as determined as we were, but it all came a lot easier for him. He had finesse and intuition, while Greg and I were kind of plodding. Joe could make these leaps, connect A and E without going through B, C, and D, and he could see both sides of any issue, which Woods always said was what made a top debater."

By the time he began his second term of freshman speech, it was Joe who partnered with Lund, debating on the squad's junior varsity. "I remember the first tournament we were in together as a team, out in Claremont," Lund recalled. "I was really into the American College of Debate style, which is to hit your opponent with a blizzard of rhetoric, just keep talking, loud and fast, through him, over him, around him. And then Joe came on almost diffident, speaking in this very hushed voice so that you almost had to strain to hear him, but with so many facts, this argument that was so thoroughly prepared and reasoned, like he was saying to the other side, 'Excuse me, but you do see, don't you, that you're wrong?' I got very upset and impatient, feeling this was far too passive an approach. But it turned out to be very successful, maybe because of the contrast in our styles, and we took first place in the tournament."

Young Joe Gamksy, though, won debates no matter who partnered him and by the end of the school year was one of the few high school freshmen in the United States accorded a National Forensics League rank of "Excellence." Joe began debating with the varsity as a sophomore and showed signs of a new aggression, a flair for personal attack no one had seen the year before, yet still won week after week. His evidence file was as substantial as a senior's, but he was one of the few Harvard debaters of any age who could run a successful "squirrel," a technique that involved approaching the assigned topic at an angle so acute that the other side could not possibly prepare for it. Joe showed a real genius for this, inventing arguments that linked penal reform to no-fault insurance or preparing for the topic of presidential politics by devising a system that eliminated any possible inconsistency between the electoral college and the popular vote in national elections.

Gamsky made a fetish of his dedication to debate, going to lengths that were extreme even by Harvard standards, devoting an entire month of lunch periods to a forced march across the entire unindexed *Congressional Record,* slogging through thousands of crushingly dull pages to cull out those two or three dozen little documentary nuggets that, if hurled at a propitious moment, would devastate another debater. He became a habitué of the forensics room, one of those boys who hauled their evidence files across campus in double-wide paper portfolios known as "ox boxes" and devoted free periods to passionate discussions about getting their SHIT (solvency, harms, inherency, and topicality) together. A tight little cadre of unofficial scorekeepers, they whiled away whole afternoons rearranging the colored pins and plastic letters of the "tab board" where the National Forensics League rankings were displayed. "I personally never thought Joe was as brilliant as some people did," recalled Peter Kleiner. "I mean, he was intelligent, yes, but the only area he ever impressed me in was debate, and even there, I wasn't impressed by being impressed because Joe didn't seem to be really enjoying himself at tournaments. I actually felt sort of sad for the guy, this driven person."

As a sophomore, Joe dominated so thoroughly that he was awarded the mark of "Distinction," just one level below the National Forensics League's ultimate accordance, its double ruby of "Special Distinction," this despite the fact that he could not afford to attend the national tournament where other top debaters piled up points. People had begun to speak of him in the same breath with Bert Bernheim, the legendary senior debater and national champion anointed by Coach Woods as the standard by whom all others must measure themselves. Bernheim fostered this comparison, adopting Joe as his disciple, driving him to debates, divulging the secrets of his tactical approach, even sharing the evidence cards of his own voluminous research file.

Joe's relationship with Coach Woods, though, was not so salutary. While Woods professed to adore all his boys, he demonstrated a noticeable tendency to cultivate relationships with those young men who came from wealthy or prominent families, fellows like Chris Escher, a debating partner of Joe's whose parents not only were Harvard benefactors but had specifically endowed a speech and debate award called the Escher Cup. The poor boy for whom victory was the ultimate personal expression offended Woods's sense of propriety, and although he professed admiration for Gamsky's abilities, such statements seemed always to come out of his mouth as concessions rather than as compliments. Joe retaliated with disdain, "pretty openly treating Woods like he wasn't good enough to teach him," recalled Taglianetti.

Woods was a teacher vulnerable to mockery, not so much because he played favorites but because he had the habit of expressing his affections physically, tickling a boy's ribs with his index finger or pinching both his cheeks between thumb and forefinger, employing such reckless endearments as "you little wienie, you." The rumor that the coach was gay had been around Harvard so long that it achieved a quasi-official status among debaters.

Of course, at the Harvard School the Advanced Examination of Homosexual Tendencies had for years been a popular course of independent study. "We were an all-boys' school and everybody was always watching everybody else for signs," explained Eric Lund. "It was the ultimate put-down at Harvard, the dividing line between the weak and the strong, the ins and the outs. If you could call somebody a fag and get away with it, you had basically dismissed them from further consideration." The irony of his campaign against Coach Woods was that Joe Gamsky was himself one of those boys around whom innuendo grew like a second skin. It was whispered that Jamie Hogan's devotion to him had been spawned by their sexual relationship and that Joe had made a pass at his debate partner, Chris Wright, or that Chris had made a pass at Joe. The rumors were fueled initially by Joe's appearance, his smooth, pale cheeks adorned not by any new growth of whiskers but by those rather prominent beauty marks, then later on by his adopted manner, a kind of fey and askance mimicry of Noel Coward's worst moments, intended as evidence of intellectual sophistication and disdain for rough sorts but interpreted otherwise by the boys who commented on the suggestive way Joe crossed his legs or upon his increasingly overwrought enunciation.

His classmates were struck as well by Joe's practice of retorting on a sexual level. During one debate trip he had walked unannounced into a motel room where two rival teams sat preparing their cases. "What do you want, Gamsky?" one boy demanded. "I want you to give me a blow job," Joe shot back. The other boys in the room all broke up at what by debate squad standards was a daring riposte, but they also all repeated this remark when they returned to school on Monday morning. In the matter of Joseph Gamsky, though, people were forced to consider the possibility that such remarks might be calculated attempts at intimidation. Everyone recalled, for instance, the debate in which Joe had interrupted an aggressive opponent to ask, "Do you masturbate?", rattling the other boy so badly that he lost not only his composure but also the debate.

As his confidence grew, Joe no longer hid his poverty but began actually to assert it, letting people know that he took the bus to school because there was only one car in his family, informing his fellow debaters of just how many hours he had worked after school as a stock boy to pay for the new three-piece suit he wore to tournaments. "Suddenly he wanted you to know how poor he was and how hard he had to work," recalled Brad Reifler. "He seemed proud of it, really, because it proved how he had gotten where he was completely on his own, without any of the advantages a lot of us had."

It remained rare, though, for Joe to invite anyone from Harvard to his home. Among the first to visit was Eric Lund, who qualified first as a debating partner to both Greg and Joe, and, more important, as one of the few students at Harvard whose economic circumstances were comparable to their own. Even by Lund's standards, though, the Gamsky home in Van Nuys was a modest place, a tiny tract house built on a lot so narrow that from the front porch one could hear the television sets of each next door neighbor. Despite its dimensions, Lund found the little living room as warm as it was cramped, with a mongrel dog that rolled over on the braided rug and a baby sister who couldn't stop smiling but was too shy to speak. The boys' mother was attentive and affectionate. There was a reedy and clinging quality to the woman, however, that appeared to make each of her sons uncomfortable. At dinner, tears seemed to well up in Mrs. Gamsky's eyes every time she looked at Greg or Joe, and she actually choked up with gratitude when all three boys pitched in to clear the table and wash the dishes. The father was "obviously absent," Lund recalled, but the circumstances were unclear; a mention of divorce and California's community property laws was followed not long after by the statement that Mr. Gamsky was off touring the country on his motorcycle.

The purpose of Lund's visit was to prepare for a debate the next day, and for that the boys adjourned to the small back bedroom Greg and Joe shared. The room was like a kid motel, Lund recalled: There were bunk beds, neatly made, and two small wooden desks, each with an identical reading lamp, a *Webster's New World Dictionary,* a gray metal card file, a stack of notebooks, a cup filled with ballpoint pens—and that was it. The walls were bare. It was a place so stark and ordered that Lund found himself tempted to peek in the closet for a glimpse of the secret chaos they must have shut away in there.

During his junior year at Harvard, Joe Gamsky's sense of self inflated to the point that he ran for class representative. The results were a revelation: Joe not only finished last in a field of three but received just two votes, one his own. He covered his wound by asserting that the position he truly desired was that of debate squad captain. It seemed his due; even the boys who disliked Gamsky acknowledged that he was the best debater at the school. Joe's problem was Coach Woods's refusal to make the position of debate squad captain an elective office, reserving his right to personally appoint the boy "best qualified" for the job. After a review of his candidates for the 1976–77 school year, Woods's selection had been not Joe Gamsky but rather Rick Berg, who did not rank among even the squad's top ten debaters. Rick was, however, Woods's special pet, a charming and popular boy whose father, Dick Berg, owned one of the entertainment industry's most powerful television production companies, Stonehenge. Well-liked by almost everyone, Berg was that rare individual at Harvard who could move with ease from clique to clique, able to stand at the very center of the wealthy group, exchanging expensive gifts with the Reiflers, Beyers, and Wymans, yet managing to remain distinct from them somehow, distanced by a sense of irony and a subtle cynicism. Rick could go straight from smoking dope with the party-hearty crowd in the senior parking lot to a meeting of the chapel committee, and an hour later leave the priests smiling and nodding, telling one another what an exemplary lad this was. A lot of debaters liked that Berg refused to take either himself or his position as captain very seriously. It was exactly this attitude, of course, that infuriated Joe Gamsky. Not to have been selected debate squad captain when he clearly was the most deserving candidate, that was an indignity, but to see the coveted honor bestowed upon a boy to whom it meant almost nothing, who was at best a perfunctory debater, a person who actually preferred original oratories, an individual more committed to style than to substance, this devastated Joe. He could sublimate his rage but not conceal his resentment, snidely referring to Rick as "Ricky" and openly deriding him at tournaments. That Rick seemed more amused than angered only increased Joe's suffering.

It began to occur to some of the boys that what Joe Gamsky really resented about his wealthier classmates was not their German cars, Italian sweaters, or Swiss watches, but rather that unshakable sense of certainty, of *belonging*, which was their finest possession. The cruelest injustice of the social order at Harvard was its ineffability, an absence of any formal standard, the unspoken but entirely conscious cloaking of a hidden agenda that no grade point average, no SAT score, no forensics tab-board total ever would alter. Popularity was not something a person might earn but rather a condition that could only be *assumed*. The evidence of this was that a social success at Harvard didn't need to be class president like Brad Reifler or debate squad captain like Rick Berg; popularity might accrue to a person who was no more than a Dean Karny.

Karny was bright but only a B student, a scrawny kid whose greatest athletic feat had been making the Harvard junior varsity in tennis. Dean debated, but only as a senior would he reach the rank of "Excellence" Joe Gamsky had achieved as a freshman. Yet Karny seemed to have been admitted to a department of the Harvard School from which the Gamskys were permanently excluded. One of the school's best-dressed students, Dean was not merely a member of the monogrammed masses but a boy who had traded in his tennis shoes for Top-Siders with a sense of timing so impeccable that it was impossible to tell whether he was following the trend or setting it, one of those boys born on the last breath of the baby boom who achieved an apparently telepathic recognition of the very instant when long hair became an emblem not of stylish rebellion but of lost causes and downward mobility, returning to school the following Monday morning with his own light brown locks cut close at the temples.

Dean not only steered his white Camaro into the senior parking lot every morning but returned to spend his free periods there as well, loitering among the right people, not merely privy to their custom-made nick-names but granted one himself—"Rothschild's Cousin," he was called. It was an acknowledgment of the vaguely old-world quality people saw in Dean, this assertion of himself as not only Jewish but also French, not merely well connected but actually well bred. He was the kind of boy who grew up knowing his great-great-grandfather's biography, rare in a community where even "old money" went back only a generation or two.

The Karny family mythology was centered on Dean's father, Sha-lom. Mr. Karny was a burly man with a big handlebar mustache, famous for having served in the Palmach, running survivors of that ultimate pogrom, Nazi Germany's, through British lines into Palestine after World War II. Though he never said so himself, Shalom reportedly had held the rank of colonel in that precursor of the Israeli army. He came to Southern California during the country's expansionary "I LIKE IKE" era and was reputed to have taken advantage of those last low land and labor prices to create his own construction company, emerging twenty-five years later a man described not merely as a builder but also as a "developer," owner and operator of several lucrative shopping centers.

It was an impressive résumé, but between the lines was a truth slightly more complicated, since the real force in the Karny family was not Shalom, but his wife, Danielle—"Danny." As tiny and fine-featured as Shalom was big and broad, Danny also was as domineering and driven as Shalom was quiet and retiring. The Karnys' real estate portfolio had been built less upon Shalom's shrewd business sense than with Danny's inheri-tance. Her father, Herz Mantchik, was among the first men in Los Angeles County to see potential in what had become the community's most profit-able blight, the shopping mall. After Shalom married Danny, the family not only continued to manage its commercial property in the San Fernando Valley but began to explore the virgin territory of condo conversions as well.

The Karnys' own home was situated high in the Hollywood Hills, in a quasi-rustic area known as Outpost Estates. Just south of Mulholland between Beechwood and Nichols Canyons, across the freeway from the reservoir and within walking distance of the Hollywood Bowl, it was a neighborhood of intertwining deer paths and leafy culs-de-sac, where coy-otes drank from hot tubs and escaped parakeets roosted in palm crowns. Many of the "estates" up along Outpost Drive belonged to people who conceived of themselves as homesteaders who happened to have six-figure incomes, and the vestiges of a rugged individualism clung to the hillsides as tenaciously as the creosote and chaparral. The chief caretaker of the little community's work ethic was Judge Ron Swearinger of the Los Angeles County Superior Court, a gregarious but crusty character who advocated such extreme measures as castrating rapists and executing child molesters. Judge Ron had built his own home, expanding and refurbishing the place over the years, amassing one of the spectacular hand-tool collections that the Outpost Traders exchanged among themselves like the precious relics of some earlier and more devout period. The judge maintained his property without hired help, doing his own painting, landscaping, and home repairs, delegating duties to his two sons as soon as they were old enough to push a soapy sponge across the hubcaps of his Dodge station wagon. That was one thing that had bothered him about the Karnys right from the start: Their kids never did a lick of work around the place. Of course, the parents didn't do much either, since just about every task was attended to by the family's famous and faithful retainers, a black couple with French accents who were reputed to have once held positions in the Haitian foreign ministry. It was Danny who did the reputing, of course, which placed the matter in some doubt, since it was the feeling of her neighbors that Mrs. Karny tended to inflate herself quite considerably. Judge Ron and his neighbors regarded Shalom as a nice-enough fellow, a bit bland, perhaps, but at least unassuming. He was a man who spent most of his days at home, puttering around the house, offering passersby a good word or two, but rarely more, seemingly devoted to minding his own business. Danny, on the other hand, was a public presence, full of opinions and self-regard. She related to her neighbors principally through the medium of her children—Dean and his sister, Laurie, two years older. The Karny kids were the most obedient and closely observed in the neighborhood, the best dressed and the most polite. Their mother, making sure of this, regularly marched her children up Outpost Drive so they might stand and listen as she informed one mother that Laurie was not allowed to eat hard candy or reminded another that Dean was not permitted to play football in the street. "I think maybe some of the parents took this as an implied criticism, like, what were they doing—raising a bunch of bad influences?" recalled Steve Bisharat, who lived on the same block.

All the neighborhood children car-pooled to school, and the ride was a lot less fun on the days Danny drove. "The Karnys had this fantastic station wagon, which they kept for years," recalled Judge Swearinger's son Rich. "It even had skylights. It was great to be in, except that Mrs. Karny was a lot more strict than the other mothers. She would be on Laurie all the way to school, and you always felt like she was yelling at you, too, like her daughter would never behave this way if you weren't around." During summer vacations, Dean and Laurie were the first kids called home in the evening, never later than six, always in bed by seven-thirty, even when it was still light out. "Me and my friends would be tearing up and down the street, screaming and yelling," Rich Swearinger remembered, "and through the window we'd see Dean in his pajamas, crawling under the covers."

Rich and his friends called themselves the Hill Rats, hiking up the deer paths toward Mulholland to build forts and stage wars. Dean Karny would stand silent on the curb, dressed in some color-coordinated outfit that looked as if the tags just had been torn off, his expression solemn as he watched the other boys pass. "I felt sorry for him, really," Rich recalled. "Laurie, too. They were always so neat and clean and polite, so perfect. You could feel the pressure they were under to achieve and perform and excel. The family was bristling, in a way, against the whole American way of life. They thought they were European or something. They had a disdain for us that we all felt."

Dean was not allowed to play Little League because his mother worried that he might be hit in the head by a pitched ball. At twelve and thirteen, the Swearinger sons and their friends asked for mopeds as Christmas presents. When their wishes were granted, the boys formed a gang their parents dubbed "the Dumb Shits," a name worn proudly by the minibikers who ravaged the neighborhood's last vacant lot. Dean was forbidden to go near the awful machines.

It was Danny's assertion of herself as an arbiter of taste that irritated Swearinger senior. In all the years they had been neighbors, the judge attended only one of Danny's dinner parties and left vowing never to return. "So overdone and grotesque," he recalled. "There's nothing worse than spending five hours locked up with a bunch of social climbers trying to impress each other."

Judge Ron and his cronies were alternately amused and annoyed that Danny subsidized such soirées by spending her weekends organizing elaborate garage sales, hauling in carloads of broken appliances and discarded clothing, posting signs down on the corner of Franklin and La Brea to attract the crowds that clamored in her driveway. Danny even got Dean and Laurie involved, training the children to manufacture pencil boxes by covering tin cans with colored tiles, selling them for a dollar and a half apiece.

Danny's canned food collection, the one she kept in case of emergency, was a neighborhood legend. This wasn't a shelf or two stocked with Del Monte green beans and Star-Kist tuna but an entire utility closet filled to the brim with such staples as vichyssoise and smoked oysters. Everyone up on Outpost knew about Danny's hoard, and jokes went around for years about how well the Karnys would eat in the event of a nuclear holocaust.

Outpost Estates was an isolated, insular little community, semirural, practically a sanctuary—"like growing up on this big ranch we all had a little piece of," Steve Bisharat recalled his childhood—yet less than five minutes by foot from the tumult and squalor of Hollywood Boulevard. By the time they turned twelve or thirteen, all of the kids up on Outpost, even Dean Karny, were sneaking down the hill to slip in among the white-kneed tourists who planted their sandaled feet beside the famous prints in front of the Chinese Theatre. Sometimes they'd even climb aboard one of the studio buses that collected people to clap on cue in the "live audiences" of game shows. Most often, though, they visited the boulevard to take in the street show headlined by that special breed of performer who fuses persona with psychosis, the Wind-Up Woman and the Coin-Operated Man, the gaudy hawkers and beer-bottle jugglers who collected nickels and dimes among the Walk of Fame tributes to Selznick and DeMille. There were biker gangs who lined their choppers along the curb and charged tourists two dollars for a snapshot, low-riders promenading past in hydraulic Impalas, thirteen-year-old professional women standing in panty hose with cut-out crotches outside the souvenir stands, goofing on the Hare Krishna street cleaners and Scientology testing service volunteers. Occasionally an Outpost kid would carry the chaos back up the hill. There was Carla, for instance, a fourteen-year-old girl who fell hard for a Hollyweird hustler ten years her senior, then tormented her parents by sneaking him into their basement to copulate on the rec room floor. One night when the couple was especially demonstrative the girl's mother had stormed downstairs, where she discovered her daughter and the boyfriend soaking the shag carpet with gasoline, planning an early retirement on the proceeds of the parents' fiery demise.

"We were all exposed to a lot, but most of us were protected by this strong sense of community that was waiting for us when we came back up the hill," Steve Bisharat explained. "Very few of us were allowed to become isolated in a way that made us so susceptible to the outside. The Karnys, though, were one of the families that never really seemed to share the sense of neighborhood, almost like being relatives, that the rest of us had."

Not that anyone on Outpost stayed up nights worrying that Shalom and Danny would be barbecued by their children. Laurie Karny was a shy, pretty blonde whose cache of lyric poetry fascinated Rich Swearinger and the other boys in her class at Le Conte Junior High. When Dean reached the seventh grade, he followed his sister to Le Conte, a feeder school for Hollywood High that stood just south of the KTLA television station on Sunset Boulevard. Though still forbidden from contact sports, Dean was notoriously competitive at those games his mother allowed him to play. Danny served as his one-woman rooting section, "an overwhelming, overbearing presence, always there, pushing him forward," recalled

Morgan Schwartz, a classmate of Dean's since second grade. The two boys never got along, and after a fight in the sixth grade, Dean convinced his mother to let him take kung fu classes, promising to chop Morgan down to size. That never happened, but Dean did challenge Schwartz to a series of tennis matches, handball competitions, and road races, losing to the taller, stronger boy every time out. "Dean wanted some acknowledgment that he could never get," Morgan said. "Being an average kid wasn't good enough for him."

Laurie's friends, though, saw a truly sweet boy, one who would dance with them long before the Chads and Thads in their own grade were ready to try. Dean showed a real interest in what mattered to girls; he could talk without embarrassment about clothes or makeup, had the nicest giggle and the best manners of any boy around. Among his peers at Le Conte, though, Dean developed a reputation as a kid desperate to fit in, to find his place not only within a group but within the *right* group. He clung whenever he could to the central figures in his class's cool crowd, Dirk Mathison and Steve Gordon, who played lead and bass guitar in Le Conte's drama department band. After school, Dean would fall in uninvited beside Dirk and Steve as they jogged the paths along Mulholland. It was Dean who conceived the idea that the three of them should start an official running club, call themselves the "Hollywood Hill Rats," get T-shirts printed with this legend. The other two boys disappointed Dean, though, dismissing the idea as a waste of money.

When they thought of Karny later, Dirk and Steve always would remember that noontime out on the quad, where the cool crowd spent lunch periods, when he had come charging up on them from behind, plunging headfirst between the two taller boys, literally wedging them apart, wearing this manic grin as he announced, "Hi, guys." Dirk and Steve merely exchanged smiles, but everyone else on the quad cracked up, and, as if by acclamation, all present understood that Karny would endure a serious image problem for the duration of his stay at Le Conte.

Dean was rescued from this fate by his parents, who never had planned to let him attend Hollywood High, anyway. The public school was still best known as the set for those scenes of discontented white middle-class youth rumbling beneath its towering flag poles and massive stone façades in *Rebel Without a Cause*. By the early 1970s, though, the campus was being transformed into the microcosmic global village it would become, filling up with the offspring of the world's political and economic refugees, the Korean, Armenian, Iranian, Filipino, Laotian, Cambodian, Salvadoran, Guatemalan, and Mexican immigrants who were making Hollywood High the most ethnically diverse school in the city. Steve Bisharat and Rich Swearinger might argue that their neighborhood school offered the best possible preparation for real life, but the Karnys had a more rarefied atmosphere in mind for their Dean and sent him to the Harvard School to start the eighth grade.

Not even his mother's scrupulous attention to detail, though, had prepared Dean for the subtlety and ruthlessness with which distinctions were drawn by students on the Coldwater campus. It was at Harvard where Dean learned the all-important difference between being merely "well-to-do," which suggested the highest strata of the upper middle class, and being "well-off," which meant really rich. Dean discovered at Harvard that his father's rust-spotted Cadillac and his mother's aging station wagon made damaging statements, so he insisted that his parents drop him off outside the front gate rather than in the parking lot. "He was the kind of guy you knew thought he was being watched all the time, and so you did sort of watch him," recalled a younger student, Allen Myerson.

Dean was still a joiner, trying out at four feet eleven inches and eighty-nine pounds for the freshman football team, crushed when the coaches cut him. He got on the JV tennis team, though, a wiry and quick baseline player who made a decent doubles partner. Dean invested his entire identity in this minor success, regularly showing up for school in Fila tennis outfits just like Bjorn Borg's. "He wore them really tight, which was weird, considering how skinny he was," recalled Steve Taglianetti.

Most classmates, though, found Karny inoffensive and amusing. His manners were flawless, his wit quick, his approach ingratiation. Dean did stir titters when he celebrated his fifteenth birthday with the purchase of twenty tickets for a performance by the Second City comedy troupe at the Ice House in Pasadena. Quite a number of the classmates he invited, it turned out, were people he really did not know very well. "I remember sitting there and wondering, 'What am I doing here?'" recalled Mike Kaplan. "We were in the same homeroom, but I don't think I'd ever had one real conversation with the guy. The feeling I got was that this was someone who wanted really badly to have friends." The most serious charge against Karny was that he could be a cheapskate. People started noticing in the ninth grade how Dean was always managing to remember that he needed a new lunch card—Harvard's coin of the realm—right after the bookstore stopped selling them, and so would be forced to borrow another student's. On a ski trip to Mammoth in his sophomore year, fellow travelers began to use Dean's last name as a verb: "Don't try to Karny me," they would tell boys who tried to borrow Chap Stick or pick French fries off their plates.

Karny's financial status became a subject of speculation when other students noticed how impressed Dean was by classmate Cary Bren's new BMW, one of the first to appear in the student parking lot. "He loved just to sit in the passenger seat," recalled Brad Reifler. "That was heaven for him." Dean's parents bought him the new Camaro for his sixteenth birthday in May of 1976, and when he returned to Harvard as a senior, Karny had become a fashion leader. He was working afternoons and evenings at Rudnick's, a haberdashery in Beverly Hills, investing his wages in the new wardrobe he purchased at cost, forsaking his Fila outfits for silk blazers he wore with khakis and Top-Siders. Dean's persona suddenly was smooth and stylish: "You had the feeling he spent a lot of time reading magazines," Brad Reifler observed. "He was the most up-to-date person around."

Dean dropped tennis as a junior when he joined the debate squad. He showed up for tournaments every weekend but explained he was using forensics merely to hone the speaking skills he would employ someday as an attorney. It fit Dean's image, this idea that cases could be won with enunciation and elocution rather than with facts and evidence. His partner that year was David Peterzell, a brainy twin from an academic family forced to dig deep to pay the boys' tuition at Harvard. "I always thought of Dean as a kind of Harvard School–style good old boy," Peterzell recalled. "He was a backslapper and a nicknamer, always complimenting people, but basically a nice guy." Peterzell's eyes opened wider, though, when he showed up for their first debate wearing his only sports coat, an ancient blue blazer that was several inches short in the sleeves, with a pair of clashing plaid pants. "Dean thought I was joking at first, then he got very upset with me when I told him this was all I had," Peterzell remembered. "It was like I had done something wrong. Dean really had this 'CLOTHES MAKE THE MAN' concept in his head. He made me try on some of his clothes and insisted I should wear them to the next debate."

In general Dean was a perfunctory debater. That year's general subject was "Scarce World Resources," and Dean grew passionate on only one occasion, at a tournament attended by his parents. The assigned topic was the oil shortage: "He insisted on turning our whole argument into this pro-Israeli position that was very unpopular," recalled Peterzell, who tried to talk his partner out of it. Dean was adamant, however, presenting an elaborate plan for the invasion of Saudi Arabia and the seizure of its oil fields. "It turned all the judges against us and we lost badly, but Dean didn't care," Peterzell recalled. "I could see how much his parents' approval meant to him."

Everyone else in his class saw, too, when the 1977 *Sentinel* was published in the spring of their last year at Harvard. On his senior page in the yearbook, Dean had been, as usual, the perfect gentleman, opening with expressions of gratitude to all his favorite teachers, then adding, "Furthermore, I must thank my parents most of all for their efforts to give me the very best." It was only fairly unusual to mention one's parents on a senior page, but Dean went further, illustrating his prose with a photograph of himself as a child, posing beneath a Christmas tree in his new gunslinger's outfit, wearing pearl-handled cap pistols, hand-tooled holsters, a brocaded black hat, and two-toned cowboy boots. Dean's final statement was a chronicle of his Harvard years by height and weight:

> 9th—tried out for Freshman football (didn't make it)
> 4'11"—tried out for Freshman basketball (didn't make it)
> 89 lbs.—tried out for J.V. tennis (got lucky)
> 10th—tried out for Sophomore football (didn't make it)
> 5'1"—tried out for Sophomore basketball (didn't make it)
> 95 lbs.—tried out for J.V. tennis (got lucky again)
> 11th—I turned my pursuits towards forensics and the
> 5'4"—cultural aspects of life, placing the greatest
> 106 lbs.—emphasis on eloquence in circumlocutionary speech
> 12th—I'm gettin' bigger and I'm still tryin'

The picture on Joe Gamsky's senior page was another leading indicator of what was due and to whom. Joe used a photograph of himself at the podium in his three-piece suit, gleeful as he emptied an evidence file onto the head of a fellow debater. Joe and the other boy had posed for the picture all in good fun, but when Gamsky made use of it a year later, adjacent to the caption "HARVARD, 'THANKS,'" classmates took it as a taunt, his final rebuttal.

Joe's last year on the Coldwater campus had been a debacle. He voiced his objections to Rick Berg's appointment as debate squad captain openly at a varsity debaters' meeting in the fall of 1976, then followed up by organizing a campaign to remove Berg from office and replace him with a "five-man elected board." Coach Woods retaliated by refusing to recognize Gamsky at debate meetings. Joe raised the stakes by recruiting supporters to his cause, "going around talking to the really humorless and driven types," recalled Mike Kaplan. The campaign culminated in the famous "Article of Impeachment" Joe prepared on behalf of the "United Varsity Debaters."

When he and his associates attempted to discuss certain "innovations" at the meeting in November, Joe explained, "we fully expected to be heartily supported by Mr. Woods, who has long requested help in the unification of the squad. We were amazed by his foreign reaction." Coach

Woods had ignored his phone calls "and would not permit the vocalization of opinions on several other occasions," Joe complained, denouncing the ideas of those opposed to Berg's captaincy as "dangerous" and "egotistical." "We were very confused at this juncture," wrote Joe, who had possessed the presence of mind to suggest a vote on the matter. "Mr. Woods responded by saying, 'Not in this room, you won't,'" he recalled. "So out of deference we moved our meeting across the hall." Woods denounced the gathering as a "Kangeroo Court." To the contrary, Joe asserted, "We were only being true to our education. After all, the purpose of the Debate activity is to aid the student in clearly stating his opinion." Thus, "We found ourselves at a crossroads," Joe explained: "We could either forget our principles or further anger Mr. Woods. We chose our ideals and our education."

The result of this noble selection was a fourteen–two vote to remove Rick Berg as debate squad captain. "Rick was laughing hysterically," his partner Peter Kleiner recalled. "Joe wanted to argue with him, but Rick just said, 'Joe, this isn't that important.' Joe was shocked that Rick refused to take the impeachment seriously. The word itself was ridiculous, but Joe never saw the humor of the situation."

Coach Woods missed the joke as well and warned Gamsky he would be dismissed from the squad for failure to cease and desist. Joe delivered his eight-page impeachment article three days later. "At Harvard we have been taught to believe in certain principles," he observed. "We have been taught that attitudes held by the majority should be recognized and taken seriously. Mr. Woods tells us we have no administrative or structural right to decide these things. We are quite truthfully shocked. The whole reason this culture exists is that a few vocal men had the strength of their convictions. Even when their life was in peril they held to these ideals. They had no administrative or structural right. They only had a human prerogative."

The first signature on page 8 read *"Joseph H. Gamsky."* Joe found fifteen other debaters willing to sign on for the ride, but not without making a few additional comments. "These were all wordy bastards, churning internally," Mike Kaplan remembered, "so everybody had to write a page or two, and the thing kept growing."

Woods followed through on his threat to throw Joe off the squad. "Most of us saw the whole thing as this big joke," Peter Kleiner recalled, but it was clear that Gamsky had been changed by his experience. The previous spring, Joe had listed Harvard, Yale, and Stanford as the colleges where he wanted his high school transcript sent; now, though, Gamsky said he would not apply to any of these schools because he didn't wish to sit in classes with the sort of people one met on the Coldwater campus.

It was at around this time that Mike Kaplan and his partner, Tagan West, devoted their weekly *Harvard Mystery Theatre* radio show to a series of faculty impersonations, mimicking the voices of various teachers raised in song. Coach Woods's contribution was "Mrs. Robinson." "When they got to the part about 'Joltin' Joe, our nation cries [*sic*] for you,' everybody on campus cracked up," recalled Steve Taglianetti. Joe no longer heard them laughing, though. He was taking classes at UCLA in accounting and economics to accumulate unversity credits, in a bigger hurry than ever. At Harvard, a circle of younger students gathered around him, seeking guidance. "He wasn't the kind of person you'd want to be close to, but he *was* the kind of person you'd want to be around," explained David Peterzell, "because you knew there was a good chance to profit from it."

Part of the fascination with Gamsky was that, while he remained a figure of ridicule for the majority, some of the school's most prominent students found themselves drawn to him. When the senior wills were published that spring, Joe's name was mentioned only twice, but both times by boys their classmates considered most likely to succeed. The first was their class president, Brad Reifler, who acknowledged the urgency of Joe's mission by willing him "the heart attack you have diligently worked for." Joe's second bequest came from the first prefect himself, Dan Greenberg.

Youngest son of the prominent attorney Arthur Greenberg, whose two older boys both had served as first prefect (the boy chosen to serve as liaison between the school's students and its faculty) at Harvard ahead of him, Dan was the class of '77's star: freckle-faced, shiny-eyed, kindhearted, an early admission to Princeton, lead actor in the school's theatrical productions, playing Puck in *A Midsummer Night's Dream* and the title role in *Peter Pan*. "Our eternal sprite," Mike Kaplan called him. It had startled nearly everyone in the class when, late in their senior year, after the attempt to replace Rick Berg, Dan developed a sudden, intense interest in Joe Gamsky. "You'd see the two of them out walking and talking alone on the lawn, and it was jarring at first," Peter Kleiner recalled. "But when I thought about it later, it fit, because everyone knew Dan was questioning a lot of things then, having a lot of doubts about himself and the whole success track he was on. He was looking for something inside himself, and we could all feel it. He and Joe were like opposite ends of a spectrum coming together: Dan had it all and wanted more; Joe had nothing and wanted more."

"Joe, I wish I could have spent more time with you. Let's keep in touch," read the senior will submitted by Greenberg, who two years later would forsake the Ivy League to follow a mendicant monk across Europe on foot.

Most of the 1977 *Sentinel*'s contents were utterly predictable: There

were the full-page "CONGRATULATIONS" ads placed by Beverly Hills investment firms and insurance brokers, the page taken out by "THE GIRLS FROM
MARLBROUGH AND WESTLAKE"—L.A.'s most exclusive skirt schools—
announcing, "WE VOTE HARVARD NUMBER ONE." There were the senior-page
pictures of boys posing with shiny sports cars and pretty girlfriends, on the
decks of cabin cruisers or in chairlifts at ski resorts. There were double
entendres and daring ditties. And then there was the stilted, arrhythmic
poem written by Joe Gamsky—who had neither girlfriend nor sports car—
to accompany the picture on his own page:

> *My favorite place is a place that is*
> *always there.*
> *For all my life it is my paradise.*
> *It is the favorite place of mine,*
> *Which can be created at a*
> *moment's thought.*
> *No one can disturb you.*
> *Not for your life, if you please.*
> *The eternal silence, which would*
> *be great for anyone to have, is there.*
> *You just have to concentrate.*
> *There are endless galaxies which*
> *are yours.*
> *You can journey to infinity.*
> *Through the endless passages of*
> *the cosmos.*
> *Even better this all belongs to you.*
> *This is your mind.*

Three years passed before Dean Karny came as close to Joe as the
seven pages that separated their senior pages in the 1977 *Sentinel*. Like most
members of his class, Dean would feel a little cheated by the commencement exercises that year: Ronald Reagan had addressed the 1976 class, and
the speaker at the 1978 graduation ceremony would be Johnny Carson, yet
the best the class of '77 could do was an assistant secretary of state named
Warren Christopher.

Dean had heard almost nothing of Joltin' Joe, other than that he
won the big Gemco Scholarship and was using it to get a biz ed or econ degree
at USC. Word was that Gamsky had refused to come back to Harvard to
pick up the plaque that went with the award, preferring to let it rest in
one of the trophy cases in the debate room like a last retort to Coach Woods.

Dean had stayed in town, too, moving just over the hill from Harvard to UCLA. He still planned to be an attorney but was majoring in English Literature. In lieu of the part-time office jobs held by most of his friends, Dean earned his spending money in the outdoors, teaching tennis to friends of the family, faculty, and fellow students on borrowed courts in Beverly Hills. His enterprise had resulted in a falling-out with Brad Reifler, who was offering tennis lessons to the same circle of people. Brad charged the standard rate, twenty dollars an hour, and was infuriated when Karny lured away a number of clients by reducing his hourly fee to fifteen dollars. "A weasel move," Reifler called it.

Dean was teaching a UCLA classmate's cousin on the family court in Stone Canyon when he reconnected with Ben Dosti in the fall of 1979. Ben had been two years behind Dean and Joe at the Harvard School. Swarthy and poker-faced, he was by reputation the sole seventh grader on campus who could read both the stock reports in the *Wall Street Journal* or the wine list at Perino's with equal facility. Ben also was the Harvard School's first Albanian, the only son of parents determined to instill in their children the sense that they were aristocracy in exile. "The Dosti name in the history of the Balkan state of Albania long has been identified with resistance to tyranny," Ben's aunt would write in a letter that traced the boy's lineage to his paternal grandfather, Hassan Dosti, who, as chief justice of the Albanian Supreme Court, had challenged the monarchy of King Zog, and later, as president of the National Democratic Front, led the battle for national independence, first against the Axis powers and then against the Communists. Hassan's son Luan was a compact and dapper man who spoke exceedingly formal English with an East European accent and wore his Savile Row suits with such panache that his horn-rimmed glasses and bulbous nose seemed fashion accessories. Luan held a degree in physics from Columbia and had worked in the aerospace industry as a designer of rocket modules, but now he was a glorified salesman, marketing defense systems to the Middle East for Litton Industries under a quasi-official license that required security clearance and carefully chosen words. Luan was better known by Ben's friends as an internationally respected connoisseur of wine and spirits, a jolly host who offered them fruity Alsatians and hearty Dortmunders that not even Beverly Hills boys had tasted. Ben's mother, Rose, worked as the top food writer at the *Los Angeles Times,* a position that afforded her an approximate celebrity on the Westside, where she could get a front table at any restaurant without reservations. Mrs. Dosti—whose dusky complexion, dark red hair worn in a tight bun, and enormous Modigliani eyes gave her the look of a gypsy orphan abandoned in the editorial offices of *Vogue*— cultivated her children by designing programs for their birthday parties that included readings by avant-garde poets and string quartet recitals. She was always saying "Voilà!" Ben's friends noticed.

In manner and carriage, the Dostis suggested the sort of people who had come to Southern California bearing letters of introduction, deftly inserting themselves into that social network outsiders called the Establishment. In truth, they were not wealthy people, not even quite what Harvard School students called "well-to-do." They lived in Hancock Park, to be sure, amidst the corniced mansions and gated grounds of those who ran the city's banks and brokerage houses. The Dostis' own home, however, was the smallest on their street, Las Palmas, south of Beverly Boulevard and west of the Wilshire Country Club, in outer Hancock Park, one might say, as more than one did. The entire family dressed beautifully, but their five drivers shared a pair of used cars, and the meticulous way they handled their Baccarat stemware or hastened to wipe a spill off a Bokhara rug suggested to Ben's friends that they were cutting it very close, living graciously, yes, but living month to month as well.

For their only son, though, the Dostis would have nothing but the best. At Harvard, Ben was renowned for showing up every week with a new pair of running shoes, carrying them around campus still in the box, perpetually on the crest of fashion as Adidas gave way to Pumas, which lost ground to Nikes, only to be overtaken by Reeboks. Certain members of the faculty designated Ben as unofficial president of a group they referred to snidely as "the Tennis Shoe of the Month Club." Dosti startled classmates, though, with his ferocity on the playing fields. One of the smallest boys to turn out for freshman football, he not only made the team but started at fullback, a power runner sent straight into the line for the tough yards. "There was a real fire in his eye when he was out there," recalled teammate Allen Myerson. "He'd run right over you."

Ben became famous at Harvard, though, for a pair of off-field performances. The first was delivered on a ski trip to Mammoth. Nine or ten eighth graders had rented a condo together, and right away Ben noticed that he was the only one who didn't have first-rate skis. His were an outdated model, inherited from an older sister. Dosti began complaining about his skis that first morning on the mountain, saying they didn't have enough camber, were binding too tightly. By midafternoon he was telling people, "It's affecting my performance." The next morning, Ben and Allen Myerson were riding the chairlift to the top of Stump Alley when Ben unsnapped first one ski, then the other, and dropped them onto a rock slide far below. When he hiked back down the hill, however, Ben discovered his second-hand skis had survived the fall. Undissuaded, he scooped the skis into his gloved hands and bashed them against the trunk of a pine tree until the fiberglass splintered. Later that afternoon, Ben showed up at the Village Sports Shop with his mother's MasterCard and used it to pay for a new pair of Rossignols. The next year, there was a girl from Marlbrough who had conceived a rather public crush on Ben, letting it be known that she was waiting for him to ask her to the school's prom. She approached Ben's best friends and asked them to intervene, going so far as to say she would rent his tuxedo. When this proposition was put to him, however, Ben's back stiffened: "I have my own tux," he said. Sure enough, on prom night, Ben arrived wearing a spectacular rig, with silk lining and satin lapels. By the time the punch had been spiked, everyone in the room was talking about Dosti's amazing tuxedo: The thing looked as if it had been cut from one of Fred Astaire's, they said. Ben never mentioned that his mother had paid seven dollars for the jacket at a Goodwill store.

He transferred out of Harvard to Beverly Hills High as a sophomore. It was the most socially effective form of economy the family could afford. Beverly was essentially a private public school, tuition-free, yet on an academic par with Southern California's best prep schools. Parents who could not afford to live in Beverly Hills engaged in elaborate subterfuges to place their children in the city's schools. Within the 90212 zip code, there were more post office boxes than people, and the school district employed a full-time private investigator to ferret out the middle-class mothers who took jobs as dental hygienists or legal secretaries in order to maintain mailing addresses in the business district along Wilshire Boulevard between La Cienega and Doheny.

The Dostis themselves lived miles outside the Beverly Hills border. Rose, though, had arranged to teach cooking classes at the high school, entitling her, under a special provision of the city's charter, to enroll her children as legitimate students. Ben's sister Marya, older by one year, also transferred to Beverly. Marya was a dancer who had been admitted into the school's artistic community. Ben spent evenings and weekends with his sister and her friends, among whom he forecast himself not as an artist but as art's future patron.

The Dostis taught their son to appreciate the business advantages of a legal background, and at sixteen Ben found work in the collections department of a local law firm, Solomon and Glasberg. By his senior year, Ben had come so far as to obtain his own credit card from Mobil Oil, inflating his age by two years on the application where he listed his car as a 1975 Porsche, his employer as a "Beverly Hills Law Partnership," and his position there as "Investigator."

Ben had just enrolled as a freshman political science major at UCLA when he and Dean were reacquainted that afternoon in Stone Canyon. The two became a mutual admiration society almost at a glance, young adepts of cultivated consumption who lacked only a suitable means of subsidizing their good taste. Dean already was a junior at UCLA, one of the best-known figures on North Campus, where the fast-track crowd, the social science majors headed for law or business school, spent their free periods. On North Campus students shared a sense they were rising with the new wave, emerging from the crash of the sixties and the trough of the seventies as front-runners of the first American generation to truly put the past behind them, whose heritage was here and now. Starting school in the years between the assassinations of the Kennedy brothers, they had borne witness to a time when TV telescoped ensuing events into a miasma of fleeting images, as much Mr. Ed as Malcolm X. Their questions were who had the time to sort it all out and why would anyone bother? They had watched Vietnam fall from front-page news to footnotes in five years, and now the war was basically a balance sheet on which the red was ink not blood. No one so much as mentioned the subject while they were in high school, perhaps because by then Watergate had replaced the war as a symbol of national disgrace.

On North Campus, students were amused by the self-appointed pundits who pointed them out as symptoms of a spiritual malaise. Every week, it seemed, you could catch some graying ex-radical on the tube railing against the apathy and materialism of this new lost generation. Who were those people to talk? Tom Hayden had become a model local citizen whose movie star wife financed his election to the state legislature and now went around telling Rotarians he wasn't a socialist. Everybody gave the sixties credit for good music, but it was duly noted on North Campus that most of the people who made those records were either dead or not feeling too well.

The seventies had been a period of recovery that somehow produced President Carter, that relic of mealymouthed moralizing who walked when he could ride and wore a denim jacket to the press conferences where he told his fellow Americans about the hard choices they had to make in this new era of limits. "There you go again," Ronald Reagan would tell Carter during their first debate, and the words were taken up as a slogan on North Campus: "There you go again," they'd tell the sign carriers from the Committee in Solidarity with the People of El Salvador who harangued them along the paths of Myerhoff Park. Fuck hard choices, for one thing. And who but a whiner would look out on Los Angeles and see limits. The city had been swelling for sixty years, climbing up the steepest slopes and creeping into the most barren gullies. Every other summer there was some dreary story about a drought up north, but no one had turned the water off yet, and Bel Air still grew grass as green as Galway's. Tract houses, business parks, shopping malls, and sprinkler systems were being poured into every dry gulch and arid arroyo from Azusa to Thousand Oaks. "Don't cry for me, West Covina," they sang out on North Campus. Central American and Southeast Asian refugees kept the supply of cheap labor and good help at an all-time high. The Japanese were rebuilding downtown, the Koreans were reviving Wilshire, and Iranians paid cash for condos in Beverly Hills. The entertainment industry's new technologies—cable TV, videocassettes, and CDs—were keeping the Westside in carpaccio and collagen. And in the South Bay, the big defense contractors who hugged the shore between LAX and Redondo Beach—McDonnell Douglas, Rockwell, Lockheed, and Northrup—were poised to pounce on the billions that would be theirs when Reagan was elected.

True, certain economic inhibitions had to be acknowledged. That same three-plus-two Tudor in Brentwood for which their parents had paid sixty thousand dollars in 1960 would cost the kids six hundred thousand in 1980. The public defender's office didn't pay that kind of money, and people who wanted to be socially relevant had to live in apartments or in Glendale. The banks were sending students an unmistakable message, issuing MasterCards upon demand to engineering and business majors, rejecting the applications of art and education majors without review. The new economic model showed a top tier expanding, a bottom rung exploding, and a middle class being squeezed out of existence. The conundrum of time and place was that there was plenty to go around, yet not enough for everyone. In the eighties, Rodeo Drive retailer and economic prognosticator Bijan Pakzad advised *Time* magazine, "the stores that do well will be the very, very expensive and the very, very cheap." Bijan was of course taking the high road, stocking chinchilla bedspreads and designer pistols in mink holsters.

"Pragmatic" was the password on North Campus. At UCLA, where a major in mass communications was the easiest way to avoid English classes, it was pragmatic to think of education as an "investment" and of the future as a "strategy." It was pragmatic to bear in mind that a sociology professor with tenure earned slightly less than a student who finished in the top third of his law school class could expect in his first year of employment. It was pragmatic to be upbeat and outgoing. It was pragmatic to network. It was pragmatic to know someone with a boat at least thirty-six feet long.

Most pragmatic of all was to admit you wanted the best of everything, then go out and get it. This was a particular advantage for Dean Karny and Ben Dosti, acknowledged experts in what the best things were. Dean and Ben could tell you what model of Mercedes had the highest resale value or distinguish an imported chardonnay from a domestic. Unfortunately, even California wines cost money, and Dean and Ben had a lot less than their admirers imagined. Dean barely could support his Fiat convertible, and both boys still lived at home.

It was the urgent need to find a place of their own, in fact, which the two of them had been discussing on that evening in May when Joe Gamsky appeared in front of them on the sidewalk outside the Village Theatre. The first thing that struck them both was that Joe had on a suit, cut from cheap cloth and a trifle tight in the shoulders, but a bona fide business suit nonetheless. He was with his brother, Greg, who also wore a suit but didn't look much different from high school days. Joe, though, had changed. He was even taller, up around six feet five inches now, and had filled out enough to make his height imposing. His features finally had formed, and he was almost handsome in some way that worked off the contrast between his finely textured fair skin and thick dark hair. Dean asked how USC was. He had been out of school for eighteen months, Joe said. After applying all his AP credits, he had started at Southern Cal as a sophomore. One of the university's progressive policies permitted students to challenge the final exams of required courses, Joe explained, and he had taken full advantage, passing tests at a rate that allowed him to graduate in three semesters. On North Campus, a lot of people were impressed to learn that Dean was planning to graduate from UCLA in three and a half years.

Joe invited Dean and Ben to join them for dinner "on me." They got a booth at the Old World, and Ben asked Joe what he had been doing since leaving USC. Had they heard about him passing the CPA exam that first summer after graduating from Harvard? Joe asked. He thought they might have; it had been in the paper. He took no small pride in this accomplishment, Joe admitted, since he had been the youngest person ever to take the test, let alone to pass it. As a matter of fact, he had posted the highest scores in the nation on a couple of sections. Greg told them how Joe's tutor, Stan Becker, was so impressed that he asked young Gamsky to pose with him in an endorsement of the course for magazine advertisements. Dean and Ben were impressed as well, not only by Joe's accomplishments but also by the way Greg—who had graduated from USC himself and mentioned he was working with computers at Southern California Edison—seemed to stand in actual awe of his younger brother. Greg told Dean and Ben how at USC Joe had joined a failing fraternity, the Chi Phis, and almost single-handedly revived the house. The other members actually elected Joe president while he was still a pledge, Greg said, yet somehow his brother found time that year to start his own newspaper, designed to rival the gossipy fraternity-row rag that printed front-page stories about beer busts and beauty contests. Joe's room in the Chi Phi house Greg described as a twenty-four-hour crisis counseling center, with other students dropping in night and day for advice and assistance.

It *had* been exhausting, Joe admitted, since during that time he also was working thirty hours a week as a trainee in the accounting firm of John F. Forbes. After graduation, in December of 1978, he had gone to work for the "Big Seven" firm of Peat Marwick Mitchell and Main, located downtown in the Arco Tower, when the company offered him an opportunity to skip their training program and go straight into the prestigious consulting options program. He was honored to have been included in the team of accountants sent by Peat Marwick early in 1979 to Washington, D.C., where they had audited the compliance of the nation's largest financial institutions with the Real Estate Settlement Procedures Act. Unfortunately, his unprecedented advancement had generated a good deal of conflict with some of the more senior accountants, who resented him bitterly. In retrospect, Joe said, he looked upon his experience at Peat Marwick as an essential lesson in the process by which corporate systems stifled the initiative of truly capable people. The problem was rooted in the very nature of hierarchies, or "ladders of progress," as Joe called them. A bright young person was hemmed in at every turn, Joe said. For example, when he made suggestions, his superiors invariably reacted in one of two ways, either by appropriating these ideas as their own or by informing him that he was employed to implement their programs, not to develop his own. People were threatened, Dean remembered Joe saying, "by an intelligent presence in the corporate structure."

It had been altogether shocking to see the ways in which grown men would stoop to petty intrigues against someone half their age, Joe said; the tremendous irony of the corporate system was how it drove out its best people. His frustration and claustrophobia increased exponentially with each month he spent at Peat Marwick, Joe said. For relief he turned to the brokers at the Paine Webber office on the tower's twenty-ninth floor, depositing a few thousand dollars of savings into commodities accounts. He had started the previous October, Joe said, trading every day from 6 A.M., when the East Coast markets opened, until nine o'clock, when he had to be at his desk downstairs. By the first of the year he actually was earning more money during the three hours he spent at Paine Webber than in the next eight he put in at Peat Marwick, Joe said; his own broker gave him a power of attorney over a personal account. Ultimately, corporate confinement had ceased to make sense on any level, and in February he had resigned to trade commodities full-time. His account was up thirty-five thousand dollars since then. Joe "kind of made an example of himself as he explained the way he thought that things worked out in real life for exceptionally bright people," Dean recalled.

His experience had persuaded him, Joe said, that if he ever could assemble enough similarly ambitious and gifted young people—"people like you," he told Dean and Ben—their combined energies would be sufficient to operate outside the corporate system while competing with it on equal terms. "A force to be reckoned with" was how Joe put it.

After dinner, as they said good-night on the sidewalk outside, Joe suggested that the three of them get together sometime to kick around the ideas they had discussed that evening. Dean and Ben wanted to set a date. "We felt flattered to be included in this type of discussion," Dean explained.

He and Ben walked in Westwood for an hour afterward, stirring the embers of the fire Joe had set under them. At Harvard, they all had known Joe was bright, but Dean felt positively dwarfed by the person he met that evening. Ben was no less impressed. On North Campus, there was incessant conversation about striking out on one's own someday, declarations of independence to be fulfilled when the opportunity "presented itself." Joe Gamsky, though, had not waited for someone to show him the way; instead he found it for himself. "And it seemed to be some incredible stroke of good fortune," Dean recalled, "that now he wanted to show us."

Within a week, the three of them were meeting almost every afternoon. Dean and Ben finished their last class at two-thirty and Joe also was free by that time, since the financial markets not only opened but closed on eastern time. Usually they began at WestWorld, the video arcade beside the Bruin Theatre. Joe could play Pac Man for an hour on one quarter, running up record point totals day after day, attracting a crowd but competing only against himself. It was awesome to observe. Joe's immersion in the games he played approached symbiosis; he did not seem to be reacting to so much as anticipating the computer's moves. As the difficulty levels increased, even the best players were forced into tactics of retreat, but Joe never let up; when he *was* caught, it almost always resulted from pressing a pursuit too far.

Afterward, Joe coached as Dean and Ben used the free plays he had accumulated. Video games were mental calisthenics, Joe said, which reinforced by rewarding the understanding that success was entirely a matter of eliminating from the mind any considerations other than one's goal and the obstacles to it.

Before dinner, they often caught a movie and Joe always paid for the tickets. They saw virtually every film in release. It was all choices in the

movies, just as in life, Joe said, but somehow the screen synthesized involvement with detachment in a way that allowed one to see those choices so much
more clearly, without inhibition or reservation. He was fascinated by the
character of Colonel Kurtz in *Apocalypse Now*. The powers that be moved
inevitably to reduce or remove a man of such stature, Joe observed, for no
other reason than that he was too large for any system they could devise.
Joe found it significant that the vestiges of conventional morality in Kurtz
were what led to his demise. Who knew what the colonel might have carved
from that jungle if he had kept the courage of his convictions?

They ate most evenings at the Old World, Joe's favorite place. He
would wait always for one of the dark-paneled booths where they could talk
privately. Dean and Ben might drink one glass of wine with dinner but no
more. Joe did not touch alcohol at all and for that matter abstained from
coffee and tobacco as well. He abhorred the use of drugs and regarded the
ingestion of any substance that diminished one's intellectual capacities as
desecration. Joe would ask about their classes, leading discussions of the
assigned reading. He was a better source than Cliff's Notes. He had committed himself to reading at least one major work every week since finishing at USC, Joe told them. Most great thinkers, he asserted, were autodidacts.
What did that mean? Dean asked. "Self-taught," Joe told him. After eating, talk turned inevitably to this idea that Joe had about gathering together
a group of other bright and ambitious and capable young people. Imagine
what might be accomplished by an organization that brought together the
best-prepared members of the most advantaged generation of the wealthiest society in the history of human evolution, Joe said, the first people on
the planet to have arrived at a genuine demystification of existence, removed
from the cycle of self-deception and disillusionment practiced by their pre-
decessors. Imagine what they might accomplish, Joe suggested to Dean and
Ben, working within a system that did not *harness* their abilities but rather
released them. Imagine not being required to adapt to some preexisting
quasi-political pecking order that was nothing more than a monument to
human limitation but instead working within a system that adapted to them,
where they were not employees but *members,* Dean remembered Joe saying, "who could do what they were capable of doing."

Such an organization should not consist of strangers who came together for eight hours a day, five days a week, to do nothing more than abase
themselves by competing for raises and promotions, scraps off the table, but
rather should be a kind of extended family, where business and social goals
overlapped, the kind of group one could join as an entire human being, not
as the compressed and cautious subject of arbitrary imperatives. Only the
young were still capable of the idealism that should inform such a group,

Joe said. And yet a profound maturity would be required as well because each member must necessarily operate with the dignity and intelligence to recognize the value of what the others in the group contributed, so that every individual rose or fell on merit alone. Dean and Ben sat rapt.

By the first of June, Joe was leaving the office earlier every day, often sitting in with Dean and Ben on their afternoon anthropology class, whispering corrections and addendums during the professor's lectures. Afterward they ate a late lunch among the outside tables in the North Campus commons. "They were like one person with three heads, that inseparable," recalled Brad Reifler, who saw them there often. "Dean and Ben had been telling everyone what a genius Joe was at trading commodities," and Brad naturally was interested, since the New York branch of his family were the founders of Refco, the country's largest commodities brokerage. "Joe said he had developed a method of inverting the butterfly spread but didn't want to be more specific," Reifler recalled. "He was like a scientist protecting a secret formula. Anyway, Dean and Ben handled his PR. They were introducing him around to all the main people on North Campus." One of these was Alan Lieban, a junior econ major who also was a Deke—"like Reagan," as he had taken to adding. "They weren't talking about an organization then," Lieban recalled. "It was just that Joe was this remarkable person and we should all meet him. The story I heard was about how Joe had gone through USC in two years and was running his own brokerage out of a storefront on Sunset Boulevard. I was more intrigued than impressed at first, maybe even a little skeptical. We were all young, but Joe seemed even younger, less worldly in a lot of ways." What did impress Lieban and a lot of other people on North Campus was Dean Karny's devotion to Joe. "Dean to me was someone who seemed to know all the angles," Lieban explained. "He was friends with everybody on North Campus. He had this air of being someone who really knew what was happening. Dean was short and didn't have the strong physical presence that Joe's height gave him, but he was stylish and smooth and . . . at the center somehow. All the people you knew came from money or were really going places would stop by his table to talk. You thought, 'This guy has connections.' There was no sense what he was going to do with them, but people listened to what he said. It was like he was biding his time, and then suddenly all he could talk about was 'Joe, Joe, Joe, Joe the Genius.' So everyone thought, 'This Gamsky must be a real phenom.'"

At the end of finals week, Dean and Ben brought Joe along to the summer-break parties in the frat houses and apartment buildings on the west end of campus. Something about the sight of Joe, with his ill-fitting suits and shaggy head, towering above Dean and Ben, the two so immaculately turned out in their brushed suede loafers, perfectly faded denims, and tailored jackets, cemented the impression that this was everyone's pet prodigy. Joe would stand there silently, sipping Sparklett's amid the beer-swilling students, watchful, set apart by his seriousness, until, one-by-one, people began to orbit around his dark star. "We were all getting ready to graduate, and everyone was thinking about their futures, about going into business and building careers," Lieban recalled. "A lot of people who might have looked at Joe as something of a nerd a year or two earlier were interested in what he had to say now." Dean and Ben learned a lot by watching Joe operate one-on-one. He assumed that all present had heard of his success and referred to it only in the context of questions he asked people about themselves. Joe took an interest in everyone, and it amazed Dean what people would reveal to him—family secrets, childhood traumas. It seemed as if all of them were worried about disappointing their parents, and yet at the same time sincerely believed Mom and Dad had sold them out to a world where little ground was left to gain.

You won power over a person through the knowledge of two things, Joe explained: One was what they wanted, the other was what they feared.

During June, Dean and Ben both brought Joe home to meet their families. While the Dostis were "impressed with the way Joe expressed himself," as Luan put it, both he and Rose felt the young man asked a lot of personal questions. The Karnys, though, were thrilled with the effect this Joe seemed to be having on their Dean. By the time he was twenty, Shalom had fought for his life and struggled to support a family. What had his son done but sell silk ties and teach tennis in Beverly Hills? Finally Dean was showing a sense of direction, a genuine interest in the family business, in how property was acquired, held, divided, and managed. Dean told them about Joe striking out on his own, about how he deplored drugs, refused to take even a sip of wine, despised idleness, and read reference books the way some people devoured trashy novels. When they finally got to know Joe, both parents were effusive, Danny especially. It was an effect Joe had on any number of older women, an appeal to the maternal instinct laced with discreet sexual overtones. There was the feeling that here was a fine and gifted young man from a less-than-ideal background who needed only care and grooming to blossom. Joe possessed a dazzling smile that outlined his beauty marks in the crescent of a deep dimple. He was surprisingly affectionate, a hugger and squeezer whose big ears and long, lanky body contributed to an impression that man and boy were equally present.

Danny adored cooking for Joe and was having him over for dinner two and three times a week, serving fresh fruit afterwards out on the patio where they caught the breezes that stirred in the hills above a city suffocating on the second-stage smog and immobilizing heat of Los Angeles in July. Dean's new friend slept over so often that Danny referred to the spare bed in her son's room as "Joe's bed." "He was almost living with us," Dean recalled. "My parents loved him. They thought he was a good influence on me."

Dean and Joe stayed up late on those hot summer nights, lying side by side in their twin beds, discussing the kind of people they would want in this group they had in mind. It would be possible to include the best individuals from every field of endeavor, Joe said, because an organization such as this need not be limited by any rigid definitions or assumed agendas. They could have attorneys, architects, accountants—even artists—all working on projects within the same system. "Everyone would be doing what they did best, and we would decide how to capitalize on the talents of the group," Dean explained.

It was important to catch people early, before they became too deeply invested in structures that crushed the spirit of enterprise. The inherent problem was that such a group might require an initial period of pre-production, a "lag time" of some months before it could begin to pay its own way. Without offering salaries, Joe noted, it would be difficult to convince people they should surrender their trainee toeholds on the corporate cliff-face to gamble on a vision. Capitalization would be required to carry the group through its formative phase. As Joe saw it, their only viable asset at this point was his ability to trade commodities. And with the trading base he had at present, it might take years to amass the capital necessary to finance their group. Joe, though, had a plan for accelerating the process: He was considering Chicago, moving there to join the big traders on the Mercantile Exchange. Not only would he pay less than a tenth of what it cost him in brokerage commissions to work on the West Coast, but on the floor of the Merc he would have direct access to moment-by-moment movements of the market, be in a position to draw not only upon the power of his analysis but upon the speed of his reflexes as well.

Joe sought to give Dean and Ben a rudimentary grasp of his trading theories so that his friends might understand how critical such access could be. His approach to the commodities market was based less on economic models than on psychological ones, Joe said. In financial instruments, he explained, "there are no crop periods or seasonality to consider. You don't have blights. You are not interested in weather. The pigs aren't being infested by a certain disease. All of that becomes irrelevant. You have a pure, smooth psychological phenomenon. As a result, you can be a little more accurate." Because financial instruments tended to rise or fall in psychological patterns, Joe elaborated, one could tie the movement of the T-bill market, for example, to the fluctuations of government mortgage bonds or even to the value of the dollar against the deutsche mark. Certain conditions invariably produced identical patterns. All one had to do was wait patiently for what Joe called "certainty periods." To Dean, "It all sounded very interesting and very scientific and very convincing."

His father's friend Dr. Milton Rubini had agreed to help finance the move to Chicago, Joe said, and he had been contacted as well by an investment group from Ohio, which was considering the commitment of as much as two hundred thousand dollars to his trading fund. If Dean and Ben could persuade their parents to contribute as well, his capital base might be sufficient to stake a seat on the exchange.

Shortly after the Labor Day weekend, Joe left for Chicago with his father to establish legal residence in Illinois while preparing for the written test and oral examination he was required to pass in order to be licensed as a trader by the Mercantile Exchange. Two weeks later, Joe called Dean and Ben to give them the address of a house in Glencoe, a suburb on the North Shore, that he and his father and his father's girlfriend Jean had rented. Joe passed the Merc's written test with a perfect mark, and by the time he turned twenty-one, on October 26, had found an exchange seat he could lease for twenty-eight hundred dollars a month. He began trading in the treasury-bill pit on the morning of November 3, 1980, the day before Ronald Reagan's election as president, with seventy-five thousand dollars that Dr. Rubini had sent east, plus fifty thousand from the Ohio group, which indicated it would increase that amount if Joe showed results. His profits were in five figures by the end of his first week, Joe reported. In three months, he had turned an ambitious idea into a fact of life, Dean and Ben marveled. "Happening" was the highest praise you could give anyone on North Campus, and they never had met anyone there half so happening as Joe Gamsky.

When Joe flew back to Los Angeles for Thanksgiving, the boys greeted him with good news and bad news: The bad news was that Ben doubted his parents would agree to put up any of their own money before they saw long-term results. Dean, though, felt certain his own parents, out of their high regard for Joe, would be willing to consider a substantial investment. With Dean's help, Joe prepared an elaborate presentation for the Karnys, producing a series of beautifully drawn graphs that charted his analysis of yield curves in the T-bill market. Joe explained to Shalom, the cautious one, that he had designed a virtually fail-safe investment, a system that tied together four or five overlapping spread positions, creating a cross-indexed calibration of market plays that permitted him to adjust risk to the point of non-existence. Profits, of course, would be shared on a fifty-fifty basis.

Shalom asked for time to think, but Danny was willing to commit $150,000 of her own money immediately. She was investing in a *known* commodity, Joe Gamsky, said Mrs. Karny, who urged her friends to do the same. Among these was Dr. Stanley Blicker, recently retired from his medical practice in Toronto and on the lookout for ways to put his capital to work. Dr. Blicker met with Joe in Los Angeles later that month and was so impressed by the young man that he not only invested $100,000 of his own money but persuaded a pair of Canadian friends to add another $150,000. Dean and Ben decided the time was right to cut their own little corners on the market. Dean put in his entire $4,000 savings, and Ben matched that amount. The Ohio group was tripling their $50,000 investment, Joe said, and Dr. Rubini had upped his ante as well. He would go back to Chicago with a trading account of more than $700,000. With that kind of capital he could hold his ground against even the investment bankers, Joe told Dean and Ben. They would have to deal with him now.

When Joe flew back to Los Angeles for Christmas, his pockets were filled with hundred-dollar bills. He took Dean and Ben to dinner at Trader Vic's, where they dined on lobster and abalone amid the torches and thatched walls of the Polynesian alcove off the Beverly Hilton. Ben was in his glory when Joe handed over the wine list and gave him carte blanche. Dean was anxious to know if their profits were large enough to permit the two of them to get a place of their own. That time was coming, Joe said. In the meantime, he wanted to treat them to a trip back east, between Christmas and New Year's Day. It would be a graduation gift for Dean, who had finished at UCLA a week earlier.

By the way, Joe added, almost offhandedly, as if it were a matter of no great importance, there was something they should probably know: He was no longer Joseph Henry Gamsky. Larry had obtained a name change in California and now was Ryan Hunt. Since he felt a son should have the same surname as his father, Joe had filed parallel papers in Illinois. His legal name at this very moment was Joseph Hunt. The news startled Dean and made Ben slightly giddy: Just like that, Dean asked, a whole new name? It was a remarkably easy thing to accomplish, Joe said, especially in California. Joe looked around the restaurant at the other diners; half the people in here, he said, smiling, probably were somebody else once. Why Hunt? Ben asked. Joe shrugged; his father had chosen it. Already, though, he had discovered certain advantages to the name: Some people on the exchange in Chicago seemed to think he was related to the Hunt brothers of Texas, Herbert and Nelson Bunker. The Hunts had been much in the news lately, ever since that "Silver Tuesday" back in March when they gained control of two-thirds of the world's privately held silver. Joe had been delighted when Nelson Bunker, called before a Senate subcommittee, asserted that he was just like any other ordinary American, concerned about protecting his interests in an uncertain economy. The brothers lost $1.7 billion when the price of silver dropped from fifty to ten dollars an ounce in the panic that had followed their attempt to corner the market. Asked by one senator how he could sustain such a loss, Nelson Bunker answered, "A billion dollars isn't what it used to be." Now those, Joe said, were words to live by.

The day after Christmas, Dean and Ben followed Joe to Chicago. They spent one night at the house in Glencoe, where Joe's father introduced them to his new girlfriend, Jean Clarke. Jean was an impressive addition to the family. An elegant ash blonde, she had been a starlet in the sixties and since that time not only kept up appearances but improved on them slightly. She had the look of a lady who devoted a good two hours out of every day to her toilette and made every second count. Larry—or rather Ryan—told them Jean had been married to the comedian-turned-agent Marty Ingels, who now was married to the actress Shirley Jones. The satisfaction his father took in dropping these names seemed to amuse Joe. Ryan Hunt would make the world forget there ever had been a Larry Gamsky, he said.

Dean and Ben flew with Joe from O'Hare to Kennedy. In New York, Joe paid cash for a suite at the Plaza. They spent three days steeping in the savor of money, sipping four-dollar glasses of orange juice in the Oak Bar, ordering hot chocolates from tables on the rail above the ice rink at Rockefeller Center. Joe had Brad Reifler's New York number and called to invite him out for an evening on the town with them. Brad was trading commodities himself these days. His stepuncle, Refco's chairman, had offered him a desk and a phone in the firm's Manhattan office if he could raise one hundred thousand dollars to trade. Brad went calling on his old tennis partners, among them the producer Irwin Winkler (*Rocky*) and former MGM president Freddy Fields, until he put together a financial portfolio. His fund had fallen promptly to less than fifty thousand dollars, but was back up to more than twice its original worth now, so he was feeling fairly flush when Joe called.

Brad told Joe that Bob Beyer was in town, too, staying with his family at their apartment in the Pierre Hotel. Joe rented two limousines for the evening. At dinner, Joe "was full of stories about all the big deals and the money he was making," Brad recalled. "He told us, 'I was hungrier than everyone else. That's why I've gotten to where I've gotten.'" As a tribute to his success, Bob and Brad decided to let Joe pick up the tab. "It was such a trip and such a treat for him not to flinch at that," Bob recalled. "We went and drank some champagne and went to the late-night clubs, and all of a sudden it became apparent that Joe was not bitter anymore, that he felt comfortable at your social level. It was really a thrill."

There was a disconcerting moment, however, at the bar in Xenon's. Joe had been standing back from the club scene, aloof behind his mineral water and his roll of hundreds. Suddenly, though, he stepped up to the most beautiful girl at the bar and asked her to dance. When she said no, Joe stared at the girl so hard she crossed her arms to cover her cleavage, then he asked— "absolutely straight," Brad recalled—"Does that mean I don't get my blow job later?" Bob and Brad, not the most sensitive of souls, shared a shiver. Joe's voice had been cold like the cold of deep space, as if in an instant he had put such distance between himself and the girl that she actually disappeared from his sight. "He was scary for a second there," Brad remembered. "But when he turned around, he was smiling."

A few days after their return to Los Angeles, Dean and Ben called Joe to ask if they might withdraw the money from their accounts to make down payments on the Porsches they had been pricing. A minute passed before Joe answered: "I'm still driving the Le Sabre I took back to Chicago in September. It's a little early to ask for something that I'm not even willing to give myself, don't you think?" The inability to delay gratification was the hallmark of the nine-to-fiver, the also-ran, Joe said. If that was how Dean and Ben saw themselves, he needed to know now, before going further. "I felt scolded," Dean recalled.

Joe had happy news when he called the Karny house a few days later, though, informing Dean, and Ben as well, that he had placed their money in a long term T-bill position where his present yield curve projected profits of 30 percent per month. Delighted, Dean was reluctant to remind Joe that his parents still were waiting for the brokerage statements on their account. Those would be in the mail by the end of the month, Joe promised.

When Joe flew into Los Angeles for Valentine's Day, he distributed profits to Dean and Ben in the form of a shopping spree, buying them silk sweaters and linen slacks. He even let himself be persuaded to inspect the townhouse Dean and Ben had found on Spaulding Drive in Beverly Hills. It was expensive, they admitted, but at 30 percent per month their share of profits would cover the cost. They pressed for permission to sign a lease. Joe warned he would not be able to send them money until he distributed profits at the end of the month. When Ben volunteered to sell his old Porsche, though, and use the money to cover their move-in costs, Joe gave in. "Nice place you have here," he said.

Joe called from Chicago a week later and said he had been wrong: The account where he held their money would not yield 30 percent this month; it would yield 40. A week into March, though, Dean and Ben were waiting for their checks. The Karnys complained they still hadn't received the statements they had asked for. It took a day or two to get Joe on the phone. He was using their money, Joe said, to hold positions that were yielding unexpected profits. The brokerage statements had been sent off a week earlier, and he couldn't imagine why they hadn't arrived. He would ask his clearing firm to prepare a second set of papers, just in case. He could send Dean and Ben twenty thousand tomorrow if they wished to cash out their position, Joe said, though he wouldn't recommend that, since the spread he had put on for them continued to yield substantial profits. "I guess we're impatient," Dean said. "I guess so," Joe agreed.

Over the next two weeks, though, Joe would become "difficult to contact," as Dean recalled it. He and Ben left messages on the answering machine at the Glencoe house, but their calls were never returned. Then the answering machine was turned off, and few days after that, the phone was disconnected.

Finally, one morning in early April, Joe called from a pay phone in the Chicago Ritz-Carlton. "He said he had lost all the money he had made," Dean recalled, "about fourteen million dollars."

2

JOE HAD BEEN ON THE FLOOR OF THE EXCHANGE ONLY A FEW DAYS BEFORE THE other members began speculating among themselves about this latest wunderkind's system. He stood out at first by standing up, literally head and shoulders above his competition in the trading floor's new hot box, the treasury-bill pit. He had just turned twenty-one and looked younger, with his pale ardent face serving up those dark omnivorous eyes, yet spent money like someone whose future was a blank check.

Most independent members of the Chicago Mercantile Exchange—"local traders" they were called—survived by "scalping," slipping into gaps created by the money management policies of the big financial institutions, betting mostly "ticks," playing off 5 percent pieces of contracts against incremental movements in market prices. The whole idea was to bid against the bankers, but carefully—"sort of coax them into the right price" was how Joe's trading partner in the T-bill pit, Richard Duran, put it—then sell your accumulated inventory at a tidy profit.

Only awareness of danger, though, made success possible for scalpers, because the banks could turn on a local trader at any time and bury him beneath their overwhelming capital reserves. The Merc's heroes, however, weren't its six-figure-a-year survivors but rather that handful of wildcatting independents who accumulated the combination of cash and courage that enabled them to play a strong hand to the hilt—"bet your left nut," as they said on the trading floor. Richard Dennis had done it: Arriving at the Merc as a teenage runner out of the South Side, Dennis leased his seat on the exchange at age twenty-one with sixteen hundred dollars borrowed from his parents and ten years later was taking in twenty million dollars per year through his C & D Commodities.

This Joe Gamsky from California looked a lot like Dennis from a distance—young, brilliant, fiercely daring, and set upon the kind of course that left a legend in its wake. Joe had come through the door buying and selling whole contracts, each with a face value of $1 million. The margin on T-bills permitted a trader to purchase the option on a contract with as little as $5,000 in cash, but along with that control came an obligation on the remaining $995,000. To well and truly inventory a position meant taking on at least thirty contracts in a given month, and the balance due on a buy that size tended to break the nerve of anyone unable to shrug off the loss of a few hundred thousand in an afternoon.

His sense of proportion was what immediately impressed people about Joe: When he liked a position, he took all of it he could get. "He would come into the pit and ask, 'What's your December six bid?'" recalled Duran. "And somebody would say, 'How many you want?' Anybody else, it would be twenty contracts, max. Joe would say, 'Oh, a hundred, two hundred— how many you got?'" The nonchalance of him was unnerving, and so was that small fixed smile, just this side of smug. "People were pretty much in awe of him," Duran remembered. "Guys would come into the pits, see him do something like this, and they'd say, 'Who is that guy?'"

It was a question Joe kept them asking. Even in the crowded and clamorous T-bill pit, he had found a small pond where he could be a big fish. Joe traded mostly in deferred months, buying options on contracts that wouldn't come to term for a year or two, selling them off as the time grew near. It wasn't a game many local traders wanted to play; there was no way to get quickly in and quickly out or to curb risk by betting red spreads. "It takes big balls to do it right," Duran said. "You have to wait out some scary swings in the market. A guy who will panic loses his ass every time."

Joe won over doubters with his willingness to balance another trader's front-market play by picking up the long-position option. This endeared him especially to the brokers, who were deluged daily with requests for back-market protection. Joe's air of magnanimity also was impressive. He refused to quibble. Never once could anyone recall Joe pushing an out-trade dispute into one of those futile arbitrations that inevitably resulted in a fifty-fifty split. Joe always accepted the other trader's accounting, even if it meant absorbing a shared loss entirely on his own.

He made himself the Merc's young man of the moment, swept into town on the currents of the born-again bravado that attended Ronald Reagan's election to his first term as president. On the trading floor of the Merc, there was a palpable yearning for deliverance from the bleak epoch of circumspection that had been upon the land at least as far back as Nixon's "PEACE WITH HONOR" pledges. During the past year, signs of America's economic decline had become fodder for the front pages of every major newspaper in the country. GM, Ford, and Chrysler reported third-quarter losses in excess of $1.5 billion, and a Detroit entrepreneur made a small fortune by charging citizens a dollar for a swing of the sledgehammer with which more than fifteen thousand of them demolished a Toyota Corolla.

In Southern California, 1980 had brought the summer of the pyramid-scheme frenzy. Out in the San Fernando Valley, Victory Boulevard was bright with the orange vans that transported players to warehouses where they assembled in groups of thirty-two to pledge their faith in a creed they called "Prosperity Consciousness." Each pyramid member put in one thousand dollars and half the total—sixteen thousand—went to the person at the top of the edifice, the one who bought in first. Its promoters pitched the pyramid as the economy's first perpetual-motion machine, a perfectly sanitary system in which the sole product was confidence and the only raw material needed was an unlimited supply of like-minded folk.

Ronald Reagan's presidential campaign was a tonic to those who talked in terms of restoring order and getting back to basics. When Reagan swept into office in November his electoral college margin was ten to one, and Jimmy Carter became the first elected incumbent to lose the presidency since Herbert Hoover had received the bill for the Great Depression.

"We are not, as some would have us believe, doomed to an inevitable decline," Reagan assured the nation during his inaugural speech. The inaugural event itself was an aggressive display of conspicuous consumption, budgeted at eight million dollars, with eight hundred thousand of that going for a laser-light and fireworks display that reduced Jimmy Carter to tears. The capper, though, came forty-one minutes after Reagan's speech, when the Iranians put those Americans who had been held hostage in Teheran for fourteen months now aboard a plane en route to Washington.

In Los Angeles, directors of the Harvard School were delighted, observing that three of the school's recent commencement speakers had played important roles in the day's events: Warren Christopher ('77) had negotiated the hostage release in Algiers, while Johnny Carson ('78) served as emcee at the inaugural ball, where guest of honor and Harvard School class of '76 speaker Reagan was serenaded by the Osmonds' rendition of "Ronnie B. Goode."

The Reagan revolution began the moment the president and his wife moved into the White House, where they reinstated the dress code, resurrected the honor guard, and replaced Thomas Jefferson's portrait in the Cabinet Room with that of Calvin Coolidge.

Reagan's incumbency heralded a new era of enthusiasm and freewheeling on the floor of the Merc. No permutation of the economy was so volatile as the commodities market, and there never had been a commodity so mercurial as those new, purely paper instruments of acquisition called financial futures. By late 1980, the main action and the big money had moved to the markets in Eurodollars, bank certificates of deposit, and, most active of all, treasury bills. The T-bill market created conditions of almost pure liquidity, where even the most microscopic shift in perception was registered instantaneously. Billions changed hands every day, and the fortunes that the most daring traders amassed were astonishing to an old guard who still associated concepts like value with real things.

The Merc was housed then in its 444 West Jackson building, an ugly squat box built of reflecting glass and crisscrossing steel girders out on the edge of the Loop, under the Sears Tower. From outside, it looked like an aquarium built to contain flesh-eating fish. Inside, the trading pits were frenzied during the first months of the Reagan presidency, soaring and tumbling ten points at a time, creating unprecedented potential for profit and loss. On the floor, every exchange member was an auctioneer, and the din approximated that of a pro football game played in an indoor stadium. Their shouts and roars only enhanced the traders' myth that they were the last freebooters, neo-buccaneers on the sea of capital that connected the countries and continents of the modern world. Class and other external distinctions dissolved on the trading floor, where Ph.D.'s on sabbatical stood side by side with tenth-grade dropouts and learned quickly that formal education meant less than nothing in the pits. The traders loved to tell newcomers that the most advanced degree Richard Dennis had obtained was his high school diploma. Character, virtually everyone agreed, was as critical to success as acumen: "The biggest single key to it may be the ability to recognize and admit when you're wrong, then get out quickly," explained Richard Duran. "Because everybody makes bad trades. The guys who prosper are the ones who learn how to cut their losses."

Duran was himself a pure scalper, jumping aboard market movements a beat behind and bailing out "as soon as I feel the wind blowing the other way." He hacked out three hundred thousand a year that way, five times what he had earned as a junior account executive at a New York ad agency. Duran's greatest fear was that he might yet yield to a fatal lapse of discretion, arrive finally at that moment when impulse overrode reason and he held on too long or reached too high, and lost it all. Yet, like all commodity traders, the players in the pits Duran admired most were the ones who took the biggest risks.

Watching the baby-faced boy from California, Joe Gamsky, saunter into the T-bill pit and pull off big play after big play, Duran was convinced this was a guy they all would be whispering about in a year or two. Duran remembered the morning he and Joe had been working side by side when a five-hundred-contract order came up on the board at a price they both sensed was a winner. For Duran, this was an opportunity to be admired from a distance but never approached. A five-hundred-contract order involved a terrifying amount of money, half a billion dollars to be exact. Joe, though, didn't think the chance could be missed. "He was moving toward it and backing off, moving toward it and backing off," Duran recalled. "Finally he comes to me and says, 'If I take three hundred, will you take two hundred?' I say, 'No, that's too much for me.' And he says, 'Okay, how about if I take four hundred and you take one hundred?' I said, 'Done.'" Within minutes the order was a big winner, to the tune of forty thousand dollars, and Duran was ecstatic. "Joe turns to me and he says, 'Do you want more of these?' I said, 'No, you put your ass on the line, they're yours.' He says, 'Well, if you change your mind, let me know.' It was hard not to be impressed by shit like that."

Joe kept his distance from the Merc's mainstream, though. For friends he chose people like David Tempkin, the spacy math genius who wanted to be a concert pianist and financed his ambition by trading in the T-bill pit, coming and going at odd intervals, arriving long enough to make a hit or two, then disappearing for days. Joe also made friends with the Merc's resident mavericks, the Crawford brothers, Andy and Sam. The Crawfords thrived on a sense of outrage and regularly challenged any form of preferential treatment for big traders, castigating brownnosers publicly. Neither brother wanted help from anyone, which made it all the more interesting when Sam allowed Joe Gamsky to bail him out of a dicey situation. This was right after Sam's wife gave birth to their first child; the elder Crawford brother had been on the bad end of an out-trade that left him looking at a thirty-thousand-dollar loss in a month when he didn't have a lot of cash on hand. Joe stepped in, took the positions himself, playing what appeared a sure losing hand, and "Sam was loyal as hell to Gamsky after that," one trader would recall. "Joe liked to rescue people, save them from themselves," his out-trade clerk at the KNS clearinghouse, Leslie Eto, observed.

Joe remained closemouthed, however, in regard to his own background. About the only socializing he did with the other traders was an occasional late lunch after the market's closing, and even then "it was always in a crowd of three or four; he never wanted to be alone with you," Duran remembered.

The other local traders assumed Joe was playing with his own money, though where it came from remained a subject of speculation. All they knew for sure was that Joe always was flying off to L.A. for the weekend to attend to his "other affairs." It was rather disconcerting for some when—two or three months after he stepped into the T-bill pit—Joe changed his last name from Gamsky to Hunt. By then there was a rumor going around that the shaggy, distracted-looking, vaguely handsome middle-aged man who turned up on the trading floor occasionally in a runner's jacket with a JOE HUNT, TRADER badge on the lapel was Joe's father.

One of the few who could confirm this was Leslie Eto, whom Joe had hired away from KNS to work as his personal out-trade clerk. He introduced his father, Ryan, as "a retired psychologist," Eto recalled. A number of times she had seen his father pull Joe aside, whispering urgently into the son's ear, after which Joe would speak to the older man in a soothing voice, as if comforting a frightened child. Joe spoke also of a brother and a sister back in California but mentioned his mother only once, Eto recalled, when he said his parents were divorced.

Early in the spring of 1981, the new rumor on the trading floor was that Joe had suffered a huge loss. The KNS Risk Manager, never among his fans, reportedly had imposed a margin call that resulted in the liquidation of all Joe's positions. Talk was of a loss in the area of a million dollars. "He got stubborn" was Duran's appraisal. Joe had jumped aboard a surge in the credit markets created by a heavy flow of money during Jimmy Carter's last year in the White House. When Reagan took office, however, the money supply was squeezed to counter inflation, and interest rates inevitably fell. Joe argued the new conditions were temporary and was right about that, but hadn't maintained the kind of cash reserve that would enable him to wait out the transitional period. When the KNS margin call came, he couldn't meet it and lost every cent in his accounts there.

Within the week, the compliance department auditors were working the trading floor, asking a lot of questions about Joe's methods and practices. This incursion into his affairs generated considerable sympathy for Joe among the local traders; those compliance spooks were always trying to stick it to some poor schmuck who gave them a bookkeeping problem. The feeling on the floor was that Joe probably had overplayed his hand, but hell, everybody did that at least once. "The other traders in the T-bill pit were contemptuous toward us," recalled one compliance auditor. "They kept asking, 'Haven't you guys got anything better to do?'"

He had been set upon by "strong and malicious forces," Joe explained to Dean and Ben, when he finally returned their calls in early April, just as the Dow-Jones was hitting its highest mark since Nixon's resignation six years earlier. His trading theories had been validated in every respect, Joe said; unfortunately he had failed to account for the political dynamic. No matter how high trading took the numbers, commodities remained a zero-sum game, which meant that for one player to win, another had to lose. "Because he was so able and quick to take advantage of any opportunities, Joe made enemies," as Dean understood it. He had committed himself to a large inventory behind a sure winner, Joe said, when two of the most powerful brokerage houses on the exchange threw the weight of their cash reserves behind a position counter to his own. Both these firms had been "stung" by a maneuver he had executed only a few days earlier, Joe explained. The new play the firms put on was ludicrous on its face, he said, but they held steady even as their losses mounted. He realized the intention was to squeeze him out, and he met margin call after margin call, Joe said, hoping to raise the price of his ruin to a point where it would be sheer folly for the other side to continue, but these brokers had been relentless, and eventually his cash reserves were exhausted. It meant the total liquidation of his own positions; fourteen million dollars was a conservative estimate of the loss.

Joe flew back to Los Angeles a few days later, lifting out of the muddy slush along the runways at O'Hare into a cloud cover from which he descended three hours later to the arena of pink-and-brown-tinted sunlight at LAX. A taxi took him straight to Outpost Drive. He wanted to look Shalom and Danny in the eye, Joe said, when he told the Karnys he had more confidence than ever in his trading approach, that in fact he regarded his failure as a form of affirmation. It was only the politics of petty malice for which he had been unprepared, and now he understood; a young person of ability must keep the noise down, win quietly, disguise his success rather than revel in it. There was an element of strategy that had to do more with appearances and egos than with anything of substance. He wanted the Karnys to be assured of two things, Joe said: One, he had other investor funds in accounts where he was earning 20 percent a month and intended to reinvest his own share of the profits on behalf of Dean and his parents; two, he would think of the money Shalom and Danny had given him as a loan, to be repaid with interest. He came prepared with a note, which Danny refused to accept. Joe's word was enough.

Dean was awed by how easily and effectively Joe had assuaged his parents. He never would be able to explain it, but somehow Joe made catastrophe seem a minor setback, an insignificant digression from the great task he had set for himself. As if to demonstrate the degree of his conviction, Joe treated Dean and Ben to an expensive meal the next night, urging them to invite friends if they liked. It was an occasion to celebrate the knowledge he had won rather than mourn the money he had lost, Joe said.

Dean and Ben both brought dates to dinner, as did their friend Ronald Pardovitch and Dean's North Campus pal Mickey Fine. Joe sat at the head of the table, the only boy without a girl, addressing the others like some warrior-philosopher fresh from the front lines of the Trading Floor War. Joe did not attempt to conceal the magnitude of his recent loss from anyone, Dean recalled, instead using it as evidence of his own effectiveness. Why else would such powerful persons lay siege to a young man less than half their age? What they did not know was that he had come away stronger than ever, Joe said, because now he understood for all time that rules were merely suggestions, guidelines to follow until you found your own way. Everyone worked in the dark on the exchange. At any given moment, no trader could say for sure how any of the others stood. Buys and sells were like the raises in some immense poker game where the only chips you saw were the ones in the pot. Time and time again, Joe said, you watched the highest fliers teetering on the brink, financing a buy here with a sell there, stacking their trades in great structures so intricate that they were impenetrable from outside, then unloading all at once, just in time to meet a margin call, leaving everyone around them wondering whether what they had just witnessed was a power play or a bluff. The perfect justice of the exchange was that only those who made bad bets were caught cheating. Real success, Joe observed, was achieved only by those daring enough to "step outside normal procedures." Regulations withered in that cool, dry atmosphere where great fortunes accumulated. At such altitudes, one simply "channeled resources" to achieve "effective utilization."

Alone with Ben and Dean, though, Joe had more bad news: His cash flow was too tight to continue paying rent on the Beverly Hills condo; they would have to be out by the first of June. Ben went back home to live with his parents. Dean moved out to Encino to take up residence in the model unit of a condominium complex his father had converted. He was just starting law school at Whittier's Hancock Park campus. Instead of the library, though, Dean did most of his studying in the condo, between the tours he gave prospective buyers. "Ben and I were kind of wavering in our faith," he recalled, but "somehow Joe convinced us . . . that these things happen when you are trying to achieve something of great magnitude."

The investigation had opened with a phone call from a woman named Lorraine Stitzlein in Akron, Ohio. It was a simple inquiry, really: The caller wanted to confirm that there was a member of the Mercantile Exchange named Joseph Gamsky.

It was the first time Tom Utrata, the compliance department's manager, had heard the name. A few phone calls to the trading floor filled Utrata in on the legend of the boy wonder who had pulled off a series of spectacular plays in back-market T-bills. The only disquieting note was the name change to Hunt and the rumor that he was somehow connected to the notorious Nelson Bunker and his brother Herbert.

The Ohio woman called back a week later. This time she was more specific about her concern: It seemed that Stitzlein and the investment group she represented, Rainbow Inc., had given Joe a sum of money in excess of one hundred thousand dollars to trade in the commodities market. "She just wanted to make sure the money was being traded as Joe had said it would be," Utrata recalled. "She knew he was a very fine young man. There was certainly no accusation." When he took another look in the files, though, Utrata found that Gamsky was not registered as a broker, meaning he had no authorization to trade an investor's money. As a precaution, Utrata shot a memo upstairs to his supervisor, John Troelstrup, the Merc's top lawyer, who worked under the title of vice president for law and compliance.

Now Joe had a problem. Troelstrup was a stickler. A rangy, straw-haired West Virginian whose severity was softened only by a faint Appalachian accent, the attorney projected the persona of a coal miner's son risen to CEO. Relaxed on the surface, he was relentless underneath, a proctor of rectitude whose nature left him little tolerance for loose ends. It was the name change to Hunt, combined with the rumor of a connection to the Texas billionaires, that initially intrigued Troelstrup. Back in the early seventies, as regional counsel for the Commodity Futures Trading Commission, Troelstrup had prosecuted the Hunts for forming illegal soybean consortiums, putting a million bushels each in the names of family members in order to accumulate what they needed to manipulate the market.

After reading the Utrata memo, Troelstrup sent one of his staff downstairs to check the accounts of this Gamsky-cum-Hunt. The records showed Joe had been trading big numbers, all right, but not nearly so successfully as it seemed to those who watched him in the T-bill pit. After some early success, Hunt had committed himself to a long-term position that was a loser from the first day he took it and by February of 1981 was eight hundred thousand dollars in the hole. Since that time, he had been in a holding pattern, maintaining his positions by depositing new funds to cover the margins but adding virtually nothing to his inventory. "It looked like his purpose wasn't to go down there to make money so much as to go down there to make a name for himself," one of Troelstrup's aides observed.

At that point, Joe might have skated to safety with little more than a slap on the wrist and a small fine. The allure of the thin ice around Troelstrup was too tempting, though, and Joe compounded his problems considerably a few days later when he paid an unannounced visit to the attorney's office. Hunt's presumption didn't bother Troelstrup; most traders—and nearly all the good ones—were arrogant. As for a twenty-one-year-old trading hundreds of thousands of dollars in the commodities market, Troelstrup had seen that, too, more than once. What set Joe apart was a peculiar shiny-eyed opacity: he was utterly unreadable except on the surface, as if beneath that lay a system of psychic self-defense so elaborate it could not be breached from anywhere but within. He understood that the compliance department had been looking at his accounts, Joe began, and wondered if Mr. Troelstrup might tell him why. Troelstrup replied that there had been "inquiries" about his trading customer money. "Has there been a complaint?" Joe asked. "No," Troelstrup said.

Better for Joe by far if he had ended the conversation there; instead he tried to impress the older man, telling Troelstrup how he had become the youngest CPA in the country, grown bored with that, then developed his theory of trading T-bills in the back markets. "He seemed to want very badly to convince me he knew what he was doing," Troelstrup recalled. Later in the conversation, though, Joe referred to himself not as a CPA, but as an "accountant." "Are you a CPA or an accountant?" asked Troelstrup, one of a handful of people on the exchange who would know the difference. Joe sat stammering for a moment—it was almost as if the question wouldn't register, Troelstrup remembered—then explained that while he had been the youngest person in the country to pass the CPA exam, he hadn't wanted to spend three full years working as an accountant, and so had failed to meet the CPA requirements. He wasn't bothered by the answer, Troelstrup said, so much as the way Joe arrived at it. "It seemed less an attempt to cover up than to readjust his own mind before he answered," the lawyer explained. "I almost had the feeling Joe was lying but didn't know it."

At his next weekly staff meeting, Troelstrup personally placed "the Gamsky matter" on the table. There was a pattern here, the attorney said: The young man who tells you more than you want to know, who contradicts himself without recognizing it, who convinces himself of the lie before he tells it. "Check him out," Troelstrup told Ed Donlan, a young law student on his staff. "Start with the name change." That was easy enough. Donlan walked across the Loop to the Cook County Courthouse, where records showed that in February of 1981, Joseph Henry Gamsky, age twenty-one, had filed for a legal change of his name to Joseph Hunt, submitting an affidavit asserting that he had been a resident of Illinois for the past year. Joe told Donlan, though, that he had moved to Chicago in October of 1980, about five months before the affidavit was signed.

Donlan brought a copy of the court records to Troelstrup, who summoned Joe to his office. "It rattled him," Troelstrup recalled, "the fact that someone had followed up on something he said. He wanted to know what I was going to do with this information. I said, 'You're a liar and I can prove you're a liar. That's all I want to do with it.' He seemed puzzled by this."

"Ask him if he's a CPA," Troelstrup told Donlan. Joe's story was congruent this time: He explained to Donlan that he had been on an accelerated program, passing the CPA exam after high school—at eighteen, the youngest person ever to do so—then graduating from USC in less than two years. He had worked as an accountant for only about the same period of time, Joe said, before leaving to trade commodities and for that reason never quite completed his requirements for a CPA certification. "He gave a very elaborate and detailed description of his employment history and of his experience as a trader," Donlan recalled, "and it all fit together, except you had to wonder how anyone who was only twenty-one years old could have done all this." Just checking, Donlan called the registrar's office at USC. A Joseph Henry Gamsky had attended the university, he was told, but the student had dropped out after the first semester of his sophomore year and never returned.

As Donlan picked his way through Hunt's story, placing calls to the various companies where Joe said he had worked or traded, the discrepancies mounted. Investigating Joe became a formal exercise: the third-year law student was taking trial practice that semester and found Hunt the ideal subject for honing his interview skills. "He told lies about little things, meaningless things," Donlan recalled. "It wasn't like he was trying to dupe you into some big hoax, it was just that he couldn't tell the truth about anything, almost like a matter of principle, or reverse principle."

Joe's area of exposure, the suspicion that he had been trading commodities as an unlicensed broker, could have been resolved quite simply, Tom Utrata thought, "analyzed as a technical misunderstanding that we're going to clear up and correct. But when we found his answers to even the preliminary questions to be false, the process snowballed."

Lorraine Stitzlein continued to call the compliance department from Ohio, seeking verification that the money she had given Joe was being traded on the exchange. She was, Stitzlein said, secretary-treasurer at Rainbow, a one-time promotional enterprise that had grown into a diversified investment group that put its money into everything from Broadway shows to blue-chip stocks. She had met Joe in Los Angeles, where his father worked as a therapist in the office of a psychiatrist who was treating the daughter of a dear friend for bulimia. The treatment was expensive, some might say unorthodox, involving hypnosis and psychotropic drugs, but the girl had improved, and as far as she was concerned Joe's father was a brilliant man. She had been introduced to the son one afternoon in the doctor's office. Joe said he was a commodities trader and was applying for a seat on the Mercantile Exchange in Chicago. She found the young man utterly charming and quite attractive. "I told Joe that if he got on the exchange, I would give him some money to invest in the commodities market," Stitzlein recalled, "because I'd never been in that, and I was willing to take a whirl."

After Joe moved to Chicago, he came down to Akron for a meeting with Mrs. Stitzlein, who asked everybody to call her Rainy, and the other partners in Rainbow Inc. She personally had signed a check to Joe for $125,000, Rainy said, upon which he promised a modest monthly return. A few weeks later, Joe said Rainbow's account was doing better than expected but the monthly payments were a short-term problem because he could not withdraw funds without liquidating profitable positions.

Even after Troelstrup told Stitzlein he believed Rainbow's money had been invested in an account at KNS under the name Joseph Hunt and that the account was a heavy loser, the Ohio woman remained reluctant to criticize Joe. "I'm sure he can explain all this," Rainy said. Stitzlein paid her first visit to the compliance department a few days later, accompanied by Eddie Elias, who was the senior partner in Rainbow Inc. as well as president of the Professional Bowlers Association. Elias was a big, bluff man who seemed to go soft on the subject of Joe Hunt. "Choey is a good boy," Elias told Troelstrup and Donlan. "I feel like a father to that boy."

Stitzlein and Elias had not come to Chicago to make a complaint. What they wanted, in fact, wasn't clear. It seemed to Donlan as if the two were more interested in pressuring Joe to account for the money than in seeing him prosecuted. Stitzlein said Joe had sent her trading statements that showed Rainbow was making a substantial profit on its investment. Troelstrup asked to see copies of the statements. When the sheaf of documents arrived at his office a week later, he was amused and appalled in equal parts. "It was obvious Hunt had turned them out on his Apple computer," the attorney recalled. "They were totally fraudulent."

With the trading statements in hand, Troelstrup authorized a formal investigation. Donlan remained on the case, assigned to trace the origins of the money Joe had poured into his account at KNS. Joe, though, refused to provide specific details. "He hinted in very broad terms that he had a network of associates and friends and he could make money appear in his account at will," Donlan recalled. Donlan heard vague references to a psychiatrist in Los Angeles, a surgeon in Florida, some people in Canada. "Give me one name," Donlan said. "All right," Joe answered. "Danielle Karny."

When Donlan followed this lead to Los Angeles, he found Mrs. Karny indignant: "It was 'Who are you to question Joe Hunt?' Joe was a brilliant boy, a fine person. She was very protective of him."

Utrata complained that his auditors were being "accosted" by Merc members on the trading floor. "There were department heads and administrators who defended him," Utrata explained, "saying things like 'Gee, this is a bright guy. Get him involved in committees, groom him for something.'" There even were traders who said they had given Joe money out of their own accounts to trade for them. When he went into the T-bill pit, Utrata said, "I would take somebody else along just so I wouldn't find myself taking up a collection for poor Joe."

Troelstrup, though, continued to press the investigation. Donlan and Utrata were confused by the attorney's fixation on Joe; they each had seen cases involving far larger sums disposed of with a ten-day suspension. At the attorney's direction, however, Donlan continued to shadow Joe, even visiting him at home in Glencoe, where they whiled away hours talking about Joe's fascination with the film *Deathtrap*. He had seen it a dozen times, Joe said, savoring the contrived plot's elaboration of double cross, one-upsmanship, and hidden meaning. As in life, he observed, nothing was what it seemed.

Surface appearances and underlying principles were converging on Joe, however. When Rainy Stitzlein next visited Troelstrup's office, she brought a tape recording of a phone conversation in which Joe assured her the positions where he had placed Rainbow's investment were performing splendidly. Troelstrup chose that moment to show Stitzlein the account statements from KNS, proving that the money there had been lost to the last penny. Stitzlein immediately filed a claim with the exchange, alleging that Joe had taken Rainbow's money under false pretenses. A customer arbitration was calendared for the end of the year. In the meantime, Troelstrup was bringing Joe before the Merc's business conduct committee, alleging that Hunt had refused to provide the compliance department with financial documents needed as evidence.

Some members of the committee were quite sympathetic to Joe, Utrata recalled: "Seeing someone so young, who showed at least the surface signs of being well spoken and well connected, it looked like somebody just getting off on the wrong foot, and they were troubled that this thing was growing into such a massive affair." Since prosecuting Joe for an illegal pooling of funds was outside his purview, Troelstrup had alleged fraudulent intent, asserting that Joe was converting the money from Stitzlein and Elias to his own use.

The seriousness of the charges forced the business conduct committee to rule it could clear up the matter only if Joe produced his financial records. Joe refused to comply, however, pleading the Fifth Amendment. On September 9, 1981, the committee posted a notice on the trading floor announcing that exchange member Joe Hunt had been suspended from trading until he agreed to cooperate with Troelstrup's investigators.

The notice did little to diminish Joe's reputation among other traders. "The compliance department was a pain in the ass for us all," explained Richard Duran, "so in a way you sort of admired Joe for his defiance, because everybody knows they like you to come in with your tail between your legs, that you get treated better that way. But Joe wouldn't do that."

After his suspension, Joe's attempts to create an appearance of co-operation with the committee only contributed to the case against him. He had made most of the money in his KNS account while trading another account at Paine Webber in New York, Joe said. When Donlan called Paine Webber, though, none of the brokers he spoke to could find any record of such an account. Troelstrup asked for an account statement. The papers Joe produced appeared to be authentic, "but we were still getting negative information from Paine Webber," Troelstrup recalled. Finally, Joe gave Donlan the name and phone number of a Paine Webber broker who had handled his account. The man would be in his office at 1 P.M. on Friday, Joe said, and was expecting Donlan's call. When Donlan dialed the Paine Webber number, his call indeed was answered by a man who confirmed that Joe had traded an account there on which his profits exceeded half a million dollars. Troelstrup, skeptical, told Donlan to phone the broker back. When he called New York this time, the phone rang for more than a minute, Donlan recalled, before it was answered by a janitor who said he was speaking from a pay phone in the basement of the Paine Webber building on Water Street.

As Troelstrup prepared for the customer arbitration, he began to push for a larger investigation, one that would involve federal agencies such as the Securities and Exchange Commission (SEC). It was during this time that Joe, always unannounced, began stopping by Troelstrup's office in the late afternoons. "He was offering me an opportunity to see the light, I think," the attorney recalled. "At first it was 'You're an important man, Mr. Troelstrup'—he always took the trouble to pronounce the name—'you have important things to do and you shouldn't be bothered with something as trivial as this.' I felt Joe saw me as an obstacle, and he seemed to have no doubt he could bowl me over. At first he seemed to think he could do it with charm, then with intelligence, and finally with intimidation." Joe's threats were subtle, usually parenthetical suggestions that "he had contacts beyond the range of my knowledge," Troelstrup remembered.

When Donlan and the other investigators confronted him with the contradictions in his story, Joe continued to insist they had misunderstood. "He would laugh at us," Donlan recalled. "He would say we had the wrong number or the wrong department or the wrong office." Alone with Troelstrup, though, Joe denied nothing. "Instead he would always say, 'You'll never prove it,'" the lawyer recalled. "I think he enjoyed the match of wits. Absolutely loved it. He just loved risk. That was one of the things that made him very comfortable trading large amounts of money at his age.

He seemed to me relatively immune to the normal fears that risk causes in most people. To him, it was a challenge."

The customer arbitration was played out in December before seven committee members who referred to it later as "the Psychodrama." "Usually, by the time they get to arbitration, customers who make a claim are ready for a knock-down-drag-out fight. They want to humiliate their opponent. But that wasn't the case here," Utrata recalled. "Elias and Stitzlein acted like at any point in time this could all be resolved, so they kept interjecting these personal pleadings. Elias kept talking about if only 'Choey' would do this, or admit that, or promise something else."

The claimants' conduct was ironic, considering that Joe's defense rested upon his contention that Stitzlein and Elias were con artists who had swindled their own investors and were attempting to make him the fall guy. Elias, whose size, swagger, and booming baritone made him an initally imposing figure, grew plaintive, even abject, as the proceedings dragged on. "He would say, 'Oh Choey, that's not what happened,' like it was breaking his heart," Donlan recalled. "'Oh Choey, I was like a father to you.'"

Inevitably, the cover-up damaged the defendant more than the crime itself. The fraudulent account statements, the tape-recorded phone conversation with Stitzlein, and the ruse at Paine Webber all proved devastating. A week before Christmas, the committee awarded Stitzlein the entire $125,000 she had invested, adding to this the maximum punishment of revoking Joe's Merc membership until the debt had been paid. The committee then announced it would be sending its findings to the board of governors, with a recommendation that a special hearing committee be formed to deal with Joe. Even Donlan and Utrata were taken aback by this development. Special hearing committees were formed at the rate of about one every two years, usually for the purpose of addressing some massive misconduct involving a number of traders or brokers and extraordinary amounts of money.

The day the business conduct committee posted its ruling, Joe told Leslie Eto he was going back to Los Angeles for Christmas. "He said I should take a vacation and we'd meet again in two weeks," Eto recalled. "He was sure this could all be cleared up."

They had agreed to meet at Lake Tahoe on the evening of the winter solstice, Dean remembered. Joe would fly in from Chicago, while he and Ben drove up from Los Angeles with a spare set of skis.

Dean left L.A. in pitiful shape. For most of the past year he had been dating his first serious girlfriend, Claudia Stillman. Wooing and winning

Claudia was the first accomplishment in his life that validated him as "a unique individual," Dean explained, whole and separate from his parents, less their boy than his own man. Ever since he'd started law school in August, though, Claudia had been slipping away. It was cruelly ironic, really; Dean had selected a second-rate school like Whittier precisely because its less demanding curriculum would leave him more time for his girlfriend. When she returned to UCLA without him in September, though, Claudia began failing to return the messages he left on her machine until the next morning, then told him she couldn't see him that night either, since she already had a date to meet "friends" for dinner. Desperate, Dean proposed marriage on Thanksgiving Day. Claudia answered that she wasn't ready to make that kind of commitment, then announced she no longer wanted to see Dean, even as friends. The rejection devastated Dean. His stomach, always weak—it was the reason he could never gain weight—became much worse. The bile began to gurgle like some subterranean geyser. He could actually hear it when he was awake, which was all the time now. He was throwing up at least once a day. Pale and sickly, so gaunt that his skull showed at his temples, Dean barely could make himself go out at night. He and Claudia went to all the same places, and every time he saw her in a bar or club, he would end up on his knees in the men's room toilet.

From that unpleasant perspective, Dean embraced with renewed fervor the idea of belonging to this elite group of bright and ambitious young men Joe envisioned. When Joe and Ben proposed the trip to Tahoe, it was Dean who suggested bringing along Mickey Fine and Ron Pardovitch. Mickey was a go-getter with a *GQ* wardrobe, set to follow Dean to Whittier Law after graduation from UCLA. Still an underclassman on the Westwood campus, Ron was a social animal who knew everybody's family history and personal finances. He lived on his cousin's estate in Stone Canyon while working nights as a waiter at the trendiest new nightspot in town, the China Club on Melrose.

At the last minute, Dean invited a third friend, Evan Dicker. Ben actually had known Evan longer, since their sophomore year at Beverly Hills High. At Beverly, as staff photographer for the *Watchtower* newspaper, Evan had served as chief chronicler and court fool to the school's social elite, attending their parties, flattering their vanities, often filling in as escort to some of the prettiest girls in school when they were fighting with their boyfriends. Evan's qualification for this last job was that he would never be a threat. Pale and owlish, he began losing his hair at sixteen and looked as if he was born wearing horn-rims. Six feet two inches tall, Evan carried most of his weight in the hips and thighs even when he dieted down to 160 pounds. He was bright, but his sly and self-deprecating humor went unappreciated by the tennis players who posed for his pictures, then called him "Dick-Head Dicker" behind his back. After high school graduation, though, the scheme of things shifted; more and more people took to observing that Evan was the son and grandson of the senior partners in the Century City law firm of Dicker and Dicker. One of those noticing Evan's new appeal was Ben Dosti, who hooked up with him at UCLA. The shared sensibility of Beverly bonded them in the belief that they already had seen everything once, and when the two began crawling the clubs together, they established themselves as astute observers of the scene, famous for their ability to dissect the regional and economic backgrounds of poseurs who paraded past in the eleven-pound motorcycle boots and leopardskin roachkillers that did nothing to disguise their origins as the sons of plasterers and insurance salesmen from Passaic and Boise.

It was not Ben, however, but rather Claudia Stillman who introduced Evan to Dean. Claudia had been Evan's girlfriend in the fourth grade at Horace Mann, and when he met her at the China Club one night and mentioned that he was interested in tennis lessons, Claudia told him she knew one excellent instructor quite well. He had liked Dean from the first day, Evan recalled. Karny's manners were exquisite, but the best thing about Dean was that he never condescended; once you were accepted as a member of the class, Dean never asked you to prove another thing. During their very first tennis lesson, Dean spoke of this genius, Joe, as both mentor and friend. Evan grew curious, because "Dean and everyone else cast such an air of mystery around Joe."

When Dean invited Evan to join the trip to meet Joe at Tahoe, Dicker accepted. The five of them—Dean, Ben, Mickey, Ron, and Evan—had driven north in the Karny family station wagon through an icy fog that slowed them to second gear as they climbed past the view of Mount Whitney at Lone Pine and crept into the Sierras. There was no new powder at Tahoe, though. That first morning they rode all the way to the top of the lift at Heavenly Valley, where the view of the lake was magnificent but the snow-pack was so thin that they could ski only a couple of hundred yards. After they grew bored, there was nothing to do but play blackjack at Harrah's. Joe arrived from Chicago that afternoon and was a major disappointment for Evan. His clothes were ghastly, his hair shaggy, his manner alternately distracted and imperious. He seemed to Evan almost entirely lacking in the social graces: "I remember thinking Joe was—dorky is too strong a word, and geeky is much too strong—but . . . he was not someone I would have expected Dean and Ben to be friends with."

While the others played blackjack in the casino, Joe wandered into the video arcade, where he set new records at Space Invaders. "He was a kid's dream," Evan recalled, "because he would work the game to the point where he had as many ships as you could possibly get, then he'd grow bored and let whoever was watching take over." The six of them agreed to meet before dinner for a workout in the weight room, where Dean fell to the floor in a dead faint when he attempted the military press. Joe was the only one not to panic, lifting Dean into his arms and carrying him like a bride back to the room, where Karny was revived with cold compresses.

They left Tahoe for Mammoth the next morning. On the drive south, there was a stop for lunch in some hamlet east of Yosemite where downtown was a café with gas pumps. A girl at the next table asked where they were from; when Ben said, "L.A.," the girl didn't know that meant Los Angeles. The girl's friend asked what part of Los Angeles they were from. Evan answered, "Beverly Hills," and then all the girls at the table began asking what movie stars they knew and who their neighbors were. Evan said he lived near Gregory Peck, since his parents' house in the flats south of Wilshire was near the intersection of Gregory Way and Peck Drive. They wasted a couple of hours in the place, goofing on the mountain girls, giggling and giddy as they invented foibles for the rich and famous, all except Joe, who seemed "really not very amused by all this," Evan thought.

At Mammoth they rented a condo where the manager said it had snowed six inches the night before and even the lower runs like Stump Alley were open. Evan and Ben and the others all headed off for the chairlifts that afternoon, but Joe said he would stay with Dean. The two of them were never apart after that. Every day while the others ran the Roller Coaster, Dean and Joe would remain behind to play billiards or take long walks in the snow, "very private, very together," Evan remembered.

Only to Joe could he reveal the "self-esteem problems" that had tormented him since Claudia's rejection of his marriage proposal, Dean explained. Joe responded by attacking the very premises of his friend's supposed inadequacy. He had incorporated into his psyche a fundamentally destructive fallacy, Joe told Dean, the idea that he needed the approval of others to function as a complete person. This was particularly absurd when one considered that the person whose acceptance and admiration he craved was a young girl who drank alcohol to disguise her consumption of quaaludes, a person whose operations were based entirely upon acquired assumptions and inherited ethos. Joe had this theory that "a woman, not so much because of her personal desires but because of her genetic function in the evolutionary scale, has the function of testing a man," Dean explained. This was the essence of the marriage contract conceived millions of years earlier when the first proto-humans climbed down out of the banana trees and ventured onto the plains, a bargain in which the woman promised loyalty in his absence if the man pledged to share proceeds from the hunt. That genetic coding in Claudia merely was filtered through cultural conditioning that equated the hunt with success and status. "I began to feel part of a larger process," Dean recalled, "this vast drama of humanity."

Even if he couldn't grasp all that was said, Dean noticed his distress seemed to abate in Joe's presence, and by the end of the second day his stomach had settled. That night, the six of them met for dinner at a restaurant where the tables were built around open grills so that diners might cook their own steaks. For the first time in weeks Dean was able to eat a full meal and keep it down. Afterward, though, when Ben and Evan and the others went off to drink in the bars, Dean preferred to stay by the fire with Joe, sipping tea.

Most modern women, Claudia included, had been conditioned to focus on what was manifest in the moment, Joe asserted. A young man only a few years older might envelop himself in an aura of accomplishment that was most misleading. Like others of her ilk, Claudia looked past the potential in a person such as Dean. To Joe, Dean's prospects were as obvious as they were unlimited, but that was not important either; all that mattered was Dean's belief. His own studies, Joe said, had persuaded him that the key to personal power passed into the hands of those who "refused to be invalidated by externality." As Sartre had written, "Man can will nothing unless he has first understood that he must count on no one but himself; that he is alone . . . without help, with no other aim than the one he sets for himself, with no other destiny than the one he forges for himself on this earth."

On Christmas Day, Joe rode with Dean in the station wagon back to Los Angeles. Two days later they flew to Florida to meet with Dr. Blicker, the Karny family friend who—with his associates—had invested $250,000 in Joe's trading fund. He had explained the loss at KNS to the doctor by phone, Joe said, and made the same promise he had given the Karnys—that the money would be repaid out of his profits from other accounts. Joe felt he should see Dr. Blicker in person, however, when he suggested that payments might be made more rapidly if he had a larger capital base with which to trade. Between meetings that resulted in the transfer to Joe's trading fund of an additional $50,000, the two young men spent their days at the beach.

Sitting with Dean in the sand, Joe expanded upon their discussions in the snow at Mammoth. He observed that Dean's emotional ache had abated enormously in just a few days. Interesting, was it not, that simply stepping back a bit to look at the small and personal through the larger lens of history could produce such a profound shift in one's feelings? You had to ask yourself how real those feelings had been in the first place. He believed this paradox was the secret of the human condition, Joe said. One must understand that a "reorientation of perspective" could produce an entirely different experience of the very same situation. That, simply, was the essence of what he had come to call Paradox Philosophy, Joe said. It was his belief that every relationship in the world was producible to paradox. Yet this underlying truth went utterly unaccounted in Judeo-Christian doctrine. The moral and ethical code of that system propounded absolutes: dos and don'ts, shoulds and shouldn'ts. Life's lesson, though, was that reality is situational. Even morality was contingent upon circumstances: On the one hand, "THOU SHALT NOT KILL," while on the other hand even homicide could be justified by self-defense or national interest. The only integrity available to a human being was arrived at by the elimination of "internal impediments," Joe asserted. Guilts, taboos and other "societal constraints" all hindered people who had to make practical decisions in the real world. The first step to freedom was "streamlining consciousness," Joe explained, in order to become "more yourself." Only then could one begin to practice Paradox Philosophy in earnest because only then could one place each circumstance in the perspective that most effectively served one's needs. Joe had a motto for Paradox Philosophy: "Black is white, white is black, and all is shades of gray between."

He had come to regard those who unthinkingly adopted traditional values as actually dangerous, Joe said. These people inevitably were bent on encumbering others with their own fears and inhibitions. They not only clung to but also imposed by law and edict their narrow and frightened point of view. He had come to call such persons "Normies," Joe explained. The hidden agenda of Normies was to suck the pure consciousness out of those around them, particularly their own young. If he truly attained to greatness, Dean must understand that his own parents were Normies. Shalom and Danny were fine people, with good intentions, but they also were the agents of their son's destruction, committed to a life within limitations that not only were unnecessary but would constrain him to a degree that robbed Dean of his true nature.

Paradox, therefore, was a path of liberation, Joe explained. The philosophy enabled an individual to find a center of focus, to become one with his purpose. No man ever had accomplished anything of importance without first becoming reconciled completely to his task, eradicating internal impediments entirely, until the only obstacles to progress were those that lay outside himself. "In other words," as Dean understood it, "you wouldn't cause yourself to fail. The only thing that could stop you would be the outside world."

***

In the compliance department, they called Joe's case 432 BILQ, for those sections of Statute 432 he had been formally charged with violating. Joe was acting as his own attorney before the special hearing committee, but his appearances at the exchange were increasingly rare. John Troelstrup assigned Ed Donlan to check out Joe's declaration that he had voluntarily removed himself from the trading floor until he was cleared of all charges. What Donlan found was that Joe's lease on his exchange seat had expired back in October. No longer a member of the Merc, Hunt could not be compelled to answer the charges against him.

He was facing this hearing voluntarily, Joe explained to the committee and intended to prove that Mr. Troelstrup was not so much a prosecutor as a persecutor. Troelstrup, smiling through clenched teeth, suspected it was all a show; if Joe sacrificed his seat on the exchange, he would be free to reapply immediately. The attorney, though, had committed himself to push for the most severe sanction the Merc could impose on a member, formal expulsion.

As had been the case at the customer arbitration, several members of the special committee were extraordinarily sympathetic to Joe, who had just turned twenty-two. There was an unspoken feeling that Troelstrup's zeal had blown the affair out of proportion. Stitzlein and Elias said they not only would repudiate their accusations if Joe repaid them but might consider giving him some of that money to trade on the exchange. None of his other investors would say so much as a word against the young man. Joe's facility for dealing with people one-on-one, Troelstrup noted, was the most impressive thing about him; he seemed almost to have been trained in it. The consensus in the trading pits was that Joe's tribulations had less to do with any infractions than with his defiance of Troelstrup's authority.

Far from the traders on the floor, Troelstrup had ample space within which to keep his own counsel. The attorney's office was in a remote corner of the West Jackson building, abutted by a loading dock and barricaded behind rows of cubicles where the compliance auditors crunched numbers. Most people couldn't even find the place without directions, and upon arrival visitors were intimidated by the long, narrow room's funereal gravity, its twenty-five-foot ceiling, heavily draped windows, and massive mahogany desk. Troelstrup was alone in his office one gray afternoon, just before the special committee hearing, reading a report from Donlan, when he sensed another presence in the room.

The man standing in the doorway was perhaps fifty years old, tall and lanky, disheveled yet handsome in an angular and ascetic sort of way, with a stand of thick, tousled, silvery black curls. Troelstrup had the sensation the man had been standing there for some time, studying him. When he looked into the stranger's eyes, the attorney experienced a sense of recognition. The eyes were a pale blue, almost opposite in color from Joe's, which were a brown that appeared black in anything other than direct sunlight. Joe's eyes always had made Troelstrup uneasy. The boy never blinked, for one thing, and while Joe looked at you very closely, his eyes never reacted, never showed any emotion at all, no matter what was said. Troelstrup thought he was myopic at first, then decided it was something else. The attorney saw that same quality—"an eerie combination of intensity and vacancy"—in the eyes of the man at his office door. "You're Joe Hunt's father, aren't you?" he said. The man, taken aback only briefly, extended his hand. "Yes, I'm Ryan," he said, and took a seat.

In Chicago to visit Joe, he had heard of "the trouble," Ryan explained, and wondered if perhaps Mr. Troelstrup might tell him what it was all about. He couldn't discuss the specifics of a pending matter, Troelstrup explained, so the elder Hunt talked a bit about his son. Ryan assumed the attorney understood that Joe was an unusual young man, exceptionally advanced in some areas, still only a boy in others. His father knew Joe had a tendency to grow bored with red-taped formalities, but if the young man took shortcuts, it was only because he saw so clearly where he was headed. The man was extremely ingratiating, Troelstrup thought: "He actually made me feel very comfortable." There was no attempt to influence, and "I gradually realized that he was there simply to check me out, to read me," Troelstrup said. After Ryan shook his hand again and thanked him for his time, the attorney sat alone for a few moments, then stepped out into the hallway to ask his secretary, then his receptionist, then four or five of the auditors if they had seen Mr. Hunt come in earlier. No one had.

The hearing was two weeks later, at the end of February, when the crust of ice on the shore of Lake Michigan was broader than the beachfront. Joe's lack of legal acumen did not prevent him from filing quite a number of briefs, although the legal authority he cited most frequently was not Blackstone but Shakespeare. The first page of Joe's final filing, in fact, consisted entirely of three lines from *Hamlet:* "This above all: To thine own self be true / And it must follow, as the night of [*sic*] the day / Thou canst not then be false to any man." "Things like that have interesting effects on laymen, though," Troelstrup observed, "and members of the exchange, even the board of governors, are laymen."

Though he supervised the prosecution, Troelstrup allowed Ed Donlan, who was in his final semester of law school, to present the case. Once again, Joe's collateral yet compound dishonesty—the false application for a name change, the claims he was a CPA and had graduated from USC, combined with the fraudulent account statements—was damning, an effect heightened by the defendant's refusal to plead for consideration or leniency. "Something in Joe wanted to be brazen, to challenge authority rather than cater to it," Donlan said. "We would ask A, B, C, and D," Utrata recalled, "and he would say, 'I'm only going to answer A and B because I can show you that the other questions shouldn't have been asked in the first place.'"

The committee turned on Joe in unison when he was caught changing his story about a meeting that preceded the phone conversation taped by Stitzlein. His problem here was that one member of the special committee had sat also on the customer arbitration panel. "Only the member had shaved his beard, and Joe didn't recognize him," Donlan recalled. "The member said, 'Hey, don't you remember me? I was there, and this was what you said then.' But Joe didn't remember because remembering wasn't important."

The hearing had commenced on a Wednesday after the close of regular business at 3:30 P.M. It was early Thursday morning and the committee still sat when Joe commenced his closing argument. "This was the kind of oration where you swear the guy hasn't taken a breath," Donlan remembered. "And then he started repeating himself." Half a dozen times the committee chairman told Joe, "Five more minutes," but Joe kept going. It was almost 3 A.M. when the committee members clambered out onto the icy sidewalk in their cashmere overcoats, coughing, watching their breath freeze as they cursed Joe for keeping them to this hour.

When the committee met the next afternoon, the proceeding moved apace: Joe was found guilty on all counts, and the recommendation to the board of governors was "Maximum Penalty"—formal expulsion from the exchange.

Every obstacle was a challenge and every challenge an opportunity, Joe said. The opportunity in this case was Ben's. Joe could coach him through the Merc's membership test. When he passed, Ben would be able to lease a seat in his name, enabling him to trade from the floor of the exchange while in constant telephonic contact with Joe. Raising a new trading fund proved no great problem. Dean's parents kicked in thirty thousand dollars; Dr. Blicker and his people came through with the fifty thousand they had promised; Ben's older sister and her husband put in ten thousand; and one of Luan Dosti's friends added another seven thousand.

Ben stayed with Joe in Glencoe, while Joe tutored him for the written test. When Ben passed on his first try, the two took an apartment in a downtown high-rise on Dearborn at the corner of Superior, with a terrace offering views of Lake Michigan from Lincoln Park to the Navy Pier. Ben began trading through the clearinghouse of Goodman-Manaster in April of 1982. Joe rented a Reuters Quotron to track the market from their apartment's living room, where he spent most of the day on the phone with Ben. In the afternoons, Joe often would walk the seven blocks of concrete embankments along the Chicago River to the Merc building, where he stood behind the glass wall of the public viewing room, watching from exile the action on the trading floor.

During his free time, Joe prepared an appeal of the special hearing committee's ruling for the board of governors. At Troelstrup's behest, Donlan still was dogging Joe, following his move from Glencoe to the apartment on Dearborn. In June, Donlan discovered that Joe had applied to the city's other major exchange, the Board of Trade. On his application, Joe left blank a question about whether he had been disciplined by any other exchange. Troelstrup not only gave formal notice of Joe's suspension from the Merc to the Board of Trade but sent copies of his letter to the major exchanges in New York and Los Angeles as well.

"I thought him doomed at that point," recalled Donlan, who met Ben Dosti soon after in a hallway off the trading floor. The two engaged in a brief conversation that Donlan could recall verbatim five years later: "'Arben, do you know Joe Hunt?' 'No, I don't know Joe Hunt.' 'Isn't Joe Hunt your roommate?' 'Oh, oh yeah.' And then he was out of there," Donlan recalled, "before I could say another word." A check at Goodman-Manaster revealed the account there was producing a small but steady profit. The Ohio people said it wasn't their money, "so we couldn't determine where the fund came from," Troelstrup remembered.

In the evenings, Joe and Ben strolled the three blocks from Dearborn to Rush Street, where singles' bars stretched from Delaware to Division. One night the two of them phoned Dean from the Bombay Bicycle Club and told him they were voting to call their group the BBC, as an homage to that establishment. Joe, however, actually preferred the bar next door. The Snuggery was a suffocating place in the summer of 1982, filled to the corners every night with well-dressed revelers crammed shoulder-to-shoulder and hip-to-thigh as they poured forth from the financial, commercial, and legal towers that ringed the Loop and lined the Magnificent Mile. It got rowdy behind the plate glass windows after the sun went down; the fine English oak bar became an atoll in the churning, groping, leering sea of frustrated ambitions and furtive consummations. Amid absurd drunken brawls between lawyers with loosened ties, the establishment employed ten bouncers to keep the peace on Friday nights.

Joe generally avoided the scene at the bar, positioning himself among the video games in a corner alcove. The Snuggery's employees called him "the Milk Man" because instead of substituting club soda or tonic water for the alcohol he refused, Joe would order only an occasional glass of whole milk. He became an inconvenience, since the Snuggery didn't stock milk at the bar but rather stored it in the basement cooler. To save themselves the trouble of a trip downstairs, all the barmaids but one took to avoiding the Milk Man.

The exception was a twenty-one-year-old aspiring actress named Shannon McMahon, a tall and photogenic strawberry blonde recently returned from New York to recover from a careless marriage. The Snuggery offered both a source of income and a salve to the ego for Shannon, who was being asked for dates by her customers at the rate of six or seven a night. None of the "slobbering jerks at the bar," however, interested her. Shannon was intrigued, though, by Joe. He was so clean-cut and clear-eyed, sober and unmussed, unfailingly courteous amid the clamor of stale lines and sly flattery. She began to volunteer to bring the young man his nightly glass of milk, never charged him for it, and always received in exchange her biggest tip of the evening. Sometimes Joe was accompanied by his friend Ben, who ordered a drink or two or three, yet remained very courtly, almost formally polite, even when he was glassy-eyed and tottering. There was a rumor around that Ben came from some sort of sheikish Middle Eastern money.

Among the other waitresses in the bar was Shannon's sister Karla. One weeknight when a summer rain thinned the crowd, the sisters loitered in the little alcove with Joe and Ben, asking questions about how it felt to buy million-dollar bonds or bills or whatever they were. Joe suggested to Shannon that he might elaborate over lunch the next day. Lunch, she thought; that was so polite.

They met at Hilary's, in the Water Tower. Joe's story was that he had come from California to trade commodities on the Mercantile Exchange, where he made and lost millions within a few months. She thought it must take years to learn the market, Shannon said, but Joe replied that it was easy once you understood the system, which he likened to breaking a secret code.

After lunch the two of them walked for hours on the lake shore in Lincoln Park. It was the longest conversation Shannon could recall with a member of the opposite sex. Joe told more of his past, explaining he had a college degree but preferred to think of himself as self-educated, since he had gone through USC during a year and a half when he spent all his time studying for final exams. Before that, Joe said, he had attended the most exclusive private high school in Los Angeles, where he was the star of the debate team. Debate was his first passion, Joe said, but the faculty advisor for forensics at the school had resented him from the first for his ability and independence and, finally, after a series of ludicrous conflicts, accused him of cheating and dismissed him from the team. Joe spoke of this incident without the slightest rancor, Shannon noticed, his tone "calm and bemused," just as it had been earlier when he described the brokers who had conspired to squeeze him out of his position in the commodities market, as if he regarded such people as foolish children.

One subject on which Joe had little to say was that of his parents. They were divorced, he told Shannon, and neither was what he could call a stable person. Joe spoke with feeling, though, of a younger sister who was very dear to him and whose future worried him terribly. He talked to the girl almost every evening long-distance, Joe said, hoping to persuade her to leave the home she shared with their mother. Joe seemed actually to dislike his mother. He said he had promised to put his sister through school if she would move out.

Shannon found herself telling Joe things she had not shared even with her oldest friends. Joe had a gift for nurturing self-esteem and seemed to see the star quality in everything from Shannon's long legs and green eyes to the blush that brought out her freckles. She told him about the breakup of the marriage born out of her first serious relationship, in New York, with another young actor. They each had succumbed to the stress and temptation of the city, but her feelings for this boy had been like an addiction, and even as he consumed her she couldn't let go. She returned to Chicago feeling like a recovering alcoholic, and was working two waitressing jobs to save money for school, Northwestern, probably. Suddenly Shannon began to tell Joe how her father, a business executive, had given up his job to start a business of his own, then drifted into an affair that almost destroyed the family, and about the hyperactive younger brother who had gotten hooked on prescription drugs in his early teens, turned to petty crime to support the habit, and now was in a rehab program up in Maine that was supposed to be the last stop before jail or death.

Joe said he had learned to look at families as laboratories for cooking up the conflicts a person had to overcome in order to grow and prosper. It required strength of will and real courage, but he saw both of these qualities in her, Joe assured Shannon. "Joe didn't really show emotion, but there was such a feeling of strength and certainty that flowed from him," she remembered, "that I felt all this confidence surging through my own self."

They saw each other almost every day after that. Joe always made plans and reservations, which was so adult, Shannon thought. After she got off work at the Snuggery, Joe would meet her on Rush Street, then walk her to the Ritz-Carlton, where they often were the only customers in the café built around the hotel's spectacular fountain. When he came into the Snuggery, though, Joe still devoted himself to Space Invaders. The suburban kids who got through the door using fake ID would gather behind him three deep, marveling at his skill.

What was odd was that two weeks passed, and Joe never asked her back to his apartment. In July she helped Joe arrange a party for Ben's twentieth birthday at Gordon's—perhaps the trendiest, and certainly the most expensive, new restaurant in Chicago. She arrived from work after dinner for dessert and was surprised to find that the other guests were all married couples in their thirties, suburban types who seemed to know Joe much better than Ben. After dinner, Joe insisted on picking up a tab that was in excess of six hundred dollars, then led them all down the street to the Baton, whose female impersonators staged the best and bawdiest drag revue in town. Afterward, Shannon walked with Joe and Ben back to Dearborn, where she saw their apartment for the first time. It was like a hotel room, Shannon thought, with bare walls and rented furniture. Joe "seemed very uncomfortable having me there," recalled Shannon, who told herself it probably was because of Ben.

Joe preferred to spend their time together at Shannon's parents' apartment, where the two of them would sit talking on the terrace for hours. Joe was such a cut above the other boys Shannon met. He quoted long passages from Shakespeare, not like an actor studying for a part but as if he remembered the words because they mattered to him. Finally, one night under a crescent moon Joe walked Shannon out onto the terrace and asked if he could kiss her. It was the first time in her life that a boy had asked permission for a kiss, and if it had been anyone except Joe, she might have laughed out loud, Shannon said, but with him it was so perfect. When their lips touched, though, she let her face show for the first time how deeply smitten she was, and in the next instant she saw Joe's own eyes retract and withdraw. I don't want to scare him off, she told herself.

Her mother was fascinated by Joe. Mrs. McMahon told Shannon that once she and Mr. McMahon had been dining out in an expensive restaurant above Lake Shore Drive when Joe came in wearing a camel-hair blazer. She had never seen someone so young in a camel-hair jacket and commented on this to him, Mrs. McMahon said. Joe's answer was that he had just come from the funeral of a friend.

One night Shannon and Joe had a double date with Ben and Karla. Karla was a vivacious girl with a raucous voice, and that summer she was always carrying her "To Go" cup, a large, lidded plastic container that she filled with wine before she left the house. Karla got them all "To Go" cups that afternoon, even Joe, and they carried them around Chicago for hours, tippling and giggling, sprinting down deserted commercial streets where they shouted at storefronts, walking along the lake shore at sunset. Joe seemed looser than Shannon ever had seen him, and she was having such a wonderful time herself that she couldn't even cry when she lost her purse with two hundred dollars in it. Finally the two of them ended up alone back at the apartment on Dearborn, sitting on the edge of the mattress in Joe's bedroom. They kissed again, but it was more intense than before. For the first time she could feel real emotion stirring in Joe, and as his face heated, the cool and charming exterior dissolved. When Shannon leaned backward, Joe's face grew suddenly strained and pale. "Let's go out," he said, and led her by the hand to the elevator, where they rode to the lobby in silence, not looking at each other. Joe headed for Rush Street, to the Snuggery, where he pushed through the crowd to the video games. Joe played Space Invaders for a while but still wouldn't look at her, Shannon remembered. Then, without preliminaries, he said, "I have to go," and left the bar alone. She walked home sobbing so loudly that people stopped on the street to ask if she needed help. The next morning she told her mother that if Joe called, she was out.

Joe got her on the phone a week later, but Shannon lied and said she had a date. Another month passed. Then one evening in mid-August Joe showed up at the Snuggery not looking like Joe. He wore a white T-shirt with greasy jeans, and his hair seemed to have been slept on. His expression was strange, like it had been that last night at the apartment, only more wild-eyed and sort of pathetic but scary too. He asked Shannon if she would go for a ride with him the next day on his motorcycle, maybe up along the lake into Wisconsin. Shannon didn't even know he had a motorcycle. "It seemed very important to him that I say yes, and his eyes, they were so sad," Shannon remembered, so she agreed to meet him at her parents' apartment the next morning. After Joe left the bar, though, Shannon felt a sudden anxiety, almost a foreboding. She actually was shaking and dropped a huge pile of dishes that shattered on the kitchen floor; when she bent to pick up the pieces, she fell among them to her knees, sobbing.

The next morning when Joe called the apartment, Shannon told her mother to say she was not home.

Joe and Ben actually were ahead at Goodman-Manaster, up by $30,000 on an investment of barely $100,000. Once again, though, the slow, steady accumulation of profit frustrated Joe, and he committed heavily to a decline in interest rates between September and December. When the market moved against him, he failed to execute the back-and-fill maneuvers that would have protected his position and later lacked funds to cover the mounting losses. To meet the margin call, Ben wrote a $9,500 check on an account that contained only a few hundred dollars. By the time the check was returned NSF ("not sufficient funds"), the account was $197,922 in the red. Goodman-Manaster liquidated the position overnight.

Joe told Dean and his investors that the loss was due to a misunderstanding by Ben, which resulted in his failure to sell off some of their T-bill options at the moment he was instructed to do so. "Joe said the loss was understandable, considering Ben's inexperience," Leslie Eto recalled. "He said they would start over again."

Ben had been suspended from trading as of August 10, 1982, however, and Goodman-Manaster already was preparing a lawsuit against him. With Ben off the exchange, Joe made a desperate bid to win his own appeal for reinstatement before the Merc's board of governors. Rainy Stitzlein, whose testimony was the core of the case against him, said she would gladly recant if Joe paid the $125,000 he still owed her. Joe answered that this was agreeable, but before giving her the money he wanted an exculpatory letter addressed to the board of governors. Stitzlein said she would give him the letter when he gave her the money.

In early October, they negotiated a meeting. Joe wanted to come to Rainy's hotel room, but she insisted on a public place. Finally, they agreed to meet on the afternoon of October 13 at the entrance to the vault of the Harris Bank on West Monroe, just two blocks from the Merc, where Stitzlein and Elias had a safe-deposit box.

Joe came in carrying a valise, recalled Stitzlein, who held her letter clasped in both hands. Joe opened the valise and removed an envelope stuffed with cash. It didn't look like any $125,000, Stitzlein observed, unless it was all in $1,000 bills. Joe said he wanted to see the letter before he gave her the money. Stitzlein wanted to count the money before she gave him the letter. Joe called the woman a con artist. She called Joe a thief. Joe stared at her coldly for a moment, then snatched the envelope from her hand and made for the exit. Stitzlein caught his arm, though, and held on. Joe literally dragged the shrieking woman a dozen feet before prying his arm loose and shoving her against a wall. He ran for the front door, where a confused bank guard lunged at him and was swatted aside by the valise as Joe sprinted out onto the sidewalk and dove into the backseat of a taxi.

One week later Joe appeared before the board of governors to present his appeal. His first exhibit was Stitzlein's letter. Troelstrup was waiting for him with a certified copy of a criminal complaint filed six days earlier at the Cook County Court, charging Joseph Hunt, age twenty-two, with simple battery and summarizing the circumstances.

The next morning, the board of governors posted its ruling in the matter of Joseph Hunt aka Joseph Gamsky. "Findings: Guilty. Unanimous." The special hearing committee had ordered that Hunt be expelled from the Merc and prohibited from reapplying for ten years. It was the longest suspension in the history of the exchange, and one effectively extended into a lifetime ban by Troelstrup, who prepared a formal recommendation that Joe never be readmitted as a member, then forwarded copies of the document to every exchange in the United States.

"Hunt literally forced us to make him a landmark case," Utrata marveled.

Joe returned to Los Angeles on October 26, 1982, more than half a million dollars in debt. It was his twenty-third birthday. He had no bank account and carried four crumpled dollar bills in his pockets.

Part Two

THE BILLIONAIRE BOYS

Accept the fact that the achievement of your happiness is the only moral purpose of life, and that happiness is the proof of your moral integrity.

—excerpt from Ayn Rand's *Atlas Shrugged*, submitted by Joe Hunt to the BBC as "Recommended Reading"

3

IN JOE'S MOMENT OF WEAKNESS, DEAN FOUND HIS STRENGTH. THE TIME HAD come to consider abandoning the BBC idea, Joe suggested when he appeared at the door of the Encino condo on the afternoon of his return from Chicago. Perhaps it would be best for them both if Dean took a job as a law clerk, while he went back to work as an accountant, Joe said. They could save money, bide their time, see what developed. Or just call an end to it.

He would not accept that, Dean said. Back in the snowplow paths at Mammoth, hadn't Joe declared as his first article of faith that there always was an alternative to surrender? And hadn't Joe said as well that it was not money but rather membership that mattered most in the formation of such a group, that only the quality of the individuals involved should determine an organization's trajectory? If that was true, then why not start with what they had—a vision? The two of them sat up all night talking it through. By morning they had arrived at a revision of the plan: Rather than make their fortune first, they would begin by gathering a group of like minds, a "core of desire and initiative," as Joe put it. "We decided that by the sheer energy of the personalities involved and the philosophy that we believed in," Dean explained, "we would create our financial success."

They presented the new and improved plan to Ben, who was amenable, to say the least. He had become bored with admitting his blunders and playing the dutiful son, Ben said, living at home, reenrolled at UCLA, hating every minute of it. His parents seemed to have his future planned for him; they even had found him a job in the law office of a friend. Looking ahead, he saw his life as a long, slow slog to security in the company of sleepwalkers.

There was the Normie pathology for you, Joe observed. What Normies believed in was sacrifice: First, they sacrificed themselves to a society for whose benumbed comfort they traded away their volition, then they sacrificed their children, out of what they called "concern." Dean and Ben were at a turning point, Joe asserted. Would they follow the routes mapped out for them or make their own ways? If they chose to join him on the path of Paradox, they must understand this meant forsaking forever the standards imposed since birth by those who feared choices and fled decisions. Joe recalled the key phrase: "Black is white, white is black, and all is shades of gray between." An adept of Paradox understood that he was at all times alone in a gray area. His perception and his focus might determine the shade of gray, but no more. This was the only real freedom a human could know, and those who seized it he called Shadings, Joe said. A Shading was everything a Normie was not, one who found in himself the wherewithal to see things not as he should but as he must, to shift or narrow or expand his focus to the point of view that best served his will in each circumstance, then gave himself to it without reservation. "Reconciled" was a word Joe used again and again to describe the mind-set of a Shading, Dean recalled: "Joe said that people who are not reconciled to their purpose would not succeed at anything."

The grand design was a transformation of the holiday season into "a recruiting drive," Dean recalled. Between them, he and Ben would receive invitations to more than a dozen parties between Thanksgiving and New Year's. They would travel in a group, gathering numbers as they went, cruise the clubs on free nights. Certain individuals had been targeted in advance; the first planned addition to the group was Evan Dicker. Evan had the family name and the home base in Beverly Hills. Also, there was a certain susceptibility, an invitation to impose, that emanated from Evan. At Beverly, Ben recalled, it had been easier to borrow money from Dicker than from anyone in their class.

It was true that he rarely objected to being taken advantage of, Evan agreed. In high school, he had been slow to sort through the gradations of Beverly's social hierarchy. In fact, until ninth grade he was completely unaware that the world attached any special significance to Beverly Hills High. It was only when he began to mix with people from the other public schools, Evan recalled, that he began to comprehend all Beverly represented to those looking in from outside. It was a bother, really; when he took up skiing and the people he met on the lifts at Mammoth or Squaw Valley asked where he was from, Evan learned to answer simply, "Los Angeles." It saved a lot of silly conversation. How could you translate to any outsider the subtle nature of status at a place like Beverly? What would other American teenagers make of a high school where substitutes on the volleyball squad stood higher socially than the stars of the football team?

His high school days seemed rather innocent from the perspective of the 1980s, of course. During Evan's years at Beverly, the dress-to-impress ethos was still in its designer jeans phase, so only occasionally did you see anyone resembling those fifteen-year-old girls in Norma Kamali originals who strolled the school's grounds like runway models these days. Cars and Cartier tank watches were the symbols of status among the class of '79. BMW hadn't yet come out with its 325 convertible—"which I will always believe they designed specifically for the Sweet Sixteen parties of the girls at Beverly Hills High," Evan observed—so the first choice in student transportation was the 320i, followed by Porsche Targas, Corvettes, and 280 Zs. Though he had a Targa now, Evan had driven a Z in high school, handed down by his older brother Layne, as was the Cartier watch he wore until the stem fell off and Evan discovered it was a fake. Evan wasn't complaining; his parents had been extremely generous within their means. The Dickers were well-to-do but not really well-off. Yes, his father's law office was in Century City, and yes, Dicker and Dicker's clients included Jerry Buss, who paid part of his fee in senate-section seats at the Forum, but all the firm really did for Buss was prepare and serve eviction notices on tenants of the rental properties that were the foundation of the Lakers' owner's financial empire. His father's other clients were Transpacific, Coldwell Banker, Cushman & Wakefield—all very impressive names to be sure, but again the firm handled their real estate matters exclusively, and while such work was lucrative, Evan discovered, it also was deadly drudgery.

His father had been a classic workaholic, in Evan's estimation, rarely around the house, and remote when he was. Yet Evan considered him a kind man: "He gave me whatever I wanted, and the only reason I didn't have more was that it never occurred to me to ask." Absentee fathers were virtually the norm at Beverly; Evan knew any number of people who received the same Christmas present each year—a check drawn on the company payroll. Evan's father, his father's father and his father's father's father all had been attorneys. "A family joke was that I turned twenty-one before I discovered that everyone didn't go to law school," he recalled.

In his mother, Evan always had sensed a certain subdued exotic quality. Perhaps the reason was that she had worked as an extra in the movies during her youth. Mrs. Dicker abandoned her screen career after she was married, of course, channeling her energies into the volunteer work she did through her social club, Wives of Beverly Hills Attorneys.

Both his parents were native Angelenos, born and raised in the old Jewish neighborhoods of the Fairfax district. The Dickers were hardly devout Jews, though. The family gathered each year at Passover, but for seder preferred takeout Chinese to unleavened bread. Evan was a college freshman before he was introduced to the concept of anti-Semitism. "After all," he explained, "I grew up in a community that is, what, ninety-one percent Jewish? If anything, you were discriminated against for *not* being Jewish at Beverly."

The family's home on South Roxbury might have been described as a Tudor ranch house, with an interior of dark mahogany panels and leaded glass windows. Evan was aware that many people might consider his home lavish, "but everything is relative," he pointed out, "and ours was like a servant's quarters compared to some of the houses my friends lived in." Evan contemplated what well-off really meant when he ventured across Wilshire onto North Roxbury to visit the home of Julie Smith (whose father, Joe, was the president of Capitol Records), or veered west to see his confidante Kathy Silvers (whose father, Phil, practically owned the show featuring his Sergeant Bilko character), or spent the night with his friend Seth Marsh (whose father, Sy, managed Sammy Davis Jr.).

During their freshman year at Beverly, students tended to separate socially along geographic lines. Among the first questions anyone asked was where you had gone to grade school. Wilshire was the dividing line: Hawthorne and El Rodeo, to the north, were where the rich and famous sent their sons and daughters, while the southern schools, Horace Mann and Beverly Vista, received the merely well-to-do. Coming from Horace Mann, Evan entered Beverly on the bottom rung of the status ladder. He was one of the Backpackers, those earnest youths who went on camping trips sponsored by the Beverly Hills Recreation Department—"the ultimate nerd group," Evan admitted. When he got into photography, though, and made the *Watchtower* staff, the conditions of Evan's life changed dramatically. By the time he was named photo editor of the school newspaper as a junior, invitations were rolling in: dinners, screenings, openings, parties. He had long since abandoned the camping trips, agreeing with his father that nature could best be experienced by driving Mulholland in an open Porsche. Social standing among his new companions depended upon any number of factors, Evan found. Being the child of a celebrity helped, certainly; Evan's friends Peter and Daisy Vreeland, whose grandmother Diana had served as *Vogue*'s editor during the magazine's most influential period, enjoyed what Evan called "definite advantages."

All their parents were pretty permissive, in Evan's opinion. Though hardly encouraged, drugs certainly were tolerated. He saw cocaine served in salad bowls at parties, and for a brief period it had been chic to shoot heroin. Only LSD, psilocybin, and the assorted psychedelics that informed the sixties were considered taboo; no one wanted to change their minds at this point. Alcohol was the drug of choice among those with whom Evan associated. They did their heaviest drinking at weekend parties in the beach houses their parents kept as second homes. That was how Evan first got to know Ben Dosti, drinking daiquiris with him out at Fred Anawalt's parents' place in Malibu.

Evan received at least his share of abuse at Beverly and absorbed by inference what people said behind his back. He knew he was mocked because he invited it, eternally affable and easy to get. "I just never minded as much as most people," he explained. He was quick with a quip but delivered the best lines at his own expense. Evan was fundamentally a gentle soul, eager to please and anxious to be included. He was brighter than most at Beverly but made almost no effort academically; as a consequence he had been unable to follow his friends from high school to UCLA, forced instead to do two years of hard time out in the Valley at Cal-State Northridge.

Evan was reintroduced to Ben when he transferred to UCLA as a junior. They exchanged greetings on campus but really got acquainted at the Fake Club, which in its earliest incarnation had been a kind of private dance party for the well-informed held Friday nights in an old Hollywood bus terminal, and in the red leatherette booths of At Sunset, the after-hours club in the basement of Whiskey A Go Go. He and Ben had decided to study for final exams together during Dead Week, observing a schedule Evan recalled as "study for half an hour, sleep an hour, go have lunch, sleep for another hour, study for half an hour, go get cookies." Ben knew how to relax; even at Beverly he had been known as someone whose greatest gift was for finding corners to cut. "He was a snob but a strange sort of snob," Evan explained. "The people Ben looked down on were the ones who worked for a living; he figured they didn't have the brains to find an angle." The image of Ben that lingered longest in Evan's memory was of Dosti reading the financial pages of the *L.A. Times* in the school's Skytop Cafeteria, raving enviously over the killing some new mogul had made. "Lazy and greedy and a great deal of fun" was his standard description of Ben.

If he harbored a secret belief that his new friend lacked a certain intellectual dimension, Evan regarded Ben as an ideal social companion: "He was witty and always got the jokes. We knew the same people and we didn't know the same people." The two of them shared as well an appreciation for what they called "the Pressure," that impacted sense of entitlement that was every Beverly boy's burden. Something Evan always felt that other people, outsiders, didn't understand about growing up in Beverly Hills was "the difficulty of coming from very successful, wealthy parents. I mean, in my family, graduating from college is nothing and graduating from law school hardly ranks as an accomplishment. To better my father seemed out of the question to me at a very early age, insurmountable without doing an enormous amount of work. And it's a double bind because you have this very high achievement that you have to accomplish, when your entire life you've had to do almost nothing to get everything."

During that summer of tennis lessons Evan found Dean especially sensitive in this regard and felt they were close friends by the autumn of 1982: "Not that we discussed a lot of intimate details, but then none of us did. We just sort of shared this point of view . . . It was very subtle, but we understood what we had in common."

Evan's home that season was an apartment in an art deco building on Spaulding Drive, where he was living on the monthly stipend provided by his parents while finishing at UCLA. The plans he and Dean had discussed for that Friday evening in early November were entirely social, Evan remembered, so it came as a surprise when Dean showed up at the door with Joe at his side. The two asked if they could sit with him for a few minutes before they went out; Evan put them in the red leather wing chairs his parents had just delivered as a housewarming gift. Joe inquired about his major at UCLA, Evan remembered, as if it really mattered: "From the moment Joe sat down I had the distinct sense that I was being felt out, tested." Since he had entered college knowing he would go on to law school, Evan explained, he chose as a major his favorite subject, history. He had made an emphasis of the Roman Empire, Evan added, and saw that this pleased Joe in some way. They digressed at length into a discussion of Rome's early history, and Evan was enormously impressed that Joe knew the Twelve Tables and how Rome's rulers had saved the city by bribing the Gallic generals who laid siege in the sixth century B.C. "For a twenty-three-year-old commodities trader with an accounting degree, Joe's range of knowledge was quite spectacular, I thought," Evan recalled.

It was Dean who raised the subject of this organization that he and Joe and Ben Dosti were forming. The group as they conceived it would be an effort to integrate the professional and social lives of its members, Dean explained, the ultimate network, really, a gathering of the bright and ambitious and well-connected. A member could choose the level of his participation in the BBC, Dean said, because one would profit by exactly the degree of one's contribution.

Joe introduced Paradox Philosophy that night as a system of thought based on "realism," Evan recalled. It was impossible to encapsulate Paradox in an evening, Joe explained, since the philosophy had no fixed boundaries but rather was an evolving interdependency of understanding and insight, one that would grow and develop within the organization. As he envisioned it, Joe said, the group would operate within the framework of a fluid hierarchy, one in which the leaders would be those individuals who at any given moment demonstrated the greatest mastery of Paradox, who took initiative in expanding and articulating the philosophy.

He was intrigued, Evan said, by the idea of living according to some creed or code—"something to sort of discipline you and guide you"—since this was an experience he had never known. The real attraction of the BBC at the beginning, though, Evan admitted, was the social network that would form around Ben, the friend he most enjoyed, and Dean, the friend he most admired. "One point Joe made that night was that, regardless of how far we got, we'll have succeeded," Evan recalled, "because we'll have formed this great group."

From Evan's they adjourned to the China Club, designated by Dean and Ben as the recruiting campaign's central staging area. The China Club had been born in almost the same moment with the BBC, and from its first night there was a sense of immanence about the place. Behind the wall of windows that separated it from Third Street, the restaurant and its adjoining bar seemed to have been designed as a display case for beautiful young people possessed of discretionary incomes, familiar names, abundant free time, and subscriptions to *Interview* magazine. The mood was cool, the tone arch, and the prospect expensive. Amid aqua and coral accents, furnishings combined mandarin elaboration with high-tech details; mood lighting was surfaces of black lacquer burnished by halogen lamps. What the China Club expressed better than any place in L.A. was that money, fashion, and video had replaced drugs, sex, and rock 'n' roll as the nightlife's holy trinity. Synthesis, not genesis, was the new engine of the cultural apparatus. The sense was that all mediums were merging, that as "standards" disintegrated certain underlying principles might coalesce. People searching for a language to describe what was happening at the China Club borrowed the art world's new catchphrase, "postmodern." "He's very PM," they said of the China Club's "creative director," Raymond Lee, as if it meant late in the day, which in fact it did. All at once, it had become hip to embrace rather than resist the inevitable.

In Hollywood, the postmodern sensibility was conveyed most effectively by those baby-faced VPs who delighted in the opportunity to tell yet another self-important writer that a summer rerun of *Three's Company* drew a larger audience than had sat through every performance of *King Lear* in history. The PM attitude perhaps was served up most succinctly by the young executive who flew into a rage one afternoon when an Academy Award–winning scenarist thirty years his senior made careless reference to Dante's *Inferno:* "I am not interested," the younger man shrieked, "in anything that existed before I did."

Already a VP for development at twenty-six, the young exec was an habitué of the China Club, arriving early on opening night to secure a prime location in that giant networking party where the BBC boys were asking for a larger table each week. Socially, all advantages flowed through Dean. "These were friends of mine, predominantly," he explained, "almost every one of them; the boys that wound up in the BBC were people that I knew, people that respected me, that trusted me." Besides introducing Evan to the group, Karny could take credit for Ron Pardovitch, Mickey Fine, and Simmie Cooper, a young South African whose family was buying into the local construction industry. Dean also delivered Joel Gelff, an ambitious acquaintance from North Campus who was now at UCLA Law School. Through Gelff, Dean brought in the Novian brothers, ebullient Farhad and canny Farid, Iranian Jews whose father owned the most prosperous rug shop in Beverly Hills. It was through Farhad that Dean was reintroduced to Alan Lieban, who had left UCLA for Fireman's Fund, where he worked as an underwriter and waited impatiently for an opening in the executive ranks. Even before they invited him to join the group, Lieban had observed the BBC's growing public presence in the after-hours clubs of West Hollywood. Watching as they occupied the power corners of the Rhythm Lounge or Club Domino, Lieban was increasingly impressed. "A conservative group, low-key," he recalled. "It wasn't as if they were trying to make a scene. It was that they had cool men acting in a certain way and attracting attention because of what they seemingly stood for as opposed to being loud or showy. What did they stand for? Success. Inevitable success, through confidence and conviction, like they just knew."

While Karny modeled the attitude, Joe Hunt was offered as evidence. "Dean and Ben and the rest of us may have formed the surface appeal of the BBC, but Joe's success in the commodities market was a big selling point for everyone," Evan explained. "It was like he was offering his coattails and saying, 'Grab on.' I was initially suspicious, because I thought, 'Why does he need us?'" When he spent time with Joe, however, Evan was won over not just by how intense and earnest Hunt seemed but by how little interest Joe evinced in anything money could buy. "By far the least materialistic of us," Evan said of Joe, "and when I saw that, he began to seem like some philosopher prince, offering us all this great gift."

It was not easy to keep up appearances. Joe still was penniless, his pocket money provided out of Dean's earnings as a tennis teacher. Their tabs at the China Club were paid for with a Visa card bearing the name DANIELLE KARNY. Hunt's ouster from the Mercantile Exchange had to be explained again almost every night. "When recruiting people, Ben and I never told them about Joe's losing money in Chicago," Dean recalled. "We just told them about the fourteen million he had worked the account up to and stopped there. This was an application of Paradox, shifting the focus from the negative to the positive." Joe actually boasted to the new recruits about having been "railroaded" off the Mercantile Exchange, Dean recalled: "He said he had so antagonized and challenged them, that he was such a threat to these older attorneys, that they had given him the longest suspension in the history of the exchange. Again, this was a shifting of focus, to the power of his personality, the fact that a twenty-two-year-old kid could drive all these big lawyers crazy."

Dean and Ben compensated as best they could for Joe's impatience with small talk. "Joe was often curt with people," Dean explained, "so he would play people off between Ben and myself, who are socially very adept, something that we endeavored to teach Joe. Joe came back from Chicago still wearing suits that were too small for him. His hair was too long. Ben and I knew all about style and the social graces, and he learned a lot from us in that regard."

By early December they were inviting interested parties out to Encino for informal gatherings, exploring what sorts of businesses interested people, who they knew, what resources were available. Those most favored were included in the tennis tournaments the boys held weekday afternoons up in Stone Canyon.

While Dean filled out the rank and file of the BBC with his friends and admirers, it was Evan who brought in the first really big name, high school classmate Alex Gaon. The Gaons were well-off, to say the least. Their home was as magnificent as any in Beverly Hills, a palace paid for with the profits from a textile business that had manufactured the first really successful designer jean, Chemin de Fer. The family's scope of influence extended far beyond Southern California, however, mainly through Alex's grandfather Nessim Gaon, president of the Geneva-based World Jewish Federation. Evan had arranged for Joe to meet Alex at a party during Chanukah. He and Alex hadn't actually been friends during high school, Evan explained, but became familiar during a trip to Europe with a party from Beverly the summer after graduation. In London, Evan had introduced Alex to his future fiancée Audrey Tannenbaum—whose father, Tom, was president of Viacom. Alex had been a bit beyond Evan's station before that, an officer of Beverly's most exclusive social group, the poker and drinking club formally called "Probability and Statistics," but better known among students as "Sit 'n' Sip." Analogous to the Argyle Balling Club at the Harvard School, Sit 'n' Sip was famous for its motto "LIQUOR UP FRONT, POKER IN THE REAR." The party the teenage cardsharps threw at the home of Norton Simon's grandson Eric rivaled Dan Sarnoff's *Deep Throat* affair as an enduring local legend.

After Evan set Alex up with Audrey, the two boys remained on the best of terms. Within an hour of introducing Alex to Joe, Evan knew he had made another match. The Gaons were a tight family, but all the boys could sense that Alex was looking for an avenue to independence. Early the following week they invited him up to Stone Canyon for tennis, to partner with Evan against Dean and Ben. When Joe arrived for lemonade afterward, Alex confided that he held more than a passing interest in the market, in fact had been dabbling with a few thousand dollars in an account at the Beverly Hills brokerage of Cantor Fitzgerald. As Joe recalled it, "Alex indicated that he felt he was a neophyte, didn't really understand the ropes of trading. We talked about some of my experiences in the market. He invited me over to Cantor Fitzgerald to meet with him a few days while he traded." It was not long before "Alex and I began to feel very similarly about the market movements," Joe explained, and "collaborated on a number of trades." Soon Joe was arriving at the Cantor Fitzgerald office on Canon Drive every morning in time for the 6 A.M. opening of the New York market, cutting himself in for a percentage of the profits Alex now was earning. Dean, Ben, Ron, Mickey, and Evan put up five hundred dollars apiece to be invested on behalf of the BBC.

With Joe back in play, the BBC was afloat, and the group's improving prospects took a spectacular turn for the better when Dean approached his old friend Cary Bren. The possibilities that arose out of this connection gave pause even to Joe. Bren was a name that inspired awe in every Californian fascinated by money and power. Cary's father, Donald, earlier that year had won control of the largest land development firm in the state, the Irvine Company, owner of sixty-eight thousand acres of almost inconceivably valuable real estate situated at ground zero of Orange County's monstrous building boom. What the Irvine Company owned was not simply one-sixth of all the land in Orange County, but the most valuable one-sixth, a vast tract of mostly undeveloped acreage spread across the inlands of Newport Beach, Irvine, and Costa Mesa. Donald Bren already held 86 percent of the company's stock and would have 92 percent before the end of the next year. What this was worth no one really knew, though county assessors were preparing an estimate that placed the value of the Irvine Co.'s land holdings at three billion dollars. Ranked by the *Los Angeles Times* as the second-richest man in California, right behind Hewlett-Packard head David Packard, Donald Bren was the most fabulously shadowy financial figure in California since Howard Hughes, quietly building a reputation as a master of timing whose veil of secrecy was his most potent weapon. Unlike the East Coast Donald, Trump, Bren was no overweening product of inelegant outer boroughs but had grown up surrounded by glamour and celebrity, raised on the Bel Air estate of his film producer father, Milton Bren. Demonstrating not the slightest interest in show business, Milton's son began laying the foundation of a real estate empire in his early twenties when he used a ten-thousand-dollar loan from his movie star stepmother, Claire Trevor, to build a single home on Lido Island, selling it for a substantial profit to Ronald Reagan's first wife, Jane Wyman. At once ruggedly handsome and abstemious, the last downhill skier cut from the 1956 U.S. Olympic Team, Bren was described then as "a leading candidate for the world's most eligible bachelor" in an *L.A. Times* article that quoted novelist Mary Anita Loos as saying, "He moves at the speed of light."

No son could hope to keep that pace, and Cary Bren never bothered to try. Quiet, shy, and unassuming, written off as "a nice guy" by virtually everyone who knew him, Cary was at least as handsome as his father but not nearly so bright or motivated. Even as Donald Bren sat on the board of directors at the Harvard School, Cary was flunking out before graduation. He made a halfhearted run at UCLA's business school, worked unhappily for a time at the Irvine Co., then elected to pursue the one line of work for which he had shown either interest or aptitude, driving Formula I race cars. It cost his father a quarter of a million dollars a year to keep Cary's cars running, but then, as one friend put it, "you're talking about a man who's making that much money every day before lunch."

Dean had been one of Cary's best friends at Harvard, and the two kept close, playing tennis as a doubles team at least once a week on the court at the Bren estate in Holmby Hills, a long lob shot from the Henry Moore sculptures that decorated the pool. Most often they were opposed by Dean's rival, Brad Reifler, and Jamie Lee Curtis's stepfather, Bob Brandt. "Cary fell for Dean's man-of-the-world act," Reifler observed, "and when he went along with the BBC idea, it was as a favor to a friend."

Whatever Cary's reasons, everyone in the BBC had been ecstatic when they learned that Donald Bren's son was coming out to the condo for an audience with Joe. "Even if all we ever got from Cary was the use of his name," Evan explained, "when you considered what that name was, it seemed we were getting something of enormous value."

While Dean and Ben brought in the big names, it was Joe who parlayed their imaginary assets into the BBC's first important business deal. Through his father's friend Frank Mingarella, he had arranged a meeting with an inventor named Gene Browning, Joe told the others, a legitimate genius who had constructed a machine out in his desert laboratory that might well be the most important new technology of the decade. This was a sensitive situation, however, Joe explained. Browning was a scientist, not a businessman, and his past experiences with investors had left him something of a skeptic.

Browning himself put it rather more plainly: "I've seen 'em all," he said, "every con man and slyster that ever came down the pike." The BBC's prospective business partner was the progeny of a family famous for its inventions, the best-known being the recoil-operated handgun patented by Gene's grandfather. Besides the line of Browning weapons that ran a gamut from 16-gauge shotguns to the 9 mm automatics favored by ghetto gangs, the family trust continued to accumulate royalties on small arms as diverse as Colt .45s and German Lugers. Gene Browning had eschewed the weapons industry as a youth, however, and was by training a biochemist. He had spent twenty-five years in medical research and was a regular lecturer at the American Academy of Medicine when he quit the field to devote himself full-time to development of the Browning attrition mill. The BAM, as Browning called it, was essentially a rock grinder, though its inventor would liken this description to calling the hydrogen bomb an explosive. Other rock grinders operated by using large metal balls or blades to cut rocks into a fine gravel. The BAM used no grinding mechanism at all but rather a powerful airstream created by vacuums that accelerated rocks to a velocity at which they literally pulverized themselves into dust. Browning was convinced he could reduce stones to molecules if he could create enough friction. Translating such notions to the physical plane required money, of course, lots of it, and Browning had run through all of his own, more than half a million dollars, in the past fifteen years.

Back when he began all this, Browning liked to reminisce, he had been earning 125,000 preinflation dollars per annum, owned a large ranch in Montana, and maintained a fully equipped laboratory within walking distance of his barn. He longed to make a larger contribution, however, something grand, enduring even, and became obsessed with avocados at one point, convinced they retained enzymes that inhibited the growth of cancer cells. The avocado idea had been abandoned, though, one afternoon when Browning was watching his assistants operate the machinery they used to sharpen microsurgery tools. The attrition mill came to him as a vision, the creative instant he had waited for all his life. As Browning conceived it, his invention would solve the acid rain problem: Millions of tons of shale coal that lay now in useless heaps because the stuff was too dirty to burn under existing environmental laws could be ground so finely that waste would be virtually eliminated; the coal would incinerate without ash, almost without smoke. Browning so far had developed five prototypes of the BAM, each one falling just short of what he hoped for.

He was without training in law or finance and had been beset by con artists. A good deal of his fortune had been lost to litigation; persuaded that attorneys took it all in the end, he sent both his daughters to law school. Now fifty-three years old, Browning was broke. Nearly all of his problems had arisen out of the machine's collateral applications, in particular the BAM's ability to separate minerals by weight, a capacity that inevitably attracted entrepreneurs invested in the new cyanide-leach method of gold mining. "The precious metals industry is an obscenity," the inventor explained. "They're all mad with greed." Yet increasingly he had turned to those with gold fever for financing. Browning's current suitor was a Rumanian count with a Ph.D. in chemistry who claimed to have come to the United States after spending World War II in a German concentration camp. The inventor's plan was to cut a deal with the Rumanian and his investors for the gold mining applications of the BAM, then use the seed money to develop the more advanced prototype that would solve the acid rain problem, revolutionize the computer chip industry, and bring its inventor acclaim as a savior of mankind. From the Rumanian, however, Browning had received numerous documents, contracts, amendments, and addendums, but none of the hundreds of thousands of dollars that had been promised. The Rumanian continued to cite sources of finance, however, and was most enthusiastic about a Dr. Frank Mingarella.

It seemed that Dr. Mingarella had an associate named Dr. Ryan Hunt, and that Dr. Hunt had a son named Joseph, an absolutely brilliant young man, a former scholarship student at the exclusive Harvard School who had assembled a consortium of former classmates looking for investment opportunities. Mingarella trotted out the names on the BBC roster, but the effort was wasted on Browning, who recognized none of them. A few days later, though, the inventor called his friend Ken Elgin, who had met Joe Hunt almost a month earlier. Ken was a kind of freelance wheeler-dealer who lived and worked out of a beach house on Balboa Island. He was a Yale man who had "been around," as Browning put it, breaking codes for the OSS during World War II and later making his fortune as one of David Rockefeller's aides at Chase Manhattan Bank. Browning was immensely impressed when Elgin described Joe Hunt as "the most articulate young man I have ever met." The inventor ran down the names of the young men Mingarella had mentioned; when he spoke the word "Bren," there was an audible gasp on the other end of the line. If Donald Bren's boy was part of this group, Elgin told him, Browning was about to enter a sphere of truly limitless possibility.

Browning endeavored to sustain his skepticism when Mingarella brought Joe Hunt up to his home in Hesperia for a meeting, but "I was as overwhelmed by the boy wonder as everyone else," he admitted. The inventor was hugely pleased when Joe engaged him in an informed discussion of the BAM's potential as a solution to the acid rain problem; the young man obviously had done his homework, arriving at the same thirty-billion-dollar estimate Browning had reached in calculating the savings to the nation's utility companies. Joe seemed to grasp the underlying principles of the attrition mill's design far better than the Rumanian, contemplating in some detail the BAM's potential applications to the manufacture of silicon chips and glass lenses. Best of all, never once did Joe mention gold. Browning's spirits were lifted even higher when his wife Claire announced she found Joe "adorable." "Always so interested in everyone else's problems," she explained, "always concerned with what's on *your* mind, what *you're* feeling."

Just after Christmas, the Rumanian phoned Browning to report that he and Joe Hunt had arrived at an agreement in principle by which Hunt and his group would commit five million dollars to the manufacture and distribution of the BAM for a 20 percent interest in the company. On December 29, the Rumanian called Browning at home to tell him, "Joe Hunt is going to be over today with a five-million-dollar check." Browning was in his truck and on the road a few minutes later, anxious to witness the event firsthand. He waited at the Rumanian's house in Pacific Palisades until well after dark, then said bitterly, "I knew it. Another phony."

A week later Mingarella called the inventor's lab in Hesperia. "He said, 'Joe would like to talk to you,'" Browning recalled. "I said, 'Why should I talk to him? I came all the way down to meet with him and he didn't show up.' He says, 'It has to do with why he wasn't there.' I said, 'Well, just for curiosity's sake.'"

When they met the next day at the Moustache Café in Westwood, Joe apologized profusely for standing Browning up, then explained that his problem was with the Rumanian. After investigating the man, he and his associates had come to the conclusion that the Rumanian was bad news, perhaps even an international criminal. No defender of the Rumanian, Browning said all he wanted was enough money to finish his machine. "We can help you," Joe said, "but without [the Rumanian] in the middle." When Browning wavered, Joe suggested bringing his "associates" to the inventor's laboratory for a meeting and demonstration. "That could be arranged," Browning agreed.

Joe gathered the group at Alex Gaon's the next afternoon. "He told us that Mr. Browning was looking to us for a good deal of money before he would agree to get in business with us," Dean recalled. "We didn't have much money at the time, of course, but we sort of put on a show like we did."

It was a performance that left an indelible impression upon Browning. The boys met that morning at the Gaons' gate to assemble a caravan of luxury cars, led by the black Rolls-Royce Alex borrowed from his father, followed closely by Evan's Porsche Targa and the Novians' Mercedes, then a second Porsche, and a BMW, both borrowed. They drove in formation up the Golden State Freeway to the top of Angeles Crest, then dropped into Antelope Valley, rolling out past Pearblossom to the edge of the Mojave Desert, where the landscape was desolate and dead level, marked mainly by dry lakes and secret air force bases ringed with electric fences, arriving just before noon in Hesperia, a tiny community of sun-dried retirees. They parked the cars in front of the town's lone eating establishment, a daylight diner. Half the local population had poured out onto the street to study the situation by the time Browning was summoned to the scene. He grew giddy, unable to keep the grin off his face, Browning would confess later, as he approached Joe and the boys: "I said something like 'Hey, guys, you're going to have to park your cars down the block, you're spoiling the neighborhood.'"

After the boys bought him lunch, Browning led them on foot to his lab, where he fired up his most recent prototype, shoveled a load of walnut-sized stones into the chute and watched the wonderment as his machine returned a powder the consistency of talc. Joe told the others to "look interested but not to talk a lot," remembered Evan, who had been up most of the night before and at one point needed to stifle a yawn. "Joe saw it and gave me this look, just a glance, really," Evan recalled, "but that was the moment when I realized how much I wanted to please him."

Dean and Ben and Alex especially were worked up after the demonstration, Evan recalled, "very anxious to sign Browning on." Joe was forced finally to tell the inventor that they did not have five million dollars on hand at present—that was one of the Rumanian's fictions—but pointed out that they did have access to such sums through their families. What was the least amount of money Browning could manage on until the new prototype was completed and they could approach their investors for financing? Joe asked. Browning's bottom line was a stipend of five thousand dollars per month, plus materials, until he completed the prototype. Alex came up with most of the money for the first month's check and gave Joe the use of the computer in his brother's bedroom to draft a contract.

Browning signed the agreement on January 15, 1983. "Of course I was tremendously excited," he recalled. "These boys seemed to have everything going for them—money, name, influence, connections, education. I don't know what more anyone could have asked."

By Valentine's Day the boys had begun to move their base of operations out of the China Club. The BBC's new preferred rendezvous was the Hard Rock Café, which had just opened on the street level of L.A.'s first showcase shopping mall, the Beverly Center. The Los Angeles Hard Rock would be the flagship of restaurateur Peter Morton's American line, the first of these establishments opened after the success of his original London location and a nifty complement to his other L.A. dining room, Mortons. The Hard Rock was a more mainstream atmosphere, a place where anyone could get a table if they were willing to wait for it. The establishment's declaration of its war on decorum was the mint green, tail-finned Caddy Coupe de Ville affixed nose-first to the club's roof, as if it had plunged onto the scene out of the astral body shop. The effect was enhanced by the Hard Rock's setting amid the neon streamers and chrome rails of the Beverly Center, where deck upon deck of escalators were decorated with lovely young creatures bearing Ann Taylor shopping bags and Frusen Gladje ice-cream cones like totems of esteem.

Waiting in the line that began forming at dusk, the boys watched with something like solemnity as that handful of young men their own age— the tribe of arriving actors who soon would be the Bratpack: Rob Lowe, Emilio Estevez, Sean Penn—were ushered without delay from parking valet to doorman to the center table where they spent the evening sipping Coronas and absorbing looks of longing. Patrons of the Hard Rock saw their place in time most clearly, though, on those nights when the star's star, Magic Johnson, swept into the room with one of his running mates, loitering at the bar just long enough to gather up the armload of sticky-haired young ladies from whom he would select his evening's company. The authority of fame finally had transcended race, lineage—even history. Magic's skin was green, the boys said. Celebrity, wealth, and power were the only measures anyone really believed in, and that threw everything up for grabs. "If I wanted to reduce the motives of the BBC to a single sentence," one member would observe later, "I'd say, 'Being able to get into the Hard Rock Café without waiting in line.'"

Only Joe was indifferent to fame and oblivious to glamour. He preferred the Hard Rock to the China Club solely because Peter Morton had provided him with a power spot, two old pinball machines pushed into a darkened corner where he could turn his back on the scene yet remain part of it, posing as the boy wonder of finance for the crowd that gathered

to watch him break the record totals he left on the machines like a signature, playing for half an hour on a single quarter, his games inevitably ending when he thrashed the apparatus into "Tilt," setting off the small siren
that became "Joe's sound." His former social superior at the Harvard School,
Bob Beyer, the insurance heir who now was working as a broker at Shearson
Brothers, watched with bemusement: "Here were all these young twenty-
year-olds, mostly single attractive girls, loud music going on, . . . and Joe
was off in a corner really determined to win at pinball."

As Beyer would observe, though, Dean and Ben did Joe's mingling
for him. Dosti, usually in a pair with Evan Dicker, became a fixture at the
bar, advertising Joe among the Beverly Hills High alums who assembled
along the rail while Karny worked the floor, known to nearly everyone,
shaking hundreds of hands each week to find those few whom he felt might
hold Joe's interest. Dean's greatest success in this regard came in early March,
when he stopped to sit for a moment with the two former Harvard School
classmates who would finance the BBC's incubation.

The May twins, Tom and Dave, were the scion of a family as well
known as any in California, the sole male heirs of their generation to a fortune founded upon the state's largest department store chain, the May Co.
Tom and Dave, however, were not the natural sons of the man they called
Dad, David May II, the family's ruling figure. Dave Two, as he was known,
had been largely responsible for diversifying the May holdings, gradually
unloading the family's interest in the department store chain to invest in
real estate, most prominently as developer of the enormous Park La Brea
apartment complex just north of the Tar Pits. Much-married and already
the father of three daughters, Dave Two had been unable to sire a son, a
situation that was the cause of such dismay that he attempted to alter it by
adopting the twins. The boys' mother was Andra Renn, a ravishing blonde
who had emigrated from Sweden as an au pair girl and within a year was
under contract at Warner's. At birth, the twins had been Jeff Orsin and John
Richard Hardin, taking the stage name of their natural father, a handsome,
square-jawed stiff who was Orsin Whipple Hungerford II before he became
Ty Hardin and jumped from a supporting role in *Gunsmoke* to the lead in
his own 1959 TV Western, *Bronco*. Neither of the twins had met Hardin,
who evaporated from the Hollywood scene after the cancelation of his television show, investing his earnings in a chain of Mexican Laundromats. His
twin sons knew him only as the object of ridicule whom they occasionally
caught hosting what Tom termed "a weekly Holy Roller show" on cable
television.

Dave Two had adopted the twins when they were eight, bestow-
ing upon them the imposing names Tom Frank May II and David Herbert

May III. So committed to the boys was Dave Two that during his divorce from their mother he went to court to plead for joint custody, and when it was granted he attached the twins to the various trusts where the family held the bulk of its wealth.

At the Harvard School, Tom and Dave's assets consisted entirely of their acquired names and inherited looks. The twins had grown into near replicas of their natural father, tall (six feet three inches), lanky, and tanned, with chiseled chins and sensuous mouths, their dazzle dimmed only slightly by small, narrowly set eyes. Being handsome Mays was enough to get by and get laid but hardly enough to get over among classmates who regarded achievement as the overriding standard of social status. Not very bright to begin with, the Mays' cheerful complacency made them objects of derision for campus leaders like Brad Reifler, who called them "probably the dumbest guys in the class."

The Mays' closest friend at Harvard was Steve Taglianetti, the class of '77's token Italian. Although a bit brighter than the Mays and considerably more motivated, Taglianetti was a boy most memorable to classmates for the juxtaposition of his rather prominent nose and considerably absent chin. His father was an attorney who also ran a lucrative auto importing business, and his mother was a pediatrician, but the rumor that Steve Tag, as he was known, had been sent to Harvard by a Mafia family would follow him to graduation. Taglianetti's one significant social coup at Harvard had been the rural driver's license his father finagled out of the family's residence on a one-acre estate in Bel Air. Tag was driving his new Cougar convertible to school soon after his fifteenth birthday, much to the consternation of the Mays, who also owned cars—a 280 Z for Tom and a TR-7 for Dave— but were restricted to driving back and forth in front of their mother's house in Holmby Hills. "They used to get furious every time I pulled into the parking lot," Taglianetti recalled, "and whenever we had a fight they'd threaten to turn me in."

Taglianetti was always willing, though, to drive Dave, the twin he preferred, to his meetings with Dave Two at the May Co. corporate offices in the big downtown store. Since Dave never could resist a display of his special "executive" charge card, Taglianetti recalled, "I got a lot of my clothes in high school just by being with Dave when he saw his father."

Though less well liked than his brother, Tom was considered the brighter and more ambitious May twin. Dave was a little leaner and a bit better looking, however, and did extremely well with public school girls behind his party-animal persona. Tom, on the other hand, had a tendency to take himself seriously, to mention right off that he was one of *the* Mays. While Dave's senior page in the *Sentinel* consisted entirely of a photo showing him aboard his snow skis, slashing through a spray of fresh powder, with only the legend "LET'S BOOGIE" for information, Tom's page was quite elaborate, beginning with a Gothic stencil of his name above a personalized crest formed from the intersection of a tennis racquet, a snow ski, and a fishing pole, with photos of his family's assorted sea craft and of his own beloved sports car, flanked by a horoscope from which he had extracted his favorite Scorpion predilections: "YOUR EXPANSIVENESS IS A WHIRLWIND WHICH IN PASSING CREATES A CERTAIN DISORDER. REBELLION, MYSTERY AND MONEY ARE THE THEMES WHICH SHAPE YOUR LIFE."

After leaving Harvard, Dave matriculated to UCLA, where he washed out within the year, then moved on to Colorado to ski for a few seasons. Tom stuck it out for nearly four full years at USC, joining the school's most elite fraternity, the Tri Delts, and passing enough classes to come within a few credits of a bachelor's degree in business before dropping out in 1982. By then the twins were sharing an apartment near the water in Newport Beach, where Dave was trying school again, a JC this time, Orange Coast College. If nothing else, the twins had at the age of twenty-two finally found an environment in which they thrived. Newport's commitment to conspicuous consumption and leisure as lifestyle outstripped even that of Beverly Hills. In the community that boasted the nation's largest Rolls-Royce dealership, most opulent pleasure-craft harbor, and busiest private-jet landing strip, the unaccredited rich could enjoy their wealth without the slightest apprehension of discomfort. It was only that you had it, not how you got it, that mattered in Newport, where local luminaries included mobile home aluminum-sash sultan Elmer Hehr, Armor All emperor Arlen Rypinich, and Veg-o-Matic magnate Samuel Popeil. Mr. Popeil had lived in the house right next to Don Bren's new digs before deciding to divorce his wife Eloise, reducing the poor woman to a point where she was forced to seek work as a dog groomer in order to support upkeep on the Rolls-Royce, Mercedes, and Jaguar that Samuel had left behind, a situation so untenable that Mrs. Popeil resorted to offering a total stranger four hundred dollars in cash and fifty thousand dollars in diamonds if he would murder her estranged husband. It was Newport Beach where Nixon's henchmen Haldeman and Ehrlichman waited out the Watergate hearings, and Newport also where—during the Mays' first year in residence—thirty members of Harbor High's graduating class would drive BMWs to a commencement exercise that included a showing of *The Great Gatsby*.

The citizens of Newport were not completely without sensitivity. Local art patrons were stunned and hurt by the clapping controversy that nearly ruined the unveiling of Orange County's new seventy-million-dollar concert hall in neighboring Costa Mesa. It began on opening night when guests who had paid two thousand dollars per ticket were invited to applaud their own generosity and responded *con gusto.* Unfortunately, the clapping continued, almost unabated, as conductor Zubin Mehta stepped to the podium to lead his orchestra through Beethoven's Ninth. Glaring and glowering, the maestro grew increasingly indignant each time the audience interrupted the performance with ill-timed ovations. When Leontyne Price stepped onto the same stage a few nights later to sing Richard Strauss's *Four Last Songs,* management had taken the precaution of including in the program a plea that all applause be held until the conclusion of her performance, but to no avail. As the final notes of each song were drowned in salvos of ovation the diva faced her admirers wearing a grimace of disdain. Isaac Stern attempted to quell the crowd with his raised bow but was forced finally to prevail upon the public address announcer for a request of silence. Critics for the Los Angeles and San Francisco papers deplored the Costa Mesa crowd, prompting an unprecedented number of letters to the editor of the *Orange County Register,* nearly every one asserting that the local audience had "paid for the right" to applaud whenever they felt like it.

The community ethos was perhaps best presented in a series of questions put by a wealthy Newport realtor to *California* magazine writer Steve Oney over dinner one evening: "What is wrong with hedonism?" the man asked. "What is wrong with clear-skinned people raising their children and living athletically? What obligation do these people have to those who live elsewhere?"

It was in such a spirit that the May twins settled into their first Newport residence, a cozy little party pad at 218 Prospect, just off the Pacific Coast Highway (PCH) and less than a minute's drive from the yacht their stepfather kept at the Balboa Bay Club. The twins' mother had remarried well; Phil Stein was a wealthy land developer who set her up nicely on an estate neighboring the Playboy mansion. It seemed the least a man could do for so serene a beauty. The Mays' friend Taglianetti was in awe of their mother—"I lost my breath and almost fell on the ground the first time I met her," he recalled—and equally amazed by the lady's bemused tolerance of her sons' antics. Neither Andra's former nor current husband was so understanding, however. Dave Two, after another marriage and two more daughters, had grown increasingly cool to the twins. "He knew what fuckups they were and was just sort of waiting to see if they ever did anything with themselves," Taglianetti explained. Dave Two's exasperation gained ground on his patience with each passing year, though, and his threats to disinherit the twins, followed by their groveling efforts at reingratiation, became a ritual of the luncheon meetings that were increasingly the only time he spent with the boys. Phil Stein, too, had grown weary of Tom and

Dave, refusing their pleas for a spare key to his yacht, incensed by their practice of smuggling dates aboard anyway.

At twenty-three, the twins' affinity for very young girls—"fourteen-or fifteen-year-olds were what they really liked," Taglianetti recalled—was notorious. It was rare for either Tom or Dave to become involved with a young woman his own age, so friends had been taken aback when both boys were moved to make a run at Alisa Goza, a blond beauty queen who only recently had arrived from Arkansas with an industrial psychology degree and the belief that anything was possible in this land where valets parked Mercedeses in the handicapped spaces at the supermarket and the airport was named for a movie star. Even before she met the Mays, Alisa was reeling from those heady vapors that scented Newport's atmosphere like an attar of money. Her new girlfriends were all LOLs (ladies of leisure) who taught her the ropes with brazen displays of avarice. "Every time you'd sit at a table with these girls, the first thing they'd do is show off their new jewelry, then tell you who gave it to them and what they did to get it," she recalled. The young lady from Arkansas was warned not to accept a date with any man until she saw his car, trained to spot a fake Rolex, and instructed in how one took advantage of the no-questions-asked return policies at the Fashion Island shopping mall's stores.

The first May Alisa met was Dave, who caught her attention with that killer smile of his one evening in a bar called Promises, offering to buy her a drink moments after establishing that she was new to the area. When he went off to fetch her a white wine, a young woman whom Alisa thought she might have met once rushed across the room to embrace her. "She asked me, 'Do you know who you're talking to?'" Alisa recalled. "I said, 'Well, his name's Dave, isn't it?' And she tells me, 'That's right, Dave *May*!'" Dave picked her up the next evening for dinner in a Porsche 911. "Right off he started asking me, 'What does your father do? What kind of car do you drive?'" Alisa remembered. Dressed in a polo shirt and Top-Siders without socks, Dave took her to a restaurant where the other male diners wore Italian suits. They got a table by the window anyway, and every two minutes there was somebody in a white jacket stopping by to ask if Mr. May and his guest were satisfied. "I was overwhelmed by it all," Alisa admitted. "I saw the way these other girls were and I never wanted to become that way, but when I got a taste of that life, I thought, 'This is kind of fun, isn't it?'"

The apartment Dave shared with his twin Tom was a disappointment, however; the heirs to the May Co. fortune had furnished their home principally with piles of dirty laundry, stacks of empty pizza boxes, and heaps of crushed beer cans. Dave drove her down to the beach the next morning to watch as he and his brother raced their Hobie Cats. "They were insanely competitive, cutting in front of each other, screaming and cursing, arguing about who cheated who for an hour afterward," she recalled. The twins spent seven days a week at the beach, Alisa was to learn, riding their catamarans, oiling their tans, and sneering at the Caspers, returning to the apartment in time to meet their beach buds for beer and pizza, playing the Blues Brothers album so often that they wore away the record's grooves. At sunset they put on fresh khakis, polo shirts, and Top-Siders—"the only clothes they ever wore," she recalled, "besides their swimsuits"—then headed for their favorite bar, Promises, to decide which party they would hit first that night. "Parties, parties, parties, every night of the week," Alisa complained. "They wouldn't even go see a movie. Finally I asked Tom, 'Don't you guys do anything but play?' He said, 'You know, we really don't have to.'"

The twins' blithe-spirit stance was becoming a bit shaky, however. Dave found that enrolling in a junior college did little to lift the weight of his adopted father's increasingly stern gaze, and like Tom he acknowledged privately a mounting sense of obligation as Mays to occupy an "esteemed function." Finding a job was out of the question, of course, which left only going into business as an alternative. The prospect of obtaining financial backing from their father was remote, though Dave Two had taken of late to suggesting that perhaps he should buy the boys an ice-cream truck, since that was about all they could handle.

The stress accumulating around their situation would be alleviated, however, by the timely death of their uncle Wilbur, kind enough to write the twins into his will's fine print to the tune of $250,000 apiece. Before considering their investment opportunities, Tom and Dave agreed, they needed new wheels. For this they turned to Taglianetti, who recently had arranged for the import of a Ferrari Testarossa that the twins' sister Kathy gave her husband for his birthday. "Dave calls me right off and says, 'Steve, I want a car, I want a nine twenty-eight,'" Taglianetti remembered. "I just laughed." Tom was more prudent, paying cash for a used Mercedes 450 SL at one of Steve Tag Sr.'s private auctions. Dave's Porsche had been a thing of beauty, though, Steve Jr. remembered, one of the very first S models, pearl white with black leather interior, tricked out front and back with spoilers and chrome spoke wheels. "The day he picked it up, Dave took me for a drive down to Newport. We were doing a hundred and ten on PCH when I asked him, 'Dave, do you have insurance?' 'I'll get it,' he tells me."

The two spoke next when Dave phoned Tag first thing the following morning. "Steve, you won't believe what happened," the twin began. He and Tom were headed up to Holmby Hills to show their mom the new cars, Dave said, when they decided to race that sweet stretch of San Vincente between the Palisades and Wilshire. The Porsche and the Mercedes were bumper to bumper, Dave said, when they tried to beat a yellow light at Bundy, hit a puddle of water, slapped fenders, and slid off the road in opposite directions. Tom came out of it with only a few thousand dollars in front-end damage, but Dave had wrapped the Porsche around a light pole and his car was a total. Anyway, they sort of wanted Steve with them when they laid all this on their father, Dave said. "Which was normal," Tag explained. "They always wanted me with them when they saw their dad. When they told Mr. May what happened, he didn't even say anything. He just sort of shook his head like 'Why bother?' Then he started talking to me like they weren't even there."

The twins already were formulating a plan for redemption, leasing a building in Dana Point, between Laguna Beach and San Clemente, where they planned to use Uncle Wilbur's money to open the splashiest new nightclub on the Orange Coast. Everyone who saw the place told Tom and Dave they had a gold mine. It was not only an immense space, but a spectacular one, alone on a promontory landscaped with royal palms and fish ponds that sparkled under the harbor lights. A wall of windows offered a Pacific view that extended all the way from the yacht basin to that exquisite haze of mist and lights enveloping Catalina. They had invested eighty thousand dollars in their remodel, the twins told Taglianetti, installing the longest bar on PCH and building a stage wired with a state-of-the-art sound system. Their private apartment upstairs had separate bedrooms and its own champagne-stocked bar.

When the Mays finally opened Jamaica West, the club was filled to capacity every evening for weeks. Even Taglianetti was impressed when he drove down from Los Angeles for a guided tour. "I thought, 'They can't lose with this place,'" he recalled. "Then I reminded myself it was Tom and Dave. And right off I noticed that the only thing they wanted to do around the place was hang out at the bar, score coke, pick up bimbos, take them upstairs. They're handing out gold passes, private memberships, to these little girls who got in with fake ID. They think they're rock stars. I told Dave, 'A cash business, you have to be hands on. Otherwise you get robbed.' 'It's taken care of,' he tells me."

Dave's date on opening night was Alisa Goza, who spent most of her time with Tom. "Dave and I weren't even talking, as usual, so I said, 'Let's dance,' and Dave said, 'I have all this PR work for the club.' So he went off to flirt, and Tom and I started talking." When Tom moved the conversation upstairs, though, "Dave got mad," Alisa recalled. "He comes up and says, 'Oh, Alisa, your friends are looking for you, but I guess you don't care.' Then he looks at Tom and says, 'And I guess you don't care either.' And Tom didn't. So . . . that was the end of Dave—and the beginning of Tom."

Tom was "much more serious and solid than his brother," in Alisa's estimation, "and a lot more considerate. He showed up on time or called if he couldn't. When he was with you he was with you, not looking ahead to see who was next." Not that her new relationship was without conflict. "It was hard for Tom because I didn't have the status that he needed in a girlfriend," Alisa explained. Tom did his best to inflate her reputation, telling friends Alisa's father was a pilot, but leaving out the air force officer part, introducing her at parties as "Miss Arkansas" rather than as "Miss University of Arkansas." Tom approved of Alisa's new job as a stewardess for JetAmerica—a good way to meet important people, he said—but was mortified by the Toyota Corolla she drove. "He said, 'You know, you really should get yourself a new car,'" Alisa remembered. "'Why don't you put some money into a Beamer?'" A used Porsche 911 was what Alisa put her money into, a vehicle that broke down approximately once a week during the nine months she owned it. "Tom loved the way I looked in it, though," she recalled.

Sweet as their beach life was, Tom and Dave discovered it could be a drag to spend night after night in the same club, even when you owned the place. By early March the twins had decided it was time to do a little research up north, check out the competition, "see what was happening at the Hard Rock," Tom explained. Joe Hunt was happening, according to Dean Karny. Tom's old Harvard School tennis teammate told the twins how the former Joe Gamsky had become a Hunt, then headed for Chicago from USC, making millions for his investors as a trader on the floor of the Mercantile Exchange, and now was back in L.A. to set up an investment pool here. Tom and Dave did not find it difficult to believe. They remembered Joe as the brightest kid in their class at Harvard—Tom had been sent to Joe for training when he joined the debate squad. It was the revenge of the nerds, the Mays told their friends; those guys were always the ones who hit it big after high school. When Dean drew Joe across the room to sit with the twins at the Hard Rock bar, the former Gamsky told them how it had been in Chicago, down there on the floor in the T-bill pit, competing against big banks and brokers, knowing that a moment's hesitation or a minor miscalculation could cost tens of thousands of dollars. To Tom "it sounded like pretty substantial stuff." The twins invited Joe and Dean down to Dana Point to see their club, maybe discuss the market over a drink.

Joe and Dean brought Ben with them when they appeared at Jamaica West a week later. In the apartment upstairs Joe explained that what he had in mind was not merely an investment pool, but rather a group of young men his own age, just out of college and brimming with ambition, who could create and operate businesses financed with the money he made trading in the commodities market. He elaborated at length, but the twins' grasp of Joe's ideas was tenuous at best. "Joe had a new type of philosophy for forming a business," Tom would explain. "It was, 'Whatever you put in, you get back.'" Well, the philosophy was new to Tom, anyway. He and Joe and Ben had spent the past three months gathering what they considered a truly impressive group of young men, Dean told the twins, and only recently had agreed that the time was right to bring them all together in one room. They had scheduled the first formal meeting of the BBC for the following Friday, March 18, and hoped Tom and Dave could be there. "My brother and I said we'd come," Tom recalled. "We figured it wouldn't hurt to listen."

4

THEY CAME TO CALL IT THE BLACK BOOK, EVENTUALLY. HE AND JOE HAD PENT themselves up in the condo that entire weekend, Dean recalled, sitting face-to-face across a pair of typewriters as they prepared the prospectus to be offered at the BBC's "inaugural" on March 18, 1983. The two of them felt it was important to give those who attended the meeting "something tangible," Dean explained. The "objects of the BBC," Joe wrote in an introductory passage of the Black Book, were "to create a system (1) where information travels rapidly and with a minimum of distortion; (2) which allows an individual to operate at the highest level of his capability; (3) which is aware of its resources and efficiently focuses them; (4) which reflects Paradox Philosophy."

Joe was afire that weekend, Dean recalled, taking off on one inspired tangent after another, ideas literally pouring off him. Yet when he urged his friend to write out Paradox, assuring him that at book length it would be a best-seller, "like *Dianetics,*" Dean remembered, Joe turned reticent. "He said it was a difficult and subtle thing to do," Dean recalled. Previous attempts at committing Paradox to paper all had failed, Joe said, and he suspected the philosophy might never lend itself to transcription, better referred to, perhaps, than explained and revealed most effectively by demonstration so that each individual could absorb that measure of understanding for which he was prepared.

Despite Joe's reluctance to expound upon the principles of Paradox, he was elaborate in diagramming a structure for the BBC. His design was a cell system. Cells—"the means of transferring information of general concern"—would consist of between four to nine BBC members led by an individual named as "Nexus," Joe explained. Above this base of the BBC pyramid would be a "Section Level" made up of between four and nine nexuses overseen by one designated as "Axis." Atop the edifice would stand the "Division Level," four to nine axes commanded by a person to be known as "Thrax."

The structure they had designed could encompass up to 2,187 individuals by Joe's accounting. While the turnout for the first Friday night meeting scarcely approached such a scale, he and Dean were enormously pleased when they counted off the eighteen young men who signed the BBC's first membership roster. Cary Bren's name appeared at the top of the list, followed closely by the signatures of Dicker, Gaon, and the Mays. "All these impressive names—there was a lot of electricity, to say the least," recalled Alan Lieban. "My first reaction was, 'Maybe I'm in over my head,' but I stopped myself and said, 'Hey, these guys are all my age. Yeah, they're from families, but I don't see their families here—I see them.' We were all a little green, and just the fact that we all had come together like this sort of signified that nobody was going to get where they wanted to go by themselves. There was hunger in that room."

Hunt did all the talking that night, Tom May remembered: "He spoke for at least three hours. It was quite a speech."

They were the culmination, Joe told them, the last privileged members of that class within an age group the media called baby boomers. The seventy-eight million Americans born between 1946 and 1964 were the inheritors of the earth, whether they wanted it or not. Those born in the forties and early fifties, yet called the sixties generation, were out in front by virtue of age, but their context hindered them. The leaders of that group strayed into metaphysical fantasy or political delusion, shielding their eyes against the hard clear light in which the human condition ultimately was cast. They had resorted to what they called maturity in the end, of course, most of them, to secure positions and authorities, yet remained divided in their minds. These people never would be free from a need to justify their existences within an artificial—actually laughable—moral context, and paid the high cost of hypocrisy every day.

The people in the room with him this evening, however, and those who would join them later, were free of such inner conflict. They were here because they felt obligation neither to deny their desires nor to subvert their ambitions, and this was their advantage. "Enlightened self-interest" was the term to which Joe returned again and again as he described the essence of Paradox. Everyone wanted what was best for him or her, Joe said; that was the natural order. Groups and organizations, like states and nations, derived all meaning from their capacity for enabling individuals to achieve private ends by public participation. The people who had come here this evening must recognize, at least subliminally, that they stood at the threshold of a historic era in which the schism between have and have-not would increase exponentially.

Those who remained alert, Joe said, who succumbed neither to bleak forecast nor to cynical ennui, would recognize the abundance of fortuity that attended the presidency of Ronald Reagan. In the very moment that they sat together in this room, opportunities for personal enrichment existed on a scale not seen since the heydays of John D. Rockefeller and J. P. Morgan. It was absolutely essential to begin by understanding that Reagan was a monetarist, tutored privately by Milton Friedman for the past ten years. During his first twenty months in office Reagan had broken the upward spiral of inflation by squeezing the money supply and raising interest rates. As a result, financial markets were flourishing. Anxious investors unwilling to commit money for the long terms required to support productive capacity had turned by the thousands to financial futures, where they were able to take advantage of a real interest rate that was higher than it had been since Eisenhower was in the White House.

And the boom in the financial markets was virtually certain to sustain itself, Joe observed. The legislation Reagan pushed through during his first year in office had been the spearhead of his supply-side attack on the progressive income tax. Now those who made the most money could count on keeping the biggest piece of it. Many major corporations were looking at "negative tax rates" for 1983; even General Electric anticipated paying no taxes at all for the current year. With more money in the hands of the well-off, and in a time of soaring interest rates, it was inevitable that billions of previously withheld dollars would be placed in the hands of those trading government bonds.

The BBC would be there, Joe promised, working through the first of the economic entities to be known within the organization as "Shapes." While operating in the public sphere as independent corporate divisions of the BBC, Shapes would remain under the authority of the organization's internal structure. Thus who was named president or vice president of a Shape's corporate shell would matter less than who was designated by the BBC as a "Factor" in the Shape. Factors would be those persons making a "vital contribution" to a Shape's success. In the "Commodities Shape," Joe and Alex Gaon were the Factors at present, trading through their accounts at Cantor Fitzgerald. The ancient adage that it takes money to make money never had been more true, and it would be the primary objective of the organization initially to generate as great an infusion of funds as possible into the Commodities Shape.

They should all realize, Joe said, that it was their great good fortune to be coming of age not only at the right time but in the right place. The malaise in the industrial East only served to underscore the surging economy in Southern California. The region's most visible industry, motion pictures, had enjoyed its biggest year ever in 1982. In purely economic terms, however, the making and marketing of films produced only a fraction—less than a sixth, in fact—of the revenue generated locally by Southern California's biggest business, defense. More than one-fifth of all the military spending in the United States had come to California in 1982. During that year, Reagan's administration awarded virtually every big-ticket contract to companies in his home state, ensuring that as much as one-third of the president's proposed $1.8 trillion military budget would be spent in California over the next five years.

In August of the previous year, Reagan had reversed his monetary policy by releasing billions of previously unavailable dollars. Within two weeks, the stock market rallied to register the largest one-day increase in its history. Even better, the 1980–81 anti-inflation policies had produced a dramatic increase in the strength of the dollar against other currencies. The dollar's surge made imported products a better bargain than they had been since the early seventies, a condition that would be sustained for at least the next three years.

The BBC was poised to pounce on this opportunity as well, Joe announced, through its "Arbitrage Shape." The Factor here was Ben Dosti, who had arranged through his father's contacts in Hong Kong to purchase Citizen watches and Casio calculators at prices substantially below the wholesale costs in this country.

The third major front of the Reagan revolution was deregulation. During his first ten days in office, the president froze more than 170 pending regulations on business; he had persuaded Congress to suspend or repeal dozens of existing statutes in the two years since. No single sphere of the economy benefited from deregulation so significantly as securities brokerage. The savings and loan industry would be the other principal beneficiary of deregulation. Free finally to offer whatever rates they were willing to pay in order to attract new depositors, S and Ls also were being allowed—encouraged, actually—to double their investments in commercial real estate, an area that Ben Dosti had been researching for the past few months. More significantly, though, billions of dollars would be available for new businesses that retained their deduction advantages under the new tax laws, in particular those that were approved as "energy-related." The BBC's third economic entity, the "Cyclotron (as Joe had renamed the Browning attrition mill) Shape," was on the verge of presenting its first stock offering on a company that would be inordinately attractive to investors scrambling to find businesses where they might unload their sudden surfeit of capital.

While the companies formed to supervise the BBC's discreet operations would be subsidiary to the organization's overall corporate structure, the Shapes that bracketed those businesses remained under the authority of the BBC's "Core," or "Main Decision-Making Council," as Joe described it. The Core would be the seat of power in the BBC. While unanimity was its aim, in no instance would any decision be made by the Core without the approval of 85 percent of its members. The likelihood of conflict within the Core would be mitigated by the requirement that each member must be a Shading. Joe read aloud from a section of the BBC manual headed "The Nature of a Shading": "Shadings must understand Paradox Philosophy. Such an understanding must go beyond mere deference and entail implementation."

Only Shadings, Joe said, would be permitted to sit on Paradox Court, the body that would decide all disputes within the BBC. "Shadings may adopt any information-gathering system that they see fit," Joe explained. "For a Shading there is no privacy from examination and evaluation by the other Shadings on any level. A Shading would not see this as a hardship."

To become a Shading, one could not be nominated or sponsored, Joe explained, but "must submit one's own name for consideration." At present, there were three Shadings within the BBC: Joe Hunt, Dean Karny, and Ben Dosti.

They should view the organization as a vehicle, Joe told those in attendance, one designed to carry them as far as they were willing to go. Evan, the one member of Joe's audience to take notes that evening, understood him thusly: "The premise was that as far as this thing gets, it gets. There's no disappointment if we can only rule the solar system, not the galaxy."

Within a week of the March 18 meeting, Joe was courting the May twins over lunch, first separately, then together. Dave went forward first, advancing $10,000 to a trading account controlled by Joe. Deeply impressed by Hunt's oration at the Friday night meeting, Tom proposed a lunch at Café Casino in Westwood. Joe arrived laden with charts and manuscripts, remembered Tom, who believed he possessed a "broad brush" understanding of the financial markets (since he occasionally scanned the May Family Trust statements sent in his name from Smith Barney) and felt he could say with some confidence that "Joe's strategy was to invest so far in the future that the market was totally unpredictable." Joe said that on the basis of current market movements he could promise a minimum annual return of 30 percent, Tom recalled. It seemed that Joe perhaps had been too modest when Dave, less than a month after his initial investment, received a "disbursement" of $5,000 in "profit." "I thought that was great," Tom remembered. So did Dave, who wrote Joe a check for an additional $70,000 a few days later. Tom matched Dave's investment with his own check for $80,000; on April 19, 1983, the twins—representing their net worth at $3.5 million apiece—signed releases authorizing Joseph Hunt to trade out of the Cantor Fitzgerald office in Beverly Hills as their "agent and attorney in fact" on an account at Drexel Burnham Lambert. Dean signed a Drexel release that same day, estimating his net worth at a more modest $310,000.

While Joe required the access to financial markets that Cantor Fitzgerald afforded, it was toward Drexel he aimed his ambition. Just two Beverly Hills blocks west and one south, atop the Gump's building at the corner of Wilshire and Rodeo, was the Wall Street firm's high-yield bond division, encampment of the most influential financial figure to emerge since the Great Depression, Michael Milken.

The parallels between Joe and Milken were striking. Each had been raised on the flats of the San Fernando Valley. Milken was in fact a graduate of Birmingham, the public high school Joe would have attended had he not won his Harvard scholarship. Their fathers each had been born and raised in eastern Wisconsin, migrating to Southern California as young adults. Milken's father was, like Joe, an accountant by training, and Michael Milken had himself worked for a year in the Los Angeles offices of Peat Marwick's rival Touche, Ross. Each had been president of his college fraternity, yet each professed an indifference to titles. Each had assembled a coterie of ambitious and mostly Jewish associates to whom they complained constantly about the "insularism" of corporate America. Each was a riveting speaker, overpowering face-to-face. And each was running what might be described most succinctly as a pyramid scheme.

Forty percent of all the original debt in existence would be issued during 1983, and Milken's company would underwrite most of it. There was room under the money tree for everyone, Milken asserted, and the escalating figures in virtually every financial market appeared to bear him out. What one might make seemed to depend upon two factors: how much cash you could raise and how quickly you invested it. The magazine that called itself *Money* would double, then triple its circulation when a new editor began running covers that depicted smiling young couples counting their cash and planning early retirements under "how-to" headlines. The chant of prosperity consciousness was gathering all of middle-class America into its chorus, clamoring for their piece of the action.

Such a man was the BBC's first outside investor, Steve Weiss. His daughter Alison was dating Mickey Fine at the time and had been familiar with the Harvard School boys since her days as a student at a sister school, Westlake. Alison first met Joe on North Campus at UCLA, where she heard all about the boy genius from Mickey and his much-admired friend Dean Karny. Her father had put Alison through private school while working as a video editor at CBS but would abandon his television job in the throes of a midlife crisis, resolving to devote what remained of his time to "making a difference." Father and daughter became college students during the same period, and Weiss eventually obtained both a master's degree in psychology and a state license as a marriage and family therapist.

Before he left CBS, Weiss's career at the network had financed the purchase of a home in Cheviot Hills, on the high ground above MGM. Like virtually every Angeleno who managed to buy a house on the Westside before 1970, Weiss was wealthy on paper from the tenfold increase in property values. His income, however, had dwindled since his departure from CBS, and it cost the man no small stress to set aside even a few thousand dollars for a planned trip to France in June of 1984, when he would join the soldiers he had commanded as an infantry sergeant to celebrate the fortieth anniversary of their D-day landing. "From the moment I first heard about Joe," Weiss recalled, "I had the feeling he might be the answer to all my worries."

Weiss was intrigued by his daughter's description of Hunt as "brilliant, but cool and distant." Joe was making money for people twice his age, Alison said; some of his investors actually were brokers themselves. A youthful fifty-eight, Weiss was a handsome, ruddy man whose flinty features had been softened by Southern California. He thought of Alison as "not at all the kind of person who could be easily impressed," Weiss explained, and "sensed there must be something very unusual about this young man she spoke of so highly. I told my daughter I wanted to meet him."

Hunt was cordial but brief on the phone, recalled Weiss, who told Joe he had five thousand dollars to invest in hopes of paying for a trip to Europe. Joe invited Weiss to drop by the Cantor Fitzgerald office in Beverly Hills the next afternoon. There was no need to come in; he would meet Weiss on the sidewalk outside, Joe said. He had been charmed by Hunt from the moment they met, Weiss admitted. Joe's articulation and confidence were enhanced by "a boyish, ingenuous quality" that made him immensely appealing. During the eighteen months he spent with Joe, Weiss said, the younger man's vocabulary sent him to the dictionary after almost every conversation. *Concatenation* ("a connected series of things or events regarded as causally or dependently related") was the word Weiss remembered looking up after that first meeting. While Joe made it plain he regarded five thousand dollars as a paltry sum, Weiss said, Hunt seemed genuinely engaged by the idea of helping Alison's father make his dream come true. Joe declined to discuss his trading method in detail, however. "He guarded his system like a state secret," said Weiss. Joe had gone so far as to say that when any of his investors attempted to discover his technique, he immediately liquidated that person's account.

He and Joe talked for nearly an hour about other, more philosophical matters that first afternoon, Weiss remembered, walking west along

Dayton Way to Rodeo Drive. Amid such opulence, the older man was won over by Joe's self-effacement: "His attitude seemed to be that he had been blessed with a peculiar genius and that what he wanted was to see something good come from it," Weiss recalled. That was why he had formed the BBC, Joe explained, to ensure that his abilities and the profits they produced were used "constructively."

The two shook hands and said good-bye on the sidewalk in front of Cantor Fitzgerald. Weiss was aglow with good feeling: "I remember thinking as I walked away, 'There's hope for future generations after all.'"

The BBC began to take on a dual aspect—private and public, business and social—after the opening of the accounts at Cantor Fitzgerald. While the official roster never would grow beyond thirty members, another two dozen or so individuals became part of the BBC entourage, drinking and dining with the boys, decorating their tables, amusing their guests, impressing their investors. These were young women, mostly, nearly all between the ages of eighteen and twenty-two, virtually every one a product of the Platinum Triangle, that mythical braid of precious metal connecting the communities of Bel Air, Beverly Hills, and Holmby Hills. Many had filtered into the BBC's circle out of the social set Evan was running with during his early China Club period, a group of young people Dicker referred to as the "Mob." They included Deborah Corday, the ubiquitous Raygo sisters, Phoebe and Daisy Vreeland, Ben's sister Marya, Evan's former housemate Maureen Burke, Maureen's acquaintance Angela Child, and Angela's dear friend Brooke Roberts. Brooke was the daughter of a major player in the entertainment industry, Bobby Roberts, a man who first had hit it big back in the mid-sixties when he cofounded Dunhill Records and licensed a string of gold records out of the Mamas and the Papas, Steppenwolf, Three Dog Night, and Johnny Rivers. Roberts also had worked as a personal manager for Ann-Margret, Richard Pryor, and Paul Anka, using the money and the connections he made in the sixties to expand during the seventies into the movie industry, producing films that included *The Gypsy Moths* and *The Hot Rock*.

Brooke's mother, Lynne, had been lifted by her husband's show business success into the most exalted strata of the Platinum Triangle's social establishment, accepted for membership in a local civic group best known by its acronym, SHARE (for "Share Happily and Reap Endlessly"). Officially the directors of a foundation for "exceptional" (retarded) children, SHARE also was the most exclusive women's club in California. Fewer than fifty members had been admitted, and simply being invited to attend one of

SHARE's luncheons represented an enormous elevation of a woman's standing in the community. Something of both the stature and the spirit of the organization might be inferred from the names used by the "Share ladies" in the group's official literature. These included: "Mrs. Jack Benny, Mrs. Milton Berle, Janet Leigh Brandt, Mrs. Johnny Carson, Mrs. Sammy Davis Jr., Polly Bergen Endevelt, Liza Minnelli Gerco, Mrs. Henry Mancini, Mrs. Robert Mitchum, Lucille Ball Morton, Mrs. Kenny Rogers, and Maria Shriver Schwarzenegger."

Before introducing Brooke to Joe, Evan had never for a moment imagined the two as a couple. Brooke seemed in fact the embodiment of all that Joe would disdain: a babbling blonde who was brazenly cute but far from bright, still seventeen when they first met, and "a snotty little snob" according even to Evan, who would add in the next breath that he had always been a little bit in love with her. Her looks were part of it, though Evan recognized that Brooke's appearance was largely a fabrication of judicious selection and lavish allowance. Every aspect of the girl's appearance had been enhanced by the best that money could buy, from the Aida Thibault facials that gave her the complexion of a shaved peach to the Jose Eber bleach jobs that left her hair with the tone and texture of a gold silk tassel.

Brooke already was preeminent among the Groovers, that coterie of teenage girls who decorated the openings of every notable new club, gallery, or salon between La Brea and Ocean Avenue. The Groovers were famous for forming like foam on the crest of each new wave, evaporating magically at the moment a trend began to weaken, only to reappear at a more current venue the next week. Brooke was traveling at the time in a company of classmates from the private school Elysée. What the Groovers did best was translate high fashion from the showroom to the street, integrating postpunk with haute couture to create an urban chic that accented Kamali skirts with Kaffaya scarves and Tiffany bracelets with thrift store lace, achieving a look that at its acme suggested fairy princesses moonlighting as streetwalkers.

Evan got to know Brooke during the opening of the China Club and found himself fascinated by her. All the Groovers practiced an indifference to difficulty, but Brooke did it best, projecting an impression that the only obstacle between her and all she wanted was remembering to ask for it. During the summer of 1982, Evan had become her unofficial escort, squiring her to premieres and receptions, hoping to be taken seriously but knowing it was not likely. The evening they attended the opening of the Palace (a once-grand Hollywood theater redone as an art deco nightclub) was the first time he saw the Robertses' home on Bellagio Drive, in the Foothill Estates section of Bel Air. The house was an English Tudor with walls of stucco and brick covered by vines. Inside were five fireplaces, a private tavern, and a world-class collection of art. "A really lovely place, even by Bel Air standards," Evan thought. As he pulled through the gate that first time, two German shepherds charged his open Targa with bared teeth, Evan recalled, "as if the Porsche was a dinner bowl and I was puppy chow." Brooke ran outside giggling at his terror and swatted the noses of the snarling dogs. A week later he received his invitation to the party celebrating Brooke's graduation from Elysée—*"It's a Sparkle at Brooke's"* read a hand-lettered card instructing guests to "dress all in white."

He had introduced Brooke to Joe in one of At Sunset's booths on a November night two weeks before her eighteenth birthday. Hunt's ability to put pretty girls in their place was part of his legend, and Joe seemed to regard Brooke at first glance as "amusing, but irrelevant," Evan thought. Joe devoted most of his attention that evening to Brooke's brother Todd, twenty-two and working as a salesperson for At Ease, the venerable preppie haberdashery in Westwood Village. When Hunt visited Todd at work a few days later, the only mention of Brooke was a joke she had made about Joe dressing in the dark. He saw no evidence of an attraction between Joe and Brooke, Evan recalled, until one night in February when the two of them were part of a crowd of people who gathered at his house to choose a movie. Evan caught just a flash of conflict—a remark by Brooke about Joe's lack of style that brought a retort from Joe about Brooke's lack of wit—and then Brooke was storming out the door, blinking back the first tears Evan had seen in her eyes. More astonishing was that Joe followed her. When the two returned half an hour later, they were holding hands.

Just about everyone thought it strange to see Joe and Brooke together, said Evan, who was most amazed himself by Brooke's posture of submission. "To understate it," he explained, "her ego was not naturally yielding, but she yielded to Joe, completely. From the start she seemed to feel her place was three steps behind him. She did his shopping, fixed his meals, answered his phone, made his appointments." Like most of the BBC, Evan concluded that being the consort of a genius satisfied Brooke's self-image. He was particularly impressed when she began to remark that Joe, unlike the rest of them, "had done it on his own."

What Evan and the others could not know was the liberation Brooke might find in the company of a young man who suspended moral judgment as a matter of principle. With Joe, Brooke felt free to divulge the secrets she grew up keeping in the family. Most of these had come down through her father's side. As a public figure, Bobby Roberts was not without taint. He had been sued a number of times, and though most of the claims against him were much like the one Richard Pryor made for failure to pay a promissory note, a few escalated into embarrassment—for example, the accusation of fraud made against Roberts by the giant entertainment conglomerate MCA, which resulted in an attachment of the family home before it was settled out of court.

The Robertses were ducking a full-blown scandal at the moment, one that went back a generation to Brooke's grandmother, Ann Roberts, a career con artist whose latest scam was particularly ambitious. Abetted by a newly acquired but ailing husband, the seventy-four-year-old woman recently had closed a deal to purchase the Pacific Palisades home that President-elect Reagan and his wife Nancy put on the market as they prepared to move into the White House during late 1980. The Reagans were asking $1.9 million, a lot for a three-bedroom home, even in the Palisades, though the place did come equipped with historical significance, having been the appliance-filled "Home of the Future" featured in *General Electric Theater* television commercials back in the 1950s, when the Great Communicator was honing his speaking skills as GE's spokesperson.

Ann Roberts's offer to the Reagans through their attorney William Miller was the crowning glory on an empire of artifice the woman had created during the course of just a few months at large in Los Angeles County. Mrs. Roberts's fabricated financial portfolio included a set of forged probate records showing her net worth as $13 million, nearly all of this in assets that were tied up in court due to delays in the settlement of the sham estate left by her recently deceased husband. The papers were quite skillfully prepared, good enough to get by the loan officers at two large Southern California banks that had advanced the woman more than $200,000 in cash. The assistant district attorney who later prosecuted her would remark that what amazed him most was that the larger the loan Mrs. Roberts applied for, the more likely she had been to get it. "The only motto I can find here is 'IF YOU'RE GOING TO STEAL, STEAL BIG,'" he observed. As an enhancement to her portfolio, Mrs. Roberts made friends with a man who owned an imprinter and persuaded him to prepare three cashier's checks totaling $800,000. All the checks were postdated and could not be cashed, but they made excellent "flash," and Ann Roberts was able to use them as collateral on another $123,000 in loans obtained from acquaintances who included her housekeeper and chauffeur.

After testing her portfolio in the real estate market with the purchase of property in Palmdale, Roberts submitted the same papers with a bid of $1.4 million on the Reagans' house. The president's attorney not only accepted the offer but allowed Mrs. Roberts to live in the house while the deal was in escrow. During her residence at the Reagans', Roberts obtained a $47,000 loan—against his commission—from the realtor who handled the sale. Her run of luck ended only when a real estate agent handling a separate deal reported her to the police.

After he was assigned to prosecute her, Deputy District Attorney Al Botello had been able to trace the woman's criminal history as far back as 1940, when she first was arrested for forgery in New York. Slogging through a blizzard of bad checks, Botello traced Roberts's route from Brooklyn to Miami to Beverly Hills, where she first had settled in the mid-1960s, just as her son was starting Dunhill Records. Despite the massive evidence file and a long list of witnesses, Botello regarded Ann Roberts as tough to prosecute. "She has a grandmother act so sweet and convincing, it's almost irresistible," he explained.

The woman whose story always began with growing up poor and Jewish in a New York ghetto got the Protestant chaplain at Sybil Brand (Los Angeles County's jail for women) to write the judge hearing her case a letter asserting that Mrs. Roberts had been born again in Christ and fully repented any wrongful acts. A former friend from whom Roberts had taken twenty thousand dollars was called to court as a witness for the prosecution, only to announce she no longer wished to press charges because "the poor woman needs the money." Several victims said Mrs. Roberts had taken their money because she wanted to help her son, whose career in show business was floundering. The plastic surgeon who had been defrauded for a face-lift dropped his claim against Roberts after he saw her crying on television. Even the attorneys who said she had failed to pay their fee refused to press charges after reporting that they had been compensated by Roberts's work for them as a bill collector—"by far the best we've ever used."

Botello, convinced Roberts had charmed the judge, was prepared to lose at trial—until the afternoon when the woman came to court wearing a new mink coat and was confronted at the bench by the furrier who held her bad check. "Even then she seemed more amused than anything else," Botello recalled. "Everything was a joke. Being convicted and sentenced, that she treated like overhead on the business she was in. When the judge sent her to state prison to start serving a five-year sentence at an age when most people are ready for a rest home, she never batted an eye."

In court, the only explanation of her conduct Ann Roberts would offer was "I'm an actress at heart."

Brooke Roberts was also an actress, though quite against her father's wishes. It was Brooke's official story that she and Bobby had fallen out after her father cost her a featured role in the television series *Different Strokes*.

She won the part at an open audition, Brooke said, but lost it the next day after Bobby called the casting director and threatened to run him out of the business. Brooke retaliated by moving out of the Bellagio house into the Encino condo, where she was living with Joe a few months after her eighteenth birthday. Furious, Bobby canceled her credit cards and charge accounts, then demanded return of the Volkswagen Rabbit convertible that had been her graduation present. "Joe has his own money," Brooke informed her mother, to whom she refused to reveal her new address. When Bobby announced he was hiring a private investigator to track her down, Brooke was delighted, recalled Evan: "She loved drama."

It seemed a function of the BBC's momentum that Dean and Ben would acquire fair-haired women of their own during this period. Ben's blonde was Julie Marks, a pretty Pepperdine student from a wealthy Sacramento family whose air of assurance was a match for Brooke's. Dean discovered his princess in the kitchen of Donald Bren's Bel Air mansion. Lisa Marie Sobel was working as the senior Bren's personal chef when Cary introduced her to his friend Dean early in 1983. A more natural beauty than either Brooke or Julie, Lisa Marie was a grown woman as well, almost twenty-six at the time, and with a past she made no attempt to hide. "She told me she had been living in New York for years with some old man who kept her," Gene Browning recalled. Dean seemed "such a sweet boy," Lisa Marie remembered. While working for Donald Bren she met many young men from wealthy families but not one who was half so polite or respectful as Dean. "He was so anxious to please that it touched you," Lisa Marie explained. Her ambition was to sing for a living, and she spent every penny she could save on voice lessons and demo tapes. When Dean said he wanted to help, the words sounded so heartfelt that tears came to her eyes. For Dean, the discovery that his stature was increased dramatically simply by walking into a room with Lisa Marie came as a revelation: this was not just another pretty girl but a beautiful woman, living proof that he was someone to be taken seriously. Out on the town together, the three couples turned heads wherever they went, and it seemed to Dean that strolling into a club with Brooke, Julie, and Lisa Marie on their arms was the most effective form of advertising the BBC had found. As he explained it later, "We tried to project this image of the BBC as being a cool group of people who really had our heads screwed on straight, who were making money and having pretty girlfriends."

The boys further inflated their public image in early June of 1983 when the BBC rented its suite of offices in the Wells Fargo bank building at 8425 West Third Street, just a block from the Hard Rock Café between the

Beverly Center and CBS Television City. Dean brought Tom May along to sign the rental agreement: "None of us had any credit history and . . . the landlord wanted a name that meant something," he explained. Dean and Tom agreed to a two-year lease at a total rent of $68,640 and took most of the building's third floor. They represented themselves as officers of Eye Contact Advertising, a company Tom had formed to sell advertising space on the garbage cans at state beaches from Redondo to Zuma.

The BBC moved in on June 10, 1983. "The offices made it all seem much more real," Evan recalled. Dean and Brooke shopped for furniture at Dania. The Novians got carpets and Levelors at cost. Ben rented a pair of Quotrons and bought an IBM computer. Joe took the largest office, with a desk outside his door for a private secretary. The Mays were rewarded for their contributions with the corner office closest to Joe's, while Ben and Dean moved into adjoining rooms across the hall. That night they celebrated by baiting Evan into one of his famous eating challenges. A month earlier Evan had won a hundred dollars by eating all the red peppers off a platter of kung pao chicken; on this evening he was offered another fifty if he could consume a plate of sweet litchi nuts ordered in from the Fortune Fountain next door. Dicker and Dicker's heir cleared half the plate before his stomach turned, then stumbled into the executive washroom to vomit on the floor as the other keyholders stood over him cheering wildly.

Evan was elevated from comic relief to indispensability by virtue of access to his father's law office. Joe designated him sole incorporator and secretary of the BBC's corporations, providing Evan with two books titled *Forming Closely Held Corporations* and *Maintaining Closely Held Corporations*. "Joe was very big on self-help books," he explained. Under Joe's instructions, Evan designed a corporate empire beneath the umbrella of a firm called BBC Consolidated of North America, Inc. Financial Futures of North America was the company formed to hold Joe's limited partnerships in the commodities accounts. Evan also incorporated General Manufacturers, created to assemble Gene Browning's Cyclotron.

The Mays, along with Dean and Ben, Alex Gaon, and Farhad Novian, became executive officers of licensed California corporations. Evan and Joe joked about how they might advertise future openings: "CEOS, CORPORATE PRESIDENTS, VICE PRESIDENTS WANTED. SHORT HOURS, HIGH PAY. NO EXPERIENCE REQUIRED." Joe's own name would appear as an officer of only one company, BBC Consolidated, where he was CEO.

Evan incorporated one other BBC company during those first few weeks, Fire Safety Inc., a business that carried the names of two employees on its books—Joe's father, Ryan, and the elder Hunt's "stylish sidekick," as Alan Lieban called him, Frank Mingarella (better known in the BBC as the 250-pound man with the $1.98 toupee). The purpose of Fire Safety's existence, as the other BBC members understood it, was to market a fire-retardant formula upon which Ryan Hunt and Mingarella had obtained a patent. A week after the offices were rented, the two older men moved into corner cubicles separated from the rest of the BBC suite by what would become the legal room. Many in the BBC were taken aback by Ryan's appearance. "Wrinkled clothes," "hair askew," "dirt under his fingernails" were among the images they called up later when describing Joe's father. "Actually, meeting Ryan made Joe more impressive to me," said Lieban. "Then I really saw Joe as a self-made man."

Everyone in the BBC was instructed by Joe's treatment of his father as an employee, nothing more. "When he spoke to Ryan in my presence, it was usually to give him orders, very cool and precise," Evan recalled. "Joe wanted to make it clear to the rest of us that this was strictly a business relationship," said Lieban, "that Ryan was there only because it was a good opportunity for the BBC."

The Third Street offices were particularly impressive to those young men who had been hovering along the BBC's perimeter. Among the first of these to be included was Steve Taglianetti. Like Joe and Tom May, Tag had gone from the Harvard School to USC, a decision that did not please his father. Steve Tag Sr. was set on seeing his son become a physician and in fact pulled Steve Jr. out of college after his first semester, shipping the boy off to the Dominican Republic to enroll at a medical school in the small, squalid city of San Pedro de Macorís. Though his father's letters reminded him that anyone who stuck it out at the school for three years "could more or less buy a medical degree," Taglianetti lasted less than three months before returning unannounced to Bel Air. Steve Sr. reluctantly permitted the boy to reenroll at USC, where Steve Jr. majored in international relations and prepared to make a career of foreign service. During his last semester in school, however, Tom May sold Tag on the May Co.'s executive training program, parroting Dave Two's recitation of former enrollees who now were CEOs or congressmen. "Just to see what would happen," Taglianetti drove downtown one afternoon to fill out an application. A few weeks later he found himself smogbound in the San Gabriel Valley, assigned to the position of manager in the Arcadia store's juniors department.

Tag had been on the job less than a month when Tom and Dave invited him for lunch at the Hard Rock Café, where they extolled a new and even more exciting opening with the BBC. "Tom and Dave sat on both sides of me," he recalled, "and they're telling me, 'This is a tremendous opportunity. We just met this guy Joe, who you know, he went to Harvard, his name was Gamsky then, he's just making money hand over fist; it's incredible. He's got dozens of investors, unlimited backing.' Dave tells me, 'I'm making tons of bucks. This thing is taking off, and you can come in on the ground floor.'" The twins took him to the Third Street offices after lunch, in time to see a sign painter put the finishing touches on the BBC CONSOLIDATED OF NORTH AMERICA, INC. logo that filled most of one wall in the lobby. "I walked around seeing these guys my age running their own show, one is the president of this company, another is the president of that company, and I'm pretty amazed," he recalled.

A week later the Mays brought Tag back to the Hard Rock for a meeting with Joe, who came in wearing a new suit and a Beverly Hills brush cut, looking as if a few hundred coats of lacquer had been applied to his surface since Steve last saw him at USC. Joe described the BBC as a fraternal organization first, remembered Taglianetti, who had been a Phi Kappa Sigma at USC. The idea of a business arrangement had developed out of a desire to make effective use of his profits in the commodities market, Joe explained, and the BBC was always open to new members and fresh ideas. Joe's tone was rather desultory, thought Taglianetti, who squirmed in his seat as he tried to catch Hunt's wandering gaze. Tag had come to the meeting expecting to be recruited but instead found himself giving the sales pitch, explaining that his father was one of the two leading gray-market importers of luxury European automobiles in the United States, and that through Steve Sr.'s West German contacts he had access to used Mercedeses, BMWs, and Porsches at the best available prices. Even after the cost of import and conversion to Department of Transportation standards, there remained a substantial margin for profit. "I was trying harder than I wanted to," Taglianetti recalled. "Joe's attitude seemed 'Yeah, fine, I'm interested, sort of, maybe we'll give it a try.' He made me feel like I had to prove I really was one of the best and brightest."

He was surprised, Taglianetti admitted, when Joe called a week later and invited him to the Third Street office for a private meeting. He had done some research, Joe said, and now understood that the gray market was in essence a form of arbitrage, a bet on the dollar's increasing strength against the deutsche mark. It was a position he liked. The BBC could offer Tag a fifteen-hundred-dollar-per-month base salary, a percentage of profits, and the position of president in whatever company they created to market the cars, Joe said. Taglianetti resigned from the May Co. the next day. Two weeks later he moved into the Third Street suite, setting up his desk in a corner of the Mays' office.

He attended his first BBC meeting that afternoon, Tag remembered, and was scandalized when Tom May presented his plan to offer Eye Contact Advertising's services to USC during the 1984 Summer Olympics.

Tag had heard the same spiel, almost verbatim, three years earlier. "It was at my parents' house," he recalled. "Tom was there one night when this guy who had proposed the idea to the City of Los Angeles made a presentation about it to my dad, to try to get backing. Tom asked my dad if he could sit in on the meeting. When my dad wasn't interested, Tom asked if he could borrow the materials the guy left. What he did was take all the papers and this eight-millimeter film the guy had, mimeograph the papers, have the film copied, and there was Eye Contact Advertising." Whatever private outrage he claimed, Taglianetti made no public objection. It was the very next day, in fact, when Tom introduced Tag to Paradox, describing the philosophy as "a way of seeing things so they work in your favor."

By June, each of the twins was far more involved with the BBC than in the management of their nightclub. Two months after its opening, Jamaica West had yet to yield a penny in profit. Tom and Dave cited start-up costs and problems with their liquor license when they asked Joe for $15,000 apiece out of their commodity accounts to purchase a matched set of Porsche 944s. He gave them the money, promising a monthly stipend of $3,000 apiece if the twins left the remaining $130,000 in their accounts.

The Mays' membership opened new and exhilarating avenues of expression for most of the BBC. All the boys maintained a certain sobriety in the company of Joe, who reminded them that every social excursion was a public appearance, an opportunity to attract the interest of those who had money to invest or reputations to lend. Rarely would anyone in the BBC drink more than a glass of wine with dinner when Joe was around. Even Ben Dosti curbed his excesses in Hunt's presence. Ben had moved into Evan's apartment after he left his parents' home, and for a solid month the two lived in a state of perpetual debauch that culminated on the evening they saw *My Favorite Year* in Westwood. So enamored of the alcoholic actor played by Peter O'Toole had the boys been that they stayed up all night after the show, shooting kamikazes to achieve a semblance of the star's besotted charm, then passing out on the floor at dawn. Ben's hangover endured for days, forcing him to explain his shakes and pallor to Joe as a case of the flu.

The Mays also drank with Evan, using him for foil at their favorite Beverly Hills fishing hole, Trader Vic's. The twins' procedure here was to obtain a large table for guests who would be arriving later, then order a Giant Scorpion Bowl (an enormous fruit punch scented with gardenia blossoms) with extra straws for any young ladies who might be persuaded to take a sip. Though they kept an apartment in Brentwood, the Mays consummated these evenings most often on the leather couch at the Third Street office. "The girls you met at Trader Vic's were a lot more interested in going back to a guy's office than to his apartment," another BBC member explained.

After Taglianetti abandoned them for the young lady he would marry, the twins began taking Evan along on those evenings when they returned to the apartment above Jamaica West. The first time he saw it, Evan was at once thrilled by the glamour of the Mays' glassed-in aerie and appalled by its squalor. "Tom and Dave thrived on accumulating filth in luxurious surroundings," he explained. Evan ended his first evening at the Mays' club by passing out on one of the California King mattresses upstairs. He was vaguely aware of other persons in the bed with him at some point, Evan recalled, but had been too ill to open his eyes. Waking at dawn, Evan staggered into the bathroom to be sick, but even in that condition could not bring himself to kneel on a floor that looked as if someone had died and decomposed on the tile. "I looked in the shower," he remembered, "and was afraid to use it." After splashing his face with cold water, Evan drove home on PCH in second gear.

Dicker's fecklessness delighted most of the BBC. He went through cars at the rate of one every month or so. After the engine in his Porsche blew, Evan sold the Targa for parts and used the money to purchase a Volkswagen Rabbit. Within a few weeks, he accumulated nearly a thousand dollars in parking tickets but assured the others this was nothing to worry about, since he never had bothered to register the car. Dave borrowed the Rabbit to meet a date one evening when his own Porsche was in the shop. The next day, Dave said he had left the VW parked outside the girl's apartment, somewhere in the vicinity of La Brea and Venice, after it failed to start that morning. Several days passed before Evan got over there with a pair of jumper cables; when he arrived, the car was gone. A letter from the city's towing company arrived within the week, informing Dicker of what he owed in parking fines, towing charges, and storage fees. Rather than a check, Evan sent in the Rabbit's title and his keys, then bought a topless Jeep to drive until the rains came.

Evan had followed Dean to Whittier because it was the only law school that would take him. "My test scores were high, but my grades were lousy" is how he explained his failure to gain admission to UCLA at a time when his father was listed among the law school's "benefactors." Southwestern and Loyola would have accepted him, Evan believed, except that he forgot to mail in the letters of recommendation they wanted. It was his fault entirely, agreed Evan, who appreciated very much that Southwestern had sent him no less than four written reminders.

For all his foibles, Evan was becoming an increasingly important Factor in the BBC. After bringing in Alex Gaon, he obtained a job for Dean as a clerk at Dicker and Dicker, and then a second position for Ben in the firm's collection department. Evan also continued to act as Brooke's escort on those evenings when Joe was doing business. He had been her date for the Square One L.A. opening party, where they were so convincing as a couple that the trendy clothing store began running advertisements featuring photos taken that evening of Brooke posing on Evan's lap. After the Square One party, Evan dropped Brooke off in Bel Air, then drove Ben out into the desert for a rendezvous with Joe in Las Vegas, where Hunt was meeting with a gold miner interested in purchasing several Cyclotrons. Evan still had his Porsche at the time; the stereo had been stolen, however, so he and Ben wore Walkmen as they crossed the Mojave. "We were passing cars so fast, they looked like they were all shifting into reverse," he remembered. Ben reached across the dash to tap the speedometer just as the needle hit 127 miles per hour. When Ben smiled, Evan pressed the gas pedal to the floor. "I had the feeling that the faster we went, the safer we were," he remembered.

The Mays drove over from Palm Springs the next day to play blackjack at Caesar's Palace and brought their friend Jeff Raymond. Tall, tanned, muddy blond, and handsome in a slack-jawed, soft-bodied way, Raymond befriended the Mays after dropping out of Arizona State to attend Orange Coast College. Jeff had grown up in Newport Beach and became the twins' tour guide after they took the PCH apartment. Alisa Goza got the impression that Tom and Dave kept Raymond on retainer: "It seemed like he just sort of followed them around, and whatever they wanted, he did his best to make it happen."

Like Steve Taglianetti, Raymond remained skeptical of Tom's enthusiasm for the BBC but was impressed that Dave—"the down-to-earth one"—seemed equally avid. The twins talked about this Joe Hunt as if he were a teacher rather than a former classmate, Raymond recalled. "And Dave bragged all the time about the affluence of the other kids who were involved. He mentioned Cary Bren's name a lot." When the twins brought him to West Hollywood to visit the Third Street offices, though, Raymond was won over. After reading the materials Joe had prepared to market the Cyclotron, Jeff said he would like to join the BBC if he could work on that project. Gene Browning was all for this. The inventor recognized Jeff's father, Lewis Raymond, as one of the finest metallurgists in the country, best known as the designer of the casings used on the nation's newest nuclear warheads. When Mr. Raymond agreed to design a casing for the attrition mill, Jeff not only was put to work for the BBC's newest company, Cyclotronics, but received a seat on its board of directors.

After Taglianetti and Raymond joined the BBC, Joe drew the May twins closer to the Core. "We were all made aware that bringing in someone valuable enhanced one's own stature in the group," Evan explained.

"And forever after, it was as if you played a part in their contribution. So the sense of recruiting was constant. The criteria? The criteria was whoever fit in with us."

By July, Joe's Financial Futures account was receiving five-figure deposits at the rate of at least one a week. The infusion of funds started with Steve Weiss's decision in late June to withdraw an additional fifteen thousand dollars from his mutual fund and invest that money with Joe. It was a choice he made after the lunch meeting where Hunt described his departure from Chicago, Weiss recalled. He was run out of town by a conspiracy of powerful forces, said Joe, who admitted in the next breath that hubris had hastened his downfall. He was not satisfied merely with beating these people at their own game but had been so brash as to rub their noses in it, Joe said, and for this paid dearly. He believed, though, that all men who grew to stature did so by learning from the follies of their youth, and for the remainder of his career Joe pledged to remember the value of low profile and impassive demeanor. "He was very convincing in this regard," Weiss recalled. "So low-key. Joe was eccentric, but he refused to be flamboyant, and that in some way made him much more appealing. I wondered how one so young could be so wise."

Within a week of his second deposit, Weiss received his first profit payment, four thousand dollars, and that week began to tell friends about Hunt: "I said I had the good fortune to meet a young man who demonstrated a know-how in trading commodities and was considering investing as much money as I could," he recalled. Others remembered Weiss describing Joe as "the goose that lays golden eggs." "I did quote Churchill," Weiss allowed: "'I feel it in my bones—our time has come.'"

The first member of Weiss's family to invest with Joe was his wealthiest cousin, Chester Brown, who had grown up with Steve in the same Brooklyn neighborhood. Chester lived in a basement apartment back then but resided now in a secluded split-level out in the San Fernando Valley's Woodland Hills, where he was making his fortune as an importer of glassware. Weiss first had mentioned Joe to Chester and his wife Mary over a poolside brunch one Sunday in July and was surprised when the normally cautious couple requested a meeting with Hunt at his earliest convenience. Joe invited the Browns and Weiss to his office on Third Street, where he explained the virtual elimination of risk from what was normally a highly volatile market by an inversion of the butterfly spread. When Mary Brown asked if he could guarantee that no money would be lost, Joe replied that this was impossible, since one must acknowledge history's lesson that catastrophic occurrences were beyond prediction. Joe devoted most of the meeting to describing such anomalies, working back from the 1929 stock market crash to the cancelation of Confederate currency at the end of the Civil War.

While Mrs. Brown left the meeting mystified by Joe's symposium, her husband, she recalled, was "dazzled." "Why didn't you tell me about him sooner?" Brown asked Weiss as they walked back to the car. "I wanted to check it out first," Weiss answered. "If you hadn't told me about this and I found out," Chester advised his cousin, "I'd never have talked to you again."

Joe's reports on his accounts at Cantor Fitzgerald were glowing during the summer of 1983. Everyone in the BBC offices was stunned and delighted, however, on that afternoon in mid-July when the normally undemonstrative Hunt strolled through the front door, removed his jacket, executed a series of cartwheels down the length of the hallway, then stood up to announce, "I made a hundred thousand dollars today."

The Mays were euphoric but confused. The twins had just received the first set of statements on their account at Cantor Fitzgerald, and while Tom and Dave were astounded to discover they now controlled on margin nearly forty million dollars in assets, the amounts at the bottom lines of the statements showed that only thirty-five thousand dollars apiece had been invested in their account. Tom and Dave were reassured when Joe said the rest of their money was in a "repo" account not included in the Cantor Fitzgerald statement.

The impression of prosperity in the BBC was heightened by Joe's habit of carrying a roll of hundred-dollar bills in his hip pocket. Dean and Ben drew two, three, four hundred dollars at a time in spending money. "All their wardrobes changed after they got the office," Lieban recalled. "They were coming in wearing these beautiful cashmere sweaters, gray flannel slacks, Cole-Haan loafers. They were going over to Westwood in a group to shop. Joe always gave you the feeling he could pull as much money out of his pocket as you needed."

Lieban nevertheless was a BBC member who hedged his bets, holding his day job at Fireman's Fund, yet stopping by the Third Street office every afternoon. Ostensibly his task was to underwrite insurance policies for the assets of the West Cars and Cyclotronics corporations, but the truth was "I just liked being around the office," he admitted. "It reminded me of when I first joined the fraternity at UCLA. Everyone was always so up and united. Also, a big part of the BBC was going out in a group every evening to Godfrieds, to the Promenade, to the Hard Rock, catching eyes, keeping in circulation."

The BBC fraternity's house mother was Danny Karny, who ordered the stationery, brought by bagels and lox or turkey sandwiches from Canter's deli, even added another twenty-five thousand dollars to Joe's new commodities account. Ben's parents, however, remained "rather skeptical of Joe," as Luan Dosti put it. Ben won his father over finally when he invited Luan to a demonstration of the Cyclotron organized by Joe and Gene Browning for a group of potential investors. While the event itself consisted entirely of converting a pile of pebbles into a mound of dust, Joe's narration lifted the moment onto a plane with "the invention of the wheel or at least the discovery of electricity," Evan recalled. "Hunt's presentation that day was very impressive," Luan Dosti agreed, "quite excellent and sophisticated. And I know because explaining advanced technology to business executives and government representatives is what I do for a living."

Joe made believers of everyone in the BBC two weeks later, when he announced that one of the businessmen who attended the meeting, Gold Sun president Michael Dow, had signed a contract obligating him to pay a $150,000 nonrefundable deposit on the purchase of twenty Cyclotrons at a total price of $4 million. "All of a sudden I have this multimillion-dollar contract sitting on my desk," Evan recalled. "It was astounding."

Collecting from Dow and his backers, however, proved difficult. The Gold Sun people actually wanted the BBC's money, two million dollars of it, to help purchase a savings and loan in Nevada. Joe, who had boasted of his organization's financial backing, feigned interest. The Dow group then proposed an even bigger deal, involving a fifteen-million-dollar down payment toward the purchase of the Guaranty Savings and Loan in Fort Worth, Texas. The BBC would receive only 40 percent of the S and L, plus management of the thrift, for its money, while the Gold Sun group would take 60 percent for brokering the deal. "These weren't exactly honest men," Joe noted. "They had inflated expectations." He encouraged those expectations by negotiating a contract on the Guaranty deal with the giant L.A. law firm of Manatt, Phelps, Rothenberg, and Tunney, whose senior partners included the former national chairman of the Democratic party and a retired U.S. senator. By the time a meeting with Guaranty's board of directors was scheduled, the Gold Sun group was "in a frenzied state," Joe said.

When he and Dean flew to Texas for the meeting, Joe explained, "my agenda [was] to walk a very fine line. Not to commit to anything orally. Not to even suggest I have the money to do so. But to walk out of there in such a position that I would have leverage on Mr. Dow." After he was introduced to the board of directors—"all these gray-haired gentlemen"—Joe recalled, the chairman asked him to tell them a little about the BBC. "I said,

'My situation, our credentials, are not at issue,'" Joe recalled. "'It's this bank.'" He had reviewed Guaranty's balance sheets on the plane from L.A., Joe explained, and noticed that the thrift was capitalizing the difference between the value of its mortgage contracts at market price and the price at which the mortgages had been issued. In short, nearly one hundred million dollars of Guaranty's claimed "assets" did not exist. "I had them on the defensive," he recalled. "And they ended up never asking me any more questions."

Michael Dow was awed by reports of Joe's performance in Texas. When Dow phoned him the next day in Los Angeles, "I told him, 'We would like to do the deal,'" Joe recalled, "'but Dean and Ben have a problem with your integrity. You haven't honored our contracts. They don't want to get into bed with you if you guys aren't going to honor your deal.'" Dow phoned again the following morning to tell Joe that his office in Santa Monica would have a cashier's check for $150,000 ready later that day.

Evan was dispatched to collect the Gold Sun check. "I remember being absolutely amazed that people who seemed so serious and legitimate would hand over a hundred and fifty thousand dollars like that," he recalled. "They were investing in a product that didn't even exist yet, but Joe had sold it to them. I thought, 'Do they know we're just kids?'"

5

AFTER THE GOLD SUN CHECK PASSED THROUGH THE HANDS OF EVERYONE AT the Third Street office, Joe and Dean delivered it not to the Bank of America branch on La Brea where the BBC had opened its corporate accounts but rather to 144 South Peck Drive in Beverly Hills, where Ron Levin lived. Screening them through his alarm-lock, steel-gate, and intercom systems, Ron instructed his housekeeper to admit Joe and Dean into the sunken living room where he sat like a pasha on a throne of raw silk. When Joe handed him the check, Ron counted the zeros out loud and smiled: "This Michael Dow must be a real fish. Give me his phone number, and I'll get a million dollars out of him."

Joe was not amused. He had been courting Levin for weeks, determined to be taken seriously. Dean and Ben were becoming jealous of the effort Joe made for this man.

The name Ron Levin had been introduced into the BBC's discussions back in March, at one of their earliest meetings, when the South African, Simmie Cooper, mentioned that the wealthiest individual he knew was a Beverly Hills businessman who "liked young men and had a number of them under his wing," Dean recalled. Simmie had been told that Levin was gay, but it seemed Ron preferred the role of patron to that of lover. Even his friends said Levin was a scammer, Simmie warned, a man who pronounced a dozen deals done and undone every day, insinuated himself into everybody's business, and boasted constantly of how he had taken this fool or that one. On the other hand, Levin talked about a million dollars like it was loose change, and "Joe thought it would be very interesting to meet this man," Dean remembered.

Simmie arranged for an introduction over dinner in Beverly Hills, and Joe returned to Encino that evening in a state of intellectual arousal, describing Levin as among the two or three most compelling characters he ever had encountered, an operator of majestic proportions, truly brilliant, obviously wealthy, and utterly addicted to the action. It was clear even then that Joe found Ron "a challenge to his personality," Dean said. Yet Joe hadn't allowed himself much hope that Levin would invest in the BBC, describing Ron as "skeptical about us." Nevertheless, Joe felt he had profited simply by spending time with this man.

Joe let his interest in Levin languish for a time, though, caught up in the trading at Cantor Fitzgerald and devoting most of the energy he had left to marketing the Cyclotron. The subject was revived at dinner one evening by Ben and Evan, who mentioned that they were acquainted with "one of Ron Levin's kept boys," Dean recalled. That young man, freelance photographer Neil Antin, seemed to be developing an ambivalence about his relationship with Levin, according to Ben and Evan. "Everyone assumed Neil was gay, but I knew he had at least some heterosexual tendencies," explained Evan, whose friend Phoebe Vreeland recently had been dating Antin. People judged Neil by his appearance, in Evan's opinion: "He looked like a model, very statuesque and very pretty." Less inclined than the others to pass judgments in this regard, Evan knew that most of the BBC believed *he* was gay, even after he denied it. "On the other hand, there were so many people being bisexual back then that you really never knew what to think," he conceded.

Joe found the situation intriguing. "He suggested we should try to get Neil into the BBC," Dean recalled, "so he would have another angle of approach to Ron." Evan brought Antin to dinner one evening. It was an education to eavesdrop as Joe worked a recruit one-on-one, Dean recalled: "Joe would become important to the person, try to identify the central aspects of their personality, the things that were important to them, [and] give them what they needed, in terms of whether it was support in a squabble they were having with their parents or whether it was aid in dealing with a girlfriend. Joe was always there to back you up. In helping you at the beginning to accomplish what you wanted to accomplish, you would identify him with succeeding at what you wanted to succeed at."

Joe offered to help Neil succeed at asserting his independence from Ron Levin. It was an advantage that Neil blamed Ron for most of his problems. Ron had drawn him in, Neil said, by promising to catapult his career. Earlier that year, after predicting that Australia was about to become a hot topic in the media, Ron had proposed collaborating on a coffee-table book featuring Neil's photographs. They flew first-class to Sydney with plans to spend six weeks touring the country, but Ron went no farther than a boat ride around the harbor before announcing that he loathed Australia, Neil was a parasite, and he was flying back to Los Angeles the next morning, leaving Antin to find his own way home.

Only a few months later, though, Ron came to Neil with a more ambitious project. This one involved the formation of a company he called

Network News, designed to shoot video footage from midnight to 6 A.M. of the murder scenes, drug raids, arsons, and assorted domestic tragedies that the union camera crews employed by local TV stations refused to cover. Ron assembled an astounding collection of state-of-the-art equipment, Ikigami cameras and Hasselblad lenses worth $250,000 at a minimum. He gave Neil a CB radio to monitor police dispatchers and a Honda Accord for transportation. It was grueling work, but the business was grossing as much as $10,000 a week by late spring. Neil remained an employee rather than a partner, however, despite Ron's pledge to "either cut him in or let him take over," as Evan recalled it. Ron was using him, Neil said.

Over dinner, Joe suggested that perhaps the BBC should consider forming a news organization of its own, "something that would compete with or replace Network News," Evan remembered. Neil and Joe even discussed creating a production company to make low-budget films for foreign distribution. "Neil was very excited about being part of the BBC at that point," Evan recalled.

Joe's ploy worked wonderfully, Dean observed: Ron Levin called within the week to say that perhaps he should hear more about the BBC. Joe drove to Peck Drive for a meeting, then went back the next night. "All of a sudden, it seemed that Ron was more interested in Joe than in Neil," Evan remembered.

Nearly all the other boys knew of Levin was what Hunt told them. Ron had graduated from Harvard Law School first in his class, Joe said, and worked as an attorney with the big downtown L.A. firm of Gibson, Dunn, and Crutcher before a tax fraud charge resulted in his disbarment. Reinstated in New York, Levin had made a fortune of twenty million dollars in commercial real estate, according to Joe, who remarked that he felt closer in some ways to Ron than to Dean and Ben. "He said Levin had an IQ of one eighty-six, even higher than his own," recalled one BBC member.

Most of the BBC met Levin for the first time when he joined them in Westwood for an advance screening of *Superman III*. It was difficult not to be influenced by Ron's appearance. He looked to be about forty, though his hair already was silver-white, swept straight back from his high brow and exquisitely arranged. His full beard was white as well and even more magnificently manicured than the hair on his head. The man had the look of a deposed monarch: aquiline features honed to a patrician edge, eyes that were a translucent blue and profoundly piercing. Tall and slender, he wore lambskin loafers with linen slacks and a loosely knit Italian sweater that had to have cost at least six hundred dollars, by Alan Lieban's estimation.

Levin was introduced to them as a very important person, Lieban remembered, "someone we wanted to spend time with, work on. I met him in passing that night, and he was impressive. He listened to these guys. And they were feeding him some of the best bullshit I ever heard in my life. I was overhearing Dean and Joe talking to him about different things, art and film and literature and philosophy, about how Superman comics and movies were the new mythology. They seemed to want to get him to see them credibly before they got down to business. You could tell by Levin's responses that he knew what these guys were up to, but the way he allowed it to go on, it was like he respected them enough to let them have their day in court."

During April and May, Joe continued to meet alone with Ron at his home on Peck Drive. "Originally, Joe wanted to keep his relationship with Levin private," Dean explained, "because he didn't know how some of us less sophisticated boys would be when we were in conversation with a guy as slick as Ron Levin, [but] then after a while, Joe began to think that Ben and I could make a contribution to the relationship, and he began bringing us around as well to Ron's house."

Most visitors found the space as imposing as the man who occupied it. Ron's residence was an immense deco duplex situated just five blocks from the corner at Wilshire where the Beverly Hills branches of Saks and Tiffany's competed for customers. Save for his beloved Shetland collie, Kosher, he lived alone on the lower floor, renting the smaller apartment upstairs to a retired actress. Levin still had more than three thousand square feet to himself and seemed to need every inch of it to contain his vast collections of modern art, electronic equipment, couture clothing, and designer furniture. In Ron's sunken living room, the Karastan carpeting was layered with Chinese rugs. The billowy couches and overstuffed chairs were done in crème leather and raw silk, separated by tables of polished chrome and beveled glass weighted with first editions and Fabergé eggs. One wall was covered with Warhol lithographs, another with Picasso plates, a third with ancient African tribal masks hung in a half-circle around a gold pharaoh's head. The sleeping chamber, as Ron called it, was equally opulent. The high bed looked as if it had been removed from Rebecca's room at Mandalay and redone all in white. Hanging behind the headboard was a huge handwoven rug of green, gold, maroon, turquoise, and black. The Plexiglas nightstands were piled head-high with reference books; Ron owned every dictionary from the *Oxford English* to the *American Heritage*. The doors on his closets had been removed so that his wardrobe might be displayed as decoration. Ron's clothing alone had to have cost a quarter of a million dollars. There were two rows solid with suits, nearly all Valentino and Versace. Ron's jackets had been divided into sections of Italian silk, French linen, and English wool. His sweaters were folded and stacked from floor to ceiling. One entire closet was filled with a collection of shoes that rivaled Imelda Marcos's, seven rows of fine loafers in every color from canary to cobalt. A coat tree was hung with cashmere, silk, and velour robes.

In the office where he kept a photocopier and a telex machine, two computers, and three telephones, shelves overflowed with law books, medical texts, and the latest *Encyclopaedia Britannica*. There was a microscope the size of a Volkswagen engine and beside it a full human skeleton wearing a safari hat, a stethoscope, and a smoking jacket, a cigar clamped between its teeth and a medical bag gripped in the bones of its right hand. The walls were hung with inscribed photographs of Ron's celebrity friends, ranging from Muhammad Ali to Bianca Jagger.

In the garage out back, Ron kept a Rolls-Royce, a Mercedes, and a BMW. It cost a hundred thousand dollars a month to cover his overhead, Ron complained, but he didn't seem to be worrying much about money. On the desk in Levin's office, Dean and Ben saw a sheaf of passbooks for accounts at banks that spanned the globe from Glendale to Geneva. Joe arrived at the Peck Drive duplex one afternoon to find Ron running off a stock portfolio on his computer's printer that "went on for pages and pages," he said, and had been there as well the day a delivery boy wearing a Ticor badge came to the front door with a check for twelve million dollars.

Dean and Ben worked in supporting roles as Joe wooed Ron with the financial histories of the families whose sons had signed the BBC roster. He explained in detail the group's corporate structure, described its far-flung enterprises, and boasted of his own success in the commodities market. Yet it seemed to Dean that "Ron was sort of laughing at the whole thing. I kind of got the feeling that he saw through Joe in a way, but at the same time, he wanted to be Joe's friend."

Joe had a real gift for flattering Ron's sexual insinuations, even as he deflected them. "Joe always looked at Ron as a potential target, and I believe that Ron looked at Joe as a sort of plaything," Dean explained. And yet "there was affection and mutual respect between them," he allowed. Joe and Ron possessed strikingly similar personalities. Like Joe, Ron was alert to sham or dissonance, eager to point out the seams of hypocrisy woven into the social fabric. Levin could reel off the names of every macho man who was a closet queen and describe the nose bobs, tummy tucks, or silicone implants of America's most celebrated beauties as if he had performed the surgery himself. Ron savored the irony of seeing champion athletes compete for shoe commercials and took pleasure in reporting that while the likes of George Lucas and Robert Redford guarded their "integrity" closely in this country, they were happy to make millions of yen by hawking Suntory and Sony on Japanese television.

Ron was not surprised when Joe told him that the majority of the BBC's members either had attended, were attending, or planned to attend law school. It seemed to be the only field of endeavor in which too many was not enough, he observed. Ron recently had clipped an article reporting that more than 275,000 young men and women had graduated from law schools in the United States during the 1970s, more than the total number of attorneys who had been practicing in 1969. California alone now turned out 10,000 new attorneys every year, he noted, loosing them upon the world to feed a mounting frenzy of litigation.

Ron joined Joe in deploring drug use—was perhaps even more adamant—and said he believed alcohol had been invented to help stupid people find one another.

Whenever Levin paused to take a breath, Joe persisted in his efforts to persuade Ron that an investment in the BBC would pay off. By May, Joe had shifted his emphasis out of the commodities market to the Cyclotron project. "Ron Levin was one of the people we knew who was rich," Dean explained. "Joe brought over marketing reports and articles written about the invention." Ron scoffed, saying he knew all about selling concepts as products. Joe was beginning to wonder if Ron took him seriously as a businessman, Dean recalled, until the Michael Dow deal convinced Levin to give the BBC a second look. "We hadn't rented our plant at that point," Dean explained. "No construction had even been started. So Ron thought it was pretty outrageous." After that, Levin "began to be supportive of the BBC idea," Dean recalled, "saying, 'Oh yeah, we'll have a party at my house.'"

The first formal function Ron arranged for the boys was a dinner at his home in early May. Taglianetti arrived before the others: "A maid answered the door, and he had a butler too. Levin told me to make myself at home, to feel free to look around. It was an impressive place, even for Beverly Hills." When the rest of the BBC arrived, Ron sat them down to a six-course meal that was interrupted by the arrival of several teenage boys who walked through the front door carrying skateboards, wearing short-brimmed caps and tank tops. "They were all very tanned and said they just got back from the beach," Taglianetti recalled. "Ron told them to eat in the kitchen. He acted like it was normal, and so did everyone else."

Ron spent the early part of the evening discussing desert real estate with Taglianetti, whose family had invested heavily in the Palm Springs area. "He seemed to know a lot," Tag remembered. "I mentioned this developer's name that my parents were involved with, and Ron said he knew him, too, and described what he was doing. It seemed he must have something going out there."

The most impressive thing about Levin, though, was the way Hunt behaved in his presence, Taglianetti thought: "Joe was different around Ron than he ever was around anyone else. He would actually sit back and take second chair occasionally, to try to absorb what this man knew, how he had accumulated all his wealth and knowledge."

Joe was not about to play a supporting role for an entire evening, however. Before the table was cleared, he and Ron began a competition that continued until the party broke up, turning the conversation into a trivial pursuit that traversed a range of knowledge from the root meanings of verbs to the process of chemical hybridization. "Then they would run to a book and look it up," Tom May remembered, "to see who was really right." Joe relished the adversary relationship, Dean explained.

Within a few days of the dinner party, Ron invited Joe and the May twins to luncheon, where he proposed formation of a company designed to take advantage of the family connection. They could call it May Bros. Land Corp., Ron said. "He said it sounded like a respectable name to use, so we lent him the name," Tom explained. The twins signed an agreement with Ron guaranteeing them a percentage of any profits the company made. As the Mays' confidant Taglianetti understood it: "They were gonna put Ron in touch with the guy in charge of Dave's father's real estate division, and they had some kind of deal where they were gonna buy up all the property in the surrounding areas where Dave's father was going to develop a mall— knowing that Dave's father was going to want it too—to basically preempt anyone else and sell it to their father's company. Basically to squeeze their dad. They thought that was great."

Joe seemed to have put together a company of players, Ron said. Even Hunt was taken by surprise, though, when Levin announced in late June that he had decided to liquidate his investment fund at E. F. Hutton and place the money in a commodities account to be traded by Joe. How much money were they talking about? Joe asked; $5,225,187, Ron answered, and 50¢.

"All confidence is false," Ron liked to say, with that heartfelt cynicism that made him at once the best-loved and most despised con artist in Beverly Hills. The character described by *Interview* magazine as "a flamboyant crony of celebrities" had been little Ronnie Glick once upon a time, back in Cleveland, Ohio, where he was already half an orphan at the age of three, after his father, Roy, was killed during June of 1944 in a battle near Nancy, France, fighting with General George Patton's Third Army. His mother, Carol, moved the boy to California during the celebration of the Allied victory in Europe. Carol worked as a bank clerk and then as a dental hygienist during those first years in Los Angeles, eking out an existence made more difficult by her son's problems at school. His teachers described Ronnie as a likable, even charming boy who couldn't be controlled. "A disruptive influence," said the instructor who complained to Carol that her son would sharpen his pencil six times in ten minutes during a spelling test. It wasn't fair to the other children, explained the teacher who reported that Ronnie asked to go to the bathroom no less than twenty times a day. He raised his hands every sixty seconds or so, said another teacher. Between the ages of six and nine, the boy was admitted to and expelled from seven schools, public and private.

When Ronnie's teachers gave up on him, his mother turned to doctors. Hyperkinesis was a tenuously accepted and marginally understood diagnosis in those days. Medication was attempted, but nothing slowed Ronnie down, and one or two prescriptions actually increased the child's agitation.

Carol had help by the time Ronnie turned nine, having taken her second husband, Martin Levin, a short, balding haberdasher who was utterly devoted to her. Carol was more than Marty dared hope for, a true tomato, in the parlance of the period, tall and willowy, with a heart-shaped face, luxuriant red hair, and a southern belle pallor that lent her the aspect of a lady born to wear the Van Cleef & Arpel jewelry she learned to favor. Mr. Levin doted on his bride, showered her with gifts, would do anything for her, even adopt her problem child.

Just before he turned thirteen, the Levins got Ronnie admitted to the Remedial Reading School on the UCLA campus. The classes were small, five or six students to a room, but the other children all were years younger than Ronnie, who was tall for his age anyway. "They'd call him dummy," Marty remembered. When the teachers at UCLA finally penetrated Ronnie's dyslexia and taught him to read, however, they discovered the boy hardly was dumb. Although handicapped by a short attention span, Ronnie inhaled books in great gulps of concentration, remembering almost every word he read. His IQ was unmeasurable, the teachers said, but it had to be in the genius range.

Despite what was already a profound estrangement from ordinary existence, Ronnie, growing up during the 1950s in an upper-middle-class Jewish family, assimilated his mother's belief that to become a doctor or a lawyer was the appropriate ambition of every bright boy. He began devoting himself to medicine during his early teens, reading *Gray's Anatomy* from cover to cover, supplementing his studies with medical texts he bought used at the UCLA bookstore and requesting a chemistry set for his thirteenth birthday. A few months later, Ronnie began to attend performances at the famous medical theatre in the UCLA Medical Center, standing shoulder to shoulder with the world's leading physicians as they observed the latest in surgical techniques from the balcony above the operating room. Ronnie was fourteen when he participated in his first operation, the removal of a brain tumor, slipping onto the medical theatre's main stage disguised by a surgical cap, gown, and mask filched from the laundry. Only as the patient's head was being closed did one of the nurses notice that there seemed to be an extra doctor in the room. Marty remembered the call from campus police an hour later: "'We have your son,' they said."

Ronnie was fifteen when he graduated from the Remedial Reading School. It was the only diploma he ever would receive. His parents enrolled him in several private high schools, including the Beverly Hills Military Academy, but Ronnie never lasted even a single semester at any of them. He was still in his teens when he was arrested for the first time, after faking a signature to rent a car. Carol and Marty sent him to a psychiatrist, who recommended a special school in the state of Washington, where Ronnie was arrested for the second time when he went AWOL a few weeks after his arrival.

Back in Beverly Hills, his parents rented the boy an apartment at 148 South Peck Drive, right next door to the duplex where he would establish his eventual domain. He continued to visit the medical center, often sitting in on classes. A number of physicians on the faculty found themselves fascinated by this strange and brilliant boy. "The only close friends Ronnie ever made before he left home were the doctors at UCLA," his mother recalled. One of these was Dr. Thomas Noguchi, the famed pathologist who would perform the autopsies on Marilyn Monroe and Robert Kennedy, among others, in his position as Los Angeles County coroner. Noguchi adored Ronnie, offering to write a letter of recommendation if the boy would apply to medical school.

Classrooms never had been happy places for him, though, so instead Ronnie used Noguchi's good offices to obtain work in a funeral home on Washington Boulevard. His work embalming corpses bored Ron after a year on the job, however. "So then he was in pictures for a while," Marty remembered. Ron's first performance on film was with Elvis Presley in the King's *Viva Las Vegas,* a job obtained when he won a dance contest sponsored by the film's producer. Later Ron would frug and twist with Annette Funicello and Frankie Avalon in their beach-party movies and even worked as an instructor at the famous Mark Boyd Dancing School. During the months he spent on and around movie sets, Ron discovered that while he would always feel outcast among the conventional, he achieved ease the moment he entered a star's orbit. He was accepted, acknowledged, even encouraged by Elvis and his entourage, Ron said; they didn't expect him to be like everyone else. "Ronnie needed to live in a kind of dream world," his adopted father explained. "Reality didn't interest him."

Yet Ron's attraction to the stage lights was countered continually by a yearning to appear solid and successful in his mother's eyes. Still in his early twenties, he started a limousine service, created a term-paper business catering to premed students, managed a rock 'n' roll group called the Time. "But he still couldn't concentrate and go with any one thing," said Marty. "As soon as he found he could do something, he was done with it," explained Carol. His parents tried bringing him into the family business. Marty gave him a job as a salesman at the men's store, Marty's (the women's store was Carol's), even bought him a good suit, but after Ron left for lunch that first day, he never came back.

However much his parents anguished over Ronnie, the young man retained a celestial sparkle in the eyes of his half-brother, Robert. Bob never would forget his fourteenth birthday, when Ronnie picked him up at home in a limousine, then directed the driver up over Sepulveda Pass into Hidden Hills, where the Dodgers lived, to keep a lunch appointment at Don Drysdale's house: "Whenever Ronnie was around, amazing things happened."

Yet Ron could not find freedom from an aching to achieve what Carol called "a professional career." Learning it was possible to be admitted to the state bar without formal education, Ron abandoned his medical texts for law books. Within a year, despite his inability to submit a transcript that went beyond the sixth grade, Ron was admitted to West Los Angeles Law School, after scoring in the ninety-ninth percentile on his law boards. He lasted less than four months. "It was too slow for him," explained Carol.

There always seemed to be a professor who recognized Ron's brilliance, however. This time, one of his teachers offered Ron a job as a clerk in his law office, promising to tutor the young man until he passed the bar exam. Ron resigned after a few weeks on the job. Coming into an office every morning, grinding out briefs in support of insurance claims and tenant evictions, that was not his idea of a life, Ron said. The experience did inspire the young man, however, to create a new business, by far his most successful, subcontracting to perform research and prepare briefs for some of the city's largest law firms. Legal Research Associates, he called it. Ron did little of the labor himself, instead assembling a staff that ranged from recent law school graduates waiting to take the bar exam to retired municipal court judges. "A Kelly Girls for lawyers," he described his business to the Los Angeles legal community's *Daily Journal*.

He had been among the earliest to rent space from Paul Fegan, the entrepreneur whose Fegan Suites approach to commercial real estate—renting out shared suites of offices—would make him one of the wealthiest men in Los Angeles. The first Fegan Suite was in the Glendale Federal Savings building, where Ron generated much of his business in the offices of neighbors Len Jacoby and Steve Meyers, who were introducing the first television-advertised, mass-marketed law firm.

Increasingly, it was Ron's appearance that put him over in person. Long and limber, his fine features always had been striking, an effect that became even more pronounced when he went prematurely gray and answered by growing a beard, bleaching it white, hot-combing and clipping the hair, adding tinctures and toners until it acquired the softness and sheen of alpaca fleece. "I used to tell him he looked like a Medici prince when accoutered," recalled Gloria Van Dyk, one of the young lawyers Levin hired at Legal Research Associates. She had taken the job planning to leave after a summer and instead stayed three years, Van Dyk reflected. "It was both the poorest-paying and most exciting office I've ever worked in," she said. Nearly all the excitement was generated by the boss. Between classes at West Los Angeles Law School (where he was admitted for a second time) and UCLA (where he served as president of the premed club), Ron worked as a notary public and a male model, on the side speculating profitably in precious metals. His various mail-order businesses offered the public everything from paperweights to performance-enhancing sexual ointments. During the OPEC oil embargo, Ron struck a blow for Yankee ingenuity by running up a thirty-thousand-dollar tab at Western Union for telegrams sent to businesses in Qatar and Yemen, announcing that his "international import firm" would accept orders for American products that included computers, aircraft, and automobiles. In the midst of all this, he found time to form a talent agency that represented the Jackson 5. "They used to come around the office when Michael was just a young boy," Van Dyk recalled. "I taught him to tango," Ron would say later.

Levin was learning a number of new moves himself during this period, picking up most of his fresh steps while playing the part of court clown at Bernie Cornfeld's palace. Cornfeld's Geneva-based Investor's Overseas Services had been perhaps the biggest financial hustle in history, organizing hundreds of subsidiary companies into investment plans offering an international array of tax havens. The former Brooklyn social worker began promoting IOS as "worldwide people's capitalism" during the late sixties. "Do you sincerely want to be rich?" was the question posed by Bernie and his sales staff of fifteen thousand as they went about selling investment plans to African tribal chieftains and Eskimo consortiums. "Possibly the world's richest man," *Newsweek* called Cornfeld at the height of his success. Nobody knew for sure what Bernie was worth, but the lifestyle he created at his Swiss castle, Château de Pelly, suggested a splendor known previously only to the readers of Jacqueline Susann novels. "We're in the business of converting the proletariat to the leisured class painlessly," the self-proclaimed "ex-socialist" had exulted in 1969. Bernie's ebullience subsided a year later, though, when European bankers staged a bear raid on IOS stock after it was reported in the press that more than one-third of the net worth of IOS had been loaned to its companies, officers, and friends. The ensuing liquidation compelled Cornfeld and Co. to pay off at a rate that reached ten million dollars a day. Exchanges in Toronto and London suspended trading of IOS stock, and in June of 1970, Bernie was deposed by his own board. In 1971 he sold his IOS shares—either to or through the international financial criminal Robert Vesco—for millions rather than billions.

Inevitably, Bernie had repaired to Southern California, where for a time he managed actually to escalate his standard of living, purchasing a mansion called Grayhall in the Hollywood Hills that became the wildest party house in L.A., a place crawling with aspiring actresses. Cornfeld had been amused and intrigued by Ron Levin from the moment they met, taking the young man under his wing, introducing him to assorted earthshakers and superstars. "Ron made Bernie laugh, for one thing, but what really made Cornfeld happy was that Levin always brought at least one woman with him when he came up the hill but never took any girls when he left, and Bernie appreciated the hell out of that," recalled a regular at the house. "Guys like Nicholson and Beatty and Pacino would come in empty-handed, then lure Bernie's girls out the door, and it drove the guy nuts; he literally got sick over it."

While Bernie envied star power, Ron basked in it, ingratiating himself to the famous at every opportunity. "At the office, he would tell us, 'Don't interrupt me; I'm on the phone with Jack, or Warren, or Al,'" recalled Van Dyk. "Ron actively courted celebrities," said another attorney who worked for him. "If all else failed, he would get them deals."

The most enduring relationships Ron formed during his Grayhall period, however, were with a loose association of lawyers who had fallen into stages of disrepute ranging from disbarment to federal prison sentences. One-by-one, Ron hired his new friends to work at Legal Research Associates. "Pretty soon it seemed like he knew every shady lawyer in town," recalled Van Dyk. What Ron acquired from these associates was an increasingly sophisticated grasp of that gray area in the law having to do with "provable intent," the hazy and malleable line dividing civil tort from criminal fraud.

He began to take advantage of those opportunities afforded by the creation of collateral corporations: Law Care, Law Clinic, Law Network, National Law Institute. It seemed that each new company he formed qualified for its own line of loan approval, its own checking accounts, and, best of all, its own credit cards. As president of more than two dozen corporations, Ron became a world-class shopper, leasing a fleet of luxury automobiles and making daily forays into the stores that lined the streets north of Wilshire between Canon and Bedford Drives. Although regularly short of cash—frequently borrowing money from Marty to pay the rent on his one-bedroom apartment—Ron was able to sell himself into almost any situation when he stepped out his front door. "It's amazing how far a man can go in this town with a Rolex and a Rolls," he would observe with that high, hysterical giggle of his.

Van Dyk and other associates at Legal Research sniffed at the scent of scandal, "but Ron had a decent sense of shame about what he did back then," Gloria recalled. "He would usually send me out of the room when he was discussing anything nefarious." Ron could not resist boasting of his more creative scams, however, describing to Van Dyk how he had raised several thousand desperately needed dollars by scraping the paint off his first Rolls-Royce with a house key for the insurance claim. When his secretary asked for a loan, Ron replied that he was a bit short of cash at the moment, "but offered to have me rear-ended instead," she recalled.

"He wouldn't steal from family members or from employees," Van Dyk observed. "He would from friends, but to him that was like a practical joke, a game of one-upsmanship." "If he did things illegal, he did it to show people how smart he was, not for personal gain," Marty agreed. "He had been bound so long that he wanted to show that he could be somebody."

"He was a thief," explained Van Dyk, who remained close to Ron for years after she left his employ, "and yet he was also one of the basically most honest people I've ever known. On an emotional level, I mean. Ronnie would share his soul with you. He had this vibrancy. It was something so real that people felt a tremendous affection for him, sometimes even after he ripped them off. I was always furious at him, but I always forgave him. I felt an almost religious love for Ronnie. I know it sounds funny, but it wasn't sexual and it wasn't the usual friendly feeling. It was something special."

The boy who had grown up unable to form even a single friendship found himself at age thirty encircled by the beautiful and dangerous. Ron's wicked grin, an affront to some, was irresistible to others. In crowded rooms he could sustain several conversations at once, shattering trust and flattering vanity in the same breath, seducing with allusions that put Dostoyevsky piggyback on Dale Carnegie, holding whole rooms enraptured as that high, nasal, manic voice spewed forth propositions, ripostes, insights, and insinuations at a rate that left listeners dazzled and dumbfounded.

The person to whom Ron granted greatest access to his private business was the friend who always had put the coldest eye on him, Len Marmor, his next-door neighbor. Marmor was a burly, balding, bearded fellow who padded around in plum velvet Gucci loafers and exquisite golf sweaters, looking from a high angle like an overdressed thug, yet exuding an ineffable air of distinction. What intrigued Ron about his neighbor was that Marmor seemed to live very well for someone lacking any visible means of support. Ron's interest turned to esteem on the evening when he invited Len to dinner at La Scala. A man in a shiny suit wearing a bimbo on one arm and a bodyguard on the other had attempted to take their table. Marmor floored the bodyguard with one punch, then turned on his employer. The man in the suit mentioned the name of a certain Italian-American business-man residing in New Jersey. Marmor replied with the name of a man from Brooklyn, observing that the second man did not think highly of the first. The man in the suit turned white, began to shake, then literally sprinted out of the restaurant. "When Ron saw the way I dealt with that type of situation," Marmor recalled, "he was very impressed."

The admiration in this regard was mutual. "Ron was a person who could not be intimidated," Marmor said. "I never saw him show fear once in the whole time I knew him. He was an aggressive fellow who projected total confidence and insisted upon people understanding this about him. He would go to any length to sell it."

While Len appreciated Ron's nerve, however, it was Levin's wit that made his company a pleasure. Ron's invention of a personal fortune was among his more amusing projects. He had begun by opening accounts at almost every bank in Beverly Hills, always using a check drawn on another local bank as his initial deposit, each one written for an amount in the neigh-borhood of half a million dollars. The accounts would be canceled, of course, as soon as the checks—the $373,648 one written on a First Fidelity account containing $82, the $641,003 one written on a Manufacturers Hanover account containing $37—bounced, but by then Ron would have added to his collection yet another passbook showing a single enormous deposit and no withdrawals. Ron found that these same banks would allow him to open accounts in the names of his corporate shells. Invariably, each company would issue its first check—somewhere in the $200,001 to $999,999 range—to one Ronald G. Levin. These Ron left lying on his desk with the passbooks, or used as bookmarks, or placed faceup on the floor under a chair in his office so that when a visitor spotted it he could say, casually, "I was wondering where that went."

While Ron "had the outward appearance of possessing wealth," Marmor said, "he was most of the time without money." Marmor could recall at least one occasion, though, when Ron not only amassed a significant sum but did so legally, selling a cache of silver purchased for five dollars an ounce when the price hit fifty dollars and coming away with a profit that was "well into six figures, though less than a million." Ron was not a man who pinched his pennies, however. "He loved to spend," Marmor explained. When he was flush, Ron would invite as many as two dozen guests to dine with him at the best restaurants of Beverly Hills, recalling these adventures according to the kind of automobile he might have purchased for what the evening cost him, memorializing such meals as the "Datsun dinner" or the "Subaru supper." He rented the largest suites at the Beverly Hilton and Century Plaza hotels to host catered parties where the bar stayed open all night, bought Swiss watches as presents for people he barely knew, flew to Paris for dinner and was back in Beverly Hills in time for breakfast on the loggia at the Polo Lounge. It wasn't long before his profits from the silver sale were gone, Marmor recalled, but Ron was a man who professed to value the money he stole far more than the money he earned. Whenever Ron opened his mail to find a new credit card issued to one of his companies, Marmor recalled, "he would bring it right over to show me. He would rub it all over his body, caress his ass with it, put it under his shirt, and the whole time he's making these sounds—'ooh, whee, ahhh.' It was like an orgasm for him. Then he would go out and run it up to its maximum the very first day."

The beauty of the man, in Marmor's view, was that Ron never relented: "His attitude toward the people he owed money was that he wanted to increase the numbers." At the same time, however, Ron was unable to spend more than a few hours around anyone without telling them he was a con man and a thief. "He couldn't contain it," Marmor recalled. "It was the thing he bragged about."

Marmor had loaned Ron as much as twenty-five thousand dollars at a time and prided himself on the fact that he got most of his money back: "I don't know of anybody else he ever paid. I took it as a sign of our friendship." The relationship baffled Ron's other friends. Marmor was gruff always and often ugly, flouting decency as if he regarded it as an affectation of the effete. While Ron was remarkably free of prejudice, Marmor was a man who called blacks "niggers" and gays "faggots," who insisted upon addressing Ron's friend Muhammad Ali as Cassius Clay and carried a handicapped sticker in his Mercedes convertible to avoid wasting time searching for parking places, dismissing inquiries into the propriety of this practice by growling, "Fuck the gimps." At the same time Ron objected to such speech, he seemed to consider it evidence of a perverse integrity, and for years Marmor was the sole person to whom Ron would confide the true nature of his financial dealings: "He told me, 'You're the only one who really knows me, the only one I can be truthful with.'"

In 1975 Ron moved from his one-bedroom apartment to the luxurious duplex next door. He had been in residence for only a few months before contriving to swindle his elderly landlady, Lillian Warner, by typing the following on the back of a rent check: "I, Lillian Warner, agree that by endorsing this check I grant to Ronald G. Levin and/or his agents an option to purchase the building at 144 S. Peck Drive, Beverly Hills, California, for a firm and final price of $30,000, such option to remain in effect for a period of ten (10) years." The building would be worth more than $1 million by the time the option expired, but the old woman had signed and deposited the check, which Ron referred to thereafter as "our contract." Mrs. Warner died soon after, leaving behind a will that bequeathed the building to the Catholic Church. "I couldn't believe it when Ron told me the old bitch left that building to the church," Marmor recalled. "I thought it was the most disgusting thing I ever heard."

The two soon conceived a plan to claim the building belonged to them. They brought in Ron's half-brother, Bob, who by then had been admitted to the state bar. "Ronnie had sold his option on that building to a number of people, but he couldn't record it," Bob recalled, "because of all the creditor claims against him. So he and Lenny called me up and asked me to put it in my name. I went over there for a meeting. This was the first time I met Lenny, and I could see right away that he was the type of person who makes me nervous. I asked him, 'You ever been in jail?' He said, 'Yeah.' The deal they had in mind was that Lenny was gonna give me the money, I was gonna record this option in my name, and somehow—it was like they were gonna make it look like Lenny was owed money by Ronnie, and Ronnie had this option, Lenny was gonna loan me money, I was gonna pay it back to Lenny in exchange for the option, and then . . . already I was getting nervous. After a few minutes I said, 'I'd like to help you out, but I don't sleep well in these types of situations.'"

During the years that Marmor believed he was Ron's best friend, there were at least a dozen other men and women—film directors, artists, actors, heiresses, and athletes—who believed the same about themselves. "Ron was many people," one would observe, "and if you gave him the time, he would introduce you to them all." Of the numerous claims made upon

Ron's affection, perhaps the most compelling came from Mark Geller. The two had met for the first time in 1973, when Geller, a recent law school graduate, went to work on a research project at Ron's National Law Institute while awaiting the results of his bar exam. Geller's first day on the job would be the most memorable of his life; in the span of a few hours Mark met both the man he considered his closest friend and his future wife, Laura, who was working as a receptionist in the office.

When Mark and Laura married in 1975, Ron was the best man. By then, Geller had withdrawn from the practice of law to compete with Michael Milken in the field of corporate finance and already was a wealthy man by the time he ascended to CEO at his Beverly Hills–based firm. Despite the obvious differences in their professional pursuits, Geller said, "Ron and I had many essential qualities in common." Like Mark, Ron was obsessed with order and cleanliness, insisting that his housekeepers wipe and dust even his unsorted mail and bedside reading each day. Levin accompanied the Gellers on shopping sprees all over the world, sharing their search for bargains on Pratesi linens, Christofle silver, and Steuben crystal. Ron delighted in playing on the greed of overzealous salespeople, Mark recalled: "I remember once I was at his house, and Mrs. Levin's houseboy Joseph was there. Ron had gone to an art gallery and bought three pictures rapid-fire, all very expensive, just to impress the salespeople. The salesman had tried very hard to sell him another, even more expensive picture. Ron called back and said he had decided to take it. He said, 'I'm sending my butler over to pick it up. Bill me on memo.' Then he'd never pay."

Mark arranged to dine out with Ron at least once a week, always in "the better restaurants"—Spago, Mr. Chow's, Ma Maison, L'Entourage, and Ron's perennial favorite, La Scala. Ron's affection for this venerable but faded establishment was for him an expression of his devotion to Beverly Hills. La Scala once had been the city's most expensive restaurant, and even in decline the place retained the shimmer of that tony glamour attaching to longtime loyalists such as Jimmy Stewart, Cesar Romero, and Lucille Ball. "This is my new home," Ron would proclaim when he truly loved a place, and all the places he loved best were in Beverly Hills. His passion for his adopted hometown exceeded all Ron's other devotions. It was the only city in the world where bomber jackets for babies could be purchased at two stores on the same block, the one community on earth that could support a thriving black market in Histoacycryl, the wonder glue that permitted plastic surgeons to close incisions without leaving scars. "Where else could I live?" Ron often asked.

He always had adored grand hotels, Claridges and the Savoy in London, the Pierre and the Plaza in New York, and yet the hotels Ron loved best were those within walking distance of his own home. When he was blue or bored, Ron would reserve a suite at the Bel Air or the Beverly Wilshire, invite friends for dinner, then suggest they stay for breakfast, running up huge tabs on fresh credit cards. Ron's favorite place on the planet, though, always would be that moldering palace of pink adobe that seemed to hover in a perpetual Pacific twilight among the towering palm and peppercorn trees on the knoll above the intersection at Sunset and Coldwater. Ron loved the Beverly Hills Hotel so dearly that even when he could not afford a room he came early on Sunday morning to rent a cabana out by the pool. Ron was on a first-name basis with almost everyone who mattered at the Beverly Hills, from its six-foot, four-inch doorman Leon Johnson to its four-foot, six-inch page Buddy Douglas.

He knew all the hotel's legends, could tell you how Elizabeth Taylor insisted upon cut crystal bowls of pistachios in the bungalows where she honeymooned with her various husbands, why Van Johnson would use only red napkins when he dined on the loggia, where the chef got the bear steaks demanded by a certain Texas oilman or the honey-glazed larks requested by a Saudi sheik. Ron knew that it was booth two in the Polo Lounge where Haldeman, Ehrlichman, and Mitchell were sitting when the call came from the White House informing them that the Watergate story had broken, and which booths as well had been favored by Charlie Chaplin and Paulette Goddard, Errol Flynn and Freddie McEvoy, W. C. Fields and John Barrymore, whose pal the cartoonist George McManus once crashed a private party in the Polo Lounge by tearing a button stamped PRESS off a men's room urinal and attaching it to his lapel.

As he assembled his company beside the hotel's pool on a Sunday morning, Ron "would tend to be noticed," his friend Geller reflected. Ron's practice was to begin his morning by ordering four grapefruits for himself, very loudly. Only when certain that he had the attention of everyone within earshot would Ron proceed through the remainder of the breakfast menu, ordering eggs benedict with bagels and lox, Spanish omelets with waffles and strawberries, surrounding himself with platter upon platter of food, eating only a bite or two from each, yet insisting they be left where they were, in display of his profligacy.

Wherever he went, Ron endeavored mightily to create a scene around himself, Mark explained. In restaurants, Ron always introduced himself—though not always by his true name—to those sitting at nearby tables, welcoming visitors, inveigling celebrities, entertaining everyone. Like most residents of Beverly Hills, Ron regarded special treatment as evidence of his standing in the community. He had appeased this conceit most satisfactorily during a period in the late seventies, when somehow he persuaded the manager and the maître d' at the Bistro Gardens to provide him with a private dining room for his luncheon at the restaurant. "He would get them to set up a special table on the second floor, where they normally wouldn't serve," Geller recalled. "Everyone would watch as this was done . . . he made a big production out of it."

Yet when they ate out together, "I usually paid for his dinners," Mark remembered. "He said, 'You're one of the few who pays for me. The rest all sponge.'"

As he moved into his mid-thirties, Ron began to surround himself with an entourage of "poor little rich boys," as he called them. "Ronnie wanted that feeling of family and closeness," Marty explained. Among the boys who formed Ron's "kiddie corps" was the son of his former friend Janet Factor, of the Max Factor family. Janet had been among Levin's intimates for years until their falling-out when Ron arranged for her to purchase a dining table at a bargain price, only to decide that the piece suited his own home so well that he should leave it there. Janet refused to speak to him after that; Ron responded by taking her son Dean under his wing. The younger Factor was a Beverly Hills High freshman at the time, as was his friend Michael Broder, who joined Ron's circle that same season. On weekdays they would walk to his house after school and spend the afternoon, Dean recalled. In the evening, Ron might take them to dinner, to a movie, or roller-skating on the disco rink at Flippers. "Ron was always doing interesting things," explained Michael, recalling the time Levin loaned him a limo for a trip to Magic Mountain.

His boys all were a little uncertain about Ron's professional status, he carried both a beeper for his medical practice and business cards from his law firm. "Most of the time he was a lawyer," Michael recalled, "but he was Dr. Levin when he wanted a good seat in a restaurant." Ron boasted often of his work with Dr. Noguchi. One afternoon when Michael and Dean challenged Ron's training as a physician, he drove them to the UCLA Medical School and "talked his way past several people," Michael remembered, until the three of them reached a cold room filled with cadavers. Ron lifted sheets off several of the corpses until he found a fellow he liked, then proceeded to cut the man open, Michael recalled, explaining the functions of each organ as he removed it from the body.

When Michael was fifteen, Ron hired him to work for the summer as an errand boy, paying him five dollars an hour to deliver an occasional package. Most of the time Michael sat around, and the benefits were fantastic: Ron took him several times to lunch at Muhammad Ali's.

Few who knew him doubted that Ron's support of black causes was sincere, and even the cynic Marmor regarded Levin's ability to be accepted as the one white face among the inner circles of black celebrities and politicians as nothing less than astonishing. Ali regularly flew Ron to his championship fights during the 1970s, providing him on each occasion with front-row seats, and often dined with Ron before his bouts. Ron donated both time and money to Yvonne Burke's campaign to become California's attorney general, keeping the letter of gratitude and inscribed photo she gave him on his office desk for years afterward. He opened his home to Jesse Jackson several times when the reverend was in Los Angeles to make appearances on behalf of Operation Push. One of the city's most prominent black physicians, Richard Hendrix, would say that he might never have made it through medical school without moral and monetary support from Ron.

Like all those to whom Ron played benefactor, his boys believed he was enormously wealthy. When Ron took them to a movie, Broder remembered, he invariably paid with a hundred-dollar bill. Ron's motor vehicles during the years Dean and Michael knew him included two limousines, a Rolls-Royce Silver Shadow, two Mercedeses, and at least four BMWs. "He liked to tell people how much things cost and where he bought them," Michael remembered. For years Ron kept the stamped and canceled one-million-dollar check he claimed to have inherited on his twenty-first birthday mounted in a gold frame on his office wall, and when he took them out to dinner, Michael recalled, he often carried one-ounce silver bars "from a bigger pile that he said he had."

Ron used his money not only to collect beautiful boys but also to attract celebrities. Sometimes the two tendencies overlapped, as in the case of his relationship with Don Johnson. The two met for the first time at Andy Warhol's Factory in New York. This was years before *Miami Vice* made Johnson famous, back when the actor's first film, *Stanley Sweetheart,* was in release. Warhol was so taken with the handsome young actor that he made Johnson one of *Interview*'s first cover boys, then invited him back to New York, all expenses paid. Ron was the Factory's criminal-in-residence at the time, often in the company of Warhol's director, Paul Morrissey. Ron "hit on me in his crudely blunt way," Johnson recalled, "and in my crudely blunt way I told him, 'Go fuck yourself.' And when he laughed and accepted that, I thought, 'You're all right.'" The two got to know one another better back in Los Angeles. Familiarity with Ron was an experience he thought of as "educational," Johnson said: "He loved running with outlaws; he loved running those scams. I was involved in a couple myself when I was between acting jobs." The actor believed Ron took as much pleasure in the sport as in the profit: "People like Ronnie, they need the rush from the action." And anyway, "most of the time you'd be taking off people who were trying to take you off," Johnson observed. After the relationship ended, "I lived in hotels for years on techniques he taught me," the actor recalled, "sending the telex to New York: 'Mr. Johnson will be checking in and bill X Corporation.'"

Ron's methods of obtaining free lodging would evolve over the years. Recalled Warhol diarist Pat Hackett: "When [Ron] was in New York he'd call me and say, 'Darling, I'm at the Pierre, but ask for Dr. Levin— they think I'm going to book the place for a gynecologist's convention.'" "Tall, thin, striking, rude and funny" was how Hackett would eulogize Ron in *Interview*. "He paced like a panther and spent his lifetime making enemies by cheating people in order to make money to buy friends."

Of all the relationships Ron formed during his association with Warhol, the most enduring was with a woman, actress/model/fashion designer Terre Tereba. They met in Los Angeles, at the Filmex premiere of a Warhol/Morrissey movie in the Chinese Theatre. "I was with Warhol, and Ron was among the people Andy invited," she recalled. When they were seated next to one another in the theater, Terre remembered, she asked Ron what he did. "I'm a thief," he replied proudly. She was shocked, Terre said, and ignored Levin until after the film, when they all went to dinner. Ron grabbed the chair next to hers at the table and spoke during the meal as if they were old friends. "It was hard to resist him," she admitted. Not only was Ron intelligent and charming, but he understood women on an emotional level most men couldn't begin to imagine. He was an adult male who would shed tears at the most minor personal slight, who spoke often and openly of his loneliness, who seemed to feel no fear whatsoever of public humiliation and in fact took enormous pleasure in any opportunity to shock the uninitiated. She always would remember her first walk with Ron in Beverly Hills, Terre said, watching him grow giddy as he pointed at the windows of Fred's and Cartier and Tiffany, shrieking, "They're my creditors and they're my creditors and they're my creditors," as if elevated by the quality of the stores he stole from.

Ron's relationship with Terre was certified when he hung a photo portrait of her in an antique frame on his office wall with Laura Geller's. While he never would know one carnally, Ron worshiped beautiful women all his life. His Warhol lithographs of Marilyn Monroe were his most prized possessions, and the snapshot taken outside Marilyn's crypt in Westwood Cemetery was the image of himself he carried in his wallet. Eventually, Ron would hang the inscribed glossy given to him by Bianca Jagger with those of Terre and Laura on the wall he had made "a shrine to my goddesses." There was only one woman, however, whose image Ron allowed into his bedroom, a lady whose grace and charm he extolled endlessly. That was his mother, Carol. "He always talked about how beautiful and elegant his mother was," Mark Geller remembered. "She was his ideal woman. He said he would never find one like her."

At the same time that Ron insisted upon his adoration of Carol to everyone else, however, he permitted Len Marmor to tell him that his mother had sent her oldest son away to boarding school in order to protect her marriage to Marty. Look at the way your parents live, Len would say: Marty drives a battered old Cadillac while Carol cruises Beverly Hills in a Rolls-Royce; at the same time he wears cheap suits off the rack, she dresses in designer originals. "He gave her what she wanted to get what he wanted," Marmor insisted. "Marrying a guy for money, it's the same as being a whore."

Carol Levin insisted she was "extraordinarily close to my son." Wherever Ronnie went in the world, Mrs. Levin said, he would call her the moment he arrived. When he was at home in Beverly Hills, his mother stopped by the Peck Drive duplex at least twice a week: "I'd see him in bed reading, maybe," Carol recalled, "give him a kiss on the head, and go right back out." Ron didn't visit Carol's house, except on Jewish holidays, but he never forgot Mother's Day, every May sending her a bouquet of flowers and a card with a lavish inscription.

His mother was one of many people who were confused about Ron's sexual nature. While he most often professed to be gay, Ron told many people he slept with women. Most of his friends agreed with Gloria Van Dyk that Ron was "ultimately asexual." "He was an adult child, really," she explained. "Ronnie never made a pass at me in the whole time I knew him," Michael Broder said, and Dean Factor described Ron's sexual interests, if any, as "a mystery." "Ron was deeply ambivalent," said his lawyer and friend Oliver Wendell Holmes III. "He had macho values and wanted to be known as a ladies' man. He was very effeminate but tried not to be. And yet his admiration for beautiful women was sincere, and he liked to be around them."

Holmes had been retained by Ron to represent him in a claim against IBM. The incident in question involved the repossession of a typewriter: Ron resisted, there was a scuffle, and he had broken a bone in his hand. The IBM lawsuit hardly ranked among his most inventive, of course, nothing on the order of the eleven-million-dollar claim he filed against a cleaning company he said had destroyed important records, or the landlord he sued for injuries suffered when he "tripped and fell violently" because an elevator had stopped two inches below floor level. Ron would stiff Holmes for almost twenty thousand dollars in legal fees when he abandoned the IBM claim, but "for some reason I was able to accept it from him," Holmes said. "I suppose I considered it the price of admission to the world of the most fantastic, complicated character I have ever encountered."

Ron had informed his newest attorney at their first meeting that he was a con man by profession. "Yet he always presented his parents as extremely wealthy people," Holmes recalled. "Part of Ron's mystique was that he was rich to begin with, didn't really need the money he scammed or stole, but liked his 'little naughties.'" He found it possible to forgive Ron's transgressions, Holmes said, because of "the childlike, naïve quality to him. For all the elaboration of his scams, Ron really didn't appreciate the moral implications in things . . . he genuinely enjoyed having certain people around him, but that didn't make him feel any obligation toward them. It was every man for himself out there, the way he saw it." No matter who Ron ripped off, friend or foe, Holmes recalled, "his attitude was always the same: 'Take your loss and move on. You got a lesson.'"

Even his celebrity friends would be burned by Ron eventually. His long relationship with Muhammad Ali ended when Ron agreed to help the fighter's wife Veronica decorate their home. After arranging for the purchase of several exquisite Persian rugs, Ron kept the very finest for himself, placing it in his dining room under the table he had filched from Janet Factor. Said Don Johnson, "I broke even, and with him, hey, that was winning."

"I always had the feeling he intended to make it up to his victims later," Holmes said. "Often the horrible things he did came right after something very generous he had done. He'd see someone in trouble, give them money or assistance, then when they were back on their feet, he'd rob them blind."

Given the amount of time he spent fielding threats from lawyers, Ron felt it was prudent to keep an attorney of his own at home. Holmes had been kind enough to arrange a meeting for Ron with an alcoholic lawyer named R. Michael Wetherbee. Wetherbee was in some financial difficulty with the wrong people; Ron agreed to pay his debts, but only on the condition that Wetherbee make repayment by giving Ron the right to use his name, along with an imprimatur of the attorney's signature. Ron became R. Michael Wetherbee on a regular basis after that, but then "Ron was a number of attorneys," his friend Marmor noted.

"Ron would do deals with people who'd make you afraid to be in the same room with them," recalled Holmes, who never had been more impressed with Levin than on the afternoon when a strong-arm man appeared at his front door to collect on a debt owed to one such individual. "Ron showed no trace of fear," Holmes recalled. "When the man threatened him with violence, Ron told him, 'You are not going to do anything of the sort. You'll have to kill me,' et cetera. Ron sat the man down to talk to him, and this person actually became one of Ron's followers. The next time I saw him, he was working as Ron's bodyguard."

Charm and nerve weren't all Ron had working for him, of course. "Triple smart," Don Johnson called him. "He was more successful for a longer time than most con men because he had a genuinely first-rate mind," Holmes agreed. "He could have been legitimately successful in dozens of fields. There was this self-destructive side, though . . . Ron would take a project that had every promise of legitimate success, and then turn it into something crooked. I feel he wanted to be successful in a legitimate way, but he became afraid it wouldn't happen—and yet by then he had invested too much to risk failure, and so would go for the sure hundred thousand dollars."

By 1979, more than a score of legal judgments had stacked up against Ron in Los Angeles County courts, and dozens of other claims were pending. He was so besieged by bill collectors that he had to change his phone number every week to dial out. The number of threatening letters made sorting his mail an all-day task. When he finally filed for bankruptcy, Ron's petition to the court listed more than 750 creditors. The attorney who handled Levin's case presented him with a framed photograph of Juan Perón inciting the multitudes from his balcony in Buenos Aires, with a caption that read, "RON ADDRESSING HIS CREDITORS."

Even his family found it impossible to ignore the scale of Ron's excesses. Bob Levin read a TRW credit rating on his brother that ran to fifteen pages—"fifteen pages of bad," he recalled—and not long after saw a report from the U.S. Attorney's office describing Ron as "a danger to the commercial community." Ron asserted his array of famous friends as a buffer against apprehension. At a time when he was the object of investigations by the Los Angeles Police Department, the L.A. County Sheriff's Office, the California Department of Justice, the FBI, and the U.S. attorney general, Ron attempted to deflect detectives with a copy of the letter he had recently received from the Southern California Safe and Burglary Investigators Association, thanking him for bringing Muhammad Ali to their August 1979 meeting as a guest speaker.

The net closed on Ron in 1980, when he was sentenced to a year in federal prison for mail fraud. The charges arose out of advertisements Ron had placed in newspapers all over the country offering arthritis sufferers parcels from a "secret shipment" of the experimental drug DMSO. It seemed Ron possessed neither DMSO nor the right to sell the drug. His partner in the venture, Dr. Presley Reed Jr., had met Ron at the home of a mutual friend, the legendary Dr. William Kroger.

Kroger was a specialist in gynecology and obstetrics by training but had become famous as an international expert in the field of hypnosis and infamous as the therapist who confiscated, then returned, the pistol with which his patient the comic Freddie Prinze would commit suicide. Kroger's home on Doheny Drive was a magnificent estate, among the four or five finest properties in Bel Air, a place where the doctor entertained distinguished visitors from all over the world. Ron had been a regular guest at the doctor's dinner parties from the time he began sitting in on Kroger's Workshop in Hypnosis and Behavior Modification at UCLA. Like so many other professors on the Westwood campus, Kroger described Ron as the most brilliant pupil he ever had encountered; he presented to Ron a copy of his book on hypnosis with an inscription that read, *"To Ron Levin, a real genius."*

A few months after their introduction, Ron called Dr. Reed to say he was starting a mail-order DMSO business. He wanted to accept American Express cards, Ron explained, but couldn't get permission without an approved guarantor. If the doctor would cosign for him, Ron promised to repay with a percentage of the profits. Reed's decision to provide Ron with copies of his financial statements and tax records would haunt him for years afterward.

His new partner hardly was the only one taken by surprise, though, when the federal government first shut Ron down, then locked him up. The same day a story on Levin's conviction ran in the *L.A. Times,* his full-length picture ran in a *Los Angeles* magazine, which featured Ron in a wrinkled linen suit from Armani above the caption "THE NEW (RUMPLED) EXECUTIVE LOOK." "He told me he would never go to prison," Carol recalled, and Ron made good on this promise, persuading the judge to send him to an "honor ranch" called Wayside. "Carol was there every day, waiting dutifully in line with the other relatives, wearing her Van Cleef & Arpels jewelry," Gloria Van Dyk recalled. Van Dyk visited Ron at Wayside as well: "He was more dour and sober in there than I ever saw him," she recalled. "He said he had seen two guards murdered, and that truly disturbed and frightened him." It was an outrage that he had been locked up with such people, said Ron, who obtained a court order compelling his jailers to provide him with a typewriter, then told them he was using the machine to prepare a lawsuit naming them as defendants.

When he was released after serving three months, however, Ron endeavored to make, if not light, at least an anecdote of the experience. "He bragged about seeing someone thrown over a wall," Dean Factor remembered, "and said he made money off a laundry service in jail." "He told me he did okay," Marmor recalled. "Claimed he got protection from some guy for sexually servicing him." "He never discussed jail with me," said Carol Levin.

Back home in Beverly Hills, Ron recuperated from incarceration by upgrading his imaginary status, becoming Ronnie Rothschild, renegade scion of the European banking family. He was quite convincing; even Dean Factor, who had known him for years as Levin, believed he was a Rothschild on his mother's side. Ron bought a limousine and persuaded his parents' driver Fabulous Howard to act as his chauffeur in the evening, promising sundry future considerations. Only a maid and butler were required to complete his new family portrait, and Ron had spotted the perfect pair. Blanche and Christopher Sturkey were recently relocated from Detroit, where Blanche had taught handicapped children. In Los Angeles, she supplemented her retirement income by hiring on occasionally with the catering company where Chris was employed as a bartender. The Sturkeys were working a private party in Beverly Hills when they met Ron, who spent more time that evening interviewing the black couple in the corner than mingling with the white guests. "Come work for me," Ron said. "I'm retired," Blanche told him. "It'll be fun," Ron promised. "I got all the fun I need," Blanche said. "A couple of hours a day," Ron persisted. Blanche said no again but let him have her phone number. Within a week, Ron had worn her down; Blanche agreed to give him three hours a morning, Monday through Friday, and to be available with Chris to serve at dinner parties. Blanche chafed, though, when Ron referred to the Sturkeys as his butler and maid, faithful family retainers he had inherited from his mother, the Rothschild heiress. "And I'm not wearing any uniform," Blanche told him. She preferred to think of herself as a "girl Friday," Blanche said, but then roles tended to blur around Ron.

"I don't think there was anything in the world that Ron wouldn't have done for me if he could," Blanche would say, adding in the next breath, though, that "ours was a very odd relationship, a kind of odd, odd, odd relationship." She would be the first to acknowledge that Ron was "the biggest liar I've ever seen in my life," Blanche said. In fact, when she thought about it, "Every bad thing that's happened to me is through Ron Levin," Blanche added. It *had* been fun, though.

She did only Ron's cleaning at first, but that was chore enough, since he demanded that the house be dusted every day, yet refused to let her touch the piles of paper stacked floor-to-ceiling in every room. After a while Ron asked Blanche to do his shopping. Then he suggested that she pay his bills as well, opening a household account in her name. "As long as I worked for him, he never questioned me about a dime," she noted. Ron paid well and would surprise Blanche sometimes with a gift of diamond-stud earrings or a bracelet of real pearls. She and Chris never minded working at his house in the evening. "He gave nice parties and celebrities came," recalled Blanche. She admired Ron's taste: "He had nothing but the best. He had everything that any multimillionaire would have. He had more clothes than a department store. He had five-hundred-dollar, one-thousand-dollar sweaters. Yes indeed."

Ron hadn't hidden from Blanche his fondness for the artful fleece. He was enormously proud of his Louis Vuitton luggage, explaining he had obtained the full set by renting a Rolls-Royce and driving it to the Vuitton store, where he persuaded the salesman to load the bags into his trunk, "to make certain they fit properly," then pulled away from the curb moments after the lid was latched. If it had been a Mercedes, Ron said, they never would have trusted him.

The Sturkeys had been in Ron's employ for about a year when he offered the couple a business opportunity. He had a chance to buy a Rolls-Royce Silver Shadow that belonged to Jerry Buss for forty-six thousand dollars, Ron said, and the car was a steal at that price. "He knew I had some money," Blanche explained. "He said, 'We can make this deal and I know where I can sell the Rolls-Royce, and in a couple of weeks we can make maybe fifteen thousand dollars.'" "This is our life savings," Blanche told Ron, when she wrote the check. "A Rolls-Royce in the garage is better than money in the bank," Ron assured her. Blanche knew she was in trouble, though, the first time Ron drove the Rolls to the Beverly Hills Hotel: "I look good in this car," he said. "Don't I?" Weeks passed. "Every time I would say, 'Ron, what is happening with this car? You were supposed to sell it by now,'" Blanche recalled, "and he would say, 'Well, I got a man and he's going to call me this day,' and 'this week.' It went on and on." A year passed before Blanche went to Marty and Carol. Ron was indignant: "I'm hurt, Blanche," he said, before coughing up twenty thousand dollars in cash and a promissory note for twenty-six thousand. Just to show her the kind of person he was, Ron threw in a pair of round-trip tickets to Detroit and the spare key to his second car. "We kept his Mercedes any time we wanted it," recalled Blanche, who never would get the twenty-six thousand dollars. What always broke Blanche down was the trust Ron placed in her. "I was the only one who knew the combination to the lock on his door," she recalled. "His mother didn't even have it."

Naturally, Ron tried to turn even Blanche's integrity to his advantage. "He would tell awful lies and then he'd go and say, 'Blanche, tell 'em, tell 'em it's true,'" she recalled. "I'd say, 'Why should I tell 'em it's true? It's not true!' We used to have arguments like you wouldn't believe. And I would start to walk out the door and he would be pulling on me, and I would say, 'Ron, leave me alone!'" Blanche would be back in Beverly Hills the next morning, though, commuting by Mercedes from her home on Crip turf in South-Central Los Angeles. "I had to check on my Rolls-Royce," she explained. The truth was that she and Ron "got to be more friends than anything else," Blanche admitted: "I really felt about him like a son. There was nothing that went on that he didn't tell me. I understood him and I knew what he was. Which was a con man. I knew what Ron stood for, but I loved him."

Dusting his art and shelving his literature, Blanche listened as Ron discoursed on synaptic connection in the cortex and plots by Japanese consortiums to buy up downtown office buildings. His lectures were better than what you would get at an Ivy League college, Blanche thought: "I told him a million times, 'If you did constructively, you could have been the president.'" "But I'm so good at what I do now," Ron would answer, grinning hugely as he stood behind Blanche at the front door, whispering in her ear while she informed yet another bill collector or process server that Mr. Levin was out of town.

What could she do? Blanche would ask her critics: "Ron Levin was no good, but he had the kind of charm you couldn't ignore. He could con you into thinking it was sunshine when it was raining if he wanted to. That's the truth. He could charm the birds right out of a tree."

Ron was growing slightly more sedentary with age, however, conducting most of his business via the six phone extensions he had installed. "He would have them all going at once, sometimes," Blanche recalled. "The man could talk to half a dozen people at one time." A good deal of Ron's reluctance to venture from Peck Drive was the result of an increased concern for his personal safety. "I saw him threatened a number of times, at least three or four," recalled Michael Broder. "People called and said, 'Give me back what you took,' or they'll send someone over." Even Ron's sense of humor failed him after he was attacked in his own home. "This is what I get for being a nice guy," he complained bitterly. A hysterical young girl had collapsed on his doorstep, Ron said, sobbing that she had been assaulted and begging to use his phone. The moment he opened his door, a man with a hunting knife leapt out of the bushes behind her. Ron not only was cut on the throat but lost two paintings, a Leica camera, and a Rolex watch he was planning to return. Thank God he had doubled his money with the insurance claim, said Ron, who shaved off part of his beard to show friends the scar.

Within a week Ron was installing an elaborate security system, sealing off the entrance to his home with a heavy steel-mesh door wired into an electronically coded alarm box. "Ron's home was almost impregnable after that," recalled Mark Geller. "He even put gates on the windows that had to be opened with a key."

Ron began eating out less and entertaining at home more often. Since becoming a Rothschild, he had taken to leaving checks lying around that were drawn on the Swiss Credit Bank of Geneva or on New York's bank of the old-money elite, U.S. Trust Co. Despite the new international scope of his financial affairs, however, Ron traveled less and less. It was homesickness, he told Blanche, that had ended his Australian adventure. "He said Australia was nice," Blanche recalled, "but it wasn't Beverly Hills."

In the psychic laboratory he called his office, Ron's doctor and lawyer poses gave way to a new identity, that of world-class journalist "R. G. Levin." It was a fantasy Ron had harbored since his early twenties, when his first published work appeared in the *Santa Monica Evening Outlook*, a social note on a hundred-dollar-a-plate SHARE dinner emceed by that old Harvard School sermonizer Charlton Heston. Ron drifted into a show business delusion for a time, forming a film company in the late seventies called American Entertainment Group, for which he produced a series of "treatments" copyrighted through the Writers Guild. His favorite was "Rosenberg and Cohen," a "comedy film about medical students who make a deal with a funeral director to supply bodies for dissection." The characters were introduced by a witty corpse named Adam.

By 1980, though, it was news gathering that again commanded Ron's ambition, which he channeled into a series of journalistic corporations: Levin Enterprises Inc., General Information Corp., and the Institute of Investigative Reporting, publisher of the *Journal of Investigative Reporting*. After the Republican landslide in the November elections that year, Ron began to conceive himself a political conservative, claiming as his second writing credit a letter to the editor published by the *Herald Examiner* during January of 1981, a missive in which the author reprimanded NBC's mild commentator John Chancellor for "critical" remarks made in the aftermath of Ronald Reagan's inaugural address. "Who cares what he thinks?" R. G. Levin demanded to know. "I liked the president's speech. It was sincere and I was encouraged."

Trading Ron's account at Clayton Brokerage was Joe's chance to prove his trading theories conclusively. Finally he would control the kind of capital required to hold highly leveraged positions in the most volatile market anyone under sixty could recall. Joe appreciated Ron's choice of Clayton, a small, prestigious Saint Louis–based brokerage devoted exclusively to commodities and favored by many of the best traders in the country.

Ron insisted upon calling Joe's positions in to Clayton himself for the first week. All three Shadings were suspicious until July 5, when Ron gave Joe the number at Clayton and said he had authorized his broker there, Jack Friedman, to take orders directly from his personal trading advisor, Mr. Hunt. Joe took the precaution of calling in through the Clayton switchboard, asking for a transfer to Mr. Friedman's office. The broker's secretary kept him on hold for a minute, then put him through. "I'm Joe Hunt," he began. "Ron Levin gave me your number." "Hi, Joe, I been expecting your call," the broker came back.

When Joe asked where the account stood, Friedman informed him that a .25 percent loss in September Swiss franc contracts purchased the previous week had reduced working capital to a little less than $5 million. Still plenty to work with, the broker observed. Friedman suggested a hedge, but Joe wanted still more Swiss contracts, buying them at $50,000 apiece in lots of four and five hundred. On a 4 percent margin, Joe controlled more than $70 million in Swiss currency by the end of his first day. He took a thousand T-bill contracts on the side. Friedman never had seen anything like it; the broker's rule of thumb for clients who put $1 million or more on account was to keep 50 percent in reserve. By Friday of that first week, Joe had put almost 100 percent of his capital on margin. Friedman urged him to consider the importance of money management; no matter how skillfully selected his long-term positions had been, the broker argued, Joe was depleting his capital to a point where even a 10 percent drop in the market would wipe him out. By the middle of July, Friedman had persuaded Joe to sell off some Swiss contracts and increase his cash reserve; it was a good thing, the broker said, since the franc closed at least a quarter point lower every day for the next two weeks. By August 2, the original $5.2 million in the account had dwindled to $462,000.

Then, suddenly, incredibly, but as Joe had predicted, his positions rallied, climbing to $2 million by the end of the next week. On August 12, Joe's T-bill contracts also surged dramatically, more than doubling the account on a single day, bringing it back to almost $5 million at closing. One week later, on August 17, the account climbed to $13,997,428.86, up by more than $8 million from where Joe had started six weeks earlier. Levin phoned Friedman's office that morning to say he wanted to discontinue trading.

"There was a big hoopla" in the BBC over Joe's stunning success with Ron Levin's account, Dean remembered. Clayton's Missouri headquarters sent a statement on the account showing the fourteen-million-dollar closing at the end of August, and Joe brought a dozen photocopies to the Third Street office. Everyone had a copy on his desk, Evan recalled. "A very exciting time," Alan Lieban remembered. "There was a snowball effect.

It seemed that everything Joe touched turned to gold." Hunt however, was nonchalant. "His attitude," Evan recalled, "seemed to be 'What did you expect?'"

It appeared for a time as if Ron Levin had replaced Dean as Joe's chief extoller. "I heard him call Joe a genius," Evan remembered. No one adored Joe more than Ron's housekeeper Blanche: "A lovely type of young man," she said of him, so clean-cut and fresh-faced, and the BBC boys were the most well-mannered group she ever had encountered. A number of the boys in the Third Street office got the idea that Ron Levin had become a BBC member: Evan seemed to be running as many errands for Levin as for Hunt, and Joe had loaned Ron the services of his secretary, Terri Phillips, a former Miss Tennessee runner-up who shared her job with Alison Weiss.

It was especially satisfying to spend those last two weeks of August celebrating the millions made in the account at Clayton, Dean recalled, "since we had just lost a great deal of money in our own commodity accounts almost at the same time." The strains had begun to show at Cantor Fitzgerald a month earlier, when Joe came in late from a meeting with Michael Dow to discover that Alex Gaon had removed nearly all of their spread positions. The action cost the BBC more than fifteen thousand dollars, Joe said. A noisy dispute between he and Alex spilled out onto the street. "I didn't argue; I inquired as to his motives," Joe explained. "Alex said that his father had sworn him to secrecy."

As Alex withdrew his money at Cantor Fitzgerald, he and Ben "shrugged our shoulders and continued to trade," Joe said. When he assumed control of the Levin account at Clayton in early July, Joe moved into parallel positions on the Karny and May accounts at Cantor Fitzgerald, doubling, then tripling the volume of his trades. He was taking as many as seventy T-bill calls in a single afternoon by early August and spent most of the morning working with a growing audience of junior brokers and independent traders at his shoulder. The crowd actually applauded at times, dazzled by Joe's daring as he leveraged his positions higher and higher. By August 3, when the Clayton account was falling to about one-tenth of the original deposit, the margin calls at Cantor Fitzgerald had climbed to $500,000. Joe regarded the deficit as nothing more than a "variation from equilibrium," but the risk manager at the brokerage was not convinced, and on August 9 he informed Joe his margins were being tripled; Mr. Hunt and his clients had until 6 A.M. the next day to deposit $1.5 million or their accounts would be liquidated.

Joe phoned Ron Levin, who offered to intercede: an hour later, the Cantor Fitzgerald risk manager received an abusive phone call from an attorney identifying himself as R. Michael Wetherbee. When that failed, Ron promised to cover Joe's margins. There was, however, a delay in transferring funds through his attorney's office, Ron explained that evening. The Karny and May accounts were liquidated moments after the market opened on August 10. The loss in Dean's account was $268,000 above his cash deposit. In the twins' account, the loss was $170,000. Joe broke the news to Dean on August 15, the day the Clayton account surged above the $10 million mark. "Joe said not to worry about the losses because the Levin profits would more than cover us," Dean remembered. They agreed, however, to "refrain from telling [the Mays] that the money had been lost," Dean recalled, until Joe had time to "decompress" the twins.

Cantor Fitzgerald got to Tom before Joe did, however. "A broker called and said I not only had lost my money but owed another eighty thousand dollars," Tom remembered. "I called Joe and said, 'What's the deal?'" Joe explained the tripling of the margins at Cantor Fitzgerald—"an unprecedented action"—then confirmed that every penny on account in Beverly Hills had been lost. As he absorbed this news, Tom remembered, "Joe said, 'I am entitled to half the money that I made for Ron Levin in his account at Clayton securities, and that should come to be about four million dollars, and out of that I not only will disburse to you what I lost in the Cantor Fitzgerald account but I will double it.' I called Dave and told him about the three hundred thousand dollars Joe was gonna give us and said I thought Joe was a good guy. Dave thought so, too."

Joe met with the twins the next morning, calling in Dean and Ben to witness his reiteration of the pledge to Tom and Dave from the Clayton profits. When Dave began to ask how soon he would get his money, Joe's gaze silenced him. Perhaps it would be best if Dave accepted a check for the amount of his loss right now and left the BBC, Joe suggested. Dave was shamefaced: "I want to stay," he said. When Dave walked out of the room alone, Joe turned to Tom with an approving nod. "You're taking this very well," he observed, then added that handling a difficult situation with dignity and responsibility was the conduct of a Shading.

After Tom left the office, Joe and Dean and Ben decided it would be best to break the news of the loss at Cantor Fitzgerald to the rest of the BBC in the context of a meeting where the main order of business would be the assignment of shares from the Clayton profits. They assembled the next afternoon in the conference room, where Joe announced that he would deposit only seven hundred thousand dollars of the more than four million due to him in his personal account. Tom and Dave were due three hundred thousand apiece, he noted, while Dean, Evan, Alex, and Ron Pardovitch all would receive smaller shares. The remaining money would be used to finance production of the Cyclotron prototype. The meeting was adjourned when everyone in the room rose to salute Joe with a standing ovation.

It was a sting of beauty, even by Ron's high standards. He had started with nothing more than a two-page treatment for a TV pilot titled "The Reporters." With this he proceeded to obtain on loan $240,000 in video equipment from companies that included RCA and Panasonic, plus $50,000 in still-camera equipment from Garden Photo. The lights, cameras, and lenses Ron used to create Network News, employing Neil Antin to film murder scenes between midnight and 6 A.M., then renting the equipment out to several small production companies during the day. He was not only amused but enriched. Within a few months, though, Ron found himself growing bored again, looking for a little reverse spin on his action.

Meeting Joe Hunt inspired him to his masterpiece. For weeks Hunt had been pestering Ron with entreaties to invest in Financial Futures, lecturing him on the opportunities in back-market inventories. "All I gamble on is myself," Ron answered. Then one evening in June, while watching *Eyewitness News* on the local ABC affiliate, channel 7, Ron happened to catch the second segment in a three-part series anchored by Los Angeles's leading TV therapist, Dr. William Rader. The doctor was focusing on people "addicted to stress" in this segment and opened by quoting a *Wall Street Journal* article that ranked professions by degree of stress; commodity traders topped the list. The psychologist then cut to his interview with a local commodities broker, Jack Friedman of Clayton Brokerage. Friedman was an amusing fellow, sardonic and sad-eyed, brimming over with anecdotes about how his wealthy clients handled their profits and took their losses.

It was one week later, on June 28, when Ron called Friedman at his office in the Wilshire corridor. Mr. Levin had introduced himself as the assignment editor for Network News, Friedman remembered. They were developing a five-part documentary series on commodities trading, Assignment Editor Levin explained. The plan was to conduct paper trading on "dummy accounts," Levin said, but in real time and under actual conditions. The documentary would examine a variety of methods, using a broker at Merrill Lynch, a computer at Paine Webber, simply "throwing darts" at Shearson. At the fourth firm—Clayton, he hoped—Levin proposed to employ an outside trading advisor, a boy wonder named Joe Hunt. For six weeks or so, Friedman would take Hunt's orders, Levin explained. When the trading was concluded, Network News would send a camera crew to shoot footage of Friedman in his office: "I'd be holding up the confirms and explaining what happened," the broker recalled. "My deal was free publicity."

Friedman called the proposal in to Clayton's legal department. The company's lawyers gave their approval, conditional upon the broker's promise to explain—on camera—that the trading was "simulated." Assignment Editor Levin had one additional caveat: "He told me to make sure Joe Hunt was not aware that the trading was not on a real account," Friedman recalled. "He said Hunt's trading decisions and emotional response wouldn't be the same if he knew."

Friedman drove from Westwood to Ron's home in Beverly Hills that afternoon to deliver a confirm contract and one of Clayton's standard outside trading advisor agreements, providing Joe Hunt with limited power of attorney over an account in the name of Ronald George Levin. It was Friedman who had suggested meeting at the Peck Drive duplex. "I should live so well," the broker thought when he arrived. He hadn't realized that television editors made this kind of dough, Friedman observed. He had spent fifteen years in corporate law, Ron explained, but being an attorney bored him, so he created a more exciting career in journalism. Ron at once demonstrated his legal acumen by inserting a number of very carefully worded amendments into the confirm contract, Friedman recalled. Levin even produced a sheet of Network News stationery, a delicate ecru onionskin bearing a letterhead with an address at 433 North Camden Drive, twelfth floor, Beverly Hills, upon which he typed: "Network News, Inc. will indemnify Clayton Brokerage Co. from all loss of any kind with respect to their assistance in the Network News, Inc. news documentary entitled 'The Traders.'" Signed, *"Ronald Levin, Assignment Editor."* "He seemed extremely cooperative," Friedman thought.

Seven days later, Joe Hunt called to begin trading the account. Friedman and Levin had agreed to give Joe the worst prices in each time period—the highest price when he bought and the lowest when he sold—the broker recalled, "so people would see we didn't get any special advantage." Though he found Joe pleasant to work with, Friedman was aghast when Hunt immediately sank four million dollars of the five million on account into Swiss francs, then put nearly all the rest of the money into T-bill options. It was a struggle to convince Hunt to pull back even to an 80 percent commitment of capital, recalled Friedman, who endured an excruciating week when the franc's fall reduced the account to less than one-tenth of its original value. "Obviously I had a real interest in seeing the account make money," he explained. "I didn't want to go on TV and say, 'We lost five million dollars—wanna invest?'" Then there had been the huge scene when Clayton's compliance department sent out July confirms stamped TEST SERIES. Levin was livid, Friedman recalled, "screaming and yelling about how I was ruining the integrity of the story. He said it wouldn't show up well on camera, that he didn't want to ruin the emotionalism."

To avoid ruining the emotionalism, Clayton agreed to send out unmarked confirms after this. When the August statement on the account arrived from Saint Louis showing a closing figure of almost fourteen million dollars, Ron was beside himself with glee. If he couldn't find a way to convert this kind of collateral into cash, then he was slipping.

The matter of Jack Friedman demanded his immediate attention, however. The first rule of his profession, Ron often remarked, was "WHEN YOU HAVE A FISH ON THE LINE, PLAY HIM." The day Levin phoned to close the dummy account, Friedman recalled, they chatted like old friends for half an hour. Then Ron got an idea: "He said, 'How would you like to trade a real account for me?'" Friedman remembered. "I said, 'That sounds great.' He says, 'Well, I've got this corporation with the May Brothers, the heirs to the May Company—they're worth two hundred million dollars apiece—and I am treasurer.'"

He sent his assistant to Levin's house with a set of account papers at nine-thirty that morning, Friedman remembered. Fifteen minutes later, Ron sent the young woman back with a fifty-thousand-dollar check, drawn on a May Bros. Land Corp. account at Progressive Savings and Loan. "By ten-thirty I had bought ten Swiss-franc September contracts," the broker recalled. The account was up about one thousand dollars when Friedman learned the check had bounced. "I called Ron Levin," the broker remembered. "He said the money was being wired in. He got indignant; he told me these guys were worth two hundred million dollars." Friedman redeposited the check and continued trading. When it bounced a second time, he liquidated the positions with a four-hundred-dollar loss. The broker phoned Ron Levin a few minutes later: "He kept saying the Mays were worth two hundred million dollars. I said, 'All I see is a bad check for fifty thousand.' Levin asked for the check back. I said, 'As soon as you give me four hundred dollars.'" Friedman deposited the check for a third time the next morning, then made a fourth deposit two days later. This time it was Ron who made the phone call: "He said, 'You're embarrassing me at the bank,'" Friedman remembered. "I said, 'Too bad.'"

Ron contemplated his circumstance: On the one hand, he did not have fifty thousand dollars to deposit at Progressive Savings; on the other hand, he did have Joe Hunt and the BBC. It was the second week in September when Ron phoned the Third Street office to offer Joe another chance to learn from his experience.

***

By Labor Day, some of the boys were beginning to wonder aloud when the Levin money would arrive. Ron's initial explanation of the delay had been that the money was still in the pipeline from east to west, being transferred from his account at Drexel in New York through Clayton's Saint Louis headquarters to his bank in Beverly Hills. "These things take time, children," he said, annoyed. Then in early September Ron was pleased to announce, as Dean recalled it, that he had used the entire fourteen million dollars to exercise his option on a shopping center in a Chicago suburb. "I've more than doubled our money," Ron told Joe when he reported that a Japanese investment corporation already had offered thirty million for the property and that the BBC's equity position now was worth nearly ten million.

Joe seemed "quite proud," Dean thought, when he assembled a second meeting of the BBC in mid-September to assign shares of the shopping center. Tom and Dave were delighted to learn that their three hundred thousand dollars was now seven hundred thousand. "That seemed pretty good," Tom explained. "My money was growing." "We of course went and told our parents, 'Hey Mom and Dad, we got a shopping center,'" Dean recalled. He and Ben and Tom all joined Joe at Levin's the next afternoon, Dean remembered, all very excited, asking Ron lots of questions about such things as square footage and lease options. "Ron said there was almost full occupancy," he recalled. Dean took it upon himself to ask for the title to the property: "Ron said the documents were being gone over by his lawyers, that they were all in boxes and he couldn't get them himself."

While awaiting delivery of the title transfer and partnership papers, Ron proposed a plan to turn a quick profit from the juxtaposition of various corporate bank accounts controlled by the BBC. In short: a check-kiting scheme. Ron set the snowball in motion when he persuaded Tom May to become the latest purchaser of his option on the Peck Drive duplex. Tom risked little, actually, since the thirty-thousand-dollar check he gave Ron was written on the empty May Bros. Land Corp. account at Progressive Savings.

On September 12, Ron deposited a $50,000 check from Len Marmor in the account of his principal holding company, General Information Corp., also at Progressive Savings. Marmor would maintain that he had gone in with Joe Hunt and Tom May as joint partners in purchasing an option from Levin to buy the Peck duplex for $350,000—"a fantastic price," Len conceded. He pulled out of the deal, however, when Levin phoned him that night and said he would get only one-quarter of the building, rather than the half-interest previously promised, said Marmor, explaining his decision to stop payment on his check the following morning. The officers at Progressive were curious about this, of course, since the Beverly Hills bank had honored Levin's deposit before learning from Marmor's bank that the check had been stopped.

Nevertheless, Ron suggested, what worked once was always worth a second try: On September 21 he deposited a check for one hundred thousand dollars written to General Information Corp. by Joe Hunt on a Cyclotronics of North America account at the Japanese bank Mitsui. Progressive honored this check as well, not learning until October 3 that Joe, like Marmor, had stopped payment. There was no need to stop payment on the third bad check Ron deposited at Progressive that month, since Tom May wrote it on an Eye Contact Advertising account that he had closed more than a year earlier.

It was Ron's position that Progressive refused to honor any of the checks, a claim Joe and Tom were in no position to disprove until almost a year later, when Progressive filed a fraud claim against them in Superior Court, alleging that Levin and his accomplices had skinned the bank for $150,000.

Jack Friedman, at least, would profit by his persistence: The broker's ninth deposit of the check Levin gave him had occurred on a morning when Ron was transferring funds through the May Bros. Land Corp. account into his General Information Corp. account. When Friedman's own bank called to say the $50,000 check had cleared, he withdrew the $400 Levin owed and messengered the remaining $49,600 to Peck Drive. Ron called him an hour later—"as if nothing out of the ordinary had happened," the broker remembered—to propose that they proceed with the taping for the Network News documentary. "I told him I didn't want the story, that I wanted him out of my life," Friedman recalled. Ron was puzzled, Friedman remembered: "He said, 'Why? What does one thing have to do with the other?'"

6

THE DEAL JOE WAS PUTTING TOGETHER WITH UNITED FINANCIAL OPERATIONS International made the Levin profits look penny-ante. The BBC could expect to clear seventy-five million dollars on the first Cyclotronics contract since Michael Dow had signed for Gold Sun back in June, Joe announced in early October, with a potential for long-term profits that was well into the billions.

It was a complex situation, however. The UFOI deal was contingent upon a contract Joe was negotiating with an Orange County company called Cogenco, a subsidiary of U.S. Flywheel, which controlled the patent on a system developed at Livermore Laboratories for converting gas and oil-burning furnaces to operate on powdered coal—hence, cogeneration. Under the aegis of U.S. Flywheels, which was developing a system for storing wind energy designed by Bill Lear, inventor of the Lear jet, Cogenco had issued more than ten million dollars in publicly held stock, obtaining research and development contracts with both the French and U.S. governments.

Acquisition of the Cogenco technology was essential to exploitation of the BBC's Cyclotron in the estimation of William C. Kilpatrick, United Financial's chief executive officer. Kilpatrick and the Denver-based UFOI were ideological heirs to Bernie Cornfeld and IOS, a gigantic tax shelter consortium whose investors included members of both the Ford and Rothschild families as well as the ubiquitous Korean-born, Geneva-based financier Winfield Moon. Kilpatrick, a former business partner to deposed Nicaraguan dictator Anastasio Somoza, was working in tandem with Saturn Energy of Vancouver, British Columbia, which owned a number of small steel and aluminum plants designed to operate on coal-fired furnaces.

Kilpatrick's plans had been on hold, however, since the late seventies, when Jimmy Carter's Department of Justice charged the UFOI chairman with twenty-seven counts of tax evasion, falsification of financial records, and obstruction of justice. Kilpatrick retaliated by freezing UFOI's assets in bankruptcy court while he fought the criminal charges in Denver.

"Six years and six million dollars later," as Kilpatrick enjoyed putting it, twenty-six of the twenty-seven charges against him had been dismissed. A decision on the lone remaining count was due any day, and the financier stood on the brink of recovering thirty million dollars in hard assets—mostly domestic coalfields—that had been tied up by the bankruptcy petition since 1978. Once grinding and cogeneration technology was secured, UFOI and Saturn could offer a complete package for conversion of power plants and factories to operate on micronized coal within U.S. environmental standards, he explained. The beauty of the arrangement, from Kilpatrick's point of view, was that his investors were winners whatever happened, since a loss on investment in the development of alternative energy sources could be written off a wealthy individual's taxes at a rate that made failure nearly as rewarding as success.

What Cogenco needed, and needed desperately, was ready cash. More than four hundred thousand dollars in bills were past due, and the company's chairman, Bruce Swartout, just had announced that he most likely would be unable to meet the payroll after October. The arrival of a financial savior for Cogenco was heralded by Ken Elgin, the Balboa businessman who had facilitated the Gene Browning/BBC contract back in February. Elgin arranged a meeting between the BBC and Swartout for August 18, three days after the last criminal count against Kilpatrick was dismissed in Denver Federal Court, arriving that afternoon in the company of Gene Browning and three young men. One was a dark courtly fellow named Dosti whose mother was someone important at the *L.A. Times*, as Swartout understood it. A suntanned surfer in an expensive business suit was introduced as Tom Frank May II of the May Company department store chain. Then Swartout shook hands with Joe Hunt. Though Hunt looked to be the youngest of the visitors, Swartout recalled, "it was obvious before he said a word that all the others deferred to him."

Cogenco's chairman was a man of distinctive appearance himself. Though past sixty and white-haired, Swartout was pink-skinned and remarkably unlined, possessed of a striking resemblance to the man behind the curtain in *The Wizard of Oz*. Hunt allowed Elgin and Browning to run the conversation at first, Swartout recalled, listening attentively as the two older men described the compatibility of Cyclotronics technology with Cogenco. Only when the UFOI/Saturn deal was introduced did Joe open his mouth, Swartout remembered, "and from the moment he began to speak, I was spellbound." Joe's description of the ways in which the Browning attrition mill complemented the Swartout power van was "astonishingly adroit," recalled the Cogenco chairman, who admitted his interest when Joe suggested that their two companies might strenghten separate negotiating positions through collaboration. When Joe produced a copy of the Gold Sun contract, showing an advance order of four million dollars for the Cyclotron, Swartout's enthusiasm mounted. The older man rose from his seat and began to pace his office when Joe asserted that a merger of Cogenco with Cyclotronics might be the key to closing a quarter-billion-dollar deal with Saturn Energy and UFOI. "I remember thinking, 'If this is real, the sky's the limit,'" Swartout said.

Joe's aim was nearly that high. The BBC secured the affection of Kilpatrick by making connections through Ben's mother that enabled the financier to celebrate dismissal of the criminal charges against him with an appearance on CBS's *60 Minutes*. Complementing his string tie with ostrich-skin cowboy boots, Kilpatrick came on like a New Age Davy Crockett, describing his triumph over the IRS to an audience of forty million as "beating the biggest bear on the mountain." One week later, after receiving a report from a physicist at Livermore estimating the value of the Browning attrition mill's immediate energy-related application at $156 million, Kilpatrick proposed the formation of forty-four limited partnerships for UFOI's investors, each committed to spending $5 million for packages of the power plant equipment developed at Saturn, Cogenco, and Cyclotronics. The BBC-Cogenco piece of the $220 million contract would be a one-quarter interest—$75 million.

By late September, Hunt and Swartout had arrived at the point of preparing a letter of intent. Joe typed the document himself, promising $2.2 million over the next six months in exchange for Swartout's pledge to transfer 51 percent of Cogenco's stock to the BBC, conditional upon Joe's ability to win approval from the shareholders at U.S. Flywheel.

Swartout agreed to grant the BBC access to all books and records at Cogenco, and Hunt spent a solid week performing an audit of the company. By October 3, Joe was ready to upgrade his statement of intent to a letter of commitment, presented in person that afternoon to Swartout's board of directors, whose approval Hunt needed to address the company's shareholders. Describing first his plans to secure Cogenco's patents and to "tailor existing systems to the needs of specific companies," Joe then explained how the contracts with Gold Sun and Saturn could be used as collateral in obtaining bank loans to cover an estimated thirty million dollars in operating expenses over the next three years.

The board members were overwhelmed by Joe's presentation, Swartout recalled: "They had never seen anyone that young that sure of himself. He was probably less than half the age of anyone else in the room, and he was talking down to them, but they didn't mind." The directors of U.S. Flywheels voted unanimously to make Mr. Hunt the main speaker at a special meeting of the shareholders scheduled for the afternoon of October 31, 1983.

More than one hundred shareholders arrived for the Halloween meeting at the Registry Hotel in Irvine, remembered Swartout, who introduced Joseph Hunt, chairman and CEO of BBC Consolidated, Incorporated, of North America, then asked him to discuss "how he foresees the future." What he foresaw was the expansion of Cogenco Systems into a corporation on the scale of General Motors, Joe advised his audience. The pending deal with Saturn Energy and UFOI would launch an enterprise capable of seizing an irreducible initiative in exploiting a source of energy, bituminous coal, that not only was more plentiful than the crude oil controlled principally by OPEC ministers, Joe noted, but far more easily obtainable, since the largest deposits in the world were located on or near the land surface of North America.

That he and his associates all were young men was to be considered not a detriment, but an advantage, Joe asserted. They were members of a generation committed to restoring the United States to its manifest destiny as the most powerful force in the global marketplace. It was obvious to them—as to everyone who was paying attention—that politics, religion, ethnicity, and nationalism all would be increasingly subordinate to economics in the world of the future. BBC Consolidated was determined to win the only war that would matter to citizens of the twenty-first century, the war for control of markets. They would not lose because they understood what was at stake.

The men and women who had gathered to hear him responded to Joe's speech with a standing ovation. When the motion to accept Hunt's letter of commitment was submitted for a vote, the ayes were unanimous. Swartout moved that the bylaws of U.S. Flywheel be amended to expand the board of directors to nine members, then submitted a slate of candidates for the new board that included Joe Hunt, Ben Dosti, Tom May, Dean Karny, and Ken Elgin. Again, all present voted aye. Two hours and fifty minutes after he entered the room, Joe walked out with complete control of two corporations carrying twelve million dollars in issues of public stock, with patents and prototypes whose estimated values were in the hundreds of millions. He had turned twenty-four five days earlier.

Cogenco's new board of directors convened for the first time on November 3 and began their session by approving a motion that read: "BE IT RESOLVED that the Chairman of the Board of Directors of Cogenco Systems Inc., shall, from this moment on, be Joseph Hunt." The vote was nine for, none against. The Cogenco board passed unanimously thirty-nine other resolutions that afternoon, consolidating authority in and extending wide latitude to the company's newly elected chief financial officer, Joseph Hunt.

When he and the three other minority members who continued to sit on the Cogenco board left the room that day, Swartout recalled, "We thought we had the world by the tail. We could now turn this over to these young men, who were going to do something for our country and for our company."

Swartout's ardor would no doubt have dimmed had he seen the "exclusive marketing agreement" Joe signed two days later in the Denver offices of William Kilpatrick. As originally prepared by Kilpatrick's attorneys, the contract described an "Agreement made this 5 Day of November, 1983, between Cogenco Systems, Inc., herein referred to as Cogenco, and United Financial Operations, Inc., herein referred to as U.F.O.I." Joe made a single change, striking out the word *Cogenco* and replacing it with *Microgenesis*. He understood, Kilpatrick explained, that Microgenesis was a manufacturing division of the new Cogenco Systems. In fact, Microgenesis had no connection at all to Cogenco, other than that both were subsidiaries of BBC Consolidated of North America, Inc. It seemed that the board of directors at Cyclotronics had transferred control of all existing technology to the newly created Microgenesis. What Joe had left of Cogenco was nothing more than a corporate shell loaded with debt and devoid of assets. In short, Swartout explained, "he slickered us."

It was the afternoon he challenged Joe on the propriety of the Cogenco merger, Evan remembered, when he began to understand the true structure of power in the BBC. Perhaps more than any other member, Evan had taken to heart the Black Book's diagram of a Nexus-Axis Cell System, the layering of Shapes and Shadings, the dominion of Paradox Court, and the ultimate authority of the Core. He did not overly concern himself with how decisions were made back when the BBC was "after-school play," Evan explained, but as five- and six-figure checks began to pour into commodity accounts and dormant corporations came to life, his role as BBC secretary assumed a significance he hadn't anticipated. So it was a sense of obligation, Evan said, that prompted him to inform Joe that the merger of the Cyclotronics and Cogenco corporations had not been strictly legal. A merger could be effected only after it had been approved first by the California secretary of state, Evan explained, when he was asked to notarize and record the documents. Joe answered that he would take personal responsibility in this instance. "I pointed out that the BBC manual stated that all decisions must be made by the Core," Evan recalled. For the first time since he had met him, Joe "showed annoyance or at least shortness," Evan remembered. "His answer was that since he was the chair of the Core, that gave him the authority to do this. That was my first indication that, without doubt, Joe was the boss."

There never was any question of that, Dean explained: "We maintained the front of the Shadings as three equals to everyone else because people wouldn't be interested, Joe said, in being in a club where one guy is the leader."

The triumvirate-of-power ruse was among Dean's more minor deceptions, really, yet it troubled him in ways he had not been bothered by lying to Cantor Fitzgerald or misleading Michael Dow. For reasons he couldn't explain, Dean felt qualms only when he was asked to deceive other members of the BBC. At the same time, though, Joe was praising his adjustment of focus and perspective—"two words that Joe used frequently," Dean recalled—as evidence of his attainment to the status of Shading. It was only their limited understanding of Paradox that made it impossible to reveal to other BBC members all of the organization's internal dealings, Joe explained. The Shadings began to integrate a "Hierarchy of Information" concept into the BBC. "Joe told us that information is power and only those who can handle power can have information," Evan remembered.

When secrets were divulged, they came most often through Dean, who presented each one as instruction in the practical application of Paradox. The first really penetrating description of the BBC philosophy that Taglianetti heard was offered in early October when Dean whispered a story in his office. At the end of the previous summer, Karny said, a personal friend and prospective BBC member (Mickey Fine, according to later court testimony) had been in trouble at Whittier Law School, totally unprepared for the final examination in a first-semester class. What this friend did know, however, was where Whittier's exam forms were kept. Joe suggested that he and Dean break into the law school office, remove the test for that class, then return it the next evening. They executed Joe's plan over the next forty-eight hours, and their friend aced the test. "Dean said it was Paradox in action," Taglianetti recalled. "'We took a risk for a friend we wanted to bring in. We wanted something from him, and this is what we offered in exchange.' The wrong was justified by their purpose. So they really had done no wrong. The big idea was that anything is possible."

Nothing rankled Joe so much as the suggestion by another member of the BBC that he was "rationalizing" or "justifying" his conduct; the very use of such language demonstrated a member's failure to grasp the essence of Paradox. Joe "reconciled," Dean explained: "Because when you justify something or rationalize something, those two words have latent implications that you justify something wrong, you rationalize away something wrong. But when you merely reconcile yourself to reality, then you haven't ever put any moral judgment on right and wrong to begin with. You just do things as they occur to you." According to Joe, "A man could commit 'immoral' acts with a pure heart, in complete accord with his inner nature and his goal," Dean recalled. "If you get into a situation where circumstances get more difficult and more trying, you reconcile yourself to more severe and extreme steps."

The steps required of them at this point were neither very severe nor particularly extreme. When Joe instructed him to begin preparing minutes for Microgenesis board meetings that never had taken place, Evan thought of it as "expediting paperwork." "You think about it," he explained: "These are closely held corporations, every one is internal, the directors all approve of this, so why in God's name should I get on the phone forty-eight hours in advance and announce, 'Yes, we're having a meeting Thursday, be there,' then get there myself, find out who waives reading of the minutes, blah blah blah, when it's so much easier just to sit down and in fifteen minutes type what Joe wants me to. At first, it was just doing away with formalities; that was an early Paradox discussion."

Paradox was introduced by Joe to most of the BBC "in terms of our ability to make our own decisions," Evan remembered, "to recognize the best course under the circumstances, the assumption being that if you are intelligent, given these blind, stupid laws that did not really see the circumstances, then you should not be concerned by them. Whatever works, works."

The Hierarchy of Information approach was to present Paradox to each BBC member in terms he could comprehend at that moment. The frat man Lieban understood Paradox as "a corporate philosophy: Fireman's Fund had its culture and so did the BBC. Paradox was what made success imaginable, manageable, achievable." Reality was contained by two entirely separate sets of parameters, Joe explained. There were, he conceded, certain "absolute margins," and "within those margins was success," as Lieban recalled it. The other set of margins, made up of the legal codes and social proprieties, was an artificial stricture designed to suppress the natures of all but the most intrepid. "If you never left the 'mainstream,' as Joe called it, you weren't going to achieve anything more than anybody else, which to him was nothing," Lieban explained.

Joe demonstrated his authority over the BBC most conspicuously at the monthly meetings where Dean and Ben regularly ceded him the chair. It had been a tenet of the BBC from the beginning that "at meetings, anyone could raise anything," Dean recalled. "Joe said everything was always subject to question, subject to reevaluation, subject to further suggestion." Yet by September Joe was regularly presenting an agenda for each meeting at its outset. Increasingly unavailable to the other members during regular office hours, he transformed the meetings into educational forums, lecturing the others on subjects that ranged from the assignment of subsidiary rights in contracts to deportment at business meetings. "Before Kilpatrick came to the office," one BBC member recalled, "Joe told us exactly how to dress, in gray or blue suits with red or blue ties, exactly what to say, what not to say. It was like he was choreographing us."

More and more often, Evan remembered, "when Dean and Ben spoke at a meeting, it was in support of Joe." On those rare occasions when Dean or Ben disagreed with him, Joe would get the other one in his corner. He often was compelled, Dean said, to face the rest of the BBC at the next meeting and refute exactly what he had said earlier. Yet Hunt didn't command him, Karny conceded. "He didn't tell me, 'Okay, go tell them you were wrong,' or something like that. But he'd tell me, 'This is no way for a Shading to conduct himself.' The threat of not being a Shading was something he was constantly using on Ben and myself. He would undermine us in the group if it suited his purpose until we came around. And what better way to get our position back but to go on our own volition to the other members and boost Joe up? Because if we boosted Joe up we were boosting ourselves up."

Hunt, however, "refused absolutely to allow anyone to come out and say they were doing anything for him," Karny recalled. "He'd say, 'Cut that out; no, you're not, you're doing it for yourself.'" Enlightened Self-Interest, Evan remembered, "was the part of Paradox Joe used to introduce the idea of weighing short-term loss against long-term gain." Trickle-down theory stripped to its essence, Joe said.

As their leader grew increasingly remote from the BBC's rank and file—"above and apart from the rest of us," Taglianetti observed—alone in his office with Quotron, computer, and telephone, trading T-bills and Ginny Maes in ten-million-dollar lots, negotiating Microgenesis contracts, meeting with investors and supervising corporations, withdrawing even at group dinners into the corner of a banquette where he monitored the others' chatter while paging through the *Wall Street Journal* or *Business Week,* reading the dictionary to unwind, his two lieutenants assumed greater responsibility for both the theoretical and the practical aspects of Paradox. If Dean was Joe's sounding board and emissary, Ben seemed to live the philosophy with greatest efficiency. While Dean described his conversion to Paradox as "less a matter of inventing a new belief system than of blocking out reactions I should have had," Ben struck the others as immune to scruples from the outset. "Dean always had more emotions than Ben," Evan reflected. "That's why he struggled more. Joe was very good at making you feel ashamed of having emotions. Because they interfered with doing what needed to be done."

Many in the BBC, however, were more comfortable with Dosti than with Karny. "Dean and Joe would have conversations at dinner about Greek mythology and the Holy Roman Empire," one member explained. "Ben was a regular guy; he was more interested in how the Rams were going to do next week than in why Napoléon lost at Waterloo." Gene Browning described Dosti as having "the best manners and the most greed. He would bring things to me, ideas or patents or formulas we could replicate—steal, that is—and ask, 'Will you look at this and tell me whether or not we can do it?' Whether or not we *should* do it was never a question. There was a total amorality to him." The inventor and his wife preferred Dean: "Like a little nymph, such a sweet personality," Claire Browning said of him. "You compared them," her husband explained, "because Dean and Ben were a strange situation, in that they were both vying for a position one above the other, relative to Joe. Not with anybody else outside, just Joe."

While Dean played the part of "Joe's fashion coordinator," as Tom May called him, Ben spent his afternoons tracking foreclosures in *Daily Commerce*. As Dean posed with Joe in matching red power ties for a portrait photograph taken in the BBC lobby, Ben culled the names of company presidents from *Who's Who in American Business*. "He'd just call 'em up out of the blue," recalled one BBC member. "'It can't hurt to ask' was his attitude. He'd get people from places like U.S. Steel to take him out to lunch."

It was Ben who extracted information from executives at firms that were manufacturing machines designed to compete with the Cyclotron, approaching in the guise of "Ben Davis" to pose as a potential customer. Yet Dean continued to "set the tone for the BBC," Lieban noted. "He was the standard-bearer. For dress, for behavior at parties, for business etiquette. Dean was the one who did the most to create the feeling of exclusivity. One of the reasons I was hanging out there so much was to be exposed to them, to learn, to become more like them."

The Shadings had secured an ideal location for their new living quarters by the first of October, renting an "elegant high-rise condominium," as the building's brochures had it, in one of the gleaming residential towers along Wilshire Boulevard between Westwood and Beverly Hills. It was Dean who put his name to the two-year lease, signing as an officer of the May Bros. Land Corp., which agreed to pay $73,584.00 in twenty-four monthly installments to house its executive officers.

The move to the Wilshire Manning was part of the BBC's bid for a more imposing public image. From their balcony on the fifteenth floor, the Shadings looked down on L.A.'s Main Street, six lanes of pavement that ran east from the palm-lined palisades above Santa Monica Beach into West Los Angeles, passing below Brentwood but above Mar Vista, in Westwood separating college students from white-collar workers and dividing Beverly Hills between apartment dwellers and homeowners, coursing the Miracle Mile between Fairfax and La Brea, marking the border between the old-money arrangements of Hancock Park and the thrifty ambition of Koreatown, then spilling through a gauntlet of paneled girders and corporate logos in the downtown office district, offering one last escape via on-ramp access to the Harbor Freeway before ending abruptly at Grand Avenue, just footsteps from that patch of earth, now covered by ten million tons of concrete, where the early hidalgos had lorded over the grubby empire of adobe huts and sandy wastes they called El Pueblo de Nuestra Senora la Reina del los Angeles de Porciuncula.

Wilshire Boulevard was the invention of a man whose story illuminated perhaps as well as any the profits and perils of a life spent in Los Angeles—romantic adventure, broad farce, and cautionary tale all at once. Gaylord Wilshire had been Joe's age, twenty-three, when a failed sawmill, a fall from a horse, and his Cincinnati banker father's fascination with Southern California's first land boom propelled him west to Long Beach, where in 1884 the handsome young rake with the Vandyke beard and panama hat purchased the ground he later would cover with Ocean Boulevard.

Less than forty years after the country had claimed California as the spoil of its war with Mexico, Los Angeles was the fastest-growing city in the United States, increasing by 500 percent during the 1880s, then another 600 percent between 1890 and 1910, when it reported a population of 319,198. While local architecture amalgamated the adobe of the Spanish Southwest with classic American clapboard, the flora of Los Angeles produced the city's atmosphere of an erotic Eden where Mediterranean met Mojave, with imported palms and pepper trees towering above native chaparral and scrub oak, coastal hills alight every spring with columbine and tiger lily yielding to year-round flowering shrubs that arrived every month in the boxcars of the Southern Pacific Railroad. "California is fast becoming the winter playground of the leisure class of Americans," young Gaylord wrote his father. "I have no doubt that [one day] Southern California will be the most thickly settled part of the American continent."

Gaylord was thirty-five when he paid fifty thousand dollars in gold coins for a barley field just west of the downtown business center where he would drive away the grazing sheep, dredge Westlake, and cut a roadway an astounding 120 feet wide, announcing his belief that no city could achieve magnificence without at least one major boulevard. He named the street for himself. Gaylord had by then become L.A.s' most prominent millionaire socialist, a leader of the local Nationalist Club movement inspired by Edward Bellamy's 1888 best-seller, *Looking Backward*. Describing a future utopia of American cooperatives, Bellamy's novel inspired the most enduring indigenous socialist movement in U.S. history. Within two years of the book's publication, sixty-two Bellamy Nationalist Clubs had formed in California, thirty-three in Los Angeles alone. Gaylord Wilshire was the Nationalist nominee for the United States Congress in 1890, an election in which his defeat devastated the candidate so completely that he exiled himself to New York and London for five years.

Gaylord initiated both construction of Wilshire Boulevard and publication of his new magazine, *Wilshire's,* within a few months of returning to Southern California. The magazine he dedicated to the proposition that the Rockefeller-run trusts would be driven by their greed to overproduction, creating an inevitable depression and the widespread unemployment that would force government to take control. Wilshire's closest friend and best-paid contributor was a then-obscure Anglo-Irish journalist named George Bernard Shaw, though American radicals Jack London and Upton Sinclair also published regularly in *Wilshire's*. Gaylord was a brand of dissident peculiar to Southern California, not at all the sort to pose as a common man, but rather "the very Beau Brummel of fashion," as the *Los Angeles Record* described him at the turn of the century. Determined to eradicate the notion that radicals must be lower-class "foreigners," Wilshire argued that socialists should be "the instructors of ignorant and immature humanity." *Wilshire's* most prolific correspondent was its publisher, whose widely admired articles would lift the circulation to a high of 425,000, making it by far the largest leftist publication in the country.

Despite *Wilshire's* apparent success, however, Gaylord would squander most of two inherited fortunes, his own and his wife's, on the magazine, boosting circulation by such reckless promotions as cutting the cost of a yearly subscription from a dollar to ten cents. In 1906, the year of San Francisco's great earthquake, Wilshire induced a number of other wealthy socialists to invest in a Northern California mining claim, persuading them that gold was the only prudent hedge against the inevitable economic collapse brought on by the Rockefellers and their associated trusts. The gold mine went bust without ever booming, and by 1915, the year his magazine ceased circulation, Wilshire no longer was a wealthy man.

Even worse, Los Angeles had permitted the rise to power of its own oligarchy, headed by a pair of conspirators who controlled two powerful local institutions, Henry E. Huntington of the Pacific Electric Company and Harrison Gray Otis, publisher of the *Los Angeles Times*. By 1913, behind the façade of their Los Angeles Suburban Homes Company, Huntington, Otis, and their associates had purchased options on huge tracts of land in the barren San Fernando Valley. At the same time, in a campaign financed by Huntington and orchestrated by Otis, the Suburban Homes Company had persuaded Los Angeles voters to pass a bond financing construction of the enormous aqueduct designed (by William Mulholland) to divert water south out of the verdant Owens Valley to the desolate San Fernando. Within a few weeks of the election, Pacific Electric was running tracks into the Valley, where the simultaneous arrival of water and transportation sent land prices soaring. Otis and Huntington got rich, and modern Los Angeles, which for the next fifty years would be the dominion of Jonathon Club officers and Harvard School graduates, had been born.

Gaylord Wilshire subsided into a decade-long lethargy following the failure of his magazine, observing but not participating in the expansion of a community promoted by Harrison Gray Otis's protégé Charles Fletcher Lummis, editor of the new magazine *Land of Sunshine,* as a refuge from "the ignorant, hopelessly un-American type of foreigner which infests and largely controls Eastern cities." Even as Lummis was making *Land of Sunshine* the most successful magazine west of the Hudson River, however, a loose confederation of those very "foreigners" he deplored had won control of the new industry that would give Los Angeles the largest part of its personality. They were Jewish immigrants, every one: Marcus Loew, Jesse Lasky, Adolph Zukor, William Fox, and Sam Goldfish (later Goldwyn), men who had made their fortunes in the garment, glove, or fur markets of New York before moving west, settling in a community founded twenty years earlier by a Kansan who had banned saloons while offering free land to any Protestant church within the limits of the new city he called Hollywood.

Thomas Edison was in large measure responsible for development of the motion picture industry in Southern California. Edison never had ranked his moving picture camera, that amusing toy he called the Kinetoscope, among his most important inventions. When his cameraman Edwin S. Porter's film *The Great Train Robbery* created a national sensation in 1903, however, Edison recognized the economic potential of the movies and moved to monopolize the industry, allowing only those companies that won his approval (i.e., paid him a percentage of profits) to make motion pictures within the United States. Bootleg movie companies, harassed by Edison's thugs, retreated steadily west, arriving finally in the promised land of Southern California, where local governments protected them from the Motion Picture Patents Company and the local climate permitted them to shoot pictures year-round.

D. W. Griffith and his Biograph troupe took up residence at the Hollywood Inn in 1910, the same year the smaller city surrendered its charter to Los Angeles. Griffith shot twenty-one films in four months in Southern California, each one worshiping the youth and beauty personified by his leading lady, seventeen-year-old Mary Pickford. Griffith and his student Mack Sennett, whose Keystone comedies all were filmed in the streets of Los Angeles, would impose the city upon the American psyche to a degree no one could have imagined twenty years earlier. By 1925, the year Gaylord Wilshire resurfaced on the public scene, the Los Angeles population had grown to more than one million, and motion pictures were the fifth-largest industry in the nation. Moroccan palaces, Greek temples, Chinese pagodas, and log-cabin mansions sprouted in the hills. Voices were louder, headlines larger, accents more pronounced, wardrobes more daring.

Into the mêlée Gaylord Wilshire plunged headlong to promote his revolutionary new healing device, the I-ON-A-CO belt, consisting of two electrical coils wrapped in a leather strap that produced a small magnetic field when connected to a flashlight battery. It was Wilshire's proposition that his magic belt could cure every disease from arthritis to cancer. "People are completely transformed," he wrote to his loyal friend Shaw, "and the turning of [gray] hair back to its original color is an almost daily occurrence." Wilshire saturated radio stations and newspapers with testimonials to his machine's powers, competing for public attention against the imprecations of the evangelist Aimee Semple McPherson by quoting customers who claimed they had been cured of diabetes and dropsy, of paranoid delusions and varicose veins, through regular application of the I-ON-A-CO.

Gaylord overstated himself, unfortunately, when he wrote an ad claiming his belt had been approved by the Rockefeller Institute for Medical Research. All the Rockefellers knew of the contraption was what they had read in a California Medical Association report concluding that the I-ON-A-CO's healing powers were equivalent to "a left hind foot of a rabbit caught in the churchyard in the dark of the moon." The Rockefellers, remembering how they had been reviled in each and every issue of *Wilshire's,* announced their intention to sue. Gaylord flew to New York to offer apologies and retractions, only to die of disappointment and heart disease alone in his hotel room. The former multimillionaire left behind an estate of seventeen thousand dollars and was dismissed as a colorful crank in most of his obituaries, although Southern California's leading organ of the social elite, *Saturday Night,* saluted him as a man who "may have been chimerical, an ultraoptimist, a dreamer, but at least lived every moment of his existence."

Alone among Gaylord's visions, Wilshire Boulevard was no chimera. The street to which the young man attached his family name not only endured but became the main artery of a heartless metropolis. The Manning's location was Wilshire corridor, the deepest and most expensive of Southern California's canyons, lined north and south with high-rise apartment buildings, towering monoliths of mirrored glass that reflected the smog-filtered sunlight in flashes of gray-green and tarnished gold, rising in bold vertical defiance of the amorphous sprawl that made Los Angeles the most horizontal of the world's great cities.

The upper floors of the building offered views that on clear days reached from Cajon Pass to the Channel Islands. The Shadings selected the most expensive of the Manning's many vistas, taking a twenty-six-hundred-square-foot, 3-bedroom, 3½-bath corner condo, with living room windows that faced the Pacific. The Manning's amenities included doormen, parking valets, security guards on duty twenty-four hours a day, TV monitors at all entrances, separate men's and women's gymnasiums, climate-control and intercom systems, wet bars and powder rooms, water purifiers in the kitchens and bidets in the bathrooms.

For all the "spacious elegance" touted in its advertisements, though, the word that best captured the ambience of the building was *faux,* from the faux marble floors to the faux crystal chandeliers to the faux sense of arrival in a lobby where the black granite floor was accented with pink carpets. The Manning attracted a goodly number of celebrity residents, among them Mr. T, who stayed in shape by jumping rope beside the swimming pool wearing thirty pounds of gold chain, director Blake Edwards and his wife Julie Andrews, who kept an apartment on the twelfth floor, and an L.A. Dodger outfielder whose filthy Rolls Corniche convertible prompted complaints from several neighbors. The preferred resident of the Manning staff was a young Kuwaiti emir enrolled at UCLA to study political science. At the Manning, the emir had rented a number of spare parking spaces from neighbors for storage of his personal fleet; any time the prince's Bentley or Ferrari or Lotus or Porsche rolled into the driveway, the Manning's valets nearly came to blows competing to be the one who made it first to his door, hoping to collect one of the hundred-dollar tips the emir handed out when ever he passed a test or seduced a coed.

The boys' condo, 1505, suggested the sort of dorm room Paramount's set designers might have created for the studio's newest teen comedy. A chocolate brown mohair sectional clashed brutally with the lime green carpet that became a grid of multicolored extension cords connecting the various electronic toys Joe and Dean collected, from the five-foot Advent television screen to the new Quotrons they used to monitor the financial markets every morning over orange juice. Dirty dishes accumulated in teetering piles, although the brand was Villeroy & Boch rather than Corelle. Joe's books and magazines were stacked and strewn in every corner, overflowing with the notes to himself he made while reading. The master bedroom where Joe and Brooke slept offered spectacular views and a California King bed but no other furniture, and was decorated usually with whatever art project Brooke had used to distract herself during the previous week; her acrylic whales series endured for most of a month.

Brooke's status was developing into one of the BBC's principal mysteries. The rejection of the three young men who had nominated themselves as the second wave of Shadings—Ron Pardovitch, Alex Gaon, and Mickey Fine—was announced at open meetings, yet not one word was said in public about Brooke's application. Even Dean admitted he did not know if she was a Shading. Other than an occasional acting class, Brooke seemed to have nowhere to go and all day to get there. Her only BBC function was to shop for the residents of 1505, an obligation she satisfied by requisitioning a roll of hundreds from Joe, then driving her Rabbit convertible off to the two most expensive markets on the Westside, Gelson's and Vincente Foods. "Brooke would pay a dollar apiece for strawberries," one BBC member recalled. Her devotion to Joe was beyond dispute. She even had taken to wearing his clothes, tromping around Beverly Hills in a tie that hung to her knees and a suit jacket that ended at her ankles. Brooke allowed her look to grow increasingly radical, in the new, nonpolitical sense of the word, leaving her short hair unbrushed, going either stark or garish with her makeup, but rarely settling anywhere between. "The only person in the world Brooke had to impress was Joe," Dean's girlfriend Lisa Marie observed.

Impressing Joe, however, was not such an easy task. Brooke's most ambitious art project had been to daub her naked body with paints in primary colors, then press herself against an immense scroll of canvas in a dozen different positions that looked as if they had been lifted from the *Kama-sutra*. "I love you, Joe," she wrote at the bottom, then draped an entire wall of their bedroom with her adoration. Joe barely glanced at it. Brooke kept trying, dragging Claire Browning along to Saks to help select a pair of silk pajamas for Joe's birthday. Claire was appalled when Brooke suggested that the tallest salesman in the store remove his own clothing to try on various sleeping costumes and was astonished when the man consented. "Brooke's attitude was 'Of course he'll do it; I want him to,'" Claire recalled. "She made him try on pair after pair of pajamas, from the paisley to the pinstripe, you name it. It was unbelievable."

The Brownings imagined the scheme of sexual liaisons in 1505 as a tangle of duplicity. Their suspicions were aroused for the first time one afternoon when Gene asked Joe if he planned to marry Brooke. "He said, 'No, never. I'm just using her for a front,'" Browning recalled. Claire was startled when "Brooke made the comment that she could not figure out why Joe would get out of bed, totally nude, go striding into Dean's bedroom and stay in there for an hour."

Dean's sexuality was suspect among the BBC's more conservative elements anyway after the Mays and Taglianetti saw photographs from the Halloween Eve party at the Manning. The pictures were taken mostly by Evan, who wore his toga that night with an expression of profound torpor. Deborah Corday created a considerable sensation, arriving in a black bra, G-string garter with black mesh nylons, silver-studded leather choker, and black stiletto high heels. Most present had posed for a group photograph, all facing the camera except Deborah, who stood in profile swallowing a toy sword in a manner that might be described as suggestive only by way of understatement. The most arresting image by far, however, was the one of Dean in drag, wearing an expensive red-knit dress with white hose and a wide-brimmed straw hat, looking for all the world like Lady Di inspecting the troops at Easter. They all had been startled, some even slightly discomfited, by how attractive Dean was as a woman. Another set of photographs displayed among the BBC featured Deborah Corday, this time wearing only a black leather jacket with white lace panties, along with the set of black leather cords that had been used to bind her hand and foot, while Dean sat in the background, regarding her with the expression of utter indifference everyone was attempting to achieve back then, though few so successfully as Karny. Evan pinned one of these photos to the wall above his desk in the Third Street office—"for artistic purposes," he would explain.

The BBC's appearances in public grew increasingly ostentatious during the last months of 1983. The Shadings would transfer from a table for eighteen at the China Club one week to a feast for twenty-four at that sepulcher of show-biz swank, Chasens, the next. On the evening after they closed the Kilpatrick deal in Denver, Joe, Dean, and Ben celebrated by assembling the inner circle for a mass supper at La Scala, where a dispute between Ben and Lisa Marie over which was the world's finest champagne would be settled by ordering a bottle each of the best Cristal, Dom Pérignon,

Florens Louis, Piper-Heidsieck, Laurent-Perrier, Krug, and Grand Siecle on the wine list. After the third bottle, the boys took turns toasting Joe's achievement. One of them proposed that he should run for president some day, and the others began assigning themselves various roles in his cabinet; Evan remembered being offered the job of secretary of state.

Joe scorned politics, however, and described his own dream for the BBC, the purchase of a Pacific island where they could create a new government, designed in accord with the principles of Paradox, a base from which they might plunder the world economy with the impunity of a sovereign nation. "Joe envisioned a secured structure, a fortified compound, where the BBC would all live together," Dean recalled. These discussions were more serious than not, Evan said: "After all, the BBC had existed for only a few months, and already we had produced contracts that showed a net worth in the tens of millions. I was twenty-two then and so was Ben, Dean was twenty-three, Joe had just turned twenty-four. If we could do this much in six months, imagine what we could do in six years."

In a furor of self-congratulation, the boys began to ascribe new and improved meanings to the initials BBC. Evan liked "Brass Balls Club." "Back Bay Club" and "Beverly Hills Breakfast Club" also were suggested. "Billionaire Boys Club," though, was the name that stuck.

The BBC were arriving at a sort of supracelebrity status in their favorite nightclubs—PG's, Voilà, and the Nairobi Room. "It was exciting, electrifying," Lieban recalled. "Because it seemed like everyone who was on the scene was trying to make a name for themselves, and we, the group, you could feel heads turn when we came in, and there was the effect of this buzzing about us everywhere, any club we went to. Even if we weren't there, you sensed it; people were talking about the BBC. You sensed also that there was a lot of envy. Even if people didn't know what it was all about, you got the feeling they wanted in or at least near. It was the way we arrived. Sometimes we'd go out and all be wearing leather jackets, or another time be coming from some business meeting and all be wearing suits, or sometimes even coming from some of the black-tie affairs that we had and all wearing tuxes. There was a sense of identity that other people could recognize and be attracted by. What was cool about it was that we didn't have to explain ourselves or do anything to get attention; it just came naturally."

Their wardrobes became increasingly spectacular as time passed, Evan remembered, and always it was one of the two subordinate Shadings who showed the way. "Ben, like Dean, had a great sense of clothes," he recalled. "Down to, like, he had this perfectly faded pair of 501s, and he had them *forever*. I don't know what he did so they never fell apart. And he wore them with this pair of nice suede loafers that he always wore without socks.

Joe, as our lead man, needed clothes, of course. I was aware of Dean as his fashion coordinator. I can remember going over and Dean would tell me, excited, 'We just got Joe this great suit' . . . They tried to get Joe a lot of Armani because he looked very good in it. It fits his size very well; tall men with broad shoulders, thin through the body—the silhouette Armani creates is unbelievable. Dean and I were both very into clothes. At that time I wore a lot of Versace that I bought at the Yves Saint Laurent store in Beverly Hills. Dean was very much into these spread-collar shirts, the English spread. There was this French store in the Beverly Center that he loved, and he adored Perry Ellis shirts too. He also got them into those tasseled loafers, with the high, business cut. Dean took better care of shoes than anyone I've ever met."

As Joe's makeover progressed, his reputation expanded. Hunt's towering height, polished appearance, and unblinking gaze made him a dominating presence in the clubs. "He still wasn't all that sure of himself socially, though," Lieban observed. "Joe was always watching and observing, looking for an opening, a chance to get ahead. Dean played it off better."

Dosti and Dicker were the BBC's most outspoken snobs, chasing away the wanna-bes with implacable stares and corrosive commentary. "When Ben and I were together, everyone was a target for satire," Evan admitted. "A lot of it is simply what *you're doing* as opposed to who *we are*. I mean, the average club you go into in Los Angeles is filled with people who hang out and wait to be discovered. So you look at the things they do to make themselves interesting or novel, and it's very amusing."

Evan remained the BBC's heartiest partyer, out almost every night of the week, in a foursome with the Mays and Jeff Raymond when he wasn't among the Shadings. "It was kind of a relief from thought to be with Tom and Dave," he explained. "I didn't have to be so on, performing the part of a BBC member."

The twins and Raymond had spent most of the summer playing on the beaches of Balboa Island, where they were living in a house along the canal, their rent paid by the BBC. Gene Browning's friend Ken Elgin had arranged, much to his regret, the twins' occupancy. "They left that place a complete disaster," Browning recalled. "There were girls' dirty underwear, their dirty underwear, rotting food, maggot-filled pizza pies, plates so filthy you couldn't clean them, piles of crushed beer cans. Ken was mortified."

After Labor Day, the twins migrated north again, taking a two-bedroom apartment in Brentwood between the UCLA campus and the San Diego Freeway. "I started going out with them a lot when they moved back to L.A.," Evan recalled. "We'd do the same thing we'd always done: go out, try to pick up girls. I thought Dave was a little more fun than Tom, and one certainly picked up more girls with Dave. Dave shot from the hip; he really didn't care if it worked or not, there was always somebody else, next in line. Tom had a lot of fraternity boy left in him: 'Hey, what are you doing here? Do you want a drink? Do you wanna go dancing?', et cetera, et cetera—more of a set pattern. I don't recall Dave ever going out with a girl on a Friday or Saturday night. He wanted those nights free to hit the clubs. If he had a date, it was in the middle of the week or Sunday night. Tuesday night was Voilà, and Thursday night was getting ready for the weekend. We went out almost every night. We didn't exactly have to be at the office early the next morning."

As the Mays began to spend their days apart—Tom remaining in the Third Street office, while Dave joined Jeff and Gene Browning in the search for a manufacturing plant where they could assemble the new Cyclotron prototype—differences between the identical twins became more apparent. While Dave continued to work the clubs in his uniform of khaki pants, polo shirt, and Top-Siders, Tom's wardrobe grew weighted with suits and ties "courtesy of the BBC," Evan noted. Which of the Mays one preferred became a way of telling "the regular line BBCers," as Evan called them, from the more marginal members. Lieban, for instance, imagined that "Tom was the more thoughtful one." Another new BBC member, however, would describe Tom as "your basic dick": "Tom had to be a May. Something was missing from his life, in that he had to have the success that his family had and he wanted it now. Whereas Dave was great: 'Hey, I'm a May; it'll get me laid.'"

Tom became Ben Dosti's collaborator in soliciting lunch meetings with corporate executives. The sole surviving letter produced during this period by the twin, then twenty-four and only a few credits shy of a degree in economics at USC, began: "I am a student in the patroliam energnearing [sic] school at USC. Currently I am working on a 2 semester long project concerning the various aspects of sinfuel [sic] production."

What mattered most among the BBC was that Tom had become the clear favorite of Joe and the Shadings, more and more often invited to attend their business meetings and dinners without his brother. Alisa Goza noticed how changed Tom was when she met him for dinner in Newport Beach one evening in October. "He had on a sport coat and tie; I didn't even know he owned a tie. He was better groomed, too, but mainly his attitude was different; he was like a businessman, so cool and collected. He told me about this BBC. . . . He said he was making money faster than he could find things to do with it." Tom gave Alisa one of his new BBC Consolidated business cards, bold black letters in a grid of intersecting gray lines. When she asked Tom what BBC meant, Alisa recalled, "He said, 'Billionaire Boys Club.' I thought that was funny and he was really offended. He goes, 'This is serious.'"

Alisa understood how serious Tom was about the BBC when he invited her to lunch in Los Angeles a week later. "He wanted me to meet him at their office in West Hollywood," she remembered. "But when I arrived, he was very nervous about me meeting Joe Hunt. He whispered through the door, 'Wait here.' It was like he wanted them to see me but not to talk to me. Then he told me, 'You have to wait downstairs; no girls allowed in the office.' I said, 'Is this a business or a fraternity?' He said, 'This is just one of our policies.' Then at lunch, all he did was talk about, 'I made a seventy-thousand-dollar deal today.'"

The divergence of the twins paralleled a heightened sense of ins and outs among the BBC, a feeling that new and subtle categories were being created within the Hierarchy of Information. The October meeting would be the BBC's largest ever, with an attendance of forty members, yet already the group was collapsing toward its center, as Joe began to distinguish between "active" and "inactive" members. Evan maintained the official roster. "As the BBC took on a more business and less social definition," he recalled, "the number of people considered active members began to shrink steadily."

Part of the reduction was the result of what Joe described as "a failure of commitment" on the part of people like Mickey Fine and Joel Gelff, who wanted "more compensation, more involvement, more power," Lieban recalled. Like Fine and Gelff, Farhad Novian was still in law school. His brighter brother, Farid, had just graduated but was giving more time to his Century City law practice than to the BBC. Simmie Cooper was relegated to the inactive list when he went to work for his family's construction business. Neil Antin became inactive because of increasingly strident demands for the film equipment Joe promised. "Neil raised his voice to Joe," Evan explained, "which simply wasn't done." Ron Pardovitch, one of the BBC's first four members, had been invited to live with the Shadings at the Manning, sharing a bedroom with Ben, but Joe began to exclude him from closed-door meetings after a BBC meeting in September at which Ron asked for a written guarantee of his share from the Levin profits. When Pardovitch took a job as manager of a restaurant on Beverly Drive, Joe suggested that he begin looking for another place to live as well. Alex Gaon's departure from the BBC was the most abrupt; after Cantor Fitzgerald filed lawsuits against five BBC members in October, demanding payment on the losses incurred in the May and Karny accounts, Alex not only stopped coming into the Third Street office but began to avoid the BBC's social functions as well.

Cary Bren ceased attending BBC meetings at around the same time, partly as a result of conversations between his father and Brad Reifler. Brad had moved by then from Refco in New York to Shearson's Beverly Hill's office, where Joe and Ben began trading Financial Futures accounts after the losses at Cantor Fitzgerald. "We were sort of friendly competitors," Reifler explained, "going after some of the same people to raise money." It was from friends in Chicago that Brad learned of Joe's suspension from the Mercantile Exchange. He passed word along to the Brens. "I don't think Don was that impressed by Joe anyway," Reifler recalled. "He thought he was bright but not trustworthy. And he saw how they might use his name, so he pulled Cary away."

Special consideration was accorded to the younger Bren, however, and the BBC continued to show Cary's name on its active roster. The three Shadings even made a special trip to Atlanta in October to watch Cary compete in his first Formula I race, posing with him for photographs that were left lying around the reception area in the Third Street office for weeks afterward. "Joe was using any name, any innuendo that he could to convince the world that the BBC had power, big clout, big money, behind it," Dean explained.

Few in the BBC were shaken by the departures of Gaon and Bren. "There was nothing ominous about it," Taglianetti recalled. "I knew Cary from Harvard, and he told me he was racing cars now, and he just didn't have time. He didn't put out anything negative about it. And even if some old members were leaving, there were new people joining."

The most highly touted recruit was the BBC's new "general counsel," Jerry Eisenberg, brought in by Farhad Novian, his friend since Hebrew school. Jerry had gained an academic year on Farhad as undergraduates at UCLA, then leaped ahead another year by pushing himself through Loyola Law School on an accelerated schedule, becoming, at age twenty-two, the youngest attorney in California. For Eisenberg, though, law was merely a means to an end. By the summer of 1983, already employed as an associate in the downtown law firm of Knapp, Grossman, and Marsh, Jerry had surmised that he would need an MBA to amass the sort of stake required to buy a seat at the main table. He was about to enroll as a graduate student at UCLA's School of Business in late September when Farhad persuaded him to meet the BBC. "Farhad kept telling me, 'You gotta meet these guys. This is the greatest thing that's ever happened to me; I made ten thousand dollars just for writing a couple of memos,'" Eisenberg remembered. Farhad failed to mention that the ten thousand dollars was not cash in his hand but an allocation from the Levin profits. "He also said he had known these people since college, that they had recruited the smartest and richest kids from all over Southern California," recalled Eisenberg, who was skeptical only because "Farhad wasn't really that hungry. He liked the action, and the money was nice, but even if he never made a dime, he liked having this great office to take girls to."

Eisenberg's own appetites were honed to a sharper edge. The young lawyer hadn't grown up well-off or even well-to-do but merely middle-class, the son of a man who made his living operating a bowling alley in the black community of Inglewood, who paid seventy-two thousand dollars for their house in Cheviot Hills, "then laid awake nights worrying about whether he could make the payments," Jerry said.

When Farhad ran down the names of the BBC's upper echelon, Eisenberg recognized only Dean Karny's. He and Karny had known one another just well enough to say hello back on North Campus at UCLA. Jerry was a frat man, pledged to the most prestigious Jewish house, Zeta Beta Tau, but still a distinct notch below the prep school boys like Dean and Ben, most of whom disdained organizations that were as easy to get into as a fraternity. Still, among those who achieved even the slightest measure of recognition on North Campus, there existed an underlying bond, a sense of common purpose and collective destiny. "South Campus was for the nerds, the computer people, the doctors, the engineers," Eisenberg explained. "Central Campus was for the Orientals. North Campus was for the fraternity and sorority people, the ones with family names, the Jewish business types, the people who figured they were gonna be running things in this town, eventually." The feeling among the North Campus students, especially strong during Eisenberg's last year at UCLA, 1980, was that they were where the country would turn the corner. "My year of people was the first year when we didn't get draft notices, the first when there was no war, no antiwar. We were interested in business and money. We brought America back into the system."

Karny showed up for their meeting at the Hard Rock looking more stylish than ever, wearing one of those chic skinny ties with an Italian jacket, Eisenberg remembered. Dean was accompanied by Lisa Marie, who made an indelible impression in "an outfit that looked like it had been surgically applied." The May brothers were there, "acting like they owned the place," along with Ben Dosti, whose presence Eisenberg found reassuring. Farhad put his friend in the empty seat next to Joe Hunt, who was being toasted with round after round of Coronas. "They were all gloating about the Swartout deal, which they had just closed," Eisenberg recalled. "They were celebrating that; this was the occasion and I had been invited. It all sounded great; they just stole this company from this guy, and Joe was the master-mind; he had perpetrated this great stock swindle, and the company was going to make them millions."

Joe ordered a cheeseburger and mineral water, "then proceeded basically to grill me," Eisenberg recalled. "He said he was forming a net-work of the best and the brightest—they all used that phrase a lot then—that many were people from wealthy families, with good connections. I recognized the May name, naturally, and they mentioned Cary Bren. Joe said they also needed talent and expertise, that they were interested in acquiring their own full-time attorney to oversee contracts, et cetera." Eisenberg, a young man not easily impressed, felt slightly intimidated by Hunt: "Joe's attitude seemed to be that they were testing me to see if I was BBC material. He wanted to know what I knew about partnerships, about real estate, about taxes. I had a fairly extensive background in all those areas, so he was pleased. Joe seemed very knowledgeable for a layman. *Very* knowledgeable. He seemed much older to me. I was at the time twenty-four, but I figured he was close to thirty. I mean, how else to explain the guy?"

Eisenberg was startled when, after about an hour of questions and answers, Joe suddenly raised his water glass "to our new in-house counsel." The BBC would pay him fifteen hundred dollars a month in cash for twenty hours of work a week while he went to graduate school, Joe said. He would get an office, a secretary, an expense account, and a fair percentage of the profits from any successful enterprise to which he made a contribution. "This was at a time when these guys were talking in the hundreds of millions," Eisenberg noted.

The young lawyer had no way then of gauging his appeal to Hunt. After surrounding himself with adoring lackeys and obedient gofers, orna-mental secretaries and stylish lieutenants, Joe found himself virtually run-ning a conglomerate single-handed. The scale of the BBC's operations now exceeded even his grasp, and what Hunt needed, above all else, was compe-tence. There was something formidable about Eisenberg. Under that pink, plump-cheeked exterior, beneath the neatly cropped curls, the tortoiseshell spectacles, the bland expression, was a young man who had been driven to finish college and law school in five years while working full-time, who during that same period had transformed himself from a fat boy into a brawny young man by finding an hour every afternoon to pump iron, a plodder whose persistence got things done, a listener who remembered what others said, an operator who made everyone he met a member of his net-work. Eisenberg didn't pretend his goal was to make the A-list or to find his photograph in the fashion magazines; what he wanted to make was money, as much of it as he could fill his pockets with. "I need someone like you," Joe told him.

A few days later, Hunt arranged to lease another three hundred square feet of space at the Third Street office, spending more than a thousand dollars to create a law library. A few days after he went to work for the BBC on October 1, Eisenberg had positioned himself among those who preferred Dosti's leadership to Karny's. "I could see right off that Dean wasn't real involved in business," Eisenberg explained. "He was the head cheerleader, basically. Dean was probably brighter, but Ben knew more about business. Ben was one of the two people in the BBC I liked, along with Steve Tag."

Taglianetti allied himself immediately with the BBC's new attorney: "Jerry was ambitious and very shrewd. I knew right off that he was just in it for the bucks, like me." Eisenberg's affection for Taglianetti would be tested, however, when he reviewed the West Car documents during his first week in the office. "Joe wanted me to transfer all their personal cars to West Cars, to show the company had assets," Jerry recalled. "He also wanted disclaimers and waivers of liability in the contracts with the people who bought the cars, which is completely illegal. The worst thing, though, was when I found out Tag was planning to import the cars and phony up the modifications. You're supposed to put steel in the doors and new windows, improve the emission system. Steve tells me the only thing the government requires is pictures of the work that's been done. So what he wants to do is modify one Porsche 928, take the pictures, then use the same pictures over and over again. I went to Dean and said, 'This is asking for trouble,' and he agreed. Joe told me he didn't know about any of this and wanted to do it right, so I was reassured."

Eisenberg's second assignment was to clean up the Mays' mess in Orange County. Four months after its opening, Jamaica West, which had operated during most of that period without a liquor license, was thousands of dollars past due on bills for alcoholic beverages. The club's gas and electricity had been shut off. Employees who hadn't been paid were filing lawsuits for back wages. "Basically, everybody along the line was milking the business," the Mays' pal Taglianetti explained. "Dave and Tom were the kind of guys no one minded screwing out of money." By the first of October, the man the twins hired to manage their club had locked them out. "He barred them from the place for three weeks, had the bouncers throw them out," Eisenberg recalled. "And they just accepted that. Then he closed the place and took all the money." It was Joe who sent the BBC attorney south to see if anything could be salvaged out of the twins' investment. Eisenberg was able to retrieve the three-thousand-dollar deposit on the liquor license, but when he confronted the Mays' manager, "the guy just denied everything and stonewalled me." After Joe ordered him to serve papers, "the guy finally said he'd give Tom and Dave five thousand dollars, out of the eighty thousand they'd put into the place," Eisenberg remembered. "Joe said to take it. He didn't want to fight it anymore; the reputation of the place had been ruined, and it didn't seem worth pursuing."

More pressing matters demanded the general counsel's attention. Eisenberg devoted his second week on the job to insulating Hunt from personal liability in connection with the commodity trading partnerships, drafting a new agreement that replaced Joe Hunt as the general partner with "Financial Futures Corporation," then adding language that warned investors that trading in futures was a speculative venture that could result in the loss of their money. Eisenberg had seen the Clayton Brokerage documents on the Levin account and was informed that the BBC's share had been invested in a shopping center where their equity was worth $10 million. The Swartout merger and Kilpatrick contract promised the BBC a minimum of $75 million. The attorney was aware that Michael Dow and Gold Sun already had paid a $150,000 option on a $4 million order for Cyclotrons and knew from the banking records he reviewed that Joe's trading partnerships were taking in more than $100,000 per month. "It looked to me like people were lined up to give the guy money," Eisenberg said.

"Everybody who got into it got somebody else into it," Mary Brown explained. "We would tell people, 'I've come across this thing and it sounds too good to be true, but I think it's an excellent opportunity.' And from the minute you start telling them about it, everybody wants to believe. People want to believe there's a money tree in the backyard. Then they'd go in and meet Joe Hunt, and the minute they would sit in his office and talk to him, they became a believer."

She had seen Joe's powers of persuasion work best on her own Chester, Mrs. Brown said: "They'd spend two or three hours in a restaurant, and my husband would come back to me mesmerized by him. He was just spellbound. He used to come home on such a high." Mary Brown was no less impressed when Chester brought her along for a lunch meeting with Joe. "My husband would ask him a whole list of questions, trying to catch him in something," she recalled. "He just would come up with answers at the snap of a finger. The way he could hold facts and figures in his head! He could add long columms of numbers without a pencil."

The numbers Joe added now included deposits of ten, twenty, thirty thousand dollars a month Chester was making in his account at Financial

Futures. By the fall of 1983, Brown was funneling nearly all of the profits from his import business through the Third Street office, delighted and astonished—as were all Joe's clients—by the 13 percent profit per month Hunt delivered. Recalled Brown's friend Al Gore (no relation to the U.S. vice-president), "We congratulated ourselves for getting in on the ground floor."

Gore and Brown had joined Chester's cousin Steve Weiss as the principal recruiters for the commodity partnerships. Weiss worked out a special arrangement with Hunt, one that assigned a majority of Financial Futures investors to what became known in the BBC as the "Steve Weiss Family Account." "I placed myself as an ombudsman for these people," Weiss explained. His work in this regard would not go unrewarded. In August of 1983, Weiss recalled, "Joe and I began to talk about how he and I viewed life. For the first time in my life I saw an opportunity to express behaviorally how I felt about money. I felt it should be used in a beneficial way. Joe seemed to espouse the same philosophy." Their conversations were consummated in an agreement to set aside a certain percentage of the profits from the Steve Weiss Family Account in a special trust fund for "people in need," Weiss explained, "those in ill health, young people just starting out." Weiss would control the fund and be provided as well with quarterly statements on the accounts of each investor. As "my friends and family brought in their friends and family," Weiss explained, the list of investors on the family account expanded to seventy-seven names.

Part of Joe's appeal grew, paradoxically, out of his indifference to the entreaties of smaller investors, those who were putting in life savings of five, ten, fifteen, twenty thousand. "Joe said he didn't like all these people coming to the office, all the paperwork he had to do," Weiss remembered. It was scarcely worth his time to handle such trifling sums, Joe warned, and those who gave him any trouble at all would be turned away. Some of the people Weiss brought through the door, however, were prospects too attractive to ignore. Stuart Robinson, the agent who recently had negotiated the richest screenwriting contract in Hollywood history, Melissa Matheson's for *E.T.*, became a Financial Futures investor, as did Marvin Spector, whose pharmacy on Olympic Boulevard was the largest in Los Angeles.

Perhaps the most enthusiastic new investor to join the trading corporation was a faded flower who introduced herself as Liza Bowman. Her name had been Dottie Bowman back in 1971, when the man with whom she would live for the next twelve years, Lou Buratti, met her, as he recalled, "in a group sex encounter at Sandstone." Dottie had become Liza by the time she and Buratti bought a four-hundred-acre horse ranch in Simi Valley. They called their spread the Lizalou and stocked the stable with pure-bred Arabians, then later bought a second ranch—"the one that made us rich," Buratti said—in the Santa Monica Mountains. The relationship began to disintegrate, however, after the arrival at the ranch of Liza's only child, a son who had been among the most prominent young physicians in Honolulu before succumbing to the manic-depressive tendencies he'd held at bay for years with self-prescribed doses of dilaudid and percodan. The doctor's addictions eventually cost him his medical practice, and, in the ensuing divorce, his house and children as well. Bereft, the young man landed at the Lizalou, taking up residence in a small trailer a few hundred yards from the main house. As he continued to come apart, Liza's son "said many blaming things to her," Lou remembered. After one especially ugly exchange, the doctor locked himself in the trailer, taped the barrels of two hunting rifles to his temples, attached lengths of twine to the triggers, then "blew his brains out from both sides," as Buratti, who discovered the body, described it.

Liza "lost her center after that," Lou recalled, experimenting with arcane therapies and spending a small fortune on cosmetic surgery in an obsessive battle against the ravages of age. They already were separated and had begun to divide their assets, Buratti recalled, when Steve Weiss introduced them to Joe Hunt. Buratti ventured only a few thousand dollars, but Liza wanted to invest her entire share of profits from the sale of the Lizalou. "The investors around Hunt were almost like the members of a cult," Buratti explained, "and Liza was looking for something to belong to as much as for a way to make easy money."

Only Dean and Ben knew for certain that Joe was trading perhaps one dollar out of every three deposited at Financial Futures, that most of the money was being used either to finance the BBC's other business ventures or to support an increasingly lavish lifestyle. Karny and Dosti not only slept in bedrooms with private balconies above Wilshire Boulevard, but shared the Mercedes 350 SL that was the first vehicle imported for West Cars. "Joe gave them hundred-dollar bills whenever they asked," observed Taglianetti, who still was living on his monthly salary of fifteen hundred dollars.

The Shadings saw the money they spent to finance their social lives as an advance against the millions due on the back ends of the Dow and Kilpatrick contracts, their equity in the shopping center, the proceeds from the sales of BMWs and Mercedeses imported by West Cars, the liquidation of the commodities positions Joe was putting on at Shearson and Paine Webber. Dean demonstrated his fidelity to the organization by mortgaging himself personally, obtaining Mobil and Texaco credit cards that were shared among the BBC's inner circle. Ben used his American Express gold card to pick up most of the BBC's restaurant tabs. Joe rewarded his lieutenants by giving Dean and Ben access to all BBC bank accounts, allowing them to write out checks to "cash" for as much as $40,000 at a time. Joe's name appeared alone, however, on the account he opened at the Swiss Bank Corporation in Zurich with an initial deposit of $58,601.92.

Even Dean and Ben were unable to follow the flurries of deposits and withdrawals in BBC bank accounts as Joe attempted to build lines of credit for the corporations, writing a series of loans modeled on the one he used to finance the start-up of West Cars: There he had provided the company with thirty thousand dollars in working capital by drafting a check against the assets of Cogenco Systems.

In November, West Cars was assigned to share the warehouse in Gardena that Dave May and Jeff Raymond had found to house the Microgenesis plant. Taglianetti wanted to continue importing classic Mercedes models, but Dean persuaded Joe to specialize in the BMW 700 series. The plan was to purchase the cars in Germany for twenty-six thousand dollars apiece, ship them by freighter to Los Angeles at a cost of a thousand dollars per vehicle, spend another three thousand to reinforce the doors and install catalytic converters, then sell them in Beverly Hills for fifty-two thousand dollars per car. Some of the boys were discouraged by an article in the *Times* predicting that there soon would be a glut of gray market cars in L.A. Joe's reply to this gloomy forecast was for Alan Lieban a revelation: "By starting up West Cars, we were making a Paradox statement," Lieban explained, "because anybody else who got into the gray market, they would bring in maybe one or two cars and say, 'Jeez, this is just a break-even proposition,' but Joe was saying, 'Well, those people are looking at it the way it is, but we're looking at it for what it should be.' Joe was saying we should not look at it as some kind of a desperate gamble, but as mind over matter."

Not everyone in the BBC needed metaphysics. Evan would join Eisenberg and Taglianetti in debunking the notion that Paradox was what bound the group. "The glue of the BBC was green," he said. "We were held together much more by greed than by any vision. And we followed Joe, mainly, because we thought he would make us all rich."

Yet as time passed, "it began to seem that everyone's principal relationship in the BBC was with Joe," Evan conceded, "and everyone's was different." For him, Joe "filled someplace like an older brother who you looked up to and took a great deal of direction from and even feared displeasing." It was Hunt's appetite for work that most impressed others in the BBC. "There weren't enough hours in the day for him," Tom May said. "Joe was putting in ten-, twelve-, fourteen-, sixteen-hour days," Eisenberg recalled, "when the rest of them were on a schedule of 'Come in at ten or eleven, leave for lunch at twelve, get back to the office by three, be out the door by four.'" Unlike the others also, Joe was not attached to objects. "He put on an Armani suit the way a mechanic puts on his coveralls," Evan said. "To him it was just the uniform he wore to work." While most of the BBC equated money with pleasure and pleasure with possession, Dean recalled, "Joe said, 'Money is power, and power is freedom, so to be free you have to be rich.' He taught us to understand that we needed economic success to buy a place in the world that we wanted."

More than two months had passed since the closing of the Levin account at Clayton, and the boys still were waiting for the promised contracts transferring their share of the shopping center. The BBC by now was consuming cash at a rate that approached six figures per month. They nearly had been forced to default on the Swartout deal, Joe told Dean and Ben, when he could not come up with the fifty thousand dollars due to meet Cogenco's October payroll. Ken Elgin wrote a personal check to keep the merger afloat, but a second, larger payment to Swartout was due by the middle of November.

The complaints that had led to the departures of Gaon and Pardovitch were taken up by a number of others; even Ben and Dean grew restive. Voices were raised for the first time when he and Ben accompanied Joe to Ron Levin's house in early November, Dean remembered: "Joe was saying, 'So let's have the paperwork.' And Ron was saying, 'Well, I have to get it from my lawyers.' And Joe was saying, 'Come on, it's been a real long time already.'" Joe's phone conversations with Ron grew increasingly heated after that. Tired of "hounding Ron for proof that we owned the shopping center," Dean recalled, "finally Joe had a conversation with a commodities broker who had dealt with Ron Levin on this particular account."

"I just asked him, 'Did you ever do that story on the trader?'" Jack Friedman remembered. Joe needed only a moment to cover his confusion. "He said, 'Yes, we did the story,'" Friedman recalled. "And I said, 'Well, I didn't see it.' And he said, 'Well, they didn't play it here. They played it back east.' And I said, 'Were you aware the money wasn't real?'" Joe took more than a moment this time. When he spoke, however, Hunt's voice was quite calm, Friedman recalled: "He said, 'Yes, I was aware that it wasn't real.'"

Ron Levin phoned him at Clayton an hour later, the broker remembered: "He said Joe was over there. Levin was screaming at me. He said he wanted to know what right I had to violate his confidentiality, to talk about his business and his money with Joe Hunt. I said, 'How could I talk about your money when there was no money?'"

Relating it all to Dean that evening, Joe refused to accept either Friedman's version or Levin's: "He thought that Ron had instructed Mr. Friedman to tell him that just so Ron could keep all of the profits that Joe had made for him," Dean remembered. Apparently, Joe said, Ron still wasn't taking him seriously.

7

IT WAS KARNY WHO FIRST BROUGHT JIM GRAHAM TO THE BBC'S ATTENTION. They all had seen him around the Manning, either in the lobby or the garage, wearing the white shirt, black tie, and blue blazer in which the building's management costumed its security guards. That lackey's uniform became a body glove, though, on the smiling, stocky black man whose principal duty seemed to be escorting older women residents from their automobiles to the elevator door. On a frame five feet eight inches tall, Jim carried 220 pounds, and none of it was soft. From a fifty-two-inch chest, he boasted, his torso tapered to a waist that measured the same thickness as his thighs, thirty inches.

Dean met Jim one evening when he accepted a neighbor's invitation to a party in the Manning's rec room. Inquiring of his host if the security guard was a bodybuilder, Dean had been told that while Jim lifted weights six days a week, he was best known as a master of the martial arts. The fellow was a black belt in Tae Kwon Do, Kempo, and Shodokan, supposedly, and had won something like seventy straight karate tournaments. Eighty-seven, Jim corrected, when Dean introduced himself. How long had he been working at the Manning? Dean wondered. Just a couple of months, Jim said; he had moved to L.A. from the Washington, D.C., area in September, taking the job at the Manning while he built a private security business in Southern California. Back east, he had worked as a bodyguard to some very important people in the government, Jim said. He also had operated a martial arts studio near his home in Virginia, where many of his best students were employed at the CIA complex in nearby Langley.

He gave Dean one of his cards. JIM GRAHAM, PROFESSIONAL BODYGUARD, it read. Dean showed the card to Joe that evening. It was a marvelous coincidence, they agreed. Only a week earlier Joe had suggested arranging some private karate lessons for the BBC. Joe thought group activities would be good for esprit de corps, and martial arts instruction had been his first suggestion. The idea of the BBC as a band of immaculately groomed white boys whose manicured hands were lethal weapons appealed deeply to Joe's imagination. He sent Dean downstairs to ask if Jim would be interested in teaching them Tae Kwon Do. The security guard was only too happy to oblige, especially after he watched Joe peel off five hundred-dollar bills for uniforms and a kicking dummy.

Class was held on the plush pile carpet in the forty-foot-long living room of 1505. Tom and Dave May, Jeff Raymond, Dean, and Joe were the first students enrolled. Brooke sat on the sectional to watch, giggling as Dean flailed ineffectually with his bony bare feet, then gasping when Jim's demonstration kick lifted the dummy off the carpet and slammed it against a wall ten feet away. It was obvious from the way Joe watched Jim that he appreciated Graham's physical prowess. All the boys were surprised, however, when Hunt invited the security guard to dinner later that week, just the two of them. "Joe's the kind of guy who can pick up very quickly on the person who is dissatisfied with his lot in life," Dean explained.

Little more than a week had passed before Joe began to prepare the other boys for integration, telling them that "Jim was a very special man and that we should all get to know him," Tom May recalled. "Joe said Jim had special talents," Taglianetti remembered, "and that these could be useful to the BBC."

The karate lessons continued all during the months of November and December. Class attendance declined for a few weeks when Dean flew to Europe to shop for BMWs as an agent of West Cars. While Dean was gone, Joe spent almost as much time with Jim as with Brooke, buying the security guard a Givenchy suit and taking him to business meetings, where Jim was introduced as Hunt's bodyguard. Brooke invited Jim and his wife Dana to dinner at the Manning.

When he returned from Europe in mid-December, Dean recalled, "Jim was not working at the Wilshire Manning anymore. He was working with the BBC. He was Joe's buddy; they were spending lots of time together. He was driving a BMW, and Joe informed me that Jim was a really great guy . . . a great resource to the BBC, as he was different than the guys we traditionally have around, the young affluent kids. Jim, Joe said, was a guy who'd been around."

He had taken the job at the Wilshire Manning a week after his arrival in L.A., Jim recalled: "I figured I need contacts, and I knew I'd meet the most prominent people that I would need to be around."

Of those prominent people he met at the Manning, Jim's favorite was Julie Andrews. "She would send down all kinds of presents all the time," he remembered. The actress's husband Blake Edwards, however, "could be a little snobby," Jim thought.

The celebrity with whom the security guard felt most comfortable, however, was Mr. T, a private bodyguard himself before making his fortune as one of television's first live cartoon characters. Graham would stand watch while Mr. T jumped rope in the Manning's courtyard. "I was going to work for him," Jim recalled, "but we had a little conflict there." The rift had opened one afternoon when the Manning's celebrity astrologer, Karen Christian, host of the local *TV Horoscope* show, stopped to watch Mr. T work out. It was a hot day and Jim removed his jacket while he stood in the sun. When the astrologer saw the body beneath the blue blazer, her attention shifted from the TV star to the security guard. After a moment she began to tease Mr. T, suggesting that Jim should take his place on *The A Team*. "She said, 'He's got bigger muscles than you do,'" Jim remembered. Mr. T was so annoyed, he told the security guard to put his jacket back on.

He was no celebrity but hadn't been some stumblebum back home, Jim said, growing up in a modestly middle-class family, the son of an electrician and a registered nurse, members of a Pentecostal congregation in New Castle, Delaware. He began to study the martial arts at age four, Jim said, was a black belt in Shodokan at fifteen, and had earned black belts in five other karate disciplines by the time he began competing in major tournaments at twenty-four. The problem was that there was surprisingly little money to be made from the martial arts, unless you were in movies.

In Delaware, he made his living with a cleaning service, starting the business while still in high school. By the time he turned twenty, he could afford to buy a four-bedroom house. He thought of himself as a businessman, wearing a suit and tie to work, covering these with a white lab coat as he supervised his five employees.

In his mid-twenties, however, Jim began to feel that the cleaning business lacked a certain excitement. "That's why I wanted to be a bodyguard," he explained. "I took a course in it in Virginia." Before long he was living a double life, the mild-mannered cleaning man in the white lab coat by night, the blue-suited aspiring bodyguard by day. He mastered the use of nunchakus and the six Chinese stars he carried in a leather pouch shoved up the right sleeve of his jacket. During the afternoons Jim applied himself to "being observant," even buying himself a pair of spectacles with mirrored rims so "I can see behind me."

In Delaware, unfortunately, as at his second home in Hampton Roads, Virginia, the market for a man of his abilities was severely limited. "I do [security] work once in a while when they have a concert or a group come to town, but that's only once in a while, not a full-time thing like I really wanted. You don't have the kind of people there that need any bodyguard." He imagined how much more rewarding life would be in California: "I figured there'd be people who'd be interested in having a person like me."

If he exaggerated his background in some areas or omitted certain details in others, who could blame him? The BBC, he pointed out, "were all white. I was the only one who wasn't. Everybody had a name. Except me." If he failed to mention to Dean that it was a cleaning business rather than security work that had supported him back east, at least he told Joe about the used car lot in which he held a half-interest, D & J Autos. He told all the boys about his work with the Blackstone Detective Agency in Norwalk, Virginia, though not about the felony warrant for receiving stolen property from which he was in flight. He didn't tell them either that his real name was James Pittman.

Under Graham, his wife's maiden name, Jim became the BBC's "director of security" in early December. His salary of $1,800 per month was half again as much as he was making at the Manning. "That BMW" Jim now drove was a mint-condition 3.0, black with gold wheels, for which West Cars had paid $14,500. Graham's first assignment was the installation of alarm systems at the Third Street office and at the Microgenesis plant in Gardena. "The idea of him doing security for us didn't seem so strange at the time," Evan said, "because I thought of the Cyclotron as this wonderful gold mine that needed protection." Of course, Evan added, "it was clear that in this elite organization based on this highly developed philosophy, [Jim] was not going to be one of our theoreticians."

If the boys doubted Jim's aptitude for abstract thought, they were delighted by the swath he could cut through the most crowded club or restaurant. And if Jim had little to say, he was at least a good listener, pleasing them with that perpetual expression of incredulity he wore. The BBC boy who fascinated him most, after Joe, was Ben Dosti. "Very confident in himself there," Jim explained. "A gentleman all the way." At dinner, even when he was listening to Joe, Jim kept his eyes on Ben, riveted by the unfolding of a napkin or the selection of a spoon, "literally miming Ben's gestures," one BBC member recalled.

While he understood that Dean's position in the BBC was at least equal to Ben's, Jim had a hard time understanding how this could be: "All he really done is tell people how to dress. And toward lower-class people, he's real snobby," Jim observed of Dean. "He think they going to look up to him."

Jim liked Evan, who at least "didn't use his father's name a lot. Other people drop his name a lot, but he don't."

The Mays, on the other hand, flashed the family name at every opportunity. He understood what being a May brother meant, Jim recalled, the first time the twins took him to the Hard Rock Café: "You know how the lines be around the block? Guess what? They just walk straight through. Everybody say, 'Who's those guys?' They think they're God when they walk in there. Everyone s'posed to jump because they're there. They'd be sending people back and forth or spilling something on the table, knock over an iced tea on purpose. Make [the waitress] come and wipe it up. They'd be making noises on the table with spoons, crazy stuff."

Like the other boys, though, Tom and Dave toned down their petty malice when Joe was with them, Jim noticed. And on those few occasions when he caught the Mays harassing the help, Jim remembered, Joe's reprimands were scathing. Joe invariably would be the first one to leave the table when he met the others for dinner in a restaurant, and their leader was almost never with the boys when they met at bars or nightclubs afterward. "Most of the free time, he's either studying or reading," Jim observed. While it was always possible to engage Joe's attention with a question about what he meant by "risk assumption" or "back-market protection," Jim recalled, "he don't pay women no mind. He just totally ignore them all the way. You can take the most beautiful woman in the world and walk straight by Joe. He wouldn't even look."

Joe seemed indifferent even to the charms of his girlfriend, Brooke. Though he was put off by her "punk rocker look," Jim thought Brooke was a doll. "She would just make a person fall in love," he explained, with a faint pang of longing. Yet the only person in the world who seemed to matter to Miss Roberts was Joe Hunt. "Joe didn't treat her perfection," Jim said, "but she didn't care." It baffled Jim that Brooke seemed not to mind when Joe climbed into the car ahead of her, without even unlocking the door on her side, or that he always took his chair at a restaurant table without waiting to see that she was seated. Brooke, on the other hand, couldn't do enough for Joe, Jim observed. She dropped by the office two or three times a week with gifts, arranging a massage for him one week, a pedicure the next, and Joe didn't even thank her, Jim recalled. To celebrate a success in the commodities market, Brooke filled the master bedroom at the Manning with ten dozen balloons, but "Joe wouldn't pay it no mind," Jim remembered. "She felt hurt sometimes. She'd ask me for some suggestions, what to do for this guy. I'd say, 'You doing everything you can do.'"

In all other regards, however, he was nothing but impressed by Joe Hunt, Jim said. On his second or third visit to the Third Street office, Jim remembered, Joe was so annoyed by the time it took two temporary secretaries to transcribe a twelve-page contract that he challenged both young women to a typing contest. Combined, the secretaries typed 110 words per minute. Then Joe sat down and "burned up that typewriter," Jim recalled. "He type 142 words per minute." Joe "said he could do anything," Jim remembered. "He said there's nothing in this world that he couldn't do if he wanted to do it."

Even as the BBC trimmed its active member roster by more than half, two new recruits were being admitted to the inner circle. Jon Allen was so completely Jim Graham's opposite that simply seeing the two side by side provoked laughter. So pale he became almost transparent in sunlight, Jon was a tall, spindly, narrow-shouldered fellow with thinning blond hair, thick bifocal glasses, and a voice that seemed to come out always on the tail end of a pant. Dean knew him from Whittier Law School, where Jon had graduated the previous August. At twenty-nine, his relatively advanced age did not weigh in his favor with the BBC's corporate counsel. "Jon Allen was one of those people you always avoided in law school," Eisenberg explained, "because you figured they had failed at whatever else they had tried to do, and now they were back, thirty years old, and this was the last hurrah."

Jon had joined the BBC in November, shortly after failing the bar exam for the first time. He was a collector of arcana who had filled his West Los Angeles apartment with antique fountain pens and early televisions, "the really old ones where the tube and the screen are up off the set," Evan recalled. The Saab Jon drove was old as well, the sole surviving asset of a failed company he had created to import parts for the Swedish car.

Taglianetti was assured that Jon's assistance would be of value to the West Cars project because of his background in foreign trade. He began to develop doubts, however, Taglianetti recalled, the first time Jon drove him to the new plant in Gardena. "I found out he was obsessed with this fear he had of running his Saab into a lightpost," Taglianetti remembered. "He was terrified whenever he saw one, and since they're everywhere, he drove very slowly, like miles under the speed limit, with both hands on the wheel, at all times."

Even Evan regarded Jon as "an enfeebled soul." "It seemed like there was something inside Jon that inhibited him from ever reaching any goal," Taglianetti reflected. Jim Graham put it more succinctly: "Jon Allen, you give him a project that takes one day, it take him three weeks."

When it was suggested that perhaps he would do better working indoors, Jon took the title of office manager at the Third Street suites.

Jon seemed to sense early on that his best hope for advancement in the BBC was slavish devotion to Joe. He called out to the deli for Joe's lunch, trotted to the corner to post Joe's mail, even drove his Saab to the cleaners to collect Joe's suits. "Jon was such a kiss-ass, he dusted Joe's desk," Taglianetti recalled. If Joe rarely found time for Jon, he was pleased to discover the new office manager had a gift for gathering information from the BBC's other members. While those in the outer cubicles of the Third Street office were wary of expressing doubt and criticism around Dean or Ben, they sensed no such threat from Jon and spoke freely, not learning until months later that every complaint was being reported back to Joe verbatim.

Steve Lopez was the BBC's ticket to the Far East. Despite his Spanish surname, the young man's blood and background were entirely Asian. Steve's father had been the first Indian M.D. in Singapore and was now the wealthiest physician in Malaysia, proprietor of a "medical enterprise" that operated twenty clinics in the Golden Triangle encompassed by Bangkok, Hong Kong, and Singapore. Lopez had come to the United States with $380,000 from his father and a long list of family friends looking for overseas investments. He realized within weeks of his arrival in Los Angeles, Steve said, that ignorance and apathy would be the greatest obstacles to his success. "The most shocking thing to me about this country when I first got here," Lopez explained, "was how little interest there is among rich Americans—especially the young—about what is going on outside their own little world. Rich American kids are the least motivated people I've ever met. In Asia, it's just the opposite; the rich kids are the most motivated, and they all want to know what's going on in the U.S. I'll say for Joe Hunt that he was probably the most knowledgeable young American I ever met about what was going on in the rest of the world. And he was always asking questions, trying to learn more. That impressed me."

Lopez had been introduced to Hunt by Steve Stockton, a young investment counselor who achieved a certain notoriety within the financial community of Los Angeles when, fresh out of Loyola Law School, he parlayed a few thousand dollars of savings into a fortune of more than half a million. "A fluke," said Eisenberg, who had been a member of Stockton's class in law school. "He bought the push on a stock where he had a tip, the price kept going down and down, and he kept making money. The price went from eighty-five dollars a share to three, Stockton makes five hundred thousand, and suddenly everybody thinks this guy is a genius. He doesn't tell them that in the next six months he proceeded to lose *seven* hundred thousand."

Two hundred sixty thousand of those dollars had been wired to Stockton from Singapore. "All my father's," recalled Lopez, who absorbed the loss with aplomb. "Stockton felt bad," he explained. "He kept apologizing. I told him, 'Steve, I *am* upset—who wouldn't be?—but if you can make it up to me, things will be square. I said, 'You've been in L.A. longer, you know the people here better than I do, you've got the contacts. He said, 'Look, Steve, there's this one guy, very young, who is the most incredible phenomenon I've ever seen. He's really unbelievable. His people don't make ten percent a year—they make ten percent a month.' He went into detail about how amazing this guy was. He said, 'Once you meet the guy, you'll understand. He's from another planet.'"

Steve's first encounter with the extraterrestrial took place at the Bistro Gardens on Rodeo Drive. Joe came in flanked by Ben and Dean, his arms overflowing with graphs and charts. "He was using language I didn't understand," Lopez recalled. "It sounded both mathematical and psychological." He was confused by every bit of it, Lopez admitted, except for a set of Clayton Brokerage statements Hunt produced: "I could read them well enough to understand that Joe had made a two hundred and fifty percent profit in about a month and a half."

Three days later, he met with Joe and Ben at the Third Street office. "They explained what spreads were, about interest rates and fluctuations of the dollar. I still didn't get it. I said, 'Maybe I'm stupid.' Joe told me, 'Don't be hard on yourself, Steve. These things take time.'" Even if he could not comprehend Hunt's trading philosophy, Lopez understood enough to appreciate Joe's promise of minimum quarterly payments to each Asian investor. In late October, Steve and Ben Dosti met for the first time with a broker in the Beverly Hills branch of Shearson, where the two applied to open an account for a company called International Marketing Fund.

Within the rank and file of the BBC, almost no one was buying Lopez. A large part of it was presentation. A short man who carried himself like he was six feet tall, Lopez encased his soft body in suits so perfectly tailored, they could have slimmed the happiest Buddha. His brown skin was as smooth and beardless as a baby's. His glossy black hair looked as if it had been freshly clipped each morning. Outlined by horn-rimmed glasses, Steve's dark eyes were pools of earnest intention. It was his voice, though, rapid without being rushed, avid without being anxious, intimate without being insinuating, that convinced most of the boys this guy was too smooth to be true. Eisenberg scoffed at Steve's claims he had access through his Southeast Asian connections not to merely millions but billions in investor funds. Evan, after one or two meetings, refused to sit in the same room with Lopez: "He'd tell us about these older women he'd go out with just to get them to invest in the BBC. I'd look around and think, 'Is anybody else hearing this?'" Even Jim could not keep a smile off his face when he was in the presence of the Malaysian Indian with the Spanish surname: "Steve Lopez, as soon as he opened his mouth, I knew right away he's a real good con," the body guard recalled.

Everyone in the office wore expressions of amazement when—three weeks after joining the BBC—Lopez waltzed into the Third Street suites arm in arm with a middle-aged divorcée who just had transferred one hundred thousand dollars in U.S. treasury bonds to the IMF account at Shearson. By late December, Lopez and his investors had deposited more than a quarter of a million dollars in the IMF account. "I was astonished," Evan admitted. Recalled Lopez: "They suddenly were all a lot more interested in what was going on in Asia."

The money Lopez delivered at IMF was being matched dollar for dollar at Financial Futures, where investors in the Steve Weiss Family Account alone would deposit more than four hundred thousand dollars during the last three months of 1983. Weiss himself made plans to refinance his home in order to raise fifty thousand dollars for an investment in gold futures Joe had suggested. Al Gore was so delighted by the return on his investment that he stopped by the BBC office to offer Joe a Christmas gift of personalized stationery. "I asked if he wanted it scripted or printed," Gore remembered. "He asked that it be printed with 'JOSEPH HUNT, SHADING.'"

Joe continued to sit at his Quotron every weekday between 6 A.M. and 2 P.M., relaying his trades by phone through Ben. Brokers at Paine Webber and E. F. Hutton, where Joe was trading the Financial Futures accounts, praised both the acumen and the audacity of Hunt's approach. Chuck LaBeau at Paine Webber recalled that Joe's first order was the purchase of 110 Eurodollar contracts valued at one million dollars apiece. LaBeau had seen the butterfly spread before but never on the scale Joe attempted. Joe made "very sophisticated trades" at Hutton, his broker there, Gene Vactor, said. Rarely had he seen worse luck, however, Vactor recalled. It seemed that every position Joe took was undermined at once by an opposing order placed by larger traders on the exchanges in New York and Chicago. While the IMF account at Shearson was slightly up, showing an unrealized profit of fourteen thousand dollars, the Financial Futures accounts accrued mounting losses. Joe held on, determined to outlast these "aberrations."

The BBC spent the last two weeks of December celebrating their seemingly endless supply of money. The Mays observed their twenty-fourth birthday with a "Tiki boat party" in Newport Harbor on December 19, sending out invitations decorated with drunken reindeer surrounding a Santa Claus who sipped tropical punch beneath a palm tree. "BY INVITE ONLY!" it read. "NO BUBS OR POLYESTER!" By "Bubs" the Mays meant overweight women, explained Evan, who missed the party because of a contracts final the next day at law school. The BBC entourage that did make the Tiki boat cruise included Joe, Brooke, Dean, Jim, and Jerry Eisenberg, who estimated the average age of the non-Bubs taken aboard by the Mays that evening at "about fifteen." "They picked them up in groups of five and six," Eisenberg remembered, "gave them coke and business cards. Joe and Dean and Jim sat the whole night together, just talking BBC. Jim I think would have liked to chase some of these girls—he had an appetite—but he was with Joe, and when he was with Joe it was all business."

The BBC's official holiday totem was a fig tree that had died in Evan's apartment a few months earlier. The boys transported it to the Manning, stripped off the last remaining leaves, spray-painted the bare branches black, then hung them with ornaments that included Neiman Marcus charge cards and BMW key chains.

On Christmas Day, in a demonstration of his commitment to the great enterprise they had undertaken, Joe met Dean and Ben at the office, where he typed out a one-page document that began, "I, Joseph Hunt, a resident of California, declare this to be my will." He bequeathed all personal and household possessions, Joe wrote, to BBC Consolidated of North America, Inc., "should it still be a California corporation in good standing." If not, those items, along with the remainder of his estate, were to be divided in equal shares between his dearest friends, Dean Karny and Ben Dosti. Dean alone, however, would serve as executor.

Part Three

LOS ANGELES, 1984

What the professional lacks is remorse.

—excerpt from Rex Feral's *Hitman: A Technical Manual for Independent Contractors,* purchased by Joe Hunt for Jim Graham in the spring of 1984

8

THE BOYS BROUGHT IN THE NEW YEAR WITH A BLACK-TIE PARTY AT EVAN'S house. Everybody they invited was either beautiful or rich, Evan remembered: "It was like the China Club had reopened in my living room." Jim Graham, wearing a rented tuxedo that lent him the aspect of an iron-pumping penguin, could not keep from calculating the cost of the affair. At least ten thousand dollars, he estimated: "Lots and lots of champagne. They wasted half of it pouring it on each other."

The only blemish on the evening was the unanticipated arrival of Neil Antin, resplendent in an Armani tux. Joe slammed the front door in his face. "Certain people became persona non grata, and that was how you knew they were no longer in the BBC," Evan recalled. "Neil was persona non grata. Ronald Pardovitch was persona non grata. Alex Gaon was persona non grata. Suddenly it wasn't a matter of active and inactive members; it was in or out, no in-between."

Jerry Eisenberg, just returned to the office after a month in bed with mononucleosis, noticed the change immediately: "The most dramatic thing was the numbers. At the first BBC meeting I attended in October, there were, like, fifty people. The second meeting, when I came back in January, there were, like, twelve to fifteen people, and they were the same twelve or fifteen people who stayed from there after."

Those who left by their own decision did so, Dean explained, "either because their parents had a very strong pull and yanked them out of their position or because they got scared, scared of Joe."

Only one parent went public with an attempt to extricate his son from the BBC—Luan Dosti. After the fiasco at Cantor Fitzgerald, Ben's father recalled, he and Rose invited several parents of BBC members to a party at their home in Hancock Park. He intended "to express my concern about Joe Hunt," said Luan, and was startled by the emphatic lecture he received in retort from Danny Karny: "How can you even doubt his sincerity?"

Shortly after the May twins gave him $150,000 to trade at Cantor Fitzgerald, Joe had rekindled Danny's affection by writing her a check for $20,000—partial repayment, he said, of the "loan" he had taken in Chicago. When the BBC rented the Third Street office, Dean's mother became the only parent who visited on a regular basis. Eisenberg recalled a Saturday afternoon after his return from sick leave when the Karnys arrived with sandwiches from Canter's for Dean and Joe: "They treated Joe like their other son, hugging and kissing him."

The alleged discontent of the Dostis, on the other hand, went unremarked. Ben continued to use his father as a BBC business consultant, even in the most mundane matters. Recalled Taglianetti: "I remember one time Steve Lopez brought in a pair of underwear from Singapore, on a line, and he wanted to know what he could sell it for. Ben suggests we go over to talk to his father. So we drive over to Mr. Dosti's office in Culver City. With these briefs. His father says, 'Let me keep them and I'll check it out.' If he had any problem with Ben being in the BBC, he certainly didn't show it."

What was behind Ben's own façade of knowing smiles and witty banter, no one could be certain. "Ben you always thought liked you, you always assumed liked you, but you never really knew," Evan explained. "Dean, on the other hand, would vocalize."

The differences between Karny and Dosti were reflected in their girlfriends. Lisa Marie bonded with Brooke to form what Eisenberg named "the BBC Ladies Auxiliary." Dean's girlfriend not only prepared meals for BBC dinner parties but contributed her savings of ten thousand dollars to one of Joe's commodities trading partnerships. While Lisa Marie was regarded by most of the BBC as "sensitive" and "serene," Julie was considered a self-centered snob. "Julie came from lots and lots of money," Eisenberg explained, "and she didn't like them because they liked to feel they controlled Ben, and I think she liked to think she controlled him. Also, she thought Ben was better than they were. And she definitely thought she was better than they were."

The others wondered how Ben could sustain simultaneous relationships with his leader and his lover, especially at a time when the BBC was closing ranks. "After the shrinkage, it definitely became more cultlike," Eisenberg explained. "By 1984, either you were with us or against us." Among those who remained on the inside, Dean recalled, Joe's stature grew increasingly exalted. "The rank of Shading was elevated to a sort of mystical level that you reached by working hard in Paradox Philosophy and spending lots of time with Joe," he explained. "Everyone came to Joe with their problems, the same way Ben and I originally had, because they hoped to gain answers to all the difficulties they have dealing with society, parents, and things like that. And, systematically, you noticed that one-by-one people would break up with their old girlfriends, would tell their dad to go fly a kite and would become more and more integrated into the BBC and more isolated from society and Normies."

While he agreed that Joe "took possession of people," Evan resisted the "cult rationale" as a whitewash: "The key to controlling Evan," he explained, "was giving him a way to succeed without having to work very hard at it." The same for the others, he insisted: "Controlling the purse strings was what gave Joe his phenomenal power." Explained Jeff Raymond: "Any negative comments, Joe would argue the point, and if you didn't come around to his way of thinking, he wouldn't want you around anymore. And social exclusion was business exclusion."

Jeff was nearly as adept as Ben at using the appreciative smile, the unblinking gaze, the slight nod of the head to suggest unqualified support. Not once did Jeff mention to Joe, for example, that he and Dave May had spent two weeks during December at the U.S. Courthouse in downtown Los Angeles, reviewing documents submitted in connection to the Cantor Fitzgerald court case and calculating that Joe had traded less than half of the money the twins gave him.

Dave was equally discreet at first, continuing to work with Gene Browning at the Gardena warehouse, convinced that the millions the BBC stood to earn from the sale of the Cyclotron made keeping quiet worth it. Taglianetti recalled bitterly that, late in 1983, when Joe persuaded Tag to invest his own savings in the commodities market, "Dave didn't say one word to me about Joe having lost his money at Cantor Fitzgerald. In fact, he and Tom both said they were doing well." The twins had not told Dave Two either about their loss. "I like to stay away from things like that with my father," Tom explained.

Tom's new project involved his plans to build the prototype of an aerodynamic yacht he called the "Swoos," featuring a hull that complemented the catamaran's open mouth with a pair of tapered pontoons designed to increase forward thrust. Once again, Taglianetti was flabbergasted by the flagrance of his friend's larceny: "He got the design from this Swedish guy, Bjorn, who we both knew at USC. Bjorn bought it from this yacht designer down in Newport and was trying to get financing. It was a registered design. Bjorn was really more my friend than Tom's, so when I found out what he was doing, I go, 'Tom, this is not your idea.' And he goes, 'Oh, uh, well, we can work around this. No problem.' And he starts writing letters to the Department of Navy, trying to sell the design to them."

Within the BBC, Tom now was regarded as next in line to become a Shading. What everyone wondered was what he had done to deserve it.

"If Tom worked an hour a day, he was pushing himself," observed Eisenberg. Yet early in 1984 Joe appointed his favorite May twin president of West Cars, a position Tom modestly described as "more of a title than an actual function." Tom used his abundant free time to cultivate what he took to be the practices of the aristocracy. Alisa Goza, who still was driving up from Newport to spend an occasional weekend with Tom at the twins' apartment in Brentwood, recalled, "One morning he asked me, 'Do you like polo?' I said, 'The game or the cologne?' He goes, 'The game.' I said, 'To tell you the truth, I don't know anything about it.' He said, 'Oh, you should learn. I'm taking polo lessons.' I said, 'It doesn't really get your cardiovascular going, does it?' He was kind of out of shape. He said, 'No, but it's a good thing to know. Everybody should learn how to play polo.'"

At the end of January, Joe countered the sense of contraction within the group by announcing an expansion of the BBC's "residential base" at the Wilshire Manning, renting a second condominium three floors down from 1505 in 1206, right next to 1208, where Blake Edwards and Julie Andrews lived. The $7,000 in cash Joe advanced for first, last, and security on the new condo acknowledged the emergence of Steve Lopez as the BBC's principal fund-raiser. Two weeks into the new year, Lopez had delivered more than $330,000 to the IMF account at Shearson, enabling Joe to control on margin more than $30 million in T-bill and Eurodollar options. That was a pittance against what he could do if they turned him loose in Asia, Lopez assured Joe and Ben. He was pleased but not particularly impressed by the $29,000 in profit Joe had produced in 2½ months of trading on the account, Steve said: "My investors weren't interested in earning interest. They wanted large profits. These were rich people who approached the commodities market the way some people approach a blackjack table in Las Vegas."

Joe arranged for West Cars to purchase Lopez's twelve-year-old BMW for twice its blue-book value, providing him with a quick fifteen thousand dollars in pocket money. Next, he suggested that Dean surrender his office in the Third Street suites, so Steve could use it to impress clients. It was to please Lopez as well that Joe gave Ben Dosti the second bedroom in 1206, knowing Ben's mastery of the social graces had been almost as important in recruiting Steve as the Clayton trading statements. Lopez dined with Ben's parents in Hancock Park at least once a week and described the Dostis to his own people back in Singapore, "the class of people I had come to the United States to meet."

During early February, Joe increased his investment in Lopez, providing him with first-class tickets to Singapore, Hong Kong, and Bangkok so that Steve could meet face-to-face with his Asian investors. Before departing, Lopez signed a series of blank checks drawn on the IMF account at Shearson so that Ben could cover margin calls.

Who would take Ben's bedroom in 1505 was the next significant personnel issue within the BBC. Joe wanted Jerry Eisenberg. The more he watched the attorney, the better Joe appreciated what they had in common. They were the only two in the office who performed without a net, lacking the family money the others could fall back on. Eisenberg was the one other BBC member who wanted success so badly that he was willing to work for it, putting in six-, seven-, eight-hour days at the office, despite his pledge to work only part-time. And Jerry got more done in an afternoon, Joe observed, than Jon Allen did in a month. He also was the one BBC member Joe could count on to attend every important meeting, always in a suit and tie, sitting across the table with an alert expression and sealed lips. "I remember being surprised again and again by how much Jerry knew," Lieban noted. "It struck me he must be an awfully good listener."

Hunt and his general counsel met privately most often on Saturday afternoons, when they generally were the only two who came into the Third Street office. "Joe used to ask me on these long walks," Eisenberg recalled, "and tell me how he wants me to be more 'involved' and take more 'responsibility.'" Eisenberg's reluctance was couched in personal terms. It bothered him, the attorney said, "that I was the only one in the BBC who liked his parents. They all hated their parents, except Dean." Eisenberg rarely socialized with the group, in part because his girlfriend ("from a family so poor, we used to joke that if some people get houses when they get married and others get honeymoons, her parents would give me a bag of dirt") was uncomfortable among the Ladies' Auxiliary. When Dean and Joe offered Jerry the third bedroom in 1505, free of charge, Eisenberg insisted he preferred to remain at home. "The two of them together would have been more than I could take," he explained. It was Karny as much as Hunt who nurtured the BBC's "mini-Mafia image," Eisenberg said. "By the beginning of 1984 they were calling themselves 'the Boys,'" he recalled. "When they were gonna go to a meeting and accomplish something, get something from someone, they became 'the Boys.' Dean started that. I didn't want to live and breathe BBC twenty-four hours a day. And to be one of the Boys, you had to."

Ben remained the only BBC member other than Taglianetti with whom Eisenberg felt comfortable. "Joe and Dean would double-team me, preach to me about the BBC and what it meant, try to talk me into a deeper commitment. Ben would play along, but you felt his heart wasn't in it." Eisenberg even liked Ben's unpopular girlfriend and prevailed on an aunt who worked in the personnel department to find Julie a trainee position at the most powerful institution in the entertainment industry, Michael Ovitz's Creative Artists Agency. The week before Julie was to start her new job, she and Ben joined Eisenberg and Jerry's girlfriend for a week at the Kahala Hilton on Oahu.

Over dinner one night, "I asked Ben whether there was a future [in the BBC] for me or should I blow it off," Eisenberg recalled. "He said no, I should stay, they had lots of things planned for me. I was really more concerned that if they make a pile of money, was it going to be Joe and Ben and Dean's money or was it gonna be everybody's money? Ben started explaining how the money would be divided, kind of like a reverse spin on the Communist theory: from each according to his ability and to each according to his ability. We talked a little about Paradox Philosophy, and I didn't get the feeling he really believed it. Ben put up his hands when I asked him about Paradox, like 'Sure, right, Paradox.' I knew he really liked Joe and Dean, but I remember thinking that he was more like me than like them."

After Eisenberg passed, Dean and Joe offered the third bedroom to Evan. While he would place himself "right on the dividing line between the inner-inner circle, the Shadings, and the next circle" in the BBC, Evan was not certain he wanted to sleep any closer to the seat of power. His position in the organization had become quite comfortable, Evan explained, after the addition of Jon Allen, "who had even less self-esteem than I did, and so ran more errands and did more chores." Evan was putting in four or five very relaxed hours, three days a week, at the Third Street office and showing up for class only occasionally, calling himself "the best joke ever against Whittier Law School" after passing a community property course he attended just twice. His BBC salary of nine hundred dollars per month was mere pocket money on top of the living stipend his parents provided. Considering his assigned interests in the Microgenesis contracts and the commodity trading profits, "I felt like I was getting a lot more from the BBC than I was giving," he said. "I mean, I pictured Joe and Ben knocking heads, making big business deals and brilliant plays in the commodity market. What the hell was I doing? Typing letters and trying to figure out how to work a computer."

He understood from the beginning that the essence of his role in the BBC was obedience, Evan admitted: "I felt like if I wasn't pleasing people, I would be left behind." From Gene Browning's perspective, Evan's principal function in the BBC was to serve as "Tom and Dave's whipping boy." "I remember he came down one day when we were sanding out the inside of the mill's tubes, and they put Evan, who was wearing a business suit, in one of those little sanding machines that he had never seen before in his life. They gave him a mask and goggles, then just stood back and laughed hysterically. He came out covered with metal dust, looking like a raccoon, but not one word of complaint."

Despite the Mays' occasionally cruel use of him, Evan continued to feel more comfortable socially with Tom and Dave than among the Shadings. It was why he turned down the offer of the third bedroom at the Manning, Evan explained: "To me, Joe was an authority figure."

The third bedroom in 1505 went eventually to Jeff Raymond. This decision not only pleased the Mays but provided Joe with daily reports on what was happening at the Microgenesis plant. Jeff was assigned to work full-time with Dave May as Browning's assistants during construction of the BAM's newest prototype, while Tom served as "liaison" between the Gardena plant and the Third Street office.

Gene Browning's revised version of his attrition mill remained the centerpiece of the BBC's financial plan. While the $200,000 paid thus far to the corporate accounts of Cyclotronics and Microgenesis was a pittance compared to the $1.5 million that already had passed through Joe's assorted trading partnerships, those sums were merely deposits against eventual payments due that now approached $100 million. The most recent check taken in by Cyclotronics had been written by Arizona gold miner William Morton as a deposit on the six machines he intended to use at his cyanide-leach mining operation in Apache Junction, about an hour's drive from Phoenix.

Joe promised Morton the first of his machines by April 1, a date Browning insisted was unrealistic, since Hunt had instructed him to assemble at the same time a manufacturing prototype for Kilpatrick as well as the first of the machines due to Michael Dow and Gold Sun. The BAM had changed appreciably since Hesperia, explained its inventor, who was working still without a blueprint, adjusting the specifications by a process that amounted to trial and error. In its present state, the attrition mill suggested the sort of robotic octopus Lex Luthor might have manufactured to menace Metropolis. The guts of the machine were housed in a cylinder of two-inch-thick, case-hardened steel designed by Jeff's father. Eight feet tall and two feet in diameter, the cylinder was attached to an assortment of hoses, pipes, and vacuum bags that took up virtually the entire building. "Big as an elephant," said Jim Graham, after reporting to the plant to install a new security system. Jim was suitably impressed, however, when he watched Browning demonstrate his previous production model for the gold miner Morton, transforming several pounds of gravel into what the inventor called "kilomesh." "Way finer than sugar," Jim remembered. "Fine-fine. So fine you can hold it in your hand and it runs straight through. Like smoke."

Extreme security measures were called for, Joe said, because he had decided not to apply for a patent on the machine. "Once you patent it, anybody can find out the information," Jim recalled Joe's explanation. Graham was more than a glorified security guard by now; Joe had appointed him, along with Jon Allen and Dean Karny, to the board of directors at Microgenesis. By giving ostensible control to his most devoted followers, Joe could administer the company without exposing himself to litigation, explained Evan, who prepared the paperwork. At the same time, Joe instructed the BBC's secretary to create a new holding corporation, Seldon Inc. Two-thirds of the Microgenesis stock was transferred to Seldon, where Joe, Dean, and Ben held proxy options entitling them to purchase a controlling interest in Microgenesis whenever they liked.

The fifty thousand dollars Joe allocated for completion of the new Microgenesis prototype was less than half what he authorized West Cars to pay for the four anthracite gray BMW 728s Dean had selected while in Europe. When Taglianetti objected that the vehicles were becoming a personal fleet for the BBC's inner circle, "Dean and Joe told me they were communal property," he recalled.

The "money flow" began to concern Taglianetti as well: "There'd be problems with our paychecks; we'd have to wait a few days," he recalled. "Then Tom would come in and tell me, 'Joe just made five hundred thousand dollars today.' I wondered where it was all going." The Mays must be getting a big chunk of it, Tag figured: "They went shopping and bought a lot of clothes. They bought Corvettes and Porsches. Meanwhile, I have to wait a week for my paycheck."

Taglianetti was aware that his status in the BBC had been eroded by a refusal to sign over his Mercedes to West Cars in exchange for the stock options the others accepted. "Everything got made into a test of loyalty, and I failed that one," he said. The practical result of Tag's exile to a cubicle in the rear wing of the Third Street office, however, was to make him the BBC member most intimate with Joe's father. For reasons he never fully grasped, Ryan and his partner Mingarella had taken to treating Taglianetti as an associate in Fire Safety, inviting him to attend their meetings with a chemical company near the plant in Gardena. He never saw a sample of the Fire Safety formula, Taglianetti remembered, but heard about a deal Frank and Ryan had made with the officials at Santa Anita to spray the racetrack's grandstands. Ryan often rambled on about the rigors of raising a genius, Tag recalled, "telling me how he had left his practice as a psychologist so that he could devote himself full-time to Joe."

If Joe appreciated the sacrifices his father made, he scarcely showed it. "Joe was really curt with him," Tag recalled. "I remember he'd always make his father wait outside if Ryan wanted to talk to him. If one of us wanted to talk to him, we could just tell the secretary and walk on in. But his father had to wait. Or Joe would say to the secretary, 'Tell him to come back later.' His father would just sort of shrug and say, 'That's the way Joe is.'" Ryan's partner received similar treatment. "Mingarella would bring Hunt these plans," Tag remembered, "and Joe would tell him, 'You can't do this. These are bad business practices.' I remember hearing Joe tell him, 'I don't know how you even got this far in life.' Then I heard Mingarella go back and tell Ryan, 'Your son is a bastard,' et cetera. Ryan would calm him down. He'd say, 'Joe is like a vampire: Morning is a terrible time for him, but at night he comes alive.'"

Joe continued to support the BBC with his commodities partnerships, though hardly in the manner the others imagined. "All during the first half of 1984, I saw a steady stream of people who wanted to write him checks," recalled Eisenberg. "They'd wait an hour for five minutes of his time." Joe was using the attorney as a sort of pseudo-associate at Financial Futures, assigning him to prepare the individual partnership agreements, to accept checks and to write receipts, even to sit in on the audiences he granted each new investor, those in which Joe explained that his trading philosophy was "designed to capitalize on human greed." What the attorney recalled most vividly was the expression of disgust Hunt wore each time he closed the door on one of these sessions: "You got the feeling Joe found the whole thing a little degrading."

Degrading possibly, remunerative certainly: During the first two months of 1984, the Steve Weiss Family Account alone received more than $280,000 in new deposits. Joe was scrupulous about paying the profits he had promised to his earliest and most influential investors. Al Gore, whose total investment at this point came to $10,000, received a check for $4,012 in late January as his share of earnings from the previous quarter. Such evidence of the boy wonder's abilities paid immediate dividends; by the first week of February, Gore had delivered the M.D. who would become one of the BBC's three biggest investors, Dr. Julius Paskan, a frail, timid man with a strained smile and substantial holdings in commercial real estate.

Ten percent of Paskan's investment, like all the money deposited in the family account, was assigned to the special trust fund controlled by Steve Weiss. Setting an example followed by a majority of Joe's investors, Weiss chose not to withdraw the $22,273.54 in profits he had earned on his personal investment during the previous quarter, opting instead for a "rollover" that added profit to principal in an account earning 17.69 percent each month, according to his most recent statement.

Many of the newer investors in the family account were people who had borrowed on homes or pensions to join Joe's trading fund. "They figured they might be able to retire in a little better lifestyle," Mary Brown explained. "That's not greed; that's just planning for your future."

Joe apparently had begun to plan for his own future, opening a second overseas account in early March at the Geneva branch of the Swiss Credit Bank, the same institution where Ferdinand and Imelda Marcos had made their first foreign deposits under the names William Sanders and Jane Ryan. Joe used his own name, making two deposits of four hundred thousand apiece in the month of March.

Within the BBC, the only objections to Hunt's control of the group's finances were coming from the plant in Gardena, where Gene Browning and Dave May complained they were not receiving the money needed to complete construction of the Cyclotron. At the West Hollywood office, Evan grew concerned that the money from one corporation was being used to pay off investors from another: "I knew that by law the board of directors must authorize officers to negotiate a loan when they want to transfer money that way." Like Dicker and Taglianetti, Eisenberg was being paid every month with a check drawn on a different corporate account—"West Cars the first month, Microgenesis the next, Financial Futures after that," he recalled. Tag received a paycheck one month written on a personal account in Joe's name. "All I know is it cleared," he said. The wad of bills Joe carried in his pants pocket grew fatter each week. "He'd hand out hundreds like a father giving his kids an allowance," Taglianetti recalled.

The scale and complexity of the financial empire Joe controlled was forcing him to go outside the BBC to find able assistants. In January, he flew his former out-trades clerk Leslie Eto to Los Angeles from Chicago, putting her up at the Manning while she prepared a cash-flow chart for the BBC. In mid-February, Eisenberg's accountant friend Mike Feldman was accorded a quasi-membership in the BBC in exchange for his services. At a price of free office space, free use of a secretary, and $400 a month in "salary," Feldman agreed to audit the BBC's business dealings.

Feldman was the first in the office to raise doubts about Joe's background, Eisenberg remembered: "They always told the story about Joe being the youngest CPA in the country, and Mike didn't believe it. Joe knew accounting procedures, but he said he worked for all these firms for a couple of years apiece, and that didn't seem possible, unless he started at fourteen or fifteen." Feldman also suspected Joe of exaggerating the size of the profits he was earning in the commodities market. "I knew that butterfly spreads were basically a hedge position," the accountant explained, "and I didn't see how he could be making the kind of money he said he was." For all his grumbling, however, Feldman proved useful, preparing the financial report for West Cars submitted as an attachment to the company's loan applications. Showing "total assets" of $897,665 (including a $469,220 investment in IMF), the report listed just $200 in liabilities.

Of all the new employees in the Third Street Office, though, none was making so immediate an impact as Joe's new personal secretary, Lore Leis. The investors, in particular, adored her. Lore exuded a professionalism so cool and impersonal that it seemed to some the quintessence of elegance. Now in her early forties, she was an ash blonde who had been a beauty once, modeling for a time in Switzerland after crossing the border from her native Germany. Beneath an accent that was especially harsh on the letter r, she spoke English as she had learned it in London, where she resided for some years after sojourns in Geneva and Zurich. New York had come next, then finally Los Angeles, where she had lived for the past decade. The years had withered Lore's looks, and while she still was quite lovely at a distance, her appearance, like her manner, was severe at close range. Lore had worked as executive secretary to doctors, lawyers, and assorted CEOs in her time, though, and was a virtual encyclopedia of proper business procedures.

She had been enormously impressed by Joe Hunt, despite his age, Lore said, almost from the moment she met him. "Joe was extremely correct and professional at all times but not warm or friendly," she recalled approvingly. "Joe never lost his temper or insulted people. Never. I took his direction, which I don't do easily, because I really admired him." What she admired most was that Joe, unlike most of the men she had worked for, "always took full responsibility," Lore explained. "Other bosses, if they forget to do something, they blame it on you later, but he was never like that." From Joe alone, Lore said, could she have accepted the instruction "Only tell me something once. If I don't do it, it means that I choose not to do it. You don't have to tell me a second time.'"

Joe's reciprocal faith in Lore was such that he gave her responsibility for the day-to-day operations of Financial Futures Corp., asking her to create proper records from the receipts and contracts crammed into his desk drawers, accept the checks that came into the office from his investors, and deposit the money herself in BBC bank accounts. The investors were absolutely delighted with the quarterly distribution sheets she prepared for each of them, Lore remembered. It was really nothing, she explained: "Joe gave me all the numbers; I just typed them up."

She never once heard Joe ask somebody to invest in Financial Futures, Lore said, although he would describe his theory of the commodities market to anyone who expressed interest. "Joe's explanations were always in big words, though, which was very confusing," she recalled. "I just sort of sat and listened."

The attorney assigned to depose Joe for Cantor Fitzgerald, Richard Levy, found himself in much the same position. "From the studies I did, statistical studies," Joe explained to Levy, "I found that when the relationship between government national mortgage association bonds, United States Treasury Bonds and Treasury Bills got cumulative, weighted against all of that, to be extraordinarily stressed in a fashion that represented a steep parameter, that a reliable prediction could be made about the movement of the Treasury Bond contract within a horizon of within a week to ten days with ninety percent reliability . . . so I employed those theoretical concepts against certain fluctuations and the constellations of different government issue bonds to pick my entry point."

Joe's defense against Cantor Fitzgerald's lawsuit was that he had been "exhorted" into taking positions of a certain size by brokers from the very company that would triple his margins the moment the market deviated, and which now was suing him. "So it's your position that you don't owe any money to Cantor Fitzgerald?" Levy inquired. "I am baffled by the fact that I am a litigant," Joe answered. Levy attempted a psychological approach of his own, asking if Joe "enjoyed" the arena of competition afforded by the market. "I like the work," Joe conceded. "You are excited by it, aren't you?" Levy suggested. "No," Joe answered. "I never say emotion enters into it at all. It's a dry business transaction." "Is there any risk in West Cars of North America, Inc.?" Levy inquired. "I would say that there is risk in any human affair that you might discuss," Joe answered. "There is the risk that a brokerage house might triple your margins, for example. There are all sorts of imponderables that can intervene and affect the best laid plans." "So there was a risk in the Ginny Mae and T-Bill transactions?" Levy tried again. "There was a risk in the sense of acts of God and things exogenous to the exchange," Joe allowed. "Risk of changing the rules of the exchange. I didn't think of that."

Joe was careful, though, to distinguish on the record between his personal mythology and the literal facts of his background. "What's the highest grade of formal education that you attained?" Levy asked. "Sophomore, USC," Joe answered without hesitation. "Are you a CPA?" the attorney inquired. "I passed the exam," Joe replied, "but I only worked a year and a half in the field, and it's required in California to have two years of experience before you are certified." "Were you ever disciplined by the Chicago Mercantile Exchange?" Levy continued. "Yes, I was," Joe answered.

Joe became obscure, however, when Levy inquired about his status in the BBC. "I'm not employed by any company," Joe said. "Was there a company that you did work for named BBC?" Levy asked. "I have done some work for a company that's first three letters is BBC," Joe admitted. "What work have you done for them?" the attorney inquired. "Oh, just a little accounting work, stuff like that," Joe said. "What is the position that you hold with the BBC?" Levy asked, finally. "Fortunately," Joe replied, "it's rather muddled in my mind which officer I am in which corporation."

Dean, who also was being deposed by Levy, proved even less forthcoming. Levy first observed that Mr. Karny had estimated his net worth at $350,000 on the original application for an account in his name, then asked, "What is your net worth today?" "I couldn't even approximate," Dean answered. On his application, Dean had listed "net quick assets" of $150,000, Levy noted: "What did those consist of?" "I would like to check my records and tell you exactly what that consisted of at another time," Dean answered. After establishing that Karny kept "probably less" than $1,000 in his checking account and "certainly less" than $5,000 in his savings account, Levy wondered where the rest of his money might be. "I would have to check my records," Dean answered.

Tom May proved easier prey, assigning himself a leadership role in the BBC and asserting that decisions within the group were made "by a quorum of Dean and I and Ben and Joe." When Levy took a moment to ask if the person before him was, indeed, Tom Frank May II, rather than his brother, David, Tom opened his jacket to reveal a hand-stitched label on the lining: "It says 'Tom' here," he noted. "Mom had these sewn in." Tom was willing even to state for the record that, yes, his net worth was $3.5 million, as he had claimed on his application at Cantor Fitzgerald. Most of that money was held in "irrevocable trusts" that were "spaced out all over the place," Tom said. The $250,000 in net quick assets he had claimed consisted of "a myriad of things," he explained, "from notes to securities to various other cash on hand—things of that nature." Tom became more cautious, however, when Levy broached the subject of his dealings with Ronald George Levin and a company called May Bros. Land Corp. After a very brief involvement, Tom explained, "I decided that I didn't want to be in business with him." "Why?" Levy inquired. "I didn't like him," Tom answered. "What did he do that made you not like him?" Levy wondered. "He's just the kind of personality that I didn't like," Tom replied. "You know how some people you just don't care for?"

Levy knew very well, having only recently deposed Levin in connection to the same lawsuit. Ron had been uncharacteristically taciturn that day, listening as the attorney who accompanied him, Jeffrey Melczer, did most of the talking. After permitting his client to identify himself professionally as a "reporter for Network News, Inc.," Melczer objected to any questions whatsoever about Mr. Levin's dealings with Clayton Brokerage. "We're dealing with freedom of the press here, reporter's privilege," the attorney explained. Mr. Levin could not answer any questions about his relationship with Joe Hunt either, Melczer added. Or about his dealings with Tom Frank May II and the May Brothers Land Corporation. Or for that matter about his business interest in Network News, Inc. "We have associational freedom of privacy in this country," Melczer asserted, as his client grinned with delight. "It may be 1984, but it doesn't give you the right to inquire into anything you want to inquire into."

When the Cantor Fitzgerald attorney attempted to determine how it came to pass that the subpoena for this deposition had been served upon a person who first denied he was Mr. Levin, then picked up a phone and made a telephone call to Mr. Levin, and yet now was appearing before him claiming to *be* Mr. Levin, Melczer objected vehemently to this "gross invasion of Mr. Levin's rights of privacy" and on grounds of relevancy as well. It was perhaps understandable that Levy grew confused: "Have you ever entered into any type of a business agreement with Ronald Levin?" the attorney asked. "He is Ronald Levin," Melczer pointed out.

The Cantor Fitzgerald lawyer's decision to subpoena Levin had been prompted by his previous deposition of Joe Hunt. Levy's insinuating questions about losses in other commodities accounts provoked Joe into the announcement that he had earned eight million dollars in the Levin account at Clayton Brokerage and was to be paid half the profits. "Did you receive any?" Levy inquired. "No," Joe answered, blushing, "I didn't."

After interviewing Jack Friedman and receiving a package of supporting documents from Clayton, Levy subpoenaed Joe for a second round of questioning in early March. "All during the time that you were having these transactions at Cantor Fitzgerald," the attorney began, "you were undertaking transactions at Clayton Brokerage on behalf of Mr. Levin; is that right?" "Yes, that's correct," Joe answered. "Were you aware at the time," Levy asked, "that the account in which you were directing transactions was a make-believe account?" "I am not aware now that it was a make-believe account," Joe answered.

Even as he denied it under oath, however, Joe began to admit privately that Ron had played him for a fish. Levin's new story, the one he would stick to, was that the Clayton account had indeed been bogus, a ruse, devised for the purpose of obtaining statements from a respected brokerage house showing a commodities account where millions of dollars were on deposit. He had used the Clayton statements to open smaller accounts on credit at several other brokerage houses, Ron explained, mirroring Joe's trades at Clayton and exiting with a profit of approximately $1.5 million. He intended to give Joe $300,000 of that money, Ron added, but no more.

"I don't think Joe ever knew for sure if either there was or wasn't [a real account at Clayton]," Dean said. "But he was sure that he'd been scammed by Levin. All that heartache, all that bringing it back to us, telling us the stories about the shopping center, the seven million dollars' worth, and he ultimately had to admit that Ron had made a fool of him. But that didn't stop him from thinking that he could ultimately get something out of Levin."

Even when Joe assembled the entire membership of the BBC in the Third Street office to tell them "there wasn't a shopping center," Tom May recalled, Joe insisted he would be paid eventually. "He said, 'I am going to get the money out of Ron Levin,'" Tom remembered. "'I know I made it for him. Here are the documents to prove it.'"

The Beverly Hills Police Department had handed Joe a perfect opportunity to turn the Boys on Levin as a common enemy. They read about it in the *L.A. Times,* which published a belated account of Ron's arrest on December 23, 1983, for twelve counts of grand theft. The police had seized three hundred thousand dollars in camera equipment borrowed from Panasonic and RCA, according to the *Times,* as well as computer equipment valued at four hundred thousand dollars. It was Dosti who brought the *Times* article into the Third Street office, Tom May remembered: "Ben said, 'Read this. It's interesting.'" Joe even persuaded the twins that Levin had been responsible for their losses at Cantor Fitzgerald: If Ron had delivered the BBC's share of the Clayton profits as promised, Joe told Tom and Dave, they could have held the positions in their accounts, even after the margins were tripled. The twins began to describe Levin as a bug who should be exterminated, Dean recalled, but then "the May brothers referred to a great deal of people in terms of insects," he noted. "They would say that they just really would like to step on that cockroach or splat that fly."

Joe alone sought to maintain an appearance of amity in his dealings with Ron, Dean recalled: "Joe never really let on to Levin how mad he was. He decided to hang in there, foster whatever relationship he could, and eventually see if there was something he could get out of Ron." Joe's demands for the $300,000 Ron promised him were answered with new excuses and fresh explanations. "Joe said he didn't believe Ron Levin was going to give him $300,000 or any other money," Dean remembered. "And besides, the $300,000 wasn't going to solve the needs of the BBC. Our monthly overhead was so high by then, that amount of money wouldn't cover us for long . . . I asked Joe if he thought Ron Levin really had the $1.5 million he said he had scammed up. Joe said he thought he did. He said he was going to find out a way of getting the money from him."

"Joe was fairly calm," Dean remembered. "And that was when he said that one of these days he would get around to killing Ron Levin."

9

LEADING THEM ONE AND TWO AT A TIME, JOE HAD BEGUN TO BRING THE BOYS along on his "hunting trips" into Soledad Canyon. "A Joe Hunt ritual," Tom May called the journey. "You understood he was taking you to a place he revered quite a bit."

Though he had assigned himself a Porsche 911 from the West Cars fleet, Joe was driving the black Jeep he bought used from Donald Bren—mounted now with a chrome-plated BBC monogram—almost exclusively these days. To reach his stalking grounds, he followed the Golden State Freeway north to the Antelope Valley Freeway, bearing north by northeast toward Agua Dulce Mountain, then veering due east to catch Soledad Canyon Road, a narrow, curving blacktop that radiated heat shimmers and tar fumes in the seam of habitation separating the old Southern Pacific railroad tracks from the Angeles National Forest. The road climbed between cut banks flecked with white agate, beneath scrub oaks and broken train trestles, past the rust-eaten remnants of abandoned camper shells, through sandy ravines where telephone poles had been planted in gravel quarries carved from cliff faces. Just beyond the scraggly copse of cottonwoods where a last outpost trailer park clung to the muddy shore of White Rock Lake, Joe turned south onto a dirt lane posted INDIAN CREEK TRUCK TRAIL.

Crushed beer cans and empty shell casings littered the steep, crumbling shoulders of the truck trail. Work gangs of prisoners in the limbo between penitentiary and parole board hacked at the creosote and chaparral. Los Angeles was the only major metropolitan area in the country where rain was regarded as a fire hazard, Joe liked to tell his passengers. The city fathers had learned from cruel experience that the Southern California climate could transform those grasses that sprouted in the wet clay of February into stacks of tinder ten feet tall by October, when the Santa Ana winds blew in to fan the flames of the most minuscule brushfire.

The truck trail climbed a hundred feet, then fell fifty. Arid wastes of alkali and hardtack were scavenged after dark by coyotes and kangaroo rats. During the day, homeless men wore wool overcoats in hundred-degree heat and carried tents for protection not from the weather but from horned lizards and western rattlesnakes. Earth could not be discerned clearly from sky among the ash-heap foothills of the Transverse Ranges on the eastern horizon. Arroyo ridges at the high point above Ravenna Alpine offered a southern view of the sulfurous pall hanging over the Los Angeles basin like the toxic fog of some mutant Brigadoon, here for five hundred years, then gone in a day. To the north, the sluice gates of the California Aqueduct flashed silver in Cajon Pass as they guided the depths of Mono Lake toward the Rainbird sprinklers of Bel Air.

From this vantage point, Joe invited the Boys to experience Los Angeles as an illusion, a mirage of plenitude imposed on a landscape of drought and erosion. "That spot was Joe's favorite in the world," remembered Tom May.

He had hiked all through these foothills as a boy, Joe told Tom as they carried a pair of .22 rifles and his prized Swiss shotgun into a ravine that ran northeast. Though there still were mule deer and mountain lions— even bighorn sheep—in the highest passes of the Angeles Crest, one was reduced most often to shooting the occasional pocket mouse or striped racer at this elevation. Like other "plinkers," they used cans and bottles for target practice, Tom remembered. On weekends, gunfire echoed in layers of sound through a national forest that was home to fourteen separate "designated shooting areas." The loudest blasts came out of Pigeon Ridge, where the birds for which it had been named no longer roosted in trees that literally had disintegrated from the impact of the armor-piercing bullets and dumdums serious shooters loaded into their AR-15 assault rifles.

It was more wildness than wilderness up here: "Superbikers" raced their Harley hogs around the Angeles Crest Highway's hairpin turns riding eight abreast; four-by-four pickups with special shocks and all-terrain tires climbed giant rockslides at the Rincon Off-Road Vehicle Area; picnickers loaded their backpacks with boom boxes and cases of Coors at Chantry Flat; campers reported rapes and robberies almost every night of the year at Crystal Lake, where as many as four thousand people a day visited, even after the polluted water forced a ban on swimming.

Joe, however, had a "special private place," Tom recalled, one they reached by hiking along Indian Canyon Creek down a narrow gulley to the base of a small waterfall where cottonwoods and wild lilacs grew so dense one could see only a few feet in any direction. "We actually had to get on our stomachs and slide through some of the foliage," remembered Taglianetti, who followed Joe next into Soledad. Joe told him how as a boy he had carved a tub out of the eroded rock at the top of the waterfall and turned it into his own private Jacuzzi, Tag remembered. Of all the Boys

Joe brought to his special place, it was with Dean he shared the most intense experience. The two had challenged one another to climb the rock face below the waterfall, and Dean was about thirty feet up when his foot slipped on a crag wet with mist. He panicked, clinging to the rocks desperately, unable to move. Joe, a little below and to one side, urged Dean to hold on, then worked his way up the rock face to the lip of the waterfall, coaxing his friend to climb another few feet until Joe could catch his hand, then pull him up and over. They lay on their backs a few feet from where the water spilled over, shaking with exhaustion, for several minutes. Finally Dean said he owed Joe his life.

Jim and Steve Tag were with Joe one afternoon when he carried not only his shotgun but also a crossbow, with which he proved himself astonishingly adept. "He's amazing, really," said Jim, who was most impressed when Joe showed off his skill with the shotgun. During the hike to the waterfall, they came upon a tree filled with roosting doves. Joe instructed Taglianetti to scatter the birds by firing off his .357 magnum, then popped two of them as they came out, Jim recalled: "It was unbelievable. He said, 'I told you I could do it.'"

He was showing them the advantage in growing up without advantages, Joe told the other Boys. While they were taking ballroom dance lessons and swatting tennis balls on private courts, he had been hiking alone through these hills, learning to face whatever came along. Joe began during this time to tell a pair of stories even Dean hadn't heard before, claiming that twice in his life he had been forced to kill in self-defense. He was fifteen, Joe said, when a Mexican gang-banger with a switchblade accosted him out at Sepulveda Dam; in the struggle that ensued, he wrestled the knife away from the cholo and killed him with a stab to the heart. He had taken a second life seven years later, in Chicago, Joe said. Al Gore heard the story one afternoon in Joe's office: "He said the Mob came to him and wanted him to work exclusively for them. His reputation had become so large, you understand. They wanted him to launder their money. He naturally refused, on moral grounds, of course, and so they sent three thugs to the place where he lived. Joe said he shot and killed one of them with his crossbow, which was silent, then fled. When he came back, the body was gone, and so were the thugs. The mob never bothered him again, but he left Chicago shortly thereafter. It sounded peculiar, this crossbow story. But Joe seemed a powerful person who could have done such a thing."

By the beginning of March, new weapons were appearing almost as often as business machines among the cubicles of the Third Street office. Adjunct to the karate lessons, Jim had begun to teach Joe to use the Chinese stars and nunchakus as well. Joe brought his Swiss shotgun and crossbow by the office on mornings when he planned an afternoon trip to Soledad Canyon. He bought Jim a bolt-action .306 Winchester rifle and a .32 Beretta automatic pistol. Jon Allen also purchased a Beretta. Taglianetti, who had owned handguns since his teens, brought both his .357 magnum and a .45 automatic into the office. Evan's pistol was a Smith & Wesson .38 police special.

Joe found it easier by far to assemble a shooting party when he was willing to forsake the harsh light of Soledad Canyon for the imported amenities of the Beverly Hills Gun Club, where the firing range was outfitted with low-slung Italian couches, backgammon tables, and a cappuccino machine. "Realism" was the catchword at the Beverly Hills Gun Club, where Joe had purchased a corporate membership for the BBC early in 1984. It was a word Joe himself used more and more often lately, the Boys noticed, especially during discussions of Paradox Philosophy. In a world of choices, Joe had taken to saying, one thing or another always was being "sacrificed." "Joe gave as an example the general of an army," Dean remembered. "Perhaps the general has a choice to save a village. He can go through the forest and risk his men. Or he can go around and risk that the enemy will get to the village before he does. Either way, innocent people will die. His point was that in the course of being a responsible leader you have to make decisions where innocent people may be hurt."

Joe introduced also during this period an economic concept he called "Piracy Principle," Dean recalled, using as his example in this instance the captain of a ship at sea, forced to attack and board a weaker vessel in order to obtain necessary provisions for his own crew. "Joe's message, again, was that a person could make a decision that might involve death or injury to other people for the sake of a long-term goal," Dean explained. "He might decide it was necessary. This understanding 'freed him up,' Joe said, to make decisions."

Something about having Jim around seemed to catalyze Joe's feeling that a show of force was a far more effective tactic than most ostensibly civilized people cared to admit. Dean saw Joe use Jim's "special skills" for the first time after Brooke's father traced her to the Manning and hired a towing company to repossess her Rabbit convertible. Brooke was incensed, screaming curses from the balcony of 1505. She muttered dark imprecations for days afterward, advising the Mays that she had "enough dirt on my father to have him put away for the rest of his life." Brooke was convinced her father had found her address through her brother Todd's girlfriend, Michelle Berenak, the one person connected to the family she had trusted with her new address. It was about a week later, Dean remembered, when Joe announced that he had sent Jim up to the Roberts home in Bel Air with instructions to firebomb the girlfriend's car. "I had my doubts," admitted Dean, explaining his decision to take one of the BMWs for a spin up Bellagio Drive, where he passed the Roberts estate in time to see two fire trucks parked beside the charred remains of a VW Beetle.

Most of the other Boys heard about the firebombing within a few days. It was obvious to everyone by then that Jim was rising more rapidly within the Hierarchy of Information than any other BBC member. He and Joe were spending lots and lots of time together, Dean noted, "just the two of them." In order to increase his control, Joe arranged Jim's appointment to the board of directors at several BBC corporations, told him he could keep the black BMW, even prevailed upon Dean to provide Jim with a Union 76 credit card. "Jim was having the time of his life," Eisenberg recalled. "What he liked were guns, little white girls, and electronic equipment. Joe was supplying him with all three."

In return, Jim was at Joe's service from dawn to dusk, picking him up at 5 A.M. each morning for the drive to the Third Street suites. The body-guard sat for hours just inside the door of Hunt's office, watching Joe scan the screen of his Quotron. When he was not reading the columns of numbers, Jim remembered, Joe generally had his head in copies of the *New York Times, Los Angeles Times,* and *Wall Street Journal* that he picked up on his way to the office each morning. His trading decisions were based increasingly on a "contextualization of news events," Joe explained.

He understood little of what Joe said and even less of what he did, admitted Jim, whose job it was each afternoon to ride with Joe to the bank in the open CJ7. "Two guys wearing a suit, driving a Jeep," Jim explained, "no one expect there's any money in the backseat." Just to make sure, Joe, who always drove, took a route that led through parking lots, down one-way alleys, and through at least one red light. Hunt would park the Jeep directly in front of the B of A's main entrance, which infuriated the elderly security guard stationed at the door, Jim remembered: "He'd be hollering [but] Joe would step on the old guy's toes and walk right in. And the security guard couldn't do nothing about it, neither, because Joe put a lot of money in that bank. Joe would walk by you just like you're no one, nobody." The bodyguard trailed behind, carrying the BBC's money in his new Halli-burton briefcase. "We don't never stand in line," recalled Jim, who was confounded by Joe's instructions to the teller: "He would give her five or six different deposit slips. He would tell her, 'I want to put $400,000 in this account here, I want to put $300,000 in BBC Consolidated' . . . One of the accounts, you'd deposit maybe, say, $520,000. That $520,000, he'd come back around and get a cashier's check for maybe $800,000. Then he'd do the same thing for another account. He'd put it in, but he'd take it back out."

The rift between those who accepted Jim's elevated status and those who questioned it became yet another line of demarcation within the BBC. Taglianetti, Eisenberg, and Dave May were the three who questioned the bodyguard's role. Jim had experience in the auto business that would be "quite valuable" at West Cars, Joe had told them. Steve Tag began to doubt this, though, after bringing Jim along to a seminar on using a computer to test European cars converted to meet U.S. emission standards: "The teacher gave each of us a chance to adjust this car," he recalled. "And when Jim got up there he was completely lost; people were sort of laughing behind the backs of their hands. It was like he hadn't heard a thing the guy said." Jim continued to show up two days a week at the plant in Gardena, however. "The one thing he could do was move pieces of heavy equipment," Taglianetti allowed.

Jim at least seemed aware that he was being "remade and made up by Joe," Tag observed: "Dave or I would say, 'Hey, Jim, nice suit.' And he'd just sort of shrug it off and wink." It was difficult, though, to be certain how much of the abashed servility Jim projected was genuine and how much was put on. At the same time he pretended to a knowledge of automobiles he obviously did not possess, Jim feigned an ignorance of weapons equally belied by his behavior. Not long after Graham went to work for the BBC, Joe invited Tag to join Jim and him for an afternoon excursion to a gun convention at the Los Angeles County Fairgrounds in Pomona. "We're driving out on the Sixty Freeway, and Joe is telling me how he used to shoot his rifle when he was a kid, hiking in the hills out there, and Jim was like in awe, saying, 'Wow, I never had a gun,'" Taglianetti recalled. "But all of a sudden when we're out there, Jim picks up this four-barrel derringer that is on display and knows immediately what it was. I know guns and I had never seen one before. The thing was, like, square, it was so thick. It looked very intimidating. And Jim bought it that day. He's telling me, 'Oh yeah, I can convert it so it fires all four barrels at once.' He explained you did it by filing down this lever. I thought, 'If you never had guns, how do you know all about them?'"

"Jim was a nice guy, always smiling, always helpful," Tag's friend Eisenberg said. "At the same time, after you spent some time around him, you knew that if you offered Jim two hundred dollars to break somebody's legs, he'd take it. He just had that look in his eye."

At the warehouse in Gardena, Jim organized athletic competitions to display his abilities, once goading the twins and Jeff Raymond into attacking him with a pair of steel pipes, Tom recalled, then "disarming us easily." Jim never forgot his place in the BBC pecking order, though, running the Mays' errands and chuckling at their jokes. He was staggered, however, to learn that the BBC's inner circle averaged about thirty parking tickets per week. The Boys' attitude toward such trifling matters was demonstrated most memorably, Jim recalled, on the afternoon when Joe, Dean, and Tom took him shopping for clothes in Westwood, parking the BMW they drove that day a few feet from the front door of the At Ease store: "We just pull up and there's a fireplug, right? You don't supposed to park there. So they park. The police say, 'You can't park there! See the fireplug?' Joe say, 'I know, I see it.' He say, 'All you can do is put a ticket on it. Do it, just write it. That's your job, write the ticket. That's all you can do.' They just hop out of the car and leave it right there. And just walk right off. And the guy, you know, with his mouth open."

Still, no white man ever had treated him better, Jim said. When they were furnishing the offices at the Gardena plant, Joe invited his bodyguard to join him at an estate auction in San Diego where Jim was taken with an antique oak desk. "Joe said to bid on it, so I kept bidding on it," Jim remembered, "and he didn't stop me. I took that desk from three thousand dollars all the way up to eighty-seven hundred." What made Joe's attention flattering, Jim said, was that he had never met anyone with a mind so amazing. Among Joe's more impressive feats was to sit behind one of the other players when Jim and the Mays and Jeff Raymond played poker in the living room at the Manning. Joe would watch the deal, wait for the discard, then tell each of the players sitting across the table what cards they were holding. "He got it right every time," Jim remembered. Yet when he and Joe, Dean Karny, Gene Browning, Tom May, and Jeff Raymond took a trip to Las Vegas for a meeting with the gold miner, Morton, Jim recalled, Joe alone refused to gamble at the blackjack tables in Caesar's Palace. "He don't believe in that sort of stuff," Jim explained. Tom May, on the other hand, "just loves losing," Jim observed. "He was playing blackjack, lost about ten thousand dollars already. He went back to Joe, said he wanted more. Joe gave him another couple thousand. We went to the airport, he put his last fifty bucks in that one-armed bandit."

Joe's indulgence of Tom's sloth and extravagance was spawning an inevitable cynicism within the BBC. The Shadings' claim that promotion and reward would be distributed on the basis of effort and accomplishment was mocked by those who kept track of Tom's day-to-day activities. Eisenberg, who had taken to observing aloud that "if the Mays' IQ was one point lower, they'd be houseplants," shook his head in disgust each time he walked past Tom's office and saw him "sitting there all day long in a suit and tie drawing pictures of yachts." Tom remained a source of financial support, however, depositing another ten thousand dollars with Financial Futures, then persuading Jeff Raymond to liquidate twenty thousand dollars in stock he had received as a birthday gift and invest it in Joe's trading fund. More valuable to Joe than the money, however, was the use of a face to go with the May name when he brought the BBC to a business meeting. Cary Bren's unavailability made it "especially nice to have a May around to shake someone's hand," Evan observed.

As much as Tom's family connection, Joe needed the twin's cooperation in his legal struggle with Cantor Fitzgerald. In order to snarl the lawsuit, Hunt had helped Tom and Dean prepare a cross-complaint in which Joe was named not as a coplaintiff but as a defendant, along with Cantor Fitzgerald and Drexel Burnham. Not long after, Joe prepared a second document for Dean and Tom, a "Settlement Agreement and Full Release," in which "Messrs. Karny and May agree to fully waive and release Hunt from any and all claims, liabilities and causes of action, past, present or future." In exchange, Joe offered to transfer his full interest in the $374,799.50 note he held on West Cars of North America, Inc., to Tom and Dean in equal shares. On February 28, Dean and Tom each signed memos that were identical except for the signatures: "Dear Mr. Hunt: After reviewing your proposal presented to me in your letter of February 12, 1984, I must say it is quite interesting and appealing. I have discussed this matter with my advisors and agree."

The pressure on the twins to produce a return on their investment in the BBC was increased by a knowledge of how Dave Two would react when he heard about the loss at Cantor Fitzgerald. After learning he would not receive the seven hundred thousand he had been promised from the profits on the Levin account, Dave's simmering discontent began to boil over. "Dave didn't act like anything was wrong until after Joe told everyone there was no Levin money," Evan remembered. "*Then* he was pissed off." As his brother's apostasy became evident, Tom's conviction that Joe was taking care of him redoubled daily. He noted that Joe had prepared yet another document designed to protect the twins' interests, sending Jon Allen to deliver it by hand to Ron Levin's front door. "Please be advised to cease and desist in your practice of suggesting that Tom Frank May II or David Herbert May III are officers or otherwise involved in 'May Brothers Land Corporation,'" it read. "We are distressed to the utmost by reports that tell of your use of our name to facilitate business transactions that we have no part in."

Even as he scrambled each month to make the "profit disbursements" due on his commodities partnerships at Financial Futures and IMF, Joe agreed that the BBC would foot the bill for the polo lessons Tom, Dave, Jeff, Evan, and Ben were taking at the Los Angeles Equestrian Center. Calling themselves "the Maulers," the Boys participated in trotting scrimmages twice a week, and "it was costing two hundred bucks per person every time they go out," Jim Graham noted. When his brother accused Joe at one practice of being a crook, Tom reported the remark to Joe that evening. "I heard Tom say several times that he believed in Paradox Philosophy," Tag remembered. "Tom was thoroughly ingrained," Gene Browning agreed. "He wanted to be a Shading."

The protective custody in which Joe seemed to place Tom mirrored the mounting paranoia and attendant grandiosity that emanated from the inner circle. Jeff Raymond recalled the afternoon in early March when he and Tom were riding back to the Manning with Joe in the open Jeep. They spotted a tourist on the sidewalk, taking a photograph of Tom's tricked-out Porsche, Jeff remembered: "Joe jumped out of the Jeep and tore the camera out of the tourist's hands, then ripped the film out of the camera." They should remember that everyone was after something, Joe said.

Joe's drain on the cash coming into the commodity accounts was making it impossible to do more than hold the positions already in place. Nearly four hundred thousand dollars in checks made out simply to "Cash" had been drawn on the Financial Futures account at the Bank of America alone during the first few months of 1984, Lore Leis remembered. "I didn't think anything of it, though," the secretary said. "That was his system. You just didn't approach Joe and question him." How could she not be impressed by Joe? Lore would ask. The statements she prepared for the Steve Weiss Family Account showed profits of more than 15 percent per month. Investors "were calling me up every day saying, 'Can I put some more money in?'" remembered the secretary, who gave Joe five thousand dollars from her own modest savings account to invest at IMF.

Few of the checks Joe wrote to his investors were cashed; most of his limited partners still preferred increasing their investment to withdrawing their profits. Nearly as often, the payments Joe made were doubled and tripled by new deposits. In early March, for example, Joe wrote a check for sixty thousand dollars to Steve Weiss—the 10 percent from the family account's profits promised to the special trust fund. Weiss not only reinvested thirty-five thousand of that money in Financial Futures, but added another thirty-five thousand to Joe's gold futures trading fund. Weiss also persuaded his sister to take a second mortgage on her home to increase her investment. The investor's "ombudsman" was not without concern, however. Whenever they met for lunch, Weiss remembered, "Joe would be complaining about people phoning him at the office, trying to see him. He'd say, 'Maybe I'll just cancel all these people out' . . . Joe didn't seem concerned about bringing people in. He didn't want to be available."

Joe was in his best boy-wonder form, though, when he invited eighty Financial Futures investors to a luncheon at the Tail o' the Cock restaurant on La Cienega Boulevard in early March. The speech Hunt delivered that day "made us feel we deserved the money we were making, as if we had earned it by placing our trust in the right man," Al Gore recalled. "It was like he was congratulating us for recognizing him." While Sunny Walton, a Financial Futures investor whose savings had been accumulated during fifteen years spent touring on the Playboy Club circuit, entertained the other limited partners with a set of show tunes and impersonations, Weiss advised Hunt that one investor's disbursement check had bounced. Joe wrote a draft to the man on the spot, drawn on his personal account.

Hunt's face never showed any "affect," Weiss explained, "so all you could observe in him was what you interpreted as 'The situation is well in hand.'" Weiss found it increasingly difficult to remain calm, however, after his home had been refinanced. A *Los Angeles Times* profile of J. David Dominelli—the San Diego–based investment counselor whose Technical Equities Inc. had drawn hundreds of investors, including seventeen L.A. Raiders, into a currency manipulation scam that swallowed more than one hundred million dollars—upset Weiss so completely that he confronted Joe with the question "How do I know you're not doing the same thing?" Hunt's answer, Weiss remembered, was "'I don't have to. I'm one of the eight people in the commodity market who has a system. If Dominelli was smart, he would have given all his money to me.'"

Only among the Boys at the Third Street office did Joe begin to let on that the BBC was experiencing cash shortages, using the other members more and more often to cover for him with investors. Joe's confidence in the "underlying long-term prospects" of the group, however, appeared unwavering. "Everyone was still very positive about things," Dean recalled, "because Joe was keeping them together just completely by the force of his rhetoric, his personality."

In response to requests for funds, though, Joe's tone grew increasingly stern. A "monthly expense report" prepared at Joe's request by Mike Feldman calculated that the BBC's general operating account alone required deposits of eighty thousand dollars per month to meet its minimum obligations. Joe allowed copies of the report to circulate throughout the office, supplemented by memos warning that waste and inefficiency no longer could be tolerated. "I was on the signature card for the [West Cars] checking account with Joe," recalled Taglianetti, "and I'd tell him, 'Listen, I need to buy some parts,' and he'd say, 'No. You can't do it this week.' Before this, it had always been 'Fine, whatever you need.' But now we always needed time, the money was tied up, the check was in the mail."

The other Boys could only guess how desperate the BBC's cash-flow problem might be, but those who heard about Jim Graham's recent sortie to New York City assumed it must be getting serious. Joe had assigned him, Jim said, to plant a voice-activated tape recorder in the office of a senior executive at Refco's headquarters on the seventh floor of the World Trade Center in lower Manhattan. From Brad Reifler, Joe knew Refco was especially active in gold futures at the time. "We may be aware of some sizable orders that could possibly increase the price temporarily," Brad allowed. All Joe gave Jim was Ben Dosti's American Express gold card, an address in lower Manhattan, and a name on a door in an office upstairs. He had gained entrance, Jim said, by donning khaki work clothes and carrying a bucket filled with shampoo and a scrub brush into the building. "If they ask me a question," he explained, "I say, 'I'm just here tonight to do spotting on the carpets.'" One security guard bought it so completely that he unlocked the door to the Refco executive's office, recalled Jim, who hid the tape recorder in an air-conditioning vent, then returned three days later in his work clothes to retrieve it. After Joe heard the tapes, Jim remembered, "he said I did an excellent job. As a matter of fact he gave me a bonus, five grand."

Jim had obtained the miniature tape recorder through his friend Gaitag Kehiahian, a slick-haired, furtive-featured "private investigator" whom the other Boys began to see around the Third Street office in early March. As proprietor of a business called Lightning Detective Agency, Kehiahian made his living, according to California Department of Justice reports, from the sale of cellular phones, electronic surveillance equipment, vehicle tracking devices, novelty weapons, and counterfeit identification. "The creep," Eisenberg called him. Taglianetti, though, was the only one of the Boys who spent any time with the man they knew as "Nick." "Short, dark, with these big wing lapels on his polyester suits," Tag recalled. "I knew he was providing Jim with his toys." Jim brought him along one afternoon when he paid a visit to Nick's small office/apartment on Western Avenue in East Hollywood, Taglianetti said: "The place was real bare, with just a beat-up old couch to sit on. There was this open closet in the 'office,' with all this electronic equipment sitting inside. Jim told me, 'I'm gonna go in with Nick for a minute; just wait here. They closed the door. I didn't know what he was buying."

Tag found out a few days later, in the parking basement beneath the Third Street office, where Jim produced what appeared at first to be a ballpoint pen. Inside the cylinder wasn't ink, though, but a single .25 bullet. To prove it, Jim cocked the spring-loaded trigger and fired a shot into a pile of cardboard boxes. "The thing sounded like a cannon inside all that concrete," Taglianetti remembered. "Jim seemed proud as hell."

It was not the only or even the first new weapon the Boys had seen in Jim's possession recently. Graham had filed down the lever on the four-barreled derringer he purchased at the fairgrounds in Pomona and was wearing it "strapped to his ankle," Jeff Raymond recalled. Taglianetti, taking a shortcut through the conference room at the BBC office one afternoon, happened upon a metal briefcase that lay open on the long table; inside was what appeared to be an automatic pistol built into a side wall of the case.

Joe paid for the briefcase gun, just as he paid for Jim's other high-tech toys, among them the minicamera built into a cigarette lighter Jim had used to snap shots of the inner offices at Refco. Joe felt it was necessary to ply Jim with gifts in order to retain his loyalty, Dean explained: "[Joe's] control over Jim wasn't as great as his control over Ben and myself. I wouldn't characterize him as being as intelligent as Ben and I, so Joe couldn't use Paradox, excite him with ideas and rhetoric. Jim needed to see rewards and results."

Of all the business reversals besetting the BBC, none incensed Joe so completely as the failure of the West Cars project. By early March, the Boys had invested more than $200,000 in the company without seeing a penny in return. Joe's budget allocated $2,500 per vehicle for the conversion of the West Cars BMWs to EPA standards. If the company sold the cars for even $5,000 less than the $52,000 asking price, they still could turn a tidy profit, Joe calculated. Unfortunately, the Orange County company with whom the BBC had contracted to test the converted cars, FCI Laboratories of Santa Ana, was refusing to certify them. All four BMWs failed their first test, conducted at a cost of $750 per vehicle. "Joe and I had our first real argument," Tag recalled. "He says, 'It's your fault the cars aren't being passed. You're the one who's supposed to have some expertise about this.'" Tag suggested hiring the outside consultant who manufactured a kit for converting the cars.

When three of the BMWs were submitted a second time to FCI, however, just one passed the lab's tests. "That was the only time I'd seen Joe show emotion," Taglianetti recalled. "He said they were thieves down there." Something had to be done, Joe and Jim agreed. "First they said they were gonna blow the lab up," Tag remembered. "But Jim said that, so I really didn't pay any attention. Then one day Jim pulls me aside and says, 'Joe and I are gonna go down and shoot up the lab, do some damage.' He asked me to come."

It was March 15, the day the Financial Futures investors expected their quarterly checks, Dean remembered, when Joe called him into his office and "mentioned that he and Jim had driven down to Orange County and shot the testing lab to pieces." As with the firebombing at the Roberts house, he doubted, Dean said. Then Joe showed him that morning's *Orange County Register,* pointing to a story on an inside page reporting that the FCI Laboratory in Santa Ana had been "riddled" by gunshots during the previous evening. An employee inside the lab nearly had been killed, according to the newspaper.

That person was John Redmond, who had been working in the lab's "soak area" when he heard what sounded like a string of firecrackers exploding outside. Whirling toward the sound, Redmond recalled, he saw a puff of white dust as a hole opened in the Sheetrock a few feet away. When he came out of his crouch, Redmond crept into the office where owner Jerry Coker kept a pistol in his desk. There was a draft in the office, blowing through a half-dozen bullet holes in the plate glass window. The floor was littered with broken glass, the steel file cabinets were dented, and the computer screen had been blown away. Instead of the gun, Redmond reached for a telephone.

The Santa Ana police officer who arrived first on the scene collected two piles of .30 caliber cartridges from parking lots on the east and north sides of the building, ejected in clumps, suggesting the shots had been fired by an automatic rifle. "The place looked like Vietnam," recalled Jerry Coker, who had spent 1969 on a river patrol boat in the Mekong Delta. Every window in the building was shattered, and the outside walls were striped with bullet holes. Two Mercedeses parked outside were perforated.

Jim described the devastation in detail at the West Cars plant that afternoon, Taglianetti remembered: "He was, like, so excited and saying it was so incredible, telling me how there was glass flying everywhere and the noise was amazing. He really got a high off it."

Joe, however, retained his composure, waiting two full days before sending Ben and Jim south to discuss the settlement of their bill with Jerry Coker. "They acted surprised by the bullet holes and asked what happened," Coker recalled. He had no idea who had done it but suspected one of his Iranian customers, Coker said: "A lot of Middle Eastern people tend to get angry if their cars don't pass."

Dosti and Graham were back two days later, Coker recalled, this time with Taglianetti and two others, Joe Hunt and Dean Karny. As they pulled into FCI's parking lot, Dean recalled, "Joe pointed out the bullet holes and we had a kind of snicker." "I had to laugh to keep from crying," explained Taglianetti. Hunt's audacity was beyond anything he had imagined: "Joe said to Coker, 'This is a terrible tragedy,' and that with the aid of Jim he could find out who did this and put an end to it. Then he started selling

Jim, telling Coker how Jim had helped his father in a military operation. I couldn't believe Joe was being so blatant, saying, 'Let us handle this matter, we can take care of it' and 'I'm sure we can work out something with the automobiles.' Then Coker called in his partner, and to my amazement, they agreed."

What Joe actually said was that among the BBC's many businesses was a company that performed private investigations, recalled Coker: "They told me, 'For five thousand dollars we'll find out who did it. They said they could put someone in a business behind us to find out. I said, 'Fine, find out and I'll pay you.'" Jim and Ben were back at FCI one week later. "They asked if they could use the five-thousand-dollar fee to qualify for a discount on test prices," Coker recalled. "I said, 'Fine.' Then they said it was my ex-employer who had done it. I said that was difficult to believe. I've known him for a long time and I didn't think he'd do that." He had tape recordings, Jim said. "Then the black guy, Graham, says, 'We'll take care of it for you,'" Coker recalled. "'We'll kill him, we'll throw the body in a barrel of acid, there'll be no trace.' I looked at my partner in disbelief. I said, 'No, bring us the evidence, and we'll either turn it over to the police department or we'll ruin him professionally.'" Jim said he would be back with the evidence the next morning, Coker recalled, "but I never saw him again."

10

LOPEZ CONTINUED TO FILL THE COMMODITY COFFERS AT AN ASTONISHING RATE.
By late March, the Malaysian had persuaded his investors to deposit more
than half a million dollars in the IMF accounts at Shearson and E. F. Hutton.
All Joe could buy with the money at this point, though, was time. The
account at Shearson had slipped into the red during February, when Joe
ceased purchasing new positions and began using the infusions of cash from
Asia to reinforce the spreads already in place. Within two weeks of the attack
on FCI, the losses at Shearson mounted to more than three hundred thousand dollars. The second, smaller account at Hutton had been accumulating losses since the day it was opened, February 28; one month later, the
"unrealized loss" in the account was more than fifty thousand dollars. By
the time he began trading at Hutton, Ben explained, "Joe had changed his
approach. It got more speculative. He was in a hurry."

Financing Lopez's adventures had itself become a major expense
for the BBC, albeit one of the few to pay immediate dividends. He flew
around the world nine times between December of 1983 and July of 1984,
said Steve. The fund-raiser's expense accounts were almost as high during
his layovers in Los Angeles. Jim reported seeing Lopez leave a five-hundred-
dollar tip after a meal that had cost half that at the Chronicle restaurant in
Santa Monica, where Steve often took female prospects.

Lopez would stop by Shearson's Beverly Hills office when he was
in town, the broker on the account, Larry Maize, remembered, but Ben Dosti
made all the important decisions. Ben seemed to know exactly what he was
doing, Maize recalled, and never once asked for advice. The broker became
actively involved in trading on the IMF account only once, in late March.
Lopez was at his parents' home in Singapore when a call came in from
Beverly Hills. "Larry Maize was panicked that the positions had slipped and
there was a margin call," Steve remembered. "He said if we didn't get a
hundred-thousand-dollar check to him, he might have to liquidate. I said,
'I need time.' He called two days later and said the positions had moved
further down and now we needed a hundred and fifty thousand dollars. I

talked to my dad, got the money from him, and came back to L.A. that week." The certified check was delivered on April 10, Maize remembered.

Hunt had let him know as soon as the account at Shearson began to accumulate a loss, Lopez recalled: Joe explained it was "a temporary aberration in the market" and promised to pay the Asian investors 10 percent interest until the situation corrected itself. "He told me, 'Steve, you don't know me, but I'm an honorable guy,'" Lopez remembered. "And when he paid the interest, even though the accounts were down, I thought he was."

Ben provided him with copies of each canceled check drawn on the IMF accounts during his absence, Lopez added. Most were easy enough to understand—the forty-three thousand dollars paid to Hutton for coverage on the spread positions there, for instance, and the twelve thousand to open an IM2 account at Shearson. The eighty-two thousand dollars in checks written to "Cash" were a bit more difficult to decipher, however, as were the checks for twelve thousand dollars to Financial Futures and for four thousand dollars to West Cars of North America, Inc. "I was told that BBC companies had put money into IMF and they just directly reimbursed those companies," Steve recalled.

If he didn't press the point, it was because he continued to believe that his connection to the Dosti family was at least as valuable as his membership in the BBC, Lopez explained. Steve and Luan Dosti were putting together an international trade package, talking to a consortium of Asian and Arab brokers about loans that would finance construction of an immense hotel and casino complex in Mexico City, preparing a prospectus to sell used American military helicopters and rebuilt Boeing airplane engines to Third World countries. As much as he appreciated access to the father, though, Lopez had begun to sense a hollow core in the son.

Steve was among those most shaken by Ben's apparent nonchalance in the aftermath of a catastrophic auto accident during the second week of April. Dosti had been driving the West Cars Porsche Targa that afternoon, cruising west on Wilshire at sixty miles an hour—checking an oil gauge, he claimed—when he ran full-speed into the rear end of a Cadillac stopped for a red light at Comstock Avenue. Two women, mother and daughter, were sitting unbuckled in the Cadillac's front seat; the impact sent both through the windshield. The older woman spent a week in a coma, waking in the hospital to discover that her daughter had died at the scene. Other than the cuts and bruises around his eyes—which he disguised with Ray-Bans—Ben showed no ill effects at all. "If he had any feelings about what happened, he never showed them," Lopez recalled.

"We were all pretty desensitized," Evan said in his friend's defense. "Remember that we were constantly being told that emotions were irrational, that you should look at something, study it, *decide* what you feel. Joe reminded us of something I had heard in a psychology class, where we learned that if you examine a feeling, the physical component of every emotion is the same: If you run across a dead body or if you fall in love with somebody, your pulse races, you get jittery, there are butterflies in your stomach. Your senses and your mind tell you what you're feeling. And so emotions are relatively easy to control; the physical component can be suppressed until you really don't feel what's bothering you anymore."

The sole BBC member to express public indignation over Ben's "indifference" was Lieban, who had written the policy under which Dosti, West Cars, and the BBC were insured. "The only thing that bothered Ben was that he might lose his license," Lieban recalled. "His insensitivity really pissed me off."

Lieban was pissed off about a number of things, actually, and during the week after Ben's accident became the first BBC member to seek redress in Paradox Court. Alan had been in limbo ever since the BBC's contraction at the end of 1983. "First, I informed Joe I wasn't going to leave the [Fireman's] Fund," he recalled, "and that put me in the doghouse." He never had been paid—as promised—for brokering the BBC's insurance deals, Lieban pointed out. And after the BBC began to close ranks in January, "all of a sudden Joe and Ben were sort of aloof," Lieban noted. "For a while I could walk into Joe's office any time I wanted. Then all of a sudden it was 'I can't see you now' . . . it hurt. I felt I was as much a member as anyone, just as devoted to the cause. So I kind of internalized it and felt I was at a crossroads—time to make some demands. For what Joe had promised me in December, when he said I was gonna get the car or the ten thousand dollars. So Dean took me aside after I had asked for a BMW, and he said, 'I'll tell you what, give me eight thousand dollars, and I'll get you a great new three twenty i.' I said, 'That sounds very, very fair.' Dean was being really cool. I went out and got Dean a cashier's check for eight thousand dollars. A week later Dean calls and says, 'It's gonna cost thirteen thousand.'"

The settlement Fireman's Fund made with the woman who had survived the collision at Wilshire and Comstock fueled Lieban's sense of entitlement. "A million bucks," he recalled, "the biggest loss since I got in the business." Yet neither Ben nor Joe seemed especially appreciative. "Ben and I would go back and forth in the office," Lieban recalled. "I'd tell him what I thought I had done, and he said, 'No, you didn't make any money.'"

Finally Lieban sat down with Farid and Farhad Novian to prepare his pleading to Paradox Court, submitting it to Dean at the Third Street office.

The document came back to Lieban with his own typed paragraphs
bracketed by Joe's handwritten notes, so dense that they virtually obliter-
ated the original text:

> This submission stems from a compensation dispute concerning
> contributions made to the West Cars Shape (*The questions of
> importance are: (1) Was the Shape profitable? and if so, (2) Was your
> contribution material?*) . . . I was deemed to be philosophically
> consistent with the BBC (*No one is "deemed philosophically consis-
> tent": that is a disposition of the moment, not a certification for life.*)
> . . . There is little doubt as to the profit-making outlook for West
> Cars, since the decisions concerning the type, number and the
> model of the cars were all considered and accepted by the Core of
> the BBC (*The Core is not omniscient.*) . . . I established a business
> relationship with Jardine Insurance brokers, the purpose of which
> was to provide very reasonable insurance coverage for the West
> Cars Shape. (*The relationship that you created with Jardine was just a
> normal business relationship devoid of any quality that exemplifies
> your work and entitles you to no more than a clerk's reward.*) The
> crucial significance of the Jardine connection is that they are one of
> the top insurance brokerage houses in the world. (*Actually, Alan, I
> am not the least impressed with them.*) I met with Jardine to negoti-
> ate terms and conditions of our now existing coverages (*Actually,
> Jardine discontinued us recently.*) . . . The Foregoing allowed the
> Core to consider the coverages which I had provided within the
> context of Paradox Philosophy (*You don't consider "coverages" in
> light of Paradox, Alan.*) . . . I make special reference to the car
> accident involving Ben Dosti, covered by both Jardine and
> Fireman's Fund. I submit that it is comforting to know that the
> insurance coverage under which Ben is protected provides for a
> unique 2 million dollar umbrella provision (*That is what insurance
> companies are paid for, Alan*) . . . I submit that the court will be
> engaging in speculation, forbidden by Paradox Philosophy (*P.
> Philosophy does nothing of the sort.*) if it is to conclude without
> supporting facts (*We conclude with supporting facts.*) that another
> person would have been able to provide the same contributions. I
> remember Joe saying on several occasions, "The BBC is only
> interested in facts, not in ifs" (*True in a sense, false in a sense,
> including this one.*) . . . On December 4, 1983, I asked Joe regarding

payments for my contributions; Joe responded I would receive "$10,000 of disposable income or a nice car" (*Liar!*) . . . In conclusion, I reiterate that in deciding the issue presented to it, the court should view the disagreement in the context of the objectives upon which our organization, the BBC, was formed (*True.*): A community of individuals established for the purpose of putting together all their resources in order to make that which is unattainable by an individual, attainable by the community, within the context of Paradox Philosophy (*Also true.*) . . . As Walter Bagehot, the brilliant Victorian banker, economist and critic once stated, "We must not let in daylight upon magic." I submit to the court that where a community fails to take its purpose for being seriously, daylight will be allowed on its magic, and the daylight may show other communities the fallacies of that magic. (*Walter Bagehot is a lout, and this quote in this context is odious.*) I will look forward to your written reply within a week's time. (*Fatuous statement.*)

Respectfully,

Alan Lieban (*Claim denied. Joseph Hunt, Shading.*)

"What hurt was Dean," Lieban recalled, "supporting Joe all the way, even that I lied. I left feeling like I had been stripped buck naked. But in a sense I kind of respected the guys; I felt like it was shame on me, I got taken. And they acted like we were still friends."

The era of three-day weeks and four-hour lunches was past, Joe told the others when he assembled them in early April for the only meeting of the BBC's entire active roster since January. "It was the first time concern about making money was openly expressed," Dean remembered. "Joe said he was disappointed in the performance of some of the businesses," Eisenberg recalled. "He put each entity under separate subheads and divided people by what they were involved with, . . . then he proceeded to show that each company had yet to turn a profit." "It was the only time I heard him tell people they weren't working hard enough, that he was carrying them," Evan remembered. "The thing the rest of them were best at was procrastination," Eisenberg explained, "and he was finally telling them so. Most of the BBC weren't interested in getting their hands dirty in day-to-day business. They weren't interested in making small amounts of money a little at a time. Everybody was counting on the one big score."

From this day forward, the BBC would be meeting for breakfast each weekday at 7 A.M. to coordinate schedules, Joe announced. "The first morning after the meeting, all the members showed up," Eisenberg remembered. "The second morning, Jon Allen and I were the only ones there, besides Joe. The third day, it was just me and Joe. The fourth day, there were no more breakfast meetings."

Joe's fatal momentum for the first time seemed to falter when he was confronted at point-blank range by the apathy of his fellow travelers. Abruptly, he abandoned his practice of arriving at the Third Street office every morning before dawn. "When I moved in, Joe would be up and gone by five A.M.," Jeff Raymond remembered. "That stopped around April. I would get up, and Joe was still there. I'd come home for lunch, and Joe would *still* be there, still undressed." "You didn't know what to think," Taglianetti said. "Maybe he was finally catching up on his sleep."

Joe emerged from his hiatus before the end of the month, however, firing off a flurry of memoranda on every subject from the conservation of office products to the latest theories on time management. "There was a constant flow of paper from him after April," Eisenberg recalled. "He gave out lists—'Things to Do'—and also 'Outline Formats.' He would also send out 'reprioritized' lists."

The implicit message in all Joe's missives was that only those who paid their way could count on keeping a place in the BBC. At the same time Joe attempted to curtail waste and inefficiency within the BBC's companies, however, he declined to cramp members' lifestyles. While Joe now "demanded an explanation for every nickel I spent at West Cars," Taglianetti observed, Ben continued to dine in the best restaurants of Beverly Hills every night of the week. The disparities grated in particular on those who worked out of the warehouse in Gardena. "They'd complain about spending five hundred dollars to get the cars converted," Taglianetti remembered, "and yet they'd spend fortunes on stuff they didn't need, just for appearances. They put a satellite on top of the office, got these portable phones, so you could direct dial within a thirty mile radius, with a repeater up on Mount Wilson, so they could switch and join their calls—all this electronic sophistication. And Jim was expensive."

It seemed to the others that Joe had bestowed upon Jim a de facto Shading status, describing him as that rare individual who need not understand Paradox on an intellectual level in order to embody the philosophy. His "director of security" had become the only BBC member other than Dean or Ben who always could see Joe without waiting, Lore Leis noticed.

The Boys watched Joe's bodyguard in action for the first time one afternoon when a process server from the U.S. marshal's office showed up in the office lobby to compel Hunt's attendance at a hearing in Santa Monica, where Eddie Elias and Lorraine Stitzlein were attempting to enter a $125,000 judgment against Joseph Hunt aka Gamsky that they had obtained in Illinois. Jim literally lifted Joe out of his chair, shielded him with his body, and pulled him out the back door, Eisenberg recalled: "The marshal went after them, but Jim got Joe out of there without the papers ever being served."

If Joe insisted on scaling back the operations at West Cars and Fire Safety, economizing even in his allotments to Microgenesis, he seemed to regard the money he spent on Jim as an investment in the immediate future. Lore Leis complained that Jim was spending a lot of money in cash, without keeping receipts, but dropped the subject when Joe told her not to worry about it. Nearly a thousand dollars had gone to double the firepower of the BBC arsenal when Joe purchased a pair of Ingram "MAC 10" submachine guns, one for Jim and another for himself, Dean recalled. Jim sported a new high-powered scope on his hunting rifle, a German Luger, and a new .32 caliber Beretta so sleek and stylish that the thing looked as if it should be kept in a case at Tiffany's. He saw the silencer on the Beretta for the first time at the end of March, Taglianetti recalled, one afternoon when Jim and his friend Nick put a pair of bullet holes in a phone book at the BBC office.

"Jim liked to show me his gadgets," Tag explained. "One time he ripped apart his BMW in Gardena and showed me where he had built a rack for his guns under the backseat, and then he had another secret compartment in the trunk." Jim took to using the West Cars half of the Gardena warehouse as a private firing range, shooting up oil cans with Taglianetti's .357 magnum. "It used to just irritate the hell out of me," remembered Gene Browning.

Jim was spending not only most of his days but many of his nights as well at the Gardena plant, "baby-sitting the machine," as Taglianetti put it. He first heard about the "outside force" that was planning to steal the Microgenesis technology, Tag recalled, when he arrived at the warehouse one morning to discover barbed wire woven into the steel fence at the entrance. Jim was just inside the gate, dripping red paint onto the driveway: "He said, 'If some prowler comes around, they'll think this is blood.'"

Joe and Jon Allen were alternating with Jim in eight-hour shifts to guard the Cyclotron, Taglianetti discovered. "We were going to hire a security service," Jim explained, "but Joe said, 'No. Anybody can pay them a hundred thousand dollars and walk off with anything they want to walk off with.' So we took turns, the three of us, going down there at night."

Joe provided a provocative collection of reading material to keep awake after dark. Most of the literature was from underground presses with names like Gnu Publishing and Roadrunner Books. Titles included *Improvised Sabotage Devices, Two Component High Explosive Mixtures, Intelligence Interrogation,* and *Getaway: Driving Techniques for Escape and Evasion.* At once the most readable and disturbing of the volumes were a pair of paperbacks penned by the pseudonymous "Rex Feral," *Hitman: A Technical Manual for Independent Contractors* and *The Black Bag Owner's Manual,* which began, "This pertains to the personalized killing which, in peacetime, is called murder."

Jim and Joe heightened the sense of imminent danger and hidden enemies when they began playing games with secret codes and midnight rendezvous. After the assault on FCI, the two began referring to a location they called the Ice House, where a BBC member could go "to cool off when things got hot." Jeff Raymond remembered the evening he took a call at the Manning from Jim's wife, Dana: "She asked for Joe, but he wasn't right there, and so she gave me the message: 'Tell him green, blue, red.' When I told Joe, he grabbed his coat and ran out of the house as fast as he could. He came back with Jim about a half hour later. Jim was laughing, saying, 'It took you 17.7 seconds; I timed it.'"

Even Evan began to think it peculiar that Joe and Jim were meeting so often in private: "Usually, only higher financial matters were discussed behind closed doors, and Jim was not part of that."

Taglianetti would begin to suspect how deeply Joe was venturing into his ALL THINGS ARE POSSIBLE philosophy one afternoon when they met in Hunt's office to discuss disposal of the West Cars fleet. "Midstream in conversation, Joe swiveled in his chair and grabbed a piece of paper with a list of names on it," Tag recalled. "He rested it on the desk between us and said that if these people were eliminated, it would make doing business a lot easier for the BBC."

Reading upside down, he could decipher only the name at the top of the list, Taglianetti remembered: "Bruce Swartout's."

The BBC's relationship with Swartout had "started to go south," as Eisenberg understated it, within a few weeks of the merger between Cogenco and Cyclotronics. Swartout, it seemed, was hardly the shaved Santa Claus his rosy cheeks and white mane suggested. The man's affiliations extended far beyond Cogenco and U.S. Flywheels into strings of financial interests so complex in their arrangement that it might have taken an entire law firm to sort them out. Which was approximately the situation: Dozens of attorneys representing scores of creditors and claimants were searching for

Swartout's assets at that very moment, poised to pounce upon anything of value. Worse, first place in line was occupied by one extremely secured creditor, the California Franchise Tax Board, which had placed liens on Cogenco and U.S. Flywheel months before the merger with Cyclotronics. "It was well known that there was a tax lien against us," Swartout would assert, but Joe and the BBC were among the last to learn of it. When the Boys discovered the state's claim against the companies, "Swartout suddenly was this terrible man," Eisenberg recalled. "They figured that they'd been swindled by the guy they swindled."

In January, the franchise tax board moved into San Juan Capistrano to close down the two companies, claiming all assets as the property of the state. With Eisenberg's assistance, Joe drafted a letter rescinding the Cogenco/Cyclotronics contract and sent it to Swartout, alleging fraud and deceit.

Swartout accepted rescission but not defeat. It was March when the Orange County man and his associates saw the press release prepared by UFOI and Saturn Energy: "CANADIAN FIRM RESCUES DENVER BANKRUPT BUSINESS—$280,000,000 AT STAKE," read the heading on a document describing the deal as "the single largest transaction in the history of any Vancouver (B.C.) listed corporation." The Boys had negotiated the final details of their deal during a trip to British Columbia, where Joe arrived with Ben, Tom May, Jon Allen, and Jim Graham to meet with Kilpatrick, Saturn president Ray Robinson, and their associates at the Four Seasons Hotel. "We got suites instead of rooms," Graham remembered. "The people up there was very impressed with us: 'These young guys from California, they're really on the ball.'" It was in Vancouver that Joe began to introduce his bodyguard as a former running back for the Pittsburgh Steelers. "The way I looked, everybody believed it," Jim reflected. "They would say, 'Yeah, I remember you!' These businessmen, some of the wealthiest people you'd want to think of, was all asking me questions."

Kilpatrick showed the BBC how Big Boys played business that first night at the Four Seasons, Jim remembered. "He come in and says, 'Well guys, where's the girls?' They didn't know anything about that kind of stuff, so he showed Ben what to do. You go through the phone book and you get these escort services . . . about fifteen girls altogether showed up, and we eliminated down to who they didn't want. 'What do you think about this one?' 'Well, she's maybe a five, no, we really don't want her.' Or, 'She's an eight,' et cetera. 'I don't like this about that one.' 'Her hips are too big.' Or, 'Her breasts are not big enough.' Ben would say, 'We'll take you, you, and you. Bye bye, the rest of you.'" While the others played, Joe worked, nego tiating a share of the three-way deal for the BBC that included one million dollars in Saturn stock due in six installments, plus a royalty of 6 percent of gross revenues on sales.

Swartout, reading of this in the press release, phoned Kilpatrick in Denver to ask where his share of the money might be. Kilpatrick said he was astonished to discover Swartout did not know Joe had substituted *Microgenesis* for *Cogenco* throughout the letter of agreement they had signed in November. Later that week, Swartout informed Kilpatrick that he and the other minority members of the Cogenco and Cyclotronics boards distinctly remembered a "special meeting" held one day before Joe and his board of directors conveyed the companies' technology to Microgenesis; there had been a unanimous vote to forbid any such action, Swartout said.

Kilpatrick recognized a serious problem: He had won approval from the bankruptcy court for the merger with Saturn Energy based on his representation that he controlled both Gene Browning's attrition mill and Swartout's power van. Swartout suggested that the two of them prepare a new agreement, significantly reducing the BBC's share.

"We had lots of discussions with Kilpatrick to persuade him Swartout wouldn't be a problem," Dean remembered. "Joe said he could handle the situation."

Jim and his friend Nick were on Swartout twenty-four hours a day during the first week of April, Karny recalled, and when Swartout flew to Colorado, Jim went after him. "Dave told me Jim had gone to 'get' Swartout," Gene Browning recalled. When Jim returned to Los Angeles, though, he said that after kicking in the door of Swartout's hotel suite he found only a pile of papers on the dresser and took those.

When Joe saw what appeared to be rough drafts of a separate agreement between Swartout and Kilpatrick, he concluded that the time had come to consider "elimination" of the Orange County menace. "Joe, Jim, Ben, and I all discussed it," Dean remembered. Jim's friend Nick offered to take care of their problem for ten thousand dollars, but Joe said that was a lot of money to spend when the BBC had Jim on its payroll. They talked a number of times about killing Swartout, in general, Dean recalled, before arriving at a specific plan. First, Jim persuaded Nick to sell him a vial of "contact poison," Dean remembered. DMSO laced with strychnine, according to Gene Browning: "I know because Jim asked me if such a formula could kill a person if it got on their skin. I told him, 'Absolutely. Put DMSO on your fingertips and you can taste it on the tip of your tongue seven and a half seconds later.'"

"I knew they were planning to do Swartout," Taglianetti admitted, "but they were so braggadocious that you could never tell if they were going to follow through on things."

Joe, Dean, and Ben continued to threaten Swartout with phone calls, letters, and telegrams, but the Orange County man was proving a dogged adversary. The BBC either cut him in for a piece of the deal or they lost everything, Swartout warned. "My dispute with Joe Hunt and the others reached a peak of tension between April 10 and 13," he remembered.

April 10 was the date on the letter Ben dispatched to Ken Elgin, advising their partner in the UFOI/Saturn deal that the BBC recently had retained a "legal counselor" whose primary assignment would be "to thwart any efforts of a possible attack by Bruce Swartout, et al., and to simultaneously launch an effrontery [sic] campaign."

Two days later, on April 12, Saturn Energy sent a Canadian physicist from Vancouver to Los Angeles for the purpose of examining the Cyclotron prototype and to consult with its inventor. Describing Browning's machine as "a simple unit based on complex principles," Dr. William E. Magee delighted the Boys by reporting back to Saturn that "the commercial potential of the attrition device could well be immense."

The next morning, Friday the thirteenth, Bruce Swartout slid his gold BMW into the president's parking space at the new Cogenco offices in Irvine. It was bright and sunny, as usual. He saw a black man in khaki work clothes leaning against the building a few feet away, Swartout recalled, holding a Styrofoam coffee cup. The stranger offered him a friendly grin, so Swartout smiled back. He made it a practice and precaution against thieves to carry his briefcase on the floor behind the driver's seat of the BMW, Swartout explained: "I always get out and open the backseat door to get the briefcase." He was leaning into the car through the open door, Swartout remembered, when he sensed a movement behind him and turned his head to see the black man "standing over me." Through the screen of sunlight on the window, he saw a flash as the man's hand came forward, Swartout recalled, "and then I felt something hit my back. I thought I was stabbed." He flailed at his assailant, Swartout remembered, then gave chase, shouting for help, as the black man fled between his building and the one next door, disappearing behind a fourteen-wheel rig as it pulled into an open bay in the back alley.

When he touched the wet spot on his back, Swartout recalled, what he saw on his fingers was not blood but a tea-colored liquid. "The sensation was colder than ice water at first, but then it began to burn," he said. Abandoning the chase, Swartout retreated to the men's room on the first floor of the building, where he removed his shirt and asked an employee to wash his back with a wet towel. That request probably saved the man's life, Gene Browning observed: "Normally you would wipe it off, and that would leave a residue. If you leave a residue, that residue will absorb and kill you."

Swartout might have killed himself as well had he slipped back into his wet shirt, "but I remembered I had a suitcase in the car with a clean shirt in it," he explained, "and I put that on."

The three Irvine police officers who answered Swartout's report of assault with a deadly weapon found the Styrofoam cup—from a Carl's Jr. restaurant—on the ground near the BMW, but the tiny amount of "brownish liquid" at the bottom made testing impossible, and by the time they thought of it, the liquid had evaporated from Swartout's shirt. "Mr. Swartout did give us three names as possible suspects, however," one officer recalled: "Ben Dosti, Dean Karny, and Joseph Hunt."

11

JOE SEEMED QUITE AMUSED BY THE INABILITY OF THE POLICE IN IRVINE TO MAKE a case in the attempt on Bruce Swartout's life, Gene Browning remembered. The first problem for the detectives investigating the incident was that Swartout had failed to identify Jim Graham as his assailant, describing the man who threw the brown liquid on him that morning as "thirty-eight to forty years of age" and "between six feet and six feet, four inches in height," according to the police report. The intended victim would prove unable as well to pick Jim out of a six-man photo lineup. A forklift driver at Rock Glass told police he was 90 percent certain that the black man he had seen carrying the Styrofoam cup before the attack was Jim, but Joe remained unperturbed. They would need more evidence than this to make an arrest, let alone obtain a conviction, Hunt assured the others. "He said, 'Because of who we are, the worst we can get out of this is a slap on the wrist,'" Browning recalled.

Joe and Jim began plotting a second attempt to kill Swartout within a week of the first, according to Taglianetti, who learned of the revised plan one afternoon while riding to Gardena with Jim in the black BMW. "I saw a small amber vial resting by the hand brake," he recalled. "I reached for it with my left hand, and Jim grabbed my wrist with his right hand and said, 'Don't touch that.'" Nick had mixed a stronger formula this time, Jim said.

Almost two weeks had passed since the first attack on her employer, Swartout's secretary recalled, when "the black guy showed up in the yard again. He was pretending he was fixing something under the hood of his car. And of course everybody who worked there just knew they had to watch out for a black guy, and a black guy in Irvine stands out." Several of Swartout's employees climbed into one of their vehicles and chased the man around the block but never got a close look at him. "Jim said 'security was too tight' when he tried to get to Swartout the second time," Taglianetti remembered. "He made it sound like the guy had surrounded himself with armed guards or something. He said Joe wanted him to back off for a while, that there were other things for him to do."

What those might be was becoming a matter of much speculation inside the BBC. Jim claimed he had spent most of that month traveling between Los Angeles and Chicago, attempting to collect twenty-five thousand dollars owed to Joe by a member of the Mercantile Exchange. All that the others found difficult to believe was the amount of money Jim said was involved. "Twenty-five thousand dollars probably wouldn't have supported the BBC for more than a day or two at that point," Eisenberg observed.

Eddie Elias and Lorraine Stitzlein still were chasing Joe to collect the $125,000 he had taken from them in Chicago. That sum, of course, was a trifle next to the losses in the IMF accounts, which now stood at nearly $800,000. The BBC would have been sunk without Lopez, who again offset the deficits with deposits from his investors. The Malaysian continued to astonish with his abilities as a fund-raiser, persuading a friend of the family to deposit more than $600,000 at the Shearson office in Singapore. "One of the two or three wealthiest men in the world" was all Lopez would say of this investor.

By the end of April, Joe had consolidated all IMF accounts at the E. F. Hutton office in Westwood. Joe and Ben continued to apprise him of the deficits at IMF, Lopez recalled: "The thing that made me trust them was that they always gave me whatever I needed. If I had to make a payment, whether it was five thousand or fifty thousand, they took care of it."

Steve was disturbed, though, that every time Joe wanted to tell him anything of any importance, Dean would quiet him. Dean would say, "Joe, I don't think this is something we should talk about now."

In an atmosphere increasingly turbid with intrigue, Lopez relied on his roommate for a fair appraisal of the situation. "I said, 'Tell me, Ben, is everything okay?' He said, 'As far as I know, it's all good.' I figured we were in the same boat; we both had money in and investors we had relationships with."

Also, if Joe conceded cash-flow problems, he at the same time was announcing an expansion of the BBC in all directions. During May, he agreed to underwrite a number of new businesses administered by Eisenberg and Feldman. These included BBC Management Inc., a company the attorney and the accountant had created to manage the assets of professional athletes and entertainers. "We called all over the country during the baseball draft," Eisenberg remembered. The two attached Tom May's name to the company to impress potential clients and began bringing athletes into the offices to show them off, Feldman recalled, eventually signing as clients an L.A. Raider, Stacy Toran, and one of the movie industry's most successful cinematographers, Michael Watkins.

Joe also spared no expense in promoting the Cyclotron. An evening demonstration at the Gardena warehouse was arranged when William Morton sent a barrel of brown gravel from his digs at Apache Junction, asking Browning to test his machine's capacity to separate the material by weight and density. Joe invited every big name on the BBC's mailing list, from Donald Bren to Dave May II, decorated the warehouse with balloons and served champagne. The Boys showed up wearing gray suits and effusive expressions, "whipped up like somebody would be whipped up for a fraternity party by Joe," Dean recalled.

Within a week of the demonstration, Joe had negotiated yet another contract for delivery of the Cyclotron, this one with a gold miner named Bill Nalan, whose huge claim lay on the edge of the Mojave Desert near the Nevada border, at Shadow Mountain. His agreement with the BBC provided Nalan with a single machine at no initial charge in exchange for a 50 percent interest in any profits from the operation. A few days later, Kilpatrick phoned from Colorado to say that the Saturn Energy people had been entirely impressed by Browning's demonstration and wanted to negotiate a new contract, with or without Swartout. He would be in Los Angeles at the end of the month and hoped to meet with Joe to hammer out final terms then, Kilpatrick said.

Joe was jubilant, organizing the boys for a celebration dinner at La Scala. While the others sipped champagne, Joe toasted them with 7-Up. "He said they gonna make billions on the machine," Jim recalled: "'Gonna be one of the largest companies in the world. Gonna be an empire.'" Everyone in the restaurant was watching them, Brooke told the others. One admirer sent their table a bottle of Bordeaux, but Ben Dosti said it was a cheap wine, Jim recalled, and sent it back.

The festivities continued with a gathering at the Charthouse later that week to celebrate Dean's twenty-fourth birthday. The entire entourage turned out for this occasion. As was so often the case, Evan provided the entertainment, accepting a bet with the rest of the BBC that he could eat an entire frozen mud pie in seventy-five seconds. "They thought I was going to get a headache," he recalled, "but I had a couple of drinks and I think that protected me." During dinner, Joe had announced his plan to make the BBC an international organization of young men who either were coming soon into large inheritances or had immediate access to family fortunes. The organization's wealth would be used to accumulate hard assets rather than fortunes in paper money, Joe said. "This was all predicated on the inevitable fall of the Third World debtor nations," Gene Browning explained. "When they couldn't pay their debts, supposedly the U.S. banking system would collapse and there would be economic chaos. A dollar would be worth ten cents, and then the BBC would move in—because their hard assets would be the world's wealth—and take over."

At the Third Street office, Joe decorated the enormous map of the world on the wall in the conference room with color-coded pins to mark the spots where the BBC would open branches: Hamburg, Hong Kong, Rio. "Mondo BBC," Evan called it. Even those who would mock or denounce Joe later felt compelled to point out that his forecasts of fiscal crisis demonstrated an astonishing prescience in some regards: One of "three basic problems" he believed would result in "a gradual erosion of the economic strength of the United States," Joe wrote in May of 1984, was "the accounting shenanigans that are taking place at Savings and Loans today. It's a time bomb."

The erosion of economic strength weighing most heavily upon Joe at the moment, however, was not the nation's but the BBC's. Kilpatrick had arrived in Los Angeles to meet with Hunt, as promised. The Boys put him up in Lopez's room at the Manning, "wined and dined him, took him everywhere, spent a fortune entertaining him," Taglianetti remembered. When Kilpatrick left Los Angeles after almost a week on the BBC's tab, however, negotiations remained open. The final draft of the contract would be completed soon, he promised, but in the meantime the Boys had yet to see even a penny of the six-million-dollar payment due on the downstroke when the document was signed.

Money was tighter than ever.

Lopez predicted he could obtain—"at the minimum"—a million-dollar loan to Microgenesis on his next trip to Asia, but for the moment Joe found it difficult to find even the forty thousand dollars he needed to finish the hydraulic and drive shaft systems on the two machines promised to Morton and Nalan by the end of that month. Furthermore, Browning again was demanding the percentage of previous payments to the company he had been promised. Joe held him at bay by persuading Jeff to convince the inventor that the BBC would buy him a house when the new prototype was completed. He knew it wasn't true but never told Browning, Raymond admitted: Undermining his position with Joe, Jeff explained, wouldn't have been good business.

Browning was working in a near frenzy now, tortured by his knowledge of how close Joe had brought him to the pot of gold that seemed to recede into the mists of "legal complication" each time he moved within reach. The back ends of the Dow, Morton, and Nalan contracts alone were sufficient to ensure that Microgenesis would be a thriving company for many years, and the UFOI/Saturn Energy deal offered the inventor the prospect of a payday in the nine- or ten-figure range of his wildest imaginings. Yet

Joe, Dean, and Ben continued to quibble in the short run over expenditures of five and ten thousand dollars, he fumed, even as they fell further and further behind on delivery dates for the first three machines. His assistants, the Mays, were all but useless, Browning said, and Jeff was not much better. The twins were driving a pair of classic Corvettes these days, one red, the other white, recalled Browning, whose annoyance mounted when he observed that the moment Tom and Dave got BBC dealer plates on the cars, they began to fill the drawers of their desk at the Gardena plant with parking tickets. "They also had the West Cars mechanic spending more time on those Corvettes than on the BMWs the company was supposed to be selling," he remembered.

Browning was more discouraged than ever on the afternoon when Ben showed up at the Gardena plant with a green cleaning formula he said was being sold in stores without a valid patent. "He wanted me to find out what was in it so they could steal the formula and patent it themselves," Browning recalled. "'This is an opportunity,' he told me. His argument was 'Well, look at the money we can make.' I said, 'You look at it.'"

He heard enough references to the "FCI and Swartout incidents," Browning acknowledged, to suppose "something might actually have happened." And the inventor could not help noticing Jim's arsenal; Browning overheard him asking the Mays and Taglianetti if they knew anyone with an Arizona driver's license who would help him buy weapons from an exotic gun dealer on a trip to meet Morton in Phoenix. Jim actually had been arrested by the Gardena police on May 12 for firing his .30 caliber carbine in the warehouse while on guard duty that evening. The suspect came out the front door of the plant with his hands over his head and a smile on his face, the arresting officer recalled: "Mr. Graham was quite friendly and cooperative. He said he was taking target practice and had no idea it was illegal." Learning the weapon was not registered in California, the officer confiscated it, releasing Jim on his own recognizance after issuing a citation.

Jim was driving a white Rolls-Royce Corniche these days. He had showed up with it at the plant in Gardena one morning, Taglianetti recalled, "bragging that he'd gotten it from some woman who was so impressed with him as a stud and with Joe as a genius. Jerry Eisenberg, though, told me Jim had stolen it." Taglianetti was inclined to accept Eisenberg's version, since Jim seemed in such a hurry to get the Rolls repainted that he went behind Joe's back to pay for the new finish with a check drawn on the West Cars account.

Jim retorted that the only stolen car to appear at the Gardena plant was a Mercedes driven onto the premises by Taglianetti. The Mercedes had been "repossessed" by his father, Tag insisted. Taglianetti agreed, though, that "a sense of grab what you can" had begun to permeate the BBC. "Joe was becoming more distant, cold," he recalled, "and showed a lack of interest in the other businesses. Dean seemed like he was trying to take over, trying to get his hand in everything in Joe's absence . . . I knew all this had some connection to financial problems we were having. Dave and I and Eisenberg were all talking about how we better be careful, leave ourselves a way out, try to get some money up front. But Dave still hadn't told me that Joe had lost his money. And Tom was still rah-rah and gung ho."

Sensing discontent in the ranks, Joe began to use Jim's skills intramurally. "I bugged the office," Jim explained. "Put little mikes around. No one knew it." Eisenberg and Taglianetti at least suspected that the bodyguard was working as Joe's informant. "Jim would come up to us, 'Hey guys, what's goin' on?'" Eisenberg recalled. "Trying to get us to talk about whatever we were disgruntled about. Which was the money, mainly." One afternoon in early May, the two went on an errand with Jim, Jerry recalled, "and during the drive, Steve and I asked some questions and did some grumbling about promises that weren't being kept, about how the democratic style and sharing of money was not forthcoming as we had been told it would be. About how we knew we'd never see the money, and that Joe and Ben and Dean were using all this for their own gain. We had a bet that they'd take off with everything in the end."

Half an hour after they returned to the Third Street suites, Eisenberg remembered, "Joe called us into his office and said, 'I understand you two have some complaints.' Then he quoted us verbatim . . . I knew we must have been taped because Joe repeated verbatim what I had said, and Jim wasn't that good." Joe's tone was neither stern nor threatening, Jerry recalled: "More like magnanimous, actually. He assured us the money was going to be divided as promised, told us we were forgiven, and he was going to give us another chance to prove our loyalty to the BBC." Still, "from that point on, anything I had to say, I said it in the hallway."

12

JOE INTRODUCED HIS PLAN TO MURDER RON LEVIN ENTIRELY IN THE ABSTRACT at the beginning, Dean remembered, more as a meditation upon the parameters of Paradox than as an actual plot. Basically, Joe "did what he advised everyone else to do, which was not to be afraid to contemplate all things," Dean explained. "He said that if you are logical, then you won't exclude from your decision-making process anything, as long as some benefit can be obtained."

This was before the attempt on Swartout's life, Dean said, so it was some time before he realized such conversations were Joe's way of "coming to terms" with murder, Dean reflected: "He was telling Ben and me that if we were Shadings, in fact, and that if we did understand Paradox Philosophy, and if we really were not limited by the contemplation of a new idea, then we couldn't be rationally repulsed by the thought of taking someone's life, that it was an option in certain circumstances and had to be considered."

Joe made no mention of Levine, Dean recalled, until one night in late April, when he announced he had decided to kill Ron. He felt it was critical to view the affair as a business transaction, Joe said, in essence a form of debt collection. Specifically, he intended to recover at least the $1.5 million Levin admitted he had earned by mirroring Joe's trades at Clayton Brokerage. The best way to accomplish this, Joe felt, was by creating the record of a formal negotiation leading to an eventual contract. He most likely would use the Microgenesis Corporation for this purpose, Joe imagined, perhaps sell Ron a nonrefundable option on the Cyclotron, something modeled on the deal the BBC had made with Michael Dow, one that would provide Levin with temporary control of some relatively obscure area of the machine's application, cement or silica rights, perhaps. If Ron disappeared, his estate would control these rights for the term of the option, but even those would revert back to the BBC if the second and far larger payment required to exercise the option was not forthcoming.

He was intrigued by the subtlety of Joe's plan but not surprised, Dean said: "Joe was never at a disposition to just kill someone gratuitously," Karny explained. "He wanted to get something out of it."

Right around this time, Dean recalled, Joe began "dropping hints" among other members of the BBC, "saying in the office, 'Maybe Levin is going to invest in Microgenesis,' sort of feeling people out. Some of the guys said, 'Oh, you're not going to get involved with Levin.' And Joe would reply, 'Gosh, if he pays, he pays.'"

Joe's method of revealing his plan was to include him in each stage as it unfolded, Dean explained: "He just sort of went ahead with what he was doing and let me draw my own conclusions." Karny saw the first tangible evidence of Hunt's intentions one evening in early May when they were the only two BBC members left at the office. "Joe showed me the handwritten drafts of some letters to Ron Levin," Dean recalled. These would be evidence of a running correspondence with Levin, Joe explained, and support his claim that the two of them were business partners. He would attach to the letters a sheaf of Microgenesis marketing brochures and other documents, Joe said, and leave them behind at the Peck Drive duplex. "When Ron was found missing, there would be a file in his house containing what looks like correspondence and, ultimately, a contract," Dean explained, "so that when a million and a half dollars—or however much was ultimately gotten from him—was missing from his account in a transaction which occurred somewhat simultaneously to his disappearance, it would look believable. That at least even if [the police] were suspicious of Joe, they would be hard pressed to make a case."

Joe showed him two letters that evening, Dean remembered. The first filled a full page torn from a yellow legal pad. "Dear Ron," it began, "One of your remarks on the telephone indicated that you had not fully grasped the theoretical advantages of the attrition mill over conventional technology." Dismissing competitors on the market as "uninspired extrapolations of the mortar and pestle approach," Joe described the theoretical underpinnings of Gene Browning's invention in agonizing detail, then ended with a postscript: "As you know, I have been researching in an effort to isolate an industry that we could most easily exploit with the attrition mill. I think cement may be the answer. I will keep you updated." The second letter would be mailed perhaps two weeks after the first, explained Joe, who began it by "recapping our discussion of a few nights ago," then explained that "you do not match our profile of a suitable Joint Venture partner."

It was the morning of May 3, Dean remembered, when he saw Lore Leis typing the first of the letters to Levin that Joe had showed him two days earlier. When Lore finished, Joe proofread the letter, as he did any correspondence, and gave it back to her. The secretary kept all office mail in a tray on her desk and, when she left work in the late afternoon, would carry it downstairs to the mailbox on the street outside. On this day, though, Dean told Lore he was on his way to the post office and offered to save her a trip, then "gave Joe back the letter he didn't want sent, and mailed the rest."

It was May 15 when Lore typed the second letter to Levin and when Dean discovered that he was not Joe's only aider and abettor. "Joe said, 'Who's going to pick up the letters today?'" Dean recalled. "And Ben said he would. That's when I knew Ben was in on it too."

Joe gave Lore a third letter to Levin on May 24:

Dear Ron,

It is 2:15 A.M. and I thought I would commit a few thoughts on matters that trouble me to paper . . . I was thinking about our conversation of a few days ago. Do you really have a contact in the glass industry who would pay you ten million for this grinding technology? I know you are a good salesman, but that is a very large sum. [Also] I do not understand how you expect to maintain the anonymity of your "secret principal" as you put it. After all, his technicians and scientists will doubtless have questions and request demonstrations before recommending an expenditure of that magnitude. Sometimes you are too paranoid, Levin. If he is a legitimate intimate contact of yours, we will respect it. However, if he is someone you reached through the Yellow Pages, I cannot make any such guarantee. Please note that we plan on sending a mailer out to the glass industry in a few months.

Ron, I meant to tell you earlier today, someone complimented me on the "understated elegance" of my watch. Thanks again for the best birthday present I ever received.

Your friend,
Joseph Hunt

Dean flew out of LAX that morning to spend the last week of the month in Mexico with Lisa Marie. By that time, he conceded, "it was pretty clear to me that [Joe] was going to kill Levin."

During the past few weeks, Joe clearly had been preparing the other Boys for far more than the resumption of business relations with Ron Levin. Six or seven BBC members were present in 1505 during Joe's famous chess game with Jeff Raymond. Only a few minutes into the game, Hunt became annoyed by Raymond's foolish attempt to protect a pawn with his bishop, thereby exposing his flank to an attack on his king. "Joe started to tell Jeff why he shouldn't have moved there," Taglianetti remembered, "and how sacrificing a lesser man could be part of the overall strategy of the game. He said sometimes you have to treat a man as if it's dispensable because the point is to win the game. And then he started talking about how chess is a meta-phor for Paradox." One might be forced by circumstances to consider the most galling gambits in order to endure in the hope of eventual triumph, Joe explained. Pawns and knights—even castles and queens—might be sac-rificed to save the single piece that was essential to survival, the king. "I re-member he kept repeating, 'The long run is what matters,'" Taglianetti recalled. In the BBC, as on a chessboard, even if "minor pieces" were lost, Joe said, it was "still possible for the rest to unite behind their leader and triumph," Tag remembered. The core issue always was whether ends justi-fied means, and the game they were playing at this moment provided a pellucid answer. Study history and you found that every man who achieved greatness had done so by looking always to the goal and by doing whatever was necessary to reach it. Only those whose personal resolve failed them pretended otherwise.

"Joe went on for like an hour," Tag remembered. "The room just stopped."

Alone with Dean and Ben, Joe's exhortations drew even more openly on the power of the infernal. "Whenever we had any difficulty with, you know, lying to people or stealing from people or whatever it was we were doing—when we had some difficulty with a dishonest aspect of it—he'd tell us that if you are truly reconciled to it, then you'll do it right," Dean remembered. "He said, 'The reason that criminals get caught and that ter-rorists don't usually wind up killing thousands of innocent people is because they're ingrained with some kind of internal guilt that makes them fail . . . He used to say that if someone wanted really to kill a hundred thousand people, they'll poison the water supply and it would happen, but he described how terrorists go through these lame plans of setting up bombs and hijack-ing planes and all kinds of really stupid things because they really don't want to kill anybody. They're not reconciled to it."

The Shading, Joe said, thought not in terms of whether an action was right or wrong but simply asked himself "whether something was Paradox or not," Dean recalled. Joe seemed to be stripping the philosophy to its essence. "He said the sole ethic of Paradox is that the individual does what is in his best interest," Dean recalled. "And that survival is the sole end."

The threats he sensed to his own survival had begun to affect Joe's appearance. "He was losing weight, getting pale," Taglianetti recalled. "He wasn't dressing up as much, either; he used to always be in a suit, but now you'd see him in jeans and a T-shirt and a leather jacket." "It was all too much for any one person and you could see it was getting away from him," Eisenberg agreed. "His skin looked like it was being stretched, it was so tight and transparent. He was quieter, more distracted. And his eyes were scary, like black holes."

In Joe's case, though, what stress produced was not retreat but cohesion. He began to address group meetings almost exclusively in aphorisms. "Rule number one was 'Never feel sorry for anything you do,'" Eisenberg recalled. "After that there was 'It's all right to lie if you know the truth.'" "One of Joe's favorite statements became 'Don't visit upon us the sins of our fathers,'" Gene Browning remembered.

Joe was solidifying the BBC as well, "forcing us to choose: 'in or out, with me or against me,'" Taglianetti recalled. Evan regarded it as a test when Joe asked him to create a new set of fraudulent minutes for Microgenesis in answer to Swartout's latest strategem. Joe had a capacity to intimidate based "not on mental fear of physical harm," Evan explained, but rather by explaining things "in a manner where it would seem the best thing for them to do."

Joe also began to use "scenarios" as a means of testing people during this time, Tom May remembered. One evening at the Manning when Tom agreed with his brother that the "contemplate all things" line should be drawn at murder, Joe asked each of the twins what they would do in a case where someone intended to kill the other. Assume first that you knew it was true and second that the police refused to become involved, Joe said: "He asked us, 'Would you go out and kill that person before they killed your brother?'" recalled Tom, who conceded that he would. "Then you can't say you're absolutely against murder, can you?" Joe said.

Joe's primary teaching tool these days was a videotape of the movie that had introduced Sylvester Stallone to the world as John Rambo, *First Blood*. Joe was screening the film regularly in the conference room at the Third Street office, "asking us to pick the place where Rambo loses his advantage," Tom remembered. "Nobody could, so Joe ran the tape back to the spot where this young boy appears." Rambo was a hunted man at that point, clad in a burlap bag and pursued bare-armed in freezing rain through a dark forest by a huge posse of police officers, tracking dogs, and reserve soldiers. "He had just escaped all these national guardsmen that were chasing him, and this innocent boy comes along and sees him," Tom recalled. "He is about to give him away, but Rambo grabs him, pulls out a knife, throws him on the ground, and is about to stab him. But he doesn't, and he lets the innocent go." "Joe turned to us and said, 'That was the biggest mistake he made,'" Jim remembered. "Joe would have killed the kid," Dean explained, "because the kid endangered his life. [Rambo] would've been scot-free if he had killed the kid."

After he shut off the film and turned on the lights, Joe explained that people were divided into two groups, Jeff remembered: "There is the intelligent person who takes control of his circumstances, and then there is the innocent who is acted upon."

Even Lopez, who missed the *First Blood* screenings as he prepared to leave for London on the first leg of his latest around-the-world trip, sensed that Joe was "playing with wild cards." Several times during the last two weeks of May, Hunt had come down from 1505 to the twelfth-floor condo at one or two in the morning, Lopez recalled, "bursting into Ben's room when Ben was in there with Julie, telling him to come out and talk." Ben acquiesced on each occasion, even when Joe told Dosti to get dressed and join him "on some middle-of-the-night mission," Lopez remembered. "Ben didn't like to do it, but there were occasions where [Joe and Dean] told him, 'Listen, Ben, we need you.'" While Joe waited in the hallway, Julie fought Ben all the way to the front door, "warning him, warning him, warning him," Lopez remembered. "'Joe is getting you in too deep. You guys don't know what you're doing.' Ben always defended Joe; he said everyone was worrying too much."

What worried Lopez, though, was that the rent on the two condos had been so late in May that the Manning's ownership posted three-day "pay or quit" notices on the doors to both units. Joe wrote a check the next morning, "but I could see they were scrambling to cover it," Lopez recalled. "Meanwhile I know that hundreds of thousands of dollars are coming into the commodity accounts every month."

Just before Dean left for Mexico, "Joe told me the Financial Futures and IMF money was all gone," Karny recalled, "that he had lost seven hundred thousand dollars in one fell swoop. He said he had traded more recklessly than he usually would—outside the low-risk parameters of his system—because the market was sluggish and he had to go for broke to make any money."

Since then, he had been forced to siphon off funds coming into the commodity accounts within a day or two after the checks were deposited, Joe said, writing more than $220,000 in checks to "Cash" on one Financial Futures account alone during March, April, and May. The BBC nearly had been broken in early May when Liza Bowman demanded the refund of her entire investment. By May 15, however, Liza not only was dating Ryan Hunt but had been persuaded by Joe to reinvest $155,301.68 in a "Future Hedges" partnership with Steve Weiss.

Two weeks later, Joe conceived his most effective fund-raising device ever, a letter sent to his limited partners announcing an impending moratorium on further investments in the Financial Futures Trading Corporation. His trading method required "the cloak of anonymity," Joe explained, and he was concerned that "we are approaching the threshold of notoriety in certain professional circles." Furthermore, Financial Futures was in danger of saturating the liquidity of its markets. "Quite simply," Joe concluded, "after June 15, 1984, there will be no additions to partnership accounts. Further, all profits will be automatically disbursed to investors." "At your service," it was signed, "Joseph Hunt."

Money literally flooded the Third Street office during the next two weeks. The largest single check came from Dr. Paskan, who raised $165,000 by taking a second mortgage on the building where he kept his medical offices. The "sense of fairness" in Joe's letter had moved him, the doctor explained, as had a recent statement on his account showing earnings at a rate of 200 percent per annum.

Joe used the infusion of cash to finance a bit of insider trading, purchasing blocks of Saturn Energy stock through an Eye Contact Advertising account opened at E. F. Hutton. Hunt called in his first order for the stock on the morning of May 24, exactly two weeks before a news release from the Vancouver company would be presented to the Canadian media, announcing completion of a contract conveying the UFOI coalfields and the BBC's Cyclotron to Saturn.

In the same week, Joe vigorously asserted his authority over the other Boys, demanding the resignations of the board of directors of West Cars and appointing himself as new CEO of the company that still held the titles to virtually every automobile driven by a BBC member. "At that point, Joe just said he wanted something done and we did it," Evan recalled. "There wasn't much pretense about being democratic. We were riding on his coattails, and we all knew it."

By the time Dean returned from Mexico, Joe had completed a draft of his "option agreement" with Ron Levin. The document was a cut-and-paste job on the contract with Michael Dow, Dean recalled, allowing Levin one year to exercise his right to control all applications of the Microgenesis technology in the silica and ceramics industries by paying seven million dollars before June 20, 1985. Joe had decided to leave a blank where the "non-refundable option payment" was specified, Dean remembered: "He said he didn't know for sure what Ron Levin had, didn't know what other things he might get Levin to sign over." Also, "Joe said that having Levin fill in the blank in his own handwriting would only strengthen his position later." There was no date either on the draft of the contract Joe showed him, Dean recalled: "He was kind of waiting for a good opportunity."

In the meantime, Joe continued to nurture his private relationship with Ron and let it be known at the office that they were meeting several times a week to hash out the details of a new business deal. Evan, Tom May, Steve Tag, and Lore Leis all were shown copies of the May 24 letter to Levin or drafts of the Microgenesis contract.

To gain Ron's trust, Dean explained, Joe agreed to accompany Levin on a weekend pleasure trip to San Francisco. By the time they returned, Joe had learned that Ron would be flying from LAX to La Guardia on the morning of June 7 for a weeklong excursion in New York. Joe "decided that would be the time to do it," Dean recalled, since no one would miss Ron for at least seven days.

The two of them were alone in the office at the time, Dean recalled: "Joe was sitting at his desk, writing on some pages torn from a yellow legal pad, working on some lists." Almost casually, Joe mentioned this was his plan for Ron Levin's "disappearance," Dean remembered. Looking over Joe's shoulder, Dean saw first the words *Jim digs pit."* They intended to dispose of the body in Soledad Canyon, Joe explained, at a location where the clay soil was packed so hard that even Jim needed a pick to break it. He had believed from the beginning that the bodyguard would be involved, Dean said: "I kind of get the impression that it was through knowing Jim that Joe reconciled with himself to take somebody's life, Jim confiding in Joe that he had done it before."

He had arranged to dine with Ron at his house on the evening of June 6, Joe explained. "He was going to get there at nine o'clock, and he was going to hang around with Ron a little bit," Dean recalled. "They were going to send out for dinner from La Scala, . . . then [Joe] was supposed to call Jim and invite him to come over." Once he got Jim in the house, it was imperative that the plan proceed without interruption, each movement occurring in a sequence coordinated down to the tiniest detail. Joe had laid it out, item by item, on a separate sheet of yellow paper, Dean remembered, this one labeled "AT LEVIN'S, TO DO": "(1) *Tape mouth,* (2) *Close blinds,* and (3) *Handcuff—put gloves on"* were the first three items on the list. He had purchased handcuffs from the remarkable selection available at a Hollywood sex shop called the International Love Boutique, Joe explained. The gloves he would wear only while creating the Microgenesis file in Ron's office, Joe said. It was irrelevant if his prints showed up elsewhere in the apartment; he was one of Ron's most frequent visitors, after all, "so it would be normal to have his fingerprints in the house," Dean explained.

As to "(4) *Scan for tape recorder,"* "Joe said Jim had a gadget that could detect a recording device in a room," Dean recalled, and they knew of no one so likely to install that sort of thing as Ron Levin. Next on the list were "(5) *Put answering service on 668 1st ring* and (6) *Get alarm access code and arm code."* "Joe was going to, since Ron Levin had made plans to leave for New

York, make it look like Ron Levin had just left on a trip as planned and disappeared in New York," Dean explained.

Item number seven was *"Explain situation."* Joe "was concerned that Ron would think, once they pulled a gun on him, that he was going to die, and that he wouldn't cooperate by signing the contracts and writing the checks that Joe wanted him to," Dean recalled. "And so Joe told me at this time that he had to come up with a scenario of how he would explain to Levin that he was in fact going to survive, in order to get him to cooperate." His story was going to be that most of the money he lost in Chicago belonged to gangsters, Joe said. They had followed him to Los Angeles, Joe would tell Ron, and he had been able to hold them off only by promising repayment from his share of the profits at Clayton Brokerage. These people decided they had waited long enough, however, and sent Jim to collect. Joe was counting on the fact that Ron had not met Jim, Dean explained, and was certain that "if Levin saw an enormous black man holding a gun on him, he'd believe." Joe said he would point to Jim and tell Ron, "'He has got his gun on me as much as he has it on you because I am in just as big trouble over this money as you now are.' And then he was going to spice it up," Dean remembered, "by saying, 'Ron, have you ever seen me without my shoes on? Because, you know, I am missing my big toe because of these guys.' And he was really going to build it up so that he could then explain to Ron, 'Now, if we just pay these guys, they will leave us alone.' And that is how he was going to get Ron to believe that both he and Ron were going to survive that night."

Once he had secured the location and explained the situation, Joe said, he could *"Create a file"* featuring the letters of May 3, May 15, and May 24, supplement them with the marketing brochures, then add the executed Microgenesis agreement. "Joe said that he had spent so much time around Ron's house that he had seen how Levin made up his filing system," Dean recalled. Ron was meticulous in the organization of his records, Joe said, and it would be necessary to date-stamp each letter and document with Ron's own implement, then hang them all in the special Pendaflex holders Levin used. He had perhaps for the first time fully appreciated Joe's own attention to detail, Dean reflected, when he read "(9) *Make a file of letters (take holes with you).*" "I asked about this," Dean recalled, "and Joe said that when making a file like Levin's you had to punch holes to fit them into the notebooks and he didn't want to leave the little circles of paper behind where someone might find them and be able to prove that the holes in the letters had been punched that evening."

Finally, he would be prepared to make a *"Determination of consideration,"* Joe explained. "Joe said that once he had a gun on Levin, he'd be able to determine what Ron was able to transfer," Dean recalled. He would first persuade Ron to reveal the amount of money in his Swiss bank account, Joe said, then force him to write a check. Joe mentioned the Swiss check for two million dollars he had seen at Ron's house, Dean remembered. It would perhaps be possible to arrange the transfer or assignment of any stocks and bonds in Ron's name as well, Joe said, and he definitely intended to force Levin to sign over the option on the Peck Drive duplex. If Ron resisted, attempted any sort of circumvention or connivance, Joe said, he would answer with (*10*) *Kill dog (emphasis)*." "This was in keeping with [Joe's] idea that Ron Levin wouldn't be such an easy customer," Dean explained. "One possibility, Joe said, was to kill the dog . . . to shake Ron up and get his cooperation. We all knew Ron Levin was very close to his dog." Joe said that "he was going to kill the dog in a grotesque way," Dean remembered, "and that was what *'emphasis'* meant."

Once Ron was reduced to docility, Joe would "(*11*) *Xerox authorizations (if any),"* then "(*12*) *Use corporate seal"* to certify the Microgenesis contract, "(*13*) *Have Levin sign agreements,"* and "(*14*) *Xerox everything so he has a copy."*

Joe still was debating whether it would be prudent to hold Ron at some remote location until the Swiss check cleared, then kill him. Dean's only significant contributions were suggestions about what to pack in Ron's suitcase before he disappeared, though "I also said that when they left Ron's house they should take his keys," Karny recalled, "so they could come back in if they wanted to."

Dean learned that afternoon he had been assigned a role in Joe's plan for the evening of June 6. "Joe said I was to go to the movies with Brooke and Jeff that night," he remembered. "There were two reasons: The first was so that [1505] would be cleared out so he and Jim could use it as their base of operations; the second was that so later Joe could say he had been with us at the movies—Joe said he'd go see the movie we saw that night within the next week, so he'd know what it was about."

Joe did not doubt that he would be a prime suspect in any investigation of Levin's disappearance, Dean recalled. It was for precisely this reason that he had conceived a plan so densely layered with alibis and ambiguities: First, there would be no body, and therefore no absolute proof that a murder had been committed. As in the case of Bruce Swartout, any number of people might have reasons for wanting Ron Levin dead, which meant that making a case on motive would be all but impossible. In addition, Levin at present was facing trial on felony charges very likely to result in a sentence to state prison—an obvious reason to abscond. On top of all that, the police would learn that Ron had been scheduled to leave LAX for La Guardia on the morning of June 7, clearly raising the possibility that he had vanished after his arrival in New York. Finally, there would be the file of date-stamped letters in Ron's office to explain any payments made to Joe Hunt and the BBC prior to his disappearance.

He and Joe discussed at length the prosecution's burden of proof, Dean recalled: "He said, all of the plans that he had so carefully laid, all of these letters he had written—who would believe all of that was a murder plan? So he was sure that a jury would have a reasonable doubt."

13

"AMERICA IS BACK" WAS A SLOGAN THE BOYS WOULD HEAR AGAIN AND AGAIN that summer, the theme not only of Ronald Reagan's campaign for reelection but of innumerable marketing campaigns conceived during 1984. The country had returned to eminence, it seemed, in the autumn of the previous year, when the administration launched its invasion of a tiny Caribbean island called Grenada.

The U.S. Army was inspired to award 8,612 medals for service in Operation Urgent Fury (a figure that slightly exceeded the total number of U.S. soldiers who had set foot on Grenada), and his great military victory lifted President Reagan to an apogee of popularity. During his 1984 State of the Union address, however, the president had preferred to dwell at greatest length on the continuing upsurge of the U.S. economy: The Dow-Jones Industrial Average had risen steeply since its 1982 nadir of 776.92, heading toward the 2,000 mark it soon would surpass and unemployment was at a comfortable 4.8 percent. "We're going *Back to the Future,*" Reagan asserted during his address to Congress, making yet another of those endearing allusions to blockbuster movies with which he superseded JFK's citations of Thucydides and Oswald Spengler. Those who had "stayed the course" through the inflation-busting recession of 1981–82 now were reaping the rewards of perseverance.

Some people were reaping a good deal more than others, of course: While the income of the top 5 percent of American earners had increased by nearly thirty billion dollars during Reagan's incumbency, the earnings of the bottom 20 percent had dropped by almost forty-four billion dollars. Among the new class of "working poor," those employed in the lower-income occupations of the service industry, were as many as a million people not only unable to buy a house but without sufficient funds even to rent an apartment.

Among the most advantaged, however, among the young especially and the Boys in particular, there was an increasingly overt conviction that those who couldn't keep up should be left behind, that their abandonment was part of the price the nation needed to pay for its transformation to a new order, the leaner and meaner machine America must become to keep its place in the world, that nation of 150 million with a stable white majority, no-frills government, and compulsory full employment. "Some people are just luckier than others," Evan would observe, with his talent for turning the blandest bon mot into a droll assertion of What We All Believe.

The Boys laughed uproariously as they watched their former Harvard School mate Ron Reagan make his inevitable appearance in an American Express commercial, the one that began with the president's son sitting in a phone booth, complaining, "Every time I appear on a talk show, people ask me about my father," then realizing, "Come to think of it, that's not so bad!" before turning away from the camera as his call is answered: "Hello, Dad?"

The rich were not just getting richer, they were becoming more interesting as well. The most compelling evidence of this were Nielsen ratings reporting that the two most popular programs on television were a pair of prime-time soap operas that observed the perpetual struggle for power and wealth among a pair of nouveau riche families, one in Texas, the other in Colorado. What made *Dallas* and *Dynasty* so successful was the formula each show had found for playing at once as melodrama to those at the bottom of the demographic charts and as camp comedy to the people at the top.

It was this balance of apparently irreconcilable elements that fixed the media's attention on the real-life saga of ambition and avarice playing at the moment in downtown Los Angeles, where would-be auto magnate John Z. DeLorean was standing trial in federal court, caught by the FBI and DEA in a twenty-four-million-dollar cocaine sting. The case came down ultimately to a choice between style and substance. On the one hand was DeLorean, tall and slender, resplendent in Savile Row suits, his surgically reconstructed chin set firmly, supported by his ever-faithful wife, the model Christine Ferrare, lovely but inscrutable behind the designer sunglasses she never removed, even indoors. The alternative was James Hoffman, a fat, failed drug smuggler who testified about a meeting with DeLorean where they snacked on "camel bear" cheese. DeLorean's attorney Howard Weitzman, sipping from a Perrier bottle between questions, portrayed his client as a naive independent businessman so desperate to save his struggling company that he had attempted to raise forty million dollars with two million in capital. One needed only to observe the alternating expressions on jurors' faces as their attention shifted between Hoffman and DeLorean to know what the outcome would be. Until a verdict was reached, however, the DeLorean trial became the event of the season in Los Angeles, a show so good that *Newsweek* suggested "if it weren't a federal trial, they could put it on the road and charge admission."

Ron Levin was there, in spirit mostly, though he had managed a physical manifestation at the last moment, taking his hard-won place among the reserved seats of the press section during the first week of June. Three months earlier, in March, Ron had wrangled an assignment from *Life* magazine for an "exclusive picture with text" featuring the defendant and his wife. Ron's journalistic ambitions were frustrated, however, by a technical difficulty: It seemed that back in January he had lost his Los Angeles Police Department press pass, seized by the Beverly Hills PD following his arrest on grand theft charges connected to the camera equipment "loaned" to him by Panasonic, RCA, et al. The BHPD had messengered not only the confiscated press pass but a copy of Ron's felony indictment as well to the downtown office of the LAPD's humorless chief press relations officer, Commander William Booth, who promptly informed Ron that his media credentials were revoked.

Two weeks later, Ron's attorney, Jeffrey Melczer, wrote Booth to demand an immediate administrative hearing so that Mr. Levin, who had yet to be convicted in court, might seek reinstatement. While this prayer languished in the police bureaucracy, Ron attempted an end run, applying to the U.S. Secret Service for a media credential to cover the 1984 presidential election on behalf of Network News, Inc. This application was denied, and Ron replied with a federal lawsuit against Treasury Secretary Donald Regan, demanding recognition as "a professional journalist for a major news organization." While his federal suit pended, Ron was prevailing at the local level, besting Booth one-on-one in a May 29 hearing before the LAPD's board of commissioners and obtaining notice of his reinstatement as a "news media member" on June 1.

Ron's story was that he had obtained access to DeLorean—persuading the auto manufacturer to pose with his family on a beach in Malibu— through Howard Weitzman. "He said, 'I own the building where Howard has his office,'" recalled one of Levin's literary collaborators, former *Newsweek* correspondent John Riley. "'He's going to have to [cooperate], or I'll throw him out into the street.'" This was an exaggeration: Ron's relationship with Weitzman was through the celebrity attorney's associate, Scott Furstman, hired by Levin to defend him against the criminal charges in Beverly Hills.

Things were not looking terribly bright for Ron on the felony front. The Los Angeles County district attorney's office not only filed ten counts of grand theft against Levin but attached "enhancements" to four of the counts, requesting an additional year of jail time in each instance for "excessive taking." Ron was facing a sentence of up to eight years in state prison if convicted, and the case against him was a strong one. The value of the camera equipment, the number of companies from which it had been "borrowed," and the aggravating existence of nearly half a million dollars in unexplained computer equipment seized during the raid on his home all boded badly.

Ron pleaded not guilty, naturally, at his arraignment on January 24, 1984, when he was released from the county jail on seventy-five thousand dollars' bail, an amount Marty and Carol secured with their home. The defendant asserted his right to a speedy trial, then immediately set about postponing it as far into the future as possible, filing a spate of motions between March and May. His client worked extensively on his own case, recalled Furstman (who would achieve notoriety himself as the attorney representing Jessica Hahn in her lawsuit against Jim Bakker and the PTL Foundation), preparing nearly all of the trial notebooks outlining the accusations and defenses for each count.

Ron remained unflinching, according to his closest friends. "He was mad the criminal charges had been filed in the first place," remembered Mark Geller. "He felt it was a civil matter." "Ron said he planned to sue the city of Beverly Hills and collect forty million dollars," recalled Terre Tereba. "He told me he couldn't wait for his case to go to court."

Alone with his young friends Dean Factor and Michael Broder, however, Ron admitted a bleaker forecast. "Ron said he didn't think [the case] was going to go well," remembered Broder, home for the summer after his freshman year at Harvard College and once again working out of the Peck Drive duplex. "He said it in an offhand manner, though, laughing." Ron conceded he probably would do some jail time, but "what really upset him was the publicity," recalled Factor, who had just finished his first year at American University in Washington, D.C. "He hated seeing his name in the newspaper."

To Blanche Sturkey, Ron confided that he expected to "be away for a while," preparing instructions for the collection of his mail and maintenance of the apartment during his absence.

The threat of incarceration, combined with the costs of his assorted litigations, had propelled Ron into a month-long frenzy of financial chicanery so complex and audacious that even his creditors despaired of untangling the skeins of scam and resorted to futile defamation. "Belligerent," "bullying," and "blustery," they called Ron later, not realizing how flattered he'd have been.

Perhaps most indignant were the people in the Boston office of Fidelity Investments, where Ron recently had opened a pair of accounts under the auspices of General Producers Corp. and International Clothing Ltd. It was the second week in May, recalled Daniel Holland, supervisor of sales and service for Fidelity USA, when Mr. Levin called his office to demand that seventy-five thousand dollars in "uncollected monies" (a Bank of America check deposited in the account two days earlier) be transferred to his Beverly Hills address at once out of his International Clothing account. It was imperative that he have the money in order to complete a business transaction, Ron explained. Holland refused, but Levin's threats of a lawsuit proved more effective when addressed to Fidelity's senior executives. "The money was wired on May 9," Holland recalled grimly. Exactly one day elapsed before Bank of America returned the Levin check stamped NSF, and Fidelity was out seventy-five thousand dollars.

Ron needed the money for, among other things, legal fees being run up by the six attorneys currently representing him in matters that ranged from an IRS assessment to a lawsuit brought by the real estate brokerage Bateman, Eichler, Hill. It was seven attorneys, actually, since Ron had retained himself, as R. Michael Wetherbee, to handle two additional court cases. He had other obligations as well, for example, the more than sixteen hundred dollars due to Topaz Auto each month for the BMW 633csi, BMW 533i, and Honda Accord he had leased from the company between December of 1983 and May of 1984. The 533i, leased in the name of Dr. Presley Reed, Ron had sold for twenty thousand to a gullible computer salesman. The Honda, General Producers Corp.'s "company car," had been leased under the name Oliver Wendell Holmes III. The 633csi Ron drove himself, under the name "Dr. Robert Levin." His personal transportation had been limited to a rented Rolls-Royce during most of May, however, since the BMW was at the Pauli Body Shop in West Hollywood, where a dent on the passenger-side door was being repaired. Ron attempted to convince Pauli's owner that his insurance company would pay for the repairs, but the body shop owner had known Levin for thirteen years and held the BMW until he was paid with a cashier's check.

The management was not so prudent at American Express, issuing Ron a gold card identifying him as president of the General Producers Corp. Mr. Levin had paid the $1,009.63 in charges on his February bill but not the $5,930.16 he owed after March and April. In May, Ron ran the outstanding charges on his gold card up to $20,159, mostly to cover the cost of the rented Rolls-Royce, though the $2,999.42 he spent on May 15 at Olympic Camera, the $3,311.14 he shelled out on May 12 at Louis Vuitton, and the $2,202 he paid for two Pan Am tickets to New York on May 11 helped inflate the total, which was still less than he went through during the first six days of June, when he added another $23,159 to his running total, spending $8,146 on clothes alone at Saks Fifth Avenue.

The Pan Am tickets were for Ron's companions—Dean Factor and Michael Broder—for a trip that they planned to take to New York on June 7. Factor had proposed the expedition ("I wanted to see my girlfriend," he explained) hoping that Ron would offer to pay, which Ron did. Ron was equally generous with Broder, who recalled an afternoon during his first week back in Beverly Hills from college, when the two of them passed by the Cartier's store while walking on Rodeo Drive: "I told him I had seen a wallet I liked, and he pulled me into the store." Ron paid with a hundred-dollar bill, remembered Broder, who had to smother a gasp when the woman behind the counter asked, "Are you Ron Levin?" "Ron said, 'No, I'm George Levin, his brother,'" Broder recalled. "She said, 'Because Ron Levin owes us a lot of money.' Ron told her, 'You should be happy because he owes Tiffany's a lot more.'"

Officially, Ron was paying him five dollars an hour for a nine-hour day, Broder explained, though he worked maybe two hours a day, mostly running errands. "The rest of the time was to be there as an audience," Michael explained. Ron was growing more rooted in his home each year, it seemed, and had become increasingly obsessed with order, insisting even that the papers on his tables be stacked at perfect right angles. "Once I was sitting at his desk, and I picked up a can of pencils and put it down in not exactly the same place," Broder recalled. "He came in screaming." Ron grew agitated whenever he was away from the Peck Drive duplex for more than an hour at a time, Michael remembered: "If we'd go out to lunch, when we came back the first thing he'd do is call in for messages." Whenever possible, Ron conducted business in his living room. Visitors came and went from morning to night, "five to ten people a day, on average," said Broder, who generally withdrew to the bedroom to watch TV when Ron's guests arrived.

This practice perhaps explained how the Harvard student could be entirely unaware that Ron had a second personal assistant working out of the Peck Drive duplex that summer, a young male model named James Foulk. Flawlessly handsome in a soft-featured Southern California paradigm that worked off the way the sun bleached his sandy hair blond at the same time it tanned his fair skin brown, Foulk was an aspiring actor who had met Ron one evening at the bar above Sunset Strip in Spago, where he and a friend were making connections while sipping from flutes of champagne. Ron invited them to share his table, and as he sat among the world's most-photographed faces and fantastic flower arrangements, dining on pizza garnished with goat cheese and duck sausage, Ron "gave me a Network News card and explained the company," Foulk recalled. Four days later, looking for part-time work, Foulk called Ron at home and scheduled a meeting. He wasn't just another actor, Foulk explained; he wanted to write screenplays, maybe even direct. "Ron said Network News was expanding," he recalled, "and would become a producer of films based on news events." When Ron suggested that Foulk "do some writing" for the company, the younger man remembered, "I said, 'Sure.' He told me to start the next Monday."

Ron paid him four hundred dollars a week, cash, and leased a white Rabbit convertible for transportation to and from Peck Drive, Foulk recalled, yet the young man did no "actual writing" for Network News. "Mostly I ran errands," he explained. "I also went to dinner with him two or three times a week. He'd call to tell me if there was a party or an opening, at a restaurant or a gallery, and I'd meet him there, maybe bring friends. We went to fashion shows, too, sometimes."

While Ron spoke of turning magazine articles into movie treatments and had writers over regularly, Foulk recalled, he talked mostly about himself, starting with the boy who had grown up pampered but lonely in Beverly Hills, an heir to the Rothschild fortune who was forced to take the name Levin when his mother remarried a commoner. Ron spoke often of his relationship with his mother, Foulk recalled, and was on the phone with her at least once a day. The one other living creature Levin seemed to love as much was his dog, Kosher; Ron even took the little Sheltie with him into the shower.

During the months he was working out of the Peck Drive apartment, however, Foulk never met even one of the five children Ron said he was supporting. Several times, though, he heard Levin screaming at their mother over the phone, Foulk recalled: "He said he and his ex-wife were fighting over the kids." His two oldest boys were going with him to New York on June 7, Ron told Foulk, describing the trip to New York as "a vacation for my kids."

The ten days prior to his departure would be among the more peripatetic periods in a life long dedicated to the proposition that crime was a more demanding field of endeavor than law-abiding people imagined. Ron's lone languid interval was a weekend he spent in the company of Terre Tereba. Ron was most upset to learn that she had attended a party without him during the previous week, Terre remembered, asking, "Aren't I your friend anymore?'" It was the same conversation they had whenever she went anywhere without him, Terre explained: "Ronnie needed more attention than anyone I've ever known. He had people around him constantly, and yet he always seemed so lonely." When they went to see a movie Saturday afternoon, she remembered, Ron not only wore his beeper but ran out of the theater to check his messages each time it went off. During their dinner Sunday at Palette, Ron told Terre of his impending trip to New York, claiming his purpose was to interview the favorite new rock star of the bored and breathless, Billy Idol. Terre told Ron she would arrive in New York herself on June 8, and they made plans to meet for lunch.

Even Beverly Hills was closed on Monday, Memorial Day, but Ron made up for the lost time by devoting what remained of the week to his two favorite business practices, shopping and banking. After the $8,000 spending spree at Saks, he ran up another $15,000 in charges at Brooks Brothers, Bonwit Teller, Maxfield Bleu, and Gump's. Thursday, May 31, Ron spent most of his morning at the Olympic National Bank branch in West Los Angeles, where he maintained three separate corporate accounts. It had been a particularly active month for him, the bank's operations manager observed: Nearly $105,000 had been deposited in the General News account alone, although $66,620 of that was in bounced checks, and most of the rest consisted of a check for $36,000 wired in from Boston. His business dealings were not only complicated but private, replied Ron, who cashed a check for $25,000, then used most of the money to purchase $15,000 in Citibank traveler's checks.

Much of that weekend Ron spent lounging outside an upper-level cabana on the deck of the Beverly Hills Hotel pool. His guests were Mark and Laura Geller, who recalled that Ron had required neither raucous demands nor expensive gestures to command the attention of others at poolside on Sunday afternoon; his wardrobe was sufficient. "Knee-length shorts with long socks and shoes he never removed, plus a long robe," Mark Geller remembered. Ron mentioned the trip to New York, Geller recalled, though not the fact that his ticket was a "free nonrefundable" one issued in Mark's name, obtained by Ron through the use of his friend's frequent-flier mileage.

Monday the fourth found Ron at the district attorney's office in Beverly Hills, negotiating a reduction of his bail on the grand theft charges in exchange for an agreement that some of the cameras, strobes, and light meters seized in the raid on his home five months earlier might be released to his principal accuser, Bob Garden of Garden Photo. Ron was adamant about reducing his bail to a point where his parents' home no longer would be required as security, noted Scott Furstman, who recalled that Mr. Levin and Mr. Garden spent no small portion of the day shouting threats at one another. In the end, though, Ron not only won Garden's assistance in persuading the DA's office to lower his bail from seventy-five thousand dollars to ten thousand but also obtained a six-month postponement of his preliminary hearing. "Ron was delighted," recalled Furstman, who made an appointment with his client to meet two days later, on June 6, to supervise appraisal of the property in police custody.

The next day, June 5, Ron paid $221 down to install a $3,500 cellular phone in the BMW he had leased as Dr. Robert Levin, then drove to West Hollywood to meet Joe Hunt for lunch. During that spring, Joe had continued to stop by the Peck Drive duplex at least once a week, Blanche Sturkey recalled, and remained her favorite of all Ron's companions. She never once saw the two argue, Blanche reflected, though she was aware from their conversations that Ron owed Joe money. "Ron would say, 'I don't have any money,'" Blanche remembered. "He'd call to me, 'Blanche, come here a minute. Tell 'im.' I said, 'I'm not getting into that. I don't know what money you have.'"

Ron was in no position to plead poverty on the morning of June 6, which began badly for him with the unannounced appearance of Len Marmor at his front door. Ron excused himself to make a phone call, but Marmor followed his friend into the back office, where he spotted a stack of hundred-dollar traveler's checks two inches high on the desk. Marmor seized the opportunity to remind Levin of an outstanding debt, "and Ron went crazy," Len recalled. "He hated to pay. I said, 'You owe me fourteen thousand dollars. Reduce that number.'" Cursing between breaths, Ron snatched two thousand dollars off the top of the pile and signed it over, Marmor remembered: "When I wanted more, he said he was never going to let me into his house again."

Ron had recovered his good humor by 9 A.M., when Blanche arrived for work. A Rolls-Royce she never had seen before was parked in the driveway, Blanche remembered, but she scarcely regarded this as unusual. Ron spent most of the morning coordinating a wardrobe for his stay in New York, according to Michael Broder, who arrived at the house half an hour later.

During the late afternoon, Ron was everywhere at once, apparently; at least five separate individuals would recall having conversations with him—three in person and two on the phone—at approximately the same time. Scott Furstman, who already had waited more than an hour for his client outside the Beverly Hills PD's property department, remembered that Ron called "around four-thirty" and said he couldn't make it. His mother, Carol, remembered seeing her son for the last time at "about four-thirty," when she spotted him walking Kosher at the corner of Peck and Charleville, and pulled her car over to the curb to talk. What she remembered best about that conversation, Carol recalled, was Ron's "irritation that I was driving [Marty's Cadillac] instead of the Rolls-Royce. He said, 'Why are you driving the old car?' It upset him to see me in it." They spoke only another minute or two, Carol remembered, mostly about Ron's plan to keep Kosher with him that night, then have Blanche bring the dog to her house the next morning. When Ronnie was out of town, he liked to call and have her put the dog on the phone, Carol explained. It was four-thirty as well, according to a Prudential Bache broker in the 9701 Wilshire building, when Mr. Levin called to say he wanted to open a General News Corp. money market account with check-writing, Visa, and international wire transfer privileges. "He was in a big hurry," the woman remembered. "He mentioned that he was traveling and needed the account right away." Mr. Levin was perhaps the most presumptuous customer she ever encountered, the broker said, "demanding that I come to his home and pick the check up myself because he was waiting for a phone call." When he appeared at her office door half an hour later, however, the woman recalled Ron was "suave, telling me he was a writer of some sort." He opened his General News account with a fourteen-thousand-dollar deposit, then assured the broker he would double this amount when he returned from a "research trip." It was also "four-thirty or so" when Michael Broder told Ron he was calling it a day and "around four-thirty" when Blanche announced she was leaving. On her way out, she promised once more to come by the house at seven the next morning, Blanche remembered, so that she could drive Ron and the boys to the airport.

James Foulk dropped by the Peck Drive duplex at about 6:30 P.M. to collect that week's wages and found Ron wearing his favorite gray velour warm-up suit as he packed a suitcase and garment bag for the trip to New York. Ron suggested he come along, Foulk recalled, but "I said I had other things to do. He said if I changed my mind he'd be leaving around eight A.M."

Carol Levin spoke to her son for the last time when she phoned him at about eight that evening. Their conversation was so inane, she scarcely could recall the content, Carol said: "It was probably 'Be sure you take a sweater' or something."

Ron called Michael Broder about half an hour after that. "He asked if I would come down to his house for dinner and said I should spend the night," Broder remembered. "I said I'd already eaten, and I'd spend the night at Dean's house." Factor phoned Ron at around 9:30 P.M. from the Beverly Hills diner Larry Parker's. "Ronnie answered on the first ring," Dean remembered. "The whole conversation was less than a minute. Ronnie just said, 'I'm sleeping. I have to hang up. Everything's fine. I'll see you tomorrow.' But he never did."

He and Joe knew it was a gamble, Dean Karny conceded, bringing Ron Levin by the Third Street suites on the afternoon of June 5: "We'd been dropping hints all around the office about the deal with Microgenesis, and

Ron Levin didn't know anything about it, so Joe was concerned that some-one was going to bring it up to Ron." Joe felt it was worth the risk, though: "Everyone would remember Levin coming to the office, being friendly with Joe," Dean explained, "and if later suspicion were cast upon him, they'd say, 'Come on, Levin was in the office visiting.' Why was he visiting? 'Because we were negotiating a contract.'"

Unfortunately, the office was virtually deserted when Joe and Ron showed up. Dean and Ben were waiting, of course, along with Jon Allen, but not another soul was in sight. Taglianetti and Eisenberg had disappeared into the legal room just moments earlier, and Lore Leis for some reason had chosen that day to go out for lunch, which she never did. "So [the trip to the office] didn't really serve Joe's purpose," Dean reflected, "because not too many people wound up seeing him with Ron Levin on friendly terms, except the people that already knew he was planning to kill him."

Joe did not actually produce a final draft of his contract with Levin until the next day, June 6, when he brought it to Jerry Eisenberg at three-thirty that afternoon "and told me to 'jazz it up' with legalese," the BBC attorney recalled: "Joe said there was a time issue . . . he had to have it that day because he was going to meet with Ron Levin that evening." Eisenberg remembered Joe as "hurried, excited, animated, which was not normal for him. Joe was always cool." The amount of money involved in the Micro-genesis deal was less surprising to him than "the suddenness of it all," Jerry reflected: "My advice was that this was a good agreement for a small amount, but for seven or eight million dollars it should have been more compre-hensive." Joe insisted a complete revision of the contract was unnecessary, however, and gave him just half an hour to make insertions and deletions, Eisenberg recalled, leaving with the document just before 5 P.M.

It was about half an hour later, according to Dean, when Joe reminded him to take Brooke and Jeff out to an early dinner, then a movie. He was "pretty sure" Brooke knew what was about to happen, Dean said. And while uncertain whether Jeff would be willing to support Joe with a lie later, neither of them imagined it mattered much: "My impression was, months down the line, who would remember whether Joe was along or not," Karny explained.

He and Joe said good-evening at about 7 P.M., when Dean saw him at the desk in his bedroom, "reprioritizing" the "AT LEVIN'S, TO DO," list.

He and Brooke and Jeff and Lisa Marie ate a light dinner at Hana Sushi, Dean remembered, then caught the eight o'clock show at the Avco Cinema. The movie they saw was *Streets of Fire,* a "rock and roll fable" set in what appeared to be the Chicago of the late 1950s as it might have looked had the Korean War ended in nuclear holocaust. Alleys were filled with fog, sidewalks were slick, and women all were streetwalkers, hash-slingers, or stars. The baddest boys in town were a motorcycle gang called the Bombers, who took whatever they wanted and trashed the rest. Easily the best thing about the film was the lead villain, a kind of Mephistophelian revision of Brando's Wild One performed by Willem Dafoe, an actor so good he could have played Joe Hunt had he been a few years younger. "I remember thinking to myself how much Joe was going to like this movie," Dean reflected.

The condo was dark when they returned at about 10 P.M., Dean remembered: "I went to bed. I don't know what Brooke did."

He was awakened at seven the next morning, Dean recalled, when Joe came to his room and shook him from sleep. Joe wore a freshly pressed business suit and his hair was wet, as if he had just stepped out of the shower. They went into the living room and sat together on the couch. Joe opened his briefcase and brought out a large check on blue and purple patterned paper, embossed with the words "SWISS CREDIT BANK, TOWN BRANCH, ZURICH-RATHURSPLATZ," bearing Ron Levin's signature and an amount of $1.5 million. Joe remained silent until he produced the Microgenesis contract, also signed by Ron Levin, Dean recalled, "then told me that he had done it, that Ron was dead." He didn't ask for details, Dean explained, "but I did ask if that was all he had gotten. I asked if he had gotten the option on the house. He said no, that he'd tell me about it later."

Joe arrived at the Mays' apartment in Brentwood half an hour later. "He raced up to the door, knocked, told us to come down to the car," Tom recalled. "Ben was there waiting. Joe pulled out the Ron Levin contract and showed it to us. He also had the check with him, carefully folded in his pocket. He pulled it out very carefully and said, 'Ron Levin signed this— that's his signature, see.' Joe seemed very happy; he looked like all his problems had been solved."

The first strange thing they noticed was the alarm light, green rather than red, Ron's young friends remembered. "Ron was very meticulous about many things, and the alarm was one of them," Michael Broder explained. "I saw him put it on if we went to lunch in Beverly Hills and were gone an hour," added Dean Factor. Neither of them could recall an occasion when Ron had retired for the evening without first arming his security system.

Dean and Michael had come to Ron's door at a quarter to seven, as promised. When there was no answer to their third ring at the steel gate, the boys circled the building, attempting to peer in the windows of the front office and back bedroom, but found the blinds closed, something Ron did only when he left town.

Blanche arrived ten minutes later, concerned herself. She had called Ron's home an hour earlier, to tell him she was on her way but heard the phone ring four times before the answering service picked up. Usually Ron answered himself on the first or second ring. When the housekeeper let the boys into the apartment with her key, they saw Kosher cowering in a corner. The dog whimpered, then retreated down the long hallway to the master bedroom. All of them began to call Ron's name, but there was no answer.

In the kitchen, the boys found a pair of chopped salads from La Scala in takeout boxes on the butcher block table, one untouched, the other reduced by only a bite or two. When they joined Blanche in the bedroom, all three noticed the smell, which they traced to a wet spot at the foot of the bed, where the dog had urinated. In the two years Kosher had lived with Ron, this was the first time the dog had pottied inside the house, Blanche told Michael and Dean.

Their search was interrupted when Len Marmor called to tell his friend good-bye, but instead got Factor, who told him Ronnie seemed to be missing. "Hey, with Ron Levin, anything is possible," Marmor observed.

Ron's wallet and money clip were missing from the third shelf of the bookcase in the bedroom where he normally kept them, Blanche noticed. His car keys were gone as well, which was peculiar, since he had promised Blanche use of the BMW while he was in New York. Even more remarkable, he had left behind his little black leather bag, the one in which he carried his cosmetics, key chains, calculator, and notepads. "Ron never goes anywhere without that bag," she said. On the other hand, Ron had so many clothes, it was impossible to say what was missing. All Blanche could be sure of were the gray warm-up suit and the white terry-cloth robe, which were nowhere to be found.

Blanche and Michael Broder both noticed the bedspread then; instead of the thick beige down-filled comforter Ron normally used, it was the thinner floral-patterned one he kept for guests. Blanche, who made Ron's bed most mornings, counted only three pillows. "Ron always keeps four on his bed," she said.

In the office, they found three Pan Am tickets to New York. At that point, Michael and Dean sat down at Ron's Macintosh computer to type out a list of "all the things that seemed strange," as Broder put it. When they counted the number, it made them very nervous, he remembered.

Blanche also was uneasy but attempted to carry on as if Ron might walk through the door at any moment. She brewed coffee and fixed a big breakfast. She didn't want to phone Mrs. Levin and alarm her, Blanche explained, but the boys kept insisting.

"At the office, of course, there was much celebrating," Dean remembered. "When Joe came in I asked, 'Did you get it?'" Eisenberg recalled. "He said, 'I got it,' then handed me the check." Joe made copies of the Swiss draft and distributed them to everyone. "He seemed very excited, very happy," Evan recalled. "Joe said, 'I did it,'" Lore Leis remembered. "He was very proud of himself."

There was much discussion about how to cash the check in a hurry, Eisenberg recalled. The Bank of America wanted six to eight weeks, but Joe said they were losing interest, remembered Evan, who that morning fabricated yet another set of Microgenesis board meeting minutes, these dated June 7, 1984, listing Directors Joseph Hunt, Tom May, Dean Karny, Ben Dosti, and Jeff Raymond as "present." "Because of the size of the draft received via the Levin Agreement, and the fact that the draft was from a bank outside the United States, the board discussed the manner in which to expedite the completion of its negotiation," Evan typed. "Joseph Hunt proposed having a member of the board travel to Europe, with authorization to open an account there . . . Ben Dosti was considered the best suited."

"I said to Ben, 'Tough duty you're getting," recalled Evan, who created a second set of fraudulent Microgenesis minutes later that day, these purporting to be the record of a board meeting held more than a month earlier, on May 2, 1984, at which a single item of business was on the agenda: "RESOLVED, that Joseph Hunt is to investigate the possibility of selling, trading, optioning or licensing the use of the BAM in the area of ceramics and silica. The corporation gives to Joseph Hunt the right to bind the company in the above mentioned areas, without further need to consult this board."

"Joe said you couldn't be too careful," Evan remembered.

The call from Blanche came at exactly eight-thirty that morning, Carol Levin remembered. "She said, 'Mrs. Levin, I hate to tell you this: All Ron's things are here, but Ronnie's gone.'" Ron's mother arrived at the Peck Drive duplex ten minutes later. Blanche led her to the master bedroom and showed Mrs. Levin the secret place where Ron cached his Swiss watches, ruby and sapphire rings, spare money clips, gold jacket buttons, and matching cuff-links. "She just said, 'Look, everything is here,'" Carol recalled.

The missing comforter was what seemed to weigh most heavily on the housekeeper's mind, Mrs. Levin remembered. Yet there was no evidence of a struggle, no ransacking, no blood. Carol phoned the Beverly Hills police to report her son missing at a little after 9 A.M., but the receptionist who took her call explained it was impossible to file a missing person report on any-one who had been gone for less than forty-eight hours.

The two boys went to the Beverly Hills Police Department in per-son after talking to Scott Furstman on the phone. They spoke to a team of detectives in one of the bungalows out back of the main building, Factor recalled. The name Ron Levin brought tight-lipped smiles to the faces of the police investigators, who appeared skeptical, to say the least, when Dean said he believed Ron might have met with foul play. One detective "told me that unless there was blood on the walls, there was no reason to suspect murder," Factor recalled.

Ben was making his Swissair reservations when the BBC's new corporate counsel, Neil Adelman, who had reported that morning for his first day on the job, suggested there might be a simpler and faster way to cash the check. At thirty-three, Adelman was older than the others and not a BBC member. He had been employed most recently as general counsel to *Hustler* magazine and its publisher, Larry Flynt. Flynt was away in federal prison at present, however, serving a fifteen-month sentence for felony con-tempt imposed by a U.S. District Court judge, who ordered Flynt bound and gagged in his gold-plated wheelchair after the publisher addressed him several times as "you cocksucker." While working for *Hustler,* he had done a great deal of business with the World Trade Bank in Beverly Hills, Adelman said, an institution that thrived principally as a result of its ability to effectuate transactions involving overseas accounts.

The attorney was accompanied by Joe, Dean, Ben, Evan, and Jerry Eisenberg when he met later that afternoon with the World Trade Bank's operations manager, who assured the Boys he could process the Swiss check within a week at most for an appropriate fee, in this case twenty-five thou-sand dollars. It was a difficult decision, Dean remembered; that amount represented nearly all the money remaining in the BBC's Bank of America accounts. On the other hand, "Joe was very anxious to get the [Levin] money as soon as possible," Dean explained. "It was my understanding he had a [June 15] payment to make to his investors."

Joe, Dean, Ben, and Evan returned to the Beverly Hills bank the next morning, Friday, June 8, with the Levin check. After opening a Microgenesis of North America account with a deposit of $25,809, they were advised the bank would be sending the check to Zurich by international courier that afternoon.

The BBC spent the rest of the weekend celebrating not only the Levin deal but the Canadian newspaper clippings they had received from Saturn Energy's offices. "1000 JOBS TOUTED FOR CITY" was the front-page headline in the *Kamloops* (*B.C.*) *News* issue reporting Saturn's plan to construct a manufacturing plant for the Microgenesis Corp.'s Cyclotron.

The Boys all agreed to meet that evening for the grand opening of Trust, a new club in the former federal bank building on Wilshire Boulevard. The line outside was obnoxiously long, however, Evan recalled, and Brooke left in a pout after waiting almost an hour. Suddenly stag, Joe suggested they try "alternate access," then led the others to the back of the building. Giddy with fear, they followed him single file up a fire escape to the roof of the building, shinnying across a narrow brick parapet to a set of steel stairs that descended through the ceiling. "We came down in a broom closet," Evan recalled. "We were all very dressed up and our clothes were all scuffed; my good pants were torn. We came out of the closet pretending to have been smoking dope in there, which was a good cover, and couldn't stop laughing all night."

The Boys attended another grand opening party the next night, Saturday, for the new club Seth Marsh had opened on Sunset Strip. Decadence, the place was called. They all were a little hungover on Sunday morning, so it was not until later that afternoon, Dean remembered, when Joe invited him for a walk in Westwood Village and proceeded to describe how he had murdered Ron Levin.

Events had unfolded exactly as imagined at first, Joe said. "He told me he had ordered a dinner from La Scala to be delivered that night," Dean recalled. "And he said that he had left dishes with his fingerprints in the sink because he intended to claim that he was there and that he had every right to be there because he was doing this deal." He considered the *"Explain situation"* phase of his plan a complete success, said Joe, whose main concern all along had been that Ron would know he was going to be killed and refuse to cooperate. "Then there would be a killing for no money," Dean explained. "And money was what was important."

Joe felt he had played Jim off very effectively as the "gruff Mafia muscle man," Dean recalled: "He told me he said, 'I didn't want to involve you in this, Ron, but they say they're going to kill me and I told them this was the only way I could make any money . . . [Joe] told Ron that Ron would be taken to a place for about ten days or two weeks or however long it took for this check to clear, and then he'd be released. He said Ron believed him. That's why Ron willingly signed the contract and signed the check, because he believed he was going to live." He wanted more, Joe said, but couldn't say so. Jim was supposed to play the part of the man in charge, so Joe asked him, "Is that enough?" Jim messed up, though, and instead of demanding more, said, "I think that's okay."

Levin had maintained his poise up to that point, Joe said, but when they handcuffed him, began to whimper, Dean remembered: "Joe said it was at that moment Ron seemed to sense he was a dead man and 'lost his energy.'" Joe said he and Jim pushed Ron into the back bedroom then, Dean recalled, and laid him facedown on the bed. He intended to gather Ron's personal possessions and pack his things, Joe said, while Jim held the gun on him. Instead of waiting as he was instructed to, though, Joe said, Jim made a second mistake and, without warning, shot Ron in the back of the head.

Joe said he would remember the noise that had issued from Levin— "the sound of a man's last breath leaving his body"—for as long as he lived. "He made the sound for me," Dean remembered, "a kind of explosive gasp," which Joe said had revealed to him for all time how thin and arbitrary was the line between life and death. "Joe went into great detail on this," Dean recalled. "He really wanted to involve me."

There was no time then to pack suitcases or organize files, Joe said, because blood from Levin's head wound was seeping onto the comforters. "So they wrapped him up in the bedspread," Dean recalled, "because they didn't want blood to get all over; they wanted it to appear that Ron had fled . . . they wrapped up Levin's body and took it out to the car, put him in the trunk. It was one of the BMWs . . . Joe said [the body] was very heavy. He described how, when a man is dead, his weight becomes what they call dead-weight. [Also,] he and Jim were nervous, and that caused them to be having a really hard time carrying it out to the car and . . . it was very difficult getting it into the trunk and getting it closed because they were so weak from nerves." Jim made a third mistake when he slammed the trunk against Ron's shoulder, Joe said, denting the lid.

They drove the freeway north and took the main road into Soledad Canyon, then turned up Indian Canyon Truck Trail to the spot where Jim had dug the pit. He and Jim laid Ron in the loose earth, Joe said, and "disfigured the body with a shotgun, so it was not recognizable," Dean remembered. "He said he just kept shooting, a lot of times. He said that at one point Ron Levin's brain jumped out of his skull and fell on his chest. Joe seemed like he thought that was kind of neat in a weird way, as if it had surprised him. He was very casual when he was telling me all of this, matter-of-fact, except when he laughed about the brain."

He and Jim went back into the Peck Drive duplex during the early hours of Friday morning to remake the bed and complete the Microgenesis file as planned, Joe said. He gave Levin's wallet to Jim and instructed him to use one of Ron's credit cards to book a seat the next morning on the first available flight to New York. He told Jim to use the same credit card to register at the Plaza Hotel as Ron Levin, Joe said, then to lose Ron's wallet in a place where it would be found "so that if foul play was suspected, it would be suspected that it had happened in New York," Dean recalled.

His last decision involved what to do with Ron's Bulgari watch, the one Levin had purchased at the jewelry store in the Pierre Hotel. Joe hated to give it up, but "he wasn't going to mess around with a clue like that," Dean explained. "Twelve thousand bucks, but he said he threw it in one of the storm drains or whatever they're called in Westwood . . . one of us said it seemed like a shame because it was such a nice watch."

14

AT THE PLAZA HOTEL ON CENTRAL PARK SOUTH, SOME OF THE STAFF HAD grown concerned with the large and unusual charges incurred by the guest in room 1071, Mr. Ronald George Levin of Beverly Hills. During three days and nights, the hotel's credit manager reported to her supervisor, Mr. Levin had accumulated a running tab that now approached two thousand dollars, most of this for a pair of limousine rides from midtown Manhattan to Wilmington, Delaware, and Philadelphia, where, according to his chauffeurs, the passenger visited an ex-wife, collected his young son, and transported a contingent of friends and relatives to dinner in a restaurant favored by the Du Ponts.

Mr. Levin was a "walk-in," the credit manager learned when she checked at the front desk, a guest who arrived without reservation, taking a single room for one night, then upgrading to a deluxe double. Because of the size of Mr. Levin's bill, the credit manager attempted to contact him all during the morning of June 10 to arrange payment. She left a number of messages for the guest at the desk, but he did not respond. Concerned, she asked the Plaza's director of security, Joe Vega, to accompany her to 1071 to determine whether the guest had left his luggage in the room. They found two Halliburton suitcases by the fireplace. She had instructed the security director to double-lock the door to the room, the credit manager reported to her supervisor, making it impossible for Mr. Levin to remove his property without coming to the front desk for a passkey.

The guest in 1071 reported to his office at six-thirty that evening, recalled the Plaza's assistant manager, Richard Liebowitz, who was taken back by Mr. Levin's dark complexion—"Levin to me is a Jewish name"— but pleased when the man said he wished to settle the account and handed over an American Express card issued to General Producers Corp. American Express refused to accept the card, however, and the MasterCard Mr. Levin offered in its stead was rejected as well. "I said we would keep the room locked with his possessions inside until he could return to pay his bill," Liebowitz recalled.

It was about 7:45 P.M., in the stairwell on the south side of the building, Joe Vega remembered, when he saw a black gentleman in possession of the two bags he had double-locked in room 1071 earlier. The gentleman explained he was taking the stairs because the elevators were out. Vega asked if he was in possession of a room key. The gentleman continued walking past. Vega asked him to stop, but the gentleman said he had a limousine waiting and began to run. By the time he reached the Plaza's lobby, the gentleman was sprinting for the three large French doors that opened onto Fifth Avenue, where Vega's four units were waiting for him. Confronted by a quartet of husky men in blue blazers, the gentleman dropped his suitcases, let out a yell, and assumed a karate stance. This was a first for the Plaza. "All of us were amazed that it was happening," Vega recalled, "but as we just closed a circle on him, he put his hands up—'Okay, you have got me.'"

As they escorted him to the hotel office, however, the gentleman was able to use the crowd of gawkers in the lobby to separate from the security staff and make a second run for it, heading this time for the main entrance of the hotel on Fifty-ninth Street. Vega remembered that he and his men gave chase knowing, "Once he hits the street, we can't grab him." They caught him at the big revolving door just outside the entrance to the Oak Bar, Vega recalled, but the gentleman was so powerful that his momentum carried them all crashing into the door, not only knocking it off its hinges, but shattering most of the glass. It took all five of them to subdue the gentleman, Vega remembered: "I grabbed him around the neck. My other men grabbed him around the arms and one had him by the leg. He was an extremely strong individual."

The gentleman became suddenly cooperative though, when they maneuvered him into the manager's office, Vega recalled: "We usually want to see ID, but he started offering before we could ask." The gentleman showed them an assortment of credit and business cards that identified Ronald George Levin as everything from assignment editor at a television news company to president of an independent film studio to CEO for an international clothing firm. When he asked how the gentleman had managed to remove the suitcases from room 1071, Mr. Levin said the maid had let him in, Vega recalled: "I knew that was impossible, so I sent one of my units up to check." The security officer reported in on his walkie-talkie a few minutes later, sounding extremely impressed: Someone had kicked in the solid-core door of room 1071 with such force that the double lock on it literally splintered. "I asked the gentleman why he had done all this," Vega recalled, "and he said if he wanted to, he could have broken us all apart, but he didn't want no trouble."

Mr. Levin offered Vega and his men five hundred dollars if they would let him go, promising to return later with enough cash to pay both his charges and any damages. "Making sure we didn't contact the police was his main concern," said Vega, who called the cops anyway, personally signing the complaint that charged Ronald George Levin of Beverly Hills, California, with criminal trespass, criminal mischief, and theft of services.

He was with Joe at the office on Monday afternoon when Jim's collect call came in from New York, remembered Dean, who heard only Hunt's end of the conversation: "It was 'Where are you?' 'What's it for?' 'What's the phone number?' When he hung up, he told me that Jim had been arrested."

Joe's aplomb and dispatch both were remarkable, Dean thought. He drove directly to the bank, cashed an investor's check that had come in that morning, stopped by the Manning to pack a bag, and went straight from there to the airport. By sunrise the next morning, Joe was on the steps of the Criminal Court building in lower Manhattan, where he spotted "the kind of lawyer that walks around the halls of the courthouse," as Dean remembered his friend's description. "He said that he really impressed the lawyer with how stern and direct he was. He just walked up to him wearing his sunglasses and looked at him and said, 'I don't want any crap from you. You're going to get paid for this. I just want this done quietly. Get in there and see what this guy is in for. Then see what it's going to take to get him out.'"

Mr. Levin's friend *had* been an unusually intense young fellow, remembered Robert Ferraro, the gray-faced, baggy-eyed attorney who met Joe outside the New York City Arraignment Court at six-fifteen on the morning of June 12. The young man demanded a business card, but Ferraro had just given away his last one, and so showed a Bloomingdale's credit card instead. Joe's "commanding presence" would not have been so persuasive were it not backed up by the huge wad of hundred-dollar bills he pulled from his pants pocket, Ferraro conceded. The attorney accepted forty-seven of those hundreds, five for his fee, plus another two as an "honorarium," twenty more to cover the damages at the Plaza Hotel, and another twenty for his friend Ron Levin when he got out of jail.

If his young friend was a bit taciturn, Mr. Levin himself proved most voluble when they met at the New York Police Department's Midtown North precinct later that morning, Ferraro remembered: "He said he lived at the Peck address, which he said was a condo worth seven hundred and eighty thousand dollars. He said he was a show business promoter, the agent for Michael Jackson, among others. He said his business was JT Productions of 9700 Wilshire Boulevard and his wife's name was Helen." Ferraro explained to his client that a criminal arraignment in New York City could take eight hours or three days, depending upon the volume of cases.

When he returned to the arraignment court, Ferraro found Mr. Levin's young friend pacing the hallway. This was going to take some time, the attorney explained; since NYPD had no rap sheet on Mr. Levin, the court was required to obtain a copy of the defendant's criminal record from Albany. The young man grew concerned then, Ferraro remembered, "very anxious to see his friend Ron Levin." By early afternoon, Ferraro had succeeded in arranging Mr. Levin's transfer from the police precinct to the Tombs, where he was locked into a holding cell at about 2 P.M. but still was waiting for the rap sheet. At the suggestion of his client's young friend, "I called the Plaza and said, 'I have two thousand dollars for you; let's get this case resolved,'" Ferraro remembered. Two Plaza employees arrived at the arraignment court less than half an hour later, and Ferraro gave them the two thousand dollars in front of the presiding judge. Mr. Levin was released on his own recognizance, and left the courthouse at once. In the defendant's absence, the judge set an August 14 trial date.

Jim was back in Los Angeles that evening, but Joe had stayed on in New York, moving from the Hilton to the Parker Meridien, registering again under an assumed name and paying cash. The complications created by Jim's arrest seemed to worry Joe far less than the prospect of facing his investors when he returned to Los Angeles, Dean thought. A number of the limited partners were pressing for advances against their June 15 disbursement, Dean told Joe when he phoned Tuesday night. During this conversation, Joe decided he would fly on to London, where Steve Lopez was ensconced at the Intercontinental Hotel. His sole purpose was to stall the investors until Ron Levin's check could be cashed, explained Dean, who arranged Joe's prepaid ticket from Kennedy to Heathrow.

During the days that followed, Dean for the first time became "disgruntled," complaining that Joe had "left Ben and myself to make excuses for him." The two of them avoided making any criminally false representations to the investors, Dean said, but feared they could be implicated: "All we said was 'Joe knows what he's doing. He's very busy, and we're sure that he'll take care of everything when he gets back.'"

While the Shadings feinted and dodged, Lore Leis bore the brunt of the investors' onslaught. Half a dozen limited partners arrived at the office in a group on the day the disbursement checks were due, Lore recalled, demanding to know what their profits would be for the quarter. Several investors persisted until the secretary consented to call Joe at his hotel in London: "I left word and he never called back," she remembered. "So one of the investors he was friendly with said, 'Have you heard from him?' I said, 'No.' He said, 'So call again.'" She explained Joe's standing order was that she should never tell him anything more than once, Lore recalled, and the man was incredulous: "I said, 'Listen, you want to call, go right ahead.'"

In London, Lopez paid homage also to Joe's prerogative. "There was absolutely no reason for him to be there," the BBC's fund-raiser said. "In fact, it was inconvenient. But what are you gonna tell Joe? He called me up from New York and said, 'I have some good news; I want to see you.' And the next thing I know he shows up at my hotel, hands me a copy of the Ron Levin check."

Joe insisted upon staying with him at the Intercontinental for the next five days, Lopez said, and "was in the way, to be honest. What looked like socializing to him was strictly business for me." Most of the wealthiest families from Southeast Asia took up residence during June and July at four-star hotels in London or the next two stops on his itinerary, Paris and Monte Carlo, Steve tried to explain: "Basically, I would just go to the places where I knew certain people would be staying, maybe go into the bar or arrive at teatime, and it would be 'Oh, what are you doing here?' 'I've got something rather interesting, really.' 'What's that?' So it was like letting them in on a good thing."

Everything depended upon playing oneself off with an implicit but clearly defined propriety, however, Lopez explained, which was what made Joe such a pain in the ass: "He went out with me when I was meeting some people and bought us all dinner. He was very serene and smooth and upbeat—it would have gone over great in L.A. But the people I was with, they thought he was a kid because he didn't have the seriousness that they expect. He laughed too much. They saw potential—I mean, he's a very smart guy—but Asians aren't too impressed with talk; they want results. Also, he didn't have the savoir faire to entice money out of people like these. These weren't your excitable and greedy American investors. These were calm, cool, level-headed Asians. Joe would try to create excitement by telling them how great he has done in the past. Throw that at an Asian and he thinks, 'If you're doing so well, what do you need me for?' Where an American will think, 'How can I get in?'"

He warned his younger associate against overreaching, but nothing seemed to faze Joe, Lopez remembered: "In London he was smiling more than I ever remember him smiling before. He made me go with him when he went shopping, which was something he liked to do less than any of the others back in L.A. He bought me a beautiful Halliburton briefcase like the one he bought himself and a raincoat, too, a Burberry. He even went out dancing one night at the Hippodrome."

The tenuous purchase of the BBC registered with him for perhaps the first time, though, Lopez recalled, as he watched Joe peel away bill after bill from the roll of hundreds he carried in London. "I don't think I was aware until then that Joe didn't have—and couldn't get—a credit card," Steve explained. "That when you got right down to it, he was just this kid carrying a lot of cash. In fact, I think that's why he finally went back to L.A., because he was out of money."

Word that the Swiss Credit Bank refused to honor the Levin check reached the BBC office on the day Joe left London. It was Dosti who took the call from the World Trade Bank. He was uncertain about precisely why the check had been denied, Ben told Dean; the Swiss bank apparently had sent a telex from Zurich that gave as its explanation "Signature Missing."

Dean drove alone to the airport to meet Joe's British Air jet late Saturday night. Joe came off the plane exhausted by the flight from London; perhaps that was why he waited until they were back at the Manning, riding the elevator to the fifteenth floor, Dean explained, to say that Ron's check had been refused. Joe was "surprised and upset," Karny recalled, in a wan stab at humor. The "Signature Missing" explanation infuriated him especially: He had watched Ron Levin sign the check with his own pen. "Joe said maybe we could find a way to cash the check anyway," Dean remembered, and suggested they meet to discuss how after he got some sleep.

Sunday morning Dean and Joe met Jim for breakfast in Beverly Hills at Shapiro's Delicatessen, next to Trader Vic's. Joe was most concerned about breaking the bad news to Jim, Dean remembered, "because he knew that Jim was not the, ah, *groupie* like the rest of us who had complete and unlimited faith in Joe . . . Jim was there because he thought he had a good friend and also because there was money involved. I think Joe felt that Jim's confidence in him had its limitation and that if Jim started to think that Joe is susceptible to making mistakes, he wouldn't be his boy anymore."

Joe said not a word during the meal about Dean's knowledge of the murder. Afterward, though, when they adjourned to a bench beside the Beverly Gardens jogging path, where voices were muffled by the splash of the huge fountain at Santa Monica and Wilshire, Joe immediately told Jim, "Dean knows about Levin." Jim said nothing, Dean remembered: "He just had a little trace of a smile, and he kind of nodded very subtly."

The bodyguard took it well when Joe told him that the Swiss check had not cleared, recalled Dean, whose own attitude was more negative: "I said that it looked like Ron had been killed for nothing, [but] Joe, who didn't want any of us to be disappointed and especially didn't want Jim's spirits to sag, said that there were still lots of other ways that we could possibly get the check cashed." Jim said he knew someone in Washington who could help, Dean remembered. This was a person who could clean out most foreign accounts if he had a number, Jim explained, and would at the very least be able to explain what "Signature Missing" meant. "Call him," Joe said.

Joe's first official act upon returning to the BBC office Monday morning was to fire his own father. "There was no big scene," Evan remembered. "Joe just came in and told me to change the locks on his father's office and on Mingarella's." The BBC's revised plan was to market the Fire Safety formula in the Third World, Joe announced, first through Luan Dosti, who was assembling a package of samples and marketing brochures for a trip to Abu Dhabi, and secondly through Steve Lopez, who would be similarly outfitted for his flight from Paris to Singapore. Mingarella met his dismissal with curses and threats of retaliation, but the other Boys noticed that Ryan's eyes seemed filled with a contradictious mix of hurt and admiration. "It was like he knew that Joe had graduated," Taglianetti recalled. Later that same day, Joe instructed Evan to turn over the keys to the new locks on the back office doors to Jim Graham.

Jim arrived at the Third Street suites just before lunch and told the Shadings his friend wanted cash up front—thirty thousand dollars. "Joe gave it to him, and Jim left immediately," Dean remembered.

Forty-eight hours later, Joe reported that Jim's friend had obtained two salient pieces of information about the Levin check and the Swiss Credit Bank account. Apparently, Ron Levin had done it to him one last time, Joe said, signing the Swiss check in the lower right-hand corner, as with an ordinary draft drawn on an American bank. "Joe said Jim's contact said that there were specific instructions on the account that the signature had to be signed in the *upper* right-hand corner," Dean recalled.

While he could not negotiate a transfer of funds, the man in Washington *was* able to persuade his contact in Zurich to arrange for the Swiss bank to send a package of new checks to Ron's post office box in Beverly Hills, Dean recalled: "We had the key, and the plan was to make sure that we would intercept those checks, [so] one of us could forge Ron's signature in the proper place." He and Ben expressed concern about putting through a forged check drawn on Ron's account after he was reported missing, but Joe pointed out that "we had the [Microgenesis] contract to support us," Dean remembered. "So we decided to take it day by day." Joe wasn't going to give up because the BBC was broke again. After his return from London, "the investors had been given pretty much the last of Joe's money," Dean explained, "in order to placate them until the next distribution period."

The four of them—Joe, Dean, Ben, and Jim—began to check Beverly Hills P.O. Box 10505 on a rotating basis, Dean remembered. While they waited on the Swiss, he and Joe competed to see who could accomplish a more convincing forgery of Levin's signature, Dean recalled: "Joe had a set of Ron's old American Express bills, and that's how he got the exemplars."

Mail continued to arrive for Ron daily, but there was nothing from Switzerland. Jim came back to the Manning one afternoon with a receipt for an "oversized package" from Levin's box. He tried to claim it at the window, Jim said, but the postal worker wanted photo ID.

They had been at it only a few days, Dean remembered, when Joe announced that they would begin hitting the post office box on an around-the-clock basis, after discovering that "somebody else, some older man" was checking the box also.

He spent two solid months examining Ronnie's papers, Marty Levin remembered, searching for a clue to where his stepson might be. Sorting through just Ronnie's files from the month before his disappearance, however, proved an enormous task. There were statements on accounts at more than two dozen banks scattered all across the country, each one in the name of a different corporation. There were letters to and from at least thirty attorneys in connection to everything from outstanding insurance claims to a lawsuit filed against the president of the United States. There were copies of lease agreements on three automobiles, only one of which was parked in Ron's driveway. There were pages-long statements on a Beverly Hills Hotel courtesy card and a Bonwit Teller 721 Club card as well as Bergdorf Goodman and I Magnin cards.

Meanwhile, Marty was watching his wife literally worry herself sick, unable to sleep or eat, carrying ninety-five pounds on a five-foot, seven-inch frame. Carol spent whole days waiting by the phone, calling Ronnie's number again and again to leave messages.

She was but one of many. Ron had begun using his answering service in late May, recalled Jerry Stone, who owned the company. Mr. Levin's instructions were to pick up on the third ring, to answer "Network News" and to accept any messages left for Ron Levin, Presley Reed, M.D., R. Michael Wetherbee, or Oliver Wendell Holmes III. For the first two and a half weeks Ron had picked up his messages—and he did get quite a few—at least three or four times a day, Stone remembered, but after June 6, 1984, Levin had not called in even once, and the messages piled up. It became the office joke: When was Ron Levin going to pick up his messages? Like Ron's mother, Blanche Sturkey phoned repeatedly. There were calls from Terre Tereba and Paul Morrissey, and from James Foulk, who had reported for work every weekday since June 12. Also, a Joe Hunt had left messages for Ron on at least four dates after June 6, Stone remembered: The first message from Mr. Hunt came on June 7 ("Joe"), the second on June 8 ("Important!"), the third on June 19 ("Call me at work"), and the fourth on June 27 ("Joe—you know the number").

Ron's parents continued to pay rent on the Peck Drive duplex, and Blanche came by every day to tidy up, though there was little left to do other than wipe the dust from Ron's lovely, stolen possessions. Marty brought in a man from the Fairfax Lock Co. to change every lock on every door and window in the house. He recoded the alarm and put on the red light whenever he left. "We never considered that he had fled," Marty explained. "Ronnie never ran before. He wasn't afraid of jail." "Ronnie and my mother had such a close relationship, we knew he would have called if he could," added his brother, Bob. "Also, we knew Ronnie would not have left one dollar behind. Or his dog." For his family, the ultimate proof that Ron could not have skipped town was a call from a tailor on South Beverly Drive who had performed six hundred dollars' worth of alterations on several new silk suits and some linen slacks. "Ronnie leave new clothes behind? No way!" his brother said.

Nevertheless, "We tried to put it out of our head, that he was dead," Marty recalled. "We kept thinking, 'Maybe somebody's got him and they want something.'" There was a strange coincidence, though, that haunted them all: His own father had died on June 6, 1944, and Ron had disappeared exactly forty years later, on June 6, 1984.

It was June 21 before Marty Levin, accompanied by Scott Furstman, filed an official missing-person report with the Beverly Hills Police Department. "The attorney advised us to wait and see if something materialized," Marty explained. The police were perfunctory, though, taking the report but making no effort beyond that. They refused even to send an officer to inspect Ron's apartment.

Discouraged, the Levins attempted an investigation of their own, making calls to everyone who had left messages for Ron with his answering service after June 6, then cross-referencing his planning diary against his Rolodex to track down each person with whom he had scheduled an appointment after his scheduled return from New York on June 13. Only two people phoned them to inquire about Ron, the Levins said. The one who aroused suspicion was Neil Antin. "He kept calling my parents, wanting 'materials' he needed for these books and videotapes he said he and Ronnie were working on," Bob recalled. In particular, Neil wanted the thousands of feet of film Ron had stored—or concealed—in an old refrigerator he kept in the garage. "My father wouldn't let anyone into the apartment after he changed the locks, though," Bob explained. The other person who called the Levins looking for Ron was a young man none of them knew, Joe Hunt. Joe was phoning back, technically, returning a call Marty made when he began responding to the messages left for Ron with the answering service. "On the desk in Ron's office I had found a contract between he and this Joe Hunt," Marty remembered. "I thought, 'What's going on here? Ronnie's buying something for seven million dollars, and he's giving him a million-and-a-half-dollar deposit down.' Usually Ronnie would say something to me; if it was something big like that, he'd discuss it with me. I thought, 'Well, maybe he knows something about Ronnie.' I called, and his secretary told me he wasn't in, but that he'd get back to me. I didn't hear from him again until two days later. He asked who I was, and when I said I was Ron's father, he seemed surprised. I asked if he had seen or heard from Ron. He said no, and then he started *asking me* questions. He wanted to know how our twenty-million-dollar real estate deal was coming along in San Francisco. I said there was no such deal. He asked if I knew Ron had a large bank account in San Francisco. I asked, 'Do you know?' He said yes, but he couldn't recall the name of the bank. He said he would get it and call me back. Then he asked if I had the keys to Ron's house; he said he wanted me to let him in to get some papers he had left there. I told him no."

Most of what the Shadings knew about the police "investigation" into Ron Levin's disappearance they obtained through Rose Dosti. "The *L.A. Times* had heard something about a TV changer and some bedding that was missing from Levin's house," Dean explained. "Joe was trying to find out what the police knew about it just so that he had an idea of where we stood as far as risk, and he told me then that the TV changer had been on the bed when they wrapped up Levin's body, and they had taken it with them as a result. It was unintentional, because they meant to leave the place looking like Levin had gone to New York, and Joe said he came back that night after they had disposed of the body and straightened things up, looked around, made sure that everything was in its proper place. And he said specifically that he remade the bed."

Joe discussed what had happened on the night of June 6 often when they were alone, Dean recalled, going over it in greater detail each time. Occasionally it would be as if he needed to reassure himself that no loose ends had been left, Dean thought, but more often it seemed Joe wanted his fellow Shading to understand that any shortcomings in the execution of his plan were due to Jim's failures. "Joe said the fact that Jim had just taken Levin, laid him down, and shot him was kind of premature," Dean recalled, "because he had intended to pack a suitcase with Levin's clothes so that it would look more like he'd taken a trip. He was all prepared to get ties, jackets, and toilet articles and things like that. He really wanted to be thorough." Because "Jim didn't play his role properly," however, Joe said, he was unable to check the alarm code Ron had given him while Levin was still alive. "And Ron had given him the wrong combination," Dean remembered. "[Joe] wanted to leave the place locked, the alarm set, but he wasn't able to because he didn't know the code, and he felt that that was a chink in his plan, that Levin would leave without setting his alarm."

What unnerved Dean was the way Joe kept talking about returning to the scene of the crime, saying he wanted to drive his Jeep out to Soledad Canyon some afternoon and see if the body was still there. Though Dean advised against it, Joe announced one evening that he had been "out there," Dean remembered: "He said that the coyotes or something had dug Levin up and left only a couple of bones."

15

IT WAS HIS IDEA, DEAN ADMITTED, TO TELL THE OTHERS. "I FELT VERY STRONGLY about the reasons why we had started the BBC to begin with," he explained, "the idea that there was a real unified philosophy that I believed in through which to look at the world and to make your decisions. And I felt very strongly about the group of boys we had gathered around ourselves, and when we had to make excuses to our own comrades because of everything that had gone on, it really didn't sit right with me at all because I felt somehow that the ideology that I had come into the situation with was being compromised."

Money was at the heart of the matter, of course. All the BBC businesses—Microgenesis included—were behind on their budget allocations for June, Dean explained, and he and Joe and Ben "were making all kinds of stalling statements about 'We're still in a position that we cannot get out of. We're still tied up. We're waiting for a check to clear.' And it became rather uncomfortable for the leaders of the BBC, especially uncomfortable to myself."

The three of them were sorting out their stories one afternoon in Ben's office, Dean remembered, when he observed that a "general malaise" pervaded the organization, a condition he felt could be traced to increased "disparities" in the Hierarchy of Information: "I said I felt bad about the deception of friends I had brought in for their own good," Dean recalled. "I said that some of them could be trusted . . . and it would be a way of building the group together so we could proceed with the noble things we wished to accomplish."

It was his opinion, Dean told Joe and Ben, that they should include the rest of the Boys—or at least most of them—in on what had happened with Ron Levin. "I said that, you know, if these guys understand the philosophy that we are advocating here and if they really are part of what we are doing, then they will understand why Ron Levin was killed, and they won't recriminate," he explained. "That they will move on with the good and great things we had planned."

The euphoria that lifted the spirits of the BBC for the first week or two after the Levin check came into the office had "dissipated," as Eisenberg put it. "The mood was still excited but also anxious," Evan recalled. "We all had heard that there was some problem or delay with cashing the check." "Joe said it was because he couldn't find Ron Levin," Jeff Raymond remembered. "He said Levin had signed the check in the wrong place and that Levin was in New York and he couldn't reach him."

Joe's commodity trading partnerships had taken in $276,746 during June, mostly as a result of the May 18 letter sent to investors, according to Lore Leis's tally, but Financial Futures accounts were virtually empty by the third week of the month. Microgenesis remained the only viable BBC company: even as he bought time with investor funds, Joe recognized it was imperative to keep Gene Browning working on the Cyclotron prototypes due at the end of June. A day or two after he returned from London, Hunt showed up at the Gardena plant "waving this option agreement with Ron Levin," Browning remembered. When he read it, the inventor was aghast; the June 6 contract stipulated that Levin would acquire 40 percent of the Microgenesis stock should the BBC default. "I was furious," Browning recalled. "Then Joe told me, 'Well, Levin has disappeared and he's probably dead. But I've talked to his mother and it's perfectly all right. She's one of the Rothschilds, you know. I really loved that man.'"

Other than himself and Joe and Ben and Jim, Dean said, the only BBC member who knew about the murder was Brooke Roberts. Joe instructed the five of them to cease speaking Levin's name aloud, even in private, Karny recalled. From now on, Joe said, they were to refer to a "Mac" whenever Ron's absence was discussed.

He was growing more uncomfortable about keeping secrets from the others with each passing day, Dean told Joe and Ben the next time they met at the Third Street office. "I felt a disclosure had to be made," he explained. Joe seemed suddenly to favor the idea, Dean remembered: "He turned black into white and white into black, felt he could lay this information on [the other Boys] and still convince them that he was a fine fellow and they should continue with the BBC." Ben had been amenable as well, but Jim was hesitant, Dean recalled, and "expressed his opinion that he didn't know any group of people that he could trust that much, that well, that way." "There's always somebody who talks," Jim warned. "But then he said, 'Well, you guys know all these boys a lot better than I do,'" Dean remembered, "'and if you say we can trust them, then go ahead.'"

Joe tested Dean's faith in their confederation the next day, agreeing with Karny and Dosti that Tom May was the BBC member "best able to handle this sort of information." He and Joe were riding in Dave's bor-

THE PRICE OF EXPERIENCE 297

rowed Porsche from the Third Street office to the Bank of America branch on La Brea, Tom recalled, when he asked what happened. "I had noticed that all the commodities trading was stopped, and it seemed like something had changed," he explained. "I said, 'Joe, something's going on. What is it?' Joe said, 'Tom, you're gonna find out sooner or later—I killed Ron Levin.'"

The twin was included when the Shadings met in Joe's office the next afternoon. "Joe, at the same time he told Tom the bad news, also gave him the good news," Dean explained, "which was that it looked like Tom was going to be a Shading. So Tom was all happy for a few days, having been elevated to the status of the inner circle." In Joe's office, the five of them discussed who else to tell, Tom remembered. The selection of which members should be summoned to a special meeting of the BBC was a process of elimination, Dean recalled: "Those who were not invited, it was because we felt they had Normie characteristics." Dave May and Jerry Eisenberg definitely would not be included, Joe said. "We didn't think Tom would tell [his twin] because Tom and Dave had been very successfully played off against each other by Joe," Dean explained. "Also, Tom seemed pleased when Joe told him he wasn't a Normie." Jeff Raymond, on the other hand, *should* be invited, they decided. "I thought Jeff had an understanding of Paradox Philosophy," Dean explained. "Steve Taglianetti was included also, because he was close with Jim. Also, in our opinion, he had showed a willingness to participate in dirty deeds. Though we didn't believe he understood Paradox Philosophy, we thought he was loyal to the group." Evan and Jon Allen would be invited as well, the Shadings agreed.

Joe continued to test Tom over the remainder of that week, letting him in on the code word "Mac," even allowing the twin to listen in when he left a message for Ron Levin with his answering service. "Joe said he had to keep up appearances," Tom recalled.

They scheduled the meeting for Friday, June 22, originally, but Ben had not returned yet from a business trip to the Bay Area, Joe explained that evening, so they would meet instead on Sunday afternoon. "The June 24 meeting was the first one that was explicitly secret," Evan recalled. "We were told that Jerry Eisenberg and Dave May not only were not invited but were not to be told about it. Which created this sense of anticipation." Joe refused to say more, however, "even when I persisted in asking what it was about," Jeff recalled. "He just said, 'You'll find out when you get there.' I asked if it was good news or bad news. Joe said it was both."

Joe did attempt to tell *him* in advance, Evan said, though he had not recognized it at the time. That was Thursday evening, when the meeting was still scheduled for Friday afternoon. "A bunch of people were coming over to my place," Evan recalled. "A couple of them were not even in the BBC. Dave May was coming, and I think Dean, Lisa Marie, and Jon Allen also. Tom too. But Joe got there first. I remember he pulled very close together with me in the settee. First he pulled down the shades and closed the windows. I knew there was something important that he had to tell me." After tomorrow, there would be two kinds of people in the BBC, Joe began. At the forefront would be those who possessed the strength of character— "the backbone," Evan remembered—one needed to achieve greatness in this world. Behind and below would be those who lacked inner resources, who preferred a comfortable mediocrity to the opportunity for preeminence. "I almost had the feeling he was practicing a speech on me," Evan recalled. "But before he could go any further the other people began arriving, and Joe just sort of stepped away from me and never said another word about it all night."

They shot an entire roll of film that evening, Evan remembered. What struck him when he looked at the pictures afterward was the difference in the aspects of the two people who knew what the next day's meeting would be about: While Tom May appeared to be enjoying himself immensely, smiling in every shot—"entirely untroubled," Evan remembered—Dean's expression was distinctly haunted; he looked hollow-eyed and even more emaciated than usual. At the same time, though, Dean was unusually demonstrative, holding Lisa Marie close to him all evening long, kissing her again and again.

His curiosity aroused by the speech Joe had started three nights earlier, Evan was among the first to arrive at the Manning on Sunday afternoon. The Maulers had met at the equestrian center for a polo lesson that morning, all except Ben, who still was in San Francisco to see some rich Iranian. It was Ben's late arrival, actually, which delayed the start of the meeting. Brooke went out for sandwiches while the Boys waited, milling excitedly about the living room of 1505. "We knew we were there because it was felt we were the ones who could be trusted," Taglianetti explained. A distinct sense of occasion, of camaraderie and common purpose, filled the air that afternoon, Jim remembered: "Everybody was walking around shaking hands and hugging each other." Several Boys formed a circle around the blue karate dummy, enclosing it like an adversary brought to bay, kicking and chopping at the thing from all sides. Someone found the two blowguns Joe and Dean kept in the apartment and started a game of tag. "People was diving behind chairs, hollering and blowing darts at each other," Jim recalled.

At one point, Joe, Dean, Jim, and Brooke all disappeared into the master bedroom for a few minutes. Evan and Jon Allen drifted out onto the balcony for a smoke, staring south across the flats of Palms and Mar Vista toward the unknown realms of darker races. The buildings on the horizon were dissolving into one of those early summer smogs that cling to the ground like a seepage of aerosol mist. The particulate in the air glittered like microscopic confetti as it caught the light of an intense but invisible sun. It was ninety degrees outside, and along Venice Boulevard the palm crowns already were wilted, hanging brown and still, looking less like tropical flora than burnt-out torches. A front of high clouds seemed to have stalled out over the Pacific. Above Inglewood and El Segundo the jets landing at LAX appeared to hover for a moment in the seam of clear sky between the brown-gray haze below and the blue-gray haze above.

Ben's arrival from the airport just before three o'clock brought the total attendance to ten: Hunt, Karny, Dosti, Graham, Dicker, Taglianetti, Allen, Raymond, Tom May, and Brooke Roberts. Joe called the meeting to order by moving the pieces of the brown velour sectional into a horseshoe shape, taking his own seat in the very center. Dean sat at his right hand, shoulder to shoulder with Ben, while Jim took the place to Joe's left. The other Boys sat facing those four. Brooke listened from the kitchen.

For the people present, this meeting would mark a turning point, Joe began. The general subject today, he added, would be discipline. "Joe was different than he'd ever been," Taglianetti recalled. "Very cold, very brief, no compassion. His face was pale and his eyes were flat. Dean was almost shaking, like a little mouse. Ben was just sort of confused-looking. Jim was the one who shocked me—usually he was really friendly, but that day he was so serious, cold-eyed, looking everybody over."

He would be discussing "some very sensitive matters" at this meeting, Joe said, matters that would bring those present to a new level of understanding about what it meant to be a BBC member. "And he said that with that higher level of information came a very great responsibility," Dean remembered.

First, it was time to apprise them all of the organization's financial condition: The commodity accounts were "depleted," Joe said. During the past spring he had taken exceptional risks in an attempt to cover the continuing losses at the other companies and had suffered a devastating loss. "He said Financial Futures was completely wiped out," Tom remembered. West Cars and Fire Safety both were deeply in the red as well, Joe added. Microgenesis remained the sole company paying its way—entirely as a function of the deals *he* had negotiated—and now even that corporation lacked funds to complete production of the Cyclotrons due for delivery.

He had not given up on the BBC, however, Joe said, and hoped the others might also find the fortitude to continue. "He began telling us about how to achieve greatness in this world you must sometimes step beyond the boundaries of the law, and that if you didn't and you possessed anything of great wealth, people would take it away from you," Evan remembered. "And that the BBC was going to take some bold steps and achieve greatness, and for those people who wanted to go along with the BBC to achieve these levels of success within the organization, they must know things and do things."

Joe spoke almost exclusively in the first person plural that day, Jeff Raymond recalled: At the beginning he seemed to be speaking on behalf of the Shadings, but gradually the "we" Hunt used seemed to take in more and more people, until they all were included.

"When you cross some lines, you can't go back," Joe said, and the line they were approaching was one such as this. "He told them that what they were about to hear would change their lives," Dean remembered. "Everyone was given an opportunity to leave at that point."

Joe adjourned again to the back bedroom, accompanied this time by Dean, Ben, and Jim. Tom had asked them to pretend he was hearing the news for the first time, Dean explained. When Joe closed the door behind them, everyone knew this was the last chance to turn back. The only real issue seemed to be Jim's consent: "So Joe said to Jim, 'Look, Jim, if you don't want to tell them, we don't have to tell them,'" Dean recalled, "'because this is as much your information as it is mine. This is something we did together.'" Dean argued one last time for disclosure: "I said it was really important for the group if we were going to live up to our high ideology about what we were doing." Ben repeated that he was in favor of telling. "Then Jim told Joe, 'Whatever you think,'" Dean recalled.

The living room was quiet, Evan remembered: "We were just trying to figure out what was going on. No one spoke, no one left."

Dean and Ben walked out of the back bedroom first, followed moments later by Joe and Jim. Taking his seat at the crown of the horseshoe, Joe waited until Jim was beside him, looked once around the circle with a stern expression, let his eyes settle on Evan and Jon, then said, "Jim and I knocked off Ron Levin."

Joe's face, Tom May remembered, was "stone-blank." Joe had gestured to Jim as he spoke, Taglianetti recalled: "I looked at Jim's eyes; he was very serious, almost glaring." In the silence, Jim "scanned the faces of the Boys who were sitting there," Dean remembered, "and it wasn't just looking around very quickly. He looked at them rather intently to see what was in their faces."

While those Boys hearing this for the first time looked "pretty shocked," Dean recalled, "they didn't say anything. Joe pretty much held the attention of the meeting." "I'm not sure anyone breathed," Evan said.

It was obvious to Dicker, Allen, Taglianetti, and Raymond that most of the others in the room already had been elevated to this "higher level of understanding." "Dean and Ben knew for sure," Jeff said. "Tom May knew—I had that impression. He was looking around at the others to see their reactions, not reacting himself." Brooke continued puttering in the kitchen even as Joe spoke, "like she already knew and really wasn't paying attention," remembered Raymond.

"Joe said he wouldn't tell us how it was done," Jon recalled, "because that wasn't something we needed to know." "He did tell us it was the perfect crime, and that there was no way 'we' could be caught," Tag remembered. "Joe said we were all part of the murder now," Tom May recalled, "and that we had a 'responsibility' to keep our mouths shut."

Now that they knew, each of them was free to make any decision he chose about the future, Joe said. "He told us we could even leave the BBC if we wanted to," Tom remembered: "Go fishing in the outer Adirondacks if you like," Joe said, using the phrase that had become a euphemism for resignation. The murder of Levin was an "act of self-preservation," Joe went on. Because of the BBC's "setback" in the commodities market, he had been forced to divert funds from his own investors into the other businesses. "Joe said we were 'feeding off each other,'" Taglianetti recalled. He had earned more than eight million dollars for Ron Levin at Clayton Brokerage, Joe said, and half of that money was his, according to the terms of their agreement. Yet Ron had refused, repeatedly, to pay. "He said Levin was a bad character who had cheated him and had cheated all of us as well," Jon remembered. "Joe said he had been 'evening the score,'" Tom recalled. "He also said he intended to use the one point five million to pay off the investors," Evan remembered. "That was when Ben stood up and said, 'This was something we had to do,'" Tag recalled.

When the floor was opened, Jeff Raymond posed the first question: "I asked if he had spent my money too. He said, 'No, I lost your money legitimately.'" Evan wanted to know how Joe had gotten Ron Levin to sign the $1.5 million check. "Joe said, smiling, 'Well, he was under a little duress at the time,'" Jeff remembered. "A couple of people laughed."

The BBC had about two months of "burn time" left, Joe told the Boys. The rent on the Third Street suites was paid in advance, they had almost a hundred thousand dollars left in assorted bank accounts, and they could sell off the West Cars fleet and the business machines at the office if necessary. "He kind of changed the tone of the meeting," Dean recalled, "so that, you know, in the first breath he said, 'Jim and I knocked off Ron Levin,' and then he immediately started building the enthusiasm of the guys as to all the positive things that were still around that could make the situation turn out better."

The Microgenesis contracts might still be met, Joe said, or at least renegotiated. And while they were experiencing some difficulties in getting the Swiss check to clear, "he said there was still a 'significant likelihood' we could cash it eventually," Dean remembered. Joe spoke of "money and resources and good prospects and great goals," Dean explained, "and he went from the bad news to a note of optimism so that by the time the meeting ended it seemed like everyone was in an up mood."

Someone suggested ordering pizza. The motion was seconded and passed unanimously.

From the first, he had looked upon the offer of an opportunity to break from the BBC as a rhetorical ploy, Dean said: Joe knew none of the Boys would leave but had to honor his instruction that no BBC member ever should be asked to sacrifice himself for the group. "He only wanted people who made their own decisions, acted on their own volition," Dean explained. "He didn't want slaves and he didn't want martyrs. This is how he talked—protested— all the time, and he was constantly reminding people that everything was their own choice and that they are always free to do whatever they wanted, and you shouldn't ask anyone to do anything you didn't want to do yourself. And of course he evidenced this by the fact that he didn't ask anyone else to go and kill Levin. He did it himself."

A number of the Boys would defend their continuing commitment to the BBC by claiming they suspected Joe had lied about killing Levin. Evan scoffed: "I don't believe that anyone doubted what Joe told us was true. But everyone wants to make themselves look better." He not only believed, but "really didn't have any emotional reaction to the announcement of the Levin murder," Evan admitted. "I realize that's shocking, but it's true. I didn't see the Levin murder at the time as anything all that bad. I saw it as in line with Paradox Philosophy. There was a necessary business purpose."

In Evan's opinion, Joe's revelation actually enhanced his stature among other BBC members: "It seemed like he had done this for us. Joe became even more guardianlike. I know I had the feeling that I now owed the group something. Because Joe had made this enormous sacrifice on our behalf." Also, "I just didn't think anything would happen to me if we stuck together," Evan added. "I thought we would all keep the secret."

In the days following the June 24 meeting, Joe labored ceaselessly to build a consensus of complicity among those who had been present. Tom May was invited to the Manning a few days later to attend what Dean called "a signing party." Joe was practicing karate kicks on the blue bag in the living room of 1505 when he arrived, Tom remembered, while Dean and Ben sat at the dining table, scribbling on a yellow legal pad. The Shadings were copying Ron Levin's signature—an exaggerated *R* trailing off into indecipherable scrawl—from American Express receipts. Dean explained to Tom that Levin had signed the Swiss check in the wrong spot and that they were waiting for a fresh batch of checks from Zurich. "We're going to resurrect Ron for a day so that he can sign the check where he should have," Joe explained. When Dean asked him to attempt a forgery of Levin's signature, he agreed, reluctantly, Tom admitted. "Had to play along," he explained. Dean remembered it differently: Tom not only "willingly" forged Levin's signature but seemed rather proud of his effort. "Tom May was Joe's boy all the way," said Evan, who learned from Dean that the twin had known of the murder a week before the others at the meeting. "After that, I considered him part of the inner circle, practically a Shading."

Steve Taglianetti and Jon Allen were with Joe when he arrived on June 26 at the Honda Del Rey motorcycle shop, where the three of them selected ten new Enduro 600 dirt bikes—one for each of the Boys who had attended the June 24 meeting, plus another for Steve Lopez. Joe left a ten-thousand-dollar deposit on the bikes, money drawn from a deposit at Financial Futures by Steve Weiss. On the last day of June, Hunt made a gala event of a trip to the Discount Motorcycle Supply Warehouse in the San Gabriel Valley, hiring a pair of limousines to transport the Boys from Westwood to Azusa, where they were invited to select their own personal accessories at the BBC's expense. "Must have spent another eighty-five hundred bucks in that place," Jim remembered.

It was July 6 when Joe met all the Boys at the Honda Del Rey lot in Culver City, where their prepped and polished bikes were parked in a row. They drove off the lot together, riding in two columns down Sepulveda Boulevard. Everyone knew the motorcycles were a bribe, Taglianetti said: "Joe took us into the store and said, 'See what we bought for you.' He and Dean and Ben never mentioned what we had been told at the meeting. They just acted like they knew we would do what we were told."

The motorcycles were not the only gifts Joe bestowed during the last week of June. "It seemed like Joe was trying all of a sudden to be my friend and bring me closer," recalled Taglianetti, who before this rarely was granted even a private audience. "One day he asked me to lunch and then said, 'Let's go see a movie together.' And on the way we passed this store, Leatherbound, in Westwood, and he pops in, pulls this jacket off the rack and says, 'Hey, this looks good,' and sort of almost throws it at me and says, 'Try it on.' I'm standing there still zipping it up, and he's at the counter paying for it. All he said was 'Steve, I know we don't get much of a chance to talk, but I really appreciate having you in the group; you're making a significant contribution. And I wish we had more time to spend together.'"

Most of those who had attended the June 24 meeting were included when Joe gathered the BBC to attend the Bolla International Polo Challenge at the L.A. Equestrian Center on July 1. Responding to the "DRESS: ELEGANT GREAT GATSBY" note on their invitation, the Boys pulled up at the entrance in a convoy of limousines and disembarked in matched ensembles of cream linen suits, jazz oxfords, pastel shirts, and solid color ties.

One evening later that week Joe treated the Boys to a bowling night at the Picwood Lanes in Westwood. The place was packed and the waiting list was an hour long when the BBC group arrived, but the Boys wanted to bowl right now, "so Joe popped that guy five hundred bucks, the guy who was running the place," Jim remembered. "And guess what? We had four lanes open right away." A few frames into the first game, one of the Boys added another name to the list of bowlers on the overhead projector: R. LEVIN. When Joe joined in the laughter, the others began to take turns bowling for Ron.

Twice a week Joe took the Boys riding on their new Hondas in the undeveloped hills at the top of San Ysidro Drive, on the northern perimeter of Beverly Hills between Trousedale Estates and Lake Franklin Reservoir. "These were big bikes, the dirt bikes that Joe bought us," Evan recalled. "Monsters. Joe, of course, and Ben were very good bike riders. I remember Ben took me for a ride on his one night after we went to this club. Scared the shit out of me." Jim was good on a bike, too, but agreed with the other Boys that Joe was best. "They all was showing off up there, racing over those hills," he recalled, but Joe alone had been willing to make a run at the steepest climb. Hunt had almost reached the crest, Jim remembered, when a frightened deer bounded out of the brush into the Honda's front wheel: "Joe came falling down the hill, the bike with him. The deer got killed, and [Joe] had to go to the hospital. His legs, he tore the skin bad; the flesh was hanging out. He didn't make a sound, though. He's a tough kid. The pain, he was holding it in."

Even on crutches, Joe continued to conduct the business of the BBC as usual. Four days after the June 24 meeting, he zeroed out the IMF account at E. F. Hutton, withdrawing the last of the money he had been using to hold up his collapsing commodities positions. After Lopez cabled from Singapore that he had elicited interest in the Fire Safety product from a government minister, Joe assigned Taglianetti to work full-time on a demonstration videotape and marketing brochure. "I had to come in on the Fourth of July to help Steve get that out," Lore Leis remembered. The BBC's new attorney, Neil Adelman, saw an office bustling with activity: "There were people working, generating business, accomplishing tasks." The only lawyer left who had been with the BBC longer, Eisenberg, knew enough to see through the charade. "Money was even tighter; there was desperation in the air," he remembered. "Joe was more forceful in being upset with people for not generating enough business and income." Microgenesis rather than Paradox was what held the group together now, Eisenberg said: "Even those of us who were disenchanted knew there was still a reasonable chance to make a lot of money with Gene Browning's machine."

The inventor himself, however, was becoming increasingly unhappy with the disarray that seemed to envelop more and more of the BBC's operation. It had become difficult just to get Joe on the phone, Browning complained; according to Dave and Jeff, Joe was staying away from the Third Street office to avoid his investors. Browning knew that Joe had signed a contract to deliver at least one Cyclotron to William Morton by July 1 and that another machine had been promised to the Mojave miner, Bill Nalan, later in the month. And now his former partner, the Rumanian, was lurking about, Browning told Hunt, demanding a percentage of any profits from the sale of the Cyclotron and threatening to join Swartout in a lawsuit. On top of all this, Browning and his wife had paid several thousand dollars in earnest money when they made an offer on an eight-hundred-thousand-dollar house in Costa Mesa early in June; escrow would close on July 6, when the down payment was due in full, and Joe had yet to come up with the money he promised.

Joe phoned him on the evening of June 26, Browning recalled, and suggested they meet the next morning at Ship's restaurant in Westwood to "inventory our assorted obligations." Over breakfast on the twenty-seventh, Joe assured him that the Levin check was about to clear, Browning recalled, and the instant it did, the inventor would receive the money he needed for the down payment on his house. They agreed that Browning would supervise transport of his latest Cyclotron prototype to Morton's mine in Arizona the following weekend. As for his former partner, "Joe said, 'Do you want me to have [the Rumanian] killed?'" Browning remembered. "I said, 'I think you've been watching too many movies, Joe.' And he says, 'Jim will do it if I ask him.' He seemed quite confident."

It was Jim who helped him load the Cyclotron prototype aboard a tractor-trailer rig and haul it out to Arizona on July 2, Browning recalled. That evening, the two of them dined together at the best restaurant in Mesa. "I told him, 'Joe told me everything would be done as far as the house was concerned,'" Browning remembered. "That the Levin negotiations were completed. [Jim] just looked at me and said, 'Levin is dead.'"

Joe was himself becoming looser with the details of Ron's "eradication." "Whenever I asked, he answered," Evan remembered. "At some point

I knew it had happened in [Ron's] apartment. I was told that the body could not be identified." A few days later, Evan asked what Joe had meant: "He said they had disposed of the body with acid. I asked where they got the acid to dissolve a body, and Joe said it was 'commonly available.'" He imagined that Jim had pulled the trigger on Ron but didn't ask, Evan said. Also, "I presumed Ben and Dean were involved to some degree but didn't discuss it with them. I figured that might be a touchy subject."

Joe had not hesitated to tell *him,* Taglianetti said, that Dean, Ben, and Brooke all were involved in planning the murder. "I thought about who might talk eventually," Tag recalled, "and the people I knew never would were Joe, Dean, Ben, and Jim. And Brooke. Also Jon Allen. Evan I thought would drop out, and it surprised me he stayed. Jeff I didn't know about, but Tom was so wrapped up in Joe that I knew he would stay."

Evan was distressed when he returned a cotton topcoat Joe had left at his apartment. "I gave it to Joe, and he mentioned that the coat had Ron Levin's brains smeared all over it," Evan recalled. "This was some time after he had told me about the acid. It made me wonder if Joe was trying to make the situation look even more gruesome than it was."

Even the most benumbed of the Boys recognized that his revelation of June 24 had delivered Joe into some new and profoundly maleficent sense of empowerment. At the same time he continued to espouse a belief system that defied morality and disputed metaphysics, Joe began to offer himself as the object of a dark and obdurate destiny. The reference to "my black soul" Hunt made in a memorandum on his plans for dealing with Swartout was among the earliest indications. Also, Joe offered increasingly elaborate accounts of the training he had received from his father, describing hours devoted to practice in the techniques of autosuggestion, of whole weekends spent inside an orgone box learning "self-control."

He also began to tell stories of his mother. "Before that, he had never mentioned her," Taglianetti reflected. Joe recounted how Kathy Gamsky had taken him to a psychiatrist when he was just five years old, Claire Browning recalled: "The woman worked with him for a couple of weeks and told [his mother] not to bring him back because he could not be helped." The version her husband heard involved a trip to a school psychologist when Joe was ten. "His mother was told that Joe was a 'time bomb,'" Gene remembered, "and to do something about it." Kathy had spent the past seven years in a mental institution, Joe told other BBC members, and what had pushed her over the edge was not a trip to a psychiatrist but to a psychic. His mother maintained a more than passing interest in the occult, Joe explained, and sought out a famous fortune-teller after learning that her younger son "had tortured and killed all the cats in his neighborhood," as Tom May recalled the story. "Joe told us that when he walked into the room the woman screamed, 'That's the evil one!' and made him leave," Tom remembered.

"Joe actually reached the point where he started talking about being the Bad Seed, the anti-Christ," Gene Browning said.

Those further from the center could observe only the physical transformation taking place in Joe. "It was more than just losing weight and looking harried," Eisenberg recalled. "There was the quality of someone who had let things get bigger than he could control. He was so intense, it was painful to be in his presence."

Joe had replaced his videocassette of *First Blood* with Brian DePalma's remake of the classic gangster movie *Scarface*. Written by Oliver Stone, the 1984 *Scarface* chronicled the bloody rise of Cuban refugee-cum-cocaine dealer Tony Montana, played by Al Pacino, beginning with a scene in which his partner's arms and legs are severed with a chain saw wielded by a Colombian supplier. "It became the BBC training film," Dave May remembered. "That summer Joe was showing it over and over in the office. You'd walk in on him and in the middle of a violent scene he'd shout at us, 'This is the real world! We must protect ourselves from outsiders!'" Joe kept a second copy of *Scarface* in his bedroom at the Manning, according to Jeff Raymond, and watched it every night before he fell asleep.

As with *First Blood,* Joe found a scene in *Scarface* where he felt the protagonist's failure of conviction was his undoing. It came near the end of the film, when Pacino's character was offered a chance to extricate himself from tax evasion charges by assisting in the murder of a Latin American muckraker. The plan was to blow up the journalist's Citroën outside the United Nations building in New York just before he delivered a speech naming the cocaine cartel's political patrons. Montana/Pacino at first was entirely willing to play his part in the murder plot, but when he discovered there were three passengers in the muckraker's car, the man's wife and two young children, he was unable to go on with it and assassinated the assassins. Watching the scene, Joe would become visibly upset, almost as if he were attempting to will a revision of the screenplay. "You couldn't tell Joe it was a movie," Browning recalled. "In his mind, this was actually happening." What upset him was the reversion of the Montana character to a conventional morality he had abandoned so completely, so long ago, that the desire for redemption at this point seemed preposterous. It was the illogic of it, ultimately, which infuriated Joe. "Joe said that he would have killed the two little kids, no problem," Jim recalled. "Pacino didn't, and Joe called that Pacino's weakness. Joe would have did the whole thing."

16

HE FIRST HEARD THE NAME HEDAYAT ESLAMINIA ON THE MORNING OF JULY 9,
Dean remembered, at a meeting with Joe and Ben on the corner of Third
Street and Kings Road, one block from the BBC office. Mr. Eslaminia was
an enormously wealthy man, as Dean understood it, a former high-ranking
government minister in the regime of Shah Mohammad Reza Pahlavi.
Forced to flee Iran during the revolution wrought by the Ayatollah
Khomeini, Eslaminia had managed to smuggle a fortune in foreign currency
out of the country, relocating eventually to an estate in the San Francisco
Bay Area's most sedate enclave of established money, Hillsborough. According to Joe and Ben, Mr. Eslaminia was an ogre who refused to share even
one penny of his wealth with his eldest son, Reza.

Reza despised his father, Dean was told, and had become concerned
that Mr. Eslaminia intended to disinherit him. Joe and Ben suggested that
Reza wanted to enlist the BBC's aid in forcing his father to turn over his
assets, Dean remembered. The plan, roughly, was first to kidnap Eslaminia,
then compel the Iranian to reveal the location of his bank accounts, here and
abroad, and, finally, force him to sign over any nonliquid assets. That first
meeting on the street corner lasted less than five minutes, Dean recalled, and
the presentation he received was sketchy at best; he believed the abduction
was Ben's idea. It was understood clearly, though, that if they took Mr.
Eslaminia, they would have to kill him.

"My reaction was that we should look into the possibility," Dean
recalled. "We needed money to keep the BBC together."

Like most of the Boys, Dean had met Reza Eslaminia for the first
time less than forty-eight hours earlier, at Evan's twenty-third birthday
party. The affair unfolded as a rather delirious combination of dolor and
festivity. The birthday boy had learned only two days earlier that his father
was being admitted to Cedar Sinai with cancer of the colon. "My parents
knew he was dying, but they didn't tell me," Evan explained. "As far as the
party, they said I should have a good time." Evan gave it his best effort,
entertaining not only the entire BBC but a considerable cross-section of the

twenty-five-and-under set from Beverly Hills, decorating his apartment with girls who came in tandems of taffeta and spandex, sporting names like Tracine, Freedee, and Martyne. The BBC arrived wardrobed in tuxedos and formal gowns. Evan saw his new motorcycle for the first time that evening, when Joe wheeled it into the living room bearing an attached card on which the calligraphed *"To Evan, with Great Appreciation, from the BBC"* had been crossed out by Brooke, who wrote *"Love, Love, Love."* "I never actually rode the bike," Evan recalled. "I started it twice, I think, and got to the end of the block once. After that it was in my living room, like a piece of furniture. It made a marvelous conversation piece."

Reza, bearing a bottle of Chivas Regal, arrived with Ben, who introduced him as the newest member of the BBC. Dark, slim, and strikingly handsome, if somewhat reptilian, "Reza struck me as very pushy and aggressive," Evan remembered. "I didn't like him much." Nevertheless, Ben brought the Iranian along when Seth Marsh moved the party to Decadence.

Joe stayed behind, huddled with Eisenberg and Feldman in the backseat of the BMW he drove that evening. It was the most elaborate and insistent Paradox indoctrination he ever received, Eisenberg recalled: "Two and a half hours he kept us in there. Joe was really working on us—me in particular—trying to pull us deeper in or at least see how far we'd be willing to go with him. I asked if you can kill somebody and be at peace with it, according to Paradox. He started by saying that of course you could if they were trying to kill you. Then he talked about how it could also be reconciled if it served a higher purpose, and he gave example after example of when this might be the case, if the person robbed you or cheated you, if this one person's death would save other lives or protect the interests of your friends and family. By the end it seemed like you could kill somebody any time you needed to. Finally he let us drop him off outside the nightclub. Mike and I drove over to Pink's for hot dogs. When we got there I said, 'Mike, we gotta get outta here.'"

It had been Jerry, technically, who brought Reza to the BBC, arranging the introduction through his aunt's fiancé, businessman Leon Kassorla, with whom the young Iranian was discussing the formation of a company that would export foodstuffs to Saudi Arabia. According to Leon, Reza had access to people at the highest levels all over the Middle East, Eisenberg recalled. The attorney met the young Iranian for lunch in early June. "Reza spoke of his privileged life back in Iran, but there were no details," Jerry remembered. "It was clear, though, that his family was well connected." Kassorla, at Eisenberg's suggestion, brought Reza by the BBC office the next afternoon. "It was love at first sight between Reza and Ben and Joe," Eisenberg recalled. The two told the other Boys that Reza's father had been the third-highest ranking official in the government of the shah and remained on familiar terms with the patriarchs whose families controlled the emirates of the Middle East.

He saw Reza with Ben several times over the next few weeks, Eisenberg recalled: "We didn't say much beyond 'Hello again.' I just assumed they had something cooking."

They did indeed. He and Joe and Ben and Jim met with the younger Eslaminia in the living room of the 1505 condo at the Manning one day after the conversation on the street corner, Dean remembered. Joe asked the questions, mostly about the extent and type of wealth Reza's father possessed and where it might be found. Most of his father's money was in Swiss banks, Reza said, but Hedayat Eslaminia also owned several homes in Northern California, including the estate in Hillsborough, and a good deal of commercial property as well. "Reza said his father was living in one of several places, and we needed to find out which one, in order to abduct him," Dean recalled. Reza also explained that his father was considered an enemy of the state in postrevolutionary Iran. This was a man whose name had been written in the blood of slain SAVAK officers on the walls of buildings in Teheran, his son said, described in indictments published under seal of the Ayatollah Khomeini as a political criminal, an agent of the Great Satan (the United States), and a "subverter" of Islam. "So when he disappeared, it would be easy to suggest that the ayatollah had gotten him, and we could avoid suspicion," Dean recalled.

Perhaps no man in the Iran of Shah Mohammad Reza Pahlavi might have been more accurately described as "self-made" than Hedayat Eslaminia. Neither well-educated nor born to money, Eslaminia had risen from the lowest ranks of the nation's civil servants to a station so exalted that the word used most often later to describe his lifestyle—"lavish"—seemed rather paltry. "Basically, he was a great hustler," explained his admiring nephew Ali Mortzavi.

A degree from Zand High School, a clerical position in the ministry of information, and a natural affinity for Americans were all that an ambitious young man such as Hedayat Eslaminia had required for advancement in the Teheran of the 1950s. Americans—CIA agents in particular—were the pillars of the shah's regime, having financed and planned the overthrow of Prime Minister Mohammed Mossdeq in 1953. Sponsored by the Dulles brothers, CIA director Allen and Secretary of State John Foster, the shah became a true monarch that year, supported by U.S. foreign aid and the formation of a repressive secret police agency, SAVAK, whose members were trained jointly by agents of the CIA and the Israeli secret service, Mossad. During his "White Revolution" of modernization in the 1960s, U.S. and European newspapers portrayed the shah as Western civilization's best friend in the Middle East. Succumbing to his sense of destiny, the grandson of an impoverished army officer traced his ancestry to the first great ruler of the Persian Empire, Darius, and in 1967 crowned himself Emperor of the Peacock Throne.

Iran's economy exploded during the next ten years. OPEC asserted itself for the first time in 1971, under pressure from the shah for increased oil prices. The Iranian monarch remained loyal to his American friends, however, selling oil to the United States even at the height of the Arab embargo. After the Yom Kippur War, the shah announced that the National Iranian Oil Company would assume control of all petroleum production in his country. Oil prices rose 400 percent, and Iran was awash in wealth.

It was not only oil but armaments as well that fed the economy. Meeting with the shah in 1972, President Richard Nixon and Henry Kissinger urged Iran to become "the policeman of the Persian Gulf," advising Pahlavi to ignore "our liberals' griping" about SAVAK's human rights abuses. U.S. military sales grew fivefold during the next year, and the American presence in Iran increased just as dramatically. Teheran took on the aspect of a giant bazaar in which weapons and oil were the principal commodities. David Rockefeller's Chase Manhattan Bank became both Iran's largest creditor and financial planner for the shah and his family. Those closest to the shah got themselves appointed as the agents of the largest foreign corporations, demanding a percentage of every important contract. Kickbacks, bribes, and huge fixer's fees were standard procedure. By 1976, when Iran ordered eleven billion dollars' worth of the most sophisticated U.S. weaponry, twenty-five to thirty agents and subagents possessed a virtual stranglehold on the nation's economy. One was Hedayat Eslaminia.

Eslaminia accumulated his first fortune in real estate, using his government position first to anticipate—then later to arrange—conversions of public land for private development. "He bought land with big shots and politicians," his nephew Mortzavi recalled, "and suddenly, the next day, it would be rezoned. Or there would be a new road going through. Or suddenly the Ministry of Power would announce it was putting in electric power lines."

Eslaminia's real estate empire expanded after his marriage to Mina Hakimi, daughter of General Hakim Koui, chief of SAVAK in Teheran. Senior officers of SAVAK were Iran's leading land speculators during the 1960s and 1970s, when they displaced more than fifty thousand villagers in joint agribusiness ventures with European and American banks. In part to please the Americans, the shah became the only Middle Eastern leader to accept—even encourage—cooperation with Israel. Eslaminia was among the first businessmen in the nation to recognize the economic advantages of friendly relations with the Jewish state, obtaining financing from Israeli banks to organize the orange growers of northern Iran into a giant cooperative, eventually building huge packing plants at his Abbas Abad Shahsavar citrus garden. "My uncle was not just very smart, he was also very good in dealing with people," Mortzavi explained. "Excellent PR. He could talk to every level of society because he had come up from the bottom. He knew everybody, and everybody came to his parties."

Eslaminia did his entertaining then on Niavaran's Golestan Avenue, among the foothills of the Elburz Mountains northwest of Teheran, where his estate sprawled to within a few hundred yards of the shah's palace, among the few homes in Iran that could bear comparison to Hedayat's. The building alone covered more than five acres, with walls and floors of Italian marble. Next to the Olympic-sized swimming pool was a front lawn bigger than a soccer field. The house contained twenty bedroom suites and was attended by a domestic staff of a dozen.

When Hedayat married Mina Hakimi, the union was dismissed by members of the Thousand Families, Iran's old-money elite, as blatant social climbing. The Eslaminia clan saw the couple quite differently. "There were better people available to him, politically and economically," Mortzavi said. "He had been dating Mina's sister Jaleh, who was a beauty, but when Mina met him she went after him. And got him." Mina generally got what she wanted. "A movie star," Mortzavi called his uncle's wife. "Mina can cry at will or be gay in a flash. In the Hollywood of the old days she would be bigger than any of them."

Mina was not only formidable but daring, one of the first women to embrace the Western modes of fashion that were sweeping away the chadors of the Persian past. "Eventually, you know, the rich in Iran got more Westernized than the Westerners," Mortzavi explained, "while the poor got more fundamentalist because religion was all they had. In those days the women wore shorter skirts in Teheran than in London. The country went fashion-crazy. We are extremists as a people: Only European fashions would do, and everyone had to go abroad to shop."

Few Iranian women appeared in public wearing Saint Laurent and De la Renta originals before Mina did, though, and when she flew to Switzerland to have her breasts enlarged, the in-laws were scandalized. "I was there for breakfast one day right after," Mortzavi recalled. "I was very shy, and all the family was there. Mina came out in this loose robe, and her breasts were hanging out. She seemed to enjoy the effect. I was so nervous trying not to look that I couldn't eat."

The marriage was a catastrophe from the start. "There was so much trouble that my grandmother, who lived with my uncle, was forced out of the house," Mortzavi remembered. "Mina insisted that she be moved. I remember one time when I was thirteen, and my grandmother came from their house in tears. Mina was at the door a few minutes later: 'Where is she?' She dragged that old woman out into the hall and beat her. She kicked her and slugged her until my grandmother wept and bled. I started to interfere, and she swore at me like no one ever had."

The problems between Hedayat's wife and his mother grew in part out of tales the elder Mrs. Eslaminia told of what went on at the house when her son was away. Mina had taken to using her husband's home to entertain her younger brother Sina and his friends from the university, according to Hedayat's mother. "Sina was a very handsome young man," Mortzavi remembered, "and he had been admitted to the architecture school, which was very prestigious. He was also a great soccer player, a talented painter, very popular at the university. This was in the Beatles' time, and he and his friends were the most hip, the first to grow long hair. He would bring all his university friends up for the weekend to the villa, and there would be girls in bikinis and lots of parties. And Mina would think she could come up and stay with all the young kids when my uncle was not around, smoking pot with them.

"By then Mina was pumping money into her own family as fast as she could. My uncle had the most beautiful Persian rugs in Iran. He had rugs that cost two hundred and fifty thousand dollars apiece. Enormous and very, very old. Anyway, they disappeared one day, and it was supposedly some thief. A very big scandal in all the newspapers. Then my uncle found out Mina had a house of her own, that she bought with his money, and she had moved all those rugs there."

The first of four separations between Mina and Hedayat ensued, but then "my mother put them back together," Mortzavi recalled, "and they made up, and then suddenly, *poof!*—Amir (the couple's third child after Reza, the eldest, and Ali). Then when the baby was born, it starts again. My uncle gave her a new car and she totaled it two weeks later. He gave her rings and minks, designer clothes, anything she wants, but she still went off with other men. After they broke up this time, my uncle got very nasty. He did things like have someone write on Mina's parents' door that they were thieves and she was a whore. And he started to pick up girls at his functions, which he had never done before." The Eslaminias did it one more time,

however: "Broke up, reconciled, and then *poof!*—another pregnancy,"
Mortzavi remembered. "Then they broke up again. Exactly the same."

Their children were not only a result of the couple's reconciliations
but also the weapons in their long and ugly war of emotional attrition. "At
a very young age Mina got the kids to start lying," Mortzavi recalled. "She
would say, 'Don't tell your father this' or 'Tell your father that.'" When he
found Mina out, Hedayat could be brutal. Reza remembered seeing his
father beat his mother with a belt and burn her repeatedly with a cigarette
lighter during an argument in his car.

Each of the parents endeavored to persuade their oldest son that the
other was depraved. "Once, after a big fight because my mother had driven
[her car] through the wall of a house where my father was having an affair,
my father took me into the bedroom and put a tape in the cassette," Reza
recalled. "It was a lady friend of my mother speaking: She said she and my
mother and her friend and another man were all having sex together." Mina
retaliated by bringing Reza along when she trailed Hedayat to his hideaway
on the Caspian Sea, leading the boy to a window where he watched his father
smoking opium with two young women.

After the birth of their fourth and last son, Mahmoud, Hedayat
broke for good with Mina, ordering her out of the house with what she could
carry in her suitcases. "Mina thought the prestige of her family name gave
her the power, but she was the end of a dynasty; they were on the way down
as my uncle was on the way up," Mortzavi explained. "And by then he had
enough power to divorce her without a dime. That was when she started to
use the kids against him. He wanted to be a good dad, but he was the type
that thought that meant buying motorboats and skis, filling the house with
pianos and organs, anything they wanted."

Eslaminia's firstborn was sent for several summers to the Swiss
school where the Pahlevis were educated, tutored in English at home in
Teheran, and given special courses in ceremonial etiquette—"how to say
hello to the shah and that sort of thing," explained Reza, whose father promised to make him prime minister someday.

By the early 1970s Hedayat was in a position to make such asser-
tions without inviting ridicule. Besides the marble palace in Teheran,
Eslaminia owned villas all over the country, including one on the Caspian
Sea that was coveted even among the Pahlevis, a property so large that it
had to be measured in hectares, noted his close friend Colonel Ali Baniamam,
the shah's tank commander and proprietor of the nearby Hotel Ghoo
("Swan"). "The most beautiful estate I have ever seen," remembered
Mortzavi, "on a dam with an incredible view. He went there every Thurs-

day with his guests in the hot season, taking at least twenty people for the weekend. He always had people bring their families, and there would be dozens of kids, also many servants. His guests would be from all walks— clergy, generals and admirals, government officials, landowners from the old families, Americans from the embassy, probably CIA. He solved problems and made connections. For example, it would take a year to get a phone for an ordinary person. But he could get it for you in a day. During the week he would go from dinner to dinner at night, three or four in one evening. At home the phone was ringing all day. He never seemed to tire of it. And his favors were always called in eventually."

Iran's economy had overheated to the point of combustion by 1974. "Billons and billions in oil," Mortzavi explained. "Everyone was coming. A middleman like my uncle could make a huge commission on a sale or for setting up a deal. Russians, Italians, West Germans—everybody was trying to make a buck. The Americans were the main ones, though."

How well Hedayat Eslaminia was connected with the Americans visitors to his Niavaran house knew by the stacked cases of Coca-Cola that filled one entire room. "He had helped them with a bottling plant," Mortzavi explained. The Coca-Cola connection suggested something far more sinister in the eyes of the servants, however, who had been told that the enormous soft-drink company was a CIA front.

Resentment of Americans among the poor and the religious grew month by month in Teheran. At the same time, rumors of obscene extravagance and debased practices in the shah's family were whispered among peasants and savored by fundamentalist mullahs. European illustrated newspapers showing the shah at play on the slopes of the Swiss Alps, where he kept a huge chalet, were smuggled into Iran at the behest of educated mullahs who translated accompanying articles that described gatherings of finance ministers and government heads from all over Europe at Pahlevi's private parties, where each was attended by a beautiful blonde handpicked from the selection available through Madam Claude's famous Paris brothel. Tales of drug use and erotic perversity were rampant.

Outside the religious center of Qom, where the Ayatollah Khomeini denounced the shah as "a servant of the dollar," few risked even the mildest public criticism. SAVAK agents were among the best educated men in the country and used the most pious language in announcing their decisions about what films might be released or which books could be published. Behind closed doors, however, their conduct was barbarous. The shah's mandate permitted SAVAK to arrest anyone on political grounds and to prosecute them at secret trials. According to those who survived, SAVAK's methods of interrogation included beatings with belt buckles, pulling out nails and teeth, pumping boiling water into rectums, hanging weights from testicles, and gang-raping female prisoners.

In an atmosphere clotted by torture and debauchery, with envy on all sides and terror at the center, perhaps no man in Iran was more successfully peddling influence than Hedayat Eslaminia. His personal affiliation with the shah's closest advisor, Hossein Fardoust, provided Eslaminia with direct access to the palace. "Now he has all the diplomats and spies coming to his home," Mortzavi recalled. "His house is the meeting place for people from all over the world, all the Arab countries, the Europeans, and of course the Americans. Now he's international. If there's a load of sugar coming in, he gets ten percent. Someone wants a new leather factory, he gets the commission. He's a monster."

Monster was the same word Mina Hakimi used to describe her estranged husband after he smuggled their two oldest sons out of Iran to the United States in 1974. His nephew Mortzavi had inadvertently given Hedayat the idea, moving to the United States in 1973 to study architecture at San Mateo College on the Peninsula south of San Francisco. "When I go home to visit in 1974, my uncle comes to my parents' house and tells us all of his problems with Mina," Mortzavi recalled. "How the kids are being ruined, how she gives them drugs, how they are in the house with all the men, how she teaches them to lie. So he decided they should go to the United States. It was outrageous."

Reza remembered leaving his home in Niavaran on a Friday afternoon during the summer of 1974: "My father put Ali and me in a car we took to the Caspian Sea. He knew my mother was following us. We went up a street where we usually turned left but turned right instead and parked the car. I asked what was going on and my father said, 'Be quiet.' We saw my mother drive up and take the left turn to the sea. Then my father started the car and drove back to the house. We parked in the garage, where the maids had our luggage ready . . . we went to the airport the next morning."

It was still Saturday morning when the plane landed at San Francisco International Airport. Eslaminia and his sons rode in a taxi to Ali Mortzavi's Burlingame apartment. "I found their schools," Mortzavi remembered. "Woodside Priory for Reza and Harker Academy for Ali. My uncle wanted them in boarding schools. After he had been there a week my uncle decided he liked America, especially California. He said he'd buy a house so he wouldn't have to stay in my dinky apartment." Eslaminia paid eighty thousand dollars cash to take over the mortgage on his first Hillsborough house, Mortzavi remembered: "Then he wanted a car, a big American car, so we bought a Cadillac, and furniture at Levitz."

His uncle virtually commandeered Mortzavi's life, which was typical of the man. "In Iran, Hedayat Eslaminia owned people," his nephew explained. Eslaminia insisted his sister's son move into the Hillsborough house with Reza and Ali. "I have to pick them up every weekend at school," Mortzavi recalled. "I have to cook them Persian food, take care of them."

Hedayat flew Reza and Ali back to Iran to spend their summer vacations at Lake Karaj, where he kept a villa and casino, telling his sons their mother "had agreed to go away for money" and never wanted to see them again. Hedayat spent most of that summer in the company of Reza's future stepmother, Simin, who was serving Mr. Eslaminia then as his English translator. Young and pretty, Simin was from a good family but had a reputation as a rather loose girl. "She was this petite thing, though, and very vivacious," Mortzavi recalled. "She tells everybody they're right about everything, and especially Hedayat Eslaminia. They would both smoke opium very heavily, together and with others. The British brought opium to Iran; they wanted people to be lazy—it was the tactic of their empire, to get our oil. It became the drug of royalty in Iran, like coke was in America for a while, an accepted thing among the wealthy. It was a big social event to smoke it, especially in the older generation. They would play ancient Persian music, dim the lamps, light candles. Much would be revealed. My uncle hosted many opium parties."

Hedayat brought "big chunks and rolls of opium" to the Hillsborough house when he came to visit with Simin and her mother in 1975, Mortzavi remembered. "He hid them in two attic accesses. Then he showed where they were to Reza; this was because I refused to promise that I would entertain his friends when they were here. So a few weeks later, the principal at the school calls and says Reza is selling opium to the other students and she can't afford to have him there. I went home and got the ladder. All the opium in the attic was gone."

America had come as an enormous shock to Reza. The eldest of Hedayat Eslaminia's sons was entirely unprepared for his precipitous reduction in status, first at Woodside Priory, then at the Fieldmore Academy in Burlingame, where fellow students mocked the Iranian's broken English, swarthy complexion, and imperial affectations. "The Geek of Araby," they called him at Fieldmore. Unlike his more gifted younger brother Ali, who assimilated by beating the Americans at their own game, becoming both a top student and a star athlete, Reza's path was appeasement. "Reza will do anything to make friends," Mortzavi explained. "He buys people if he can, either by telling them big lies about who he is and what he'll do for them or by giving them drugs. I know of times when he bought weed from one person and then gave it to another, just to make friends with both."

The opium episode infuriated Hedayat, but it was the unannounced appearance of Mina Hakimi at his Hillsborough house that roused Eslaminia Senior to fly to San Francisco from Teheran. "When my uncle arrives, there are big fights over the kids' hair," Mortzavi recalled. "Reza wants it long, my uncle wants it short. Reza runs to the bathroom angry, crying. He swallows a bottle of speed, falls on the floor, foaming at the mouth. I drove him to the hospital. My uncle was terrified, but they pumped his stomach and he survived."

Mortzavi moved out of the Hillsborough house to Berkeley, where he had just started school, and was replaced a week later by Simin and an Iranian nurse flown in from Teheran by the boys' father. Mina continued to appear at odd intervals, meeting her sons at San Francisco hotels and San Mateo coffee shops. Hedayat still brought the boys back to Iran every summer but rarely found time to visit them in California, increasingly consumed as he was by affairs in his own country.

By the mid-1970s, Eslaminia's economic power was equaled by his prominence in Iran's political apparatus. Renowned as a devout Muslim who strictly observed a dawn-to-dusk fast during Ramadan, Eslaminia became chief advisor for religious affairs to Prime Minister Amir Abbas Hovedya and was given responsibility for the Iranian pilgrimage to Mecca. His tactful handling of internecine squabbles among the assorted ayatollahs enhanced his reputation as the one man who could mediate among the separate sects. He was elected to the Majlis, the Iranian parliament, as representative of Shahrey, the capital's religious center.

The religious center of the nation, however, remained Qom, led—even in exile—by the Ayatollah Khomeini. For nearly twenty years Khomeini had been a symbol of resistance to Western materialism, emerging in the late 1950s as an immensely popular lecturer on Islamic law and ethics. Corruption could never be reformed, the ayatollah taught, but must be attacked and eliminated. His best-known parable was of a pure spring flowing into a stagnant pool; unless the pool was drained first, Khomeini preached, the fresh water could only be contaminated by the foul.

The ayatollah's stature had merely increased when he was banished from Iran in 1964 for incitement to riot, and Khomeini's followers grew in number each month as the hyperboom of the mid-seventies collapsed into a national recession. By 1977, Iran's population could be divided roughly between two classes: above, five thousand enormously wealthy families; below, millions of people struggling to feed themselves. The workers who toiled sixteen hours a day constructing the villas neighboring Hedayat Eslaminia's marble palace slept either in lean-to sheds or holes dug along the roadsides at those points where Teheran's streets were crossed by the city's open sewers. Overextended credit forced Iranian banks to seek larger and larger loans from the financial consortium headed by David Rockefeller. Land prices doubled and tripled every month. Jimmy Carter's inauguration as U.S. president compelled the shah to mitigate the savagery of SAVAK, but it was far too little, much too late.

The Ayatollah Khomeini now lived in a Paris apartment, from which he read his sermons over the telephone into tape recorders at the other end of the line in Teheran. More and more Iranians had the time and inclination to contemplate revolution as the recession deepened. By January of 1979, power cuts and food shortages were commonplace. In a nation where a handful of families had grown wealthy from the foreign sale of oil, hundreds of thousands of displaced peasants stood in lines to collect paraffin.

The rich, sensing the inevitable, scrambled to evacuate the country. The villas of Niavaran were stripped and abandoned. Banks in Teheran were overwhelmed by requests for transfers of funds by telex to Switzerland and the Cayman Islands.

His father at first had been one of those to whom the revolution "didn't seem convincing," Reza recalled. "The attitude was that the peasants are unhappy and they'll calm down." As he watched his friends fleeing or falling all around him, however, Hedayat Eslaminia summoned his eldest son back home to Teheran at the end of 1978. "My father was negotiating with the American government—the CIA—at the American embassy," Reza recalled. "He didn't trust anyone else, so he wanted me to translate for him with these people."

The urgency of Eslaminia's desire for a U.S. immigration visa increased dramatically at the end of January 1979, when the shah boarded a private jet at Meherzabad Airport and flew to Morocco. The Ayatollah Khomeini arrived in Teheran from Paris on February 1, his plane greeted at Meherzabad by an exultant crowd of three million.

Eslaminia drove his sons to the airport while Khomeini's plane was in the air. The boys stayed one night in London, then flew the next morning to Washington, D.C., where they spent several weeks at the home of John Golden, a former attaché at the U.S. embassy in Teheran who "was very big in the underground government of Iran," Ali Mortzavi recalled. The scene in Washington was hardly encouraging: The shah's ambassador to the United States, Ardeshir Zahedi, a dashing ladies' man whose conquests included Elizabeth Taylor, had been displaced by militants who poured his Chateau Lafite into the embassy fountain, then denounced him for bribing congressmen with drugs and call girls. Mina arrived in the U.S. capital with Mahmoud later that week, followed soon by Simin, who took the three younger boys back to Hillsborough. John Golden enrolled Reza at Rollins

College in Florida. The teenager who still expected to be prime minister of his country one day lasted less than two semesters before dropping out, eventually making his way to Beverly Hills, where he would live with his mother for the next year.

Hedayat was at a loss. Eslaminia's attempts to liquidate his assets came too late for one who had spent most of his fortune purchasing real estate that had been seized by Khomeini's revolutionary government. His Hillsborough house was Eslaminia's only property outside Iran, and though he recently had opened accounts at banks in Switzerland and Germany, Hedayat claimed to have deposited only a few hundred thousand dollars. Even after learning that Prime Minister Hovedya had been executed by a firing squad, Eslaminia insisted he would return to Iran when the time was right. That it never would be—not as long as Khomeini lived—became evident when Hedayat's name was published in the book *Nest of Spies,* identifying those Iranians who had worked with or for the CIA. After the book's appearance, the names of the accused were written in the blood of slain SAVAK agents on a white wall in Teheran, their deaths decreed by the Ayatollah Khomeini; Hedayat Eslaminia was listed in the first column.

At the suggestion of his American advisors, Eslaminia traveled to Baghdad to work for Saddam Hussein, delivering radio addresses intended to foment counterrevolution among Iranians still loyal to the shah. When he learned of Saddam's plans for a military offensive against Iran, however, Eslaminia returned to Hillsborough, where his neighbors were the lace-curtain Irish of the Burlingame Country Club, people who encircled their estates in hedges filled with razor wire and elected Shirley Temple Black to represent them in Congress.

"He felt he had four options," Hedayat's nephew Mortzavi remembered: "One, go back to Iran, try to work with the ayatollahs; two, work with the shah's people to overthrow the ayatollahs and seat the shah's son on the throne in Iran; three, work with the West; and four, forget it all and go into business with me. First, he didn't think he could make a deal with Khomeini; second, the shah's son was too young; third, he did what he could for his friend John Golden, but what he really needed at the moment was a way to use the money he had left to make more."

Eslaminia's first American transaction, the sale of his Hillsborough home, produced a profit of $300,000, but he immediately invested the capital gains in a second, larger Hillsborough house on a two-acre estate one block away. "Which he kept mainly to save face," Mortzavi said. "Understand, he sees guys who begged for his help in Iran having homes in Beverly Hills because they got their money out of the country in time, and it's just killing him." Eslaminia turned another quick profit on his second real estate deal, going in with his nephew to buy a property in Hayward for $190,000, then selling it ninety days later for $320,000. "After that, though, everything he did here failed," Mortzavi recalled. A gas station and diner in Santa Rosa remodeled by Eslaminia and two partners showed losses month after month. Worse by far, soon after he married Simin, Hedayat was served with a petition for divorce filed in Beverly Hills by Mina, demanding half or more of his assets and custody of their children. Eslaminia argued that he and Mina had been divorced in Iran but could produce no document as evidence. Mina, moreover, asserted that Hedayat had hidden millions in banks and property partnerships all over the world.

The fortunes of Reza and Ali mirrored their father's. Following the takeover of the U.S. embassy in Teheran during November of 1979, even his closest friends turned against Ali; within a year the straight-A student was drinking a case of beer a day and flunking every class. By the time he turned twenty, most of the Americans Reza knew best were drug dealers. Addicted to a cycle of uppers and downers, Hedayat's eldest child attempted suicide by overdose a second time before his father sent him to a "treatment facility" in Texas, where the young Iranian promptly fell in love with another patient. Opposed by the staff, the two eloped. Within a few months, however, Reza's bride abandoned him. "He believed that his wife had left him to become a prostitute," Reza's psychologist, Stephen Bindman, wrote. After this, Reza began to blame his father for all he had lost, according to the psychologist, cultivating a rage so consuming that Bindman felt obliged to write Hedayat a letter warning, "You are in danger of potential loss of life and property from your son."

Reza moved to Beverly Hills to live with Mina in 1980. He was arrested three times that year, first for possession of a deadly weapon, next for possession of narcotics, and finally, in September, for an attempted robbery in Palm Springs plotted among a group of Beverly Hills High students. The presiding judge in this case allowed Reza to return to Hillsborough and live with his father, on the condition that he receive drug treatment at a local clinic.

In San Mateo County, Reza set about becoming a useful member of society by turning snitch, working for assorted police agencies as a drug informant. His first filing with the DEA identified "the Opium Distribution Center of Northern California" as a house at 3300 Ralston Avenue in Hillsborough belonging to Hedayat Eslaminia. His father shipped his opium sticks into the country concealed in bags of pistachio nuts, Reza said.

The DEA suspected there was something to the accusation, especially after learning that in 1977 a young woman employed at the U.S. embassy in Teheran had been apprehended in Seattle, en route to San Francisco, carrying 247 grams of opium concealed between two separate frames on a large oil painting. She had been given the painting by her friend Hedayat Eslaminia at his home in Teheran, the young woman said. The DEA's investigation was abandoned, however, when the drug agency learned that Eslaminia had friends in high places.

Reza and Ali were by then the principal witnesses in the divorce trial pitting their father against their mother in Los Angeles Municipal Court. Reza was most outspoken, writing in one affidavit that Mina was "rotten to the core" and "I wish I never had a mother." Mina confiscated the money sent by his father for his education, Reza said, using it to buy sex and drugs. His mother was "a compulsive liar and sex maniac," Reza added, who regularly paid a former *Playboy* centerfold to participate in three- and four-way sex. Mina's steady boyfriend was Ed Singleton, partner with former pro football star Jim Brown in a Los Angeles security business. That Singleton was black horrified Hedayat, who prevailed upon Ali to prepare an affidavit alleging that Singleton and Mina regularly had sex with the bedroom door open. Reza swore that he once had caught Mina in bed with not one but three black men, a scene that so upset him, he ran outside and threw rocks at her bedroom window. Later, both boys recanted, testifying this time for Mina, claiming their father had persuaded them to exaggerate their mother's activities.

The even worse news for Hedayat was that his young wife Simin wanted out of *their* marriage, filing for a legal separation in San Mateo County and placing Eslaminia eventually in the unique position of being sued for divorce by two women in the same state at the same time.

During 1982 and 1983, Eslaminia began using more and more of the opium he kept for guests. Ali, seventeen at the time, recalled returning home late one evening from a date to find Hedayat in a drug delirium. "My father refused to let me in except on one of two conditions," Ali remembered. "Either he would shave the hair from my head or press a burning cigarette against my hand." He chose the cigarette, Ali said, "and my left hand still bears the scar from this burn."

Simin won both a lien against the Hillsborough house and a monthly alimony check in her divorce action against Hedayat. Mina, meanwhile, continued to press her suit for custody of the children and whatever remained of the man's assets—which she insisted still were vast and carefully concealed. To top off his troubles, Eslaminia's oldest son was dunning him for money as well, claiming that his father had defrauded his girlfriend Debi Lutkenhouse and her family out of nearly twenty thousand dollars. One argument between father and son became so intense, Simin said, that Reza ended it by bashing his father in the face with a telephone, chipping the older man's front teeth. "They fought constantly after that, mostly about money," she remembered. "Reza wanted it and Hedayat say he didn't have any. Their fights scared me enough that I hid the kitchen knives."

Reza was often in the employ of government agencies during this period, most frequently the San Mateo Sheriff's Department and the California Bureau of Narcotics Enforcement. While money and a sense of importance were contributing factors, it was freedom from the consequences of his own crimes that principally motivated Reza's work as an informant. He was arrested seven times for possession of narcotics or theft in one eighteen-month period during 1981 and 1982 but spent only ninety days of "diagnostic commitment" behind bars.

Reza enrolled at the College of Recording Arts in San Francisco during January of 1982. School not only revived the young man's hopes but kept him out of trouble for most of the next year. After his graduation in 1982, however, Reza's applications for employment at recording studios were rejected routinely.

"It seemed like nothing he did worked out," said Debi Lutkenhouse, who had been a classmate at the San Francisco school. At the beginning of their relationship, Reza had boasted constantly of his family's wealth, remembered Debi, whose own father had made a fortune as the owner of a moving and storage company. "He said in Iran he lived next door to the shah," she recalled, "that his father owned a lake and casinos."

She realized the shadow world in which her boyfriend now dwelt, however, Debi recalled, when she visited the Eslaminia home in Hillsborough: "The place wasn't well kept once you were inside. The kids didn't have clothes, but worse than that I saw they didn't even have money for soap and toilet paper sometimes. The house was a shell of wealth, nothing more."

"All I know is that every time I went up to the mansion on Ralston they had a maid to answer the door," countered Jeff Steele, Reza's accomplice in a Foster City burglary. "The chimes on the doorbell played, like, this classical music, and I could put eighteen cars in that driveway, easy."

And Reza was not like any other criminal he ever met, Steele added: "Some sweet sweet poison, that guy. He can tell you a lie, and you know it's a lie, no doubt, and yet he'll leave you wonderin' like 'I don't know, I still have this feeling that maybe red is green.'" That Foster City job had looked like such a sure thing when he and his friend Steve Selby brought Reza in on it, Jeff recalled: "Like, these people were gone, and this girl I was goin' out with, her parents were watchin' the house. So it was an inside job. We could sort of steal at our leisure." They took computers, TVs, a mink coat, and some jewelry that first night, Jeff recalled. Then Steve and Reza went back two nights later and drove off with the vacationing couple's brand-new Chrysler New Yorker, kept the car for a few days, then rolled it off a cliff.

A year and a half passed before Jeff was arrested. "What happened was, Reza got in trouble in San Mateo, and he went to the special investigations unit in Redwood City," Jeff explained. "They had him buyin' coke, settin' people up. Then he told them about the burglary." When Steele's lawyer showed him Reza's statement, "I couldn't believe how he'd done me," recalled Jeff, who paid a visit to the Iranian after his release on bail: "He tells me, 'Oh, I won't go to court against you,' made all these promises. So I go to my preliminary hearing, thinkin', 'This guy is gonna get up there and totally clear me.' But when I go to court he's surrounded by cops, protectin' him. And he spills his guts on me but leaves himself out. That's the part that really got me, to tell you the truth. I mean, it's one thing to turn snitch, but to turn snitch and then lie, that's truly bogus."

On the basis of his success as an informant in San Mateo County, Reza applied to work for the state in March of 1983, shortly after his twenty-second birthday. He was "debriefed" at that time by California Department of Justice Special Agent Xavier Suazo. San Mateo sheriff's detectives assured Suazo that Eslaminia had provided them with information leading to arrests in fifteen cases; Reza claimed it was his ambition to relocate and work for the Bureau of Narcotics Enforcement in Los Angeles. Suazo recommended hiring the young Iranian but changed his mind two months later when Reza was caught stealing one thousand dollars from the petty cash box at the sheriff's narcotics bureau. The San Mateo detectives said they would continue to use him, however, Suazo recalled.

Reza still was living with his father at the Hillsborough house, where the Eslaminias spoke incessantly of the life they had left behind, Debi Lutkenhouse remembered. Inside the steel gate surrounding the six-bedroom house with its vaulted ceilings and wall-to-wall views of San Francisco Bay, the atmosphere was something akin to the festal gloom of a gypsy funeral. The filling of a hookah pipe or the cooking of kabobs became elaborate ceremony, intended as much to push away the present as to preserve the past; and as the damask wall coverings absorbed the odors of opium smoke and sesame spatter, the mentalities of siege, relinquishment, and grandiosity seeped into a common pool of paranoia. Police officers and firefighters were called often to the Ralston address due to Hedayat's habit of burning leaves in a pit he had dug in a corner of his lawn. Yet even as he was cited and fined, again and again, Eslaminia persisted in building his backyard bonfires, seeking some solace in the towering flames he could find nowhere else. Hedayat's housemate, confidant, and errand boy, Colonel

Baniamam—better known as Ali Bani—recalled that he and Mr. Eslaminia worked constantly on plans to overthrow the Ayatollah Khomeini. Hedayat continued to fly to Washington at the expense of the State Department every month or two. Both the colonel and Eslaminia were warned that their executions had been decreed by the revolutionary government in Iran, and "We often had the feeling we were being watched or followed," Bani said. "The FBI suggested, almost ordered, security for the Hillsborough house."

The colonel's escape from Iran had been even more harrowing and ignominious than his host's. Though not wealthy in the manner of a Hedayat Eslaminia, whose fortune he estimated at $100 million, Ali Bani had been a man of some stature in prerevolutionary Iran, trained for his job as commander of the shah's tank divisions by the U.S. Army at Fort Knox. He was best known in Iran for commanding the troops that surrounded the shah's palace during the 1978 pro-Khomeini demonstrations. After Khomeini's return to Teheran, the colonel was arrested, tried before a panel of mullahs the next morning, and sentenced to death that afternoon. While he awaited execution, Bani's relatives paid a bribe of $150,000 to a pair of revolutionary guards who transported the colonel to the Turkish border, where he joined dozens of senior military officers who were assisted through mountain passes by the Israeli agents of Mossad. Once a man who estimated his wealth "in the low millions," the colonel arrived in California without a penny. Ali Bani's only hope was his old friend Hedayat, who hired him at once as "translator."

Even in enormously reduced circumstances, Eslaminia could not resist playing patron to other Iranian exiles. When a former reporter from the largest daily newspaper in Iran proposed publishing an anti-Khomeini periodical from his new home in California, Eslaminia readily provided start-up money for the *Teheran Tribune* of San Jose. Despite how his friend labored to keep up appearances, though, it was evident to Ali Bani that most of what remained of Mr. Eslaminia's fortune was being taken from him by his ex-wives. He and Hedayat attempted to restore their wealth by brokering international loans for American land developers from Middle Eastern oil emirs, Ali Bani recalled, but were unsuccessful, in part because Mr. Eslaminia refused to try anything involving a sum of less than one billion dollars. "In business he was always thinking very high," the colonel explained. "For him it was either millions or living poor. What was a few thousand dollars to a man like Hedayat Eslaminia?"

Eslaminia was discovering that such pittances added up, however. Drawn by Mina and Simin into the sinkhole that is the American system of civil litigation, Eslaminia soon was spending more on attorneys in one month than it cost him to live for a whole year in Hillsborough. Cursing the blue-suited bloodsuckers and the women who had loosed them on him, Eslaminia watched the last vestiges of his splendor vanish when he was ordered by the court to put his Hillsborough home on the market in order to pay Simin her share of its value. His lawyer advised settling with Mina as well, assuring him that a trial would cost a fortune whether he won or lost. Hedayat grew despondent, Ali Bani recalled, and "sometimes talked about suicide; he had lost so much."

Moving from his estate in Hillsborough to a condominium at the Davy Glen Apartments in Belmont, Hedayat had no choice but to put the colonel out on his own, weeping when he learned that Ali Bani was working as the manager of a squalid apartment-hotel in San Francisco's Tenderloin district. The man who had promised his son the prime ministership was himself reduced to such sordid acts of desperation as shoplifting Johnnie Walker scotch and chicken patties from a San Mateo Safeway.

Despairing of his two oldest sons and denied custody of the two younger boys, Eslaminia had only one light left in his life by the time he turned fifty-six in March of 1984—Olga Vasquez, the young woman who was living with him at the condominium in Belmont. Doll-faced and soft-bodied, with long legs and tapering ankles, Olga was thirty years Hedayat's junior, the half-Russian, half-Spanish daughter of Puerto Rican immigrants who had raised her working class in Oakland. Their meeting was arranged through another "Persian expatriate" in August of 1983, Olga recalled, when she and Hedayat met for a blind date at the Velvet Turtle in Burlingame. Even as he succumbed to defeat and dissipation, Eslaminia remained a handsome man, hair combed straight back from his broad smooth face and streaked with perfect sweeps of silver; while no longer slim, he carried 185 pounds on his five-foot, ten-inch frame with formidable bearing and continued to dress elegantly. Olga was swept away by her introduction to a world larger, grander, and more momentous than she had heretofore known. Just a week after they met, Hedayat whisked her off with him for a trip at the expense of the U.S. State Department to assignations in Paris, Cannes, and Cologne, where Olga sat beside Hedayat as he met with men introduced as generals and admirals, listening in as they discussed international trade and billion-dollar bank loans, plotted the overthrow of Ayatollah Khomeini, or pleaded with Eslaminia to meet with the shah's son.

Hedayat arranged a number of transactions at banks in Switzerland and Germany while they were abroad, Olga said; she herself had been involved in the transfer of seventy-nine thousand dollars to his account at a Geneva bank. Olga had no real idea of his worth, but Hedayat spoke far more often of what he had lost than of what was left. While he and his friends in Europe discussed plans to inveigle hundreds of millions from Saudi sheiks,

Olga saw Hedayat agonize over spending ten thousand dollars in Germany for a shipment of Pakistani rugs: "He said he needed to invest, that he was running out of money." Eslaminia still had his home in Hillsborough, but the estate was falling into disrepair and would be listed AS IS by the realtor hired to unload it.

The ambiguity of Eslaminia's status in the United States would penetrate Olga's pretty fog when they returned from Europe and were held up at the airport in Los Angeles after a customs officer discovered a small chunk of opium in his suit jacket. They were detained for three hours, Olga recalled, but in the end Hedayat's "friends in Washington" saw to it that he was released without criminal charges.

It was clear to her that Hedayat's affairs were fraught with intrigue, perhaps peril: He regularly took calls from a man in Washington who spoke Farsi and used the code name "Mel," Olga remembered, and "reimbursement checks" came to the Davy Glen condominium from the U.S. State Department each time he traveled. While Hedayat assured her he was in no danger, she could not help noticing that he took precautions. When a package from Germany arrived for him after their trip to Europe, his young girlfriend remembered, "Hedayat told me not to open it; he said it could be a bomb." Their condo was rented in the name of his business partner, Olga would learn, and Hedayat's American bank accounts all were in the names of either his sister Fatima Mortzavi or his friend Edgar Safarian.

Olga had known of the estrangement between Hedayat and his two older sons from the time she began visiting him at the Hillsborough house. Still bitter about Mina's victory in their battle for custody of Amir and Mahmoud, Eslaminia was inconsolable after learning that Reza and Ali had recanted their earlier affidavits and now were testifying for their mother. He wanted nothing further to do with either of them, Hedayat said.

Whatever his demeanor before her time or outside her presence, Hedayat remained a perfect gentleman while she lived with him, Olga said: "Ali Bani told me he was surprised by how much better Hedayat treated me than he had Simin." In the eyes of his friends, Eslaminia was a man who at last had achieved the serenity of resignation, humbled by being broken, perhaps, yet still clutching at whatever morsels of satisfaction remained for him. His diminishment was shocking to some, though, including Ali Mortzavi, who remembered receiving the first call from his uncle in more than three years during the spring of 1984: "He phoned first, then came over to my office. As I was parking the car, I saw him standing there, waiting. I thought to myself, 'This is the end of the man. He was so powerful, and now he has to come after me.' Knowing his pride, I listened; he has a deal for me, but I am not really interested. He told me he bought these carpets, said they were very fine, and insisted I had to see them."

The carpets, unrolled and unsold, were piled in the spare bedroom at the condominium. Olga kept her job as a receptionist in San Francisco, at the Sutter Street offices of a spice company. Hedayat's last remaining consolations, aside from his young mistress, seemed to be his waning influence among Iranian expatriates, his opium pipe, and the unceasing devotion of his sister Fatima, who lived with her husband in an adjoining building. Hedayat now prayed for hours at a time in the back bedroom beside his stack of carpets, wrote in his blue diary every day, rearranged and dusted those last few treasures and mementos he kept in a Fendi case, like the curator of a miniature museum.

His young girlfriend met Hedayat's eldest son for the first time that spring. She was on her way to the market one Saturday morning to buy steaks for kabobs when she noticed a stranger sitting in a gold Porsche near the entrance of the Davy Glen condo, Olga recalled. She thought the young man looked very like Hedayat, "especially his eyes. I approached and asked if he was Reza Eslaminia. He was stunned, nervous. He said, 'Who wants to know?' When I told him who I was, he got out of the car and shook my hand, said he had heard a lot about me and that I seemed very nice, and that his father was fortunate to have someone like me. He said he was waiting for his father, that he had just talked to him on the phone and Hedayat was busy, so he was waiting for him to finish." When Olga returned with the groceries half an hour later, the gold Porsche was gone. Hedayat became quite upset when she told him about the encounter, Olga recalled: "He said, 'Did you give him the apartment number? Did you tell him where I live?' He was very firm; he told me, 'Don't ever open the door for him.'"

Other people were opening their doors for Reza, though, among them Xavier Suazo, the California Bureau of Narcotics Enforcement agent who had rejected his application to work as a "special operator" eight months earlier. Reza did not come to him empty-handed, Suazo remembered, calling in February of 1984 to offer "compelling details" in connection with an L.A. County case involving a gruesome acid attack on a fourteen-year-old girl, ordered, Reza said, by a drug dealer named James Nelms. Reza agreed to wear a wire when he met with Nelms at the Hamburger Hamlet in Brentwood; he obtained a full confession, Suazo recalled. Working in tandem with the L.A. County district attorney's office, Suazo arranged for Reza's admission into the California Witness Protection Program. The state's department of justice gave the young Iranian money to rent an apartment in West L.A. and put him to work as "Operator Reza Eslaminia."

Reza proved himself immediately, setting up a cocaine dealer for an arrest that led to the seizure of 3.5 kilos. The only real problem in dealing with the young Iranian, Suazo recalled, was that "he kept trying to supply information about his father, with regard to the import and use of opium . . . Reza told me he hated his father, whom he said had abandoned the family after they fled from Iran."

Reza's complaint to Marge Pierce, the woman through whom he would find his way to the BBC, was that his father refused to provide his younger brothers with the advantages he had enjoyed as a child. Marge was forty-six, exactly twice Reza's age, when she met him one evening at the Tennessee Gin and Cotton Club in Reseda. The young man became quite interested in her, Marge recalled, when he learned that she made her living as a manicurist at the Century West Club, an exclusive establishment that catered to visiting corporate executives. Reza took her to dinner several times during the next two months, remembered Marge, who suspected that the young man was after a peek at her most valuable asset, the Rolodex in which she kept the phone numbers, addresses, and relevant personal information of her clients at the Century West Club. He had many Middle Eastern business contacts, Reza said, and would be able to take advantage of them if he could establish similar relationships with important business executives in America. They quarreled when she refused Reza's blunt request for a look at the Rolodex during their fifth date, Marge recalled, and she went home alone. Three days later, though, the young Iranian phoned to propose a "make-up dinner" in a suite at the Beverly Wilshire Hotel, then sent a limo to collect her. That had been a lovely evening, Marge said, but Reza called the next day and confessed he had paid the bill at the Beverly Wilshire with his mother's credit card. She softened when Reza said he was desperate to find a job, explained Marge, who agreed to arrange a meeting between the young man and her client Leon Kassorla.

Kassorla had been so impressed by Reza's background that within a week of their meeting he had submitted a test order for five tons of peppers to his U.S. suppliers, recalled Eisenberg, who was introduced to the young Iranian in late May. Ben Dosti got so excited about Reza when Kassorla brought him by the BBC office in mid-June, Eisenberg remembered, that he paid Leon a finder's fee.

Reza arrived on the scene almost at the moment he and Dean learned that the Ron Levin check had bounced, Ben recalled: "He said he had just moved to his mother's house in Beverly Hills and didn't know anyone in Southern California."

To Reza, this seemed the break he had been waiting for, especially after Eddie Singleton "told me the BBC were like the Kennedys of California, the royalty of America," he remembered, "that someone from the company was heir to the May Company. He said it would be good for me if I could get involved."

It was an appointment Reza had set up with Debi's father in San Mateo County that had delayed Ben's arrival at the June 24 meeting. "I was so happy to see that Reza had met a person of Ben's caliber," Debi recalled. Ben seemed to value Reza equally, paying full fare to fly him back to Los Angeles. Reza had been "instrumental," Ben explained, in closing a deal with Eddie Singleton's company, Time Productions, to market the Fire Safety product: Singleton's group agreed to pay the BBC a fee of $250,000, plus $11 per gallon for the formula. They signed the contract on July 9, barely an hour before Ben would join Joe and Dean on the street corner outside the BBC office, where the three considered a separate proposal involving their new Iranian connection.

By the end of the second meeting with Reza, Dean remembered, Joe had reduced their agenda to a single sentence: "First to do some reconnaissance, to find out what Mr. Eslaminia's habits were, where his place of residence currently was, and then to find a way to take him from there to a hidden and remote place so that he could be interrogated and forced to turn over his assets."

The last part of this plan would be the most difficult to execute, according to Hedayat's son. "Reza said his father was a very tough man," Dean recalled, who "would lie over and over if he thought he could get away with it, so he would have to be very well convinced of the seriousness of the people involved." They decided that torture would be an inevitable recourse, remembered Dean, who was relieved when Joe announced he would handle this portion of the program personally. Joe felt "he had more the stomach for that sort of thing," Dean explained, "and the psychological presence of mind so that he could do something like that without having the kinds of problems the others of us might."

This decision led to a discussion about the nature of the place where Mr. Eslaminia would be held. "We decided it must be remote," Dean recalled, "because of Mr. Eslaminia's screams." They briefly considered renting a residence in the Bay Area, Dean remembered, but eventually decided it would be best to transport Reza's father to Southern California, where "the Olympics were an advantage for us because of all the short-term rentals around. Also, we wanted to keep Mr. Eslaminia near Los Angeles so we could shuttle back and forth to the office without creating suspicion."

The Shadings would scout Southern California for a suitable site, Joe decided, while Jim went north with Reza to locate Hedayat Eslaminia and study him at close range. Reza told them that his father's old friend Colonel Bani would know Mr. Eslaminia's whereabouts and travel plans,

Dean recalled, and that the colonel was a drug addict whose cooperation could be bartered with opium. They should have opium for his father as well, Reza said, or risk losing him to withdrawal during his confinement. Joe advanced two thousand dollars to Reza for the purchase of opium before sending him north, Dean recalled.

He indeed had spoken to Reza sometime during the second week of July, Ali Bani remembered, but there was no mention of opium. "I didn't even see Reza in person. He called me at work, said he wanted me to talk to his father and arrange for Hedayat to meet him." Ali Bani was happy for the chance to mediate the dispute between the Eslaminias, but Hedayat remained unyielding, and "I was embarrassed to tell Reza that his father refused to see him," the colonel recalled.

It was Jim who traced Mr. Eslaminia to the condominium in Belmont where he was living with a young woman named Olga Vasquez, Dean recalled. Reza explained this relatively humble abode by telling the others that his father maintained an almost spartan lifestyle in the United States, Dean recalled, but was lavish in Europe. While Bani was unwilling to provide his father's phone number, the colonel did reveal to Reza that Hedayat was planning a trip to Italy and Turkey at the end of July. "When Joe heard the news of the trip," Dean remembered, "he/we decided it would be a good time to carry out the plan. Reza said his father frequently took sudden trips, and if he disappeared, perhaps the investigation would be delayed—it would camouflage us. Also, we were in desperate financial condition and had no idea when he'd come back."

Once they had a time and a place, the abduction scheme grew quite detailed, Dean recalled. Reza moved into the Manning, taking Steve Lopez's bedroom in 1206. "We were in a flurry of activity," and Joe, their "coordinator of discussions," was thorough as ever, suggesting that they make notes of every meeting, Dean remembered: "We each had legal pads, and each person wrote a list of what they were going to do. Joe had his own list and a master list . . . we divided the things to be done into two stages. The first was in preparation for the abduction, and the second was for when we had him." Jim was sent north again to case the condominium complex in preparation for the planning of Phase One. Ben checked with the U.S. Immigration and Naturalization Service to confirm the dates of Eslaminia's intended absence from the country, then set up an account at a Sacramento company called Data Search to run a check on Eslaminia's assets; the Hillsborough house and two pieces of commercial real estate were all they could find in California, Dean remembered. Ben flew to San Francisco, taking a suite at the Saint Francis, then drove to Hillsborough the next afternoon to inspect the house. The estate was unkempt and the house empty, Ben said, but he had found a flyer on the front lawn offering the place for $795,000.

Joe assigned to himself most other aspects of Phase Two, Dean recalled: "Aside from the torturing, Joe was to check at the BBC offices for various forms, forms of contract, blank forms for loans, for transfers of property, for anything that he could think of that might be helpful in making the forced transfer of Mr. Eslaminia's assets look as though they were just business transactions." Also, since Reza believed that his father kept most of his wealth in assorted safe-deposit boxes and numbered Swiss bank accounts, Joe's task as "interrogator" would be crucial, Dean explained.

Joe instructed them to begin referring to the Eslaminia abduction as "Project Sam," Karny recalled, "so we could talk about it and no one at the office would know." While the other Boys could hardly help observing that the Shadings seemed to be keeping Reza to themselves, meetings with the BBC's newest member were enveloped in the odor of legitimate, even lucrative, business dealings. It helped that he was always with Ben. Dosti would say later that he "really didn't see that much of Reza," but the notes Reza made in his own blue diary described a relationship verging on the obsessive: "Call Ben about reservations"; "Call Ben to confirm reservations"; "Go see Ben"; "Call Ben"; "Be Nicer to Ben"; "Be Ben's friend"; "Call Ben in the morning"; "Call Ben in the afternoon"; "Give Ben his money back." It was Ben whom Reza brought to meet with his advisors, Reza Palezi and Jay Stein, who had employed him as a favor to Mina at their company Coefficient Coatings. "Reza seemed to be in awe of Ben, watching every move he made," Stein remembered. Even the two older men were taken by "the air of confidence and business acumen Ben exuded." They went so far as to negotiate a deal with Dosti to import an entire tanker-load of coconut oil purchased through the BBC's "Singapore sources," Stein recalled.

At the Third Street office, the Boys saw copies of the Fire Safety contract signed by Ed Singleton, heard reports of plans to export DC-10 airplanes and Bell helicopters, caught glimpses of telexes to Riyadh and from Kuwait City. While most of the BBC got no closer to Reza than standing over a drink with him at Decadence (as Tom May recalled his lone encounter with the Iranian), "there was a lot of buzz and excitement in the BBC about Reza's Middle East connections," Mike Feldman remembered. Feldman, who had a number of Iranian clients, recalled being summoned to Joe's office to discuss Reza's background during the second week of July: "He asked me to check with some of my clients to see if Hedayat Eslaminia was as wealthy as Reza said he was. I said I would, but I never actually did. It would have put me in an awkward position. So I just said I understood [Reza] came from a lot of money. Joe seemed glad to hear it."

For his part, Reza appeared to buy the BBC sales pitch without reservation. "All they talked about was business," he explained. "They were the kids my mother and father had preached about making friends with." While Ben offered Reza the bedroom in the condo at the Manning, it was Joe who made the newcomer feel welcome, inviting him upstairs for a one-on-one chat the first evening after he moved in. They stayed up past 1 A.M., and he shared intimacies that he had kept even from Debi, Reza said: "Joe could have made a fortune as a counselor."

Only a few days after the younger Eslaminia had moved into the Manning, Joe sent him off for a weekend with Debi at the Stanford Park Hotel in Palo Alto, where Reza was to assist Ben in the investigation of his father's assets and habits. Debi flew to Los Angeles the following weekend; Reza met her at the airport in Joe's Jeep and brought her back to the Manning. The BBC Boys "had to know what they were doing, or they couldn't have financed the kind of lifestyle they had," in Debi's opinion. That evening most of the BBC met in Beverly Hills for dinner at the Bistro Garden. Ben's command of the situation was breathtaking, Reza's girlfriend thought, and afterward she couldn't stop talking about how their table had received far more attention from the maître d' than one where three members of the *Hill Street Blues* cast were seated.

After Debi flew home on Sunday evening, the Project Sam conspirators resumed their meetings. It had been Joe's hope at first that they might lure the elder Eslaminia to an after-dark meeting with his estranged son at some relatively secluded site and take the man by force from there, Dean recalled, but when Reza said this would be impossible, Joe decided that Mr. Eslaminia must be abducted from his residence. Jim's surveillance report described the Belmont condominium complex as secure but breachable; anyone who got inside the gates could open the door to the parking garage and admit others. The building where Eslaminia lived was among the most solidly constructed on the Peninsula, another advantage: Individual units were so well-insulated as to be virtually sound-proof, meaning that once the door was shut behind them, the man might scream at the top of his lungs without being heard. Finally, their way out was a dark stairway leading to the gate that opened onto Davy Glen Road. All that left to decide was "a way of gaining access into his home and what we'd do if anyone else was there—his girlfriend, specifically—and how we'd get him out," Dean recalled. Reza warned that his father was highly suspicious, convinced the ayatollah's agents were trying to kill him, and wouldn't easily admit strangers, Dean remembered. Joe winnowed their suggestions down to two main contingencies, Karny recalled: "We could enter as policemen or enter as deliverymen." There were advantages and disadvantages to each alternative: "We were sure he'd open the door for the police," Dean explained, "but not necessarily for deliverymen. On the other hand, we wanted to be quiet and police would be more conspicuous." They should prepare to play either part, Joe said. If Olga Vasquez was at home when they entered the condo, Dean remembered, there again were two contingencies: "We could either abduct her also or kill her in the apartment and make it look like Eslaminia had done it, and then fled." As for Eslaminia's removal, "Joe decided we should take him out in a trunk," Dean recalled. "He said to look around and see what we could find."

Joe announced three weeks into July that it was time to begin preparing for Phase One and began to assign responsibilities, Dean remembered. "What we did, basically," he explained, "was make shopping lists."

Among those Boys "not far enough along to understand this sort of situation," as Dean described them, suspicion, shifting loyalties, and secret meetings seemed the BBC's new dynamic. The Shadings spent a lot of time behind closed doors during July, remembered Tom May, who was offended by his exclusion. Also, it was obvious to everyone that Joe was using those most loyal to him to spy on members he suspected of subversion. "Jon Allen was Joe's personal tattletale," Eisenberg recalled. "Every time you said anything bad about Joe, he ran and told. It got to a point where you would tell Jon Allen the wrong things just so he would go back and tell Joe." Like Eisenberg, Taglianetti suspected that Jim was recording conversations at the office. The two confirmed their fears in late July when they broke into the office Jim had inherited from Ryan Hunt and found the desk covered with technical manuals describing the use of voice-activated recorders and wireless microphones. "We figured they had the whole office bugged," Taglianetti recalled.

It was a recording of Taglianetti's angry remarks that ended his employment at the BBC, according to Eisenberg. "Steve Tag told me that he had been fired," Eisenberg remembered. "His conversations with me were cited. He said that Joe and either Jim or Dean showed up at his house at six A.M. and took back the dirt bike they had given him. He was officially a 'suspended BBC member' after that. They didn't want to lose him completely."

By the end of July, Dean explained, BBC members were resigning mainly because they couldn't afford to work for free anymore. Joe and Ben scrambled to keep enough cash coming in to support the BBC until the payoff from Project Sam; Dosti even negotiated the sale of the BMW 728 that had been used to transport Ron Levin's body into Soledad Canyon, closing a deal for $27,500 with a Culver City businessman on July 19. He wanted the dent in the trunk fixed first, though, the man said.

Joe had made an even bolder move one day earlier, on July 18, when he sent out a letter informing his investors of an amendment to his May moratorium announcement. Wrote Hunt (who had liquidated the last of the BBC's commodities accounts more than a month earlier):

> That moratorium on investment remains in effect. However, due to an increase in liquidity, it appears that distributions will not be mandatory at quarter's end, as I had earlier feared. We are enjoying the fruits of an expansion in the size of the markets in which we participate, making it possible for us to invest larger amounts as a group. I had anticipated not being able to gainfully reinvest the profits likely to be made in this quarter. I now believe I can.

Furthermore, he had begun organizing trading partnerships for "an entirely different type of speculation," Joe announced. "While this investment has a somewhat greater degree of exposure than the spread system has, it may be of interest to those parties who have confidence in our organization's trading ability and who have been frustrated in capitalizing upon their confidence because of the previously discussed moratorium." Finally, "I would like to thank you all for allowing me to trade in relative peace," Joe added. "You have checked your curiosity admirably. No one has called as yet to get advance information on the coming distribution. I hope this doesn't mean that such performance has become taken for granted. I suspect not. In any event, the quarter does promise to be a good one."

Joe's July letter, though, would not produce anything like the results that attended his May missive. Part of the problem was the absence from Los Angeles of his principal promoter among the investors, Steve Weiss, who was spending the summer in Europe, enjoying the "profits" generated by Hunt's genius. When he told one old friend how well he was doing, Weiss recalled, "she became Victorian about it. She said, unfairly, 'You've changed. You think you can make demands with all this money.' I answered her, 'Spend it. Enjoy it. It's there to grease the wheels.'"

By the time Al Gore flew to London in mid-July to shop for a flat in South Kensington, however, Weiss was apprehensive. During a meeting near Victoria Station, Gore recalled, "Steve said Chester [Brown] had called with unspecified problems. I couldn't reconcile this with the news that a check representing a sixty-eight percent return on my investment had just been deposited in my account." He returned to Los Angeles on July 24, Gore remembered, and phoned Hunt the next day: "Joe told me the account was performing well, that 'There's no way the account will pay less than thirteen percent per month,' and that we could even expect a return of more than twenty-five percent." Gore presented Joe with a check for eighteen thousand dollars, and agreed as well to roll over his profits from the previous quarter. Even at 13 percent, he would earn the twelve thousand dollars he needed every three months to pay for his new flat in Kensington, Gore explained.

Al's faith was shaken a few days later, however, when his actor friend Bill Smith described a meeting with Joe at the BBC office. He had always thought of Hunt as "impenetrable," Smith said: "You couldn't see into his eyes, and he never spoke above a whisper; you had to strain to hear what he was saying. And there was never any accommodation for what may or may not have been the limitations of a person's vocabulary, so you always felt slightly off balance and doltish. Anyway, on this day he made a demonstration for me of the Microgenesis machine. He had two glasses on his desk, one filled with gravel and one filled with sand. He said, 'This glass with the gravel is a symbol of the finest texture that can presently be created by any grinding machine. And this one with the sand is a symbol of the fineness in comparison that our machine can create.' He said, 'I would show you a sample of the ground material that our machine can create, except that if I tried to put it in this glass, it would flow through the molecular structure.' That was the instant when I realized I was talking to a person who was incapable of distinguishing between fact and fiction, or right and wrong. Until that moment, I had never detected anything in Joe Hunt's eyes. Then I knew: Joe really believed you can make it up as you go along."

Mike Feldman found himself thinking along the same lines as he prepared the prospectus Joe had requested as an appendix to his application for a $10 million bank loan to the Microgenesis Corporation. Hunt had attached copies of seven separate Microgenesis contracts, including the one signed by Ron Levin on June 6, 1984, but relied most heavily upon the agreement with Kilpatrick. "In about a year, our management team has been able to earn a little more than $13 million, pre-tax," Joe wrote in his introduction to the prospectus.

"Meanwhile, Lore Leis is complaining that we don't have the money to pay for paper clips and rubber bands," Eisenberg recalled.

Still nearly as essential as Kilpatrick to Joe's plan for a BBC bailout was Steve Lopez. Lopez was living at his father's home in Singapore during late July, preparing for the flight to Madras that would initiate the last leg of a two-month-long lap around the planet that took him from Los Angeles to Boston to Paris to London to Saudi Arabia to Singapore to India

to Indonesia to Hawaii and back to Los Angeles. His skill at selling the Fire
Safety product astonished even Lopez: During a week of meetings with
senior officers from the armed forces of Singapore and Malaysia, Lopez had
submitted the Fire Safety Manual a chapter at a time as it arrived by air
courier, hot off the presses and covered with apologies for the delay, from
the BBC office in Los Angeles. "I didn't know what to think about what
must be happening back there," he recalled. "First I was dealing with Ryan
Hunt and Mingarella, then all of a sudden it was Taglianetti, and Steve's a
little out of his depth. Finally Ben takes over." When the military requested
a demonstration, Lopez asked Dosti for a dozen cases of the fire retardant
and received three. "Ben had the stuff flown in," Steve recalled, "and I got
it cleared through Singapore customs, and then tested and approved by the
government in what was probably record time. In one week I sold it to both
the air force and the navy of Malaysia. I also had the Indonesian military
lined up; we're talking millions and millions in orders out of Southeast
Asia alone."

He asked for more samples so that the military men could test the
fire retardant by setting fire to abandoned barracks, but "Ben said they didn't
have any more of the product available at that time," Steve explained, "so I
was afraid to sign the contract they were drawing up. I sensed hesitation on
Ben's part, so I made a verbal agreement with the Malaysian military, but
we had nothing on paper."

A Swiss banker in Singapore informed Lopez that the Levin
check had not been honored, and when Ben and Joe sent him to South
India to procure coconut oil in thousand-ton lots for a shampoo manufacturer, "it began to dawn on me that what they wanted from me now was a
way to produce a payoff immediately," Steve recalled. "Another contract
promising millions over the next five to ten years meant nothing to them at
that point."

Most upsetting of all was the missed opportunity at the Public Utili-
ties Board in Singapore, where the agency's two chief engineers had given
Lopez all of one day and parts of several others to make his Microgenesis
pitch. "I had very little understanding of the Cyclotron," Steve admitted,
but the engineers became very excited after viewing a videotape documentary on the machine written and narrated by Joe Hunt. "I called Joe in L.A.
and told him [the engineers] wanted to fly to Los Angeles and see what the
machine could really do," Lopez remembered. "He said the machine had
been moved from Gardena to another location, and I should come back to
L.A. and we'd put together another machine for the Singapore people.
So the next thing I know I'm on my way back to California via India. Here
I am flying out of Singapore without a thing on paper at the same time I

have people who are ready this minute to sign contracts committing tens of millions of dollars to BBC companies. I have to suspect there are problems in L.A."

It was worse than Lopez imagined: The one member the BBC could not afford to lose, Gene Browning, was bringing his dispute with Hunt to a climax. Tensions between Joe and the inventor had been building toward confrontation since the second week in July, when Claire Browning called the Third Street office to complain that the down payment on the Costa Mesa house was a week past due and they were likely to lose the place. "I got Joe on the phone, finally," Claire remembered. "And he said, 'I don't want you to get upset.' I said, 'I'm not upset; I'm very calm.' He said, 'There's not going to be a house.' I said, 'Oh, really.' He said, 'I'm sorry. We just can't do it right now.'" If Claire kept her composure, the same could not be said for Gene. He met with Hunt face-to-face for the last time on July 24, the inventor recalled: "I was going to have it out with Joe and went charging into the office, but lo, who should be there but the whole damn gang: Jim, Dosti, Karny. I said, 'I want to see Joe Hunt.' They went into his office and said, 'Browning is here.' And even at that he kept me waiting."

Joe would not admit him until he had finished "what by then must have been his twentieth viewing of *Scarface*," Browning remembered, but "I went in anyway. Right as I came through the door, this girl walked in and shot Pacino. 'That's trash,' I told him. 'This is the real world,' he answers. Joe got Karny in there, and he said, 'Go get Jerry Eisenberg, I want him here.' So Jerry came in, and Joe immediately switched the point of the conversation, and he got off on this business of the machine that was down in Arizona. And with Eisenberg there he said, 'Well, what do we do about the machine down there?' I told him, 'Well, we have this contract,' and he turned to Eisenberg and says, 'You think we can repossess the machine?' And Eisenberg says, 'Well, he hasn't paid in any more than fifty thousand dollars.' I said, 'He's not obligated to.' And Joe says, 'I think we should get that machine back.' I said, 'Well, it's up to you, I have nothing to do with it.' And he says, 'Okay, that's all I want to talk about.' And he got up and left. Left his own office. I never even got to talk to him about the house."

"What I know now, of course," Browning added, "was that Joe had more pressing matters to attend to."

17

DEAN DID ALL HIS SHOPPING IN HOLLYWOOD, AND ALL IN ONE DAY, MAKING A map of the Yellow Pages, then following it north along Gower and Vine. He stopped at each of the big boulevards—Beverly, Santa Monica, Sunset— paying his way with new hundred-dollar bills and piling his purchases under the black camper shell that covered the bed of the yellow pickup they had borrowed from Joe's father.

His first stop was Western Costume, six stories of dusty pink granite just down the street from the wrought-iron gates hung like measures of heavenly music at the entrance to Paramount's lot. Western had been wardrobing the entertainment industry out of this location for fifty years, and the shelves of its storerooms were a museum collection of cultural icons that ranged from Count Dracula's cape to Tarzan's loincloth. Merely mounting the old oak stairs to the second story office created a palpable sense of connection to that great tradition of lavish predicament and perfect resolution.

Humility was required, however, when Dean introduced himself as the employee of an independent film company, BBC Productions. They were shooting a low-budget feature, he explained, and required three authentic San Francisco Police Department uniforms to be worn by the actors in a crucial sequence. The stock clerk pushed a shopping cart past rooms stuffed with shiny silver space suits, plumed pirate hats, and fur-covered chaps to a corner of the building filled with the uniforms of all nations: army, navy, air force—police. It was ninety-two degrees outside, not much cooler indoors, and Dean was sweating patches through his summer suit as the clerk piled blue wool jackets, blue wool shirts, and blue wool trousers by sets of three into the cart. To these were added blue wool caps with black leather visors, three black ties with silver tiepins and three Sam Brown belts, each with black leather holster, manacle, cartridge carrier, nightstick, and key ring. Details made the difference, the clerk said. The costume company could not give him official insignia, however, without written permission from San Francisco city officials. Shooting already was behind schedule, explained Dean, who accepted instead three standard costume badges, silver shields engraved POLICE. Western could not give him guns either, the clerk said. For firearms, he should go to Ellis Mercantile.

At Ellis, Dean rented not only three "replica police revolvers," .38s with blue metal barrels, but another item that caught his eye, a white canvas straitjacket with stainless-steel buckles and double-stitched straps.

If they went in as delivery men, Joe felt the brown uniforms of United Parcel Service would attract least attention. Dean stopped at California Surplus next, where he picked up three pairs of Dickies pants and matching shirts, then drove four blocks east to Val-U-Shoe Mart for rubber-soled work boots.

Bernard's Luggage was at Hollywood and Vine, catty-corner from the Brown Derby. Set in the sidewalk directly in front of the entrance was the Walk of Fame star of John Ford, the great director who once explained that his art had been inspired by "the consequences of a tragic moment—how the individual acts before a crucial fact, or in an exceptional circumstance." Twenty years later, the rosy marble of John Ford's star was smeared with a gray film of spilled soft drinks and fast-food grease. Dean stepped across it and went inside, where he told the owner, Bernard, of his need for a large and extremely sturdy steamer trunk. He was taking a long voyage, Dean explained. Bernard had three models in stock, and Dean's first choice was the biggest and best made, half-inch plywood with hard blue veneer and brass corners, reinforced with rivets and vulcanized fiber. What were the dimensions? Dean asked. Thirteen-and-a-half inches wide by thirty-nine inches long by twenty-two inches deep, Bernard told him. Dean studied the trunk, unable to conceive a discreet way of asking whether a human being might fit inside, and finally said he would take it.

Dean's last stop was the Pleasure Chest on Santa Monica Boulevard, a cinder-block building without windows just east of the Gay Parade, between Fairfax and La Brea. Bachelorette party buyers and cross-dressers browsed a selection of merchandise here that was breathtaking. One entire wall was paneled with prophylactic penises, including such structural elaborations as the Corkscrew, the Squirmy, the Prober, the Plunger, the rippled Veined Dong, and the spiked Ladykiller Dick, culminating at the top of the line in a pink plastic mold the approximate size of Arnold Schwarzenegger's forearm and fist, set in purple velveteen and labeled "HIS MAJESTY, THE KING." Dean paused only briefly at the penises, though, before he went on to the wall of leather and chrome, where eighteen different kinds of whips and sixteen sorts of masks were hung in glass cases, along with a varied selection of Slave Door Hangers and Wrist Suspender Restraints as well as assorted Twister Chains, Ball Socks, and Body Bags. Dean told the salesman he had mouth gags in mind and listened to a lengthy dissertation on the merits of each model before deciding he would take one of each, including the Rim Ring Gag, the Rubber Ball Gag, the Slave Bit Gag, and, particularly effective-looking, the Big Gulp Gag, a rubber dildo with leather laces that tied at the back of the head. He was shocked when the bill came to nearly two hundred dollars.

The early stages of midafternoon gridlock slowed Dean's return trip back through Beverly Hills into Westwood. He parked on the street outside the Manning to load the trunk and lock the latches, then drove into the underground garage. Watching the valet park the pickup with what remained of the West Cars fleet, Dean was troubled briefly by the way it stood out among the BMWs and Mercedeses, the last Targa and Jim's new Rolls. He shook his head against the whispers of apprehension. Worry was a form of procrastination, Joe had reminded him more than once, and deliberation did not involve doubt.

All five of them met that evening in the condominium on the twelfth floor to inventory Dean's purchases. Joe, Jim, and Ben tried on both the police uniforms and the UPS outfits. There was no need to decide upon costume until the last moment, Joe said. At least all the clothes fit, except Jim's brown pants.

The bodyguard was the one who tried the trunk, climbing inside to recline with his kneecaps and forehead flush against the lid as they closed it on him. A sure-enough tight fit, Jim said, when they let him out a few moments later. Not much air in there, either. They all were interested in the mouth gags. Each of them wanted to see how the dildo worked, but no one would volunteer as victim. Finally, they drew straws. Ben was the loser, which was distinctly ironic, considering that no person they knew groomed either his appearance or his dignity so assiduously as Dosti, and the other four broke up at the sight of him sitting there with his eyes goggling, gagging on the rubber shaft in his gullet.

Jim was sent north the following morning to continue his surveillance. The others added their acquisitions to the chest over the next couple of days. Reza surprised them all by delivering the bottle of chloroform he had promised and contributed as well a plastic bucket filled with cat litter, which would serve as his father's toilet during confinement. Ben, true to form, added precautions: a spray-on Band-Aid he said would enable them to avoid leaving fingerprints in the condo and an industrial deodorizer powerful enough to absorb even the reek of chloroform. Joe had organized a portable office, stocked with an IBM Selectric and an entire library of BBC stationery, legal forms, standard sales agreements, property transfers, loan documents, letters of incorporation, stock offerings, and power-of-attorney nominations. Joe still planned to perform the interrogation personally and said he had researched the subject of torture thoroughly in the UCLA student library. You could find anything in a library, Joe said.

The morning after his privacy and business torts final, Dean went back to Bernard's with Ben for a second trunk, in case the girlfriend stayed home from work that day. Any successful plan was essentially a matrix of contingencies, Joe said; the winners in the end were those who had calculated the highest percentage of possibilities. Everything they might need was piled in, on, and around the two trunks, which were being kept by the bed in Reza's room. Hedayat's son must be having some terribly interesting dreams of late, Joe remarked.

They were left then with only the problem of finding a suitable location. For this the Shadings separated: Ben drove alone into the desert, while Joe and Dean scouted the San Bernadino Mountains. The brokers ran to the window at the Four Seasons Realty office in Lake Arrowhead when the big BMW sedan pulled into the parking lot. "Any time a really nice car like that comes in, we all look and wonder who'll get them," explained Jill Lawler, that day's lucky winner. Lawler spent most of one day and part of another in the company of the two young men but scarcely could remember "the little one," Dean. Joe, "the tall, dark, curly-haired one," though, was unforgettable, the realtor said. She could not recall meeting anyone so young with such "self-possession," Lawler explained. "And he knew exactly what he wanted," she remembered, "a big secluded house where he could write." He was a political economist, Joe explained, at work currently on a treatise involving the relationship between interest rates and foreign investment from the historical perspective, due to the Federal Reserve Bank's board of governors by the second week of September.

Joe dismissed place after place, Lawler remembered, showing interest only in a large, empty A-frame on several wooded acres, well back from the lake. Even the pine plank floors were bare, but Joe seemed almost pleased that the house was unfurnished, the realtor recalled: "He said he just needed a table and a place to plug in his computer." The Olympic Games, which would begin in Los Angeles the day he wanted to move in, Joe treated as a distraction to be avoided. His one request was the installation of a phone, but Lawler had been unable to secure permission from the owner of the house in time to satisfy Joe's schedule.

Ben phoned from Palm Springs to say he had found a huge hacienda on a cul de sac, surrounded by a high adobe wall. There was a swimming pool, a central courtyard, and—more to the point—a climate-controlled wine cellar under the floor in the hallway. The two other Shadings drove south that afternoon, but Joe decided the wine cellar was too small. Then Dean was stopped for speeding by the highway patrol while returning to Los Angeles in Brooke's convertible, and Joe decided it would be best to avoid the desert altogether. Also, it occurred to him that it might be best to take a place in town after all, so they could shuttle back and forth to the office without extended absence.

By the morning of July 29, though, barely more than twenty-four hours from the time Joe had scheduled for Hedayat Eslaminia's abduction, the Project Sam team still was without a secure location where the man might be held. The *L.A. Times* classified section indeed offered an unprecedented selection of short-term rentals to out-of-towners attending the Olympics, but Joe and Dean were unable to find anything in the newspaper that suited their purpose. They used the *Times* instead to compile a list of every real estate office on the Westside offering Olympic accommodations and began calling them one-by-one. Joe repeated his political economist story again and again, explaining that he would be working sixteen-hour days for the next six weeks to meet a deadline and required an atmosphere of silence and seclusion. The first encouraging word they heard came from a broker at the Merrill Lynch office in Beverly Hills. The realtor who took their call, a lady named Bernice, was intrigued by Joe's presentation and knew of a place she thought might meet their needs. It was on North Beverly Glen, the dividing line between Bel Air and Holmby Hills, set deep in a large lot on a street with no parking. The new owner had obtained the property on foreclosure and listed it as a fixer-upper but had yet to make any repairs; frankly, it was not in perfect condition, Bernice warned. They would meet her there in an hour, Joe said.

The Boys arrived in one of the big BMW sedans, both wearing business suits. Brooke had come along in shorts and a striped blouse. Dean was not sure how much she knew, and so he said very little during the drive. The location on Beverly Glen looked ideal. The rock retaining wall in front had been planted with jacarandas that grew thick as a hedge, screening the house from the street. A two-lane driveway and another tall hedge separated the property on the right, and the enclosed tennis court was a comfortable cushion against the neighbors on the left. The backyard ended at the base of a long sloping hill surmounted by what once had been the Mattel mansion.

The house on Beverly Glen was itself nothing special, two stories of white clapboard with a Georgian façade, red brick and square pillars, the sort of generic suburban family-of-four home that might have sold for eighty thousand dollars in Seattle, but which in this neighborhood went onto the market at a million five. Bernice brought along another realtor, a lady named Ruth, and both women were fascinated by Joe, who towered above them smiling sweetly, speaking in a vocabulary of long-term equilibrium rates and parabolic curves that had the two ladies leaning forward, heads cocked, wearing that expression Dean had seen so many times before, at once quizzical and enthralled. As Joe had predicted, his identity was not questioned. Bernice even mentioned that she had rented to a number of East Coast writers over the years, most out here to work in the movies, of course, and without exception they had requested seclusion.

Bernice, though, did appear nonplussed when Joe stopped just inside the front door to ask if there was a basement. She had no idea, Bernice said, but knew that often in these houses the entrances to basements were concealed in coat closets. Sure enough, behind a door in the hallway, on the other side of a wooden rod dangling a dozen wire hangers, they found the trap door. Joe and Dean went down the stairs alone. Below, they found the perfect space, a square hole in the ground with six-inch-thick concrete walls and a cement floor, soundproof and secret. There was even an electrical outlet. The two of them stayed down there for almost ten minutes, pacing off the dimensions and congratulating themselves, then climbed back up the stairs.

"We'll take it," Joe said. Bernice was reluctant now, though, insisting that it wouldn't be right to let them rent a house they really hadn't seen. "We'd like to move in tomorrow," Joe told Bernice. She would have to talk to the owner, Bernice said. "We'll pay cash," Joe told her. In that case, Bernice said, she didn't expect there would be a problem.

The "chrome yellow" and "bright vermilion" flags posted along Wilshire Boulevard by the Los Angeles Olympics Organizing Committee one week earlier were hanging limp when the Boys returned to the Manning that afternoon. A breeze had begun to lift the tips of the pennants by 6 P.M., however, when Joe assembled the others in the parking garage to load their gear and gas up for the seven-hour drive north. The main roads all were unnervingly pristine. Los Angeles had been ridding itself of eyesores for the past month, a process that climaxed in the assignment of thirty LAPD officers mounted on horseback to drive the transient encampments off the sidewalks surrounding city hall.

Joe was right about the Olympics making good cover. The city's attention had been riveted by the opening ceremonies at the Coliseum the previous evening. As motorized platforms lifted eighty grand pianos playing "Rhapsody in Blue" out of the cheap seats and onto the world's laser-lit center stage, it was clear that the next three weeks would be the acme of the Reagan era.

Los Angeles refused to be deflected or deflated, even when, on the eve of the opening ceremonies, an enraged black man from Inglewood drove his red Buick onto a sidewalk in Westwood, injuring forty people and killing three. Soviet correspondents sent by Tass to subvert an Olympics their government was boycotting found more muck than ten of them could rake. Yet while stories of athletes narrowly avoiding death during training runs along freeways or being forced to abandon their gold medal dreams because of "smog-induced migraines" grabbed headlines in *Pravda,* the best-selling T-shirt at the concession stands outside the Coliseum read "TO HELL WITH THE RUSSIANS."

The LAOOC had ensured that the 1984 Summer Olympics would be remembered as "the Capitalist Games," the first Olympics run as a private enterprise, tightly packaged and aggressively marketed by self-made millionaire Peter Ueberroth. The Los Angeles games would cost less than six hundred million dollars, compared to the nearly seven billion the Soviets spent for the 1980 Olympics in Moscow, Ueberroth reported, and the Olympic Committee already was projecting a *profit* of twelve million dollars after selling sponsorships to thirty major corporations, among them Levi Strauss and McDonald's.

The LAOOC was able as well to circumvent or suppress those logistical nightmares Southern Californians had been warned of for weeks: There were no squads of Crips mugging tourists outside the Coliseum, no day-long gridlocks. Traffic actually was lighter than normal by the time the first four Boys began the trip north. Joe drove the pickup, with Jim as his passenger, while Ben and Reza followed in the BMW. Dean watched them turn west on Wilshire, then rode the elevator alone to the fifteenth floor.

Cooling winds off the Pacific had taken daytime temperatures down into the eighties just in time for the Olympics, and though some foreign athletes complained of breathing air they could see, anyone who had spent a summer in Southern California knew it was remarkably clear for Los Angeles in July. From the terrace, for the first time in days, Dean could see the sun set full on the ocean. As daylight dimmed, the mantle of smog on the horizon seemed to ignite, all livid glows and smoldering shadows. A fusion of cumulus mist, contaminated atmosphere, Pacific surf, and the sun's fading effulgence brought dusk to a visual crescendo, until the whole western sky seemed to fill with flames of pink and purple, like some impossibly vast special-effects explosion, a disaster so gorgeous that it was almost a privilege to stand among the victims.

***

Dean was up early the next morning but barely had time to glance at the *Times*'s banner headline: "SOUTHLAND CHEERS FIRST DAY'S GAMES; TRAFFIC, PARKING PROVE NO PROBLEM." Pairing his best gray business suit with a skinny silk tie, he called for a taxi, arriving at the office on Sunset Strip just before ten and instructing his driver to keep the meter running. The owner of the Beverly Glen house and the realtor from Merrill Lynch both were waiting for him.

On the Westside of Los Angeles, the line between illusion and reality was the one that formed at the bank, in the opinion of Bernice Rappaport. Joe's and Dean's youth was only sort of unusual, she thought, and the story about writing for the government was believable because they both seemed so brilliant, especially Joe. Their interest in the basement was novel, but in her time Bernice had fielded requests that included one for a hermetically sealed, germ-free doghouse and another for servants' quarters that could contain a staff of thirty-seven. Bernice had been selling real estate in Beverly Hills for twenty-five years and planned to have "I'VE SEEN IT ALL" carved on her gravestone.

The lady's passion for property and its play in the market was only marginally a function of her career. No subject—not development deals at Disney or three-pic packs at Paramount, not how the Dodgers are doing on the road or what the waves are like at Zuma—so consumes conversation and speculation in Southern California as does real estate. Owning one's own piece of paradise remains the central fantasy of the place, and a person's abode defines his or her position in the pecking order as nothing else can. The housing market in Los Angeles commodifies not only "entitlements" like public education and adequate health care but even such essentials to life as clean water and fresh air. The desirable neighborhoods on the Westside, laid out along the slopes south of Mulholland Drive from Laurel Canyon to Calabasas, then down the coast from Point Dume to the Santa Monica Pier, cover less than one-thirtieth of the land surface in Los Angeles County, and competition for high ground and grand views among those who could afford them had, by 1984, begun to transform the spectacle of unearned wealth and insipid celebrity into something so grotesque that one required a case-hardened sense of humor just to get up and face it every day. The newest and nastiest trend was the "teardown," the practice of outbidding all others to purchase a sought-after estate inside the Platinum Triangle, then demolishing the original mansion to make space for construction of an even larger and more opulent abode. The process would peak with the acquisition of the six-acre Bing Crosby estate in Holmby Hills by *Dynasty* producer Aaron

Spelling, who leveled the old crooner's palace in order to erect a residence of some 56,500 square feet. "It's a free country," Spelling pointed out.

It was one of *her* clients who started the price jump in Beverly Hills, Bernice liked to inform newcomers to the scene, an ex-fiancé, in fact, who put his house on the market for two million dollars in the days when there was no such thing as a two-million-dollar house in Beverly Hills. "I'd go there to show it on the weekend, and there'd be a hundred, two hundred people in the house at a time, all waiting to see what a two-million-dollar house was like," Bernice remembered. Ironically, the place wasn't worth half that, but then her ex-boyfriend really didn't want to sell it, Bernice explained, "he just wanted to play big shot, say, 'I have my house on the market for two million.' But then all of a sudden people started asking that same kind of money for *their* houses, saying, 'Well, if that thing's worth two million, imagine what I can get for mine,' and it just took off from there."

The houses on North Beverly Glen Bernice considered nothing special, even by the inflated standards of 1984, and the particular house Joe and Dean selected had no real history, she noted. Furthermore, she regarded the owner as "a very bogus guy, one of these wheeler-dealer types who buys run-down houses and overfinances them, gets money from banks in the East to remodel or add on or whatever after he has gotten a phony appraisal, which is not that difficult to do. Then he does just a little bit of work on the place and lets it go into foreclosure. And meanwhile pockets most of the cash."

The owner was in no position to play hard to get with renters by the afternoon of July 29, Bernice recalled. The games had commenced at the Coliseum that morning, and his house still was empty. The nine thousand dollars for six weeks that Joe and Dean were offering seemed a more than fair price, even during the Olympics. Their indifference to the dilapidation of the place was to her the most striking quality of the three young people she had met at the Beverly Glen house, Bernice thought. Joe's attitude was that he had neither time nor attention to spare for anything so trivial as an unfurnished room or inoperative appliance. "All he seemed to care about was his work, and all the other two seemed to care about was him," she observed.

Though Bernice "still had [her] doubts about those three" when she called the owner to say that Dean had offered cash and would be bringing the money by early the next morning, he said they sounded perfect.

The owner did look pleased, Dean recalled, as he counted out ninety hundred-dollar bills, then witnessed Karny's signature on the six-week lease. His taxi took Dean from Sunset to LAX, where he caught a PSA flight to

San Francisco International, arriving shortly after noon. There was another long cab ride out to the Peninsula, then south on San Mateo County's main drag, El Camino Real, to the Villa Hotel in Belmont. "SPEND A NIGHT, NOT A BUNDLE" read the sign out front. Joe had begun keeping a strict account of Project Sam expenses during the previous week, Dean remembered, urging them all to cut corners where they could.

At the desk, Dean asked for Ben Dosti's room, but the clerk found no Dosti on the register. "What about Ben Davis?" Dean asked, trying the name Ben still used to screen his calls at the office. There *was* a B. Davis, the clerk said; he had arrived the previous evening with a party of four, taking two rooms, 141 and 148. All four were waiting in 148, sprawled across the twin beds. Joe and Ben already were dressed in the brown uniforms. They had decided to do it as deliverymen, Joe said. Jim would go in first, wearing his gray sweat suit, to clear the way. The U-Haul was rented and parked across the street. It had occurred to Joe that the trunk should be properly packaged, though, before they brought it to the door, so Dean was sent out to a stationery store, where he bought a roll of paper, masking tape, and a felt tip pen. When he returned, they wrapped the trunk together, then Dean addressed it to HEDAYAT ESLAMINIA, 400 DAVY GLEN ROAD, #4322, BELMONT, CA.

They killed half an hour in front of the television, then carried the trunk downstairs and loaded it into the pickup. The condominium complex was just around the corner and up the hill, Joe reminded them, so it all would be happening very rapidly now. Jim and Reza led the way in the BMW, while the three Shadings followed in the pickup. Reza pulled over to let Jim out at the entrance to the underground garage, then drove to the top of the hill, made a U-turn, and parked on the other side of the street. Joe parked the pickup as close as he could to the side gate at the west end of the building. As he and Ben climbed out to pull the wrapped trunk from the bed of the pickup, Joe directed Dean to slide over under the steering wheel, since a driver sitting alone would attract less attention than a passenger. He never stopped thinking, Dean marveled. Jim already was at the gate, holding it open for them. Dean watched Joe and Ben carry the trunk through the entrance and disappear.

It was a quiet Monday in Davy Glen. Sitting beside the open window, Dean heard wrens warbling in the oak grove across the street. There was an instant when he thought he detected the sound of shrieks or screams, so faint and far away that it was possible he imagined them. He and Reza stared across the road at one another, able only to see the shape of the other's head through their shaded windshields.

Joe and Ben were back within five minutes. Jim held the gate as they lugged the trunk, unwrapped, toward the street. The two were red-faced and sweaty, their breathing labored as they carried the trunk to the back of the pickup. Joe told Dean to get out and help, but Jim already had opened the camper, and Dean could only stand there pushing air as they slid the trunk under the black shell. He smelled the chloroform then, emanating as pungently from Joe's clothing as from the trunk. Ben rode back down the hill in the BMW with Reza and Jim. Joe, driving the pickup, still was out of breath and didn't seem to want to talk, reporting only that it had been more difficult than expected. At the bottom of the hill, though, Joe said something that happened inside was bothering him: On their way out, Ben had stopped to wash his hands. "Joe thought this was a symbolic guilty gesture that demonstrated weakness," Dean explained.

They turned onto El Camino and drove a quarter-mile to the spot where a U-Haul was parked on the shoulder of the road. The pickup pulled in behind the U-Haul, and the BMW parked behind the pickup. The five of them met at the BMW, standing right out in the open, in plain view to six lanes of afternoon traffic. Joe thought Reza should stay behind to watch the girlfriend, Olga; they still might have to deal with her, and Reza's remaining in the area would increase their options. As they moved the trunk from the pickup to the U-Haul, Dean heard a knocking against the lid, then a man's voice saying, "Please, sir, please let me out." The words were repeated as Jim and Joe shoved the trunk toward the inner wall of the moving van, up by the truck's cab. Dean climbed in behind it. When they closed the doors, he was alone in the dark with just the knocking against the trunk lid for company. Then the voice, amplified by enclosure, begged again to be let out.

Dean was looking for a flashlight when the U-Haul lurched forward, and the doors of the van began to swing open. He barely caught the handles before the doors were too wide apart and nearly was pulled out into the street by their weight and momentum. In their haste, Jim and Joe had failed to secure the latch. It was impossible to do this from inside, so he had no choice but to stand like that, holding the doors shut. At least the voice from the trunk had ceased for a moment. Dean's sensation was of stop-and-go traffic for the next twenty minutes. By then the ache that started in his shoulders had descended into his hips, and his suit jacket was soaked with sweat. The knocking started up again, and then the desperate voice repeating those same words: "Please, sir, please let me out." Over and over, Dean remembered.

It was another half an hour or so before the truck stopped. The muscle spasms were running like a current from Dean's calves into the back of his neck. He gasped for fresh air and stifled a sob when the doors were pulled open from outside. Ben stood there looking at him, unable to speak, then threw in one of the blue Fila bags Dean and Lisa Marie had purchased during their vacation in Mexico. It was filled with "tools and supplies," he recalled: the flashlight, the bottle of chloroform, a wet rag, the mouth gags and handcuffs, pliers and screwdrivers, Jim's silenced Beretta.

Squinting into the white haze of sunlight, letting the hot wind dry his face, Dean made out that they were at some sort of truck turnout along the shoulder of the freeway. "Joe thought you might need help," Ben explained, and climbed into the back of the U-Haul. Jim appeared a moment later to toss in a six-pack of soda. Dean told him to make sure he shut the doors right this time.

Dean and Ben sat on unassembled cardboard packing boxes covered with moving blankets, as far from the trunk as possible. Each could barely make out the other's face in the strobe of the flashlight's beam. It took him some time to ask what happened in there, Dean remembered. Eslaminia—they no longer called him "Mister," Dean noticed—opened the door as soon as he saw the brown uniforms, Ben said, but he and Joe had barely carried the trunk across the threshold before Jim came charging in behind them, gun drawn. The man went to the floor facedown when ordered, pleading with them to take everything but to spare his life. When Jim tried to chloroform him, though, Reza's father struggled furiously, writhing and kicking, scratching at their eyes; for a person that age, his strength was amazing. Then Jim spilled the chloroform and tried to beat the man unconscious with his fists, but it was as if his punches had no power behind them—he was woozy from the chloroform or something—and just sort of flailed away. For a moment it looked as if the older man might actually overpower Jim before Ben and Joe jumped in, and all three of them pummeled Eslaminia to the ground. In the end, it was Joe who got the chloroform on the rag, covered the man's face, and put him under.

Dean and Ben had stopped speaking by the time the truck rolled into the San Joaquin Valley. It was more than 95 degrees outside, at least 110 in the back of the U-Haul, and God knew how hot inside the thirteen-by-thirty-nine-inch box. Joe's plan was that once they had Eslaminia in the U-Haul, he should be removed from the trunk, handcuffed, and gagged. They could use the chloroform if he struggled, Joe said, and always had the Beretta if needed. Ben and Dean, though, found they lacked the courage to open the trunk when they were locked up in the dark with it.

The noises were starting and stopping in cycles now: The knocking and pleading would last as long as ten minutes at a time, Dean recalled, subside for a minute or two, then start up again. Gradually, though, the voice grew fainter, until the cries were whimpers, and the knocking became a sort of scratching. When the noises stopped altogether, Dean found the man's silence more unbearable than his struggle.

Frantically, Dean probed the Fila bag with the flashlight and found a Phillips screwdriver. Ben seemed suddenly inert, as if paralyzed from the waist down, but held the light as Dean used the tip of the screwdriver to bore one hole after another in the lid of the trunk, sixteen of them in all, only a couple of inches apart. He was astonished at his own strength. After a few minutes, the air revived the man in the trunk and he began to cry out again, but from deeper inside himself this time, howling first in English and then in Farsi, alternately invoking the mercy of men and the justice of Allah. "There was a point at which the noise got very loud," Dean remembered. Sitting there in the dark, he and Ben began to imagine that the man's screams were penetrating the walls of the U-Haul, being heard by the drivers of passing cars. They warned the man to be quiet, but he would not: The wailing went on, becoming a kind of chant, echoing and expanding, combining repentance with terror and adding prayers for deliverance to cries of despair. Unable to stand it, Dean used the masking tape to cover the holes, plugging them one by one, while Ben held the light. A minute later, it was quiet again.

He and Ben looked at each other across the top of the trunk. "About how far are we, do you think?" Dean asked.

After a while they removed the tape from the holes, but only a few minutes passed before the man revived and began again to shriek and howl. Dean covered the holes again with the tape, and the noises ceased.

The truck stopped about twenty minutes later, off the freeway on a farm road somewhere near Fresno. It was just getting dark out, Dean remembered, when Joe opened the doors and told them the U-Haul's rear lights weren't working. Joe was concerned about being pulled over by the highway patrol, Dean recalled, so they moved the trunk to the back of the pickup again.

He and Joe rode up front, while Ben climbed into the back of the camper behind the trunk. Jim drove the U-Haul. They kept the sliding glass window between the cab and the camper open, Dean recalled, so Joe could listen. Even after he removed the tape again, though, the noises from the trunk grew fainter. When the sounds stopped altogether, Joe ordered Dean to open the trunk and check on the man. Leaning through the open window, half in the cab and half in the camper, he opened the trunk lid for about a second, Dean remembered. Hot air and the odor of vomit rushed into his face, and he closed the lid fast. A moment later he lifted the lid again, slightly, fanned it up and down to cool the air inside, then opened it wide to look at what was inside, using the flashlight Joe handed him. This was the first time he had ever seen Mr. Eslaminia, Dean reflected. What he observed now was a middle-aged man in a fetal position, eyes closed, drool on his chin. The man's stomach was moving up and down, though, so Dean told Joe he was breathing. Five minutes later, however, Joe instructed him to open the trunk again and check for a pulse. Dean couldn't find any but wasn't sure he knew how. He put his hand in front of the man's lips but felt no breath. Eslaminia's stomach was still moving, but Dean realized then it was from the jounce and jiggle of the road, and told Joe he thought the man was dead. Joe said to check once more, to try mouth-to-mouth resuscitation. Dean felt Eslaminia's wrist again but wouldn't try mouth-to-mouth; he said he was sure the man had died. "Oh shit," Joe said, very quietly. The two of them sat in silence for a minute, Dean recalled, until "I said, 'I guess we blew it.'"

Joe remained silent for some time, as if in assent, but when he spoke finally, his voice was calm, even kind of soothing: "Joe pointed out that we still had within our ranks the firstborn son of Mr. Eslaminia," Dean remembered, "and that provided there wasn't any particular suspicion cast on him, we could make him the conservator of his father's assets and ultimately we could probably gain control over all of the assets that we could find anyway."

Since Joe "seemed to be trying to be positive about the situation," Dean explained, "I tried to do the same." The sole concern Joe voiced during the rest of the drive into Los Angeles was that it would be best if Jim were not told that Eslaminia had died en route.

They left the 405 Freeway at Wilshire and drove directly to the Manning. Joe parked a half-block off the boulevard just long enough to let Dean out, instructing him to prepare a meal for three and bring it to the Beverly Glen house. Then Joe and Ben drove off so that Jim wouldn't learn that Mr. Eslaminia had died, explained Dean, who filled a brown paper bag with food, sent Jim home to get some sleep, and drove his Fiat convertible to the Beverly Glen house, arriving about ten-thirty. Joe and Ben were sitting on the trunk in the entry hall when he came in, surrounded by the handcuffs and mouth gags. They ate in the living room, about ten feet from the trunk, Dean recalled, discussing the disposal of the body inside. "According to Reza, lots of people might want to kill his father," Dean explained, "so there was no real necessity of destroying or concealing the body. The finger would point to other people."

Joe chose Ben to help carry the trunk to the basement. While Dean kept a lookout at the window, the two of them removed the body from the trunk, laid it on a blue tarp, uncuffed its wrists, and searched it. Joe and Ben lugged the trunk back upstairs ten minutes later and loaded it into the pickup under the camper shell, then showed Dean a key chain with a small notebook attached that they had found in Eslaminia's hip pocket.

In the end, they decided Soledad Canyon still was the best place to dump a body. Dosti then was sent home: "Since Ben got to go to the basement with Joe, I got to go in the pickup with Joe," Dean explained.

They traveled south on Beverly Glen, west on Sunset, north on 405, east on 14, under street lamps all the way. The drive was into darkness, though, after they left the Antelope Valley Freeway. To their right, the glitter of the L.A. basin dimmed as the canyon road descended, fading to a pale bluish border—like the afterglow of a flash—that outlined the Santa Susanas against the night sky. To their left, the Vasquez Rocks were Stygian silhouettes, black and encroaching. The brightest reflection off the headlamps was from the white agate that filled the cut banks along the roadside like a billion unblinking eyes.

Joe turned onto the fire lane and began the climb into Indian Canyon. Dean recognized the dirt road from a shooting excursion six months earlier. Up about five miles was where he and Jim had buried Ron Levin, Joe said—might as well dispose of Eslaminia in approximately the same place.

They had traveled only about a mile and a half, however, Dean recalled, when the truck's lights shone on another pickup and camper parked along the side of the road. He was terrified to imagine the kind of people who chose to spend the night in a place like this. Joe braked to a full stop. It was so dark that they couldn't turn their headlights off to drive past, Dean explained, but with lights on, the license plate would be visible: "So we decided to turn around and leave the body at a lower area."

They rolled back down the canyon to a plateau opposite a hillside that fell into a ravine so steep, the chaparral grew at forty-five-degree angles. Joe parked the pickup and said this would be as good a place as any. When they lifted the trunk out from under the camper shell, Dean was astonished by its weight. They barely got the thing to the side of the road before his strength gave out. Joe opened the lid, and together they tilted the box. Dean saw the body spill out stiff and folded, first rolling, then sliding into the ravine, dislodging rocks and loosening dirt until it stopped abruptly.

They disposed of the other evidence during the drive back to the city, stopping in Sylmar to toss the blue tarp into a trash can outside a truck stop, then in Mission Hills to discard the handcuffs in the Dumpster behind a minimall. The mouth gags they threw out the windows, Dean recalled.

Joe drove straight back to Westwood, agreeing with him they could clean up at the Beverly Glen house the next day, Dean remembered. And yes, Dean admitted, he was able to sleep.

In the full dark of Soledad Canyon, coyotes emerged from their burrows to practice what had been the province of high priests two thousand years earlier: haruspex, they were called by the ancient Romans, those who foretold the future by examining the entrails of sacrificial animals.

18

THE FIRST ATTEMPT TO REPORT HEDAYAT ESLAMINIA AS A MISSING PERSON came into the Belmont Police Department at a little past ten on the evening of July 30. The caller was Olga Vasquez, who introduced herself as Mr. Eslaminia's fiancée. She had seen Hedayat last at about seven-thirty that morning, Olga said, when she left for her job at Specialty Brands in San Francisco. They spoke on the telephone twice during the day, the second time just before 2 P.M. She returned home at a little past four that afternoon and immediately noticed all the curtains in the apartment had been drawn and the rooms were dark, even the kitchen, where Hedayat ordinarily would be preparing dinner at this hour. Yet the windows were open, something Mr. Eslaminia never permitted when he was gone from the condominium. She walked down the hallway flipping on lights and calling his name, Olga said, and was startled to discover the master bedroom door open: "He always locks it when he leaves the apartment." In the back bedroom, where Hedayat napped following his afternoon prayers, she could see the imprint of his body still showing in the spread. All that Olga found reassuring was the wallet in the ashtray atop the dresser in the third bedroom, bulging with ten- and twenty-dollar bills. Hedayat's keys, though, were gone.

The Belmont police were unimpressed with Olga's catalog of oddities. They could not initiate any investigation of a disappearance until a person had been gone at least forty-eight hours, the desk officer told Olga, though he was kind enough to provide her with a list of local hospital emergency rooms.

Olga phoned Ali Bani, who said, "He's just scaring you," she remembered. The colonel and Olga's Chilean friend, Veronica Fonseca, had been their guests the previous evening. For reasons she did not understand, Hedayat's mood was melancholy all day. Olga thought it had started with Bani's recollection of his most prestigious assignment, safeguarding the shah and the Empress Farah Diba whenever they went out in formal regalia to a public function. From there, the conversation degenerated rapidly into a contemplation of all that the two had lost, and Hedayat began to drink heavily, tossing down six or seven of those Sambuca and Coca-Cola concoctions he favored. Even Veronica became upset. "Mr. Eslaminia was just looking through the walls and drinking," she recalled.

It was a discussion of what Mina had taken from him that really set Hedayat off, Ali Bani explained. His friend became perhaps even slightly unhinged, announcing he intended to write the solicitor general in Washington, seeking relief from a court order that not only awarded custody of his sons to Mina but compelled him to pay alimony and child support as well. They all thought he had hidden a fortune, Hedayat complained bitterly. "He asked, 'Would I be living in this place if I had millions?'" the colonel recalled.

Ali Bani came to her just before dinner to prepare her for a talk with Hedayat, Olga remembered: "He said Hedayat didn't know what was wrong with me, that I hadn't been enthusiastic that week, and he was worried. So later we talked, Hedayat and I, with Bani in between. Hedayat said he had the feeling I was fading away, losing interest in him, and that in three or four months we'd be apart." Olga said she would marry Hedayat tomorrow, but he remained inconsolable, ending the evening when he staggered off down the hallway and fell face-first into bed.

Hedayat was still under the covers when Olga left the next morning. He had awakened but was hungover when she phoned at eleven to tell him the Italian embassy had called to say his visa was ready. Hedayat did apologize, however, she remembered, and said they would talk about their relationship that evening. When she phoned a second time at two, Hedayat mentioned he might meet Veronica's boyfriend, Rakhim, later in the afternoon at his carpet shop in San Francisco.

Alone in the condo after work, Olga phoned Veronica, who said Rakhim was not home, either. Olga poured a glass of wine and told herself Hedayat had stayed late with his friend. She kept calling back, though, more agitated each time, Veronica remembered. Finally Rakhim returned home, alone: "He said, 'Tell her I am with him, so she doesn't worry,'" Veronica recalled. "So I did. And Olga says, 'Oh, okay,' like now she can breathe. Then she called again around nine o'clock and said, 'What happened? He's not back yet.' And I go, 'Rakhim, he's not back yet.' And he goes, 'Well, tell her the truth, that I am not with him.' So I did, and she starts to cry, very upset. We drove over there so she would not be alone. I stayed with her all night."

Unable to sleep, Olga got out of bed and began to search the condo but couldn't find Hedayat's passport or green card. She also went through the closets and told Veronica that only his black slacks, black loafers, and favorite brown shirt were missing. She called the Mortzavis, who sent Hedayat's niece downstairs to sit with her. "I went to the security office to ask for the names of any new Iranians in the building, then went door to door, asking people if they had seen Hedayat," Olga remembered. "I showed them his picture, but people seemed not to want to get involved."

It was 5 A.M. when Olga phoned the Belmont police a second time: "I told them about the Khomeini hit squads, just to get a reaction, and they came right over." The patrol officer who arrived first at the condo noted an autographed picture of the shah in the living room but no signs of struggle or forced entry. He did find a .357 magnum revolver under the mattress in the master bedroom. Olga told the officer about the night before but said she was certain Hedayat would not leave in anger, adding that he never went anywhere without his diary.

The Belmont police sent two more officers to the Davy Glen condominiums at about nine that morning to conduct a foot search of the surrounding area. A canine officer showed up a short time later, leashed to a German shepherd that was allowed to sniff one of Mr. Eslaminia's shirts, then led police on a hike into the shallow ravine separating the condominium grounds from the Davy family estate.

The first TV news crew came out that afternoon, followed by reporters from the San Francisco newspapers, all attracted to the ayatollah angle. "KIDNAP, MURDER FEARED AS LONG KHOMEINI FOE VANISHES IN BELMONT" read the headline over the story in Hearst's *Examiner*. "He had been very active in going against the ayatollah," a spokesman for the Belmont police told the newspaper. "We got some information he probably was kidnapped out of there."

It was more like coming to than waking up, Dean remembered, when he rose from bed on the morning of July 31. He and Joe and Ben met in the smaller condo at the Manning, where they told Jim that Mr. Eslaminia had died of a heart attack during his interrogation in the basement of the Beverly Glen house. "So that Jim would not think we had messed up our plan," Dean explained.

Joe cut quickly from Eslaminia's demise to the issue of his estate, Dean remembered, outlining a plan to obtain the Iranian's assets by arranging for Reza's appointment as conservator, and said it was essential to present a united front when they met with Reza that evening.

Dean's attempt to recover the nine thousand dollars they had paid for the Beverly Glen house consumed most of his morning. The call from "Joe's assistant" was the first she took that Tuesday, Bernice Rappaport remembered: "He was very upset, almost in tears. He said, 'We've changed our mind—the money for our project has been withdrawn and we've just been transferred back to Washington, and we no longer need the house. Can we get our money back?'" She would have to talk to the owner, Bernice replied. "I thought it was a little odd," she explained, "that they had been so free with their money the day before and now they were so desperate to get it back." Half an hour later, Dean walked unannounced into the realtor's office at Merrill Lynch. "He looks terrible," Bernice recalled. "His suit is wrinkled, his tie is undone, he's sweating and pale—I felt sorry for him. He said, 'Can you please help us out, help us get our money back?' I told him I thought he could get half back, and that seemed to calm him down a little, though he wanted it all."

He and Ben returned the U-Haul to the rental agency in Santa Monica that afternoon, Dean recalled, then got back to Westwood in time to meet with Joe and Jim again before Reza arrived from Northern California. The three told the younger Eslaminia the same story Jim had heard. "Reza said, 'You're kidding,'" Dean remembered. Once they convinced him it was true, Reza wanted to see his father's body, to make sure that he was dead. The Shadings already had decided that there could be no good reason to show Reza where Mr. Eslaminia's remains had been discarded. "All it would do is give him possible information that he could later hold over our heads," Dean explained. Reza then asked if his father had said anything before he died, recalled Dean, who answered that Hedayat had mumbled something that sounded like *"Vi, vi, vi"* over and over again. Reza nodded, then said, "He was hypnotizing himself to death." It was an ancient art practiced among Persians, Hedayat's son explained.

Joe presented the conservatorship plan, and Reza readily agreed but said he was sure Olga would grab whatever she could. The Shadings decided Jim would return to the Bay Area, Dean recalled, to keep an eye on the girlfriend. "We also discussed that we couldn't do anything meaningful right then," he remembered, "because if we were going to act as though we didn't know how Mr. Eslaminia had disappeared, we would have to just stay quiet for a while."

The next morning, after Jim departed for Belmont, Ben and Dean headed for the Beverly Glen house to retrieve the second trunk—the one intended for Olga—as well as the brown uniforms, business papers, rope, tape, and kitty-litter toilet still piled in the basement, then drove through the alleyways of Westwood, tossing it piece by piece into various Dumpsters.

That same morning, Bernice Rappaport received a call from another realtor who said she had a doctor from Pasadena who was looking for a house on the Westside but couldn't find anything he liked. Bernice told her friend about the Beverly Glen house, said that it was empty and that the key was under the mat. "She calls me back an hour later and can barely get the words out," Bernice recalled. "She said, 'I've never been so frightened in my life. I heard this shuffling and moving, all kinds of noises, from the basement. But I couldn't see anyone, there was no car in the driveway, there was nothing.' She was imagining all kinds of things, like maybe the house was haunted. She said, 'I got so scared I just ran out of there. Bernice, there's something going on there, something horrible—don't even go look.'"

He saw a lot of the Olympic boxer, Jim Graham, during the first week of August, remembered Ken Hickson, the maintenance man at the Davy Glen condominiums. It was at the tail end of July, actually, when he met Mr. Graham. Hickson had been painting in the second-floor lobby that morning when he saw a stocky black man whose muscles bulged under a Nike warm-up suit approaching the elevators. "He sort of poked his head through the door from the parking garage, saw me, and stopped," Hickson recalled. "He said, 'Paintin' 'em up?' and I said, 'Yep.'" The two of them stood talking in the lobby for perhaps ten minutes, Hickson recalled, about the Olympics, mostly: "I joked and asked if he was in them. He looked like an athlete to me. He said he was and made it very convincing, that he was a light heavyweight fighter. He said his name was Jim Graham and he could get me tickets at the Stanford Stadium, where they were holding the boxing matches."

That was the morning of July 30. Hickson was sure of the date because the next afternoon Mr. Eslaminia was reported missing. Not that he had connected the appearance of the first man with the disappearance of the second. Maybe this was because there had been so many other odd events that week. When the police interviewed him, Hickson told them first about the very tall and expensively dressed young man he had encountered in the Sky Room on the afternoon of July 28. He was sure of that date, too, because the opening ceremonies of the Olympic Games in Los Angeles had been held that evening. The Sky Room was a huge space atop the 300 building, Hickson explained, reserved for special functions such as wedding receptions and meetings of the homeowners' association, off limits to everyone else. The young man, dark-haired and darker-eyed, wearing a suit and tie, was standing in front of the floor-to-ceiling windows that faced the 400 building, where Mr. Eslaminia lived, the maintenance man remembered. There were papers and a travel alarm clock on the coffee table by the couch that seemed to be his, Hickson recalled. "He seemed nervous; it made me feel like I had interrupted him, so I left after a minute." Later, "I thought about reporting him to the office," Hickson explained, "but he was so well dressed that I let it go."

The two Iranians in the BMW also were well dressed, Hickson recalled. He had seen *them* not long after he met Jim Graham on the morning of July 30. The BMW was a luxury model, brand-new and without license plates. He saw two strange men in the front seat, both with olive complexions and coarse black hair, but thought little of it, Hickson explained: "There are a lot of Iranians in that building." The BMW drove into the parking garage, then right back out, and turned left on Davy Glen toward El Camino. Hickson locked the gate behind them.

The maintenance man never saw the tall fellow or the two Iranians again, but Jim, the boxer, showed up a second time on the afternoon of August 1. It was about 4 P.M. when he saw Graham walk into the lobby of the 300 building and waved him over to introduce the manager of the Davy Glen complex, Jerry Miller, Hickson remembered. Jim said he was staying with a friend in the building and promised to bring by some tickets to the Olympic boxing matches so that Miller could pass them out among the residents and staff.

While the Belmont police took their time about interviewing the maintenance man, Hickson, they came straight away to Jerry Miller. It was Miller, little more than a month earlier, who had tipped off the Belmont PD to his suspicion that Hedayat Eslaminia was dealing drugs out of his condo in the 400 building. His misgivings had been aroused by "excessive foot traffic" in and out of the Eslaminia unit, Miller explained, and complaints from the man's neighbors about strange dark men appearing at their sliding glass doors "looking for Hedayat." The president of the homeowners' association, who lived directly above Eslaminia, persuaded the residents' board to authorize the manager's call to the police. He believed the Iranian had brought the drugs into the country concealed in a load of rugs, Miller informed the sergeant who took his call.

International intrigue, Iranian hit squads, Asian drugs, and Arab rugs, the Eslaminia case had it all, and if the local police were leery about proceeding with so complex an investigation, the local press was all over the story. The *Examiner* expanded on its original report of the disappearance with longer articles each day. "MISSING IRANIAN LEADER FEARED DEAD OR HELD BY KHOMEINI" read the headline on the paper's August 5 story, which led with an assertion that Hedayat Eslaminia had worked with both "U.S. intelligence agencies" and Saddam Hussein of Iraq to overthrow the ayatollah. "Police fear that Eslaminia may be dead or that agents of the ayatollah have kidnapped him and returned him to Iran," the newspaper reported, adding that "it would be the first time they have carried out such a kidnapping in the United States." While spokesmen for the CIA and FBI declined comment, a U.S. State Department spokesman conceded it was "possible" that such meetings between Eslaminia and U.S. officials had taken place.

Two days later, Ali Bani informed the FBI that Mr. Eslaminia had spoken of an impending big meeting in Europe with various important politicians and Muslim clergy and said he thought it conceivable that Hedayat had decided to travel undercover. Bani then offered three alternate theories to explain his friend's disappearance: Most obvious was that agents of the ayatollah had indeed kidnapped Hedayat in order to try him in Teheran, but the colonel noted also that Eslaminia's articles criticizing Saddam Hussein had resulted in threats from the Iraqi government, then added that he believed it possible that Hedayat's eldest sons, Reza and Ali— who hated their father—had taken him.

Olga was the one who revealed to the newspapers that Hedayat's name had been inscribed in blood on a wall in Teheran, said that he had made four trips to Europe during the past year, and confided that "people often called him using codes and fictitious names," as the *Examiner* reported it. The role of damsel in distress came easily to Olga, a woman who instinctively sought the protection of authoritative men. After San Francisco newspaper reporters, Olga found Belmont police officers most sympathetic. The sergeant in charge of the investigation listened attentively when Olga informed him that a Mr. Shiarzi had called on August 1 from Mecca, Saudi Arabia, to tell her he was taking a Lufthansa flight to Frankfurt, Germany, where he hoped Hedayat would arrange for someone to meet him at the airport, and also that a Mr. Alaivi had phoned to request that Hedayat send a translator to meet him at Heathrow when his flight from Jidda arrived in London one day later, and that a Mr. Farazian from Los Angeles had passed along a rumor that Hedayat was in Washington meeting with officials of the State Department.

"Olga was spinning" as suggestions and speculations poured in, her friend Veronica recalled: "So many stories. Olga couldn't sleep, she was crying all the time, calling people over and over." Among the first calls she made was one to Mina's house in Beverly Hills, Olga remembered, to ask for Reza: "I felt, as Hedayat's eldest son, he was the one I should notify on behalf of the family. I spoke to Mina, said I needed to talk to Reza. She said, 'He doesn't live here anymore.' I told her why I wanted to talk to him, and she asked why I was telling her."

A laughing Reza phoned her at the condominium three days later, Olga recalled: "He said, 'What do you mean, my father is missing?' I said it wasn't funny and told him what happened."

Olga next heard from Reza on August 5, the same day her photograph appeared in the *Examiner*. Hedayat's son said he had come up to inspect the apartment and wanted the access code to the building, she remembered. He was calling from the 7-Eleven down the street on the corner of El Camino, Reza added. Olga told him to wait there.

Ten minutes later, followed at a discreet distance by an officer from the Belmont PD, Olga drove down Davy Glen to the convenience store, where she found Reza sitting in Debi's gold Porsche, accompanied by a tall, lanky, dark-eyed young man he introduced as "my associate Joe Hunt." They both were in suits, Olga remembered: "When he saw the police officer, Reza got very defensive—'What's going on? Why do you need the police?' I said I just needed them to be with me; I didn't give any details. Reza was indignant, he seemed a little out of control, but Joe calmed him down. Joe was very calm; he had a face you could trust."

They drove back up Davy Glen to the condominium complex, where Olga asked the police officer to stand watch at the apartment's front door. Joe followed as she escorted Hedayat's son into the dining room, Olga recalled: "I said, 'This is between Reza and I; it's a family matter.' Reza said, 'No, I can't talk without my associate present.' He became hysterical, said he was going to come back with a court order . . . but his associate Joe was soothing, saying, 'No, that's okay, Reza. I understand how she feels. You two talk.'" When they were alone, she tried to tell Hedayat's son about various phone calls she had received, Olga remembered, but all Reza seemed interested in were his father's assets: "He wanted to know about safe-deposit boxes, about jewelry, about any overseas accounts, about real estate. I told half-truths. I knew more than I said, but I didn't trust him. Then he said, 'I know my father loved you.' I reacted to the past tense: 'What do you mean, *loved*? Do you know where your father is?' He leaned back in his chair and said, 'I made a mistake; I mean 'loves you.' Then all of a sudden Reza was saying he wanted to take care of me. He said, 'Can I stay here tonight?' I said no, and he acted totally surprised."

Before the two young men left, Olga went to the bedroom for her camera and snapped a picture of Reza standing in the living room. "I was suspicious after the 'loved' remark," she explained. "I said I wanted a recent picture of him, but what I really wanted was a picture I could show to the neighbors and ask if they saw him on the day Hedayat disappeared." She saw Joe signal with his eyes, Olga said, and a moment later Reza snatched the camera out of her hands, tore open the back, and ripped out the film. "You're playing games!" he shouted. "Reza was violent; I thought he was going to hit me," Olga recalled, "but then Joe stepped in, very calm. He said, 'Reza, can't you see the lady's upset? Let's just leave.'" As he turned to go, Reza handed Olga a BBC Consolidated business card bearing Neil Adelman's name and said he could be reached through his attorney.

***

Olga Vasquez was proving more formidable than they had imagined, Dean recalled. Reza dismissed her as a bimbo, but the young woman's use of the police boded badly. On the other hand, the publicity Olga drummed up was working to their advantage: Several family friends who read about Eslaminia's disappearance in the newspaper "called and said, 'Reza, you have to do something,'" Dean remembered. "It seemed an opportune time for Reza to take the helm of responsibility and start to act as though he were going to take care of the affairs, like a son should."

At the Third Street office, the Shadings spread the word that Mr. Eslaminia had disappeared and said the BBC should do something to help Reza gain control of his father's affairs. Within a day or two, the attorneys in the office had begun to prepare conservatorship applications.

The one area in which the BBC had continued to expand was the size of its legal staff. The newest attorney was Jon Allen's girlfriend Lauren Raab. Of the ten people still coming into the Third Street office every morning, Evan noted, three were lawyers, two were law students, and one was a law school graduate: "We were in a position to tie an enemy up in court for years."

Even as Project Sam proceeded apace, Joe led the Boys into battle on a number of other fronts, most involving disputes connected in one way or another to Microgenesis. Before leaving for Belmont on the evening of July 29, Joe had dictated a letter to be sent by certified mail on the date of the abduction, July 30, to the board of directors at Cogenco, "warning us to back away from our own technology," Bruce Swartout remembered. On the morning of August 1, as Dean and Ben discarded the physical evidence connecting the BBC to Hedayat Eslaminia's disappearance, Joe was meeting with the BBC's attorneys to prepare a Mailgram that he sent to Denver twenty-four hours later, threatening to cancel the November 1983 agreements between Microgenesis, UFOI, and Saturn Energy. That same day, Joe organized a party of BBC members for a flight to Arizona to repossess the Cyclotron from William Morton's mining site outside Apache Junction and return it to the warehouse in Gardena.

Joe flew to San Francisco with Reza the next morning. After the rebuff by Olga Vasquez, Joe decided Reza should take his complaints directly to the Belmont police. The younger Eslaminia came in alone for that first meeting at the station house and agreed without hesitation that the police could tape the meeting. He was convinced his father had been abducted by pro-Khomeini terrorists, said Reza, waxing indignant: "This is not Iran! This is the United States! How can someone just walk into a security building and take someone?" When Lieutenant Jim Scales suggested that Hedayat "might have just walked out," Reza shook his head, informing Scales, "My father called a month ago and said he was involved in some dangerous business" connected to negotiations with "pro-shah people in Paris." "We know all about your father," the lieutenant advised him. After asking for a cigarette, Reza turned the conversation in the direction Joe wanted it aimed: "How much do you know about this Olga girl?" he asked. "Some of the things she says seem a little funny." The claim that his father locked the bedroom door bothered him especially, Reza said: "Why was he locking his bedroom? Against her?" "Either she's extremely confused or she's after his assets—or she's involved," he surmised.

When the detective who had interviewed Olga just a few hours earlier asked whether there were problems between father and son, Reza allowed that "after the revolution we had our spats." Hedayat was moody, his son explained, and in business wanted to do things "hanky-panky." He assumed the police knew his father once had offered him fifty thousand dollars to kill Mina, Reza said: "I objected, and he thought I was not enough of a man." His father had been "blackmailing some Iranian people," hadn't he? Scales suddenly asked. "We know this," the lieutenant added. Reza scarcely could conceal his amusement: "Do you? You're surprising me." On his way out, Reza gave the two officers Mina Hakimi's home phone number but reminded them, "I am the head of the family. According to my father's instructions, I am handling his affairs. Please keep me informed."

Reza was back at police headquarters the next day, accompanied this time by Jerry Eisenberg and Neil Adelman. The number of law enforcement officers on the scene had increased as well: Sitting in on the meeting were a pair of FBI agents who gave only their last names, McCann and Buchanan. The appearance of the feds was his first indication of "what big shit we had stepped into," Eisenberg recalled. "Before that, as far as I knew, the only reason I had been called up there was to negotiate entrance into Eslaminia's apartment."

It was Joe who explained to him that Reza's father had disappeared, Eisenberg recalled: "He said, 'We need to go up there and help out, see what we can do to get the police active." After Joe and Reza flew ahead on August 5, Eisenberg followed them north with Adelman, Karny, and Jon Allen on the morning of August 7. The six met at the Stanford Park Hotel. According to Reza, Olga Vasquez had helped the kidnappers, Eisenberg recalled, and was keeping documents in the Belmont condominium that gave her access to Hedayat Eslaminia's assets. Joe suggested having Jim Graham seduce Olga, Eisenberg recalled: While Jim "occupied" the girlfriend, the others would break into the condominium and sort through Eslaminia's papers at their leisure, removing what they needed. What Eisenberg wondered was why Joe or Ben didn't do the seducing, since their chances of succeeding were a lot greater than Jim's. "I didn't want to ask questions, though," the attorney explained. "I wanted to get back to Los Angeles and watch the volleyball finals at the Olympics." Eisenberg was delighted when Joe elected to try the police one more time: "The story I was supposed to go in with was that Olga Vasquez was this horrible woman who probably had collaborated with the kidnappers."

Reza arrived at the Belmont Police Station at just past two o'clock that afternoon, flanked by a pair of attorneys, Detective Peter Keehn remembered, and delivered a handwritten letter. "I have contacted numerous people in the Iranian communities of both Los Angeles and San Francisco," Reza's letter began. "Those contacts have led me to believe that serious foul play has befallen my father and that his disappearance was by force and under no circumstances voluntary." The account offered by Olga Vasquez was "riddled with inaccuracies," asserted Reza, who then listed three groups that had threatened either to kill or kidnap his father: Mujahadeen, Fahadaez, and the Brotherhood of Moslems. "It is my firm belief from communication with sources in the Iranian community that actions by one of these groups has led to the kidnapping or death of my father," Reza's letter explained.

> It is my belief and the belief of my sources also that there are personal documents of my father's, including, but not limited to: A personal diary, financial documents, bank statements, deeds, certificates, letters, telexes, telegrams, stock certificates and handwritten notes, which all directly relate to the reasons for his disappearance. I personally helped my father hide most of these documents in the home he shared with Olga Vasquez and am also aware of the places my father independently hid sensitive documents. I further believe, based on my sources, and the actions taken by Ms. Vasquez, that the above-mentioned documents will be taken or destroyed some time this afternoon and that it is imperative that they be retrieved by the proper law enforcement agencies in order to insure the safety of my father.

"Eisenberg wrote all that," Reza would explain later.

The FBI agents were only too happy to agree that Hedayat Eslaminia's "sensitive documents" should be removed from his apartment but had no intention of allowing either Reza or his attorneys to handle such papers before they were reviewed by the federal government. "That was the first time I heard—from the FBI—about who Eslaminia had been back in Iran," Eisenberg remembered. "They said he had disappeared before, to go to France to meet with [Shapour] Bakhtiar, and that he was involved in drugs in Iran, and also with SAVAK and the CIA. They also said, though, 'We don't believe he was taken by any of these groups,' and I was taken aback by that."

Agent Buchanan would accompany Detective Keehn to the condominium on Davy Glen to supervise seizure of the documents and would hold them personally until the matter of Hedayat Eslaminia's estate was resolved in court, it was agreed. "I was elated," Eisenberg recalled. "Reza and I and Neil met Joe and the others at a coffee shop on El Camino, and when I told him the police had the documents now, Joe wasn't pleased at all. He didn't react, but I could tell he wasn't happy. That was when I began to suspect a hidden agenda."

19

JIM WAS RIGHT: "SOMEBODY ALWAYS TALKS." FIRST TO BREAK THE CIRCLE WAS
Jeff Raymond, who had waited no later than Monday morning, June 25, to
tell Dave May of the previous afternoon's secret meeting at the Manning.
The two spoke in private at their office in the Gardena warehouse, but Jeff
didn't tell his friend about the murder of Ron Levin. "I thought Dave would
react emotionally," he explained, "so I only told him about Joe losing our
money in the commodities accounts." Then Dave agreed to set up a lunch
meeting with the twins' father, Jeff recalled, to get advice about recovering
their investments.

That afternoon, Jeff returned to the Manning early to avoid Joe.
When he arrived, though, Hunt was waiting. "He asked for my impressions
of the meeting," Jeff recalled. "I said I was a little worried about this—all
the little details. He said, 'Don't worry; it was a perfect crime.' Then he said
the body would never be found. I said, 'But you have the contract and the
check. It will be obvious you saw Ron Levin last.' He said he had planted
letters in the office to make it seem like it happened over time. Then he said
he shouldn't tell me more, that there was no reason for me to know."

On Wednesday, June 27, he and Dave met with the senior May at
his office in Beverly Hills, Jeff recalled, and at that time told both of them
about Joe saying he had killed Ron Levin. It was the loss of the twins' two
hundred thousand dollars, though, that infuriated Dave Two, Jeff remembered: "Dave's father said Joe had stolen the money and was trying to use
the murder story to scare us off. He wanted us to find out if Ron Levin was
missing."

Jeff's talent for wearing two faces served him well in the weeks that
followed. "Jeff Raymond I always thought of as being much more involved
in Paradox Philosophy than he really was, apparently," Evan recalled.
Though Raymond later would describe Dave May as his best friend, "I
thought at that time he was much closer to Tom than to Dave," Evan
remembered. "Whenever Joe criticized Dave—which was often—Jeff never

said a word to defend him. And I certainly never thought Jeff would tell Dave or anyone else about the meeting. He just seemed so much a part of what was happening. You had no idea that he was in any way disenchanted. In fact, he seemed particularly attentive to Joe during the time he was living with him."

Jeff's opacity was such that he managed to make even his decision to move out of the Manning a nonevent: He went to stay with his girlfriend Renee Martin in Newport for a few days at first, returning to Westwood during the day to remove his belongings a few items at a time while Joe and Dean were at the office. He asked Hunt to send documents showing how the money had been lost to his parents' house, Raymond recalled, but Joe said these could be viewed only at the Third Street office, "and I didn't want to go up there," Jeff explained.

Early in July, Ron Levin's disappearance was verified by a brief article in the *L.A. Times*. Still, Dave Two was reluctant to bring in the authorities as long as Tom's involvement put him at risk of an accessory charge. The elder May arranged a meeting for Jeff and Dave with his corporate counsel, Arthur Crowley, who said he would look into the matter, Raymond recalled.

"I had to play along" would be Tom's story later, but no one else in the BBC believed his Shading-in-the-making stance had been a performance. During the weeks immediately after the June 24 meeting, the others recalled, Tom turned his twin in to Joe for accusing Hunt, Karny, and Dosti of "pocketing our money," denounced Dave at the office as a Normie, openly shunned his brother at social gatherings, and kept secret from Dave what Joe had told him about Ron Levin's vanishing act. "Tom likes to say he was duped," Gene Browning would observe, "but that's a crock. He was indoctrinated." Not that Dave or Jeff did much more than grouse about the money they lost, the inventor recalled: "Even in July, Dave's only real ambition was to come out of it with something he could show Daddy May."

Both Jeff and Dave continued to work with Gene Browning at the Microgenesis plant. Jeff not only held his own tongue but counseled against Dave's impulse to foment discontent among BBC members. As far as Evan could tell, "Dave still seemed along for the ride, counting on getting the money Joe said he would get."

Like everyone else in the BBC, Dave believed that what counted now was control of Gene Browning's machine, and by the end of July he was angling to pry the inventor loose from Joe and the Shadings. July 22 was the date on the "loan" Dave made to Browning and his wife so that the couple could purchase a new home in Irvine. In repayment the twin was promised an option on the gold mining rights to the Cyclotron in the event Browning rescinded his contract with Joe Hunt and BBC Consolidated. Early in August, still brooding about his aborted confrontation with Joe at the Third Street office, the inventor learned Joe was threatening to cancel the Microgenesis contracts with UFOI and Saturn Energy; Browning wrote a termination of his own agreement with Hunt on August 3.

It was the very next day that Joe dispatched a four-man BBC team to Arizona with instructions to repossess the Cyclotron at Morton's mining site. "Everyone was supposed to go, and then hardly anyone went," Eisenberg remembered. "In the end it was Jon Allen, me, Dave May, and Steve Tag: Jon to be the errand boy, me if they needed legal counsel, Dave because he knew the machine, and Steve, even though he was suspended, because no one else was available." The four flew on the same plane to Phoenix, rented a Lincoln Town Car at the airport, then drove an hour and a half east through the Pinal County desert to the furnace of sand and stone that was Apache Junction. They found the Cyclotron surrounded by chain-link fence and attached to a cyanide tank, with drainage beds laid out on all sides.

"This machine is gigantic, though," Eisenberg explained. "So what to do? I said, 'Leave the machine, and we'll just take the working parts.' Jon Allen didn't think that's what we should do; it wasn't what Joe had told us. So he took off in the car to go call Joe at a phone about ten miles away. We're just out there in this desert, and we start to take the machine apart, the three of us. I was soaked through. Jon Allen came back. He had been trying to get ahold of Joe but could only get Dean, and by then it was lunchtime. So we went back to Apache Junction." Jon finally got through to Joe, who instructed Allen and Taglianetti to meet him at the airport in Phoenix. This left the only two active BBC members excluded from the June 24 meeting alone at the mining site.

"We were sitting in the shade, where it was about a hundred and ten," Eisenberg remembered. "Dave started telling me, 'There's a lot of things going on.' He wasn't sure about me and I wasn't sure about him, but we started comparing notes, about the commodities trading, mostly. Then the next thing I know, he's telling me about the Levin murder. I believed it the moment I heard it." He and Jeff were worried about what would happen to Tom if they went to the police, Dave explained. And yet, the two of them didn't trust Tom, either, Eisenberg recalled: "Tom was still hanging in the balance. He didn't know Dave had talked to an attorney. At that time, Tom was definitely on Joe's side, but Dave said he was convinced he could get him to come over, with some additional information." Eisenberg provided what he could, describing Joe's fabricated trading statements on abandoned commodity accounts.

Joe arrived in Phoenix accompanied by Jim and Dean. By the time they reached the mining site to join up with Eisenberg and Dave May, mine owner Morton had showed up, "He came out and began to explain his operation," Taglianetti recalled. "I think he thought we were out there just to look and talk. Joe said he wanted to see inside the machine, see the wear or something. A few minutes later, Joe pulls us aside and says, 'Let's go into town and see if we can get a truck.' I went with them, to this rental place. We found this forklift, a tremendously huge thing, and Jim gave the guy like five hundred dollars to have him drive it out and help repossess the machine. Jim and I rode on the forklift with the guy, and Joe took off in the rented car. So we get out there, Jim and I hop off, and the guy puts the forks right through the chain-link fence and lifts it out. We loaded it onto the truck, which Joe and Jim drove back to L.A."

On the plane back to L.A., Dave confided to Tag that he had told Jerry about Levin. "So now there were four of us," Eisenberg recalled. "The only ones we trusted were each other." The number was six, actually, since not only Dave May II but Steve Tag Sr. as well had learned of the murder. "When I told my father, he was shocked," Steve Jr. recalled, "but he had always felt something would happen. He said, 'Everything Tom and Dave touches turns to shit.' He told me just to stay away, not to confront [the Shadings]. He asked for their numbers, Jim's in particular, since I had implied that he was the one who would do it if they decided to kill me."

By then, Dave had passed along to his twin the information from Eisenberg about Joe's misuse of investor funds and the inevitable SEC investigation. This turned Tom's head only a degree or two: he admitted knowing for almost two months that Joe had killed Ron Levin but refused to abandon the BBC. Frustrated, Dave tried to reach several of the other Boys, Evan in particular. "Dave was trying to talk to me about all the things that were going wrong, without alluding directly to Levin," Evan remembered. "He was complaining that they weren't getting the money for the Cyclotron, things weren't going well, Joe wasn't handling things well, this whole Paradox thing was bullshit. He never tipped his hand directly, though, except for one or two blunders, like telling Daisy Vreeland and [her friend] Penny Mathews. He told Daisy something like 'We have enough to put Joe away forever.' Daisy said something to me, which I related back to Ben. So I'm sure Joe did have reason to imagine that someone had told Dave and that Dave was telling other people."

At the end of the first week in August, after giving up on Evan, Dave spilled his story to the one individual whose control over the future of the BBC rivaled Joe Hunt's. "I came up to the [Gardena plant] one morning," Gene Browning remembered, "and the Mays were sitting around there rather solemn-faced. And Dave said, 'These are the circumstances. What in hell do we do?'" This was the first the inventor had heard of Ron Levin's murder. It was obvious to him, Browning said after he thought about it for a while, that Joe Hunt's announcement at the Manning had been an attempt to make accessories after the fact of those who attended the June 24 meeting; they better find a good attorney, pronto. Dave's twin, though, remained reluctant, Browning remembered: "Tom was still loyal to Joe. I told him, 'Do you know what the penalty is for accessory to murder? You're looking at fifteen years.'" At that point, "Tom panicked," Browning recalled, "and decided all at once that what Dave had told him was true. It was one of those PROTECT YOUR OWN ASS syndromes. Tom was still in the office, still an accepted person, still had the keys. He went into that office and went through those files with a fine-tooth comb to pick out everything that he could find that had his name on it so that he could not be implicated in all of this. He also got the contract with Levin and a copy of the check."

The Mays did nothing for the next two days, however. It was Eisenberg who made the first contact with law enforcement. Though he would do his best later to obfuscate the fact, Eisenberg had been aware of the Levin murder for several days when he traveled to Belmont on August 7 to help Reza gain access to his father's condominium. He had not begun to suspect "something amiss" up north, however, the BBC attorney swore, until after the meeting at the Belmont Police Department: "That scared me," he explained. "I had gone in there expecting just the city police, some kind of Mayberry, RFD, outfit, and then I find the FBI saying, 'Interpol's been contacted, the CIA knows about your father.'"

He saw an opportunity to "find out for sure what was going on," Eisenberg explained, when Jim came into the Third Street office alone on the evening of August 8: "I said, 'Jim, this doesn't smell right. Do you know the FBI is in on this? The CIA? Interpol?' And he told me, 'Yeah, you're right—there's more to it.' Then all of a sudden he says, 'We knocked him off.' His story was that he was with one other guy—Nick, I figured—and they hid and they got the guy and they grabbed him." Rambling a bit, Jim made reference to "Steve Taglianetti's concerns for his physical safety," Eisenberg remembered, "then said words to the effect, 'We're living off the investors' money. If things don't get better, we'll be closed in five months. We're going to get a lot of money from Reza, though, and that should solve our problems.'"

Eisenberg was on the phone to the FBI an hour later: "I told Buchanan everything Jim had told me, and he was buying it." From the Third Street office, the attorney drove to the Mays' apartment in Brentwood. "Eisenberg told us, 'They've done it again,'" Tom remembered. Dave May called Gene Browning in Irvine that evening to ask if the inventor would join the twins and Jeff Raymond for a meeting with Arthur Crowley at the attorney's office in the penthouse of the 9200 building on Sunset Boulevard.

It was obvious to him the next morning, as he sat with the three young men in the lobby of the law office, Browning recalled, that the twins "were scared to death, and mostly of their own father. When Daddy May found out about Cantor Fitzgerald and what they had lost there, he all but disowned them. Daddy May never thought much of his boys, but after that he was thoroughly disgusted with them. He told them, 'Why don't you two get jobs at Baskin-Robbins? That's all you're qualified for.'" Tom's tension was palpable, as was Dave's dolor. "Dave told me, 'We're getting a thousand dollars a month, and I don't think we're even going to be in Dad's will,'" Browning remembered. Jeff also seemed obsessed with the money he had lost. Browning suggested he consider it well spent: "Jeff had borrowed twenty thousand dollars from his dad, but his father got a fifteen-thousand-dollar consultation fee from Joe, so I told him, 'Five thousand dollars is cheap education.' My God, they could have thrown you off the balcony."

When the four of them were admitted finally to the inner sanctum of the senior partner's office, it was Dave who attempted first to explain the situation, Browning remembered: "Mr. Crowley, in his own pious and arrogant self, was sitting there in his gold cufflinks in this huge office, and he listened for a little while and then sort of shrugged his shoulders and called in another attorney." This was an associate at the firm, Paul Tobin. "Crowley told him, 'Go listen to this story and see if you can make anything out of it,'" Browning recalled. "And [Tobin] listened. Tom had this big box of documents and [Tobin] said to me, 'Can you make sense out of these things?'" After the inventor explained how he imagined the Microgenesis contract dated June 6, 1984, had figured in Joe's plan for the murder of Ron Levin, the attorney stared at the four of them for a moment, "then said, 'Sit. Don't move. Don't say a thing,'" Browning remembered. "He walked out of the office and after a while he came back and said, 'Two people from the Beverly Hills Police Department will be here in five minutes.'"

A murder investigation, under ordinary conditions, was like gathering grains of sand to assemble the boulder of a case, Detective Les Zoeller would explain to Gene Browning, "but you guys sat there at that conference table and dropped the boulder on us. So we had to break it down into the grains of sand."

The Beverly Hills PD sure took its sweet time with the sand collection part of the process, the May twins complained. "The police didn't even believe us when we gave them the [Swiss bank] check and the [Microgenesis] contract," Dave May griped. "They thought we just wanted to get Hunt for losing our money." The character of the victim was a major impediment to the case, Detective Zoeller explained. The department's "Ron Levin Task Force," as it amused other cops to refer to Detective Paul Edholm, informed Zoeller early on that Levin was facing felony charges for theft of camera and computer equipment and most likely had fled to avoid prosecution.

Zoeller officially had been the lead investigator on the Levin case since June 23 but did nothing before July 7, when he spoke with an FBI agent who informed him of Levin's involvement in a check-kiting scam at Progressive Savings, a scheme involving the very same Tom Frank May II who one month later would present Zoeller with copies of the Microgenesis contract and Swiss bank check. On July 17, Zoeller's partner sent Levin's dental charts to the Missing and Unidentified Persons Program in Sacramento: The pathologist who ran the computer check reported back that Ron Levin had a great deal of dental work, unique and quite expensive, and that he had been unable to make a match with any of the thirty-five hundred John Does reported in the United States during 1984. That was the sum of Zoeller's efforts before the August 9 meeting at Paul Tobin's office.

Only thirty at the time, Zoeller already had been a detective for five years. Red-haired and bland-faced, with a bushy mustache that looked pasted on and a Kmart wardrobe, Zoeller suggested a junior college student majoring in real estate appraisal; in fact, he already had conducted more than a dozen murder investigations in Beverly Hills, where virtually every homicide carries the freight of notoriety or political sensitivity. This one had both, obviously, and Zoeller intended to proceed with appropriate caution.

Frustrated by the reluctance of the police to take immediate action, the Mays arranged for Zoeller to interview Steve Tag and Jerry Eisenberg at Paul Tobin's office on August 14. Taglianetti directed his remarks mainly toward the subject of Jim Graham, "who sometimes uses an alias, is a body builder, holds seven degrees of proficiency in martial arts, and looks like a football player," Zoeller wrote in his notes. "He usually wears a bullet-proof vest and carries a 'pen gun' in his shirt and a knife strapped to one leg." Like Gene Browning, Eisenberg claimed credit for the Mays' decision to take their story to the police: "They never would have done it if I hadn't made them," he said. "I gave them numbers, names, told them what to say." While he was willing to make allowances for Dave and Jeff, perhaps even for Tag ("I don't think they knew what to do or who to go to because it was such an unbelievable story"), Tom May "was just as culpable as Joe Hunt" Eisenberg asserted.

No matter what his prior involvement, however, Tom now was law enforcement's mole inside the BBC, still coming into the Third Street office every other day or so, free to gather whatever papers had been requested by investigators. When his Newport Beach girlfriend, Alisa Goza, drove up from Orange County to meet him for lunch in Los Angeles, she found Tom "looking awful, really pale and out of shape. He was always tan before he went in the BBC. I said, 'You must not get outside much,' and he kind of laughed. When I came up to his apartment, he was getting a lot of phone calls, and he always took them in another room. If I was in the room, he'd ask me to leave. I finally asked what the big secret was. He said, 'Well, this club that we're in, there's a lot of money involved.'"

A lot of money *was* involved, even now. While they sweated out the police investigation, Tom, Dave, and Jeff collaborated to form a business partnership with Gene Browning; they then signed their own contract—superseding the BBC's—with the Las Vegas gold miner, Bill Nalan.

At the Third Street office, Joe was growing concerned that "people had kind of strayed," Jim explained. When Tom began spending more time at the Gardena plant than in West Hollywood, Joe's concern turned to suspicion. He sent Jim south "to see if I could find out what they was doing down there," as Graham recalled it. Tom, Dave, and Jeff definitely were up to something, the bodyguard reported back. "I could tell," Jim explained. "When I pop in they would be quiet, real quiet, then change their subject altogether. Didn't show their emotions."

At the Third Street office, the scramble to secure the assets of Hedayat Eslaminia was in close competition with the Summer Olympics for the Boys' attention. Jerry Eisenberg, instructed by the FBI's Buchanan to "stay put and tell us what's happening," barely found time to stop by the BBC office during the games. "I was really caught up in them, attending as many events as I could, and so were a lot of the others," he explained. "As much as the excitement, there was this feeling of comfort and security I got from them."

Eisenberg could not avoid making at least one brief appearance at the office each day, however, since Joe had assigned him as the lead attorney to represent Reza at his conservatorship hearing in San Mateo County Superior Court, scheduled for the afternoon of August 16. The FBI suggested pumping Jim Graham for more information, the attorney recalled, but by then "Jim apparently had let Joe know what he told me, and Joe was not happy about it. When I asked Jim questions, he said I knew too much already and he wouldn't tell me more, except that Eslaminia's body had been disposed of in a vat of acid."

Both Neil Adelman and Lauren Raab were working with Eisenberg on the conservatorship application, assisted by Evan and Jon Allen. Dean "played cheerleader" and met privately with Joe to pass on what he had learned in his wills and trusts class, which was that a conservator "has a fiduciary duty to the people who would be the beneficiaries of whatever property he is charged to administer." This meant the cooperation of Reza's mother and brothers would be necessary if the eldest son were to win control of his father's assets, Dean explained. The court's award seemed assured when Mina Hakimi submitted a declaration supporting Reza's conservatorship claim.

As Eisenberg prepared for his court appearance on the sixteenth, he continued to confer with the FBI from his home phone and contacted the SEC as well. "I didn't tell anybody [about talking to the SEC] but Mike Feldman," Eisenberg remembered. "Tom was still with them, I thought, Dave and Jeff were on the outs, and Steve Taglianetti had been fired, but they were, like, still around. So I wasn't sure who could be trusted with what." A meeting with the FBI in Los Angeles did nothing to encourage him that the situation would be resolved any time soon, Eisenberg said: "They didn't really care. It was like the Olympics were going on, and 'We got other things to take care of.'"

The investigation in San Mateo County was being handled still by the Belmont PD, which conducted a second interview with Jerry Miller on August 14. It was then that the housing manager mentioned "a large black male resembling Mr. T" whom he had seen at the condominium complex around the time of the Eslaminia disappearance; this revelation sent detectives to maintenance man Ken Hickson, who remembered the black man's name, Jim Graham, then added that he had seen Graham for the first time on July 30. Eisenberg knew none of this when he flew to San Francisco on the morning of August 16 en route to a meeting with Reza and Ben at the San Mateo County Courthouse. "I had informed the FBI that the conservatorship hearing was happening, told them what chambers, what judge, and that if they were interested, they could take action," Eisenberg recalled. "They didn't." He attempted to make the court papers ineffective, Eisenberg explained: "I didn't check certain boxes and used improper form and language, but the judge granted it anyway. It was a temporary conservatorship; you're required by law to obtain a bond. We went across the street after the hearing and got one with nothing but a California driver's license, no financial statement, nothing. I headed back to L.A. Ben and Reza went across the street to have a drink and celebrate."

That same day, August 16, more than two months after Ron Levin was reported missing, Beverly Hills Police Department officers finally entered the Peck Drive apartment to search for clues that might explain the missing man's abrupt departure. "Until then, the police just weren't interested," Bob Levin recalled. "The easiest explanation of Ronnie's disappearance was that he had run away to avoid prosecution so that was the explanation they chose." When Les Zoeller phoned on August 15 to ask if he might inspect Ron's apartment, the detective made no mention of Joe Hunt, Marty Levin recalled: "He just said they wanted to go in the house, take pictures, do some investigating."

Marty's own investigation during the past ten weeks had confirmed much of what he feared and most of what he suspected about his adopted son. The number of people who claimed to be Ron's creditors was astounding. "No one can tell me Ronnie didn't work hard at what he did," Marty said. Ron's stepfather read demands for payment from virtually every haberdasher and jeweler between La Cienega and La Peer, received "past due" bills from three accountants and six attorneys, opened threatening letters from dozens of caterers, computer salesmen, and art dealers who said Ron had taken them for rides in the guises of Presley Reed, M.D., Ronnie Rothschild, Dr. Robert Levin, and R. Michael Wetherbee, Esq. Within weeks of his disappearance, criminal and civil charges had been filed against Ron by banks in Boston and Beverly Hills. The police assigned to investigate his disappearance described him in the newspaper as "a con man and a thief." And yet, even among those who claimed Ronnie had scammed them, there were more than a few who said they missed him, Marty remembered.

Two months after Ron's disappearance, the Levin family refused to forsake him. It was, in fact, the possibility of the prodigal's return that prompted Marty to consult with Scott Furstman before admitting Zoeller into the apartment, and then only if he could supervise the search and approve the removal of any items taken as evidence.

Zoeller arrived at the Peck Drive duplex accompanied by Detective Edholm and began his search in the larger of Ron's two offices, where the date stamp on Levin's desk still was set at June 6, 1984. The detective found no entries for that date in Ron's planning diary, but there were notations entered for June 5 ("*People v. Levin:* Motion") and June 7 ("NY"). In Ron's portable phone book, Zoeller found the numbers of Tom May, Evan Dicker, Joe Hunt, and Rose Dosti on the same page. Among Levin's meticulously kept files, the detective discovered the Microgenesis contract signed by Ron and Joe Hunt as well as correspondence sent to the Peck Drive apartment by Hunt from the BBC's office in West Hollywood. There was another file marked MAY BROS. LAND CORP., where Zoeller found documents involving the Progressive Savings scam attached to letters signed by Tom Frank May II and David Herbert May III informing Ron that they were withdrawing from the company and warning him not to use their names.

There also were statements on a fourteen-million-dollar commodities account at Clayton Brokerage in that file.

As the detective shuffled through the bills and receipts on Ron's desk, Marty Levin came into the larger office from the smaller one down the hall, carrying seven sheets of yellow legal paper folded in half. He had discovered these a few weeks earlier, Marty said, on the floor between the far wall and a wastebasket in the small office. The scribbling on the seven pages struck him as "nonsensical," Marty said. "I almost threw them into the wastepaper basket where I found them," he recalled, "but instead I left them on the desk."

Marty asked, "What do you make of these?" as he handed the legal pad pages to the detective. When he opened the papers, Zoeller remembered, what first caught his eye was a heading that read "AT LEVIN'S, TO DO." Below that was a list of fourteen items. *"Close blinds," "Scan for tape recorder," "Tape mouth," Handcuff—put gloves on," and "Explain situation,"* the list began. He decided at once the seven pages had "evidentiary value," explained Zoeller, who used a pair of tweezers to turn the pages as he read. *"Jim digs pit"* was the most striking entry on the second page. Behind that was a crudely drawn map notated with the words, ROAD, EAST, and RANGER STATION. On yet another page, there was a list under the heading "PACK SUITCASE" and below that a signature: *"Joe Hunt,"* it read.

It was August 16 also when another vector of apprehension converged on Joe and the Boys, this one out of Sacramento, where the California attorney general's special prosecutions unit was about to dispatch the agent who eventually would assume command of the investigation in Northern California, Oscar Breiling. The Eslaminia case had been assigned first to an old friend from the A.G's organized crime unit, Breiling remembered, Dick Trimble: "Dick is walking by my office that afternoon, and he says, 'I'm on my way down to Belmont to kiss off a case. Wanna go for a ride?'"

The meeting at the Belmont PD included a detective, a sergeant, and a lieutenant from the city police, plus a pair of FBI agents. "The sergeant explained the situation," Breiling recalled. "He said, 'We have an informant, but it's complicated. Looks like there's going to be a lot of work in Los Angeles, and we sure could use the help.' I immediately got interested. The way it was presented was: They had a kidnapping, they believed, resulting in a death that they weren't sure of because they had no body. They believed it was for money, but they didn't know how much or where it was. I thought, 'This is a real whodunit.'"

From his office in San Francisco, Breiling lobbied to get the case transferred to his unit. The FBI ordinarily would have handled the investigation, "but during the Olympics their manpower was stretched," Breiling explained. "So as soon as the information came in that it was apparently not an international incident, they wanted out. Which left poor Belmont asking, 'What do we do?'" Persuading the AG's office to take the case, however, proved no simple task. "Some of the administrators have the attitude, 'Big case, big problems; little case, little problems; no case, no problems,'" explained Breiling, who proposed to pursue the investigation by classifying the BBC as "Conspirational Organized Crime." "I knew in the back of my head that what the bosses had to see is that this case is going to get a lot of press, make the AG look good, et cetera." Using a proposal composed largely of newspaper clippings, Breiling persuaded his supervisor to suspend the initial inquiry and preliminary review phases that would have limited him to twenty-one days on the case: "We had never done that before. So I called the FBI and they gave me Eisenberg's name, but they wouldn't give me the file; they would only feed me information in bits and pieces, because of 'national security' issues. The Belmont PD, though, they gave it all up. It was like they had this flaming rock in their hands and didn't know what to do with it.

"So I had the case. The first most logical thing was to go down and talk to Eisenberg, but I didn't do that. What I did was a lot of prayin' about it. I said, 'I have never turned a case over to You before. But I know I'm going to need help with this one. So please show me The Way.'"

While Breiling sought guidance from God, his single source inside the BBC, Jerry Eisenberg, decided on his own that the time had come to leave the organization. Though urged by the FBI to remain at the Third Street office, Eisenberg could offer little to either the Levin or Eslaminia investigations. He did, however, dissuade Chester Brown from delivering an additional six hundred thousand dollars to the new "investment opportunity" Joe had mentioned in his July letter to the investors. "Chester came to me and asked me what he should do," Eisenberg explained. "This was other people's money: should he bring it in? He wanted to know about liability. I told him, 'Chester, believe me, don't do anything now. Let me research it, okay?' I kept pushing him off and pushing him off, and finally I told him, 'Just don't do it, okay? I can't tell you why.' He said, 'Is there something wrong?' And I said, 'No, just don't do it now.'"

Knowing how desperately Joe needed the money and figuring he was in real danger if Brown talked to Hunt, Eisenberg decided to resign from the BBC the moment his August paycheck cleared at the Bank of

America: "I went down to my own bank first, just to make sure the money was in my account, then came back to the office and wrote out a letter of resignation. Before I left, Joe told me that if anything got out about what was going on he'd 'take care of me.'" When he heard that Mike Feldman also wanted to leave, "I told him to stay," Eisenberg recalled. "He certainly couldn't leave the same day I did."

As the BBC's lead attorney walked out the office door, Dean, Evan, and Jon Allen were assembling in Belmont, where they identified themselves to city police as Eisenberg's "clerks." The three had arrived with Joe and Ben at the condominium complex on Davy Glen bearing a court order permitting Reza Eslaminia and his legal representatives to enter the apartment where Olga Vasquez still was living. There was no one home at the condo, Dean recalled, so they found a security guard and showed him the order. Joe suggested that Evan and Dean keep a lookout in the lobby. "We were told that Olga Vasquez would not know Dean and I," Evan remembered, "so we could wait inside." Not long after Joe phoned for a locksmith, though, Olga arrived and promptly summoned the Belmont police. Detective Keehn and his sergeant arrived at a little past two but instead of approaching began to take surveillance photographs of the Boys from a distance of about seventy-five feet. A uniformed patrolman arrived ten minutes later and told the Boys he could not admit them without "clarification." As soon as the police showed up, Jon Allen remembered, Joe and Ben left. Keehn came to the door then, read the court order, and explained that the language was "too vague" to be enforced.

Denied entry to the apartment, the same group, plus Jim, met the next morning to plan an "asset search." "We went around to all the various banks in the area from Redwood City to Belmont with certified copies or xeroxed copies of the conservatorship documents," Dean recalled, "saying that we were representing the estate of Hedayat Eslaminia and asking did these banks have any information about any accounts that he may have." They stayed at the Amfac Hotel, out by the airport, where Ben's room served as a base of operations. "We had a large map of the area, divided into quadrants," Jon Allen remembered, "with each team of two assigned to an area." Evan was with Joe most of the day: "All I knew was that Reza's father had disappeared," he said. "After we all met for lunch, a tiny alarm did go off in my head, though, and I asked Joe, 'We didn't have anything to do with this, did we?' He said, 'No—you know I would tell you if we did.' And I thought, 'Well, of course, since he had told us about Levin.'" They all met again in the afternoon to compare notes, Dean recalled: "Between us, we found a couple of closed accounts and one that had a few hundred dollars left in it, but that was all."

Within a day or two after they returned to Southern California, the schism in the BBC was obvious to everyone. "Dave, Jeff, and Tom now had their own little fortress down in Gardena," Evan observed. On August 17, Dave took the risk of forging Ben's signature on a check to the company hired to recoat the innards of the Cyclotron while he and Jeff and Gene prepared the machine for its move to Nalan's Shadow Mountain mine. The check was denied for insufficient funds, but Joe recognized the degree of "disloyalty," as he termed it, demonstrated by so brazen a move and responded by beefing up security at the Gardena warehouse. Besides the chain-link fence around the building, the dead-bolt locks on the doors, the coded motion detector at the entrance, and the motion detector inside, Jeff Raymond recalled, Joe added padlocks to the machine itself, "so you couldn't open it."

Nevertheless, it was "the Three Stooges" (as he had taken to calling Dave, Tom, and Jeff) to whom Joe assigned the task of transporting the Cyclotron from Gardena to Nalan's property outside Las Vegas. Ben rented a flatbed to carry the machine across the desert on August 21, then left the Stooges to load the two-ton contraption. "Even with a forklift, it took us two days," Jeff recalled. That same afternoon, a Friday, Evan informed Joe the Microgenesis Minutes Book was missing. "I mentioned that Tom had been looking at me as I prepared the [fraudulent] minutes and filed them," he explained, "and also the fact that I left him in there with the cabinet un-locked. So I suggested it had to have been Tom who had removed them. Joe took the news calmly, the way he took everything. But he said he wanted to talk to them. I told him they were coming over to my apartment that evening." Before he left the Third Street office, Joe learned from Lore Leis that for the past week Tom had been requesting and receiving copies of each Financial Futures limited partnership agreement as well as copies of the Microgenesis contract with Ron Levin and the Swiss bank check.

When the Stooges arrived at Evan's place on Swall Drive in Beverly Hills, they walked in and found Joe sitting on the floor in the living room. Dean Karny was sitting in a chair nearby, and Evan Dicker was standing behind them in his library. "We got a little scared," Jeff admitted. "We knew it was Joe's last chance to do something before we left." Tom went into the kitchen and poured a drink. Joe waited until the twin returned to the living room, then said he had discovered that some documents were missing from the office and wondered if they knew anything about it. This was news to him, Tom answered. Joe took a sip of orange juice, stared at him a moment, then said that if he found out who had taken these documents, he would personally break their hands.

Jeff said the three of them had better get going. As they headed for the door, Tom remembered, Evan removed his Smith & Wesson .38 from a cabinet drawer, slammed it on the countertop, and said, "I'd rather go to hell than fuck with the BBC." Joe didn't move, but Dean followed them to the door: "He yelled out, 'Remember, guys, you can't beat a good conspiracy,'" Tom recalled. "We all smiled to each other. His conspiracy was his conspiracy, and ours was ours."

From Evan's the Stooges headed straight to the Gardena warehouse, where they discovered that a chain with fist-sized links had been used to secure the gate they left open earlier that afternoon. Fortunately, their welder was storing his equipment inside the building, Jeff recalled: "We jumped the fence, went inside, got a torch, and cut off the chain." It was still morning when they reached Nalan's site. At a pay phone in the desert, they called the BBC office. "Just to keep up appearances," Tom explained. "We figured Joe had left the lock on the gate." It was Karny who answered the phone, he recalled: "Dean said, 'Somebody put a lock on it? God, I'm glad you guys got the machines out in time.' He made out like the landlord did it because we were behind on the rent."

Less than forty-eight hours after executing their private joint venture agreement with Gene Browning in Gardena, the twins and Raymond delivered a second contract to Bill Nalan at Shadow Mountain, excluding Joe Hunt and the BBC from future consideration. "We thought since Joe stole the money to build the machine, and hadn't paid Gene the money he owed him, and said he had murdered someone, we shouldn't be in business with him anymore," Jeff explained.

When the Mays failed to phone Joe at the Third Street office, as promised, Joe called the Shadow Mountain site and learned from Nalan that the twins had delivered the Cyclotron less than an hour earlier. He and Jim drove out into the desert to verify this and found the machine at Nalan's mine. "We even took pictures of it," Jim remembered. The twins and Jeff, though, were gone.

The Stooges were by then back in Gardena, dropping off their flatbed truck at the rental agency in Gardena, then loading up the Oldsmobile ragtop from the West Cars fleet for a second trip to the desert. By the time the three arrived back at Shadow Mountain, Browning had spoken by phone to Nalan, confirming his contract with the Mays and advising the miner to hide the machine from Joe. Dave, Tom, and Jeff moved the Cyclotron themselves, using a forklift they rented in Las Vegas. At Shadow Mountain, the Stooges discovered Joe and Jim had ransacked the mobile home where they intended to wait out the police investigation. "They took several things," Tom remembered. "One of them was the shotgun Dave had borrowed from Joe earlier." After concealing the

Cyclotron ("We put it behind these mountains," Tom explained), the Stooges decided it was time to hide themselves as well. It would be the Mays' story that the three of them spent most of the next month in a remote cabin near Mammoth Lake. "Joe said, 'You can go fishing,'" Tom explained, "so that's what we did."

"The Mays didn't spend any month at Mammoth," countered Eisenberg, who spoke on the telephone to the twins several times during their absence. "I think they went to Las Vegas for a couple of weeks and gambled. Maybe they went to Mammoth also, but I doubt it. Everything they say is half made-up."

Wherever the twins were when they finally phoned the BBC office, it was not Baker, where Joe had instructed them to remain until the attrition mill was assembled. The moment Tom hung up on the other end of the line, "we checked with the operator for time and costs," Evan recalled, "and ascertained that they were not where they were supposed to be. We figured they had the Cyclotron with them."

It was Evan who suggested breaking into the Mays' apartment: "I was driving Joe home when I said we should do it. I often broke into the Mays' apartment. Whenever I was in the area and felt like watching TV— they had more cable channels than I did. They always left the screen door unlocked because one of them always forgot their keys. The front door was locked, but Joe had a key. So we got in, and it was my suggestion that we listen to the messages [on the answering machine]. And there was one that said, 'This is Les,' and then gave the number.

"The next day, Joe told me he had called the number, and it was the Beverly Hills Police Department detectives' bureau. He may even have said it was the homicide investigators. He was matter-of-fact about it, though. No fear, no anger. Just Joe, considering his options."

Hunt in fact appeared more concerned about recovering the Cyclotron than with apprehending the Mays. That weekend he and Jim hauled two of the Enduro dirt bikes out to the desert and conducted a ground search of the Shadow Mountain area. "He went in one direction and I went in another," Jim recalled. "We rode all over the desert trying to find the machine . . . then I rented an airplane, a little Cherokee one forty. Flew over the whole place, pretty low. Still couldn't find anything."

As Joe and Jim were returning to Westwood, Evan was phoning the LAPD to report a burglary at the Third Street office. The BBC's alarm company had left a message on Joe's answering machine at the Manning about a "malfunction," Evan remembered: "Joe called me at my apartment, and I went over to the office. When I arrived, I saw the alarm box torn out of the wall. I went inside, saw what had been taken, then called the Manning. The message I left was 'We've been robbed.'" The audio and video equipment, the computers, the Quotrons, the copy machine, the telex, and the typewriters all had been taken, recalled Evan, who estimated the loss at more than one hundred thousand dollars on the report he made to the police Saturday morning.

The thieves had to be BBC members, Evan said, "because before the alarm was torn off the wall, it had been turned off. I didn't think it was [Joe, Dean, or Ben] because of the papers that were left behind, apparently dealing with wrongdoing involved in the commodities trading, that had been scattered on the floor in Ben's office. Ben took those papers out the back way on Saturday." Jim's prime suspect was Steve Taglianetti: "He knows the code; it's one way he could get even." Joe insisted the Mays had done it. Evan, though, argued that the finger pointed toward Eisenberg and Feldman. "What cast suspicion on them was that Feldman took his computer out that Friday to be reprogrammed over the weekend, which tended to suggest the obvious," he explained. "It's obvious who it was, all right," Eisenberg scoffed. "Not only did they need the insurance money, but all BBC records disappeared that same Saturday, August 25, which was when I finally convinced the SEC to call Joe's investors and let them know there was an investigation going on."

Nearly every one of Financial Futures limited partners sided with Joe initially. "Before the SEC got to us, Joe wrote us a letter to say he was under investigation because of his huge success and not to be concerned," Al Gore explained. "It was all an SEC 'fishing expedition,' he said. I was upset not at Joe but at the SEC, outraged that someone would dare to incriminate our benefactor. 'Joe,' I said, 'what can I do?' He told me not to give them anything, so when the SEC called, I told them nothing, refused even to give them the names and numbers of the other investors."

Steve Weiss, though, was concerned enough to make an unannounced appearance at Hunt's office door on Monday morning. "I had decided to test him," Weiss recalled. "I said to Joe, 'I thought things over in Europe, and I'd like to retire there.'" A friend had offered him a bargain price on a villa in the South of France, Weiss explained: "I said, 'I'll need another couple of hundred thousand to consummate the deal,' and Joe said, 'No problem. We can take care of that.' He didn't have a tremor or a twitch. I said to Chester, 'If that guy is lying, he's a better man than I am.'"

"Olga has suspect for Reza," Veronica Fonseca remembered, after the younger Eslaminia's appearance at the Davy Glen condo in the company of his associate Joseph Hunt. "The way he show up very fast and the way he's coming, approaching her and me very violent, like we did something wrong to him." It was Veronica who confronted Reza on his fourth and final visit to the condominium. Olga was back at work, leaving her alone at the apartment with two of Rakhim's Iranian friends who were terrified when they heard someone pounding at the door, Veronica remembered. Through the peephole, she saw Reza and two other young men, Veronica recalled. "I say, 'What do you want?' And he say, 'Let me in!' And I say, 'No, I can't let you in because Olga's not here.' And he goes, 'I have an order from the court, so you better let me in.' And I go, 'I have to call Olga.' And he starts screaming, 'You better open the door!' I was very afraid. I called Olga right away, and she said to call the police."

The locksmith summoned by Reza and his companions arrived at the front door before either Olga or the Belmont police. "They are forcing open the door," Veronica recalled, "and I have these two Iranians inside who don't speak English, and I can't explain, so they are very frightened." Olga and her escorts, Detective Keehn and Sergeant James Goulart, stepped into the hallway just as the locksmith was opening the door. Those attempting to enter the residence were Reza Eslaminia; his attorney, Neil Adelman; and yet another "associate," Steve Lopez, Keehn recalled. Reza, Adelman, and an investigator for the attorney, Jim Graham, had come to the condo just the day before, August 20, only to be denied entrance by Keehn, who pointed out that while Reza's court order bore the judge's official stamp, it lacked his signature. He had adjourned that confrontation from the front porch of the condo to his office at the Belmont police headquarters, Keehn remembered, where Adelman presented a business card bearing the address of *Hustler* magazine's editorial offices, then demanded that the detective surrender all documents seized from Hedayat Eslaminia's apartment. Those papers remained in the custody of the FBI, which had determined that there were issues of national security, Keehn explained. ("The FBI agent who took Hedayat's diary winked and told me, 'I won't say anything if you won't say anything,'" Olga remembered.) His client was interested not in matters of national security, Adelman replied, but rather in bank records, safe-deposit box keys, deeds of trust, and certificates of stock, all of which should still be in the apartment.

When they came back to the condo the next afternoon, Reza and Adelman had a new court order, signed by the judge. The claimant's ex parte motion had been supported by a declaration from Joseph Hunt:

1. On or about July 30, 1984 I travelled to San Francisco at the request of Reza Eslaminia to assist him in investigating unconfirmed reports of his father's disappearance.

2. We went directly from the airport to the home of Reza's missing father at 400 Davy Glen Road, Unit 4322, Belmont, California.

3. We were met at the apartment by an officer of the Belmont Police Department and Olga Vasquez. Reza and I supplied the police officer, at his request, with our identification, which he noted.

4. When we were shown into the apartment I observed three stacks of Persian rugs, each stack approximately 2½ by 3 feet in size. The rugs were folded and the stacks were about waist high. I counted the rugs in one stack and there appeared to be six.

Reza's own declaration read, "My father's business and personal affairs need to be maintained during my father's absence and I believe that I am the most capable of preserving my father's estate."

Keehn had no choice but to admit Reza and his attorney into the apartment. Hedayat's eldest headed straight for the master bedroom, Olga remembered: "Reza was a real pro, stripping the bed and removing the mattress, looking through closets and drawers, in the toilet bowls, behind dressers, pulling out panels." Reza became enraged when he learned Olga had removed the rugs two weeks earlier. Rakhim told her worms were nesting in the carpets and they needed to be ventilated, she explained. Reza began then to rifle through the master bedroom closet, checking the labels on her clothes, Olga remembered, and demanding to know how she had paid for them. Discovering a case of perfume in a closet, "Reza said, 'See, she's spending his money already,'" Veronica recalled. "Reza was making many remarks about his father also to the police. When he found his father's pipes, he showed them to the police and said, 'See, he is a big drug user.' When he went into the second bedroom I followed him in and said, 'Reza, I don't understand what you're doing. Your father is missing, but he's gonna be back.' And he goes, 'How long have you known my father?' And I say, 'About one year.' And he goes, 'Well, I have known him for twenty-five.' And the way he said it, I knew. I knew he had killed his father."

Reza's sole significant find that afternoon was a deposit slip from the Dresdner Bank of Frankfurt he found in the second bedroom. Hedayat's son seemed more excited, however, when he discovered twenty-two hundred dollars in American Express traveler's checks concealed inside the panel on the back of the dresser. After that, though, the pickings were pretty paltry: fifty dollars in cash, a pair of antique Korans, a checkbook on an account at a Japanese bank, a photo album, a box of business cards, and the keys to the baby-blue Cadillac Seville, which Lopez drove to the Belmont PD, where Detective Keehn reminded Reza that his driver's license was suspended.

Olga's suspicions were further inflamed when Ali Bani called to tell her that Hedayat's son had just paid him a visit in San Francisco. "There was another gentleman with him," the colonel remembered, "a tall young American, dark-haired. He said very little, but he listened carefully. Reza told me he was very sorry for missing his father, and he's trying to find him. He asked me all kinds of information: Who were his father's friends outside of the United States? Who was he meeting in Europe? Where is his banking account? What kind of assets does he have? I told him whatever I knew."

Olga saw Reza again about a week after his search of the condo. Returning home from work that afternoon, Olga explained, she had been alarmed to discover Veronica's pet parrot outside its cage, flapping about the living room in a panic, and drove down to the 7-Eleven store on the corner to call Sergeant Goulart from a pay phone. Goulart had just come on the line when Olga saw Reza and Ben Dosti cruising up El Camino in Hedayat's Cadillac convertible. Reza spotted her a moment later and pulled into the 7-Eleven lot. "Ben got out of the car," she remembered, "handed me some papers, and said, 'Here, princess.'" The document in Olga's hand was a subpoena for a deposition the next day in connection to her court motion opposing Reza's appointment as permanent conservator of his father's estate. She told Reza that he was not going to get the conservatorship and that his father was still alive, Olga recalled. Reza answered that his father was a drug dealer who smuggled opium into the country concealed in Oriental carpets. She climbed into her car and drove half a block up Davy Glen, Olga recalled, but was so angry she made a U-turn and headed back to the 7-Eleven to tell Reza what she thought of him. Reza replied that he could prove Olga also was a drug dealer.

The two of them were shouting at the top of their lungs by then, almost to the point of blows, Olga remembered, when a stocky black man wearing a sweat suit walked out of the 7-Eleven store sipping on a giant Slurpy. The black guy asked if Reza and Ben were bothering her, and when she said yes, Olga remembered, offered to take care of them. Reza responded with a one-finger salute but looked a lot less cocky when the black guy picked him up by the shirtfront and threw him onto the Cadillac's hood. Ben Dosti stepped in then, Olga recalled, and backed the black guy off by saying, "I'm an attorney and I'm going to sue you." Instead of demanding the black guy's name, however, Ben climbed into the Cadillac and drove off with Reza. She was wobbly when she walked to her own car, Olga remembered, grateful for the escort of the black man, who introduced himself as "Jim." "I said, 'Thank you so much.' He leaned on the side of the car, asking my name through the window. He was very smooth, asking me to lunch and where do I live. I almost said yes to lunch. I was thankful. I said, 'I appreciate it, but no.' He said, 'I'd like to get to know you better.' I said thanks but that I was married. As I drove away he said, 'Are you sure? I'd really like to get to know you.'"

It was Joe rather than Ben who accompanied Reza to a meeting with Ali Mortzavi three days later at the Casa Maria in Burlingame. "They started a casual conversation—'How's the family, et cetera'—but Mr. Hunt was taking notes even then," Mortzavi recalled. "Reza told me the court had appointed him conservator of his father's assets. He said Mr. Hunt was his lawyer." When Mortzavi denied knowledge of Hedayat Eslaminia's hidden assets, Joe prepared a handwritten affidavit to this effect and asked him to sign it. Joe and Reza both seemed disappointed when he did so, Mortzavi recalled: "Suddenly they were tired and wanted to turn in. I asked Reza if he knew where his father was. He said he was trying to find out."

Ben was again Reza's companion when Olga Vasquez met with them the next day. "By now, Olga think Reza is involved, but she doesn't think Hedayat could be dead," Veronica explained. "We were talking: 'Maybe Reza gave his father to the Khomeini people, to get even.'" Olga's income wasn't enough to pay the rent on the Belmont condo; Hedayat's friends in Los Angeles had to see her through August. "She didn't know to move out because 'What if Hedayat come and he has no place?'" Veronica explained. But she couldn't afford that place, and I had to go back to my home, so Olga know she has to be out by the first of September."

Ben appeared much more in control of himself than did Reza that afternoon at the Amfac Hotel in Burlingame, Olga recalled. "Reza wanted to sit at a table away from the bar," she remembered. "He was very nervous and spilled over his beer." Reza's condition stabilized, though, when Olga gave him the name of Hedayat's Swiss bank, even providing a deposit slip. "I felt that was the last hope for finding Hedayat," she explained. She wanted to discuss how Reza might use the Swiss account to locate his father, but the two young men cut her off, Olga recalled, and began to ask about a safe-deposit box key: "They kept saying, 'Are you sure?' when I said there wasn't one."

They agreed to divide what was left in the condo: Reza would let Olga keep the furniture if she surrendered his father's "personal effects." It was Ben, however, who came to the Belmont apartment on August 28, loading Hedayat's books and his wardrobe into a Porsche convertible.

Olga vacated the premises two days later, and her hope seemed to give way all at once when she and Veronica found Hedayat's green card and reentry permit hidden under an end table in the living room. "Such a sad day," recalled Veronica. "It was like Olga finally admitted to herself that Hedayat wasn't coming back."

Now in possession of deposit slips from banks in Frankfurt and Geneva where Hedayat Eslaminia maintained accounts, the Boys decided it would be a good idea to send someone to Europe to see if they could get control, Dean recalled. The BBC's need for ready cash never had been more urgent. The investors were clamoring for information about the SEC investigation, and quarterly disbursements were due September 15. Not only the one fully functional Cyclotron but both of the partially assembled models as well had disappeared from the Gardena warehouse. The Boys were without funds even to order a new batch of the Fire Safety flame retardant for Lopez's military clients in Malaysia. Joe's "ACCOUNTING OF PROJECT SAM" showed they had spent five thousand dollars for "Supplies and Set-Up," four thousand dollars for the lease on the Beverly Glen house, and six thousand for "Cash, Trips and Reza," with virtually nothing to show for it. The only Eslaminia assets the Sacramento company Data Search could find were two closed safe-deposit boxes at the Burlingame branch of Glendale Federal, an almost-empty checking account at the Exchange Bank of Santa Rosa, and a depleted commercial account at the Mitsui branch in Encino.

They still had no idea how many accounts or what amount of money might be held for the Iranian in European banks, Dean recalled, and so decided that Reza would need a general power of attorney signed by his father. It was Joe who forged Eslaminia's Arabic signature on nearly a dozen copies of the document, dated April 16, 1984.

Brooke was at his side when Joe showed up at the Swall Drive apartment early Friday evening with several copies of the power of attorney and asked Evan to accompany them to the Third Street office, where they could compare signatures and choose the most accurate. Applying his notary stamp to the forged signature would be the most serious overt act Evan had committed, yet at the time it didn't seem like much to get worked up about, he remembered. "Joe could explain things in a way that didn't offend your values at that point in time," Evan reflected. "For instance, he said Eslaminia had already signed a power of attorney but it had been lost, so it didn't seem so dishonest to help Reza create a replacement." Evan at least recognized that Joe had brought Brooke "because he knew having her there would make me more inclined to go along." When they arrived at the office, though, Brooke wandered off to watch television, leaving Evan alone with Joe in

Hunt's office. "Joe at one point said that he had been present when Eslaminia signed the original power of attorney," Evan recalled, "so I suggested that maybe he could be a subscribing witness and I could notarize *his* signature, but he didn't think that was good enough and just sort of ignored me." In the end, Evan not only applied his notary stamp to the forged power of attorney, but drove to the Swiss consulate to have his signature authenticated.

Even as he was committing crimes in furtherance of the Shadings' conspiracy, though, Evan, like Jon Allen, would not be included in the core discussions of Project Sam. The only BBC member added to the original five was Steve Lopez, invited to participate soon after his return to Los Angeles from Asia on August 19. "I was just a guy trying to make the best of a bad situation," explained Lopez. "The first day I got back I found out they had lost the money in the commodities accounts, but then they said they were going to make a lot of money with Reza. They said his father had been kidnapped in the Iranian situation and he had thirty million dollars and they were going to help Reza recover it and he would split it with them. They were trying to calm me down. Ben and Joe said, 'Steve, don't worry, we'll take care of you.' And I saw there was a lot of money around—well, not a lot, but there was money around—and so I figured they were going to pull through." Nevertheless, he wasn't pleased to discover Reza living in his room at the Manning, Lopez conceded: "It was like 'What's this bear doing in my bed?' Then they moved him up into Jeff Raymond's bedroom on the fifteenth floor. They were buying him clothes, giving him cars, taking him to dinner, telling me he was going to make us all rich. Ben seemed certain of it."

Lopez was alarmed, though, when he visited the Third Street office a few days later and discovered the depletion of the BBC's ranks: "Joe's father and Frank Mingarella were gone. Eisenberg was gone. Taglianetti was gone. The Mays and Jeff Raymond were gone. Half the rooms were dark; they never even turned the lights on." Most defections were attributed to the twins' influence, Lopez remembered: "They said the Mays were trying to steal the machine, that they were trying to make their own deals and were making up stories to cover themselves. Brooke was telling me a lot of this. She acted really furious at Tom and Dave."

While he denied knowledge of the Eslaminia kidnapping, Lopez would admit hearing "a rumor" that Joe had murdered Ron Levin within a day or two of arriving back in Westwood. "Ben told him," Evan confirmed. "I asked Joe about it," Lopez recalled. "I said, 'I heard you shot Ron Levin.' He said, 'Oh, I just told them that to see how they'd react.'" The meeting at the Manning had been a loyalty test, Joe explained, intended to separate "true BBC members" from those who were just along for the ride. He did accompany Reza and Neil Adelman during the search of the Belmont condo, Lopez allowed, but "only to keep Neil company."

Lopez was present again, as were Dicker and Allen, when the Shadings met in late August to discuss how best to deal with the Three Stooges. "We weren't sure how far the Mays had gone with this," explained Dean, who with Jon Allen had broken into the twins' apartment about a week after Joe and Evan went in. Among the items he and Jon removed were "some lists with [the Mays'] handwriting, demonstrating that they had had contact with Les Zoeller of the Beverly Hills Police Department," Dean remembered. The two of them found Microgenesis minutes as well, he recalled, along with a copy of the Levin contract and records of phone calls to Nalan's Shadow Mountain site and to Kilpatrick's office in Denver. They left most of the documents behind, but Dean took Tom's California driver's license, which he discovered in a desk drawer. "I thought we might find some use for it," he explained.

Joe received it all quite calmly, Dean remembered: "He thought that even if some of the Boys had gone to the police, we had enough members remaining loyal that there would be conflicting stories." Still, the tension was mounting, Dean conceded: "We thought the place we lived and the place we worked had both been bugged. It was clear an investigation was going on and that the Beverly Hills Police Department and the SEC were part of it."

His suspicion that the twins were conspiring with Gene Browning to steal the Kilpatrick contract, though, was what truly seemed to concern Joe. Jim was dispatched to Denver to spy on the UFOI executive and returned to L.A. claiming he had tape-recorded part of a conference call between Kilpatrick, the Mays, and Browning.

Joe at once announced they needed to "handle the situation," Dean recalled, and proposed several plans to discredit the Stooges, perhaps even implicate them in Ron Levin's murder. At first, his primary target was Dave May. "Joe said we should stick to the story that Dave had borrowed the gray BMW [on the evening of June 6]," Dean recalled, "and that he came back late and some of us were standing around and saw the damage to the trunk and smelled what seemed to be vomit. That Dave gave us a lame excuse about being drunk, and when we opened the trunk, we saw the TV remote control inside."

Hunt had formulated a more elaborate scheme by the time he brought Dean, Ben, and Jon Allen to Evan's home in Beverly Hills a few days later. Joe suspected that even the Swall Drive apartment had been bugged, Evan recalled, and instructed them to communicate by "literally going up to a person and pressing your lips against his ear when you spoke because a bug couldn't pick that up." Joe passed his new plan from person to person that way, Evan remembered, cradling their heads in both hands and cupping one ear as he whispered into the other, explaining that he believed it would be better to point the finger at Jeff Raymond than at Dave May. First, though, it would be necessary to kill Jeff's Newport Beach girlfriend, Renee Martin, Joe said. The idea would be to "make it look like it had been done in some sexual frenzy," Dean recalled, "and then we would all tell stories about Jeff's disgusting habits. Brooke would say that Jeff had attacked her after he made sexual advances toward her and she spurned him."

Frustrated by what was being lost in translation—"I think at some point I thought we were going to say Jeff had killed Renee to cover up the fact that Dave had killed Ron Levin," Evan recalled—Joe moved the meeting to the delicatessen in the lobby of the ICM building on Beverly Boulevard. It would be Brooke who reported Jeff to the police, Joe explained as they took seats at a corner table; either the channel changer and the bedspread from Ron Levin's apartment could be planted on Jeff, or Brooke could say she had seen him with them. Brooke also would say that Jeff had confessed the murder of Ron Levin to her at the Manning and that she had phoned the office, frantic, afterward. Joe would say that when he checked out the story, he found vomit in the trunk of the gray BMW Jeff had borrowed on that evening in June.

As he "elaborated upon his ideas," Evan recalled, "Joe was, as always, totally composed. Obviously he was concerned, but there was no squirm in him, ever. The threat seemed very real to him, I know, but if he had fear, he never showed it. It was strangely calming to be in his presence. Nothing seemed impossible." After lunch, they agreed that further consideration was necessary before proceeding. While neither he nor anyone else at the table objected to the plan, Evan admitted, the part about murdering Renee had caused him to "react emotionally" for the first time in months. "I didn't know her very well, and I wasn't all that fond of her, but she struck me as being somehow innocent," he explained, "which was something that set her apart from the Mays, in that she just did not have this coming."

Oddly, it was the BBC member he liked least to whom Evan confided his apprehension: "Lopez gave me a ride home the next day or the day after that, and when I brought up the Renee plan, he said he knew about it. We both agreed it was the most absurd thing we'd ever heard. Lopez wasn't objecting on moral grounds, though. He just didn't think it would work."

Lopez claimed to recall only the "general atmosphere" of BBC meetings during August and September: "Joe was way out there, saying things like 'Nobody can touch me,' talking about 'erasing' people or 'expunging' people." Yet Lopez remained a BBC member in good standing. "It had occurred to me that if Joe went down, my chances for getting the money back were gone," he explained. "Ben pointed that out."

Evan's commitment to Joe and the organization went much deeper, as he proved once again at the end of August, giving Joe five thousand dollars out of his own savings to buy off an agitated investor. "I felt too far in to go any direction but forward," he explained. "Polo lessons were my last link to sanity. After Tom and Dave left, I had started taking my lessons alone. I know what people's impression of polo is, but for me it was better than psychotherapy. I had no other outlet. My mom was still dealing with my dad's death. And I wasn't very close to my law school friends because I was in the BBC and they all thought I was very standoffish. So I just kept playing polo and imagining that things would work out for the best."

He and Ben also continued to believe that "Joe would lead us out of this and into glory," Dean said. All three Shadings recognized, though, that several hundred thousand dollars would be needed to keep the BBC afloat until the collection of the Eslaminia assets, the recovery of the Cyclotrons, and the consummation of Lopez's Asian negotiations delivered them from catastrophe. By the end of August, Taglianetti, Eisenberg, and Feldman all had been cut from the payroll. Joe next suspended the salaries of Jon Allen and Lore Leis, each of whom chose to stay on "until the difficulties could be resolved," as Lore put it. In early September, Joe sent Lauren Raab to tell their landlord at the Third Street office that the BBC would be unable to pay its rent for the next month or two and to negotiate a deal to pay all sums owing, plus a late charge, by Halloween.

On the Monday following Evan's initial police report of the burglary at the office, Lauren and Jon Allen nearly doubled the BBC's original insurance claim with a supplemental report to the LAPD alleging that nearly ninety thousand dollars in "electronic spy equipment" had been stolen as well. Lauren informed police that the telephone scrambling system and vehicle tracking devices had been purchased from the Lightning Detective Agency. The LAPD began investigating the burglary as a possible insurance fraud the next day. Their suspicions hardly were allayed after detectives interviewed "Nick" at his apartment in Hollywood. "He stated he was a master at building electronic detecting devices, and that he had personally built this equipment for Joe Hunt," the lead investigator on the case noted. "When asked for a bill of laden [sic], however, he stated he keeps no records. He stated he always deals in cash and has no bank account. Asked about his supplies of electronic equipment, he was vague and evasive as to where he had purchased the raw materials." When the detectives learned that Lauren Raab was pushing for a quick settlement from the BBC's insurance carrier, threatening a "bad faith" lawsuit if the check was not issued at once, they urged the company to delay.

Frustrated one more time, Joe confided that he and Brooke had conceived a plan to hasten her inheritance by killing every member of her immediate family, Dean recalled: "Joe said Brooke could invite them all to a kind of family powwow at the house in Bel Air and they could be killed then." Brooke began to boast that she was a Shading. She and Joe made an inside joke of their new nicknames for one another, the Empress Falgon and the Great Rahzuli, arrogating the titles of the supernatural villains from that summer's hit movie *Ghostbusters*. "Brooke was ready to follow Joe to hell, if that was what it took," Evan observed. "I suppose that became the dividing line ultimately—who would go to hell for him and who wouldn't."

Ben's girlfriend Julie Marks had been warned as early as Evan Dicker's birthday party that appearances might be deceiving. It was Jeff Raymond who advised her "strange things" were happening in the BBC and suggested Ben might be involved. Jeff refused to provide details but made Julie promise not to discuss with Ben what she had been told. The relationship was coming apart by late August, when Ben announced he was leaving with Reza for Europe. The others had no idea how much Julie knew but were aware she had accused Ben of "hiding things," recalled Lopez, who heard Julie tell Ben several times, "You're letting Joe make up your mind for you." A few days before Ben's scheduled departure, over dinner at a restaurant in Westwood, Julie brought matters to a head by telling Ben that if he wouldn't trust her enough to reveal his secrets, she had no choice but to end the relationship. Ben's reply was that he believed it would be best for Julie if they *did* end it, now. "He chose Joe over Julie, is what it came down to," Lopez said.

While Julie mourned, Ben appeared unmoved, Lopez remembered, preparing for his trip to Europe by "shopping for two solid days before he left." At Joe's instruction, Reza obtained powers of attorney from each of his brothers, and on September 1 Hedayat's eldest son executed his own power of attorney, agreeing to "grant, nominate, constitute and appoint Joseph Hunt, Lauren Raab, Jon Allen and Jim Graham as my true and lawful attorney(s)-in-fact."

Ben paid for their plane tickets with the American Express gold card that became officially delinquent on the date of their departure for London, September 2.

At the Third Street office, "it had come to the point that there wasn't much for the rest of us to do but wait and see what Ben and Reza could find in Switzerland," Evan explained. "By then, people weren't even coming in that much. Joe was just about the only one there on a regular basis, besides the lawyers and Lore Leis. Even Dean was coming and going."

The plans to murder Renee and the Roberts family had convinced his chief disciple that Joe truly *was* willing to contemplate all possibilities, and "I began trying to disengage myself from the situation," Dean explained. Disengagement became more difficult, though, when the May twins and Jeff Raymond returned to Los Angeles during the second week of September. "We were out of money and clean clothes," Tom May explained. The Stooges parked the Oldsmobile around the corner from the Brentwood building, then crept to the front door of their apartment behind a hedge of cypress trees. While Tom dumped his dirty laundry in a pile on the floor, Dave listened several times to a message from Les Zoeller on his answering machine. Joe knocked at the front door five minutes later. With him was Jim, who had spent most of the past week watching the twins' apartment. "Tom played like 'Everything's okay, everything was normal, he didn't know what was going on,'" Jim recalled. "'They just came back from Lake Tahoe. They were tired, needed a little rest, went fishing for a few days.'" Joe's own tone was more terse than threatening. "He wanted the keys to the Olds," Tom remembered. "He said it was a BBC car, and we were no longer BBC members." While Jeff called Renee for a ride, Tom and Dave protested they were being left without transportation. Joe offered them a ride in his Jeep, but first Tom phoned his mother and said, "If I'm not there in twenty minutes, call the police." Renee arrived moments later, and the twins asked her to follow the Jeep to Bel Air. "My parents said we should be safe there," Tom recalled, "and if not, 'We have other places for you.'"

It had begun to look to the Stooges as if they were going to need safe havens for some time. The Beverly Hills police not only were reluctant to arrest Joe but actually seemed inclined toward the theory that Hunt had been set up by the "AT LEVIN'S, TO DO," list. Their most likely candidates were the Mays themselves, "who had bad business dealings with Levin in the past," Gene Browning recalled. The Beverly Hills detectives even proposed the possibility that the twins and Levin had conspired to implicate Joe as part of some elaborate con. "Les Zoeller told us, 'Ron Levin's involvement makes anything possible,'" Browning recalled. He had probable cause to arrest Joe Hunt, Zoeller said, but nothing like the kind of evidence required to win a conviction in court. And without a body, the detective observed, it was not possible even to establish beyond a reasonable doubt that a murder had been committed, let alone that Hunt had done it.

The Mays, meanwhile, hadn't received any indication that Joe knew they had spoken to the police and decided it would be safe to stay in town. Joe's last lever of control over the twins was that West Cars held title to their cars. They were keeping the Corvettes at their mother's house in Bel Air, but Jim was able to snatch the most valuable of their vehicles, Dave's 1939 La Salle. "A classic," Browning recalled, "fully restored, white with a red interior. Just gorgeous. Dave took it to Daddy May's, but he wanted to impress some girl and took her out in it. He left it in the driveway at the apartment that night, and by the next morning it was gone." Joe suggested he might return the title on Dave's car, Jeff remembered, when he phoned one day later "to say he wanted a final meeting before we were out of the BBC." Joe proposed a rendezvous that evening at the Gardena warehouse, but the Stooges suggested instead meeting for a drink at the Charthouse in Westwood. "A very public place," Jeff noted.

Joe came into the restaurant alone and immediately got down to business, informing the Stooges that the Microgenesis Corp. and the BBC retained all rights in the Browning attrition mill and would take legal action to protect its interests. The twins insisted they had delivered all three Cyclotrons to Bill Nalan's mining site in the Mojave, as instructed, and couldn't imagine where else they might be. Joe replied with that cold stare/warm smile combination he used so effectively, then said he knew what was going on. Tom and Dave should be more careful to whom they gave their phone number, Joe observed. And it was probably not a good practice either to leave messages on their answering machine for just anybody who wandered in to hear. "He said he wanted to know who Les Zoeller was," remembered Jeff. "Joe told us, 'The police aren't your friends,'" Tom recalled. "'You shouldn't talk to them.'" They should bear in mind that the district attorney's office didn't pay well enough to attract top law school graduates, Joe added, and that it would be easy enough to persuade prosecutors that the three of them were responsible for Ron Levin's disappearance. "He wanted us to go to the police and retract our statements," Tom remembered. "He said, 'Tell them that everything you've said up to this point has been a lie,'" Jeff recalled. "He also said, 'Ron Levin's a very good friend of mine, and I'm very sorry he's missing, and I don't want you to say anything bad about him.'"

Through West Cars, he held the title to every one of their cars, Joe reminded the twins, but was willing to trade these for certain documents. "He said, 'You know which ones,'" Tom recalled. When the Stooges refused, Joe ended the meeting with an ultimatum: "He said, 'In that case, I declare war on you,'" Tom remembered.

There was no overt threat, however, in the note Joe sent a few days later, dated September 17, 1984: "Tom, Your Texaco card turned up. Do you know where the mills are? Expectantly, Joseph Hunt."

Tom remembered the sign-off as "Respectfully, Joe Hunt," but then Tom was confused about many things. What, for example, he had been doing with Joe and Jim when they came to Orange County looking for Gene Browning. Dave May already had warned him, in a tape-recorded conversation, Browning said, that "Joe was hiring a contract killer from Canada to come down and eliminate me." He assumed this was a scare tactic, the inventor said, after Hunt began calling him at his new home in Irvine to make a series of veiled threats. "He had gotten our phone number, which is unlisted, out of Tom and Dave's book when he broke into their apartment," Browning explained. "At first it was the 'I'm unhappy with you' sort of situation. Then he called and said, 'Remember what I said about [the Rumanian]? That can happen to you, too.'" According to Joe, he had asked Tom and Jeff to show him the Brownings' house. "Jeff wouldn't go, but Tom did," Gene recalled. "Tom of course said he had come along for my protection, not his own." The inventor hardly was assuaged, however, when the twin boasted that he had directed Joe and Jim to a house on the other side of the lake: "Tom was rather pleased with himself until I said, 'My God, Tom, do you realize that they can come down here and this poor man can come to the door very innocently and run into a shotgun blast?' Tom said, 'Oh. I never thought of that.' I went to the Irvine police that night; they had to move those people out of their house for three days."

While the police were at his own house, Browning recalled, "I inquired whether it might be permissible to shoot Joe Hunt if he came on my property. And they said, 'If the man puts his foot on the sidewalk out in front of your house, shoot the sonofabitch.'" The police were fascinated by his arsenal, Browning recalled: "The sergeant said, 'Well, you have these weapons, but do you know how to use them?' And I said, 'Look at the name on the side of this gun. The guy that made this gun was my grandfather.' He got quite a kick out of that."

The inventor's wife was not so amused: "Literally, we were locked in the house for a week, waiting for him," Claire recalled. When Joe finally found his way to the proper address, she remembered, "Gene went to the door with a gun in one hand and my Doberman on a leash in the other." It was not possible to shoot Joe at the time, however, Browning explained, since Hunt was both unarmed and accompanied by a pair of uniformed police officers. He was there to take possession of the BMW sedan and a Subaru pickup that were the property of West Cars of North America, provided for Browning's personal use only so long as he remained in the employ of BBC Consolidated, Joe explained. "But we had moved those two cars to another location," Browning recalled. "Joe then had the audacity to tell me I was a car thief. I thought that was a fairly amusing statement, considering the context."

20

"WHAT ALWAYS CALMED ME," EVAN EXPLAINED, "WAS THE WAY JOE KEPT taking care of business." By the middle of September, though, it was obvious to all but the most devoted that Joe had lost control of everything except his emotions. Convinced he now was the main target of the Beverly Hills police investigation into Ron Levin's disappearance, Joe also suspected that Reza had been implicated in San Mateo County, where Neil Adelman's motion to force the release to the younger Eslaminia of "any and all documents" seized by the Belmont PD from the Davy Glen condominium was answered not by a local lawyer representing the city cops, but by a pair of San Francisco attorneys speaking for the California Department of Justice and the U.S. attorney general's office.

All that masked the state's criminal investigation was the silence of the DOJ attorney, Ron Bass, who declined even to explain his appearance in court. The federal government's lawyer announced, however, that he was "here representing the interests of the United States of America." Mr. Adelman's motion was moot, the Belmont PD's own lawyer informed the court, since earlier that day a pair of FBI agents, two attorneys from the U.S. Justice Department, and an unnamed man dispatched by "a sister agency" had arrived with a pair of interpreters fluent in Farsi at police headquarters, where they proceeded to confiscate the several cardboard boxes, numerous paper bags, and two briefcases filled with papers belonging to Hedayat Eslaminia that had been removed from the condominium. He was one of those who had "reviewed" the disputed documents, the federal lawyer advised the court, and could attest that there were indeed national security problems presented by the case."

Joe now had little choice but to turn back from the government blockade in Northern California and make one last attempt to stabilize the situation in the south. The quarterly disbursements from Financial Futures were due two days later, on September 15, and investors were milling about the Third Street office like a herd of lowing cattle on the verge of stampede. "First the SEC calls, then Lore tells us the police are coming in to investigate, after the break-in at the office," Al Gore remembered. "Everything was uprooted all at once, as if a precursor to disaster. But I had such confidence in Joe Hunt that I kept quiet."

Joe continued to keep up appearances, providing Lore Leis with an accounting for the quarter that showed a profit of 68 percent in the past three months and instructing her to prepare the investor checks on schedule. Steve Weiss was the first to arrive at the office on Monday morning, when the disbursement was due. Joe was not in, but Weiss saw the checks in their envelopes, waiting to be signed and subdued his misgivings.

Joe at that moment was locked up in a hotel suite on Century Boulevard in Inglewood, by the airport, where he would spend a long day in fierce session with William Kilpatrick of UFOI, Ray Robinson of Saturn Energy, and Bruce Swartout of Cogenco. Cogenco had negotiated a new agreement with Saturn and UFOI, Swartout explained, after Joe's rescission of the 1983 contract. "Joe told Bill, 'I have a much larger deal on the technology out of the country, and the BBC would like to cancel,'" Swartout recalled. Yet Hunt kept making threats, the Cogenco chairman explained, so that Kilpatrick became reluctant to sign the revised contract absent an agreement among all parties. At the hotel by the airport, Joe's refusal to step aside forced a compromise that divided the $220 million contract between Cogenco and Microgenesis.

Joe, though, still wanted it all, as Swartout discovered when he met Hunt at the Third Street office the next afternoon: "He offered me two million in cash to forget the deal. When I refused and started to leave, Joe became wild-looking. I thought I was going to get killed before I got out of the office."

Swartout was protected in part by the unannounced arrival of Steve Weiss, Chester Brown, and Lou Buratti at the BBC office. Joe kept them waiting for half an hour, then said he would speak to Steve alone in his office. After he shut the door behind them, Hunt produced a letter from the SEC, Weiss remembered, informing him that he was the subject of a criminal investigation and demanding all trading records of the Financial Futures and International Monetary Fund corporations. "I said, 'I think you've got a problem; I wouldn't want to be in your shoes,'" Weiss recalled. "Joe said, 'Oh, I've been involved in things like this before. My lawyers will take care of it.'" Hunt's aplomb infuriated Weiss: "I said, 'Why don't you cut the bullshit, you sonofabitch. There's just the two of us in here. There's no third party to bear witness. So why don't you come clean and tell us you ripped us off?'" Joe opened the door a moment later and stepped outside. "Steve's trying to psychoanalyze me," he told Brown and Buratti, smiling.

Weiss was back at the BBC office the next afternoon, accompanied this time by Brown and Gore. "Steve called and said, 'You better come with me to the office,'" Gore recalled. "'Something very bad is happening.' So we arrive the next day, walk into Hunt's office. Joe sat behind his desk. We reminded him it was time to pay, the middle of September. Suddenly he's telling us, 'There is no distribution. There is no money. The money was all wiped out in the marketplace.' His voice was absolutely flat, no fear, no concern, no regret. I said, 'Joe, how could you possibly lose it?' He said it happened in April on a day when Dosti had an accident and he was unavailable and they had to send Lopez, and Lopez misinterpreted the instructions, liquidated prematurely or something. A million and a half dollars was lost in a single stroke. Joe said he had invested the money that was left and that came in, and that was also lost. Then Steve became enraged." "I said, 'You cheated us!'" Weiss recalled. "Joe remained calm," Gore remembered. "He said, 'Steve is dysfunctioning.' He told us he would repay the money we had lost, but not the rollovers. It's difficult to explain, but his very indifference was reassuring. My attitude was that it was unfortunate, but the man will generate some more money and reinvest, and we'll all make profits again."

He had scheduled an assembly of the limited partners for the afternoon of September 22, Joe said. Later that day he sent out a letter inviting all investors to a meeting on Saturday where he would "delineate significant problems the corporation is facing."

The problems facing Financial Futures seemed not so significant to Joe by the next evening, September 19, when Jim called from Los Angeles County Jail, where he had been an inmate since early that afternoon. Joe reassured the other Boys with word that Jim had been picked up on an old Virginia warrant for receiving stolen property, but news of their bodyguard's arrest "sent shock waves through the BBC," Evan remembered. Only the involvement of the Beverly Hills police, though, gave any indication that there was some connection between Jim's arrest and the Levin investigation. "All I remember is that Joe seemed very concerned about getting Jim out of jail fast," Evan recalled. As they scrambled to raise the money to make Jim's bail, "Joe went to great lengths to tell us how we had to show solidarity, show Jim support," Evan remembered. A mass visit by what was left of the BBC was arranged for Sunday morning, September 23, less than twenty-four hours after Joe was scheduled to address his limited partners in Beverly Hills.

More than two hundred people showed up for the investors' meeting on Saturday afternoon, Mary Brown remembered: "They had this huge room in an office building on South Beverly Boulevard. [Joe and the BBC] were sitting at a long table in the front. I had met very few of the investors, and I was astounded at the caliber of the people who were taken in by this man. There were attorneys and doctors, writers from the studios, producers and directors, a variety of people. It was amazing." Joe opened by "recapitulating the three main points he had made to Steve, Chester, and myself a few days earlier," Gore remembered: "That the money had been lost in the marketplace, that he was let down by someone named Steve Lopez, and that he would repay." He had come to this meeting with copies of a "Promissory Note and General Release of All Claims" for each investor, Joe explained, his written pledge to make good on all investments within one year. "He encouraged us to give him a breather to go over the accounts and reinvest the balance of the money," Dr. Paskan remembered. Joe "mentioned the big deals with Microgenesis that were going to bring in money," Weiss recalled. "He spoke of million-dollar options and the Kilpatrick contract." Joe also showed his investors a Swiss bank check for $1.5 million. "He told us that the person who wrote the check, Ron Levin, had skipped town," Gore remembered. "Then he said the Levin family owned three-quarters of a billion dollars in real estate in Zurich, and he would get some of that to pay the debt Ron owed him."

Only one investor, the writers' agent Stewart Robinson, called Hunt a liar to his face. "[Robinson] was pounding the table with his fist, really challenging him," Mary Brown remembered, "but [Joe] never gets rattled." "Joe was in total control of that whole room," Lore Leis affirmed. "I was right by his side, and it was like he was not shaken by anything."

Joe's composure was even more remarkable the next morning, Evan remembered, when he assembled the BBC for the trip to county jail: "We all went in Dean's mother's car, that big old Country Squire station wagon. I remember Joe giving us this pep talk on the way there, about how Jim really needs our support and we have to get him out of there." Nevertheless, the trip to county jail affected Evan so deeply that he quit smoking. "Because Jim told me that it cost a dollar a cigarette in there," he explained. "And at that point I really expected to have to go to jail. What I remember most is that Jim looked really scared and that Joe did not look scared at all. Not even a little. I think that's why we all clung to him. Brooke was being very upbeat and supportive: 'Jim, we love you, and everything will be okay. Don't worry, we're taking care of Dana,' et cetera. We all tried to be very positive, as Joe had said we should, but it was hard for me because I found even the waiting room scary. I mean, they shuffle them all in wearing chains and facing the wall, and there are all these signs about not touching. Jon and Dean were scared, too, but I was afraid to look at them, and them at me, because we might lose it if we did."

Jim was out on bail two days later. "We had to turn over all the pink slips on the cars we owned to the bond company," Evan recalled. By then, though, surviving the siege at the Third Street suites had become almost as grueling as confinement in county jail. "It was like a battle line in the office," Jim remembered. "We had about fifty investors . . . Brooke was there and she sweet-talked a lot of people. Lore was taking care of things, too."

Joe instructed his still-loyal secretary to compile a list of all investors in the Steve Weiss Family Account. Bank deposit slips showed that Weiss and his investors had brought in $1,584,730.52, while only $428,028.18 had been paid out from the $1,240,374.02 in "total profits" Joe reported, leaving a balance owing to the family account's limited partners in the amount of $2,397,104.52. "Joe wanted each person to know exactly what they had coming if they signed the promissory note," Lore explained.

With Joe flying back and forth from Las Vegas for meetings with Bill Nalan and the rest of the Boys afraid to come into the office, the secretary was left alone to face an onslaught of sob stories. "Everybody had an emergency," Lore remembered. "They all came up with something. House payments. Operations. Kid that stutters that was supposed to go to school and learn not to stutter."

Joe was a lot less interested in his investors than in what the Beverly Hills police were up to by that point, however, Evan recalled. He summoned Jim, Dean, Evan, and Jon Allen to the Manning for a planning session on the afternoon of September 26. "Joe called us up to 1505," Evan remembered, "then moved the meeting to the exercise room in the basement." The case against him was at best a weak one, Joe told the others when he had locked the door behind them. There still was no body, and it could be shown that Ron had a compelling reason for skipping town. There was no physical evidence and no eyewitness. It was still only the Stooges—and possibly Taglianetti—who had talked. Even if Jeff, Steve, and Tom testified that Joe had confessed to the killing at a meeting on June 24, there still were seven other BBC members who could contradict this story. Nevertheless, it was clear that the Mays and Jeff Raymond "pose[d] a threat," as Evan recalled Joe's words, and it was time to "eliminate that threat."

Joe's first idea was to invite the Stooges along on a deep-sea fishing trip, Dean recalled, get them out on the ocean, kill them aboard the boat, then throw the bodies over the side. When the others objected that even Tom and Dave would never be so stupid, Joe outlined several other possible plans for killing the twins and Jeff. Running them off the road with a "large weighted truck" seemed to be the one he liked best, Evan remembered: "We were going to watch them, find out where they were hanging out, what

THE PRICE OF EXPERIENCE 401

bar—because they *would* be at some bar—and get them on the way home, after they'd had a few."

For the first time in months, Dean dared to disagree with Joe in the presence of others. All that killing the Mays and Jeff could accomplish, he said, would be to make Joe a suspect in four murders, rather than in just one. The others remained silent. "In hindsight, I think Joe was unraveling," Evan reflected. "Because what he said was crazy. Yet the way he said it was not. The most amazing thing about Joe, to me, was the way he handled stress. It had no visible effect. None. He gave you the feeling he enjoyed the challenge, that he knew he could handle it."

Joe's first lieutenant, however, had reached the limit of his endurance; Dean announced that evening he was moving out of the Manning. "Some of the things Joe was contemplating, the lengths to which he was willing to go—I was scared," Dean explained. "I was losing confidence in him personally . . . I was feeling more and more uncomfortable, and I couldn't overcome it just by hanging around with Joe, which is how I'd always done it before."

Les Zoeller's decision to arrest Joe Hunt at the end of September was considered a tactical error by some colleagues: The evidence against Hunt at this point, they noted, was not enough to prevail even at a preliminary hearing, let alone in a "no body" murder trial. Zoeller's explanation had been that taking Joe into custody was the only way he knew to get enough of the suspect's handwriting for a credible comparison with what was on the seven pages.

Zoeller was carrying a photograph of Joe but no arrest warrant when he drove to the Wilshire Manning in an unmarked car with two other detectives on the morning of September 28. The officers had been parked on the street outside the building for less than twenty minutes when they saw Joe's black Jeep pull out of the Manning's parking lot onto Wilshire, heading east. The detectives gave chase, but the Jeep was traveling at high speed, weaving from lane to lane. A red light at Beverly Glen Boulevard stopped Joe finally. Zoeller pulled the police car up next to the Jeep and blocked it in. Joe, wearing a gray Armani suit, handled his arrest well, Zoeller conceded: "A moment after he was handcuffed, he requested that we secure the briefcase he had with him in the Jeep."

Zoeller brought Hunt to the Beverly Hills Police Department at a little past 10 A.M. and within the hour had ensconced him in the adjoining jail. "When he was booked, we saw the Rolex on his wrist, and he said, 'Oh, that's the watch Ron Levin gave me,'" the detective remembered. Zoeller let Joe sit in his cell until 2 P.M., then had him moved to an interview room. As a police officer in Beverly Hills, Zoeller had been afforded an unparalleled opportunity to observe white, well-dressed people responding to their virgin experience with incarceration. The majority of suspects faltered visibly when they were led from lockup to a room seven by eight feet, with poor ventilation, blinding fluorescent light, no windows, a concrete floor, and a pair of police officers for company, but Joe Hunt "appeared very confident," Zoeller recalled, "very sure of himself."

The suspect nodded as the detective read his rights, then said he was willing to talk "about certain things" without a lawyer present. Informed he had been arrested on suspicion of murdering Ronald George Levin, Joe didn't react, Zoeller recalled: "I asked him when was the last time he saw Ron Levin. He said it was some time in early June, but he could not give an exact date without a calendar." Joe readily admitted negotiating a deal with Ron Levin involving the silica rights in the Cyclotron and that Ron had paid him with a $1.5 million check drawn on a Swiss bank. Throughout the interview, Zoeller remembered, Joe replied readily to some questions but simply ignored others: "He gave quick, snap answers, then expounded on whatever he wanted to talk about until I interjected a question. He said Financial Futures was his commodities trading company. He said he had lost money—$1.1 million—and had returned $455,000 to his investors, but that he was under no obligation to cover the losses under his agreement with his investors."

It was perhaps Hunt's hauteur, the slight smirk that played across his lips each time he changed the subject, that prompted Zoeller to pull the seven sheets of yellow legal paper out of the file folder in his lap. The detective's satisfaction with what happened next was still audible three years later: "I put the pages on the desk in front of Joe and asked, 'What do you know about these?'" Zoeller recalled. "He looked at them and stopped talking. A blank look came on his face. He was suddenly very solemn, going through them page by page, reading fast. He went through them over and over without speaking, forward, backward. I sat and watched him for seven to ten minutes, then I asked Joe again, 'What do you know about these?' He said, 'I don't know anything about these.'" "Did you write them?" Zoeller asked. "On a subject like this, I want to confer with my attorney," Joe answered, and ended the inteview.

Joe phoned Dean at Lisa Marie's apartment that evening, said he was in the Beverly Hills City Jail and there was not much time to talk, Karny remembered: "He began by telling me that my recollections were going to be important testimony with regard to the events at the office relating to the $1.5 million option agreement with Levin and also with regard to the night that Levin supposedly disappeared. He said that he thought that he and I might have been at the movies that night. I replied, 'I think that's right.'"

News of Joe's arrest reached Evan an hour later: "I was at home. Brooke called me and said, 'You gotta get to the office.' I think Jon and Lauren and Brooke were all there, and they told me what had happened. It was a big shock. I didn't expect Joe to be arrested. I knew the Mays had gone to the police, but no one held Tom and Dave in any very high regard, mentally. Could they arrest Joe just because the Mays said Joe had told people at a meeting that he had killed Ron Levin? If the rest of us said it wasn't true? I didn't think so."

Joe phoned from jail a few minutes later and asked Evan to spend the night with Brooke at the Manning. At this point, the condo seemed more drab than deluxe, Evan remembered: "The furniture was gone, so my bed was a mattress on the floor in the living room, with just some blankets. We watched TV and hardly said anything; we were being careful about what was said in the apartments at the Manning. It was very solemn. I remember being distant toward Brooke. I didn't know how much she knew or didn't know. We couldn't eat much. We looked at some photo album, from one of our parties, some black-tie affair. I don't know why pictures of us in our tuxedos were reassuring, but they were."

Evan joined Dean and Jon the next morning at the Third Street office, where the three of them cleaned out the file cabinets, filling fifteen fruit crates that Dean hid in his parents' garage. Neil Adelman had submitted his resignation earlier that week, when Joe told the attorney he no longer could pay his salary. That left Lauren Raab as the only lawyer in the BBC. "The Beverly Hills Police must still be laughing about the calls they got from Lauren," Evan reflected. "I was working with her, and we thought we were so fucking tough. We threatened them with lawsuits. We were trying to get the Jeep back and the briefcase that Joe had in the Jeep."

At least Lauren's bar card got her into the BHPD Jail for a meeting with Joe, who sent out notes for the other five:

Dear Brooke,
    I won't have a clear idea of my situation for about a week. I understand you have been very strong and I am proud. I carry a strong remembrance of you. My love goes with you.

                                                                    Joseph
P.S.—Don't make yourself available to my investors too much.

Dean, My First Friend,
   Don't Recoil! You are very able. Interview, Investigate,
Research.
   Look after yourself.
   I am coming back.

Love,
Joseph Hunt

Evan,
   Be aggressive.
   Apply your sense of humor to this with a passionate application.
I am not around to pat you on the back or to center you on this, so
work without an audience.

Joe

Jon,
   Bite the head off the grinch that stole Christmas.

Love,
Joe

Jim,
   I am pleased I met you. Take initiative on selling the assets.
Also sell the Lincoln Continental. And the Oldsmobile. See about
$6,000 on watch or some Reasonable price. Sell excess furniture
and odds and ends.
      STAY ON TOP OF YOUR CASE!!!

Your Home Boy (like only you'd know)
Joseph

Brooke had written a note of her own during the drive with Lauren
from Westwood to Beverly Hills:

Hello My Darling Joseph,
   I wanted to be close to you so I'm here with Lauren. I love you
Joe. Last night I had sweet dreams of you. I wore one of your
shirts so I could smell you and feel you. This is difficult to write
because I'm driving in the car. I love you so much Joe. I will be
with you forever. We've been doing terrific work. Everyone is
staying together. Don't worry about me. I am the Empress Falgon
and you are the GREAT RAHZULI.

I will see you in the window. I love you and sleep well my love.

Your precious,
Brooke

They read the notes Sunday morning at the Third Street office. Evan took comfort: "I still had so much faith in Joe, I thought, 'Fuck it, he can beat this.' I figured, 'Tom and Dave, what do they know?' And comparing the police to Joe in a battle of wits, I'd definitely take Joe. Joe had said that as long as some of us said there hadn't been a meeting where he confessed to killing Levin, then it didn't matter what the Mays said, that we could show they had their own selfish motives, that they were trying to steal the Cyclotron."

Evan, Dean, Jon, and Lauren met again that afternoon at the UCLA Law Library to research Joe's case. "Lauren and I were the first ones there," Evan remembered, "and she told me about the seven pages, that they were in Joe's handwriting. I'm not sure what Lauren's motivations were. I think she liked Joe a lot, even though she knew he was not going to be romantic toward her. I assumed she knew he was guilty—Jon Allen must have told her—but I didn't press."

Evan's assignment that day was to research murder cases where a conviction had been obtained without a body. "There were two main cases," he recalled, "one where some guy threw his wife in the river and another where he dropped her in the ocean. I remember I got dinner for everybody. Somebody—Lauren, I think—told me that Joe wanted me to spend Sunday night with Brooke, and again I obeyed. I still wasn't terrified. That came Monday morning."

It was Tuesday, actually. Joe's refusal to provide a sample of his handwriting was playing into Zoeller's hand. "Your affiant believes that the suspect wrote the 7-page list, which were [sic] found at victim's house," the detective noted in the application for a search warrant he submitted in court on Monday morning, "and as the suspect refused a handwriting exemplar, your affiant can find handwriting by the suspect in the briefcase, his house or his office." Warrant in hand, Zoeller and two other Beverly Hills detectives, backed by a pair of LAPD officers, reached the Wilshire Manning at a little past seven on the morning of October 2.

"I was still asleep on the floor," Evan remembered. "Lauren's big female German shepherd was there, for protection, and it went berserk. She was like a guard dog, trained to attack intruders. They banged on the door very hard, said, 'This is the police. We have a search warrant. Open up.' I was just sort of waking up and trying to get some sweatpants on, and they banged again and said, 'If you don't open the door right now, we're going

to break it down.' I got to the door before they forced it. The LAPD officers put the dog in one of the bedrooms, and Zoeller showed us the warrant.
I started reading it, asking a couple of questions, but I was pretty feeble.
Zoeller asked who I was, and when I told him, I could tell he recognized
my name. For some reason, that scared me."

Brooke came out of the bedroom wearing only a T-shirt and refused
to tell Zoeller anything. "The police started in the kitchen and searched
everything, very neat but relentless," Evan remembered. "They even
searched my bed. All I remember them finding was this book that had been
shot. They were carrying a lot of papers out. They took Brooke and I into
Dean's bedroom to question us. The first thing Zoeller asked me was
whether I had ever been at a meeting where Joe told me he murdered Ron
Levin. And I very matter-of-factly said 'No.' Then he asked me if I knew
anything about the disappearance of Ron Levin. And I said, 'I heard he
disappeared' or something. I was very nervous, not shaking or anything, just
not making eye contact. Then right at the end when he read me a minor
version of the riot act, telling me, 'We know what happened and we know
what you did and you'll be arrested and you're going to jail,' I did shake. I
was probably as scared at that moment as I've ever been in my life, convinced
that, if I wasn't an accessory before, I was now."

When the police left, Evan phoned Lauren at the BBC office: "She
told me they were searching there also. And she said, 'Why did you even
talk to them?' She was reassured, though, when I told her what I'd said."

The detectives had done better at the Manning than at the BBC
office. The pantry in the apartment was filled with papers, Zoeller recalled,
including "Bearer of Arms" applications for the right to carry concealed
weapons in the names of Joseph Hunt and James Graham. Among "mis-
cellaneous items" police collected were a box of shotgun shells and an empty
nine-millimeter ammunition box. Joe's passport, stamped only once
(HEATHROW, 13 JUNE 1984) was in the master bedroom, where detectives
discovered assorted "yellow and white papers with writings on same." Two
were selected to serve as exemplars of Joe's handwriting. The first was a
personal note: "Dear Brooke, You no longer anger me. I see how hard you
try. Now, I just feel annoyed that you do not allow yourself to enjoy your
deserved reward: Peace, my love, and joy in yourself. Love, Joe." The second sample was Joe's latest last will and testament:

I give all my personal and household effects to Brooke Roberts . . .
nominate Dean Karny as the executor of my estate [and] direct him to
assist in every way that the corpus of my estate reasonably allows him,
to nurture, comfort, house, equip, feed, clothe, educate and protect

Brooke Roberts (as well as to provide for her future in the event of his death). If my estate is large enough, I direct him likewise to provide for Ben Dosti, James Graham, Himself, Evan Dicker, Jon Allen, Steven Lopez and Reza Eslaminia.

The search team at the Third Street office could find no copies of the Microgenesis contract, the Swiss bank check, the letters to Levin, or any May Brothers Land Corp. documents. While most of the file cabinets were empty, however, in Lore Leis's desk police discovered a set of Wings Travel Agency receipts for HUNT, JOE, MR. and GRAHAM, JIM, MR. dated June 12, 13, 19, and 21, for flights between Los Angeles, New York, London, and Washington, D.C.

After the police left the Manning, Evan remembered, he and Brooke walked the dog around the block so they could talk about what he had told the police: "She wanted to know if they'd asked about the meeting and was very pleased by what I said. We reassured each other a lot. Again, it was that we could get through this, that the police didn't have a case, that Joe could beat it. I still believed that. I mean, Joe had made such a big deal of how solidarity was our protection, and if the rest of us stick to our story, they'll never be able to pin anything on us. If it was seven against three, or six against four, or even five against five, we still had conflicting accounts and reasonable doubt."

As he predicted, Joe was released from custody on Tuesday afternoon, when the district attorney's office refused to accept the case. "Insufficient evidence" was the explanation. Joe wore his best summer suit and an expression of bemusement when he returned to the Third Street office Wednesday morning. "Business as usual," Lore Leis remembered. Several investors were waiting in the lobby, there to obtain Hunt's signature on the promissory notes he had given them at the meeting on Beverly Drive two weeks earlier. "Lore told us the day before that Joe had been arrested for something, but that it would be cleared up," remembered Al Gore. "She didn't say it was for murder, and the way Joe looked when he got out, you would have thought it was jaywalking they were after him for. He didn't carry any impact. Anyone else hammered by such circumstances, it shows on his face. Not Joe."

Gore and Dr. Paskan were permitted a private audience, at which Joe repeated his claim that the Levin family owned hundreds of millions of dollars in Swiss real estate: "He said he had been told this by one of his investors, who happened to be chief of police for the Canton of Zurich," Gore remembered. "He said he would be able to get the money and pay back all the people by the end of 1985. I didn't even ask what he had been arrested for; I was so mindful of his feelings." Dr. Paskan not only presented Joe with a signed copy of the promissory note but also handed him a personal check for two thousand dollars to help Lore Leis buy a car.

Joe gave his secretary seven hundred dollars, then ate lunch with Evan at Godfried's, where they sat at their favorite outside table. "Joe was very confident," Evan thought. "He said, 'Look, they couldn't even hold me.' He sort of mocked Zoeller. I didn't want to know about being in jail. It helped steady me, though, to see how sure of himself Joe seemed." Joe joked about the expression of terror worn by Zoeller's partner during the arrest, Evan recalled: "He seemed pleased to know he had made such an impression."

Joe's pleasure no doubt would have doubled had he heard what the police were saying about him among the BBC's defectors. "We had the Beverly Hills police, the LAPD, the Gardena police, and the Irvine police all coming to check on us," Gene Browning recalled, "warning us, 'This kid is the most dangerous criminal walking the streets. The kid is totally amoral, he has absolutely no reservations.'" "The terror we lived through," Claire Browning added. "We wouldn't walk into our house for weeks without thinking, 'Is he gonna kill us tonight?'" Like the Brownings, the May twins were waiting for Joe with loaded arms: Dave carried a .38 police special even when he went to the bathroom, while Tom slept with a 12-gauge Remington shotgun. They were warned by Steve Lopez (who had approached the twins to suggest a new deal to market the Cyclotron in Asia) that Joe "planned to lure us to some party and kill us there," Tom remembered. "So the two of them went out and bought that shotgun," Gene Browning recalled, "then immediately came home and shot a hole in the wall. It scared hell out of me to think of those two carrying weapons."

The Mays were in less danger than they imagined. Joe's suspicion now centered on Jerry Eisenberg, whom he surmised must be the opposition's mastermind. "He could not have known that I had talked to the police," Eisenberg reflected, "but maybe he figured the others weren't smart enough to know what evidence would hurt him." Joe had been out of jail only a few days when he phoned Eisenberg at home to ask for a meeting at the Hard Rock Café. "For once I came early," Eisenberg remembered. "I brought Mike Feldman to be a witness and had him stand way in the back, where he couldn't be seen. It was a hot day, but Joe came in wearing a trench coat. He was sweating, but he didn't take it off, which made me wonder what was under his coat. He had Jon Allen with him, and Jon stayed by the door, like he was keeping watch or something. Joe sat down at my table and got right down to it: 'What do you know about what's been happening?' I said, 'What?' He said, 'Don't try to lie to me. Tell me what you know about all this.' I said, 'I have no idea what you're talking about.' He looked at me, then said, 'Well, okay. But if I find out you do, I'll kill you.' Then he got up and walked out. I took it seriously. Mike and I waited in there for another hour before we left."

Joe had begun to suspect that even his closest allies were wavering. When he met Dean for dinner at the Old World in Westwood, "Joe said he had been hearing things I had been saying about him that suggested I was not completely on his side anymore," Dean remembered. It wasn't true, Karny insisted: "I was still with Joe. My plan was to tough it out and keep my mouth shut." They spoke like old friends after that. When he asked what jail was like, Dean recalled, Joe said not that bad and described washing his socks in the sink. He still seemed sure of himself: "Joe said Detective Zoeller wasn't very smart, and that he, Joe, had made him look stupid. He said he had been so bold as to tell Zoeller that he hadn't done good police work. He said he got particular enjoyment out of saying that." Joe admitted being taken aback by the seven pages but said he had managed to mask his reaction. "He thought the fact that he had been released meant that even the list couldn't prove the case," Dean remembered. "There still was not enough evidence."

Joe was "supportive" when Dean suggested it might be best to go his own way for a while. "We agreed we'd get together in the future and maybe pursue our dreams together," Karny recalled. "We would take some time apart, but we'd stay together on hiding our secrets."

Evan, too, now wanted "distance." "I kept having the feeling that I was being watched whenever I came in to work," he explained. "We weren't talking about anything in the office anymore. Nothing. I was just going through the motions, waiting to get some money from Eslaminia." After Joe's arrest, Evan had returned to the law library, not to research Joe's case this time, though, but rather to study the statutes on accessory after the fact. "It said you had to do whatever you did or say whatever you said with the 'specific intent' to help the person escape justice," he recalled. "I didn't think I'd done that yet, and I didn't want to." Also, his attempts to recover Joe's Jeep and briefcase had been "traumatic," Evan said: "Every time I'd call, they'd try to question me or make threats." Finally, a week after Joe's release from jail, "I told him I wanted to continue to be part of the BBC, and I wanted to be his friend, but I didn't want to work in the office anymore," Evan recalled. "He said that was fine. We talked about my getting a job clerking."

Before he left the office, though, Evan destroyed the forged minutes of the Microgenesis meeting that had authorized Ben's trip to Europe, tearing them up into tiny pieces and tossing these into a toilet. Only they wouldn't all go down the drain, so he kept flushing again and again, Evan remembered, and was soaked with sweat by the time the last little scrap of paper went down.

Even Joe's confidence might have been shaken had he known that, less than an hour after he was released from custody, the Beverly Hills police obtained a search warrant to open his Halliburton briefcase. The contents of the case proved a trove of treasures: scores of file folders, legal pads, and loose documents were piled under Joe's personal planning diary. The titles on the folders alone made interesting reading: "SWARTOUT," "REZA: ASSETS RE CONSERVATORSHIP," "SWISS BANK CORP.," "MAYS," and "MICROGENESIS" were but a few. Both the scope of the BBC's operations and the scale of Joe Hunt's ambitions were outlined in hundreds of handwritten entries on dozens of "To Do" lists. There were addresses in Abu Dhabi, Madras, Frankfurt, and Paris. Under the heading "JOE MUST CALL" were the names and phone numbers of potential witnesses who ranged from Bernice Rappaport to John Golden, as well as for the hotels in London and Zurich where Reza Eslaminia and Ben Dosti could be reached. There were an original of the Microgenesis contract with Ron Levin, a Home Savings of America withdrawal slip for fifty-eight thousand on an account bearing Joe's name and the address of Shalom and Danny Karny, a copy of Hedayat Eslaminia's probation report, and the original of Tom May's California driver's license.

Joe's portable office proved perhaps less useful to Zoeller's investigation in Southern California than to Oscar Breiling's in the north. The state's agent nevertheless was among those who believed the detective's decision to arrest Hunt had been a hasty one: "When I found out Hunt was almost immediately released, I went bonkers. I still hadn't gone near the BBC, wanting them to think it was just Podunk PD on the case, and I figured that when Les interviewed Joe, Hedayat Eslaminia's name must have come up. So I was very upset with Beverly Hills PD. I went to my boss in Sacramento and said, 'Is there any way we can take that investigation away from them?' I cooled off when I learned Les had avoided mentioning the Eslaminia investigation."

Breiling himself had avoided speaking even to the inside source handed over by the FBI: "I was concerned about talking to Eisenberg because I had been told he was very actively involved. And I just didn't trust anybody with the BBC. So I concentrated on Olga and what I could learn from her." After Olga described the appearance of Reza and his "associates" at the Belmont condo, and the help they gave Reza in winning the conservatorship, Breiling obtained pictures from the department of motor vehicles for a photo lineup. Olga calmly identified Joe Hunt, Dean Karny, and Ben Dosti but lost her breath when she came to the picture of Jim Graham.

On his last day in the office before leaving on a two-week vacation at the end of September, Oscar found the state narcotics agent who had used Reza Eslaminia as his snitch in Southern California. He last had seen Reza on August 2, Xavier Suazo said, when the Iranian approached him with a bizarre tale of "two individuals whose principal activity involved the kidnapping, torture, and subsequent killing of wealthy individuals after the individuals had been forced to turn over their assets." Was Reza attempting to set up the Shadings and provide himself with an alibi, Breiling wondered, or just smoking the mirrors in general? "I didn't even know he had gone to Europe with Ben at that point," Oscar said.

Breiling found this out on his first day back in the office, October 9. "The morning didn't start out too well," he remembered. "Before I went on vacation I had asked Ron Bass to find someone who could translate the papers that had been found in the apartment, most of which were written in Farsi. But when I came back, Ron told me the feds had come in, claimed national security, and taken it all. I was probably just as unhappy as the BBC about that." Breiling's disappointment was forgotten an hour later when he took a call from Hedayat Eslaminia's friend Edgar Safarian, a resident of Beverly Hills who had been the Chrysler Corp.'s agent in Iran during the last decade of the shah's reign.

He had received a package by international courier that morning from a Swiss banker named Victor Benjamin, with whom he had been friendly in Teheran, explained Safarian. Benjamin now worked as vice president at the Trade Development Bank in Geneva. The package from Switzerland contained copies of a conservatorship award to Reza Eslaminia and a general power of attorney signed by Hedayat Eslaminia assigning control of all his assets to Reza. In an attached note, Benjamin explained that Reza and another young man were in Geneva with an attorney, attempting to force his bank to surrender all monies held in the name of Hedayat Eslaminia. Safarian insisted the power of attorney must be a forgery because Hedayat never would have turned his money over to Reza. When he received copies of the documents, Breiling noted the date on the power of attorney was April 16, 1984. According to Olga Vasquez, she and Hedayat were in Mexico on that date; the two had been stopped at the border for bringing too much alcohol into the country and strip-searched at the San Ysidro crossing. U.S. customs documents confirmed this.

"That's when I started calling Victor Benjamin, telling him, 'Don't release the money,'" Breiling recalled. "He said, 'Well, these fellows are here, and they have a conservatorship from the state of California. We're advised by our attorneys that we have to give them the money.' I was calling Benjamin at home and at work, and he was very good about confirming that there was an account there that had X amount of dollars and even that there was a second account, which was unusual, because Swiss bankers don't even like to give you the time of day. I remember telling Benjamin that if, as I believed, Hedayat Eslaminia was dead, then there was nobody left to speak for him. And I felt I was his voice. That it was my responsibility to see that the people who had done this were brought to justice ... anyway, Benjamin gave me the account number, how much money there was, who the beneficiaries were. I'm sure he could have gotten in trouble. But he said, 'We have to release the money.' And I said, 'Can you at least delay it?' And he said, 'I might be able to hold them off for another day, but that's all.'"

Recovery of the Eslaminia estate was the last real hope for the BBC's survival. The Boys had the Third Street offices only until the end of October and were facing eviction at the Manning on November 3. Money was so tight that Joe assigned Jim to sell off the motorcycles. At the Honda dealership in Van Nuys, Jim used the BBC Productions cover story, claiming the bikes had been driven just once, during a scene in a low-budget movie. "He wanted to know the name of the movie," Jim remembered. "I said, *Hell on Wheels*."

Most of the cash was cabled to Zurich, where Ben and Reza spent it to obtain legal counsel. Penetrating the strict secrecy laws of the Swiss banking industry required more than a power of attorney notarized by Evan Dicker and copies of a California conservatorship award, Ben and Reza had discovered. Every document they submitted had to be sent by courier back to Los Angeles, where the Swiss embassy demanded verification of each date and every signature. Lore Leis did most of the paperwork, while Evan ran back and forth between the BBC office and the embassy. "Verifying my notary signature with the Swiss was another harrowing experience," Evan recalled. "I figured that at least a European prison would be safer than San Quentin. Joe said we had to have the Eslaminia money, though, and we had to have it now."

The only Swiss account the Boys had evidence of was the one at the Trade Development Bank branch on the Place du Lac in Geneva, where Ben and Reza went first from London. After submitting their documents at the Geneva bank, they took the train to Zurich, where Reza opened an account in his own name to receive transferred funds. They spent two weeks in the city inquiring after accounts in the name of Hedayat Eslaminia but found none. In Zurich, Ben retained attorney Fritz Keller to compel release of the $147,000 in the single Swiss account he and Reza were able to confirm. Keller accompanied them by train to Geneva on October 15 to meet with officials at the Trade Development Bank.

It was that evening when Oscar Breiling received Victor Benjamin's warning that the funds would be transferred to Reza's account within twenty-four hours. "So I said, 'I'm gonna get the conservatorship pulled in the morning,'" Breiling remembered. "'As soon as I get it pulled, I'm gonna call you, and that call will be followed by a Western Union Mailgram, which will be followed by a cover letter with documentation of the fact that the conservatorship has been revoked.' I called Ron Bass at home in the middle of the night and told him, 'We've got to pull a conservatorship.' He says, 'It can't be done, not once it's been assigned by a superior court.' I says, 'Don't tell me it can't be done. It was obtained under false pretenses. Get your ass down here and let's make some law.' He wouldn't get up, but he said he'd be in early the next morning. I said, 'I'll be waiting for you,' knowing Ron's not exactly your early riser. I spent the night at the office, drafting a chronology of events for Bass and a declaration by me.

"He comes in, goes down to the sixth-floor library, and pretty soon he's back, big smile, going, 'Hey, there's a way we can do this.' I said, 'I told you.' So he filed a brief with the court that afternoon, and I phoned Victor Benjamin at home, early in the morning their time. He said, 'The lawyers say we have to release the money now. It will be transferred to Reza's account first thing this morning.' I said, 'I'm giving you the information over the phone that should allow you to refuse. You were shown a power of attorney that I have proven is fraudulent, the conservatorship is being revoked and the money in that account was the motive for the murder, and the people you're giving it to are the ones who killed this man. If you release that money to them, after I have told you this, I will try to get a warrant for your arrest as an accessory to murder after the fact.' It was a complete joke, but I think he half bought it. I sent the Mailgram as soon as I hung up. Then when I called him later in the day and asked if he got the Mailgram, he said yes, they weren't going to give Reza the money."

The revocation of Reza's conservatorship left Joe with only his theory of reasonable doubt to play out. Since he had not been formally charged at the time of his arrest, Hunt was unable to obtain a copy of the Beverly Hills police report and thus had no certain knowledge of Les Zoeller's case against him. He would have been astonished to learn that the detective's investigation—still officially a missing-person case—had not been undertaken in earnest until the afternoon of Hunt's release from the Beverly Hills City Jail, October 3, when the detective for the first time interviewed Blanche Sturkey.

Finally on the record, Blanche scoffed at the suggestion that Ron Levin would leave behind his wardrobe and other valuables, no matter what was at stake. Ron's possessions were everything to him, she told the detective. Len Marmor used virtually the same words when Zoeller interviewed him six days later. Marmor mentioned also that he knew Joe Hunt, in fact had seen him about two weeks earlier, at Ship's restaurant in Westwood, among the crowd that filled the venerable diner on the last night it was open. He remembered discussing Ron's boasts of wealth, Marmor said, and Joe Hunt asking if he believed they were true. "It seemed to [Marmor] that Joe Hunt was genuinely concerned that the victim was missing," the detective wrote in his notes of the interview. What he told Zoeller, literally, Marmor recalled, "was that I thought Joe Hunt was one of the mildest people I ever met and that I was ninety-five percent sure it wasn't him [who killed Ron]. And Zoeller told me, 'I'm ninety-five percent sure it was.'"

Zoeller's interview that same afternoon with Dean Factor was actually discouraging. He had spoken to Ron Levin by phone at 9 P.M. on the evening of June 6, said Factor, who added that "Ronnie was in bed while talking to him and that everything appeared to be normal." Jerry Eisenberg was interviewed for the first time on October 9 as well and advised the police that everything he knew about Ron Levin's disappearance had come from either the May brothers or Steve Taglianetti.

The technician's reports comparing Joe's handwriting and fingerprints with those on the seven pages reached Zoeller's desk on October 11 and October 14. Joe's habits of connecting some letters in a word but not others and of alternating script with printed words were quite distinctive, noted the analyst, who was willing to swear in court that Hunt had authored the "AT LEVIN'S, TO DO" list. The fingerprint technician was more equivocal, however, reporting that he had found twenty-five latent prints on the seven pages but could identify only two as Hunt's.

With what was at best circumstantial evidence, supported by testimony not only uncorroborated but actually refuted, Zoeller recognized he had barely enough to indict Hunt and not nearly what the DA's office needed to win a murder conviction in court. A warrant to search the Westwood apartment of James Pittman aka Jim Graham was executed on October 15, but the detectives who ransacked the place found nothing more incriminating than a closet "packed full of what I would consider very expensive clothing," as Zoeller described it.

Steve Taglianetti, describing Joe as "another Charles Manson," told Zoeller on October 17 that "the people around Hunt will say anything he wants them to" and that even those who might waver—Jon Allen and Evan Dicker—were convinced that they would "go down" if Joe did. Two days later, on October 19, Taglianetti and Tom May took Zoeller on a tour of Joe's shooting range in Soledad Canyon, leading the detective up the dirt fire lane that wound to the top of Indian Canyon. There the detective noted not only the "bleak vistas" but thousands of arid acres in the foreground where a body might be buried.

By the morning of October 22, Zoeller had decided that the only real hope for a case he could take to court was to harrow those Boys who still stood by Joe until, one-by-one, they broke. Just before noon, he phoned Lauren Raab to tell the attorney that Joe could retrieve his briefcase from the Beverly Hills Municipal Court building. Joe had Lauren with him when he arrived an hour later at the courthouse, where he was formally charged with the murder of Ronald George Levin and arrested. In his wallet were a California driver's license in the name of Joseph Henry Gamsky, a bank deposit slip in the name of Mina Hakimi, and a bank statement in the name of Hedayat Eslaminia.

It was no big deal; Joe would be out in a few days, Brooke assured Jim when the bodyguard stopped by the Manning that evening. She gave him a blue Fila bag filled with Joe's things and said to stash it someplace safe, Jim recalled. He drove straight home, parking outside his apartment building on Midvale at a little past 7 P.M. Eight detectives from the Beverly Hills PD's crime suppression unit awaited his arrival, hidden in shrubbery or behind parked cars. Taglianetti's description of the BBC's bodyguard as "armed to the teeth" had been taken to heart. "All these police jumped out of nowhere," Jim remembered. "Not in uniform at all. I didn't know they was police until they started pulling guns . . . and they said, 'Halt,' 'Freeze,' 'Don't move or I'll blow your head off!'"

Jim had dropped the Fila bag when he fell to the ground. Inside, detectives found Dean Karny's Union 76 gas card, pink slips on the black BMW and a West Cars Mercedes, a manila folder labeled "JOE HUNT," a "JIM GRAHAM, PROFESSIONAL BODY GUARD" business card, and a dozen books, including *How to Survive in the Slammer*.

It was 2 A.M. when Joe called Dean's parents' house from the Beverly Hills City Jail to say he had been arrested again. "He started out by saying that I should come and visit him," Dean remembered, "and he made mention of some supposed conversation wherein I said that I could come up with ten thousand dollars for his defense." He didn't want to talk over the telephone, Dean said. Whether Dean liked it or not, he was involved in this case, Joe told him, and they were going to speak at this time about some of the areas where his testimony would be critical. Most important, Joe explained, was whether or not there had been a meeting at which he announced the murder of Ron Levin. He couldn't remember, Dean said.

The police left Joe's first friend alone for the time being, concentrating instead on the BBC member they were told was the weakest link in the human chain around Joe. A team of LAPD detectives assigned to investigate the burglary at the Third Street office knocked at the door of the West Los Angeles apartment where Jon Allen was living with Lauren Raab on the morning of October 23, less than twenty-four hours after Joe's second arrest. When Jon and Lauren opened their front door, a detective informed them he understood that a video camera Lauren had reported stolen two months earlier might be found in their apartment. Both Jon and Lauren denied that the camera was inside but refused consent for a search. The detective in charge informed the two that he intended to secure the premises until a warrant could be obtained. "Allen then became very cooperative," the detective noted, "and produced one Sony Beta video camera."

Jon paid his last visit to the BBC office the following morning, typing out a letter of resignation addressed to Joe Hunt: "Dear Joe, This must signal the end of our business relationship, legal relationship and parts of our personal relationship. I still consider you my friend, but we must do some talking in future times. Jon." "I guess I basically just got smart at that point," explained Allen, who had dated the letter "June 30, 1984."

From the office Jon drove to the Beverly Hills Police Department and told Detective Zoeller he had attended a meeting on June 24 at which Joe Hunt informed nine other BBC members that he and Jim Graham had "knocked off" Ron Levin. He had refused to cooperate with the investigation earlier, Allen said, because Joe Hunt was threatening his life. Jon also informed Zoeller that Joe had asked him to cache some items in the boiler room at his apartment building, among them the shotgun retrieved from the Shadow Mountain mining site.

His margin had been cut from seven–three to six–four, but Joe was still ahead. "Joe told me, 'Big deal. Nothing to worry about. The charges will never stick,'" Jim recalled. "So I didn't worry."

Jim looked worried enough to Les Zoeller when the detective ordered the suspect he knew now as James Pittman moved from the cell adjoining Joe's to an interview room early on the morning of October 23. "They said, 'You're going to spend the rest of your days in jail,'" Jim remembered. For someone whose first words were "I don't know anything about anything," Jim revealed a fair amount. Describing himself as a private investigator, Pittman denied ever working as a bodyguard and insisted his primary employer was not Joe Hunt but another Wilshire Manning resident, former Wisconsin Lieutenant Governor Milton Polland. "When asked what kind of investigative work he does for Mr. Polland, [Pittman] stated that he followed people around for him," Zoeller noted. He occasionally followed people around for Joe Hunt also, Jim admitted. Was he working for Hunt when he had "the confrontation" with Bruce Swartout in Irvine? Zoeller asked. Yes, Jim answered. Zoeller chose that moment to tell Jim he had been significantly implicated in the murder of Ron Levin. When was he supposed to have killed Levin? Jim asked. Sometime during the night of June 6 or the morning of June 7, Zoeller answered. Jim said he wasn't even in town during June, that he had spent the first half of the month in Washington, D.C., and the second half in Maui, working for Milt Polland, and didn't get back to L.A. until June 29.

Half an hour later, Zoeller was on the phone with Polland, who confirmed that Jim had spent two or three days working for him in Hawaii but said this had been at the very end of June or in early July. Later that day, Zoeller obtained a Wings Travel receipt for a Western Airlines flight by TRAVELLER: GRAHAM, JIM from Los Angeles to Honolulu, dated July 3, 1984.

Confronted with the discrepancy, Jim retreated into silence. "Joe told me, 'There's nothing there. Hold steady,'" he remembered. It was not so easy for Jim to lean on Joe after Thursday, though, when the two were separated during the transfer from their comfortable stucco chambers with a rose garden view to the tiers of steel cages at the Los Angeles County Men's Central Jail. Joe lost not only his Beverly Hills address that day but his legal representation as well; Lauren Raab met him in the attorneys' room to announce that she was resigning from the BBC. After Lauren confirmed that Jon Allen had spoken to the Beverly Hills police, Joe said he intended to have her boyfriend executed, Raab recalled. There were lots of people in here who would do it for a hundred dollars, Joe observed; the same people would sodomize her for free.

Raab was on the phone to Oscar Breiling early the next morning. "Before this I was her worst enemy, and then suddenly she wants to talk," Breiling remembered. "Things do change." The one important piece of information Lauren provided was the number on Ben Dosti's American Express card. "I run a search warrant with American Express," Breiling recalled, "and I find receipts and charges for the Saint Francis Hotel, the Villa Hotel, and the U-Haul shop in Belmont. Now I can place at least one of them in the area at the time."

While Raab was on the phone with Breiling, Joe's last two loyalists were closing down the Third Street office. "His father, Ryan, was there—with Liza Bowman, I think—and Brooke was there too," remembered Evan, who had come by to clean out the drawers of his own desk. "They were loading everything into the back of the yellow pickup. I hadn't seen

Ryan since the day Joe fired him. He was very orderly and matter-of-fact. Brooke said something about what a weak case they had against Joe, but I didn't want to speak to her. I picked up my stuff, took some annotated codes that I thought might be useful, and just sort of hurried out the door."

Evan saw Brooke next on Sunday morning, when she showed up unannounced at his apartment. "She told me that Joe wanted me to sign a declaration saying that there was no June 24 meeting, which I refused to do," he remembered. Evan was on the phone with Dean moments after his guest departed. Dean convinced him it would be a good idea to find some place more secure, maybe move back into his parents' home for a while, Evan recalled. "One of the reasons I wanted to move out of my apartment was to get away from Brooke," he explained. "I didn't think she knew my parents' address, and they had an unlisted number." Three days later, he and Dean rented a truck, Evan remembered, and moved everything he owned from Swall Drive to the Roxbury house.

That weekend, the two attended a Halloween party together, both going as Ronald Reagan, wearing a pair of rubber "Rapmaster Ronnie" masks with the bootblack pompadour and 'What, me worry?' smile, as if they hoped the Teflon master's stick-proof powers might accrue.

They were meeting almost every day now on the campus of Whittier Law School, surrounded by but separated from the once-scorned classmates whose conventionality they had come to envy. To avoid eavesdroppers, he and Dean usually carried on their conversations in an open courtyard or on the lawn in the shade of a big eucalyptus tree, Evan recalled, waiting for one another in the cafeteria between classes, then stepping outside to talk. None of this was planned, he reflected: "We just sort of did it without needing to put the idea into words. Who else was there for us at that point?"

It was the day before Reagan's reelection when Dean finally told Evan the truth about Reza's father. "He just looked me straight in the face and said, basically, 'Look, the BBC was involved,'" Evan recalled, "or he might even have said, 'The BBC killed.' Dean also said he was 'involved.' My feeling was he needed to tell me. I think I was the first person he told. All I remember blurting out is 'Don't tell me anything else.' We were outside one of the big lecture halls, and I just turned and ran inside the building to get away from him. I stood there trying to catch my breath while all these people were passing by, on their way to class, and I wished I was one of them."

Evan ran into Dean again later that evening: "I told him, 'I don't want to know anything else that could possibly implicate you.' Because by then it had occurred to me that going to the police might be the only way out for me. It's difficult to describe what Dean was like. He wasn't in tears, but he was like someone who would have cried if he had been able. I don't think either of us were capable of tears. That might have been the first time in my life I envied people who could cry."

Autumn is the season when people pay for living in Los Angeles. The chemistry between heat and smog comes to a climax in late September. Leaves may be crimson and gold in Boston, but in Beverly Hills the imported maples and elms along the avenues that bear their names turn swiftly from yellow to brown, yet another dissonant amenity, as out of place as that Santa Claus with the reindeer-drawn sleigh the chamber of commerce hangs every Christmas between the two tallest palm trees astride Wilshire at Rodeo. In Southern California, the most vivid colors of fall are the shades of heliotrope and mauve in the poisoned sunsets. During daylight hours, the horizon is an enclosure and the sky a vapor of ashes, with only wisps of blue directly overhead. Air becalmed for months, collecting the emissions of ten million automobiles and cooking in one ninety-degree day after another, achieves a harrowing density, like some fugitive element capable of passing from gas to solid without liquefaction. It is a time of shallow breathing and suspended animation, when only the truly driven wear jackets to meetings and police form new task forces to track down the latest serial killer. In early October, the L.A. basin is an arena of perfumed toxins and pretty lies where one falls asleep at three to the drone of a neighbor's air conditioner, then wakes an hour later to the siren of his car alarm. All anyone can do is wait, mainly for those sirocco winds Southern Californians call Santa Anas, hot, dry blasts of air that yowl out of the east each November to sweep away not only the pollution but the last traces of moisture in the atmosphere as well, reminding even people who can afford ocean views that they are dwellers in a desert. By Columbus Day, a pall of actual despair hangs over the city. The beaches are bearable, but all inland is hell, with isolated exceptions nestled among the upper reaches of the canyons connecting Sunset to Ventura. On that high ground, at dusk, when the Rainbird sprinklers water lawns laid over the crushed stubs of creosote and chaparral, there is the sensation of a breeze cooling the brow as one watches darkness permeate smog. Those who raise their eyes may even detect a few spectral stars, pinpricks of brightness flickering on the margins of the sky, bearing no comparison to the towering firmament one is awed by in the Rocky Mountains, yet no less stirring, their very faintness a reminder and a reproach.

No one in all of L.A. was aching for a change in the weather more desperately than Dean. In a season when the days drag on and on, his only hope seemed time's swift passage. He was at his parents' house "laying low," numbed by terror and drugged by denial, sleeping sixteen hours a day. Joe continued to place collect calls to the house on Outpost Drive after his transfer to county jail, but Dean no longer accepted them. Up to the time he revealed his involvement in the Eslaminia abduction to Evan, "I was still sort of believing I could just walk away," Dean explained, but by the middle of October that fantasy was untenable.

What Dean needed first was not a defense but an explanation, one his parents could live with. His sister, Laurie, was working as an intern at the *Herald Examiner* and dating the paper's best reporter, Andy Furillo, son of *DodgerTalk* sportscaster Bud Furillo. "The first time I was told about it all was one night when I came over and they had all these books on cults and mind control and programming and deprogramming spread out all over the living room," Furillo remembered. "Dean and his mom and dad, and Laurie, too, were all reading them, comparing notes on how being in a cult can change a person and how the leader can get a person to do things they would never do otherwise. I knew a little bit about the BBC, that it was some kind of combination social club and business group. They hadn't made it sound like a cult before, but now they did. I never had liked Dean; he seemed like a snobby little wimp to me. He still seemed like a snobby little wimp, only now he was a scared snob. I don't think his family knew then that he had been involved in murder. They said the worst he had done was ride in a car with the body of someone the leader of the group, Joe, had killed. It was all Joe, he was responsible; Dean didn't know what was going on until later. I don't think he'd told his parents much."

Dean had told his parents enough, however, to persuade the Karnys they should hire a criminal lawyer, Jan Handzlik. "I wanted to know what my exposure was," Dean explained. "I got the number from Brooke of the guy who was representing Joe. I called him to ask what he wanted me to say. I was going to stick with Joe. He wouldn't talk to me, though, so I got my own attorney."

One day after Joe's lawyer, Ed Masery, refused Handzlik's request for a copy of the Beverly Hills Police Department file on the case, Brooke showed up at the front door of Dean's parents home on Outpost. "She told me that things were getting worse for Joe because more and more people were coming out against him and making statements that there was, in fact, a meeting in which he admitted killing Ron Levin and that he had threatened them," remembered Dean, who began to make notes of each conversation he had with a BBC member. "She said it was very important for me to make a statement which contradicted those other statements, or Joe might not get bail set. Then she said that if I did not want to 'go in' and make such a statement, Joe's attorney would write up an affidavit for me to sign stating that (one) there was no meeting where such an admission was ever made; (two) Joe did not kill Ron Levin; and (three) I was never threatened by Joe.

"I replied that I couldn't and wouldn't do anything or say anything, on my attorney's advice, at the very least until I was able to give my attorney a copy of the police report to read so that he might be better able to evaluate my position. She said that for me to just sign an affidavit would help Joe *so* much and couldn't really hurt me. I replied, 'An affidavit is a statement, and it becomes a record, and it has consequences.' Again I told her that I most certainly was not going to do or say anything unless I had a copy of the police report to give my attorney.

"Brooke then told me that 'they' want to send Joe to the gas chamber and that if he gets convicted, then 'they're going to come after you.' She also said that if I talked to Ben, I should tell him that it is safe to come home and that he should come home and help Joe. She also said that the evidence against Joe is insufficient because one, the 'list' had been tampered with and would be excluded from evidence; two, the supposed fingerprint which had been found on the 'list' was not specified as to page; and three, the Mays' statements could be shown to be motivated by their desire to steal things that didn't belong to them and would therefore be excluded too. All of this and more—which she said she wanted to but was not allowed to tell me— meant that Joe was going to get out on bail if only I'd make a statement."

The next day, November 14, Brooke called to tell Dean he could pick up a copy of the police report from Joe's father at Ryan Hunt's office in Van Nuys. When he read the Beverly Hills PD file that evening, "I became much more frightened," Dean said. "I realized the police knew a lot more about what had happened than I thought they knew." The most disturbing page in the police report was a copy of the flyer Oscar Breiling had been circulating to police departments throughout the state for the past ten weeks, emblazoned with a photograph of Hedayat Eslaminia over a request that any information concerning the Iranian's disappearance be forwarded to the California Department of Justice office in San Francisco. "I had no idea that law enforcement had connected the Ron Levin case to the Eslaminia disappearance before I saw that flyer," Dean explained. "I got pretty upset then and scared for my own sake."

Dean's fright increased as he read the only other reference to Eslaminia in the Levin case file: "The police report mentioned Jerry Eisenberg having said that Jim Pittman said the BBC was involved in the Hedayat Eslaminia disappearance. This convinced me that Eisenberg had told the police everything he knew, and I felt that could be a great deal with regard to me. I figured law enforcement must know about our attempt to locate and seize Mr. Eslaminia's assets."

The scope of the investigation that engulfed the BBC was intimated most comprehensively in an LAPD report included in the Beverly Hills case file, written by the detective who had confronted Jon Allen and Lauren Raab at their apartment on October 23: "This is a tale of intrigue that involves several law enforcement jurisdictions," the report began. "Crimes committed include murder, stocks fraud, attempt [*sic*] murder, assault with a deadly weapon, grand theft auto, insurance fraud, etc. BBC is (was) a parent conglomerate founded by a man named Joe Hunt, AKA Joseph Gamsky, D.O.B. 10–31–59, FBI # 4032511AA1. BBC Consolidated (commonly and kiddingly referred to as Billionaire Boys Club) was formed as an investment corporation with promises of high yields for investors . . . "

Many of the dots were connected for Dean the next day, November 15, when Jon Allen called—as a friend, he hoped, Dean said—"and told me that he had decided to make a statement to the authorities rather than to potentially 'get in trouble' for things he was not responsible for. He advised me that I also should seriously consider making a statement, as he felt it would alleviate both my emotional stress and the potential risk of becoming a target for prosecution. He said he preferred not to come over and visit me when I asked him to, but said he did want to acquaint me with what he had said and with whatever other information he had concerning the overall situation."

To begin with, Dean should know that far more than the Beverly Hills Police Department was involved in the investigation, Jon explained: The LAPD, Gardena PD, Irvine PD, and Belmont PD were part of it, as were the FBI, the California Department of Justice, the SEC, the California Corporations Commission, the IRS, and Interpol. He had told the police about the June 24 meeting, said Jon, who claimed he hadn't been sure Joe was telling the truth about the Levin murder, imagining it might have been some sort of test. Jon told the police he had no notion of whether Dean had been involved in planning the murder but said Joe ran the BBC, despite how it might have appeared. While he was definitely fearful of Joe and Jim and somewhat fearful of Ben and Reza, Jon had told the police, he was not afraid of Dean at all. Jon had claimed he knew nothing about Hedayat Eslaminia's disappearance but acknowledged his involvement in the search for the missing man's assets. He spoke also to a state investigator named Oscar, Jon told Dean, explaining that the police and insurance reports he had submitted were written at Joe's instruction.

The Mays had spent two hundred thousand dollars in legal fees already to keep the family name out of the newspapers and to make sure the twins got immunity on all charges, Jon said; now Tom and Dave were boasting that they had made sure Dean and Evan never would become attorneys. The twins called him "a little fly," Jon told Dean. Zoeller knew Dean had been involved to some degree with the Levin murder and might arrest him at any time, said Jon, who urged Karny to contact the police first. "Jon thinks Zoeller sees the Mays 'for what they are,'" Dean wrote in his notes of the conversation, "but Zoeller is more concerned with nailing Joe than in discrediting Joe's detractors."

Jim Graham had been warned he would be charged with the attempted murder of Bruce Swartout, Jon advised Dean, and might go state's evidence. Steve Lopez had spoken to the SEC for eight hours and with Zoeller as well, Jon added: Lopez claimed Joe told him where the body was and was taking Zoeller out to look for it. Steve Tag also had talked to Zoeller, Jon said.

The next day, Dean told Evan he had hired an attorney. "By that point, my discussions with Dean came down to 'We've got to go to the police,'" Evan explained. "It was obvious the tide had turned. Paradox Philosophy was out the window; we treated it almost like a dirty joke. Joe was still Joe, but he wasn't the same Joe he had been. I don't recall Dean blaming Joe, but it was now clear that Joe was no longer to be admired, deferred to, loved, supported. I mean, we were talking about selling Joe down the river."

It wasn't only Joe whom Dean was thinking about selling down the river but Ben as well. Twice during the third week of November Karny dialed the number of a pay phone in Zurich where Dosti awaited his call. Ben had learned of Joe's second arrest from his parents, after Rose Dosti was advised by Les Zoeller "that Ben could have been involved in Ron Levin's disappearance," her husband recalled. According to Zoeller, he had nothing against Ben and would give him immunity if he testified, Luan Dosti remembered. The father spoke to his son a few days later when Ben phoned from London and passed along Zoeller's offer. "He said, 'I have nothing to hide, nothing to tell,'" Luan recalled. "'Why would I need immunity?'" Ben's father remembered him saying. "'I have done nothing wrong.'"

Ben was not so serene after November 20, when Reza took a phone call from Debi Lutkenhouse, who told her boyfriend she had just come from an interview at a Foster City coffee shop with an investigator from the State of California named Oscar Breiling. "Debi told me Oscar thought I was involved in my father's disappearance," Reza remembered. "He said God had told him so, and that my only hope was to go to him and talk to him, or he was going to crucify me."

Dean, convinced there would be limited seating in the lifeboat, advised Ben this might not be the best time to come home, warning that he and Reza would be arrested if they returned. Get an attorney, Dean suggested.

Karny was replacing his own lawyer, Handzlik, who had not been entirely successful in concealing his horror during Dean's description of the Eslaminia kidnapping, with an attorney who was not so squeamish, Ron Morrow. Together, they compiled a list of what Dean might be able to offer the Beverly Hills police. "There was no reference in the police report to Jim's trip to Washington, D.C., or to Michael Dow and that contract, or to Joe's conversation with Jack Friedman, or to Jim and his silenced pistol, or that Jim had been sent to New York City," Dean recalled, "or to the dent in the [BMW] trunk, or to the plans to kill the May brothers and Jeff Raymond's girlfriend, or to Joe going back to Ron Levin's house to make the bed that night, or to the use of the term 'Mac' for Ron Levin, or that Joe went to New York to get Jim out of jail."

It was only corroboration, of course, that Dean could offer in the Levin case, where his maximum exposure would be as an accessory. He was an eyewitness, though, in the Eslaminia case, where a conviction might mean the death penalty. Morrow hired a former L.A. County sheriff's deputy to help prepare a proffer for the state attorney general's office.

Evan, meanwhile, was "getting real antsy," pressing for Dean's permission to talk to the police himself. Dean continued to insist that Evan let him approach law enforcement first. "Dean said if I went to the police, it could severely compromise his ability to make a deal," Evan explained. "His point was that because my exposure was so minimal, I could follow him, but he might not be able to follow me."

Morrow flew to San Francisco on the morning of November 26 to meet with Ron Bass at the attorney general's office. "I was beginning to have an emotional reaction," Dean explained, "feeling terrible, starting to lose weight, throwing up again. I sort of cowered in my bed for days."

Dean was cowering, specifically, in a back bedroom at his parents' home in the Hollywood Hills when Les Zoeller arrived there at about noon on November 26 with a subpoena. Danny Karny answered the door and let the detective in. A moment later, Mrs. Karny handed Zoeller the phone in her living room so that the detective might speak simultaneously to Morrow, who was in San Francisco, and to Dean, who was in the next room. After Zoeller assured Morrow that his subpoena was only to take Karny in for questioning, Dean came out from behind a closed door and accepted the document.

Dean called Evan at his parents' house that evening. "He was very nervous, unable even to speak in complete sentences," Evan remembered. "He said Zoeller had been to his parents' house. He said he was trying to make a deal in Northern California first. He promised to call me back. I didn't hear from him, though, and I was going crazy, so I finally called his parents, and then later that day Dean called and we met, just the two of us, and he told me he was going to San Francisco."

Debi Lutkenhouse had warned Reza from the first that Oscar, the special investigator from the attorney general's office who said he had been sent by God, seemed slightly crazy. The characterization elicited a delighted grin from Breiling, who admitted freely to "fanaticism." "It's the only way to the Lord," he explained. Breiling was a law enforcement officer who claimed to have spoken fluently in a tongue he had never heard—an obscure Corsican dialect, to be precise—and to have assisted in the healing by hands of a woman with congenital heart disease during services at his Pentacostal church in Pleasanton. Ever since his surrender to Jesus Christ, Breiling maintained, he had been witnessing miracles and receiving messages. He knew that there were people in his own office who snickered behind his back, Breiling said, "and I don't mind at all."

He liked to tell nonbelievers about that Sunday when an elderly woman he had never seen before got out of her car in front of the church and asked if he was Oscar Breiling, the policeman. When he admitted he was, Oscar recalled, the woman handed him two packages wrapped in brown paper, addressed to a small Bible college in Oregon. They were precious books concerning the true nature of Christ's mission, which she had mailed to her alma mater, the woman said. "Weeks passed, she thought they had been delivered, and then one day she heard a loud thump on her porch and went outside and found the books, with this UNABLE TO DELIVER stamp on them," Breiling explained. "She told me, 'I fell on the floor and prayed on the spot until I heard the Lord tell me to come over to this church and deliver them to a policeman named Oscar.'" It was her mission to inform him he had a teaching ministry, the woman told Breiling. "'So here you are, God bless you,' she says, then gets in her car and drives away," he recalled. "It was the only time I met her."

Those two slim volumes had changed his life, Breiling said. What he came to understand was "the true impossibility of human perfection," Oscar explained: "Man is inevitably sinful and will always fall short of divinity. This must be recognized. Those who teach to emulate Christ are arrogant and misguided because Christ suffered and died for the sins we have committed and the sins we will commit. It is only in recognizing our fallen nature and turning our redemption over to Christ that we can be saved." After beginning with a private study group, Breiling splintered from the Assembly of God when he began to hold his own Sunday services, shepherding a flock he liked to describe as "half Hell's Angels and half little old ladies." His first biker was a young man Oscar arrested and helped send to San Quentin. He converted the biker during his prosecution, Oscar explained, then later introduced him to Jimmy Lee Swaggart, who took the Angel on tour when he was paroled.

Moving on from the Fremont PD to the attorney general's office in the mid-1970s, Breiling retained the beard and mustache he had cultivated as an undercover narcotics agent, continued to wear cowboy boots, and hung out at the same East Bay honky-tonks where he had cultivated most of his drug sources. Among the Hell's Angels, Oscar's reputation as an asskicker was a distinct advantage: "They are constitutionally incapable of listening to anyone who is afraid of them," he explained. It was his contempt for mere piety that drew the bikers, though, who responded to Breiling's teaching that the most terrible transgressions were washed away by sincere surrender, while even the pettiest crimes brought retribution in the absence of atonement.

He had sensed an unprecedented moral conceit in the Eslaminia case from the first moment he heard about it, Oscar said, and for the only time in his career asked the Lord to take charge of an investigation. He had discovered during prayer, Oscar advised his colleagues, that one of the BBC Boys—"someone close to Joe"—was going to break, so all he needed to do was form a perimeter around the inner circle, then close in until Joe's Judas came forward.

He even had known in advance that it would be Dean, Oscar said: "When Morrow came up with his private investigator to make an offer of what his then-confidential client could do, we all met in Ron Bass's office. Now, Morrow was cute at playing games, and he was making comments to the effect that 'I represent an individual who is involved in a crime that you're investigating.' So I said, 'Oh, how is Dean?' And he goes, 'What are you talking about?' I say, 'You've got to be representing Dean Karny.' He doesn't confirm this, but says, 'What do you think happened?' I outlined what I thought, that these BBC people had come up to the Bay Area, kidnapped Hedayat Eslaminia, taken him down to L.A., killed him, and disposed of the body, then gone off to Europe to get his money. He says, 'Well, you got the big picture, but I think we can fill in the holes.' Then Morrow's investigator handed Bass, who handed me, a report he had prepared."

"What I knew that Oscar didn't was about Lake Arrowhead and Palm Springs," Dean explained, "the purchase of the trunks and the delivery uniforms, the bucket and the cat litter, the Ozeum and the chloroform, the U-Haul and the Beverly Glen house. And where we had disposed of Mr. Eslaminia's body."

After asking the attorney and his investigator to wait outside, Breiling read the proffer. "Bass, who hadn't read it yet, says, 'Well, what do we give him?'" Oscar recalled. "I said, 'Complete immunity.' He says, 'Are you kidding?' Who knows, maybe if I'd said, 'Let him plead to second-degree [murder],' we might have got him anyway. It just popped out of my mouth. Why Dean? Because the first one through the door gets the prize, basically."

Karny flew to San Francisco the next morning, September 27. "So young, so bony, so frail-looking," Oscar remembered. "The suit he had on may have fit him once, but it hung like a tent now. He was this almost-emaciated kid." Pitiful as Dean was, however, he showed little or no remorse, Breiling recalled, insisting upon promises from Bass to intercede with the SEC and to support his application to the California bar when he graduated from Whittier Law School in December.

Dean's home-study course in cult psychology helped him direct Breiling's attention in the direction he intended that blame should flow. Joe had introduced the Boys to Paradox Philosophy, Dean began, by "giving us legitimate answers to situations that we found troublesome." Eventually "everyone came to Joe with their problems," Dean explained, and "as we got more and more involved in Joe's plans, we became more and more isolated from the environment. We all came from good environments. We never had to do much hard work in our lives. Our parents were taking care of us, but [Joe] isolated us from that environment and from any other environment, and gradually anesthetized us to anything that—that had to do with right and wrong, and everything just became situational."

As he considered his coconspirators in Project Sam, Dean took a position that was coldly neutral toward Reza, who after all had sanctioned the abduction, torture, and assassination of his own father, while remaining sympathetic but distant from Jim, whose skills and ambitions Joe so successfully exploited. Ben, like him, had been "dutiful" in his obedience of Joe, Dean explained. Even as he played the part of apologist for Dosti, though, Karny betrayed his friend when it mattered most, advising Breiling and Bass that he had thrown away the European phone numbers where Ben could be contacted—and possibly offered a deal of his own.

While Dean was questioned by Breiling, Ron Morrow got on the phone with Les Zoeller and negotiated a separate grant of immunity in the Levin case. Dean flew back to Los Angeles on the morning of the twenty-eighth, then met with Zoeller at Morrow's office in Century City the next day, explaining in detail the lists on the seven pages and the formation of Joe's plan to commit the perfect crime. He knew Joe had to be kicking himself again and again for leaving behind the seven pages, Dean told Zoeller, after explaining Hunt's theory that only "internal guilt" caused a criminal's capture: "I'm sure it's a great blow to Joe's ego when he found that he had made a serious mistake like that. He felt that he had planned this brilliantly, and as you can see, he *did*."

At the end of Dean's recorded statement in Century City, Zoeller phoned Breiling in San Francisco and agreed to drive Karny to the Soledad Canyon area, in the hope that Dean could find the spot where he and Joe had dumped Hedayat Eslaminia's body.

Zoeller and Karny drove north by northeast in an unmarked police car along a route the detective would come to know well. Dean directed him to a fire lane that led into an area called Indian Canyon, Zoeller recalled, then asked him to stop at a truck turnout just inside the Angeles National Forest. Dean needed only a moment to study the slopes opposite the ridge where they stood, then said, "This is the spot where we threw him over."

Zoeller and a second detective, Dennis DeCuir, slid through shale and sandy loam to a clump of creosote sixty-five feet from the edge of the truck trail before they found the first human bones—an ulna, three ribs, and four vertebrae, all showing signs that they had been chewed by wild animals. Fifteen feet deeper into the ravine, they found another arm bone, then fifteen feet beyond that a scapula. Ten feet farther away were a tibia and a fibula, near a pair of shredded black trousers. Less than thirty feet away were a femur, another ulna, a complete pelvis, the upper part of a skull with several vertebrae attached, and a scrap of white cloth with a label that read JOCKEY CLASSIC BRIEF, SIZE 36. The detectives very nearly had assembled a complete skeleton by the time they found the only piece of Hedayat Eslaminia that mattered anymore, a lower jaw containing fourteen teeth that matched exactly the missing man's dental charts.

Part Four

SHADES OF GRAY

There is nothing in this world that a warrior cannot account for. You see, a warrior considers himself already dead, so there is nothing for him to lose. The worst has already happened to him, therefore he's clear and calm.

—excerpt from Carlos Castenada's *Tales of Power,* Joe Hunt's

primary reading material during his trial in Santa Monica

21

JOE WAS OUT OF SIGHT BUT HARDLY OUT OF MIND. BY THE TIME EVAN DICKER submitted to separate interviews with Les Zoeller and Oscar Breiling in early December, every Boy left unindicted had come over. There remained just one BBC member who would be joined to Joe until the end, Brooke Roberts.

Brooke had moved out of the Manning about a week after Joe's arrest, staying for a time at the home of the young "personal manager" she began seeing after Halloween. She was still Joe's girl, though. "He winds her up every day and plugs her in," said Steve Weiss, who had accepted a call from Brooke in early November, when she asked if they might meet for dinner. Brooke "said she wanted me to know that Joe was a good man," Weiss recalled, "that he was sensitive and knowledgeable and would make a marvelous contribution to society [and] that he wanted me to come visit him at county jail."

Brooke still was estranged from her family on November 12, her twentieth birthday. It was shortly after the Thanksgiving Day she spent with Shirley MacLaine, Lynne Roberts remembered, that she received the first call in weeks from her only daughter. The rest of the family learned Joe was in jail the next morning, when Lynne assembled them to announce that Brooke needed help.

Bobby Roberts, who had spent the past two years denouncing Joe to anyone who would listen, began visiting him in jail, as did the other family members, even the oldest son, strange but handsome Kurtis, who was living in Dallas at the time. "My father said Joe was innocent, that he had been abandoned and somebody should stand by him," Kurtis explained. Brooke's other brother, Todd, came to county jail almost every day, usually bringing that morning's *L.A. Times,* reading headlines and leads through the phone as Joe listened from the other side of the six-inch-thick pane of glass that separated him from visitors. Joe wanted all the information he could get about what was going on outside, Todd's girlfriend Michelle Berenak remembered: "Movies we saw, books we read, clothes we wore, work we did, relationships we were in." She was touched that Brooke's boyfriend did not wish to burden them with a description of conditions on the inside.

By the beginning of 1985, Bobby and Lynne were trying to find Joe a new attorney and promised to consider putting up the house on Bellagio as security for his bail.

Former BBC members traded speculations about the Robertses' improved relationship with Joe. Gene and Claire Browning became a kind of clearinghouse for rumors. "The story we heard most often was that Brooke has something on Bobby Roberts," Gene recalled. "She told this to Jeff and Dave and Tom." The Mays' theory of the Robertses' rallying around Joe, though, was that Hunt had signed over his film rights to Bobby Roberts and together they were working on a multimillion-dollar movie deal. Oscar Breiling heard that Joe and Brooke had been married in a secret ceremony. There was a puzzling tendency to overlook the most obvious explanation: that Brooke—a legal adult at the time the crimes were committed—could be implicated as an accessory to murder. The district attorney's office already had enough evidence to indict the young woman, though not enough nearly to convict her. Everyone in the BBC believed Brooke had been involved to some degree in the planning of the Levin and Eslaminia murders, though not even Dean could be certain. Only one person was in a position to say for sure, and that was the Great Rahzuli.

"Joe had dirt on all the people in the BBC," Evan observed, "but couldn't use any of it without implicating himself."

Evan had met finally with Les Zoeller on December 7, telling a story that began with his introduction to Joe on the ski trip at Lake Tahoe and ended with Hunt's plans for pinning the Levin murder on the Mays and Jeff Raymond. "Evan Dicker told [me] that he was scared to speak with [me] regarding the Levin murder," Zoeller wrote that afternoon, "because he considered Joe Hunt a very powerful person and didn't want any repercussions."

It was an explanation they all gave, even Jim, who was interviewed also on December 7, by Detective DeCuir, just back from New York with confirmation that Pittman had been arrested at the Plaza Hotel on June 10, 1984, while posing as Ronald George Levin. "I'll admit that I was in New York," Pittman said when DeCuir handed him the form for a handwriting exemplar. "I was supposed to guard a guy named Ron Levin, but he never showed up at the hotel, so Hunt just told me to take a few days and have a nice little vacation." As he completed the exemplar, Jim paused after each sentence to insist he had been a minor figure in the BBC. "You've got the heavies on this case," he told DeCuir. "Hunt and Karny and Dosti and Lopez got me into all of this. I would never kill anyone. In fact, I hate violence."

Jim stopped writing again a few moments later: "I heard that Karny showed you where the bones were," he said. "Of course he knows where the bones were; he was there, and he's not in jail. I didn't do anything, and I've been in jail for five weeks." Jim became very emotional then, DeCuir recalled, and began to cry.

While Jim wept, Steve Lopez expressed aggrieved astonishment that he had been named by Pittman as a "heavy" in the Levin case. Lopez was the last BBC member to move out of the Manning—"only because I had nowhere else to go," he explained. A return to Singapore would be ill-advised, Steve had concluded, after contacting several of his Asian investors: "Everyone wanted their money, and everyone wanted it now." He asked E. F. Hutton for a statement on the IMF account, Lopez explained, "to show the people in Asia, so they'd know the money had been lost in trading and I didn't pocket it. After I sent copies, I called people up and told them that the money was lost but that I would make it up to them. What else could I do?" The call he made to his largest investor, the man who had given him six hundred thousand dollars, was the one Lopez dreaded most: "He's not a person who needs to get angry to make an impression," Steve explained. "He just listened while I talked, without saying a word, until I told him I was going to pay the money back. Then he told me, 'That's right, boy, you'll pay me back.'"

After speaking to his Asian investors, Lopez felt he had nothing to fear from them: "These are very practical people," he explained. "They didn't want to kill me, because then I couldn't pay them." Americans, on the other hand, tended to react more emotionally, Lopez observed: "When Joe told the investors here that it was my fault the money had been lost, I began to get phone calls. Someone would say, 'You're gonna die tomorrow!' Bang! Hang up. I'd say things to these people like 'You better make your first shot count.'"

Lopez had at least one piece of heavy artillery with him at the Manning, the MAC 10 submachine gun left behind by Ben in his clothes closet. "Ben called me from Europe right after Joe was arrested for the second time and asked me to hide that gun," Lopez recalled. "I said, 'No way.'" Rose and Luan Dosti showed up at the apartment a day or two later. "They said they had come to get his things, but it was mainly to get the gun, I could tell," Lopez recalled. "They were very sad. I gave them the gun, and they were really upset when they saw it. I told them Ben wanted me to hide it, and they looked shocked."

Ben phoned him from London the next day, "yelling and calling me names," Lopez remembered. "He said I should have taken the gun out and buried it or something. I said, 'What, and get arrested myself? No way.' That was basically the end of our relationship."

Lopez moved out of the Manning ten days later, borrowing a bedroom from a friend in an apartment on Beverly Glen. He was interviewed at length by Zoeller and Breiling in early December. "The SEC called and I had a talk with them, so we were square," Steve said. "And the FBI, I gave them whatever they wanted."

The threats against his life continued, though. "I didn't know who was after me," Lopez said. "My own people, the investors here, Joe and the BBC. It could have been any one of two hundred people. I told Zoeller, and he gave me permission to carry a gun." The Walther PPK Steve wore strapped to his ribs scarcely seemed enough, though, when he returned to the Beverly Glen apartment one afternoon to find the place "shot to pieces" with an automatic weapon. In his absence, Steve's roommate and his girlfriend had seized the opportunity to make love on the living room floor, an impulse that probably saved their lives. "If they had been standing—or even sitting—they'd have been dead," Lopez said. "There wasn't a bit of the place that wasn't shot up—every window, every wall."

Still, "I was barely scared," Lopez insisted. "I was so low when I moved out of the Manning that I didn't care if I died." In his own mind, Steve had become a victim: "It doesn't matter in L.A. if you play straight and deal fairly, people don't appreciate it. The only issue is how much money you have and what you can do for them."

"Lopez thought it was the BBC," Jerry Eisenberg said of the shooting. "And he's lying if he says he wasn't scared. He was shitting. He moved out of there the very next day and he's been *so* quiet ever since."

No other BBC member had so successfully insulated himself from allegations of wrongdoing as Eisenberg, who already was practicing law out of a new office in Encino. The worst any of the other Boys could say about the attorney was that he had known Joe was deceiving his investors long before contacting the SEC. Jerry's air of sanctimony, though, made him perhaps the most despised BBC member. "My biggest complaint about the whole thing is that a lot of people are being let go, not held accountable," Eisenberg explained. In his opinion, everyone who had attended the June 24 meeting should be charged as an accessory, the attorney added: "I think Joe is most culpable, along with Dean. I think Jim is after that, with Reza. Ben would be after that. Then Jon Allen and Tom May. And Evan. Brooke, I don't know. My belief is that after you screw a girl, you own her, most times. And Brooke was a kid. Jon Allen getting off is the one that really pisses me off. He has the Nuremberg defense: 'I was just following orders.' As far as I'm concerned, he's an accomplice."

According to the May twins, it was Dicker who deserved to be charged as an accessory. "Tom and Dave were telling the police that Evan was second after Dean among Joe's intimates," Gene Browning explained. "They said he was Joe's sounding board, and that he had become a Shading by the end." In Browning's opinion, if anyone was getting off easily, it was Tom May: "Tom was in it up to his eyeballs and only pulled out to save his ass. Yet he's walking away scot-free." The walking-away part of Browning's complaint was certifiable. After the L.A. County district attorney's office decided against indicting Tom as an accessory in the Levin murder, the SEC allowed him to skate their investigation of the securities fraud at Financial Futures. At almost the same moment, the FBI agreed not to arrest Tom in the 1983 check-kiting scheme, after the May family settled with Progressive Savings out of court.

Jim Pittman, meanwhile, was trying to raise money for an attorney with his story that the Taglianettis were a Mafia family who had used the BBC as a front for a stolen car ring, with assistance from Jerry Eisenberg. "Jim called me up once from jail and threatened me," Eisenberg acknowledged. "He wanted money, said I gotta give him five hundred dollars or a thousand dollars right now or he was going to make my life miserable. He sounded desperate. I put him on the speaker phone with Mike Feldman, said, 'Jim, fuck you!' and hung up."

No one in law enforcement, though, was very interested in what the Boys said about each other; the priority the police placed on obtaining a conviction against Joe Hunt was working to the advantage of every other BBC member. Evan, who still expected to be charged in connection to either the Levin or the Eslaminia investigations, or both, was profoundly relieved when Les Zoeller offered him a grant of immunity in exchange for his cooperation. "The SEC was still after me," Evan recalled, "but I was a lot more concerned about Oscar Breiling." Evan met with Breiling in Beverly Hills a few days after speaking to Zoeller. "Oscar was pretty forceful," Evan recalled, "saying that he could arrest me if he wanted to. He scared me, to be honest. Zoeller was matter-of-fact, nice and easy, but Oscar wanted to make goddamn sure that I knew what I did was wrong."

"That I did," agreed Breiling, who went straight from the office of Dicker's attorney to his first meeting with Shalom and Danielle Karny. As Breiling and Ron Bass drove their motor-pool Dodge back to the Ramada Inn, each was aware that their superiors in Sacramento were not happy that Dean Karny had been given "Walk for Talk"—a grant of total immunity in exchange for his testimony. "The bosses feel 'He's a no-good murderer and he got one helluva good deal,'" Oscar explained. "And I understand that point of view. It made me feel a whole lot better, though, when I saw what kind of a family Dean had come from." Mrs. Karny's determination to stand by her son, no matter what he had done, was what made it possible to live in peace with his decision, Breiling explained: "That mother was not going to quit on this boy, ever. The father wasn't, either. If there's one thing I respect, it's loyalty."

Dean was allowed to continue living in his parents' home while he finished at Whittier Law School during December and applied to the state bar in January. The only BBC member with whom he kept in regular contact was Evan, who recalled, "We would stop, start, stop, start up again, go out to clubs, parties, lunches, dinners. We went to a few polo games. But I didn't even know where he was living. He had been at home, and then he was sort of disappearing. I understood his circumstances, that he was at some risk. I mean, Joe is Joe. Dean seemed to handle it pretty well when Lisa Marie told him she didn't want to see him anymore, after he confided to her that he was involved in the Eslaminia thing."

Alan Lieban encountered Dean on the driving range at the Encino Country Club and saw him a couple of times at parties. "He always seemed very reserved but very together," Lieban remembered. "I ran into him once on Rodeo Drive, and we went into Theodore's together. He bought some new clothes, even knew the salesman. 'He's quite a guy,' I thought. We didn't talk about the situation much—I didn't want to put him in an awkward situation, and I really wasn't sure I wanted to know. But once the subject was raised, Dean didn't totally avoid it. He just said he had a lot of misgivings about what was happening and couldn't see siding with the group any longer. He didn't seem at all emotional about it."

Dean was not yet so free and clear as it looked to Lieban. His application to the state bar was being held up by a "moral character" review. He had been added as a defendant in the lawsuit filed by Progressive Savings, which offered him a chance to settle for one hundred thousand dollars. The investors in Financial Futures were demanding money as well, alleging that Dean had helped defraud them, and attorneys for the SEC named him alongside Joe and Ben as the primary subjects of their inquiry into the securities crimes committed by the BBC. Evan let Dean know that he already had been subpoenaed as a witness by the SEC.

As always, Dicker was doing his best to mend relations. "I reinitiated contact with David May sometime around Christmas," he recalled. "I was in the neighborhood and just ran by his house. We had lunch. He was obviously very shaky about talking to me, so we stuck to small talk. Jon Allen I saw on New Year's Day; I ran into him on the street and we had a hamburger together. I think we both wanted reassurance that life would go on, that the BBC part of our lives was going to be more of a detour than a roadblock. I ran into Lisa Marie not long after that. I was on my way to the equestrian center when I saw her on the road. We had a cup of tea together and talked for maybe half an hour without saying a word about any of what had happened. She didn't even speak Dean's name.

"I think everyone who had gotten out early was feeling very fortunate," Evan explained. "I know I thanked my lucky stars a thousand times that I hadn't been asked along on the Eslaminia thing. Because I might very well have gone along with it. I think some others might have as well. That was how I thought of Ben, as just sort of going along."

Ben had continued to call Evan from Zurich and London through the end of 1984. "We would have brief conversations about what was going on—Joe's arrest, Jim's arrest, et cetera," Evan recalled. "Ben as usual was closemouthed. The one thing he did say to me that I was grateful for was 'Do whatever is best for yourself.' After I gave him the number at my parents' house, he called a couple more times. He was on the run by then and I was talking to the police, and I just decided that I didn't want to talk to him anymore. I don't know if I said it outright or just made it clear, but I never heard from him again after Christmas."

Ben was aboard a jet on the tarmac at Heathrow—en route from London to Newark, New Jersey—on the afternoon of December 1, 1984, when a flight attendant advised him there was an urgent phone call. It was his parents. The attorney they hired to represent Ben, Richard Hirsch, had called that morning, Rose and Luan explained, to alert them that, according to the *San Francisco Examiner,* a warrant had been issued for their son's arrest. Ben got off the plane and checked into an airport hotel. He reached Hirsch by phone the next day and set up a meeting in New York.

"SHAH'S 'RICH' AIDE FOUND SLAIN IN L.A." read the headline on the *Examiner* article. Datelined BELMONT, the story began: "A body discovered yesterday in a remote hilly area of the Angeles National Forest in Los Angeles is believed to be that of Hedayat Eslaminia.... Eslaminia's estranged son and three other men connected with BBC, a Los Angeles–based investment corporation, have been charged with his murder."

While the lawyers representing Arben Dosti and Reza Eslaminia could not be reached for comment, the *Examiner* reported, attorneys for Joseph Hunt and James Pittman were most outspoken. Joe's new lawyer, Arthur Barens, called the charges against his client "completely unfounded," while Jim's court-appointed attorney, Douglas Young, described the investigation as "a witch-hunt."

"The son and Dosti are still at large," the article ended, "and are believed to be in England." Oscar Breiling's information had been accurate. Aware by the end of October that Interpol agents were looking for them in

Switzerland, Reza and Ben returned to London within days of Joe's second arrest. The two were down to less than one thousand dollars in cash, though, and worried about where they would find free housing once the Iranian exiles in London learned of Reza's involvement in his father's disappearance.

After advising him several times earlier in the month that it was not a good time to come home, Ben recalled, Dean reversed himself on November 29, the day he obtained his second immunity agreement at the meeting with Les Zoeller. "Now Dean said I *should* come back, to corroborate his story," Ben remembered. What he told Ben, Dean explained, was that he had done his best to convince law enforcement that, like him, Dosti was "misled" by Joe Hunt, encouraging Breiling and Zoeller "to give as much consideration as possible to Ben." Dean "didn't say I'd get complete immunity, but that I'd have to do a little time," remembered Ben, whose parents told him to stay put.

Danny Karny phoned the Dostis at home that evening and invited them to breakfast at her house the next morning, Sunday, December 2. The meeting was Dean's idea. Danny and Shalom were in another room, Dean recalled, when he told the Dostis of his and Ben's involvement in the abduction of Hedayat Eslaminia. The Karnys all were there, Luan later insisted, and Dean's parents had listened attentively to Dean's tale until he got to the part about loading the trunk into the back of the U-Haul. "Then Mrs. Karny said, 'I don't want to hear! Stop talking!'"

He didn't describe Ben's involvement in detail, Dean recalled, telling the Dostis only that their son had "participated." What Karny told them was that Joe and Jim had gone into Hedayat Eslaminia's apartment, Luan recalled, while Ben was merely "in and around" the condominium complex. "Dean said, 'Ben can corroborate my story and add more details,'" Luan remembered. "'He can say he saw Joe and Jim rough up Hedayat Eslaminia, that he saw Jim with a Beretta' . . . he said Ben should come in because the authorities are going to be very lenient. He said they were more interested in Joe, Jim, and Reza, that they have nothing against Ben."

The Dostis drove directly from the Karnys' home to a meeting with Richard Hirsch, who had been referred to them through Rose's literary attorney. The lawyer agreed to fly with Rose to New York for a meeting with Ben on December 7.

Oscar Breiling would not formally apply to the court in San Mateo County for warrants in the Northern California case until the next afternoon, December 3, when he submitted a forensics report matching the teeth from the lower jaw found in Soledad Canyon with the dental charts of Hedayat Eslaminia. "Affiant believes Hedayat Eslaminia is now dead," Breiling wrote to the court, "and that the direct and proximate cause of

his death was being forcefully abducted against his will, then tortured by
manacled confinement in a restrictive container of limited size."

Ben and Reza flew to New York from London two days later, on
December 5. Rose Dosti and Richard Hirsch arrived in Manhattan the next
evening. The attorney advised them never to discuss the case with anyone,
including their son, Luan explained, so it was Hirsch alone who met with
Ben the following day. Rose phoned from New York afterward and said
Hirsch had told her Ben's story was "dramatically different" from Dean's,
Luan remembered.

The Dostis met with Hirsch again in Los Angeles on December 8.
"[Hirsch] said the authorities have already got Dean's story, so they were
not interested in Ben's or in making a deal with him," Luan remembered.
"But he did say that if Ben can corroborate Dean's story, he will negotiate
the best deal he can, from a short time in prison to total immunity." Rose
and Luan phoned their son in New York that evening. He told Ben what
Hirsch had said and urged his son to come in, Luan recalled. If he corroborated Dean's story, Ben replied, he would have to lie.

Faced with their son's refusal to admit he had participated in the
Eslaminia abduction, Hirsch gave the Dostis the impression that it would be
best for Ben to remain at large "until things could be cleared up," Luan remembered. "I told the Dostis that I had a legal obligation to tell them Ben should
surrender," Hirsch demurred. "It's like a doctor who wants to say you have
to have an operation but can't say that," Luan countered. Among the options
the Dostis discussed with their attorney was "Ben changing his identity," Luan
remembered, and it was this that he and Rose advised their son to do.

Ben did not require much persuading. He and Reza were sharing
a tiny room at a cheap hotel in midtown Manhattan, closer to Times Square
than to the Fifty-ninth Street fountain. With the aid of a book titled *The
International Man,* Ben began poring through the obituaries in the back issues
of out-of-state newspapers on file at the New York Public Library. He was
at it for almost a week before finding an article describing the crash of a
private plane on January 3, 1965, in Kentucky that had claimed the lives of
an entire Minnesota family, including two small boys, ages four and two,
named Lansing Lee and Christopher Lee Potter. Using first one name and
then the other, Ben wrote to the state registrar in Minnesota to obtain copies of birth certificates for each dead boy. With these documents in hand,
he and Reza secured ID cards from a Manhattan department store, Ben
recalled, "then went after Social Security numbers and driver's licenses before applying for passports."

Ben stayed in New York for Christmas, spent New Year's Eve with
his grandmother at her apartment on West Thirty-second Street, then left with

Reza for Florida the next day. They went to Fort Lauderdale, for the weather, Reza recalled: "Ben said if we ran out of money, we could sleep on the beach."

While Ben darkened his tan, grew a beard, and avoided arrest, his parents were attending Jim Pittman's preliminary hearing in Beverly Hills. The day before the chief witness for the prosecution was to testify, Luan remembered, he and Rose ran into Karny at a restaurant near the courthouse. "Dean told me, 'Ben hasn't come to the authorities yet, and he should come forward,'" Luan recalled.

Dean spoke to the Dostis a second time three days later, when he phoned them at home, according to Luan: "He said his attorney and Hirsch were good friends and also that the authorities are eager to make a deal with Ben. I told him Ben would come in, and that he would tell the truth. Dean got very emotional. He raised his voice and said, 'Truth has many forms.'"

Joe's preliminary hearing in Beverly Hills Municipal Court during late March of 1985 was reminiscent of those by-invitation-only private parties that had been essential events at the China Club back in 1982. Many of the same people—no longer needing fake ID or dark glasses to get through the door—were in attendance, savoring the spectacle as one of those few delicacies that might still be enjoyed by appreciative cognoscenti.

The saga of the BBC was not yet public property, having been all but ignored in the Boys' backyard. The media's indifference could be attributed almost entirely to a decision by the most powerful institution in Southern California, the Los Angeles Times, to shun the story. The only coverage accorded to Joe Hunt and the BBC in the Times was a single brief article that ran on a back page of the paper's Metro section on December 8, 1984, under the headline "2 CHARGED IN MURDER OF FORMER IRANIAN OFFICIAL." The "2" were Joe Hunt and James Pittman. The newspaper's source, Oscar Breiling, "has also issued a warrant for the arrest of Eslaminia's son, Reza," reported the Times, which failed to mention that a fourth young man had been charged as well.

The Times would not touch the story again until almost two years later, after it had been featured on the covers of magazines headquartered in New York and London. "For the longest time I was wondering why there was nothing in the Times about any of this," Evan reflected. "I mean, it seemed like the sort of story they would go crazy over, considering who were the people involved. But there was nothing. And then it dawned on me, and I thought, 'Ah, what a small, wonderful world it is.'"

Despite the absence of the media, spectator seats at Joe's preliminary hearing were filled to capacity each day. It felt a little like a class reunion,

Evan said, when he was led into court to take the stand as a witness for the prosecution on March 25. "I found the big crowd surprising, since there hadn't been anything about the trial in the newspapers," he recalled. "I saw a dozen, fourteen, familiar faces in the first few rows. Deborah Corday was there with one of the Raygo sisters. There were lots of people who had just been sort of around, not members of the BBC but more like members of the entourage. You had the feeling this was our own private theater."

It was a jolt, of course, to see the leading man step onstage wearing manacles and a blue jail jumpsuit. "Joe and I had eye contact but no words," Evan remembered. "He wasn't bashful about the way he looked at me. It wasn't so much trying to intimidate me as to make sure I knew he was there, to acknowledge what he had been to me."

That no reporters were in attendance seemed even more remarkable after the attorneys who were defending and prosecuting Hunt identified themselves. The prosecutor's fame was a reflection from his father, Judge Joseph Wapner of *The People's Court*. Fred Wapner owned none of his sire's fiesty certitude or imperious airs, however: Slender and pale, with wire-rimmed spectacles and close-cropped graying curls, the younger Wapner, then thirty-five, came across as exceedingly earnest if a bit bland, scrupulous but prissy, more like a middle-aged boy than an aging bachelor. "Low-key and methodical," his father described the prosecutor.

Low-key was scarcely the style of the lead defense attorney, Arthur Barens. Trained as a divorce lawyer by Marvin Mitchelson, for whom he represented the wives of Groucho Marx and Beach Boy Dennis Wilson, Barens had come to the attention of the Los Angeles media in a major way less than two years earlier when he accepted his first criminal case; at that time he agreed to represent Marvin Pancoast, the young man accused of murdering Vicki Morgan, mistress to department store heir and Diners Club creator Alfred Bloomingdale, an inner-circle member of Ronald Reagan's "kitchen cabinet" whose wife, "Best-Dressed Betsy" Bloomingdale, was Nancy Reagan's closest friend. Alfred and Vicki had been careening across the front pages of the newspapers since 1981, when the young woman, twenty-eight at the time, filed a palimony lawsuit against the sixty-five-year-old Bloomingdale, accusing Alfred not only of reneging on financial promises but of using her to satisfy his craving for young women he could bind with silk ties and beat with alligator belts.

Pancoast had confessed to murdering Morgan with a baseball bat during an interview with Laurie Karny's boyfriend Andy Furillo two days after his arrest in July of 1983. Loaded already with salacious intrigue, the story became a media sensation forty-eight hours later when Pancoast's first attorney, Robert K. Steinberg, called a press conference to announce that he had just viewed videotapes of Morgan engaged in sex acts with prominent members of the Reagan administration. Steinberg expanded in an interview the next evening with Ted Koppel on *Nightline,* offering the tapes to President Reagan to spare the administration further embarrassment. The Los Angeles County district attorney's office asked the next day if it might see the "Morgan sex tapes." An hour later Steinberg phoned the Beverly Hills Police Department to report the tapes stolen. When Barens took over the defense, he at first said of the tapes (which never were produced), "I doubt they exist," then proceeded to make them the crux of his case, claiming their "suppression" had been the motive for Morgan's murder. Marvin Pancoast withdrew his earlier confession (though he did admit killing Marvin Gaye, the Motown singer actually shot to death by his own father) and swore he also had seen the sex tapes.

Until it was overtaken by the DeLorean trial, the Pancoast-case circus had been the hottest ticket in town, and Barens was its ringmaster, combining Acapulcan tan with Anglophile affectation as he held forth to the assembled media day after day. "Arthur talks a better game than he plays," groused the prosecutor on the case, who was borne out when the jury convicted Pancoast of murder in the first degree.

In a city where people remember better how you appear than what you accomplish, however, Barens emerged from defeat with a reputation as a winner, and the conventional wisdom was that such a slick and savvy character would eat a wimp like Wapner's boy whole when the Hunt case came to court. The preliminary hearing was no test of this theory, though, since the prosecutor at this stage was obliged only to show evidence of probable cause. Dean Karny's testimony alone was enough to accomplish this, but Wapner also called Tom May, Jeff Raymond, Evan Dicker, and Steve Taglianetti to testify that Joe had admitted killing Levin at the June 24 meeting. "Wapner was kind of weak, and Barens was very abrasive," Evan recalled. "He called me a liar in the elevator."

Joe's only supporters in court, the Roberts family, were outnumbered by the single faction of his detractors who identified themselves as limited partners in the Financial Futures Corporation. Hunt's former investors crowded eagerly around Gene and Claire Browning, who recycled the unsubstantiated rumors that "Ron Levin was a terminal AIDS case and there's a good chance Joe Hunt caught it from him," and that Joe had been raped in county jail. The Manson metaphor was already a cliché among the older crowd in court. "Charley's second coming," said Gene Browning, who snorted derisively at attempts by the other Boys to disavow Joe, the BBC, and Paradox Philosophy. "They were a family," the inventor said, "and they all feel for it."

The bitterness in Browning grew out of the inventor's realization that he remained bound to the BBC even as those who had aided and abetted Joe were escaping without consequence. Within a few months of Hunt's arrest, the Arizona gold miner, Morton, obtained a $1.64 million default judgment in Phoenix against the Microgenesis Corporation and seized all three functioning attrition mills from Bill Nalan's mining site in the Mojave. Browning sued to recover and continued with plans for a partnership involving UFOI and Saturn Energy. By early 1985, though, the inventor was thigh-high in a morass of lawsuits, cross-complaints, and appeals involving Morton, Nalan, Kilpatrick, Robinson, Ken Elgin, and Bruce Swartout, all fighting for control of Browning's machine. "Apparently, my function on this earth is to pay for the European vacations of Los Angeles lawyers," the inventor, now fifty-eight, observed.

The one figure in the tableau who seemed still able to stiff the legal profession was the "alleged deceased." Ron Levin's unpaid attorneys' fees were but one facet on the Hope diamond of debt he had left his family. The Levins hired Ron's favorite Southwestern School of Law professor, David Ostrove, to act as conservator of the estate. Assigned to "marshal assets," Ostrove collected a total of $36,410.07 from U.S. banks, which was almost exactly $20,000 less than Ron owed on his American Express bill alone. He discovered dozens of passbooks for bank accounts in Ron's apartment, Ostrove said, most of them opened with a huge initial deposit—$1.5 million at American Savings, $850,000 at Glendale Savings—but invariably he found that the sums still on deposit were but a pittance: $1 in a Network News Corp. account; $1.01 in a May Brothers Land Corp. account. An auction arranged to dispose of Ron's personal property netted only $58,476. Ostrove raised another $50,000 by settling Ron's claim against the estate of his former landlord, Lillian Warner, in connection to the "contract" written on the back of a rent check. The $140,000 in total assets the conservator collected, however, made barely a dent in the claims against Ron's estate.

Ostrove prevailed upon officials at Wells Fargo to deal with the Swiss Credit Bank branch in Geneva where Ron had drawn upon his account for the $1.5 million check he wrote to Joe Hunt on the evening of June 6, 1984. His hopes had been raised by a pair of checks drawn on the account he found in Ron's desk drawers, the law professor explained, one for $500,000 and the other for $980,877.83. Once again, however, Ron's reach eluded his creditors' grasp: After the Swiss bank's fees and the Wells Fargo processing charges, Ostrove reported, the final statement on the Geneva account showed it $4.31 overdrawn.

22

MOST OF THE BOYS FOUND IT INCREDIBLE THAT BEN DOSTI REFUSED TO "CUT the best deal he could and come in," as Eisenberg put it. Perhaps only Dean and Evan understood. "I'm sure Ben thought that if he confessed, he might lose the one thing he believed he always had to fall back on," Evan explained, "the support of his parents."

Rose and Luan indeed were clinging to their son's claim of innocence. Although Richard Hirsch warned them to avoid contact with Ben and not to support him, said Luan, he and Rose made a conscious decision to disobey the law: "We felt Ben needed us more than anything else."

After splitting with Reza on the beach in Florida, Ben headed back up the East Coast to Waltham, Massachusetts, where he lived in an apartment on College Park Road rented by his father. From the Boston suburb, Ben managed to spread his alter ego Lansing Lee Potter across half the world. Using a post office box on Seventh Avenue in Manhattan, he obtained a New York City Board of Elections voter registration card the same week he used the Potter name to apply for a library card in Cambridge, Massachusetts, that showed his home address as a post office box in Harvard Square. Admitted on a part-time basis at NYU, Ben carried student ID for Lee Potter in his wallet with a Massachusetts driver's license issued under the same name. He used a post office box in Lexington to negotiate with a banker in New York and his parents' home in Hancock Park as the return address on the letter he wrote suggesting "the possibility of business cooperation" to a Vancouver entrepreneur. Both Massachusetts mail drops had been rented by Luan Dosti.

By the time Hunt's preliminary hearing had ended in Beverly Hills, Ben was engaged in a new arbitrage deal, attempting to arrange a five-billion-dollar loan to a Houston land development firm through the trustee of an enormous West German investment fund. While he waited for his five-million-dollar loan commission, though, Ben was supported by his parents. It was Rose who set up the Bay Banks "Harvard Trust" account for her son in Cambridge and gave him the MasterCard she obtained from

Shawmut Bank in Boston. Luan provided Ben with a Litton Industries ID card so he could obtain medical benefits. In a *Los Angeles Times* envelope addressed to LEE POTTER, Ben's mother sent a fresh batch of bank checks wrapped in an article about "skimpy plates" she had written for the front page of the newspaper's Food section. The note Rose scribbled in the margin was her signature: *"Voilà: XXXXXXX."*

Ben and Reza kept in contact through a complicated set of telephone codes. He would call Debi at her office, Ben recalled, leave a number, then the code they were using, and she would pass the information along to Reza.

Reza made his way back to California through Las Vegas, where he flew from Florida on a ticket Ben had purchased, carrying $500 cash in his pocket and a Minnesota birth certificate for Christopher Lee Potter. Ben explained how he could obtain a birth certificate on his own, Reza remembered, and suggested he look for a Hispanic name. The Potter ID, Ben added, should be used only in an emergency. It was as Chris Potter, though, that Reza registered at the Dunes Hotel in Vegas, and he gave the same name as he drifted up and down the strip looking for work in casinos. By early March, Reza was on the run again, heading first north to Reno, then west across the California border to Lake Tahoe, where he went to work for the Sugar Bowl Corporation as a ski-lift operator, earning $4.25 an hour. Debi helped him through the last weeks of winter, sending $2,000 in cash through Western Union.

By the beginning of April Reza was officially Chris Potter in California, obtaining a driver's license under that name. He was scrounging for money, unable to persuade Mina to send more than a few hundred dollars. Late in April, as Mr. Christopher Potter of 110 Montague Missions, London, Reza attempted to raise a fast $2,310 in cash by claiming that a new Nikon camera, a Dictaphone, and a pair of ostrich-skin cowboy boots had been lost with his luggage on a Frontier Airlines flight from Reno to Sacramento.

Reza had visited California's capital to set up a mail drop he and Ben could share behind the screen of Debi's new alias, "Pamela Johnson." Even as the Potter brothers continued to track each other by telephone, though, Reza began to devise a scenario to explain Hedayat Eslaminia's death, one he hoped would allow him to sell Ben to the authorities for a deal like Dean Karny's.

A *60 Minutes* segment on San Francisco's "counterculture counselor," Tony Serra, persuaded Reza this was the lawyer who might present him sympathetically. Serra took the Iranian's case after Reza passed a lie detector test but delegated negotiations with the California Department of Justice to an associate, Larry Lichter. Reza by then had moved once more, this time to Santa Cruz, an hour south of San Francisco on the Monterey

Peninsula, registering at his motel under the name Lee Chen. Reza was Chris Potter again, though, when he interviewed for a job with the concessionaire who operated the perpetual carnival along the beach town's boardwalk.

Larry Lichter met with Ron Bass finally in early June, but reported back that the state attorney general's office refused to deal. Now that they had Karny, Bass explained, no one needed Eslaminia. He and Tony thought the best course for Reza was to negotiate a surrender to the FBI, Lichter said. When Bass and his superiors refused even to promise bail, however, Reza committed himself once again to life as Christopher Potter. Soon after obtaining a Social Security number, he prepared applications for MasterCard, Visa, Sears, and Macy's credit cards, listing himself as an executive of the MSI "computer software" company headed by president Ed Singleton. Christopher Potter also applied for a U.S. passport in July, stating he intended to travel to England and France for four weeks.

Even as he planned his escape to Europe, however, Reza pressed Larry Lichter to continue negotiations with the FBI. "I want to be in a federal institution, not county and under extreme protective custody," Reza wrote under the heading DEMANDS in his new green notebook. "Also, they have to give my family the same protection the Carneys [sic] have been getting."

Ben Dosti still showed no sign *he* intended to surrender. At the same time Reza was reduced to his last $50, Ben had $8,218.79 in the account Rose opened at Bay Bank. He scanned the newspapers constantly for business opportunities, Ben said, and in his oxblood portfolio carried contracts for international loans, advertisements for bulk perfume sales, and notes on the various apartment buildings he inspected as "investment opportunities for my parents." Even as he applied for a Massachusetts driver's license under the name L. Lee Potter, however, Ben endeavored to establish other identities, submitting a series of requests at the Cambridge library for issues of the *New York Times* from the early 1960s. He planned a trip to Europe in September, Ben said.

While Lansing Lee Potter had obtained his U.S. passport in Boston more than a month earlier, however, his brother Christopher's application still was being reviewed at the passport office in San Francisco, where certain "irregularities" had come to the attention of Agent Steven Mullen. It was mid-July when Mullen made contact with the registrar of vital statistics in Minnesota: Christopher Lee Potter had died with his parents and older brother in Kentucky when their light plane crashed into a farm pond and burned in the water, the passport agent was informed. A copy of Christopher Lee Potter's birth certificate had been requested six months earlier by a Mr. Robert Hoffman, of 701 Seventh Avenue in New York City, who identified himself as a "genealogist," the Minnesota registrar added. Robert Hoffman also had asked for the birth certificate of Christopher Potter's older brother, Lansing Lee.

The home address listed on the passport application submitted in Carmel by Christopher Lee Potter was 1008 Tenth Street in Sacramento, which, Mullen discovered, was the location of a business bearing the name Your Mail Box.

July 26 was the date on the arrest warrant issued by the federal court in San Francisco for "the unknown individual using the identity of Christopher Lee Potter." That same day, Mullen sent a letter to the Sacramento address, informing Mr. Potter he could collect his passport at the federal building on Market Street in San Francisco during the afternoon of August 1, 1985.

Reza spent the night of July 31 with Debi, who let him sleep when she woke to leave for work the next morning, propping a note against the lamp on the nightstand: "Peeshin, Here are your morning kisses—XXXX!! I love you. Porsche's been fed—Call me at work (toll free)—I'll be home earlier today. Love, Moosh."

It was just past 2 P.M. when Mullen phoned the FBI office to say that Christopher Lee Potter was waiting for his passport in the lobby of the Market Street office. Special Agent Stockton Buck and three other FBI men arrived five minutes later, carrying the photograph Chris Potter had attached to his passport application. Buck approached a young man who resembled the person in the photograph and asked if he was Christopher Lee Potter. Reza stood up and said yes. "You're under arrest," Buck told him.

Lansing Lee Potter's passport application had listed his home address as a post office box in Harvard Square in Cambridge. Two FBI agents were waiting outside when the doors opened the next morning. The proprietor recognized Ben Dosti from his passport photograph and said "Lee" came by to pick up his mail every morning at around eleven. It was barely five minutes past the hour when Ben, still bearded, strolled through the door carrying his oxblood portfolio. Dosti looked more sad than surprised when he was arrested for "unlawful flight," the FBI agents noted. As usual, Ben kept his mouth closed.

Good news for all the accused awaited Ben and Reza at the San Mateo County Jail: A jury that listened for three months to the state's case against Jim Pittman in Santa Monica Superior Court had declared itself unable to reach a verdict. The final vote was ten to two in favor of conviction, but those numbers had to be weighed against a largely incoherent defense.

Licensed in California and Florida, Douglas Young was a criminal lawyer best known for his handling of drug cases, though the attorney's personal consumption of cocaine had begun to rival his legal practice as a topic of courthouse conversation. Young's eyes glittered and his complexion was dull; he was sweating one moment, shivering the next. "The defense will argue that Ron Levin fled to avoid prosecution," Fred Wapner had predicted in his opening statement, but Young did exactly the opposite, all but stipulating that Ron Levin had been murdered and that Joe Hunt had committed the crime. Young's only significant divergence from Wapner's narrative of the case concerned the part played by the poor black man who had attempted to better himself in the service of several spoiled rich boys who called themselves the BBC. Pittman was "a fall guy," Young asserted, "in Joe Hunt's plan to commit the perfect crime."

"The prosecution's case is Dean Karny," the defense attorney began his opening statement to the jury, "and Karny has agreed to testify as part of a dirty deal." An admitted accomplice to murder, Dean had helped Joe— "the mastermind"—implicate Jim as the killer as "part of their paradoxical philosophy [sic]," Young told jurors.

Despite Young's agreement that Ron Levin had "died at the hands of another," Wapner plodded ahead with the case as planned, calling bank officers, cellular phone salesmen, optometrists, and attorneys in an attempt to demonstrate that Ron's actions during the first week of June 1984 were not "consistent with the actions of someone about to flee the country."

Young called no witnesses for the defense, preferring to pick at the prosecution's case. Tom May, Evan Dicker, Jeff Raymond, and Steve Taglianetti chronicled the rise of Joseph Gamsky and the formation of the BBC, describing one after another the meeting at the Wilshire Manning on June 24, 1984, where Joe told them, "Jim and I knocked off Ron Levin," as Jeff recalled it. "Or bumped off," Steve said. "Or did away with," said Tom. "Or took care of," Evan added. Jim had remained silent that afternoon, they all agreed.

Young ignored several obvious discrepancies in the Boys' testimony, aiming only to establish that a belief system called Paradox Philosophy existed and that at least two BBC members, Joe Hunt and Dean Karny, subscribed to it. This was true, Tom, Jeff, and Steve hastened to affirm. And no, they all agreed, Jim never joined in any Paradox discussions. For that matter, none of them ever had seen him read a book or even any part of a newspaper but the sports pages.

Young's best work was his cross-examination of Karny. It was Dean's demeanor that undercut his testimony. Even Oscar Breiling, who wanted badly to believe in "my witness," as he called Karny, would admit "there was a certain smugness in Dean on the stand, an 'I've got mine' attitude that came through." After the trial, jurors described the state's star witness to Wapner as "cold." Young persuaded Dean to admit he had lied to Michael Dow, William Kilpatrick, Milton Rubini, Steve Weiss, Gene Browning, even "to my parents and to a lot of the other young men that were in the BBC." Most of the jurors assumed Karny was lying still and gazed at him with naked contempt as Dean explained his decision to approach the state in hopes of making a deal: "The time I spent by myself [after Joe's second arrest] is when I really realized how wrong [Joe] was about so many things and how I had been twisted around his finger, like all of the other nice boys who really weren't knowing what they were doing, as I didn't," Dean said, "and I just decided, if there was any possible way, to testify against [Joe and Jim] without incriminating myself for anything that I might have done." Young was only too pleased to accept Dean's description of the BBC as a cult: "Did you seek any professional help," he asked, "to deprogram yourself from [Paradox] Philosophy?" No, Dean replied, "at the time I decided to go to the police I had my thoughts recollected, and I had my head back together, so I didn't need deprogramming." "Let me ask you this question," Young said. "Wouldn't your going to the police be consistent with the Paradox Philosophy, in the sense that you would not sacrifice yourself because of your loyalty to Joe Hunt or to any of the other members of the BBC?" "I couldn't begin to answer that question," Dean responded, but for the jury, he just had.

In the end, the prosecution's strongest witness was a Puerto Rican from the Bronx who had not set foot in California before the morning he flew to Los Angeles to testify at Jim's trial in Santa Monica. Joe Vega's description of Pittman's attempt to sneak out of the Plaza Hotel on the afternoon of June 10 was proof of his complicity in the murder of Ron Levin, Wapner argued before the jury in his closing argument. "It took five men to subdue him," the prosecutor noted.

An inevitable undertone of racism crept into the prosecutor's summation when he told the jury that Jim had been "recruited by the BBC specifically for doing things like this. . . . The BBC was a group of young, fairly wealthy kids," Wapner observed. "It didn't contain, until [Pittman] got there, anyone suitable for doing something like this."

Young agreed with Wapner that his client was like no one else in the BBC. "Jim Pittman had no understanding of Paradox Philosophy," his attorney told the jury. And the numerous "stupid things" his client had done were evidence of his innocence, Young argued, scoffing at the idea of "Pittman, a black man, posing as Ron Levin, a Jew." On the other hand, Jim never admitted to anyone his involvement in the murder of Ron Levin.

Neither Pittman's fingerprints nor his handwriting had been detected on the "AT LEVIN'S, TO DO" list. Joe's statement that Jim had helped him "knock off" Ron Levin meant nothing, since "Hunt is a pathological liar," and Karny's testimony should be disregarded also, Young contended, because Dean remained "under the spell of Paradox Philosophy."

The fundamental injustice of the situation Young saved for his summation: Could the jury accept as just an outcome in which the BBC's first lieutenant, a well-educated young white man from a wealthy family—an admitted accomplice in the murder of Ron Levin—walked away from this crime without serving so much as a single day behind bars while the state sought the death penalty against the BBC's black bodyguard, an obvious "dupe"?

This was the argument that hung the jury. The first vote had been eleven to one for conviction, the single ballot for acquittal cast by an elderly black woman. The holdout refused not only to budge but even to explain her position. Several other members of the jury signed an angry note sent to the chambers of Judge Lawrence Rittenband complaining that juror number two "refused to communicate" with the other members of the panel and devoted her time during deliberations to crossword puzzles or romance novels. The woman told them, "'I don't have to say anything,'" the irate jurors wrote Rittenband. "'I am here. I can read and hear you. Do you want me to look at you when you're talking?'" Rittenband had little choice but to leave juror number two in her seat, though, after the panel's other black member switched her vote to not guilty as well, deadlocking the jury at ten to two. On July 27, the judge declared a mistrial.

23

THE DEFENDANT WAS PREPARED TO TESTIFY THAT, IF GRANTED REASONABLE bail, he would be living in the home of Bobby Roberts, Arthur Barens informed Judge Rittenband at Joe's hearing on September 27, 1985. "Mr. Hunt is engaged to Mr. Roberts' daughter," the attorney explained. "They plan to be married immediately upon his release."

Joe's application for a reduction of his bond requirement from a total of four million dollars in both jurisdictions to one million apiece in Los Angeles and San Mateo counties, coming so soon after the conclusion of Pittman's trial, unnerved nearly every one of those Boys who remained at large. "When Jim's first trial ended with a hung jury was the first time it occurred to me that Joe might actually beat the charges against him," Evan explained. "I mean, the evidence against them was exactly the same, and Joe was certain to put on a lot better defense than Jim had."

The obvious hole in the habeas corpus of Fred Wapner's case was the continued absence of the corpus itself. Les Zoeller spent nearly as much time digging with a shovel in Soledad Canyon as with his computer in Beverly Hills but had yet to come up with so much as a bicuspid that could be identified as Ron Levin's. The lack of either an eyewitness or a body, combined with the prosecution's failure to convict Joe's codefendant on its first try, provided Barens with reasonable grounds to argue that a reduction in bail was warranted.

Bobby Roberts was the principal witness at the September hearing, testifying that his "English Tudor Country Estate" in Bel Air should be sufficent to secure a bond, then submitting an appraiser's report placing the market value of the Bellagio property at $2.3 million.

Judge Rittenband took the matter under advisement but appeared to agree that a bail reduction was appropriate under the circumstances. Wapner, adamantly opposed, fumed over Rittenband's rapport with Barens. "This is the one person I've ever prosecuted who actually scares me," he said outside the courtroom. The judge, though, was impressed with the defendant when Joe represented himself (during a trip out of town by Barens) at

a hearing on October 22. Arguing the reasonableness of his request for reduced bail, Hunt cited case and precedent so skillfully that Rittenband first
complimented his "acumen," then engaged the defendant in a discussion of
his legal theories so protracted that Wapner felt obliged to intrude an objection "just to remind you I'm here."

When the judge agreed to Joe's release on a bond secured by the
Roberts estate eleven days later, Wapner sulked shamelessly, suggesting
that Barens's pending application for membership to the country club
where Rittenband ate his lunch each day, Hillcrest, had influenced the
judge's decision.

Unlikely as that seemed, Rittenband's fascination with the case had
increased enormously over the past three months. It was the appearance
of the news media rather than the involvement of Barens, however, that
intrigued the venerable jurist. While Pittman's murder trial had not
attracted a single reporter, Joe Hunt's bail hearing alone drew half a dozen
journalists representing CBS, the *Los Angeles Daily News, Playboy* and *California* magazines. Rittenband, at once flamboyant and unflinching, savored
the spotlight as did few other judges, even in Los Angeles. The plaintiffs
and defendants who had appeared in his Santa Monica court included
Marlon Brando, Cary Grant, Ann-Margret, Liza Minnelli, and Kareem
Abdul-Jabbar. Rittenband had performed the marriage ceremony of Ronald
Reagan's daughter Maureen and delighted in reminding the press how
he settled the divorce case of Elvis and Priscilla Presley during a private
session with the couple in chambers. He became the first judge in L.A. to
call his own press conference, when, in 1977 film director Roman Polanski
fled the United States to avoid a jail sentence for having sex with a thirteen-
year-old girl. "He doesn't belong in this country," Rittenband told reporters. That statement, though, was nothing next to the judge's outburst at
the end of a 1973 trial, when he was so enraged by the acquittal of a man
charged with stabbing a woman seventy-four times that he flung the case
file across the courtroom, informing jurors, "because of you, a man got away
with murder."

The senior member of the Los Angeles Superior Court at age
seventy-eight, Rittenband routinely won reelection by huge margins against
opponents who used the incumbent's age as the central issue of their campaigns. What made it so difficult to overturn the elderly judge, politically
or legally, was his undiminished intellect. A native of New York City,
Rittenband had entered NYU's law school at fifteen, straight out of high
school, finishing at the top of a class whose other members nicknamed the
teenager "Judge." Too young to take the state bar exam at age nineteen,

Rittenband killed the next two years at Harvard University, where he graduated summa cum laude. First a federal prosecutor for the city of New York and later the most successful sole practitioner in Southern California, Rittenband had been appointed to the Los Angeles Municipal Court by Governor Edmund Brown Sr. in 1961, ascending to the superior court ten months later.

Diminutive and spry, with twinkling blue eyes and a piercing wit, Rittenband had tempted many reporters to describe him as a "leprechaun." "Curmudgeon" was more like it. On the bench, Rittenband was known to assert judicial privilege more frequently by far than any other superior court judge in California, regularly assuming control over the direct examination of witnesses, making spectators of prosecutors and fools of defense attorneys. The judge mocked questions he regarded as "idiotic" (a favorite adjective) and rarely made a secret of his thoughts on any important matter. His conduct of cases was challenged more often than that of other judges, yet his winning percentage on appeal was the highest of any superior court member in the state. "He misreads everything but the law," one embittered defense attorney said of him.

Even Rittenband, though, recognized that his tenure on the bench was near an end. The judge seemed to sense early on that the Hunt trial would be his last big case and became intent on doing it his way, now more than ever.

Joe's release from Los Angeles County Jail on November 3, 1985, was an occasion for festivities at the Robertses' Bel Air compound. "It was as if he'd come home from war, the long lost brother," Todd Roberts recalled. The family decorated the Bellagio house with a big HAPPY BIRTHDAY banner, balloons, and streamers, then ate an early Thanksgiving dinner at the Old World in Westwood.

While Brooke and her family celebrated, others shuddered. "He'll kill somebody else, no question about it," Gene Browning predicted. Browning had little trouble believing the stories he heard about what Joe had accomplished during the year he spent behind bars. "We were told [by the police] that he taught himself French and Japanese while he was in county jail and is now fluent in both," the inventor reported. "He also is supposedly prepared to pass the bar exam. He still has big plans for himself, of that I'm certain."

The Beverly Hills police were convinced Joe's biggest plan involved fleeing the country at his earliest opportunity. "Les tells us, 'He's gonna skip,'" Gene Browning said. "The Beverly Hills Police Department has someone on him every day."

Most of the BBC were less concerned about Joe's disappearance than with the possibility they might meet him again. "He still wants to kill us," Dave May insisted. Evan Dicker admitted that Joe's power "continues to fascinate and frighten me."

Evan still was testing his standing in the community. He was especially relieved that Alex Gaon seemed friendly when they ran into each other at a party. Those who had been part of the BBC tended to talk only to one another, Evan noticed, and relied on gossip rather than on reports in the media to keep abreast. "When we saw that there were no stories about the BBC in any of the papers," he recalled, "we all began to believe that this might remain a nice quiet little thing, something we kept to ourselves."

By the autumn of 1985, though, it had become obvious this wouldn't be the case. The *Playboy, California,* and *Daily News* articles were scheduled to appear in early 1986, and Jim Pittman was selling his story to any number of people. The first to make a deal with Pittman was a "producer" named Frank Cutler, introduced to Jim at the Hall of Justice Jail by Michael Canale, a former American Nazi party commander. Canale, who had spent several months in the same cell block with Pittman, persuaded Jim to sign an "option" agreement giving Cutler ninety days to peddle the BBC bodyguard's story. Canale and Cutler then brought in journalist John Sack to conduct a videotape interview with Pittman at the Hall of Justice Jail. Soon after, Sack proposed to Pittman that they sign an agreement of their own to market "The Jim Pittman Story" when Cutler's option expired in November. One day after Pittman, Sack, and Canale executed a "joint venture" agreement, however, Pittman signed a third contract with yet another would-be film producer, Frank Touch, who promised to pay for a private attorney if Jim gave him an option on his "rights."

Most of the other Boys avoided reporters. Several who had left early on denied ever belonging to the BBC. This tactic infuriated those whose avenues of escape had been cut off by subpoenas. Even Evan did not conceal the contempt he felt for those who repudiated their involvement. "There were no 'semi-BBC members,'" he said. "A Mickey Fine, an Alex Gaon, a Joel Gelff, a Cary Bren were all most definitely BBC members." "If those guys want to pretend they weren't part of the BBC, fine," added Jerry Eisenberg, "but the truth is, they were." Eisenberg, shrewd enough to recognize that cooperation with the media was a wiser course than antagonism, had been the first of the Boys to make himself available for interviews. "I told the reporters who came around at the beginning, 'You gotta eat this story, you gotta breathe this story, you gotta live this story,'" he explained. "'That's the only way you can get it.'"

***

By the time Joe stood to argue his own case before Judge Rittenband in late October, bail requests by Arben Dosti and Reza Eslaminia were pending in the San Mateo Superior Court of Judge James Miller. Associated Press advisories on the capture of the pair, ignored in Los Angeles, were snatched up in San Francisco, where the *Examiner* ran front-page mug shots of Ben and Reza.

Ben's apprehension in particular had produced mixed emotions among those who knew they would be seeing him in court. The state's star witness was suffering terribly at the thought, according to Oscar Breiling: "Dean told me during the initial stages of this investigation that I could count on him to tell the truth, no matter how bad it made him look, to the slightest detail, and that the reason for this was his hope that Ben would come forward and fill in the blanks."

Ben chose to remain mute, though the same could not be said for Reza. According to one fellow inmate at the San Mateo County Jail, Reza boasted of beating the polygraph by swallowing several hits of a methamphetamine just before entering the "Truth Verification" company's office. He had been marked as a snitch the moment he set foot in the Redwood City jail, answered Reza, whose big toe was broken fifteen minutes after his release into the general population. Guards arranged to have the Iranian transferred to an isolated section of C Wing after Reza sought medical attention for a dislocated shoulder and three bruised ribs, incurred when he "fell out of bed."

Among the Iranian's new neighbors in C Wing was his old partner-in-crime Jeff Steele. Jeff had been in Soledad Prison during Reza's months with the BBC, sent away by Eslaminia's testimony against him in court. He lasted on the street for about a year, Jeff explained, before being arrested in October of 1985 for "stealin' a drug dealer's drugs." At the San Mateo County Jail, he and Reza were assigned to the same neighborhood, a wing of three two-man cells the jailers called "celebrity row," less in tribute to Eslaminia than to a pair of other inmates, Cameron Hooker, "the Red Bluff Sex Slaver," and Jack Sully, "the Golden Gate Barrel Killer." "Me and my buddy Larry more or less ran the place, though," Jeff explained, "because we had done so much time there. Reza was kissin' my ass, tellin' me how sorry he was. It got to the point where I started rappin' with the guy."

Reza was out the door by November 1, though, when his $250,000 bail was secured with $25,000 in cash from Debi plus the title on Mina's house in Beverly Hills. Ben also was free, released three days earlier on a $500,000 property bond secured by his parents' home in Hancock Park.

While the Mays, Eisenberg, and Taglianetti all complained that setting the Shadings free would endanger their lives, no one took the news so badly as the one BBC member who remained behind bars. "All I did was work for the people," Jim Pittman sobbed during an interview at the Hall of Justice Jail in L.A. "And here I am sitting in jail. I been mistreated all around, used by Joe. Everybody using my size and my strength and my karate expertise to be killing a person. That's probably why they hired me in the beginning, 'cause they figured they could use me."

Jim was given something to celebrate on November 25, though, when Joe, Ben, and Reza were summoned back to court in San Mateo County for a hearing to consider a motion by the state to revoke their bail. The principal witness for the prosecution was Jeff Steele. "I wish I'd had a camera," Steele reflected, "'cause Reza didn't know nothin' about me, and all of a sudden a door opens on the side of the court and here comes Jeff, walkin' in chains, up to the witness stand. This courtroom, it was like out of a movie, cops and guards all over the place, guns everywhere. Like the Mafia was on trial. The BBC guys and their lawyers are all lookin' around like, 'Who is he?' And Reza was green, just fuckin' green. Before he could even bat an eye, I was sworn in, and before he could even grasp the situation, they were askin' me about this plan to kill Dean Karny."

It was about three o'clock on the afternoon of October 16, according to Steele, when Reza began to complain about "this guy" who was getting immunity to testify against him. "First he asked if I knew anybody from the streets—maybe somebody I met in Soledad—who would hit the guy," Steele remembered. "Then he says that when he was released from jail, he was gonna hire someone to do it because without this guy, there was no case."

Since no evidence was offered to show that Joe or Ben had communicated with Reza after his capture in August of 1984, they were permitted to remain free on bail. Reza, however, was remanded to custody that afternoon. "They put him right into Protective," Steele recalled. "That's the most kicked-back part of the jail. Everybody there is either a snitch, or killed a Hell's Angel or molested some little kid, or has got a prison gang after him. Nobody wants to talk about nothin' back there, 'cause they'll all tell on you. I used to walk by him every day, and I'd smile at him. Finally one day he goes, 'You asshole.' And I said, 'Hey, Reza, have a nice day.'"

The Shadings were together again for the first time since 1984 at the preliminary hearing in Redwood City during January of 1986. While Jim waited in Los Angeles for a retrial on the Levin charges, his codefendants in the Eslaminia case wore their best charcoal and navy suits—an Armani for Joe, a Valentino for Ben—to court in Redwood City. Reza's attire was equally striking, if somewhat less stylish: an orange jail jumpsuit accessorized with manacles and leg irons.

The new prosecutor on the San Mateo case, Deputy Attorney General John Vance, led a procession of coroners and detectives who had found the gnawed bones and gold-filled teeth in Soledad Canyon, and then of dentists and forensics specialists who had identified them as Hedayat Eslaminia's, through dilatory and largely unchallenged testimony. Olga Vasquez was worked over for an hour and a half by defense attorneys, who managed at a minimum to insinuate her involvement in opium smuggling and a romantic interlude with Jim Pittman. All other witnesses, however, were but a warm-up for the last one, Dean Karny, whose direct and cross examinations consumed most of the three-day hearing.

While Dean's face was still gaunt, his gray suit fit him more snugly than in Santa Monica, the torso under it beefed up by a bullet-proof vest. The body armor was provided by Oscar Breiling, who during November had enrolled Dean in the California Witness Protection Program, using Jeff Steele's testimony for justification. Breiling told one reporter that Karny was staying with friends in Oregon, but Dean actually was living in a Sacramento apartment Oscar helped him find. The two had met regularly during the past few months to discuss not only the facts of the case but the perspective of Joe Hunt. Dean suggested that Breiling read the works of Ayn Rand, *Atlas Shrugged* and *The Virtue of Selfishness* in particular, if he wanted to understand Joe's belief system. He felt certain Hunt would flee the country if released on bail, said Dean, who explained that Joe was without physical vanity and would have no problem with radical plastic surgery to change his appearance. Joe would keep his true first name, however, Dean predicted, changing only his last.

As Dean began his direct testimony with their meeting at the Harvard School in 1972, Joe made careful notes, assuming a pose that combined incredulity with bemusement. Karny refused to look at Hunt—or at Ben Dosti, who appeared alternately sad and bored, depending upon the observer's proximity. Reza's incessant grin, an overshot effort at ingratiation, made him the most disconcerting defendant.

The state's star witness continued to refer to himself as a "boy," but Dean was almost twenty-six now, an age Joe had reached three months earlier. Karny seemed not nearly so cocky as he had been six months earlier, matter-of-fact—detached even—in describing the planning and execution of Project Sam, as if it were the plot from a movie he and Joe had watched in Westwood one evening back in the summer of 1984. Only Dean's omission of self-incriminating details—telling the court how he punched holes in the trunk so Mr. Eslaminia might breathe but neglecting to mention that he later had covered those holes with tape—betrayed any sense of personal connection to the Iranian's death. As Vance brought the witness to his discovery that the man in the trunk was dead, however, Dean's face first tightened, then paled. When the prosecutor asked him to identify the dead man as Hedayat Eslaminia, offering a photograph for comparison, Dean would not accept it into his hand, forcing Vance to hold it in front of the witness stand. As he agreed that the man in the photograph was the same person he had seen in the trunk, Dean's voice broke. He lowered his head, unable to continue.

Joe also reacted then for the first time, with an expression of disgust that seemed to reveal the part of him most approximate to a sense of ethics: he might endorse dishonesty and encourage venality, but such maudlin hypocrisy sickened him.

Vance requested a recess so that the witness might regain his composure. Dean was led to an anteroom in a rear corner of the courthouse where "he broke down and began bawling," recalled Breiling, who felt, rather than discomfort, relief. "This was the first time I had seen any remorse, and it was the real thing," Oscar explained. "I got choked up myself. He was sitting in a chair, head in his hands, elbows on his knees, crying, saying, 'What have I done? What have I done?' Ron Morrow was there, but he didn't know what to do, and, after cracking a few jokes that weren't funny, ended up just sort of staring off at the walls. So I put my hand on Dean's shoulder and told him, 'If God can forgive you, so can I.' And he looked up with this expression that I'd never seen—relief, thanksgiving, and peace all combined. I pulled out a handkerchief and gave it to him. He dried his eyes and stood up, but his lower lip was still quivering, and it wasn't phony. I knew in that moment the total realization of what he had done had hit him, and from this point forward, Dean would be the one who suffered most— more than Joe, more than any of them—because he would be the one who understood what it meant to have taken a human life."

Dean would have to deal first, however, with what it meant to face cross-examination. Each of the four defense attorneys (one apiece for Ben and Reza, two for Joe) wanted a turn at this witness. Barens asked Dean to explain again his decision to make a deal with the state and "go on with life as usual." Had he considered Joe his closest friend? Barens inquired. "Yes, I suppose I did," Dean answered. "Did he stop being your closest friend when he got arrested, sir?" Barens wondered. "I thought differently of him," Dean conceded. After outlining the terms of his immunity agreement, Dean confirmed that he had passed the bar examination on his first try but currently was being denied admission to the state bar on grounds of "moral turpitude." Yes, his parents had hired a former officer of the Los Angeles Bar Association to represent him in his suit to overturn the state board's ruling, Dean agreed, and yes, he had asked the California attorney general's office to assist in this effort.

He would go over the immunity agreement with each attorney, occasionally confused but rarely ruffled by Barens's absurdly decorous phrasing, more admiring of than offended by the pointed questions of Ben's gentleman lawyer, Hirsch, exasperated to the brink of contempt by the repetitious flailing of Larry Lichter. The one interrogator who seemed capable of unbalancing Dean, perhaps even of breaking Karny if he got the chance, was Barens's new cocounsel, Richard Chier. Short, fat, and strutting, with flaming red hair and watery blue eyes, Chier was not only a borderline grotesque but a shrewd lawyer, one who had been remarkably successful as an advocate for accused drug dealers in federal court, "known for coming up with things that will make trouble for the other side," as a federal prosecutor said of him. Wearing an insolent expression and speaking from the corner of his mouth like a stage actor sneaking in a lewd aside, moving close on cross-examination, Chier hunched his shoulders and pumped his arms, suggesting a street-fighter looking for the chance to pull an opponent down off the sidewalk into the gutter. After Olga Vasquez testified that Mr. Eslaminia prayed for as long as an hour and a half every day, Chier cut quickly to the subject of her boyfriend's opium use, forcing Olga to admit that Hedayat liked to smoke a pipe in the evening. "Was that before or after he prayed?" Chier asked, turning to the defense table with a leer of delectation.

Given the limitations of a preliminary hearing, however, even Chier could make little dent in Dean, though Joe's second attorney managed at least to intimate the flogging that Karny could expect at trial, forcing the witness to describe in detail the mouth gags he had purchased at the Pleasure Chest, "the dildo one" in particular.

While Joe disappeared from sight during adjournments, his attorneys were only too happy to hold forth with the press. Chier demonstrated a particular talent for suggesting that there was much more to this case than the court files showed. All sorts of shocking revelations would surface at trial, he implied, especially in connection to the sexual predilections of Dean Karny. "You should see what Karny looks like in a dress," said Chier, who asserted that Dean's "obsession" with Joe motivated his appearance as a prosecution witness. As to how Hedayat Eslaminia had come to his death, Chier promised that the Iranian's blue diary would explain this: "It's the key to our case."

In Los Angeles County, Barens said, Joe's defense would stress the elaborate guile of "the purported victim": "Our contention relative to Mr. Levin is that he is not dead, but rather has voluntarily absented himself from the jurisdiction," Barens explained. "He had a lot more motive to flee than he did to stay. And I believe he took advantage of a rather gullible group of young men whom he went to lengths to set up, to make it look like they had disposed of him, so that he could shill anyone tracking his whereabouts."

Observing that the Roberts family had occupied front-row seats for the final day of the preliminary hearing on January 24, Barens professed perplexity. "Bobby Roberts's involvement is as much a mystery to me as it is to you," he told reporters during the morning recess. There was no mystery about the outcome of the prelim: Moments after Dean Karny examinations concluded, Judge Miller ruled that the state had shown probable cause that the defendants were involved in the abduction and death of Hedayat Eslaminia, and so must stand trial in superior court.

Joe accepted the news without change of expression. Barely a tremor of concern rippled his aplomb even when John Vance moved for the revocation of bail. As Judge Miller began his response by pointing out that "the defendants are innocent until proven guilty," Joe glanced over his shoulder to nod at Bobby and Lynne Roberts, who beamed back at him. Watching from the prosecution table, Oscar Breiling was struck not so much by the absence of relief as by the presence of resolve in Joe's expression. "Right then was when I knew we probably didn't have to worry about Hunt leaving the country," Breiling observed. "I could see it in his face: Joe was playing to win."

24

HIS NAME WAS JOE ROBERTS WHEN THE TOWERING YOUNG MAN WITH THE sculpted dark hair and obsidian eyes was introduced at the Lifespring semi-nar on La Cienega Boulevard in March of 1986. Of 130 people in attendance, he was singled out, remembered Steven Cowan, who joined the class that same evening. "It was explained he was in some kind of trouble," Cowan recalled, "but they didn't elaborate. The instructor just told us, 'Joe is here because of a court matter.' But there was this reference to the Roberts fam-ily being very important in Lifespring, so he was like a celebrity."

A "system of mind reform" was how Lifespring had been described by its founder, John P. Hanley, who had conceived the workshops not long after leaving the Mind Dynamics Institute in Marin County, where he had worked with est's Werner Erhard.

Cowan, a year older than Joe, was taking the Lifespring seminar "under protest," urged on by the friend who paid his fee. "The instructors first try to convince you how fucked up your life is so that by the time they're done, you're convinced you've got to do something to change," he explained. "They got to me through my indecision, the fact that I had no specific goals." Three years earlier, Cowan had walked away from his job as a travel agent in San Francisco to try the life of an aspiring actor in Los Angeles. He spent a small fortune on pictures and classes, was working out at the gym every day, saw a stylist once a week to keep his blond hair at the ideal length, maintained a year-round tan—even resorted to cosmetic surgery to improve his leading-man looks—yet had failed to land the smallest speaking part. Now nearly twenty-eight, Steven was unemployed and living off what was left of his savings. "A very lost period," he conceded.

He and Joe spotted one another as skeptics during the introductory lecture, Steven remembered, and later, during the advanced course, when-ever the group leader began to go off again on how the course had helped her discover she was the author of her own life story, the two would look at one another and roll their eyes. "I just didn't feel like I was on an equal basis with anyone else there," Steven explained. "The guys were drabbers, schlubs, nobody you felt like you could experience an intense relationship with. But Joe, he gives that off right away. He was preppie, Top-Siders, no socks, but expensive slacks, Ralph Lauren, and he was handsome. When the instructor was talking, he would sit there with his legs spread, elbows on his knees, staring down at the floor, like he was saying, 'I gotta get out of here.' And I was feeling the same thing."

Steven was delighted when he and Joe were assigned to the same small group for the Intense Sharing Experience. Even at close quarters, though, Joe set himself apart. "You were supposed to let it all go," Steven remembered, "past history, personal problems, family issues. Joe was the one person who wouldn't give anything. He just had this attitude that you don't share your feelings with a bunch of strangers, that people who need to have this reinforcement are pathetic. You either know what you're doing, or you don't. And it was like he *knew*."

Other pockets of resistance surfaced early on in the advanced course, but the accumulating force of cathartic experience absorbed them one-by-one, Cowan included, until only Joe was left outside the emotional consensus. Even when he stood alone, though, Joe remained unbending, mocking the fetish for confession that led others to believe they could solve their present problems by looking backward. All this weepy examination of childhood traumas, of hurts inflicted by unloving mothers and controlling fathers, was a way of avoiding not only the responsibility but the opportunity of existence, Joe said. And these unceasing references to the "Life Force," he added, were nothing more than a pseudoscientific substitute for faith in God—the ultimate escape from Self. "Joe already had a system," Cowan recalled. "Rationality was his god." What impressed Steven, though, "was the way Joe more than held his own, even when everyone else in the group ganged up on him. He would just talk people under the table. They literally couldn't speak anymore because he was so good at running a conversation. They had to shut up and consider what he had just said because it was so detailed, so intricate. People were getting to where they were more interested in what Joe had to say than what the teacher said."

The intent of the advanced section was to achieve a "total breakdown," as Steven understood it: "No matter what It was, It was supposed to come out. You were supposed to clear the air and get rid of It. We were supposed to walk out of there like new people. And Joe was fighting this every inch of the way. The staff tried to get into his psyche, what made him cry and what made him laugh, and it was basically nobody's business, was his answer. They'd say, 'What are you hiding?' And he'd laugh. They couldn't get to him."

Joe got to them, though. "You could see him having fun pushing people's buttons," Steven recalled. "He had this ability to see people's weaknesses and bring them right to the surface."

By the fifth day, the whole Lifespring staff was working on Joe, "trying to make him cry, telling him how much everybody loved him, and asking why he wouldn't share that experience of compassion and emotion," Cowan remembered. "Then somebody noticed how he avoided talking about his family, especially his mother, and they went after him on that. And it did seem like he might really have been touched. He even managed to muster up a few tears, but he and I kind of had a smile about it later, and it was like he had only done that to get them off his back."

The climax of the Lifespring course was an exercise called "Stretch," in which each student was to make a public performance designed by the other members of his group. The goal, instructors explained, was to create for each individual the role that would most profoundly challenge his or her "assumed identity." "Embarrassment was supposed to be a big part of it," Cowan explained. Steven nearly refused to participate after he was assigned to the "Gay Ensemble": "One guy had to be Anita Bryant, another guy had to be Peter Allen. I had to be Ronald Reagan." The young man playing the part of Nancy Reagan attacked him on a sexual level, threatening repeatedly to "'tell people what only I know about you,'" Steven recalled, "and I really started to be afraid. I got through it but only because I had several people up there with me." Joe's Stretch, though, was to be a solo. The other members of his group had decided that young Mr. Roberts should play the part of a prima ballerina, outfitted in tights, tutu, and toe shoes. "He was amazing," Steven recalled. "Really. He went through it without any problem at all, twirling and leaping, and was, like, perfect. He never blinked or flinched. You could see all the people who wanted to humiliate him just sort of wilting in their seats. Everybody else gave him a standing ovation."

"Fascinated by him now," Cowan was thrilled when Joe pulled him aside on the last day at Lifespring and asked for his home number. Only a few days passed before Joe phoned to invite him for dinner at the Old World in Westwood. "We sat in a booth and he told me how he had just been through this really rough period in his life," Steven remembered. "He didn't go into detail, just that there had been some trouble, and he had spent a year in county jail. And now he was out. He did say it had to with business, and that he couldn't get too involved in projects until it was all settled, but he had this idea."

Since his release from jail, he had been adopted by the family of his girlfriend Brooke, Joe explained, taking their last name as his own. Fortunately for him, it was a name that meant something in this town. Joe ran down the résumé of Bobby Roberts, Steven remembered, then explained that among his future father-in-law's many irons in the fire was a nifty little opportunity at Capitol Records. Bobby had been offered a seven-year option on the complete music library of Judy Garland, Joe explained, and believed that a collection of the singer's work might sell in the millions of units if marketed properly, perhaps through commercials on late-night television. "I'm sitting there questioning: 'Why would somebody like that want to get involved with a nobody like me?'" Cowan recalled. "Joe explained that the Garland project was sort of a gift from Bobby, that Bobby was involved in so many things himself that he couldn't do everything, and that he had said if Joe and I could pull it together, he would guide us through, but that it would be our project. I thought, 'This sounds too cool.'"

Steven's enthusiasm mounted when Joe invited him up to the Bellagio estate for a meeting: "All around me are these fantastic symbols of Hollywood success, pictures of performers Bobby had managed on the walls, gold records, platinum records, posters from Bobby's movies, and signed photographs from the stars—Robert Redford, George Segal, Charles Bronson. We walk into Bobby's office and I'm thinking, 'This is really happening.' Everything about it was so perfect. I met Brooke and I thought she was beautiful, so young, studying to be an actress, the daughter of a rich show-business family, with the fabulous home in Bel Air, and it was all very cliché, but the dream cliché.

"So we met with Bobby, who explained the Garland deal very briefly. Bobby was kind of curt, but it seemed like he just wanted his privacy. I met Lynne, and she was the same, nice but distant. To me, this was the way glamorous people were."

On one point, Bobby was very clear: He wasn't putting in any of his own money. "He had already given us this gift, right," Cowan recalled, "and anything we could make of it was ours. I was pretty much in awe of him. I imagined Bobby as this very busy but incredibly kind and giving person because he was one of the heads of Lifespring, had run some of the classes, and so had Lynne. I had to keep looking down at myself to make sure I was really there."

That same week Steven and Joe began doing demographic studies at UCLA, studying telemarketing techniques. "Joe seemed like he always knew which direction to turn next," Cowan recalled, "and we were both getting very excited." After finishing at the UCLA Research Library, the two would spend the rest of the evening in Westwood Village. "Joe loved movies," Steven recalled. "He could memorize lines of dialogue from just seeing a movie once. Video games, he was the best; people in that one place,

WestWorld, stood in line to watch him. I was just amazed by him. I kept asking myself, 'Why does he want me?' But Joe told me he knew I had no money, but he also knew I had a lot of ambition and drive, and he said those were just as important as money if you wanted to make something happen."

The two named their company Garland Inc. and began to work out of Joe's office in the Bel Air house. "Joe had a computer," Steven remembered, "and we spent several days just burning. By the time we finished the prospectus, though, we realized we were going to need a lot of money to do this, like a couple hundred thousand. That was when Joe said, 'Why don't we talk to Brad Buckley?'"

Brad had been another student in the Lifespring course. Lanky and bearded, a laconic yet genteel presence, he hadn't made a particularly deep impression on Cowan. "I said, 'Why do you think Brad?'" he recalled. "And Joe says, 'Because I think Brad has a lot of money.' See, Joe knows; he can just tell. Brad has that top-drawer air, I guess, though I didn't recognize it. Joe had noticed that Brad drove a Jaguar, and so had I. But in L.A., so what? What Joe had noticed that I hadn't was this gold ring Brad wore, with a family crest on it. And that meant something, though not to me."

Joe's surmise was on target: The ring on Brad's finger bore the crest not only of his clan but of their company, Buckley Broadcasting, owners of radio stations stretching from Connecticut to California. Brad had worked selling air time for several family stations but at twenty-five felt it was time to "obtain a position of my own," as he expressed it during the Lifespring course. He had been interviewing at record companies since arriving in Los Angeles several months earlier, yet still was without work. "Joe and I sketched the idea for him," Steven recalled, "and you could tell even over the telephone that the idea of owning his own record company really excited Brad. Joe was pleased but not too surprised because he had sensed during the Lifespring course where Brad was coming from."

Brad agreed to meet them for lunch the next day at the Hard Rock Café. "A fabulous afternoon for me," Cowan recalled. "Joe and I drove over in the big BMW sedan. He was recognized when we came through the door, and we got a great table. We were all wearing suits. Joe had on that gray Armani and I had an Armani on too. Brad was really dressed, and we looked so cool. Everyone was watching us, I noticed, and it was like being at the Center all of a sudden, on some sort of stage. We all shook hands, sat down, and I felt like my life was finally happening."

Brad was more reserved. He had been equally impressed with but rather less taken by Joe than Steven during the Lifespring seminar. "Joe stood out because he was like this rock-hard wall," Brad remembered. "He didn't reveal himself to anyone. I recognized that he really knew how to play people, though: whatever type of person someone was, he could adapt, sort of tailor his approach. There was this extreme arrogance, also, a kind of holier-than-thou expression he wore during Lifespring, only in his case it was more like a smarter-than-thou expression. Anyway, I felt his power, and that made me cautious."

When he and Joe showed Buckley their prospectus, however, "Brad was flabbergasted," Steven remembered. "We had really done our homework, covered all the bases, and Brad saw that."

They took him to meet Bobby Roberts, "and Brad was sort of reassured by the house on Bellagio," Steven recalled, "because that was the style he was accustomed to." Brad seemed eager in spite of himself, Cowan thought, "like he was making himself wait, wondering if maybe all anybody wanted from him was his money." To prove this wasn't the case, Steven went to his own family first, borrowing twenty thousand dollars from his grandparents. "That was part of the high, too, feeling they believed in me more than I ever thought they did," he remembered. "Joe and Brad were really impressed with me. When I came in with this check that day, it was the high fives and the long lunch—our lunches were always at the Rock—and toasting each other, grins from ear to ear."

Brad immediately matched Steven's twenty thousand dollars. Garland Inc. registered with the state as a California corporation, even obtained stock certificates. Steven and Brad admired him more than ever when Joe announced he did not wish to be an officer of the company, ceding the positions of president and vice president to Buckley and Cowan. The two young executives were startled, however, when Joe explained that Bobby Roberts and his partner David Semas would own 56 percent of the stock in the company—"for bringing in the rights and the expertise," Brad recalled. Furthermore, Joe wanted to hire Bobby to work for them as a consultant at six thousand dollars a month for three months. "Also, we had to hire Kurtis Roberts as our 'administrator,'" Steven recalled. "Bobby wanted someone with experience in the music industry and said Kurtis had worked for him at Dunhill Classic Discs." "We went along because we figured it could only help to have Bobby Roberts, Mr. Film Producer–Record Company President working with us," Brad explained.

By April they had rented the largest suite in the Valley State Bank building on Lankershim Boulevard, opposite Universal Studios. "We already had a couple of other investors by then," Steven explained. "People were excited by the idea of Judy Garland's music, by Bobby Roberts's impressive résumé."

After they moved into the North Hollywood office, Joe suggested Garland Inc. might be but the cornerstone of a corporate empire, one that could include other collections of classic songs, perhaps a music video pro-

THE PRICE OF EXPERIENCE 467

duction company—maybe even a real record company someday. Joe even had a name for their holding company, Brad remembered: "He wanted to call it Basic Business Consolidated."

People who were not close to him often misinterpreted Joe's unruffled appearance, Michelle Berenak had noticed: "He's calm, not cool," Todd's fiancée explained. Like the rest of the Roberts family, though, Michelle was delighted by how Joe "got more in touch with his feelings and vulnerabilities" through the Lifespring course.

Joe had endeavored to make a whole new set of friends after his release from county jail, Michelle observed, among them Steve Solomon, the young "personal fitness consultant" who operated the Sunshine Health Bar at the Century Health Club. Solomon, an ebullient and brawny twenty-five-year-old who suggested what Howdy Doody might have grown into on a diet of steroids, had met Joe for the first time when Bobby and the rest of the Robertses, who were regular customers, brought him in to the health bar for a carrot juice and spinach shake one afternoon. "I could relate to Joe right off because we were from similar backgrounds," Solomon explained. "Joe said he had had a simple upbringing, like mine, that he had an educated but not financially successful father and was only able to attend the Harvard School on a scholarship."

Solomon, recently reborn in Christ, also appreciated Joe's personal habits. "I'm a very moral person," Steve explained. "I study the Bible, like, four or five times a week. And I liked that Joe didn't have the typical male characteristics you see around the club. He didn't discuss drinking or drugs or women like others did."

Joe kept the relationship simple: "Basically," Solomon said, "we played a lot of video games and went to a lot of movies."

Joe's former out-trade clerk, Leslie Eto, flew to Los Angeles from Chicago for a visit later that spring. Joe had called her collect from Los Angeles County Jail every day for weeks during the summer of 1985, Leslie recalled: "The only thing he told me about his situation was that he had done nothing dishonorable." After she arrived in L.A and slept off her jet lag, Leslie said, Joe took her straight to the Lifespring seminar. What she admired about Joe, the young woman explained, was that he refused not only to feel sorry for himself but even to cast blame upon those who turned against him. Joe quoted, "'The rarer action is in virtue than in vengeance,'" Leslie remembered.

He knew Joe as a wonderful listener, Steven Cowan recalled, full of advice and insights: "He said we had led parallel lives because we both had grown up as loners." Steven traced his own alienation to his parents' divorce when he was six years old. "I had spent my whole childhood pulling away from everybody," he explained, "because I didn't want to get hurt again." Joe, on the other hand, insisted that his sense of separation had less to do with family dynamics than with class consciousness. "Joe spoke very little of his parents," Steven remembered. "There was this tone of dismissing his father, and he never talked about his mother at all." When Joe spoke of isolation, "he put it mostly in terms of what it was like being the poor boy at the Harvard School and how that had held him apart," Cowan recalled. "The one positive thing he said about that whole experience was how great he had been on the debate team there. You had the feeling of him doing it all by himself, with no help at all. He had a way of making it seem like being the loner had made him strong, self-sufficient, capable."

Joe explained that he had developed a philosophy of life—Paradox—out of his experience at the Harvard School, Steven remembered: "He told me how he had come to believe that there is no supreme being, no ruling force, and to understand that we are 'the masters of our own universe'— a favorite phrase of his. He also used to say that we each create our own impediments, and if we remove them, they aren't there."

Joe permitted Steven to meet Ryan Hunt on several occasions. The first time was when the two drove out to Calabasas to pick up some computer software they needed for the Garland Inc. prospectus. Their destination was a new tract house near the Old Abercrombie Ranch, where Ryan was living with Joe's former investor and new stepmother, Liza Bowman Hunt. "It looked like they had just moved in," Cowan recalled. "They were redecorating, but they also treated the place like it was just temporary. They were talking about this cabin on a lake in Idaho they were going to buy. Ryan reminded me of a mad scientist, with that curly hair and rumpled clothing. He seemed like a genius type because he was incredible with the computer, even better than Joe. I understood that Joe and his father and Liza were involved in various deals together, and Joe and his father acted more like business partners than father and son. They treated each other as intellectual equals and were very in tune on that level, but there was no emotional connection that I could see. I really didn't feel comfortable there."

Steven now experienced not only discomfort but a mounting sense of unreality each time he visited the home of his silent senior partner, Bobby Roberts. "Basically, I didn't trust him," Cowan explained. "I couldn't figure out what it was, so I thought it had to be me. Brad kept telling me, 'Open your mind. Open your heart.'" Even Brad was becoming uneasy, though, about Bobby's lack of enthusiasm for the Garland Inc. project: "He wasn't putting in any effort at all. Yet at the same time he was constantly pressuring us about bringing in money more rapidly."

Joe's relationship with Brooke was a mystery to both young men. "A guy with his intellect running around with a girl who seemed almost moronic?" Steven asked. "She sat around drawing whales with crayons all day, like that was her occupation." "Mostly, Brooke was silent and meek," Brad recalled. "She would scream and curse at her mother, sometimes, though, and it was unbelievably crude, some of what she said, like she had another personality in there." "Finally I told Joe I just couldn't see the relationship," Steven recalled, "and he told me, 'I love her.' There wasn't much feeling in his voice when he said that, but there was when he told me she had been his big support while he was in jail, had come down every day to visit him, that she never left his side and he would never forget that. And yet in the house they never seemed together, never hugged or held each other."

Of all those living in the Bellagio house, Brad observed, the two who seemed closest were Joe and Lynne. "Joe hugged Lynne more often than he did Brooke, and it was obvious she was very fond of him," Steven agreed. "But Lynne seemed off to me, too." "Lynne struck us as being very nervous, always trying to say what you wanted to hear," Brad explained. "Out front, she was Mrs. Lifespring, and yet the things that came out of her mouth were a total contradiction of the philosophy, about how you were supposed to take responsibility for your own life and let other people take responsibility for theirs."

"After a while, the Roberts household started to seem like this put-on because there was no real closeness," Steven said. "They all had the same last name, but you felt like they were only together for a reason," Brad agreed, "and we could never figure out what it was."

The two had little time to ponder, though. "We just kept raising money," Steven recalled. Cowan borrowed fifteen thousand dollars from a friend he had made during the Lifespring course, an amount that was again matched by Buckley. "Brad was willing to stay in step but not to get ahead of us," explained Steven, who turned next to the person he admired and trusted most, a Catholic priest. "I told Father Steve how much this meant to me, how it was the opportunity of a lifetime and I had to take it, and I was asking the people who cared about me to have the kind of faith and trust in me that I finally had in myself," Cowan recalled. "He gave me thirty-five thousand dollars, and it was actually the church's money for the summer fiesta at the retreat. I promised him—and so did Joe—that the money would be repaid before then. I felt in way deep after that."

Even as the water rose to his chin, though, Steven explained, "what made it possible to keep an optimistic attitude was the relationship I had formed with Joe." While Brad was "intrigued" by Joe, he preferred to spend social time with his fiancée. Steven, though, considered Joe his closest friend. "Joe knew from Lifespring that I was bisexual," he recalled, "and after we had known each other awhile, I let him know that I had an interest in him on that level. He didn't get upset at all, but he told me he was completely straight and completely committed to Brooke. Joe didn't have any judgment of what other people did in private, though. And whenever he'd see me or we'd say good-bye, he'd always give me a hug and it seemed very natural. There aren't that many heterosexual men who can hug a guy who's physically attracted to them and not feel a little uncomfortable, but Joe was completely cool about it. And that was great for me because it was like I finally had this regular friendship."

What made his nights out on the town with Joe so memorable—even thrilling—though, Steven admitted, was "the incredible attention he got. We went to all the fad places, and everywhere we went, Joe was the center of attention. We were with all the *très chic* in town and Joe knew them all, all the kids whose parents ran the studios and television networks and all of that, and I felt like 'Wow, I'm in with the Group' because he knew all the hottest-looking people, the greatest-looking girls, and everybody would come up and hug him and kiss him, and they were all the son of this movie producer, or the daughter of that record company president, Walter Matthau's son, whatever. I remember one night Belinda Carlisle from the Go-Go's came over to give him a big hug and a kiss, and Joe didn't bat an eye. He had this, like, *immunity* to beautiful women and famous people. It was always like he had the power, he was the center, the main person, everywhere he went, and he just overpowered the whole room. He was like this secret celebrity—the star's star.

"After a while, he started to reveal himself, in bits and pieces, like 'I got myself into some trouble, and you'll find out eventually.' It was this mystery. He explained about the BBC, this conglomerate of companies he had, with all these young entrepreneurial types—guys like Brad, basically—who were from affluent families with fathers who wouldn't let them be on their own and were looking for a way to make something for themselves, to show their parents what they could do. He told me the May Brothers were in it and Donald Bren's son was in it, and I was just overwhelmed, thinking, 'What a mover and shaker,' and it seemed even more like our own company had to be going places. Then he told me how these kids he was in with had started embezzling from the companies, and there had been a falling-out. And then this Ron Levin, who had set up this bogus account Joe traded for him, disappeared, and they had all taken advantage of it, making accusations against him. He mentioned Dean Karny but said just that they had been close and Dean betrayed him."

Steven didn't let the revelations shake him: "Okay, he had spent a year in jail, but now he was out, and everybody we met, the people who would know, I figured, treated Joe like he was a victim, like he had been framed or set up. Then one night we went to the City Restaurant." The City was unsurpassed among Los Angeles restaurants for cachet among clientele in the under-thirty category, a stark, crowded room where the placement of one's table registered social standing with an exactitude only approximated in other venues. "Everybody is watching everybody else but pretending not to," explained Cowan, who always had been intimidated by the place.

"So Joe and I walk in that night without a reservation, our first time together there, and we get the best table, right in the middle of the room. Marya Dosti sat us, though I didn't know who she was at the time. And I look around, and I can't believe what's happening: Everybody in the place—everybody—is looking at us. There were famous people in the room, but they were all watching Joe. And I can hear them all talking about us because it's so close in there. Every eye is on us, and this name—'Joe Hunt'—is on everybody's lips. So I say, 'Who's Joe Hunt?' Joe says, 'I am.' Then he tells me, 'You better get used to this because there's been some publicity.'"

An article previously rejected by *Playboy* was the first into print, appearing in the May 1986 issue of *Los Angeles* magazine under the title "THE DEADLY PIED PIPER OF BEVERLY HILLS." "Was Joe Hunt's Billionaire Boys Club a social plaything that allowed rich, young Westsiders to dabble in commodities brokering," the article's subhead asked, "or was it a breeding ground for murder?" Among the Boys themselves, the most affecting aspect of the article was a panel of photographs lifted from the Harvard School's 1976 *Sentinel,* showing Joe and Dean alongside Tom and Dave May as fresh-faced young teens.

"For me, the *L.A.* magazine piece had the most shock value," recalled Evan Dicker, who had been mentioned by name but quoted anonymously ("What do you wear for cross-examination? Is black too morbid?"). "Because it came out first. Up until that time, not many people knew about my involvement. Someone I played polo with called up and said, 'I thought you were lying.' He figured it had to be made up because it was too incredible to be true."

The *L.A. Daily News* article ran at the top of the front page on Sunday, May 4. This was the version Brad Buckley saw first: "I didn't know anything about the BBC, really, until I read the *Daily News,* and their article blew me away. I called Steven up that morning and told him, 'You better look at this.'"

By late May, a "soon to be a major motion picture" label had attached to the BBC story. "While the jury will be asked to determine the question of Hunt's guilt or innocence," wrote Greg Kilday in the *Herald*'s Page 2 gossip column, "Hollywood is already asking the bigger question: Who will make the movie?" Previewing the film as "The Brat Pack Meets the God-father," Kilday reported that the rights to the *Los Angeles* magazine article had been "acquired" the day before by ITC Productions, which also had purchased the film rights to the stories of Tom and David May. "These guys are modern-day heroes," enthused the project's executive producer, Donald March, who, Kilday added, saw the twins as "sympathetic protagonists."

Several other studios were "circling" an article scheduled for publication in the September issue of *Esquire,* wrote Kilday, and "there's also the question of how other principals in the case will choose to dispose of the film rights to their stories. Hunt's bail has been posted by music manager Roberts, the father of Hunt's girlfriend, who—the speculation goes—could also be harboring designs on the story. And Dean Karny, Hunt's chief lieu-tenant, who has been granted immunity to testify, could also provide yet more rights."

The next to make a movie deal was none of the above, however, but rather the joint venture threesome of Jim Pittman, Mike Canale, and John Sack. Early in June, Sack had negotiated an agreement with a produc-tion team composed of actors Rob Lowe and Cary Elwes, as well as Joe's old Harvard School classmate Brad Wyman, whose participation must have come as a surprise: Five months earlier, Wyman had refused Sack's request for an interview "because speaking on this matter wouldn't be right until Joe's trials are over."

The *Esquire* article appeared in late August and gave the Billion-aire Boys a national audience. "One of those wild Southern California sto-ries that could never have been invented and can barely be believed," said *USA Today.* By the time jury selection for Joe's trial began in Santa Monica on November 4, articles about the BBC had appeared in publications as disparate as the *New York Times* and the *National Enquirer,* along with *Time* and *Newsweek.* CBS's *60 Minutes* and ABC's *20/20* each initiated BBC seg-ments. The *Los Angeles Times,* however, had yet to report the story.

Joe remained a local celebrity—only now more notorious than eminent. "Everybody still stared, but all of a sudden he wasn't getting the center table or being kissed on the cheek by Belinda Carlisle," recalled Steven Cowan. Joe had warned him over dinner at the City Restaurant that the publicity "would definitely sway people's decisions about him," Steven remembered. "But I told him, 'Look, you're my friend and that's that.' Then a few days later I get this call from Brad that the story has come out in the *Daily News*.

It was a lot clearer than the *Los Angeles* article and I was sick when I read it. And Brad was losing it. I knew most of the story by then, but from Joe's point of view, and this was *their* point of view. It scared me. I still wouldn't consider, though, that Joe actually had done it."

"Graciously," it seemed to Steven, Joe announced a few days after the *Daily News* article appeared that he would be withdrawing from the Garland Inc. project. "He says, 'Now the tough part's coming,'" Steven recalled. "'I'm gonna be involved in a lot of court situations, and I don't think you want to be publicly associated with me.' Like he's concerned for us. But I'm getting this big knot in my stomach, thinking, 'If he pulls out, the whole thing crumbles.'"

Cowan and Buckley had just invested twenty thousand dollars of Garland Inc.'s funds in a side deal at the urging of Bobby Roberts—"to earn some money on our investment capital in the interim," Steven explained. "We were at sixty thousand then, and we needed one fifty at least for Judy's record. So then Joe told us about this friend, Frank Mingarella, who had a video distribution market where we could purchase a collection of ninja movies from the Orient, then put them on cassette. There would be a relatively quick turnover, we were told, in and out in three months with a hundred percent profit at the very least." When Steven and Brad met Mingarella, they were taken aback by the squat body and cheap toupee, but Joe assured them that Frank knew his stuff.

Cowan and Buckley signed a contract with Mingarella and rented him space in the Garland Inc. office. Three weeks later, Frank informed the two that there had been "complications" in Taiwan, Steven recalled. One week after that, "he said there was a problem in Hong Kong also," Cowan remembered, "that his principals had sold our movies to another company."

When Mingarella said he needed an additional nineteen thousand to buy a batch of other, better movies, Steven pulled Brad away for a private meeting. "I said, 'No way! No more money! I'm not writing any more checks,'" he recalled. "And everybody said, 'Look, this is just the way it's happened, let's take care of it.' I wanted to trust, but I was torn. Finally, like a fool, I said 'Okay' and wrote the check."

The *Daily News* article came out only a few days after the check cleared. "Brad was so sick, he couldn't even talk about it," Steven recalled, and avoided any social encounters with Hunt from that point forward. Cowan and Hunt, though, became even better friends. "Once the stuff starts to break in public, he becomes more vulnerable and more attached to me," Steven explained. "He's coming over more, spending whole evenings at my house, watching movies on TV, sprawled across the bed, talking about what he's going through, saying he felt like the whole world was against him and no one would listen to what he had to say. Joe had told me several times how close he and Dean had been and how he had been betrayed by Dean, and that he really hadn't had another friendship that close, so it made him reluctant, but by that summer he was admitting he needed connection."

Even the Robertses were reeling from the impact of the publicity. "You could see the whole family was affected," Steven remembered. "Bobby was worried about his reputation. They were tired. Then Brooke moved out of the main house into the guest house above the garage. Joe said she couldn't handle the stress and needed to have space away from him."

Joe continued to protest his innocence and predicted that a lot of people were going to be ashamed to show their faces when the truth came out in court. His trial had been set to begin during the first week in November, and by June Joe was working full-time on his case, Steven remembered: "He said he was going to pop these surprises on people in court and it was all going to start making sense to them. The one thing he said was that Dean had done all this to him and was out to get him because Joe had in some way rejected him. He gave me the impression that there was this sexual thing between them."

At the Garland Inc. office, Steven and Brad began to chafe at paying Kurtis Roberts two thousand dollars a month as their company's "administrator." "Kurtis would come in just before lunchtime, go out to eat with us, then leave for the gym shortly thereafter," Brad recalled. "He always said he had this going and that going, but nothing ever materialized." "Also, whenever we had a meeting with Bobby," Steven remembered, "he'd never discuss our business. Instead, he always had some new idea he wanted us to raise money for, like this Coleco Toy project."

In August, Joe and Frank and Bobby explained that there had been unanticipated delays in obtaining the new batch of ninja movies and proposed buying ten CBS movies of the week. Frank had arranged to acquire the cassette rights on the TV movies, it was explained, and Garland Inc. could distribute them on home video, but it would cost another fifty thousand dollars. Joe took him into the conference room alone to sell the idea, Brad remembered: "That's what he always did, get one of us on his side first, then go to the other one. He drew up this contract saying I would own the films, with provisions for a refund, with interest, if the deal fell through. So I got a cashier's check for fifty thousand from my own portfolio, made out to this company in New York."

Joe and Bobby suggested that Frank should fly to New York alone to purchase the CBS movies, "but I said 'No,'" Steven recalled. "'Brad and I will go to New York, and we'll decide what to buy.'" "Bobby told us, 'If you can get ten movies for fifty thousand, you can make a fortune,'" Brad remembered.

The Garland Inc. partners were uneasy, though, when Bobby's son Todd showed up at the office, proposing to write life insurance policies on the two of them worth five hundred thousand dollars apiece. Joe explained the policies could be listed on their books as corporate assets and "enhance the company's balance sheet." "Todd was a real hard-sell artist," Brad recalled, "but we decided to wait until we got back from New York."

Mingarella had flown east ahead of them to meet with his "liaison." On the morning after Steven and Brad arrived in Manhattan, they agreed to meet Frank for breakfast at his hotel, which turned out to be some shabby semi-dive at Ninth Avenue and Forty-fifth Street, Brad remembered. Mingarella took them first to meet his "liaison." "We went to his apartment in the fifties around Sixth Avenue, this crummy place," Steven recalled, "and he was flipped out of his skull, running into the bedroom to do lines between sentences and frantic because he couldn't reach the owner of this movie company on the phone. He was desperate, you could see that. He was going to make a quick commission of like ten grand on the deal and so excited, he couldn't control himself." "Finally he said, 'I'm gonna take you downtown to meet some people,'" Brad remembered. "So we went down to the garment district, up this narrow staircase to the top, where there's this tiny sleazy little office. And this guy has these duffel bags filled with old videos, mostly dubs, with a few porno thrown in. Here we are in our suits, sitting on these rickety chairs, in this, like, two-by-four room." "Frank said, 'We're just warming up,'" Steven recalled. "He said he was testing us. By then, though, we were ready to get on the next plane out."

Brad had started looking over his shoulder, Steven noticed. "The thought kept flashing through my mind that they were planning to kill us for the insurance money," Brad explained. "I told Steven how glad I was we hadn't signed the policy, but he said, 'That's ridiculous.'"

"When we got back to Los Angeles, though, I wasn't so sure," Cowan admitted. "The *Esquire* article had just come out, and Brad and I both found it difficult to disagree with. Still, when I looked at Joe, the last thing I saw was a murderer."

Steven reminded Brad of the generous deal Joe had given him on his new 700 series BMW, a sale price of twelve thousand dollars, no money down, with payments of four hundred dollars per month. Several weeks passed, though, and Cowan still hadn't seen the title to the car. "Supposedly the papers were coming, and then they weren't coming, and then they were again," he explained. "Finally Joe came up with this excuse that I was renting the car, not buying it. I blew up at him. Joe couldn't believe it. I was raging; things were just spewing out of my mouth. And Joe denied everything. He said he was *embarrassed* for me, acting like this."

When Bobby Roberts discovered that Cowan and Buckley had hired an attorney to sue Mingarella, he summoned them to a meeting at the Bellagio estate. "We went over," Brad remembered, "and Bobby really castigated both of us for pulling such a stunt. 'Why didn't you talk to me about this?' he said. And, 'If I were Frank, I'd say, "Fuck you guys," and walk.' He tells us, 'You should have used your Lifespring training to see where you were coming from and how to handle this.'" "I'm sitting there thinking, 'I don't believe this,'" Steven recalled. "I'm out thirty-nine thousand dollars, and Bobby's trying to tell me that I should sign up for another Lifespring course."

Mingarella signed a contract promising either to deliver the ninja movies or fork over forty-five thousand dollars within two weeks "but never paid us a penny," Brad said.

Worse news was still to come, however, when Brad phoned an executive at Capitol Records—"Jack Reynolds, who used to work for my family in Philadelphia," he explained—and set up a meeting at the record company's Hollywood offices to discuss obtaining a letter of credit on the Judy Garland library. "I arrive with my attorney, meet with the people at Capitol, and they tell us not only that the rights to the Judy Garland material have never been optioned by Bobby Roberts but that they have been optioned that morning by a man named Mike Howard," Brad remembered. "It turned out that Bobby and Mike Howard had been in association earlier but broke up."

"I get a call from Brad that night, saying, 'You're not going to believe this,'" Steven recalled. The two young men met the next morning at the Garland Inc. office. "We were totally lost at that point," Cowan remembered. "We were so in debt—we could have ended up going to jail. I couldn't believe Joe would do this to me. I was on the verge of a nervous breakdown."

Steven called Joe a few days later to arrange "a last meeting." He hadn't seen his friend since November 4, the day jury selection for Hunt's trial in Santa Monica commenced, Cowan recalled: "I asked Joe to meet me in Westwood. He suggested the video arcade. He was playing when I got there, and he wouldn't look at me. He just said, 'You have to look at this as a lesson in life. It'll be valuable later on.' He told me, 'I can get you a job at the Palm Canyon Hotel,' which Bobby and David Semas were buying. I was really annoyed by that and tried to get into it, but he cut me off with 'Hey, look at what I'm dealing with.' And he said, 'I can't believe you're coming to me with all this petty stuff when I have the problems I do.'"

Steven's stuff did not seem so petty on the morning of December 3, 1986, however, when he stepped out of his apartment and was surrounded by a team of LAPD detectives who came out of the shrubbery flashing badges, then told him he was under arrest for suspicion of murder in the the first degree.

Those pressing the cases of *People v. Hunt aka Gamsky* began their journey into the darkest gray area yet at a little past 1 P.M. on the afternoon of October 18, 1986, when a Salvadoran maid at the Hollywood Center Motel on Sunset Boulevard entered room 304 and found it orderly but filled with a sickening stench. The odor seemed to be emanating from the clothes closet, where the maid found a large steamer trunk, latched and locked.

The call to the Los Angeles Police Department's Hollywood Division came in at 1:45 P.M. Officer William Massa was dispatched to investigate, and it was he who opened the trunk. Inside was the partially decomposed body of a young man wearing only a clear plastic rainsuit, wrapped in two large green garbage bags.

Room 304 had been rented on the evening of September 27 by a bearded, silver-haired gentleman who gave his name as Tim Mill and paid cash for one full week's rent, the motel's night receptionist explained. The day his week was up, Mr. Mill sent a money order to the office, covering his rent into early November. Attached to the payment was a note in which the guest stated he was in San Francisco for a few days and did not want anyone to enter the room while he was away. They were accustomed to unusual arrangements at the Hollywood Center Motel, the manager explained, but no one had thought to tell the new maid of Mr. Mill's request.

Forty-eight hours later, coroners from the Los Angeles medical examiner's office and detectives from the LAPD's Hollywood division had determined that the young man stuffed into the trunk was Richard Keith Mayer, five feet six inches tall, 130 pounds, and six weeks shy of his twenty-first birthday. Mayer's mother, who lived among the scorched foothills of Sun Valley, gave her son's occupation as "factory worker," but by then police knew that the young man had been employed most often during the past three years as a roadie for the heavy-metal rock bands Leatherwolf and Whitesnake. "A shy, timid guy who would do anything for us," said one band member. His only goal in life, Mayer had boasted to the musicians, was to sleep with as many girls as possible. Neither band could afford to pay even subsistence wages, however, and "anonymous sources" told the LAPD that Mayer had been moonlighting for months as a streetwalker on Santa Monica Boulevard, selling himself to motorists in passing cars.

Death had been caused, an autopsy revealed, by asphyxia. Examination of the body was made difficult by the deceased's several tattoos, including a pair of black crosses and a blue bird roosting upon three red roses, but the coroner had discovered hemorrhages in the strap muscles on both sides of the neck, indicating that young Mayer had been strangled. Also, shortly before his death, the coroner reported, Mayer had injected cocaine cut with heroin, a "speedball" in the vernacular of the street.

Now officially classified as a murder, the case was assigned to Hollywood homicide detectives David Diaz and Robert Rozzi. By October 22, the investigators had obtained an artist's sketch of the man who had rented room 304 on September 27. Diaz and Rozzi also inventoried the "personal effects" found in the drawers of the dresser and vanity in the room where Richard Mayer's body was discovered. Among these were a transistor radio, a pair of Nike running shoes, a syringe with needle cap, a tin of "La Vosigenne" pastilles, and several scraps of paper with writing on them, including a Mobil Oil credit card slip bearing the signature *Dean L. Karny*.

"I got a call in Sacramento from John [Vance], saying, 'Get back to the office, we've got to go to Los Angeles right away,'" Oscar Breiling remembered. The two walked into the district attorney's office at the Santa Monica Courthouse little more than three hours later. "Les Zoeller comes up and says, 'Here's a composite of the suspect,'" Breiling recalled. "I looked at that and my eyeballs almost jumped out of my head; it was me."

The man who rented room 304 wore sunglasses even indoors, the motel's receptionist remembered, and the artist had drawn him that way. "So before the LAPD people come in, I borrow John's dark glasses," Oscar recalled. "Rozzi and Diaz just about swallowed their tongues. They sit in these chairs along the wall in the office and they're trying to act nonchalant, but every time I turn my head, they're looking at me. So then they give us a very limited briefing about what's happened, and it's obvious that after seeing me they're playing it close-in. Rozzi was too cool. He says, 'Can I get a couple of pictures of you? My lieutenant's not going to believe this.' I say, 'Sure.' So they stood me up against the wall, and first they wanted a front, then a right profile, then a left profile, and I start thinking, 'Should I get ahold of my lawyer?'"

They needed to speak to Dean Karny, obviously, Rozzi and Diaz said, and Breiling was the only person outside his family who knew Dean's location. "I said, 'I'll get him to our headquarters in Sacramento and you can interview him there,'" Oscar recalled. "Sacramento was aware of what was happening, and the order came down from the boss personally to go out and arrest Dean." The attorney general wanted Karny in "protective custody," Breiling was informed. "He felt Dean would run as soon as he found out," Oscar recalled. "And I said, 'No, he won't.' My boss said, 'Well, what do you think he'll do?' I said, 'I think he'll come to me.' The top brass were really upset—they think I'm gettin' too close to my informant. I said, 'I'm the agent on the case, and you either trust my judgment or take my badge.' They said, 'We'll get back to you.'

"In the meantime, I realize I'm officially a suspect. [Diaz and Rozzi] not only take new pictures for a photo lineup but take my finger and palm prints, too, then ask for a complete accounting of my activities and locations during this week in October."

Breiling phoned Karny and picked him up personally at his apartment: "I felt the LAPD should have the opportunity to hit Dean cold, so I invented something bogus about the driver's license I was having made up for his new identity. I also called Morrow in L.A., said I wanted a meeting in Sacramento, and got him over to the office. I introduced Morrow to my boss, knowing how Ron likes to talk. Then I brought the two dicks down to the interview room, introduced them to Dean, said, 'They've got something they want to talk to you about,' and left the room.

"I was worried, but even I had misread Dean, because I thought the first thing he'd do is panic out and demand to see his attorney, which I knew would make the dicks suspicious. So I'm upstairs BSing with Morrow, and the whole time I'm watching the clock. Fifteen minutes pass, and I know Dean hasn't panicked. Finally I say to Morrow, 'Obviously you're aware that the LAPD people are interviewing Dean.' He immediately gets his back up: 'What interview?' I told him there had been another homicide and Dean's name was mentioned. He says, 'I want to see my client right now.' We go downstairs, knock, open the door, and Dean is sitting there talking to these guys, very calmly."

He was scared, Dean admitted, but not shocked. "I knew Joe would try something like this," he told the detectives.

The impeccable logic of the crime was the most compelling evidence that Hunt had committed it. Killing Karny would have accomplished very little, Breiling reminded the Hollywood detectives, since Dean's sworn statements and testimony from previous proceedings could then be entered as evidence at trial. Discrediting Dean, however, would serve Joe's purpose precisely.

"I felt a real revulsion when I recognized the obvious," Oscar recalled. "To kill a completely anonymous person just so you can use his body to incriminate a witness, I'd never dealt with anything like that before. Dean wasn't as horrified as John and I were, though. He said he was convinced that Joe was capable of *anything*. He basically said, 'I told you so.'"

Before the Hollywood murder, though, Dean had seemed to imagine he might yet return to the course he had abandoned back in 1980 for the BBC; early in 1986 Karny asked his attorney to set up a meeting with the SEC in Los Angeles, attended by Fred Wapner and John Vance, at which he sought a "reevaluation" of the federal government's suit to enjoin him from future stock and commodity sales. Dean had continued to visit his parents' home on Outpost Drive all through 1985 and into 1986, spending several days at a time in Los Angeles. "My father said he was always seeing this Honda with Oregon plates parked outside the Karnys' house, and he knew it was Dean's," Rich Swearinger recalled. "So he must not have been too terrified."

Alan Lieban remembered meeting Dean with Farhad Novian for a dinner at the Cheesecake Factory in Marina del Rey during April of 1986, four months after Karny had entered the California Witness Protection Program: "Dean was talking very openly about being under the program, admitting he was uncomfortable about looking over his shoulder. The one thing he did express, though, was how frustrated he felt about having trouble being admitted to the bar," recalled Lieban. "All he wanted was his life back."

The Mayer murder, though, would force Dean to recognize that it wasn't going to be that way. Oscar Breiling, convinced the state's witness program would never be enough to ensure Karny's safety, contacted the U.S. Department of Justice to seek Dean's admission to the Federal Witness Protection Program, where he would receive a "permanent replacement identity," a new Social Security number, and relocation to another part of the country, plus an escort of U.S. marshals each time he surfaced to testify in court.

In the meantime, Dean remained the primary suspect in the Hollywood murder: He provided Diaz and Rozzi with palm and fingerprints, then agreed to a search of his residence on what would have been Richard Mayer's twenty-first birthday, December 1, 1986. The DOJ agents who searched Dean's apartment had, at the request of Diaz and Rozzi, removed a Smith Corona typewriter, taken to match it against an unsigned letter the detectives' supervisor had received two weeks after the discovery of Mayer's body: "NOT A JOKE," shouted the caption above a text reading, "Mean Dean Karny is at it again."

The same day Dean's apartment was searched, Arthur Barens phoned the Beverly Hills Police Department to report that he, too, had received a letter—stenciled in this case—reading: "COVER UP AT HOLLYWOOD P.D. ABOUT DEAN KARNY AND HOMICIDE AT HOLLYWOOD LAND [SIC] MOTEL. HONEST COP'S FRIEND."

Steven Cowan was arrested two days later. "Diaz and Rozzi didn't tell me anything on the way to the police station, except that it was 'Joe Hunt–related,'" he recalled. "Then, when I got down there, they started to interrogate me. I figured my phone was tapped. Joe had told me the phones were tapped at the Roberts house and 'Don't be surprised if they tap the phones at the office.' It didn't really bother me because I think, 'This is Joe Hunt,' and that comes with it.

"What got to me, though, was when they threw a blue book on the table at the precinct, about six inches thick, and it was a whole history of me. It turned out they had had me under surveillance for months. And I never had a clue. I don't think Joe did, either. They had all these photographs they'd taken of me and of Joe. They told me, 'We know all about you, fella.' They knew I was gay, they knew about this automobile accident I had in Philadelphia, about when I moved to California, about the Judy Garland business. They said I was protecting Joe because he was my lover. They were really trying to intimidate me. There was this big two-way mirror on the wall with the rest of them—Zoeller and whoever else—right behind it, I knew. I went up to it and I was almost laughing because it seemed so bizarre. They started to soften, once they knew they weren't going to intimidate me. They wanted to know why Joe spent so much time at my apartment, and they listed all the places we went, and they told me, 'You guys have something going together, don't you? You can tell us.' They told me Mayer's name and asked if I knew what speedballs were. Then they asked about my car, if it was this make and color—a Datsun 310 GX, gold with black trim. They told me the license number and said I might have been seen in this car on such and such a date. Then they asked, 'Did you ever loan Joe your car?', and they saw the look on my face because I was going, 'Oh, my God,' and so I had to tell them because they caught it."

Joe *had* borrowed his Datsun, Cowan admitted, one night late last summer when Hunt said his BMW needed repairs. "He returned the car at like five in the morning," Steven remembered, "and left the key on my doorstep. I was pissed because he brought it back damaged; there was this dent in the side on the right rear panel. I told Joe about the dent, and at first he denied he had done it, then he apologized if he had and wanted to pay to get it fixed. He also had left a black flashlight under the seat of the car, but I didn't tell him that."

Cowan told Rozzi and Diaz about the flashlight, however, and about the dent and also about the contact lens case he found later. "They were all over me then," he recalled, "threatening, 'Do you realize you could be an accessory if you're withholding anything? We know you know something. You've got to tell us. You could be harboring a murderer; you have no idea what this guy has done.'

"And it was getting to me. All kinds of images were flashing in my mind, one of Joe sitting on my bed spilling out his heart and then another of some kid killed in a motel room. I remembered Joe telling me that there was going to be a surprise that was going to come up within the case. I was shaking. The detectives finally told me that they thought Joe had set this up to make it look like Dean had done it and that they were sure my car had been used. They even tried to bribe me: They said, 'We know you're in a really difficult situation right now. What would it take for you to talk?' I couldn't believe they were offering me money. They wanted Joe that much. I was in custody most of the day, but I got out by late afternoon because they had nothing real to hold me on.

"I called Joe, but he was still in court, so I left a message. He called me from Arthur Barens's office that evening and they said, 'Come over,' so I went over there for a meeting. I told them I had been taken in. They wanted to know everything, and they were very nervous about it. Joe was actually the calmest of the three. Barens said, 'We should sue the city for taking you in under false circumstances.' Chier was there, too, asking questions and raising eyebrows. The funny thing is, they all knew what Hollywood Homicide was up to and were all making jokes about it. Arthur said, 'I'm surprised it took them this long.' Bobby Roberts wanted to know the whole story, too, so they got him on the phone. Afterward, Barens made several phone calls to the city attorney, threatening to sue, but he seemed sort of halfhearted about it. And Joe just said, 'I told you there was a lot more to this.'"

25

THE BEGINNING OF THE END FOR THE REAGAN REVOLUTION ARRIVED ON November 4, 1986, when the Lebanese magazine *Al-Shiraa* reported that the United States secretly was selling armaments to Iran to raise funds for *contradora* "rebels" in Nicaragua. The outer layer of the president's protective coating flaked away overnight, and his approval rating in the polls plummeted by 20 percentage points in a month.

Suddenly, the news was not so good: The U.S. trade deficit for 1986 was almost $170 billion. Total debt in the United States had doubled to more than $7 trillion between 1980 and 1986. More than thirteen hundred S and Ls had allowed their capital reserves to fall below federal requirements.

Back in May, Wall Street had been shocked by the FBI's arrest of a young investment banker named Dennis Levine. "The biggest insider trading scandal in history," it was called in the press, but by November Levine's was not even the biggest insider trading scandal in the past six months. Desperate to save himself, the banker had rolled over on the self-styled artiste of arbitrage, Ivan Boesky, whose limited partnership listed $3 billion in assets. Charged by the SEC with pocketing $50 million in illegal profits through tips delivered by Levine, Boesky enlarged upon his junior associate's example, not only agreeing to testify against former associates but wearing hidden microphones to business meetings. In exchange for his "cooperation," the arbitrageur was permitted to retain most of his personal wealth while serving a three-year sentence at a minimum-security federal prison camp in California.

"The financial world gasped," according to *Fortune,* but Boesky's downfall was already less interesting than the speculation about who he might take with him. Among those served with subpoenas in connection to the case was the young maestro himself, Michael Milken, whose bond department at Drexel had raised a reported $640 million for Boesky's newest investment fund during 1986. Nearly everyone agreed Milken was too smart to involve himself in insider trading, but there was no telling what the feds might turn up once they got in the door at Drexel. "WHIZ KID OF

JUNK BONDS A FIGURE IN INSIDER PROBE" announced the headline on the front page of the *Los Angeles Times* on November 20, 1986. "MOOD AT DREXEL IS 'DISMAY' AS PROBE SHIFTS TO FIRM" read a headline in the same day's Business section.

Thorough though the *Times* had been in covering Michael Milken's predicament, it had come to the attention of many in the local media that the most powerful newspaper west of the Mississippi was refusing still to address the criminal charges involving another overachiever from out of the San Fernando Valley, young Joe Hunt, whose murder trial in Santa Monica had begun two weeks earlier, on the very day the *Al-Shiraa* article was published.

Ignoring Joe was becoming difficult, however. Boy Genius Gone Bad and Rich Kids Run Amok articles in *Time* and *Newsweek*, as well as requests by *60 Minutes* and *20/20* to bring cameras into Judge Rittenband's courtroom, tended to undermine the "We can't cover every local crime story" argument *Times* editors had offered to explain the absence of even a single article on the BBC during 1985 and 1986. Joe now was an official icon of the eighties, a "yuppie Charles Manson" in both *Time* and *Newsweek*.

The *New York Times* entered the arena on November 6 with a long article that described the BBC as "a group of well-educated and affluent young men, whose parents are among the most prominent in Los Angeles." At the *Los Angeles Times*, it became clear that a response to the incursion of the eastern elitists was required. L.A.'s *Times*, however, needed breaking news to cover its arrival in the courtroom at this late date, and the most dramatic development of the past two years provided a perfect opportunity. "NEW ALLEGATIONS SURFACE IN 'BILLIONAIRE' CLUB MURDER CASE," announced the headline on the *Times* December 7 story: "The name of Dean Karny, the prosecution's star witness," the *Times* reported, "has come up in connection to the murder of Richard Mayer, 21, whose decomposed body was found Oct. 18 stuffed in a trunk in a room at the Hollywood Center Motel." Both Arthur Barens and Ben Dosti's new attorney, Tom Nolan, were quoted suggesting the police might be concealing evidence that would discredit Karny. "Careful scrutiny is in order," Nolan said.

Barens and his client certainly hoped careful scrutiny of the *Times* article was in order among members of the jury about to be empaneled in Santa Monica. Judge Rittenband had indicated already that nothing connected to the Hollywood homicide would be admitted as evidence in his courtroom, leaving for the defense only the hope that Dean's testimony would be tainted by newspaper accounts of his "alleged involvement" in the Mayer murder.

Rittenband did more than indicate his loathing for Barens's cocounsel; the judge could not look at Richard Chier without curling his lip. Rittenband barely had commenced the proceedings when Chier rose to object that the television crews in the courtroom created "a pejorative impression" of the defendant. The judge's "overruled" was barely out of his mouth before Chier demanded hearings on the process by which potential jurors had been selected. Rittenband could barely contain his irritation. "Clearly improper," he snarled. "Denied."

Before Rittenband finished his ruling, Chier was standing again, this time to suggest that the trial should be in three parts: guilt, special circumstances, and penalty. "Keep quiet," Rittenband warned through clenched teeth.

The judge smiled only once, when Chier announced that he had attended high school with one of the potential jurors and "she doesn't like me."

The trial was nearly a month old and the jurors still were waiting outside when the judge agreed to conduct a "Livesay hearing." The evocative name belonged to the number three man in the DA's office, Curt Livesay, charged with making "special circumstances"—death penalty—determinations for the county's prosecutors. Was this the first "no-body murder case" involving an adult victim in which the L.A. County district attorney's office had requested the death penalty? Barens asked Livesay when he was summoned to the stand shortly after Thanksgiving. It was, answered Livesay, who explained that he relied on three primary factors in deciding whether to seek the execution of a killer: "one, the circumstance of the offense; two, the age of the defendant, and three, the background of the defendant."

Barens inquired about a case heard in Judge Rittenband's court that same morning, involving a twenty-five-year-old Chicano named Acosta who had beaten a man to death with a twenty-inch steel bar during the course of a robbery: Why hadn't the DA's office sought the death penalty in that case? Acosta had been in tears and appeared remorseful when he was arrested, Livesay answered. There was another murder trial in the court adjoining Judge Rittenband's that morning, Barens noted, involving a twenty-two-year-old black man named Anthony who had shot a grocer in the head during a robbery. He hadn't been convinced there was premeditation in that instance, Livesay explained. And while Anthony showed no remorse, "in Mr. Hunt's case there was a great deal more sophistication in the planning." Asked to define "sophisticated planning," Livesay answered: "Planning that is sophisticated is planning that almost succeeds." Wouldn't it seem logical that a more intelligent person would be more sophisticated about planning a crime? Barens asked. It would, Livesay answered. Then wasn't Joe Hunt in a sense being penalized for his intelligence? Barens suggested. In a sense, Livesay agreed, he was.

It was early December when jurors who had been waiting outside for five weeks were informed they would at last be admitted to Department C. Joe was posing for the cameras in the hallway when those who would judge him arrived at the courthouse the next morning. He promenaded arm in arm with Brooke through a media hail of clicks, whirs, hot lights, and blue flashes, then stepped into the courtroom just ahead of the jurors. Brooke waited outside, reading Sam Shepard's *Fool for Love*.

The 130-odd souls on the other side of the double doors were only now discovering what those who were selected would be in for. Curious already about the cameras in the courtroom, jurors began to cock eyebrows at one another as Judge Rittenband informed them, "The defense in this case will want to know, 'If you found that a murder had been committed during the course of a robbery, and in cold blood, would you automatically impose the death penalty?'" Chier objected, then objected again. Rittenband ignored him. After the attorney's third interruption, the judge spat, "Shut up!" "I believe I have a right to be heard in this courtroom," retorted Chier, still standing. As the jury sat rapt, Rittenband waved over his bailiff, lanky marathon runner Pat Quinn, and roared, "Put him down!"

Mr. Barens, Rittenband informed the jury then, was quite competent and would handle any addresses to the court from this point forward. Anointed a knight of the bar to Chier's overdressed troll, Barens was in high unction as he faced the first twelve prospects seated in the jury box on the morning of December 10. "Good morning, ladies and gentlemen," he greeted them. "We now have a little time to get to know each other." Joe's attorney was not subtle, however, about using the process of voir dire to outline his defense. "Do I need to bring someone in here to prove he's not dead?" Barens asked the entire panel, letting them know in the same breath that the prosecution would be unable to produce any physical evidence of Ron Levin's death. By the time Barens reminded the jurors that the FBI currently listed fifty-five thousand U.S. citizens as "missing," a retired fireman named Piker was prepared to say that, to win a conviction in a case built on circumstantial evidence, without a body, Fred Wapner "is gonna have to be a Houdini."

Consider what the term "circumstantial evidence" meant, Wapner suggested when it was his turn to ask questions. Dropping his pen just beyond the barrier that separated him from the panel, Wapner asked a juror in the first row if, even though she couldn't see the pen, she was sure it lay on the floor. Of course, the woman answered. "You have just reached a conclusion based on circumstantial evidence," Wapner told her.

The prosecutor was not so satisfied, however, when he ventured on to more apt examples: "Mother Jones bakes a cherry pie and leaves it on the kitchen table," he hypothesized. "She comes back and a slice is gone. She calls her son Johnny and he's covered with cherry pie." Wouldn't they agree that there was proof beyond a reasonable doubt that Johnny had eaten the missing slice of pie? Wapner asked. Not all the jurors were sure: "What if somebody threw it at him," Mr. Piker asked. Straining to keep his good humor, Wapner submitted an example even better suited to the case at hand: "There's a boat in the middle of the ocean with two men in it. One man goes to sleep, and when he wakes up the other is gone. The boat is big enough to have a dinghy, but that's still there. The boat finally gets to shore—say it lands in Hawaii—and the second man is never heard from for months or years." Could they reasonably conclude that the second man was dead? "He could be on land, in a city somewhere," one woman answered. "A helicopter could have taken him," added another. "People watch too much television," the prosecutor muttered to Les Zoeller. What about a man who fell out of an airplane without a parachute? Wapner asked another woman. Would she conclude that this man was dead, even if his body were never found? "I think the man on the boat has a better chance than the one who fell out of the airplane," she answered.

Despondent now, Wapner turned to his other big problem, the character of Dean Karny. The prosecutor broached the subject by pointing out that Ollie North had received immunity to testify before Congress about what was now the "Irangate scandal." Did any of the jurors object to immunity as a general principle if it helped people arrive at the truth? he asked, pleased at last when no one answered yes.

While Barens asked each of the jurors for the titles of the most recent books they had read and Wapner posed questions about men who fell out of airplanes, what Judge Rittenband wanted to know was how many of the twelve people in the jury box had been victims of a serious crime. The answers were at least as revealing as the latest Gallup poll: Mrs. Ewell's brother-in-law had been murdered in 1971, and the killer was never caught; Mr. Taub's ice-cream store had been robbed five times; Mrs. Shelby's purse had been snatched on the street; Mr. Cannady had had three cars stolen; Mrs. Hofer had been burglarized; Mr. Geratti had a hammer thrown at him in a hotel room; Mr. Walker's house had been broken into on New Year's Eve; and Mrs. Karkas said that not only had she lost her entire family in Nazi death camps forty years earlier but her furniture store in South-Central L.A.

had been robbed three times before it was burned to the ground during the Watts riots.

In the end, most jurors whose wit or imagination distinguished them were challenged by one side or the other, most often the prosecution's. A woman who edited the *Ayn Rand Newsletter* and who "ardently" supported the capitalist system was swiftly removed by Wapner, as was the young man who admitted he was homosexual. An English major from UCLA whose voir dire digressed into the "moral pragmatism theme" in *The Great Gatsby* was dismissed as well. And Mr. Piker, of course, was among the first to go. Mr. Taub, whose son was a pastor in the Reunification Church of the Reverend Moon and who believed "cults stink," was challenged by the defense, as was the woman who had served as foreperson on the jury that ruled in favor of Dodgers' announcer Vin Scully in his lawsuit against neighbor Sylvester Stallone over the *Rambo* star's additions to his Brentwood estate.

What they were left with, by early January, was a jury that gave neither side much cause for complaint. The conventional wisdom was most reassuring to the defense: Female jurors, according to the lore of the law, were less likely than men to convict in a capital case, and ten of Joe's twelve jurors were women, as were all four alternates. Wapner's compensation was that a majority of the jurors were Westside residents, both more well-off and better educated than he would have dared hope had the trial been held in downtown Los Angeles. "The brighter these people are, the more likely they'll see through Joe Hunt," he explained.

Finally, the "LONG-DELAYED TRIAL," as a *Los Angeles Times* headline had it, was scheduled to begin January 20. Jurors already on duty for two and a half months were sent home once again that morning, however, when Barens and Chier introduced a motion to have the charges against Joe Hunt dismissed. The grounds were that the Roberts estate had been subjected two weeks earlier to a surprise search conducted by a team of California Department of Justice agents accompanied by Les Zoeller and Detective Rozzi of the LAPD's Hollywood division.

"My way of answering back," explained Oscar Breiling who had organized the raid. "Even if I didn't have a chance in hell of finding anything, I was saying, 'I'm still on your ass, Joe. I wasn't scared off.' And then we got some good stuff."

Rittenband agreed a hearing would be necessary. Brooke Roberts testified first. She was asleep in her private guest-house room at 10 A.M. on the morning of January 8, 1987, when the search team arrived at the Bellagio address, Brooke began: "I was awakened by a banging on my bedroom door and a voice shouting, 'Police! Open the door or we'll break it down!' " Zoeller and Rozzi had ransacked her room for more than an hour, Brooke recalled, before Oscar Breiling appeared in the doorway and summoned them to the main house. She followed them to Joe's office, Brooke remembered, where she found Agent Breiling on his knees, sorting through the contents of two cardboard boxes filled with manila folders and a trash receptacle, from which he removed several sheets of discarded computer paper and legal pad pages. "Concerned," she climbed into Joe's unmade bed and took notes, Brooke explained, until Richard Chier's arrival.

The "good stuff" Breiling and his search team found on the second floor of the Bellagio house included the original of the rental agreement on the Beverly Glen house, dated July 30, 1984; four checkbooks bearing Hedayat Eslaminia's name and an address in Hillsborough, and a handwritten note that appeared to be a list of expenses for a project called "Sam"— "5,000, Supplies, setup"; "4,800, Lease"; "$6,000, Cash, trips, bail, Reza."

According to the defense, the evidence seized during the search also included nearly four hundred pages of "confidential communications" written by Joe Hunt for his attorneys, including sample cross-examination questions. "This trial has been tainted beyond repair," argued Barens. Joe himself took the stand at the January 29 hearing on the dismissal motion and "gave a foretaste of his style as a witness," reported the *L.A. Times,* now covering the trial's every development. "The lanky, self-confident Hunt contended that his fear of another search has had a 'chilling' effect on his ability to work with his lawyer to prepare for trial" the *Times* recounted. "Hunt delivered a rapid-fire discourse on case law, causing the surprised judge to smile." "You see what I mean about not needing any associate counsel," Rittenband told Barens, cutting a glance at Chier.

During a meeting in chambers one day earlier, Rittenband had informed Chier he was "abrasive" and would not be permitted to question witnesses because "he would antagonize and alienate the jurors." He could whisper to Barens and argue motions, but that was all, the judge reminded Chier in court, then ruled that the motion to dismiss was denied and that the trial would commence "irregardless" on the following Monday.

One more bolt of bad news rocked the Roberts compound over the weekend when the *Times* reported: "Hollywood police confirmed that the prosecution's star witness in both murder cases, former BBC member Dean Karny, has been eliminated as a suspect in the killing of 21-year-old Richard Mayer . . . police said that the state's attorney general's office has told them that Karny could not have been anywhere near the murder scene at the time."

It was standing room only in Department C on the morning of February 3, 1987. Six months after Jim Pittman's trial for the same crime had ended without attracting a single reporter, four rows of seats were occupied by "media representatives" assigned to report the opening statements at Joe Hunt's.

Joe's face was bright red, not in embarrassment but rather from the effects of a sunlamp burn suffered over the weekend. "Nonchalant," "composed," and "expressionless" various reporters described the defendant.

Fred Wapner's face was red as well. Clearly—vocally—uncomfortable with the media siege, convinced that the presence of so many reporters in court had put him in a position where the jury's verdict would affect his future almost as profoundly as it would Joe Hunt's, the prosecutor promptly registered his objection to the TV cameras by refusing to stand at the podium during his opening statement. "I am nervous enough as it is," Wapner explained. Possibly it did not help that his mother sat in the front row taping the prosecutor's two-hour speech for his father.

Absolutely essential to the prosecution case, Wapner told the jury, was that they understand the unique personality of Ron Levin. Levin was a creature of Beverly Hills, the prosecutor explained: "He liked hobnobbing with very rich and influential people. You will see pictures of him with Muhammad Ali and with Andy Warhol. Terre Tereba will tell you that at one time over a six-month period Mr. Levin was a constant companion of Bianca Jagger. He was the kind of person who liked to be surrounded by these kinds of people . . . and if Mr. Levin were alive anywhere in the world, he would contact these people. And, for sure, he would contact his mother."

No one who knew him even slightly could comprehend Levin leaving behind thirty-six thousand dollars in bank accounts that were untouched after June 6, 1984, Wapner said. Ron had been scheduled to leave Los Angeles for New York on the morning of June 7, the prosecutor allowed, and in fact a person registered at the Plaza Hotel as Ronald Levin had been arrested in the hotel lobby on June 10. "This is him," Wapner said, displaying a snapshot of Jim Pittman.

It was essential also that the jurors understand the BBC, Wapner said. The story began back in 1980 when Dean Karny and Joe Hunt, who had been classmates at the exclusive Harvard School, got reacquainted: "Joe Hunt talked to Dean Karny about his philosophy of life, how the system keeps good people from getting ahead. He talked about forming an organization where he would get the best and the brightest young men and put them all together and let them do what they were good at, what they could excel at. If you left them to flourish in this environment, and you got a whole bunch of people together, you could build a strong organization and take over the world, in essence." Joe and Dean recruited classmates and friends who included the May twins, Alex Gaon, and Cary Bren, Wapner explained, "people with *lots* of money."

Even with his color-coded charts, it was not easy for the prosecutor to avoid entanglement in a narrative so convoluted. By the time

Wapner got to the scam Ron Levin had run at Clayton Brokerage, several jurors were shaking their heads in bewilderment. Sensing he had lost them, Wapner cut to the climax: "Toward the end of April, 1984, most of the [BBC's] money was lost," he explained. "Joe Hunt then formulated a plan to kill Ron Levin." Joe not only explained this plan in detail to Dean Karny but wrote it out on seven yellow legal pad pages, Wapner told the jurors, then showed them the "AT LEVIN'S, TO DO" list. Less than three weeks after Levin's disappearance, Joe summoned most of the BBC to a meeting at the Wilshire Manning to announce that he and Jim had "knocked off" Ron Levin. Unfortunately for Joe, "a lot of people just weren't up for that kind of thing and realized they were in over their heads," said Wapner, who would adhere—with obvious discomfort—to the Mays' version of events. The twins had "decided they were going to tell their father, which they did," the prosecutor explained. "He said, 'You better have some proof.' They collected a copy of the contract and a copy of the $1.5 million check. They talked to a lawyer. The lawyer called the police." Then "one by one . . . people started coming forward. You will hear from a lot of these people that they didn't come forward right away because they were scared to death of Joe Hunt."

Barens began his opening statement after the noon recess: "At long last, ladies and gentlemen, I am going to tell you what this case is all about . . . the prosecution tells you about an adventure in murder. We're going to look at the evidence and see if we have an adventure in murder or an adventure in illusion."

Mr. Hunt certainly *was* unlike any other member of the BBC, Barens agreed with Wapner, but the contrast the jury should bear in mind was the one between Joe and Ron Levin. While Hunt and Levin were each "eccentric, exotic, different people," Barens allowed, jurors should understand "the differences in their differences." Ron Levin was "a pariah in society, a mako shark preying on everyone he met." Joe Hunt, on the other hand, had been "the high school nerd, dropped among a bunch of boys who are socio-economically greatly different than Joe, boys that the evidence will show ridiculed him, made fun of him in high school. The same boys who will be here testifying in this courtroom."

Even through his lamp burn, Joe's humiliation showed. His expression of indifference was restored, though, when Barens explained that by the time Joe returned to Los Angeles from Chicago in 1982, the ex–teenage geek was a "budding financial genius" and "driving power" who fascinated his former classmates, that "bunch of self-impressed, indolent young men, overindulged, having a future of hollow inheritance and passive experience" he formed into a cohesive organization.

The prosecution deliberately had avoided serious examination of either the alleged victim's character or his "pressing need to leave," Barens observed. In Ron Levin "what you have is a man who is going to con and create an illusion—*an illusion*—to make something look like something that it really isn't, with everyone that he encounters," Barens said. "A sociopath. A defrauder . . . a single man, a homosexual, a man with no ties, a man like the mythical Narcissus, who fell in love with her [*sic*] own reflection in a pool, loved only himself, cared only of himself, thought only of himself."

Levin had fled Los Angeles because he was scared, Barens explained: "He was facing a high probability of conviction for stealing over one million dollars in equipment from a photographic facility. Just plain stole it," Barens added, at once arch and aghast. "Well-known to police and to creditors, like a lion in the Serengeti that moves on after exhausting the prey in that area," Barens told the jury, "so too has Levin moved on to more fertile grounds."

His own client had one big problem, of course, Barens acknowledged, the seven pages: "You probably thought I didn't know about the seven pages. The seven pages that you were *told* are a recipe for homicide, a detailed alliteration [*sic*], writing by this genius: 'Things to do at Levin's.' I anticipate that during this trial we're gonna go through that seven pages, that list you saw this morning, word by word. I ask you to look at every word on those pages. Let's see if the things on that list were done . . . we'll see if it's a list for murder or if it was intended for another purpose."

There was as well the small matter of a June 24 meeting, Barens conceded, "this incredible meeting in which, supposedly, this boy genius tells the members of the BBC 'we'—me and Pittman—knocked off or took care or *something* Levin. Now I put it to you like that because the evidence will show that no one's quite sure what he said. So we'll ask the guy who said it what he said. And we'll ask him what he meant."

What the jurors hadn't heard, Barens told them, was that it had been Dean Karny, the state's star witness, who called that June 24 meeting, suggesting to Joe Hunt that "the BBC was falling apart right beneath their feet and that they needed some drama to galvanize them back together and get things moving again. Well, they all knew by that time, three weeks later, that none of them had seen old Levin, 'So we're gonna take credit for it.' The evidence is gonna show that they falsely took credit for his disappearance, in an attempt to—in some crazed macho way—get these boys back into action. The key to all that business is going to be: What did the people act like that heard this story? Does anybody act like they believe it?

"And who's Karny?" Barens asked. "A well-rehearsed, professional witness. A witness who's here pursuant to an immunity grant." The jurors should know, Barens went on, that prosecutors had "let Dean Karny go from a murder he admits he committed in the Bay Area"—raised eyebrows from Rittenband and an audible gasp from Wapner, each astonished that Hunt's attorney would open the door on the Eslaminia abduction—and that he had agreed to testify against Joe Hunt in the Levin case only after making a deal up north.

"What you will hear [from Dean] are the desperate words of a desperately troubled young man," Barens forewarned the jury. "Perhaps Oscar Wilde, in "The Ballad of Reading Gaol," told us what's going on with Karny when he said that each man kills the thing he loves."

Did they want an alibi? Barens asked, then nodded: "While not one prosecution witness saw Joe the night he's allegedly over killing Ron Levin, the defense will bring forth witnesses that will verify for you where Joe Hunt was the night in question and what he was doing." Wapner's head jerked, but he caught himself in an instant. "Joe Hunt's not gonna hide from you," Barens assured the jurors. "He's not gonna try to disappear. He's gonna answer all the questions."

Joe would explain to them how his words had been twisted, Barens promised. Take Paradox Philosophy, for example. "Catchy phrase, novel," the attorney allowed. "But nobody seems to know what it means. Yet we're told that Hunt leads all these boys around by the nose through the use of a philosophy that nobody understands." Those who claimed the essence of Paradox was "the ends justify the means" were distorting a philosophy that had its origins in transcendental existentialism, "an entirely moral system of belief," Barens noted.

"So what do we end up with?" Barens began his summation. "Nobody saw this alleged murder. There were no bloodstains, no evidence of a struggle or harm done to anyone. What we're left with is speculation." Then the bombshell: "The defense will bring in two witnesses who will say they saw Ron Levin alive *since this trial began*."

"The evidence will show there is neither sufficient proof that Levin is dead nor that Joe Hunt killed him," Barens ended: "Not proven, not guilty."

Heavy-set, handsome, bewigged, and a bit sullen, Blanche Sturkey came across as a proud woman and not at all timid, letting it be known immediately that she resented being described as the missing man's "maid." She was Ron Levin's "girl Friday," Blanche corrected. Wapner, happy to call the lady Ruby Tuesday if she liked, took Blanche back to the afternoon of June 6, 1984. Ron—"wearing a white terry robe, that's all"—had been on the phone when she walked out of the Peck Drive apartment at 4 P.M., Blanche recalled. "He was on the phone most of the time when he wasn't eating," she explained. Ron asked her to be at his door by seven the next morning, Blanche remembered, and she got there five minutes ahead of schedule. Michael Broder and Dean Factor were waiting outside, "worried that Ron was not there and the dog was acting peculiar." The missing comforter alarmed her, Blanche said, but it was the failure of her employer to phone her at home that evening that convinced her something must have happened to him. "Ron would call me whenever he left town," she explained, "as soon as he got into his hotel." Much as he loved to travel, Ron couldn't bear being out of Beverly Hills for any length of time, Blanche added, and "he would never give up that apartment."

Dean Factor told the jury about tooling over to Muhammad Ali's house for lunch one day, about finding Bianca Jagger asleep on Ron's living room couch another, and about a man who stuck a gun in Ron's face only to be "conned out of killing him."

Terre Tereba was defensive about her relationship with an "admitted thief." "Well," she explained, "we've had an impeached president, and I'm sure Ivan Boesky still has friends."

Ron was revealed most poignantly in James Foulk's recollection of a phone conversation he overheard between Levin and "his kids' mother." Barens took a chance on cross-examination, offering Foulk a police photograph of the bedroom as Blanche had found it on the morning of June 7. Joe's attorney asked the young man if he could see anything that was "different about the room" from what he had seen on the evening of June 6. Other than that the bed was made and the clothes were put away, no, Foulk answered. Barens asked again, then a third time, then a fourth, his anticipation mounting as he displayed to the jury the floral print spread in the foreground of the picture. Unable to quit while he was ahead, though, Barens asked the question a fifth time. Foulk finally took a closer look. "I don't think it was that comforter," he said.

Len Marmor took the stand carrying the current issue of *Golf* magazine, described himself as "Ron's best friend," and backed this up by telling the jury how Ron had given him two thousand dollars in traveler's checks on the morning of June 6. "I don't know anybody else he ever paid," Len explained, scowling at the jurors when they chuckled. Marmor was better even than Blanche, however, at convincing jurors "Ron had no fear" of returning to jail.

Scott Furstman, Levin's criminal attorney, explained that his client faced serious criminal charges in 1984 that could have sent him to the penitentiary for as long as four years but agreed with Wapner that Ron might have put prison off until at least the spring of 1985. On cross-examination, Barens went straight at Ron's June 4 request for a bail reduction. Wasn't it true, he asked, that Ron's bail had been secured with property belonging to Martin and Carol Levin, who would have been out $67,500 if their son had skipped town? It was, Furstman agreed.

Michael Broder was another prosecution witness who seemed to serve the defense case better, recalling that in May of 1984, "Ron once joked that if his trial didn't go well, he was going to medical school in the Caribbean."

Carol Levin suggested a 1950s movie star emerging from retirement as she took the stand, wearing a beige silk suit over a leopard-skin blouse, her upswept hair tinted the color of rare coral and her heart-shaped face like a mother-of-pearl mask that sagged slightly at the corners. The rose-tinted sunglasses Mrs. Levin wore indoors on a dark and drizzly day were the signature of her appearance in Department C. Protecting Ron's mother from sordid details had become her family's ethos. "My mother is a very delicate person," Bob Levin explained.

Mrs. Levin's voice shook as she gave her full name, swore to tell the truth, and introduced herself as Ronald Levin's mother, yet her affect seemed strangely flattened, as if palliated to a Valium trance. Wapner had committed himself to convincing the jury that Ron Levin's failure to contact this woman even once in the past two and a half years was the most compelling evidence the state could offer that the missing man was dead, and the prosecutor proceeded gingerly, almost timidly, with his questioning. Despite her hebetude, however, no witness would prove more effective in presenting Ron as a sympathetic character. Describing the death of her firstborn's father and the ordeal that public education had been for the hyperactive boy, his mother laid a foundation for those who described Ron as a liar they loved and a thief they adored. Her son's attachment to her had been that of a small child even when he was past forty, Carol said; they saw each other two or three times every week and spoke at least that often on the phone. Ron never once in his life had left Los Angeles without calling her upon arriving at his destination, Mrs. Levin said. Wapner brought out the Mother's Day cards Ron had sent Carol over the years and Polaroids of the bouquets that accompanied them. She read the jurors her favorite inscription, on the card Ron had sent in 1971: "Doubt that the stars are fire / Doubt that the sun does move / Doubt that truth be a liar / But never doubt I love you."

During the break between direct and cross-examination, Mrs. Levin stared through her tinted glasses straight at Joe, who returned her gaze with a blank expression, then went back to his note-taking.

If Barens's tone was gentle, deferential—even apologetic—his questions were brutally direct. What had Ron told her when he was arrested for mail fraud back in 1979? the attorney asked. "He told me everything was all right, that he would never go to jail, and I was surprised when he did," Carol answered. She couldn't remember what the charge against Ronnie had been, Mrs. Levin said: "I was so upset." And Ron's second arrest, in 1983? Blanche had told her about it, at Ronnie's instruction, Mrs. Levin explained: "I called my husband—I rely on my husband for everything—and he posted the bail."

Marty Levin had been blacking out the most gruesome details in newspaper and magazine articles he allowed his wife to read. "But then she sees them on television or hears them on the radio," he explained. "When she hears how he whimpered for his life, it's devastating for her. She's constantly looking at pictures, going over all his good qualities."

The Levins only recently had consecrated Ron's passing by posting a memorial plaque at the Temple Isaiah, asking that those who wished to make donations in Ron's name—and there were a surprising number—send checks to the Trees for Israel fund. Still, how could his wife help but have her hopes raised by the defense assertion that a Robert Levy recently taken into custody in Kentucky might in fact be Ronald Levin? Marty asked: "She knows he's dead, but she doesn't want to believe it. What mother would?"

Carol's condition worsened with each day of Joe Hunt's trial: "There isn't a night that goes by that my wife doesn't turn to me and say, 'Do you think Ronnie suffered too much before they killed him? Do you think he was dead when they buried him?' Every night, the same questions."

Every insinuation of the defense Ron's mother took personally; Barens's suggestion that Ron had plagiarized a Hallmark poet for the inscription on the Mother's Day card she read in court wounded her especially. "One of the most terrible things anyone has ever said to me," sobbed Mrs. Levin, unaware—as was Barens—that Ron's lines were cribbed not from Hallmark but from Shakespeare. Carol was upset even by the "unflattering" photograph of her son that Fred Wapner was using in court, reproduced in the newspapers and on television. His mother kept showing people what Ronnie looked like without a beard: "As handsome as any fellow you've seen."

Her husband, a man so plumb plain that he might have introduced himself more convincingly as Carol's chauffeur than as her husband, still was handling the settlement of his adopted son's "complex finances." After Marty advertised for creditors, the number of people who claimed Ron owed them money had been "unbelievable," said Marty, who felt "a lot of them were con artists themselves."

All the Levins were outraged by the deportment of the Roberts clan in court. Todd, they agreed, had been particularly aggressive, "glaring daggers at us," Marty recalled. "Like *we* had done something to *him*." Brooke was the one they couldn't bear, though. Marty recalled how, at the first day of the trial, he had asked Joe's girlfriend to slide over so that he and his wife might sit together in the center section: "She wouldn't budge. She just glared at us like 'Who are you to me?'" Marty felt certain Brooke had been involved in Ron's murder: "We think the Robertses are helping Joe to protect Brooke and also because Bobby has a piece of the movie deal."

Though discreet, Brooke's parents were a decided presence in Department C. Lynne, the best-dressed spectator in court, her hair magnificently frosted and her narrow face pulled tight at the temples, conducted herself with some dignity, taking a seat in the back row, where she slipped on a pair of round-rimmed spectacles and made copious notes on the testimony of one prosecution witness after another. Bobby was not so prepossessing, small and slightly bucktoothed, at once conservative and casual in the seersucker and khaki suits he wore *sans* socks with Top-Sider boat shoes.

The Roberts entourage included one new principal, Rudy Durand, a figure of some notoriety in show-business circles. A few years earlier, Durand had pulled off one of the great coups in Hollywood history when he was allowed to write, direct, and produce his first feature film, *Tilt*. The story of a teenage girl turned pinball wizard had come to the attention of studio executives when Orson Welles opined on the Merv Griffin show that *Tilt* was the best screenplay he had seen in years. Among the many absurdities that ensued was the fact that, while the great director was unable to obtain financing for his own projects, Welles's endorsement of Durand had set off a bidding war for the rights to the *Tilt* script.

A tiny man who managed to speak rapidly with a Texas accent, Durand was an individual of diverse accomplishments—a scratch golfer, for example, who recently had become the Riviera Country Club partner of Columbia Pictures President Guy MacIlwaine. Rudy needed friends in high places at this juncture in his career, having suffered a singular calamity in the aftermath of *Tilt*'s abortive theatrical release. Convinced that "chickenshit distribution" by Warner Brothers had killed his movie, Durand responded by filing a lawsuit that would consume the next five years of his life. He became slightly obsessed, admitted Rudy, who had pressed his claim all the way to the Ninth Circuit Court. In the end, opposed not only by Warner Brothers but by the superpower law firm of Loeb and Loeb as well, Durand lost his court case *and* his house in Beverly Hills, reduced at one point to sleeping in the backseat of his baby blue Mercedes convertible.

After a year spent reading and meditating in his native Houston, Rudy returned to Los Angeles in 1986 to "reenter the arena." MacIlwaine, the much-married ex-ICM agent said to have inspired the apocryphal "If my wife calls, get her name" story, had become by the autumn of 1986 not only Durand's golfing partner but his closest friend as well. "Guy calls Rudy up six or seven times a day," said Durand's twenty-one-year-old live-in assistant Pam Dickerson. "You get the feeling all those meetings make him lonely." The Columbia chief at his side, Rudy began to mix socially with that coterie of studio chiefs, impresarios, and superagents headed by MacIlwaine and Twentieth Century–Fox president Alan Ladd Jr. A self-styled "street guy," Durand regaled the moguls with tales of backstage liaisons and hand-to-hand combat not always received in the spirit they were offered. The best example of what could be lost in translation was Rudy's introduction at a private screening to the most powerful producer in the business, Ray Stark. After a series of flattering questions, Durand suddenly announced to Stark, "I may not have the money or the power or the standing you other guys have, but I'll tell you what: If everybody in this room was stripped naked, dropped without a dime in the middle of Harlem, and told that one hundred million dollars was waiting for the first one who made it back to L.A., I'd beat the rest of you by three days." Stark, momentarily stunned, considered this for a moment, then smiled: "What a marvelous idea for a movie," he said.

What Rudy needed at the moment, though, were not ideas but "properties." It was to this end that Durand entered the chase to bring the BBC saga to the big screen. Durand's first objective had been the *Esquire* article described by the *L.A. Times* as "the hottest property in town." Unable to make a deal, however, Durand recovered from his disappointment by arranging an introduction to Bobby Roberts, who only a few days later brought Rudy home to Bel Air for a meeting with Joe Hunt.

To Joe, Durand sold himself as a survivor of these same slings and arrows, repudiated by allies, betrayed by friends. "There's nothin' you need that can be taken from you," Rudy advised.

By the time the Hunt trial began, Durand was not only Hunt's personal advisor but Bobby Roberts's business partner as well. The two had signed their first deal during jury selection, when Durand, the designated "packager," helped negotiate a contract under which Roberts and David Semas would make "negative pickup" on the partially filmed *Return of Billy Jack,* hoping to revive the popular character—written and performed by Tom Laughlin—who had been a sort of Rambo with a peace sign, circa 1970. Joe Hunt was among those included when Laughlin screened his rough footage for Roberts and Durand. He and Bobby thought the film was terrific, Rudy said, but Joe felt it was far too violent, lowering his head and covering his eyes during the goriest scenes.

"When you're around the kid," Rudy explained, "you realize he's nothing like what's been portrayed. He's a gentle guy, maybe too sensitive for his own good." Guilty, innocent—he couldn't say, Rudy added, "but I do know it will be a tragedy if the world never gets a chance to use the talents of Joe Hunt. Say what you want, but the guy is brilliant." And if Hunt was acquitted, Rudy added, no BBC movie could be made without him.

It was Bobby Roberts's public position that he had no interest in the film sale of Joe's story, but Roberts's attorney had mailed a rough-draft contract naming Bobby as a "co-producer" of a film about the BBC to a producer at Paramount. And Roberts personally had arranged for the meeting between Joe Hunt and his agents, Burton Moss and Sy Marsh (the father of Evan Dicker's old friend Seth Marsh).

"Have we reached the point where Joe Hunt needs an agent?" Judge Rittenband asked a reporter when he heard about it. The judge's conduct was by then consuming almost as much media coverage as the defendant's. All three metropolitan dailies ran profiles of Rittenband during the trial. The least flattering appeared in the *Times,* under the headline "CRUSTY JUDGE RULES HIS COURT WITH IRON HAND."

What the newspapers loved almost as much as the Irascible Judge was the Absentee Corpse angle: "WHEN VICTIM IS A 'NO BODY'" read the headline produced by the *Herald'*s clever copy writers. Articles in both the *Times* and *Herald* discussed at length the precedent-setting case of *People v. L. Ewing Scott,* the Los Angeles man who thirty years earlier had become the first U.S. citizen convicted of killing a person whose body the prosecution could not produce. The victim in that instance was Scott's wealthy wife, who disappeared from their Bel Air home without leaving any trace of struggle or bloodshed. The Scott trial would make a legend of Assistant District Attorney J. Miller Leavy, who based his case entirely on circumstantial evidence. The oft-cited "climax" of the trial was a bit of dramaturgy repeated so often in law school classes and *Perry Mason* episodes over the years that it became a kind of official apocrypha: Reminding the jurors for the umpteenth time that the absence of a body was grounds for reasonable doubt, the story went, the defense attorney had suggested that Evelyn Scott "might walk through this courtroom door at any minute." "Ah-ha," he added a moment later when jurors turned toward the doorway. "That shows you are not convinced beyond a reasonable doubt that she is dead." To this Leavy reportedly replied, "Every head in this courtroom turned toward that door just now except one—that of the defendant. And he didn't bother to look because he *knows* she's not going to walk through that door." "Never happened," Leavy said thirty years later. What he *had* used to convict L. Ewing Scott was "the suddenly interrupted life pattern" of the missing wife, the old prosecutor recalled, "re-creating the victim in the jury's mind," a tactic that now was standard procedure in such cases.

The same strategy had been used successfully by a second L.A. County prosecutor, Stephen Kay, in the late 1960s, when he won a conviction against Charles Manson's Dean Karny, Bruce Davis, for the murder of ranch hand Shorty Shea, establishing that the two things Shea did every year—send his mother a telegram at Christmas, then a box of candy for Mother's Day—had stopped at the same time he disappeared from the San Fernando Valley's Spahn ranch.

As the *Times* noted, however, in both of those cases the evidence was "more clear-cut" than in the trial of Joe Hunt: Unlike Evelyn Scott and Shorty Shea, Ron Levin had obvious motives for engineering his own disappearance; and Barens's contention that he could produce a pair of credible witnesses who would say they had seen Levin alive in the autumn of 1986 tipped the balance even more in Joe's favor. Of course, in those earlier cases, the killers had not made public proclamations of a perfect crime, nor had they left lists of "suspicious-sounding notations" at the scene of the crime, the *Times* noted. "But defense attorney Arthur Barens, who calls his client 'brilliant, a genius,' said Hunt '*must* testify' and will explain," the *Times*'s story added.

It was the constant complaint of Hunt's attorneys that Joe had been convicted in the media. Headlines on articles published just before the start of the trial inevitably exploited the youth–greed combination so emblematic of the eighties, from *Time* magazine's "BAD BOYS" to the Santa Monica *Evening Outlook*'s "BOYISH GURU TAKES EASY STREET TO MURDER TRIAL." Even at the Mercantile Exchange in Chicago, the accusations in California against Joe eclipsed Eurodollar fluctuations as a topic of after-hours conversation. "I can't recall any kind of exchange matter that now takes on such a large importance," said Tom Utrata, still the Merc's VP for operations. "There has been a general recognition that what happened on the West Coast, the seeds were sown here," Utrata added, and not without a certain pride.

Those young men who once had been BBC members found their fears of stigma were largely unfounded. In fact, the reflected glow of Joe's fame was a light in which many now chose to bask. "The disbelievers, before the articles came out, were always scoffing at my stories, saying, 'Yeah, sure—you?'" Alan Lieban said. "But then when they read what went on and found out I really was involved, they thought that was pretty hip, and all of a sudden it was like 'Hey, you were a part of *that*?'"

***

Ron himself might have appreciated best the conundrum of the prosecution's case: The most compelling proof of Levin's death, Wapner would argue, was the evidence that Hunt killed him.

Barens had warned the jury in his opening statement, "The prosecution will attempt to anesthetize you with data," and for the last two weeks of February Wapner seemed determined to do just that, summoning to the stand a parade of bankers, salesmen, and phone company officials whose testimony was intended to prove that Ron had "gone about business as usual" during the days immediately preceding his disappearance. What the facts and figures added up to, though, depended upon who did the math: There was as much reason to read Ron's behavior as the activity of a felon about to flee as that of a scam artist playing the oblique angles against the acute. The testimony of an American Express security officer that Ron had run up more than twenty-three thousand dollars in charges—mostly for clothing purchased in Beverly Hills—during the first six days of June 1984 seemed to support the defense case better than the prosecution's.

The transition of the *People*'s case from pro-Ron to anti-Joe was where Wapner turned the corner. This commenced in earnest with the production of Jim Pittman as a prosecution exhibit prior to testimony from the Plaza Hotel staff. That was the man he had met in stairway seven and pursued into the hotel lobby on the evening of June 10, Joe Vega assured the jury.

Explaining Jim's Manhattan excursion, however, was not nearly the problem for the defense that the next prosecution exhibit posed. This was the seven pages of lists and notes Marty Levin found in the Peck Drive duplex more than a month after Ron's disappearance. The little haberdasher was wearing a cheap brown jacket with a pair of tan slacks as he took the stand. Bald and bespectacled, with short legs and big feet, Marty's homeliness lent him inimical credibility in an atmosphere overheated by the bright lights and inane interrogations of the TV crews. Referring to the missing man simply as "my son," Marty explained that he had secured the Peck apartment by June 18, when he had the locks replaced, then spent the next several weeks sorting through Ron's papers and making phone calls to his friends. When he found an original of the seven-million-dollar Microgenesis contract, signed by Ron and Joe Hunt, on the desk in the small office, "it was absurd to me," Marty recalled. "I knew Ron didn't have that kind of money."

It was maybe two weeks later, Marty recalled, one afternoon when he was straightening up in the small office, that he spotted the sheets of yellow paper on the floor, folded in half and standing on edge, trapped between the wastebasket and the wall, almost as if they had been slipped into the one cranny where they would not be seen yet were likely to be found. He laid them on Ron's desk and forgot all about them, Marty explained, until the afternoon when Les Zoeller arrived at the Peck Drive duplex to search the premises. The detective mentioned several possible suspects "and asked if I found anything with their names on it," Marty remembered. "Joe Hunt was one of the names. I said I had found a folder with a contract in it [bearing Joe's signature]. I went into the smaller office to get the folder, and while I was there I recalled that I had seen Joe Hunt's name on one of the sheets of yellow paper . . . I said, 'I have a sheet of paper I'd like you to look at.' I showed Zoeller the 'AT LEVIN'S, TO DO' paper," Marty recalled. "He seemed glad to get it."

The chuckling jurors seemed the chorus of doom, yet Mr. Levin's testimony had moved an astonishing number of "court watchers" in Department C to conclude that Joe Hunt was the victim of a fantastic frame-up. The only issue the pro-Hunt spectators debated was who had planted the seven pages in the apartment. Dean Karny was the leading vote-getter, followed by the May twins and Ron Levin himself.

Having presented the seven pages to the jury, Wapner brought on the BBC to profile the author. Jeff Raymond led the parade of Boys to the stand. Fatter but better formed, still splendidly tanned, though now a muddier shade of blond, Jeff had been working for an Orange County company that manufactured steel wire, was about to marry Renee Martin, and had applied to a graduate business school in San Francisco. He stared at Joe with a flat expression, then identified Hunt as someone "I knew in business and socially." By the time Raymond's chronicle of events had climaxed with Hunt's description of the Levin murder as "a perfect crime," the jurors were no longer watching the witness but instead studying the defendant.

Even Barens was not received so cordially as before when he rose to conduct cross-examination. It had been obvious since the opening statements that the defense attorney could count on the warm regard of at least one juror, the lone black panelist, Gloria Shelby, who greeted Barens with an appreciative gaze each time he stood to speak, clearly preferring his worldly charms to the priggish sanctimony of the mama's boy, Wapner. It was as much to Mrs. Shelby as to Jeff Raymond that Barens addressed a series of questions about whether the witness even once had seen Joe Hunt "hit," "beat," or "threaten" a BBC member. No, Jeff admitted. "Did you ever see him shoot anybody?" Rittenband cut in sarcastically. Joe's attorney got Raymond to agree that Ron Levin was a "cunning falsifier" who "led Joe Hunt down the garden path" and welcomed Jeff's assertion that Paradox

Philosophy "had no reality." "Everything's Disneyland," Barens agreed. The attorney riled the witness only once, when he asked if pretending to like and admire someone he actually loathed and distrusted had been hypocrisy. Jeff was indignant: "I think of it as normal social behavior," he said.

If Raymond's testimony was damaging, Evan Dicker's would be devastating. "The scene at Joe's trial was a big shock," Evan said. "The mob of cameramen and reporters and sound people, and some blonde with a motor drive going, 'There he is, get him!' And then inside, the place is filled. I mean, I'd been to Jim's trial and to the prelims, and it was not that big a deal. When I got to court in Santa Monica, I had to wait for two days to go on. They let me wait in the DA's office, fortunately, where I sat in the law library and read books. I wasn't expecting to be called that morning, though, so I was taken by surprise. And then those goddamn cameras—you know your face is going to be on the news that night. Even worse than the cameras were the people sticking their heads against the windows in the doors, trying to see in. It hit me then that I was never going to put the BBC behind me, not really, and that shook me."

Evan had lost more of his hair and was half-bald at twenty-five, though slimmer than in high school. He had grown a full beard, which was about all that gave shape to his soft pale face. If his gray eyes were frightened and furtive, though, Evan's deep voice was clear and strong. He made no attempt to stare the defendant down and spoke of him with abiding regard, even while slipping the blade under Joe's ribs. No, he did not think of Paradox as "a bunch of bull," Evan said: "I don't know if I understood it or not," he explained. "All I know is that at the time I began to feel less obligated to follow rules. I was doing more what seemed acceptable under the circumstances."

Dicker's description of the June 24 meeting differed from Raymond's in several respects: Joe made no threats during his prologue and had used the phrase "knocked off" rather than "took care of." Evan told the jury of Joe's plan to pin Levin's murder on Jeff Raymond by killing his girlfriend, then added that Joe had discussed killing the Mays at a meeting a few evenings later.

Barens used Evan mainly to lampoon the BBC. Leading Dicker through the Black Book's structural chart, the attorney mocked his own client's creation at every opportunity. "Joe didn't introduce himself as a friend of the thorax [sic], did he?" Barens asked, but only Mrs. Shelby seemed amused. The attorney was delighted when Evan likened Joe's announcement at the June 24 meeting to "an eagle returning to the nest with food." "Absolutely," Barens enthused. On the other hand, Evan added, "I thought,

'Why bother committing the perfect crime if you can't tell your friends.'"
Barens asked the witness to agree that Joe had been "boasting." "He certainly didn't seem to be ashamed," Evan allowed.

Of all the BBC Boys to take the stand, the most insufferable was
Tom May. Dave's twin admitted he was advised by Joe of the murder at
least a week before the June 24 meeting but explained, "I thought it was a
lie at first." "Joe had told us stories the whole time I knew him," Tom added,
as Barens nodded approval. Tom apparently forgot—and Wapner willingly
ignored—Dean Karny's recollection that the twin had asked the Shadings
to conceal his prior knowledge of the Levin murder at the June 24 meeting. It was one week after the June 24 meeting, Tom said, when he told
Dave that Joe had confessed to murder and at once set about "gathering
papers at the office" for the police. How it was that another five weeks passed
before he and his brother actually spoke to anyone at the Beverly Hills Police
Department, Tom not only didn't say but wasn't asked.

Barens nevertheless seemed pleased by Tom's appearance in court;
the twin was the prototype of that "self-impressed, indolent, overindulged
young man" he had described in his opening statement. Joe, however, began
to wear an odd expression—martyred irony might be the best description—
as it dawned on him during Tom's testimony that the jury cared little
whether the Boys lied about themselves, as long as they told the truth about
Hunt. Even more galling, there was no way to retaliate, short of admitting
his own crimes in order to prove their complicity. Joe shook his head—more
in rue than in disagreement, it seemed—as Tom told the jury of their hunting trip in Soledad Canyon and how Hunt had boasted "he could hide anything up there and no one would ever find it." Joe channeled his fury into
note-taking, flipping the pages of his yellow legal pad so loudly that Wapner
paused in the middle of a question to stare at him, scoring a point without
saying a word.

The prosecutor elected to save the four other BBC members he
intended to call as witnesses—Lopez, Taglianetti, Eisenberg, and, of course,
Karny—for later, interrupting the parade of Boys to bring on the Clayton
broker, Jack Friedman. A witty fellow who spoke in the staccato of Chicago's
South Side, Friedman was the most entertaining witness the jurors would
hear, regaling them with an abashed but hilarious description of his passage from Dr. William Rader of KABC to Ronald George Levin of Network News. There were titters as Friedman recalled Ron's explanation that
Network News had chosen Clayton because "we don't want to get sued for
discriminating against smaller firms," then howls of laughter when he remembered how concerned Ron had been about "the integrity of the story."
What seemed to interest the jury most, though, was Friedman's recollec-

tion that Joe Hunt "didn't react emotionally" upon learning that the Clayton account wasn't real.

"Aggressive and arrogant" was how Steve Weiss described Joe's attitude at the September 1984 meeting with the investors in Beverly Hills. Joe had promised him a return of 18 percent per month on his investment, recalled Weiss, who estimated his loss at fifty thousand dollars. The computations of their "ombudsman," though, were suspect in the minds of other investors in court, who noted that Weiss included not only his "reinvested 'profits'" but also money from the "special trust account." The jurors giggled behind their hands when Weiss described the trust account as "an opportunity to express behaviorally how I felt about money," and the entire courtroom erupted into laughter at Weiss's explanation of his willingness to meet Joe Hunt for the first time on the sidewalk in Beverly Hills: "I feel that lots of things happen in Los Angeles that might not happen in other cities."

Al Gore, offered by the prosecution as "a more typical investor," had attended the trial since opening statements. Arriving each morning in time to take an aisle seat, Gore issued an embittered but occasionally keen commentary on the testimony, referring to Joe most often as "the Gamsk," though occasionally appending such specifications as "that no-good bastard," as in "The Gamsk, that no-good bastard, had the nerve to tell me this morning, 'I hope you saved your promissory note, because I intend to pay my investors every penny I owe them.'" Husky, hard-faced, with gray skin and sunken eyes, Gore was a surprisingly effective witness on the stand, reporting that the thirty-three thousand dollars he had lost represented "my life's savings" in a tone of finality that hushed the courtroom.

The testimony of Joe's limited partners set up appearances by a series of stockbrokers from Shearson Lehman and E. F. Hutton, who explained to the jury that Joe had invested only about half of the more than two million dollars he took in from investors at Financial Futures and IMF, and lost all of that in overmargined accounts. Lore Leis confirmed these figures, then hurt Joe badly with her recollection of the three letters to Ron Levin he had dictated in May of 1984. At the same time, however, Joe's former secretary made it clear she bore him no ill will and actually regarded Mr. Hunt as the best boss she ever worked for. Lore disputed Steve Weiss's testimony that Joe had blamed the investors for the loss of their money at the September 1984 meeting and scoffed at Tom May's contention he had risked his life by breaking into the file cabinets at the Third Street office.

The second block of BBC Boys was led to the stand by Steve Taglianetti, who had come to court accompanied by the venerable Beverly Hills attorney Paul Caruso. Waiting outside in the hallway, Taglianetti seemed most interested in the terms of the Mays' movie deal. Sensing he might yet profit from his BBC membership, Tag let it be known that he would be pleased to grant interviews for a fee of ten thousand dollars per and seemed sincerely surprised when there were no takers. Now employed as a controller at Cannon Films, Taglianetti had been called by the prosecution to describe the activities of his friend Jim Pittman. Tag had his own agenda, however, which was to obfuscate—even falsify—the terms and timing of his departure from the BBC. It was Taglianetti's preposterous story that he had abandoned the BBC immediately after the meeting at the Manning, sleeping that night in an apartment where he placed three loaded pistols between the bedroom and the front door. He phoned his father the next morning "to tell him what had happened," Tag said, then contacted the Mays that afternoon to "set up a meeting." Even Tom hadn't been so brazen, but his old "Maytag" debate team partner wasn't finished: He typed a letter of resignation from the BBC that day and sent it by registered mail, Taglianetti said.

His testimony naturally made it difficult for Steve to explain what he had been doing at Del Rey Honda with Joe and the rest of the BBC when they picked up their dirt bikes on July 6, 1984, two weeks after the meeting in the Manning. The evidence showed, in fact, that Taglianetti had been present at the motorcycle dealership as well on June 26, less than forty-eight hours after the meeting, to help Joe and Jim select their bikes. The trip to Arizona to repossess the Cyclotron at William Morton's mining site had come a full month later than Taglianetti recalled, it was proven, and Les Zoeller's notes showed that the witness was not interviewed by the Beverly Hills Police Department until October of 1984. Much as Barens appeared to enjoy proving the witness a liar, Joe's attorney could not impeach Tag's recollection of Jim Pittman's elaborate arsenal.

Steve Lopez had been through several wardrobe changes by the time he was summoned to the stand after three days "on call." Lopez was willing to talk movie deal but little else in the hallway outside Department C. The past two and a half years had been "devastating to me personally," he explained, and quite credibly, for how else to explain the uncontrollable tic Steve had developed in his left eye. Not only was he deeply indebted to his Asian investors, but now his family had forfeited its sinecure in Singapore as well. The details were hazy: Eisenberg spread the story that the senior Lopez had fled the country after being charged with peddling pharmaceuticals on the black market. Steve denied this, vehemently, but admitted there had been "some trouble at home" and explained his father was "traveling" at the moment. He had not been back to Singapore himself since the fall of the BBC, Lopez said, "and I'll probably *never* go. I just want to pay everybody off and get on with my life." To this end, Steve had formed a company to broker Asian loans for American real estate developers, taking half a point commission when the "one out of twenty I try pays off." What he had learned was "life isn't fair," Lopez said: "I mean, I personally didn't want to be damaging to anybody, but look where I am."

Never one to burn bridges, though, he "tried to stay friends with everybody—except Eisenberg—from the BBC," Steve explained. Even Joe Hunt: "We've talked on the phone a couple of times. Joe wants to get together to discuss some real estate deals he has going." Lopez and Ben Dosti had spotted one another on the street in Beverly Hills recently, "so we pulled over to talk—about business only," Steve explained. "Ben said he wanted to do some real estate with me, also. Everybody wants to do real estate with me."

He had spoken to neither Joe nor Ben about their trials, Lopez said, but it was easy to spot the signals—a subtle shaking or nodding of the head— Hunt sent Steve as the witness described for the jury how he first confronted Joe with "the Ron Levin rumor." "I asked Joe about it," Lopez recalled. "I said, 'I heard you shot Ron Levin.' He said, 'Oh, I just told them that to see how they'd react.'" Wapner, who had brought Lopez to the stand to describe Hunt's sudden appearance at his hotel in London during June of 1984, massaged his forehead as Steve explained to a smiling Barens that "Joe said his reason for telling the others he had killed Ron Levin was to see which ones were true members."

The young man Lopez called "my only enemy in this world" passed him on the way to the witness stand. Pink and plump, At Ease from head to toe in cashmere sweater, crisply creased chinos, and tasseled loafers, Jerry Eisenberg's deadpan, down-to-earth delivery made him the BBC member one juror called "a man among Boys." By the time he took the stand at Joe's trial, Jerry had been threatened by the Mays with a malpractice lawsuit, described as a "conniving opportunist" by Evan Dicker, accused by Jim Pittman of writing paper for a stolen car ring, and reviled as "a corner-cutter" by Steve Lopez, yet emerged unscathed in the media. Furthermore, the attorney had been striking it rich since the day he left the BBC, amassing the seed of his fortune during late 1984 and early 1985 by taking over where West Cars left off, selling gray-market BMWs to customers ranging from relatives to L.A. Raiders. He maintained a law office but devoted most of his time to real estate development at present, acquiring a number of properties in the San Fernando Valley. "I'm doin' well," Jerry admitted.

By comparison to the other Boys, Eisenberg looked good, and he knew it. Yes, it was he who had written the clauses in the limited partnership agreements that justified Joe's use of investors' money to finance BBC companies, Eisenberg agreed, but "I was just doing what an attorney does." And if he fudged a bit on the sequence of his conversation in the desert with

Dave May and his call to the FBI, the few days' difference was a fraction of the time the others had taken to come forward. Eisenberg played it right to the edge of smug, and Joe's expression as he watched the young attorney on the witness stand was troubled in ways it had not been during the more damaging testimony of Jeff Raymond, Evan Dicker, and Tom May. The difference was perhaps a measure of envy; Eisenberg had achieved at least a semblance of what Joe wanted for himself. Throughout the trial, those on all sides—lawyers, cops, witnesses—had spoken repeatedly of what Joe might have been: "The CEO of a major corporation," according to Barens, or "a senator, at least, if he had gone into politics," said Gene Browning. For Joe, the successes and evasions of those Boys who possessed not only less ability but more modest ambitions exceeded mere rebuke to his conduct, went beyond even refutation of his theories; the worst part was the implication that he had lost not due to overwhelming odds but because of internal impediments.

For the Boys themselves, of course, the beauty part was that each finger they pointed at Joe sent scrutiny away from themselves. "The BBC was Joe Hunt's baby," Eisenberg told Wapner, no matter what appearance the other two Shadings had helped him create. When Wapner suggested that Hunt's position in the BBC was analogous to that of a fraternity president, Eisenberg answered, "Joe demanded a higher level of loyalty than that." Wapner amended his metaphor from frat house to football team. "Only in this case," Eisenberg quipped, "the coach was the owner." The BBC's former in-house counsel had become the Billionaire Boys' principal debunker. Jurors were amused when Eisenberg described the first BBC meeting he attended in October of 1983 as "a pick-a-company convention," chuckled when he compared the mental capacities of the May twins to those of houseplants, and laughed uproariously when he described how the breakfast business meetings Joe initiated in the spring of 1983 had ceased after three sessions. Better than any other witness, Eisenberg communicated Joe's financial predicament in the spring of 1984, describing Hunt as sunk in a mire of idle BBC members and unproductive companies, compelled to come up with seventy thousand dollars every month just to cover "basic expenses." Jim's surveillance equipment and exotic weapons were "toys," in Eisenberg's version of the BBC, and Joe was the leader of "a mini-Mafia" whose members referred to people over thirty as "grown-ups."

About all Barens could get from Eisenberg on cross-examination was agreement that money had not been Joe Hunt's motivation: "Power was the main thing," the attorney explained.

Wapner brought his case to a climax with three days of cop talk and in camera hearings concerning the appearance of the prosecution's final witness, Dean Karny. The procedural matter that occupied most of the court's time was how the identity of Dean Karny would be "masked" when he took the witness stand. An attorney representing ABC and CNN informed the court that the networks had agreed Karny's face and voice would not be broadcast. This was not enough for Wapner, who demanded that "the image and voice of Mr. Karny be distorted *while he's on the stand* and not later at the studio." Dean's own lawyer asserted that even a distorted videotape could create a "monetary incentive." "This case will be of public interest twenty years from now," Ron Morrow reminded Rittenband, and the order to alter Dean's image would be unenforceable then: "Mr. Karny could be in Massillon, Ohio, years from now," Morrow warned, "and someone could recognize him and kill him there."

That the threat to Dean was taken so seriously seemed to amuse Joe and his attorneys enormously. When Chier's chuckles and muttered asides grew loud enough to distract the court reporter, she snapped, "What's so funny, Mr. Chier? Do you mind?" Rittenband, seizing the opportunity, ordered Pat Quinn to remove Chier from the courtroom. "Take him by the back of the neck and throw him out of here," the judge urged his bailiff.

After Rittenband ruled that no videotape copies of Dean on the stand could be made until the original had been altered, a second scuffle ensued in the hallway outside, where the ABC lawyer accused Wapner of reneging on a promise and was called a liar. "You're the liar," the lawyer told him. Wapner had become increasingly petulant as the trial progressed. That the pressure was getting to the prosecutor showed in the astonishingly rapid silvering of his hair since November, accompanied by a weight loss of fifteen pounds. The prospect of "reliving this nightmare" (because of an appeals court ruling) spooked Wapner into arguing that Chier should be permitted to make the closing argument for the defense. Rittenband refused, adamantly: Chier was "abrasive and obnoxious," the judge said. "I am protecting myself against an appeal on the grounds of inadequacy of counsel."

Joe's troubles would increase, though, no matter who made his final argument. The Beverly Hills PD's "handwriting examiner" assured the court that the seven pages recovered from Ron Levin's apartment had been authored by Joe Hunt. When Wapner offered Joe's "Dear Brooke" letter as a sample of the defendant's handwriting, Barens stood at once to "stipulate that the seven pages were written by Joe Hunt." The BHPD's "identification technician" reported that, of the three fingerprints he lifted from the documents found in Ron Levin's apartment, two belonged to Joe Hunt and the other was Les Zoeller's. Barens was able to muddy the waters a bit when he—and the jury—learned that the twenty-two other fingerprints still had not been identified. The fingerprint expert was recalled the next day to report that he had reexamined the unidentified prints and was able to determine that, of those on the Microgenesis file folder, most were Ron Levin's. He had identified also one print on the yellow pages, the technician said—the right index finger of Dean Karny. There were gasps from the audience.

Les Zoeller was the last police officer summoned to the stand. The detective explained how he cracked the case by doing nothing for two months, becoming "active" only when he met with the Mays and Paul Tobin on August 8. His next move, one week later, was the search of Ron Levin's apartment, where he had been handed the seven pages that were the state's strongest evidence against Joe Hunt. Zoeller betrayed emotion on the stand only once: An unmistakable relish crept into the detective's voice as he described the "blank look" and "solemn expression" that swept away Joe's smirk when he was shown the seven pages at the Beverly Hills Police Department on September 28.

The courtroom was jammed with spectators—so many that those turned away at the door stood watching TV monitors in the hallway—by the time Zoeller completed his testimony. The crowd had not assembled to hear the detective, however, but rather in anticipation of the witness who would follow him to the stand.

A limousine filled with federal marshals delivered Dean Karny to the Santa Monica Courthouse that afternoon. Dean entered Department C through the door that opened from Judge Rittenband's chambers, wearing a blue blazer and a red tie with a white button-down shirt, "all Mom and apple pie," as one juror would observe. Dean had changed during the fourteen months since his appearance on the stand in San Mateo County. His old "Hollywood Hill Rats" running partner Dirk Mathison, now on hand as the correspondent from *People* magazine, described Dean as "less mouthy," but it went beyond that. About to celebrate his twenty-seventh birthday, Dean was more manly than he had been back in January of 1986. The most striking alteration of Karny's appearance, however, was the way tension drew a face that looked as if its features had been formed by a clenching of the teeth. Dean sat inhaling deeply and sighing heavily as he watched the bailiff check the cameras, then listened to the whispered consultations of the attorneys. He blinked into the TV lights and stared in pained resignation at the three dozen men and women scribbling in reporters' notebooks from seats in the courtroom's right-side section.

Breiling and Vance, who had spent a good deal more time with the state's star witness than had Wapner and Zoeller, admitted they were worried about "what might happen to him later." During their interviews with

Dean during the past year, each had noticed that Karny now spoke of himself in the third person when he recalled events from the summer of 1984. "He'll say, 'Dean Karny did this,' or 'Dean Karny did that,'" Vance noted. "A bad sign," agreed Breiling, "because he makes it sound like somebody else, that *other* Dean Karny, did all the bad stuff." It seemed to both men that Dean's profound animus toward Joe was the main thing that kept him going, and each wondered what their witness would use when the trials were over. "I'm afraid that when Dean realizes what he's going to have to live with, he'll eat his gun," Breiling said.

From the witness stand, Dean took the jury through it from the start, beginning back in 1972 when he met the thirteen-year-old he knew as Joseph Gamsky at the Harvard School, then jumping from graduation in 1977 to their meeting on the sidewalk in Westwood three years later. He told the jury how close they had grown that summer, how they talked into the night of the ways in which the corporate system stifles the initiative of bright, capable people, and how Joe began to talk about forming a group of these capable people, an organization "not bound by outside structures."

Witness Karny wore the same outfit when he returned to Department C the next morning, escorted by three armed men who positioned themselves at preselected sites around the courtroom. When he took the stand, Dean did something he had not done the day before—meet Joe's eyes. The defendant's former "first friend" glared at him with unblinking hatred and a curled lower lip, sneering in his face. Joe, on the other hand, remained impassive, at least on the surface, returning Dean's gaze with an expression that suggested a careful balance between pity and contempt.

Karny's testimony that morning began with the trip to Tahoe and Mammoth at the end of 1981, when Joe had introduced Paradox Analysis. From the Florida trip three weeks later, Dean leaped a year to Joe's return from Chicago at the end of 1982 with four dollars in his pocket. After a three-month "recruiting drive," he recalled, they had assembled the early membership of the BBC for that first meeting at the Encino condominium: "Joe and I and Ben and Ron and Evan and Mickey Fine and Cary Bren and Alex Gaon and Simmie Cooper and Tom and Dave May are the ones I remember being there," Dean said, generously omitting nearly a dozen names. Alex got them in the door at Cantor Fitzgerald, Dean recalled, and soon after that Joe began trading the Ron Levin account. In contrast to Jack Friedman, Dean described Ron's scam from Hunt's perspective. There was no doubt Joe had been taken, Dean said: Even when he learned from Friedman that the Clayton account had been been a fake, Joe believed Ron's new story that he had used the Clayton confirms to scam up $1.5 million at other brokerage houses, and Hunt said he was going to find a way of get-money from him. "Joe also said Levin was going to die someday," Karny recalled.

He began to believe Joe meant what he said, Dean recalled, when Hunt showed him three letters written to Levin involving a nonexistent Microgenesis deal. He and Joe then discussed for the first time burden of proof: "I said, 'That means there's going to be a reasonable doubt'—because of the letters. Joe said no court in the land would convict him with all of the confusing stuff around." The jurors began to shift in their seats; several glowered at Joe. Wapner's appearance was transformed; he looked ten years younger than he had the day before.

It was when he returned from a one-week vacation in early June that he first saw Joe writing out his murder plan on yellow legal-size pages, Dean recalled. Dean was able to recall conversations in connection to virtually every item on the "AT LEVIN'S, TO DO" list. The jury, though, reacted only once, when Karny answered Wapner's question about the *"Make a file of letters (take holes with you)"* notation. "I commented that that was a very nifty touch," he recalled, but when the jurors laughed, Dean was appalled, covering his face with his hands. He needed a pause before continuing, and a five-minute recess was called. Rittenband's clerk Diane Tschekaloff opened the door to the judge's chamber, and a gust of wind lifted the top page off the pile of yellow papers stacked on the rail of the witness stand, depositing it at the prosecutor's feet. "One down, six to go," Joe cracked. He and Chier flashed grins at one another as the three armed men escorted Karny out of the courtroom.

He saw Joe going over his lists for the last time on the evening of June 6, 1984, Dean said when he resumed his testimony, just as he was about to leave to see *Streets of Fire* with Brooke and Jeff. He and Hunt spoke again the next morning at about seven; Joe showed him the Swiss check and said Levin was dead.

Dean still could recall in detail Joe's description of Ron's death. Marty and Bob Levin had left Carol at home that day, but Ron's brother was himself unable to sit through this part of Karny's tale, storming out the courtroom door as Dean recalled what Joe said about denting the trunk hood when they loaded Levin's body into the BMW. Joe was matter-of-fact as he described the disposal of the body in Soledad Canyon, Dean remembered. "We talked about [Ron's death] a few other times. I really didn't like to talk about it, though," Dean explained, and choked up again. Joe could not contain his contempt, scribbling so hard that he split the top page on the legal pad in front of him.

When Dean returned to the stand for his third day of testimony, Wapner wanted him to explain Joe's introduction of Paradox Philosophy in greater detail. "Getting rid of internal impediments was the first step," Dean answered, speaking directly to the jury. "Joe said the best way to find happiness, fulfillment and peace was to 'streamline all aspects of your being,' so that the only impediments were external, not internal." At the same time, however, "Joe said to be aware of societal constraints and guilts and emotional reactions to things," Dean explained, "so that they wouldn't hinder you in making practical decisions," and also because such knowledge could be useful in "situations where you might seek to manipulate people." Joe spent months demonstrating how dangerous Normies were, Dean recalled: "He would find people, see a hostile reaction or dislike—it might be a girlfriend or your parents—and 'freeze it' as an example of what happened when the Normie lost control. He used to say that 'every moment is a window on all time.'"

"I was the one who started the idea of telling the others," agreed Dean, who admitted that the murder of Ron Levin had not troubled him nearly so much as lying to the rest of the BBC. His description of the June 24 meeting disagreed with that of the other Boys in just one regard: Joe had not threatened anyone with death if they talked, Karny recalled, his tone disgusted as he dismissed Tom May's claim.

He began to distance himself from Joe only after the discovery that the Mays and Raymond had spoken to the police, Dean said. When Joe began to propose plans for eliminating the Stooges, Dean said, "I got scared about what was happening. I didn't want to be part of anything else . . . Joe was still willing to contemplate all things and I wasn't. The internal impediments I was feeling were some pretty serious ones." Still, he had no plans to contact the police, even in September and October, Dean admitted: "I just wanted to walk away and start my life again."

"Joe Hunt was your best friend, right?" Barens began his cross-examination. Yes, Dean agreed. "It was a relationship of trust and confidence?" It was, Dean said. Having constructed his platform, Barens dove headfirst for the ring of fire, asking Dean if he had received immunity "for a murder in San Mateo County initially, and then for this one." The jurors wore expressions of dread as they waited for an answer. He didn't want to put either killing ahead of the other, Dean said: "My attorney decided who to talk to first."

"I wanted to save myself," Dean admitted, and yes, he knew "it had to be at the expense of somebody else." Immunity for testimony? Barens asked. That was the deal, Dean agreed. There was no shaming this witness; Dean seemed almost to appreciate the pillory. It was true, Karny agreed, that he never felt any pang of conscience before reading the Beverly Hills Police file.

Barens shifted direction then, aiming once more to debunk the "myth" of the BBC: "Wasn't Paradox Philosophy," he asked, "a survivalist philosophy?" Dean looked at him for a moment, then at Joe, a faint smile playing on his lips. "I don't know how to answer that question," he said.

It was Wapner who first spoke the name "Hedayat Eslaminia." "The man we killed in Northern California," Dean called him. "Who are the other defendants in [the San Mateo] case?" Rittenband asked. "Ben Dosti, Jim Pittman, Reza Eslaminia, and Joe Hunt," Dean answered.

Brooke Roberts was the first witness for the defense. Joe's girlfriend wore a pink linen suit with a white silk blouse, loose and flowing, as she took the stand, her white-blond hair pulled back in a plait bound by an enormous pink bow. Brooke appeared tiny and perversely innocent as she took the stand, swearing her oath in a high, breathy singsong. She sat with her shoulders slumped, looking, if anything, too relaxed, sunk so low in the box that her chin barely cleared the top of the rail, putting the microphone nearer to her forehead than to the lips she pursed in a pouty replication of prime-time sex appeal. Brooke turned then to smile cheerfully at the jurors, who did not smile back.

It was hot that day, more than ninety degrees outside, and the air conditioning in the courthouse had been shut down for repairs. Beads of sweat formed on the brow of Judge Rittenband, but Brooke's polished complexion suggested the skin of a fruit that had ripened in the refrigerator. One entered a sort of toxic reverie, listening to her tell the jury about meeting Joe back in the red leatherette booths of At Sunset, about how different he seemed from anyone else she had ever met—different especially from the other BBC Boys. Brooke explained that she had moved in with Joe and Dean when she was just past seventeen and lived with them for the next two years. Dean was a person who had problems, Brooke explained, sexual problems. Many of the jurors were breathing through their mouths now in the hot, stuffy room. It hadn't bothered her that Dean liked to make himself up as a woman, Brooke said, or even that he sometimes seemed jealous of her relationship with Joe, "but when I found the handcuffs under his bed . . ." she said, and shook her head.

"What happened then?" Barens asked. Before Brooke could answer, though, the elderly woman in the fifth seat of the jury box, Emma Becking, the lady who wore the same purple hat to court each day—who during voir dire had identified her hobbies as gardening and listening to the radio, adding that she didn't watch television because of the prurient content—reared back in her seat and gasped loudly. Clutching at her chest and turning gray in an instant, Mrs. Becking collapsed into the arms of the women who sat beside her. As Rittenband banged his gavel, Pat Quinn carried the old woman into the hallway, where she lay upon a green Naugahyde couch breathing with audible desperation, staring at the ceiling as if she could see through it to the other side. "Where's Dr. Levin?" Chier cracked. "We need Dr. Levin." Paramedics arrived moments later, reviving the woman with oxygen. Mrs. Becking was strapped to a stretcher when she demanded that they let her go. She did not like hospitals, the woman explained.

A three-hour recess ensued, during which time Mrs. Becking insisted she could continue as a juror. Judge Rittenband, advised by other members of the panel that juror number five was hard of hearing and might not have understood all the testimony in court, summoned the elderly woman—six years his junior—to a private audience. "I understand you're hard of hearing," he began. "Excuse me?" Mrs. Becking answered. It was one-thirty when Rittenband announced he was excusing juror number five "for health reasons," replacing her with Dr. Juel Janis, a Bel Air resident and assistant dean at the UCLA School of Public Health. As she left Department C, Mrs. Becking was followed by reporters who wanted to know if she had been inclined one way or the other. "I was leaning strongly toward not guilty; I just don't think the prosecutor has proved his case," the woman answered, then disappeared down the courthouse steps.

Everyone but Brooke seemed at least a little rattled when court reconvened at one forty-five. She turned to smile at the jury when Barens began with the question, "By the way, how old are you, Brooke?" "I am twenty-two," she answered, batting her brown eyes at the jurors, who seemed a little frightened by her now. It was back to the handcuffs then: What happened after she found the manacles in Mr. Karny's bedroom? Barens asked. "Dean ran to the bathroom and started vomiting," she recalled. Joe and Dean stayed alone in the back bedroom for a few minutes after that, but her boyfriend would say afterward only that Dean "was having some problems," Brooke explained: "He said, 'Listen, Brooke, you know I don't gossip about people.'" "Did you see Dean Karny with handcuffs on any other occasions?" Barens inquired, prompting Brooke's description of the photograph Evan Dicker had affixed to a wall at the Third Street office, the Halloween night bondage shot in which Evan and Dean posed with Deborah Corday.

Brooke's biggest problem as a witness was that she had over-rehearsed: She answered questions too quickly, undermined by her facility. Occasionally she caught herself and performed memory-jogging pantomimes, rubbing her cheeks or pointing at her temples with the index fingers of both hands.

RANDALL SULLIVAN

Barens asked for an example of Joe's Paradox discussions. "I remember Joe had a meeting at the house once with Evan, Jeff Raymond, Tom and Dave May," Brooke answered, "and that was because, at the time, Tom and Dave May were dealing cocaine—" "Objection," Wapner broke in. The prosecutor requested a conference at the bench, where Rittenband did most of the talking and made no attempt to lower his voice. Brooke "looks at you as if she had been completely coached," the judge snarled at Barens. "I beg your pardon," the attorney replied. "That is a good comment in front of the jury, that the jury heard." Wapner attempted a legal argument, but Rittenband waved him off like a gnat. "She is up there for the purpose of character assassination," the judge told Barens. "I want you to admonish this witness to stay away from any of these characterizations . . . I won't use her as a hatchet woman."

Denied his one route to revenge, an opportunity to reveal in open court the nasty habits of the Boys who betrayed him, Joe became demonstrative for the first time, slapping the sheaf of papers in his hand against the tabletop in front of him. His discomfort increased when Brooke attempted an explication of Paradox: "It wasn't like this whole philosophy thing," she said. "It was just, you know, different ways of looking at things, like if you are having a bad day, you know, and you think—it was like that expression— what is that expression? Black is white, white is black . . . it means, it is like— let me give you an example: Like if you are having a bad day, you know—'Oh, God, my life is over; it is the worst day of my life'—and then the next day it is fine. It is not a bad day anymore. Things are brighter. Or vice versa: One day, your life—everything is going great. And the next day you're totally—you can look at things and weigh them and be objective about it."

Several jurors were looking at the witness with undisguised derision now, yet even these members of the panel appeared uneasy. What Brooke suggested was a small pink balloon as it withered and blackened in the air; she was so cheerfully stupid and easily corrupt that it became a kind of agony to observe. She billed and cooed, chirped and trilled, flirting with the one man left on the jury whenever she got the chance. The most bizarre aspect of the entire examination was the supporting role played by her family, who all were present, yet sat apart, spread about the courtroom among the spectators, chuckling loudly and in unison, shrill like the laugh track imposed upon an idiotic sitcom, each time Brooke made some small and pitiful stab at humor, apparently unaware that not another person in Department C was laughing.

The Robertses fell silent, though, as what at first seemed a brief digression by Brooke into her parents' Alaska trip during the late spring of 1984 grew too detailed to be anything but the setup for an alibi:

She remembered very well the afternoon and evening of June 6, 1984, Brooke said. She had passed Joe on her way out the door, just as he arrived home from the office at between five and six. "He said he was going to have dinner with Ron Levin," she remembered. "He said that he was working on a business deal and he was supposed to get some money from Ron." She drove her own car that night, Brooke recalled, dining at Hana Sushi with Dean and Jeff, who were with her when they met Renee at the Avco Cinemas in time to catch the second showing of *Streets of Fire*. She returned to their apartment in the Manning between 9:30 and 10 P.M., Brooke said. And there was Joe, "in the bathroom brushing his teeth."

"What did he say to you?" Barens asked. "Objection as hearsay," Wapner interrupted. Rittenband's shrug was so insouciant that his clerk had to stifle a giggle. "Go ahead," the judge told Brooke. "It doesn't make any difference. Go ahead. Tell us what he told you."

Brooke gathered herself: "Well, he was really excited and I had— I was in the bathroom, too—and he said, 'Oh'—he was talking with his mouth full of toothpaste—he said, 'I got this check. Ron gave me this check.' So he went—I said, 'Well, slow down, slow down.' And he ran to the bedroom and he got this big check and he said, 'Look, look, look what Ron— he gave me this check.' And I looked at the check . . . it was for a million and a half dollars." Joe was "ecstatic," Brooke remembered.

Before going to bed, she had taken time to phone her parents' home in Bel Air, Brooke recalled: "I was writing on my calendar a few things and I saw that my parents got back from Alaska, so I called my mom." When she got Lynne on the phone, "Joe was going, 'Tell your mom about the check,' tell your mom about the check,'" Brooke remembered. "So I told her, 'Guess what? We have great news.' Because I wanted my mom to really like Joe. She said, 'Let me talk to Joe.'" Joe and her mother spoke for several minutes, Brooke recalled.

After taking time to establish that Pittman had been arrested at the Plaza Hotel because "[Ron Levin] tells Jim to meet him in New York, and then his credit cards bounce," Brooke was ready to move on to the June 24 meeting, stopped only by Rittenband's call for a fifteen-minute recess. "I need to catch my breath," the judge explained. When the principals reassembled in the courtroom, Barens requested a hearing at the bench. "Although I have the greatest respect for Mr. Wapner and Your Honor," Joe's lawyer began, "it was brought to my attention that during the witness's testimony the district attorney had been making pejorative faces towards the jury [Wapner was rolling his eyes], and I might say, Your Honor, although I do this with the greatest of respect, that it occurred to me at least that perhaps Your Honor had looked either amused or amiss at some of the testimony. All I am here to ask, Your Honor, is that we proceed with some restraint." "Restrain yourself, will you?" the judge retorted.

When Joe returned from London in the second week of June, Brooke recalled, she found him "in our bedroom, laying face down on the bed . . . crying. And he told me that—first he said, 'I don't want you to see me like this,' because that was the first time I had ever seen Joe cry, and I was stunned. And he said, you know, 'Please just leave me alone. I have got to get myself together.' And I pleaded with him, you know, 'Tell me what is wrong.' And so he said that the check didn't go through, and he said, 'How could Ron be so cruel?' And, 'What am I going to do about the investors?' He was, like, rambling, and saying about the BBC, 'All of the Boys are going to laugh at me.'"

More than at any time since he first strolled into Department C back in early November, Joe's face betrayed an emotion—embarrassment: His cheeks were bright red, and his jaw looked a little caved-in on one side. Brooke, though, remained oblivious: "I can remember saying, 'Don't worry, they are your friends,'" she recalled. "And he is like, 'They are going to laugh at me. I don't know what I am doing and—,' you know. "I said to him, 'Have you called Ron?' He said, 'I have. I have driven by his house. I can't get ahold of him.' That is what he said." While one or two jurors were attentive, the majority had taken to squirming again, turning in their seats to look at Brooke from the corners of their eyes, as if they believed a glancing blow might do less damage. Their suffering only increased, however, when the young woman began to describe the conversation between Joe and Dean she overheard a few days later: "I was walking to the kitchen. I heard them laughing and planning something. And I heard—it was all muffled. But the first thing I heard was—I was listening because I heard Dean talking, saying, 'Well, who could we say did it? Could I say I did it?' And Joe said, like 'Yeah. But they wouldn't believe that.' I was listening because I was like 'What are they talking about?' And then I remember Dean saying, 'I know. I know. You could say that you killed Ron.' Joe says, 'Could I have done it with you?' And they were, like, 'No, no.' Then, they were laughing, like, walking because they had a hallway. They were walking back and forth, to do this thing. I didn't want them to hear me. So then I remember hearing them say—Dean said, 'I know. I know. I know—you could say you and Jim did it.' And then I got really, like, you know—'What the hell is going on here?' And then I heard them say, 'Yeah, but you can't just tell them. They will never believe that. They will never believe that. You have got to make details, details.' I didn't know what they were talking about. Then Joe opened the door when I was listening and he goes, 'Yes?' And I said— I was embarrassed—I said, 'Joe, what are you doing?' I said, 'I want to talk to you in the bedroom.' He said, 'Okay. I will be in in a minute. Don't worry.' He was, like, 'Don't worry.' And, like, half an hour later, I was in the bedroom waiting for him. [When he came in] I told him not to say that. He said not to worry, that he is only going to say it for effect. He doesn't want to lose his business. He doesn't want the Boys to know there were—they were planning to do something to the offices. Joe had found some notes and there was going—"

"Objection, non-responsive," Wapner interrupted. "Are you going to break in?" Rittenband asked, more amused than interested. "Motion to strike," Wapner answered, but Brooke was determined to finish her story: "I said, 'But you can't say that about somebody,'" she recalled. "'You can't make some things like that up.'" Wapner was listening again, his objection either forgotten or ignored. "And [Joe] said, 'I just want to keep everything together, so, you know, I don't lose the business,'" Brooke explained. "'I can pay back the money because I have another deal going through. It will just be for effect.' I said I was against it. I said, 'Well, if you are going to say something like that, I want to be there.'"

"Did you threaten to leave Joe?" Barens was asking, but the dreaded moment had arrived; Brooke was dissolving into tears so horrifically contrived that one shivered in a kind of warped homage. "Could I have a Kleenex, Your Honor?" Brooke asked. Rittenband's mock chivalry was matchless as he deadpanned, "Oh yes," and handed her a tissue. "(Laughter in the courtroom)" was how the official transcript of the proceeding, succinct to understatement, described the moment that followed. Joe, his face bright red again, looked into the jury box, where at least half the panel had given in to giggles. Even Mrs. Shelby pursed her lips, and if she went, so did Joe.

Barens, too tan to blush, pressed forward to the June 24 meeting: "What was the mood when everyone arrived?" he asked. "Happy," answered Brooke, who denied she had been included in any of the meetings in the back bedroom. Joe's exact words when they came back to the living room, Brooke said, as if removing all doubt, had been, "Jim and I knocked off Ron Levin." The first BBC member to respond, she recalled, was Tom May: Tom "was like 'Oh, wow! That is so cool. Really? Wow!'"

Between Brooke's breaths, Barens jumped ahead to August, when "Joe learned he had become a suspect in the eyes of the law." "He said Ron Levin was missing and that Tom and Dave went to the police and told them that Joe killed Ron," Brooke remembered. Joe had tried to tell the Beverly Hills police what was really happening inside the BBC, Brooke said; the detectives not only refused to listen but threw him out of their office.

She was following his black Jeep east on Wilshire Boulevard when Joe was stopped by Zoeller and King on the morning of September 28,

Brooke recalled: "Police guys jumped out of the car and caught him. I have a convertible; my top was up so I was trying to see what was going on. And it was traffic. Jammed. And I pulled up and I just saw Joe's Jeep. They were putting Joe in the car. You know, they drove away. I saw Joe's keys in the car. They were searching the car. And these two policemen pulled me over because I said, 'What is going on?' They pulled me over. They said, 'Pull over.' So I pulled over. And they questioned me: 'Who are you?' And then the guy reached in my car and says, 'Do you have a gun in the car?'"

The indignation in her voice as she described the police search of her convertible was the first really convincing emotion Brooke had produced on the witness stand; her voice literally shook with rage, and the abrupt shift in persona was riveting. She lapsed back into singsong, though, to describe the scene at the Manning after Joe's arrest. "There were lots of people that came over," and some of them took things, Brooke recalled; Jon Allen removed several boxes.

It was true she met with Dean Karny in Ryan Hunt's office during early November of 1984, Brooke said. Dean had come in with his mother to pick up a copy of the police report. "I said, 'Why have you not called me?'" she remembered. "I kept pushing him and pushing him, saying, 'You have got to tell us. You have got to come forward and tell the truth.' I said, 'If you don't want to talk to me, call Joe's attorney. But you have to come forward.' He got really annoyed. He said, 'Look, I can't say anything about what I am going to do right now until I read the police reports.' And I said, 'The police reports mean nothing. You have got to come forward.' And he goes, 'Listen, I have a lot of problems.' He started yelling at me. We were in a parking lot while this was going on. 'I have a lot of problems,' [Dean said]. 'I have a problem in San Francisco nobody can help me with.' I said, 'What are you talking about?'"

Wapner began his cross-examination with the question, "What is your current profession, Ms. Roberts?" Brooke answered that she was working as a cocktail waitress (at the Ivy in Beverly Hills). "Are you kind of between jobs with another occupation?" Wapner pressed. "Yes," Brooke answered, pleased he had put it that way. "What is that?" Wapner asked. "Acting," Brooke told him, then performed an impromptu parody of vexation when the prosecutor suggested she had "practiced or rehearsed" her testimony on direct examination. Yes, Joe had been living at her parents' house for almost two years, Brooke agreed, and Bobby and Lynne were paying for his defense. "They also used their home in Bel Air to secure Mr. Hunt's bail, didn't they?" Rittenband put in. She had been in love with Joe once, Brooke said, but not anymore. Their "romantic" involvement had ceased a year earlier, Brooke explained, and in fact she had a new boyfriend, a young man named Grant, who had showed up in court for the first time that morning.

No, she never had approached the police with her story during the year Joe spent in jail, Brooke conceded. Wapner produced a letter he had dictated on September 19, 1986, inviting her to make a statement, hand delivered to her home by Les Zoeller. "I gave it to my father and never even read it myself," she explained.

She was hazy on most of the details from her BBC period, Brooke explained, and answered "I don't know" to most questions involving time, distance, or money. "You have to tell the truth," she explained, turning to Judge Rittenband, who could only nod his head in droll solemnity. "If you don't know, you don't know."

From her elevated seat on the stand, Brooke looked less often at Joe than at her brother Todd, who stood in the back of the courtroom, guffawing loudly at every girlish little thing his baby sister said. Brooke had become more extemporaneous on cross-examination, less Bel Air princess than Val Gal, hammering with her little manicured fist (though never quite making contact with the wood rail) to emphasize a point, snapping her fingers when she recalled a detail that had slipped her mind earlier, simpering and sighing one moment, seductive the next, flirting even with Wapner. When the prosecutor demonstrated that Joe had stayed in London only a few days, rather than the "week or two" Brooke remembered, she batted her eyes and explained, "Well, it seemed like forever."

Rittenband responded to Barens's frequent objections mostly by ignoring them, occasionally cutting the attorney off in mid-sentence with a curt "Overruled." "It looks better if you allow me to finish my objection," Barens said.

Brooke handled it herself when the judge asked if Joe had showed Dean the Swiss check at 7 A.M. rather than at 10 P.M., as she had testified: "Are you believing Dean or are you believing me?" she asked. As the answer became clear, Brooke grew openly contemptuous toward inquiries from the bench, exasperated by questions about "little details." Rittenband, who had dominated the proceedings up to this point, seemed resigned to Brooke's impervious sass. When Wapner asked the judge to "instruct the witness to stop arguing with me," Rittenband answered, "Have you ever tried to shut a woman up when she's in a mood?" Brooke sparked with feminist wrath: "Your Honor, this is a terrible thing that's gone on! I'm not in any mood!"

On re-direct, Barens moved swiftly to rehabilitate Brooke's failure to inform the prosecutor that Joe had an alibi. "It was your idea," Brooke told the attorney: "You told me that you were saving my testimony, and that I was not to talk to anybody but my family about all this."

Wapner wanted re-cross, but Brooke made him wait while she moistened her lips with Chap Stick. Wapner watched her for a few moments, then said, "When you're finished putting on your makeup, I'll ask a question." "This isn't makeup," Brooke snarled. The prosecutor turned his head to see if the jury had caught her expression, then smiled as he told Rittenband, "Nothing further."

Wapner's smile vanished when he heard Lynne Roberts called as the next witness. Brooke's mother was elegant, almost stately, as she ascended to the stand, complementing an exquisite canary cashmere sweater with a skirt of yellow linen and an immense white crysanthemum affixed to the back of her pale bunned hair. Mrs. Roberts was composed as she described meeting Joe during Christmastime in 1982, then sad but forbearing as she recalled Brooke's decision to move out of the Bel Air house into the Encino condominium four months later. "I thought she was much too young," Lynne admitted. "I wanted her to go away to college and get her education. I was very upset, and our relationship became strained."

Barens skipped over the next fourteen months and brought Brooke's mother to the evening of June 6, 1984, a night she, too, remembered well. She and her husband had planned to return to Los Angeles from their Alaskan expedition on that date but were forced by her summons to jury duty to come back one week earlier, recalled Mrs. Roberts, who produced her diary as evidence. She lay in bed watching the ten o'clock news on TV when a call from Brooke came in on her private line during the evening of June 6, Mrs. Roberts remembered. "Brooke told me she had this wonderful news," Lynne recalled. "Joe had made a big deal—one point five million—and they were all celebrating. Joe got on the phone and asked about Alaska and then told me about the check."

Mrs. Roberts looked tense but betrayed none of the synthetic emotion that made her daughter suspect. Lynne's face, lifted to an unnatural tautness above her cheekbones, sagged to withered spokes around the sockets of her blue eyes. Something so crushed and tragic emanated from those eyes that it was impossible to dislike the lady. She seemed entirely sincere in her effort to recall exactly what had been said, chewing on her lips and grimacing. If it was an encore of Brooke's performance, then the mother was a far better actress than the daughter. The jurors wore sympathetic expressions; Mrs. Shelby seemed almost admiring. Bobby sat in the front row twirling a rabbit's foot on a silver chain.

Wapner went at once to the use of the Bel Air estate as security for Joe's release from jail. Lynne was not at all perturbed when Wapner pointed out that the defendant had gone by the name Joe Roberts for a time: "Joe is like a son to me," she said.

Judge Rittenband asked whether Mrs. Roberts realized the significance of her testimony: "You have provided the defendant with an alibi," Rittenband told her. "I know it's significant," Lynne replied calmly, "because it's true, Your Honor." The judge asked Lynne if she had discussed her recollection of their phone conversation on that evening in June with the defendant. She had, Lynne said, but Joe "only said to tell the truth." Rittenband then produced a clipping from the *Daily News* chronicling the mad scramble for movie rights to the BBC story. According to this article, he noted, Joe Hunt was being represented by theatrical agents Sy Marsh and Burton Moss. Was she aware, Rittenband asked Mrs. Roberts, that her husband had introduced these gentlemen to the defendant? It was her understanding that Mr. Marsh called her husband to ask for an introduction, answered Lynne, adding that her family had not profited by a penny from their support for Joe: "All this has done is cost us a lot of money."

It was, appropriately enough, April Fools' Day, Rittenband noted before convening court the next morning. The arrival in Department C of those two witnesses who claimed they had seen Ron Levin "quite well alive," in Barens's words, only a few months earlier, was heralded by a delegation of assistant district attorneys and police detectives ushered by the bailiff to front-row seats. John Vance and Oscar Breiling arrived from San Francisco a few moments later, looking grim. It would be difficult for any jury to convict in the face of what they were about to hear, Vance said. Hunt and Chier were leafing through a copy of the September 1986 *Esquire* as Barens stood to announce, "The defense calls Carmen Maria Canchola." A stocky, sweet-faced, and decidedly unadorned young woman wearing a cotton dress entered the courtroom, looking plaintive and tired. She was twenty-three years old, Carmen said, and lived in Tucson, Arizona.

She had been a student at the University of Arizona in September of 1986, the young woman explained. One Thursday evening near the end of that month she had cut her economics class to dine with her boyfriend Chino Lopez at a place called Café Napoli. After they left the restaurant, she and Chino drove back to her apartment near the U of A campus, where they loaded some lamps into her Honda Prelude (Carmen was moving out to Chino's ranch in stages). Chino was driving as they pulled into the Vicker's self-service gas station on Campbell, right across from the university's basketball arena, Carmen remembered. While her boyfriend pumped gas, Carmen had spotted "this real attractive older gentleman. He was about six-one, slender, wearing very nice, expensive clothes." The man "looked kind of old and young at the same time," Carmen recalled: "He looked young at first and then I saw the silver hair."

As she watched the man fill the gas tank of his own car, "I became very attracted," Carmen explained. "There was something so different about him; he had a regal manner." The silver-haired man passed within a few feet of her as he walked to the cashier's cage, Carmen recalled, and her stare followed him back to his car, where he stopped to talk to his companion, who stood on the passenger side of the vehicle drinking a soda. The friend was tall, too, "but kind of paunchy," Carmen recalled, yet looked fifteen or twenty years younger than the silver-haired man. When they climbed back into the car, the younger man "said something angry," Carmen recalled, "because the older man had been looking at my boyfriend." Did the two men "appear to be of the homosexual persuasion?" Barens inquired. Oh yes, Carmen said; the younger man, especially, was "effeminate." It was the older man, though, who "kept staring over at us," Carmen recalled. She locked eyes briefly with the silver-haired man, Carmen remembered, while Chino, oblivious, was checking the oil and transmission fluid. When her boyfriend got back in the car, though, he saw the older man looking over and asked if Carmen was flirting with him. "I said, 'He wasn't looking at me; he's looking at you,'" she recalled.

As the silver-haired man drove away, he made a U-turn around the gas pumps and stopped directly across from their car, Carmen recalled: "He kept looking at Chino . . . I said he was very attractive for a man of his age, and 'It's too bad he's gay.'"

She and Chino continued to speak of the silver-haired man for the next few days, Carmen recalled: "We made jokes about Chino looking pretty when we were going out." It was almost two months later, on November 20 to be exact, Carmen remembered, when she began to leaf through the back issues of her brother's *Esquire*s. She was looking for an article she could use for an econ class project, Carmen recalled, when a pair of features touted on the cover of the magazine's September issue—R. Foster Winans's confessions of his role in an insider trading scheme while working at the *Wall Street Journal* and the "Billionaire Boys Club" article—caught her attention. She grew bored before she could finish the Winans article, Carmen recalled, but read the BBC piece from beginning to end. She barely noticed the picture of Ron Levin that accompanied the article, Carmen said, but was "affected" by the writer's description of Levin—"especially the part about his eyes." When she finished the story, she turned back to the page with the "sketch" (a mug shot–sized, hand-painted photograph) of Ron Levin, Carmen recalled, and studied it more closely. Then she reread the description of Levin in the article and had a very strong sensation that the man she and Chino had seen at the gas station eight weeks earlier was the same man she saw now on page 87 of *Esquire,* Carmen said. The article seemed to suggest he was gay, she noted. The only thing that bothered her was that the *Esquire* piece "said that he had a beard, and our guy had no beard."

She couldn't sleep at all that night, Carmen recalled, and in the morning confided to a friend what she suspected. By lunchtime, Carmen was wondering whether to go to the police or to a friend who was a newspaper reporter: "I thought it would be a big story for her."

She went to the Tucson police the next day, November 21, a Friday. A detective interviewed her for nearly an hour, Carmen remembered. On Saturday, November 22, the detective phoned her and asked if she could come to the police station, Carmen recalled, explaining that some people from Beverly Hills would like to talk to her. She met Fred Wapner, who was accompanied by a pair of Tucson detectives, that afternoon, Carmen remembered. She and Chino were questioned for nine hours.

The length of Carmen's interrogation, and Chino's, resulted from a photo lineup arranged by Wapner. There were six pictures of bearded men with leonine hair, Carmen recalled, and it had taken her about five seconds to select the man in the lower right corner, who was Ronald George Levin. Wapner wouldn't tell her if she had picked the right person, Carmen remembered: "I said then I was ninety percent sure, but that the man I saw didn't have a beard and had shorter hair." She was shown another lineup of six photographs that evening and told Wapner that none were close, Carmen recalled.

Her next contact with law enforcement came on November 26, when a female prosecutor from the L.A. County district attorney's office showed up at her parents' home. "She said I better be sure," Carmen recalled, "because I was messing up all the investigation that had been done. She was trying to intimidate me."

Carmen heard from Joe's attorney, Richard Chier, for the first time in March of 1987, when "he came to Tucson to see me." She wanted no part of testifying at a murder trial, Carmen said, and spoke to the lawyer only when forced to by a court order. The same judge had compelled her trip to Los Angeles to testify at this trial, Carmen said, then blurted, "I wasn't going to come. I was going to disappear and only came because I was forced to." She broke into tears. Rittenband dismissed the jury an hour early, advising them to return in the morning when Ms. Canchola was feeling better.

Carmen seemed to have recovered some of her confidence but none of her composure overnight. Agitation, though, lent the witness pathos, and Wapner advanced on her with obvious trepidation. Carmen reiterated that it was not the picture of Levin in *Esquire* so much as the writer's portrayal that first caught her attention. She recalled that Ron's eyes were described as both piercing and shifty, just like the eyes of the man at the gas station.

The young woman grew more garrulous as her nervousness increased, breaking into tears each time Wapner interrupted her. Chier, tasting victory at last, stood to object that the prosecutor was not allowing the witness to finish her answers and was "outraged" when Rittenband replied, "Quiet, you!" "I'm a lawyer, a member of the bar, and you can't speak to me this way," he informed Rittenband, who responded by ordering his bailiff to "remove this person from my courtroom."

Carmen was in tears once again as she watched Chier waddle-strut down the aisle, her voice breaking as she recalled her interview with the prosecutor at the Tucson Police Department. She spoke to Wapner for more than two hours, Carmen said, then waited outside for Chino while he was interviewed. "Mr. Wapner didn't want me to have a break," she told the jury, and sobbed again. It was the witness who interrupted the prosecutor now, accusing him of "telling us the defense would be even worse." "That's why we avoided them," she explained. Carmen alternated now between glaring at Wapner and weeping. The prosecutor and his staff had "hounded" her, she said: "I wish I had never said a word to anyone."

The next morning, Carmen explained that she had told the police she never would be able to say for certain that the man she picked from the photo lineup was the same person she saw at the gas station until they showed her what he looked like without a beard. She said the same thing to Chier when he came to see her in Tucson, Carmen remembered, and to Barens when she visited his office two days before her appearance in court. Joe's attorney invited her to view three photographs of Ron Levin submitted in court as evidence, Carmen recalled: "The first two, I didn't react, because he had a beard in those. The third one, though, I reacted. He had no beard in that one and I could see his jawline. I got sick to my stomach. I started crying and I got real scared, because I was almost ninety-nine percent sure it was the person I saw before."

When Wapner asked "what's the same" about the man in the picture and the man at the gas station, Carmen grew impatient: "I guess the way he's staring," she said. "I don't know—his eyes." "What more do you want from me?" she demanded, and then was sobbing again. "I tried to be helpful," she told Rittenband. "I came forward and I didn't have to." Carmen turned to the jury: "Everybody around me kept pushing me to get out of this. My parents were upset with me. Chino was upset with me. Everyone was upset with me. My neighbor across the street got a call from someone asking weird questions about me. A little girl on our street said she saw a man dressed like a jogger looking in the windows. There were anonymous phone calls, reporters calling."

Then Wapner got her, though the young woman seemed not to notice: "Have you ever in your life had the experience of mistaking someone for someone else?" the prosecutor asked. Never, Carmen answered.

On re-direct, Barens allowed Carmen to let it be known that she was not some impoverished little Chicana whose mother cleaned white people's houses. Her father, in fact, was a wealthy man who owned McDonald's franchises in Tucson and Nogales.

"The only issue now is whether it's a hung jury or an acquittal," predicted John Vance as Carmen left the stand. Wapner had made the young woman look, at worst, a sincere hysteric. And the fact that she had picked Ron Levin out of a photo lineup on her first try most likely would override that impression.

Whatever description one cared to offer of Jesus "Chino" Lopez, "pretty" was hardly the first word that leapt to mind. Twenty-five years old, Chino was stocky and swarthy, with a fleshy face and pockmarked cheeks. He worked for Mr. Canchola managing the McDonald's franchise in Tucson, and Chino's recollection of their encounter at the gas station in September matched Carmen's in virtually every respect. He had not read the *Esquire* article, Chino said, and probably never would. Yet he, too, had picked the man in the lower right corner out of the first photo lineup as the one most like the silver-haired fellow at the gas station. He had told the police then he was 65 percent sure, Chino recalled, but now, after seeing three other pictures of Ron Levin in Barens's office, "I'm ninety-five percent certain." Barens's last question to the witness was "How far is Tucson from the Mexican border?" "Sixty miles," Chino answered.

The couple from Tucson had set the stage for the fifth and final defense witness, Joe Hunt. It was Joe's job to tie the loose ends and stitch the seams: profile the BBC, interpret Paradox Philosophy, impeach Dean Karny, describe that last night at Ron Levin's, and retract his statements at the June 24 meeting. Most critically, of course, only Joe could explain the seven pages, and how Hunt would account for the "AT LEVIN'S, TO DO" list was what those who had followed the case were waiting to hear.

Department C was crowded with more spectators and reporters than had been in court since opening statements on the afternoon of April 6, all there to hear Joe work his magic. This climax to the trial had been anticipated in the press for weeks: "HUNT'S CREDIBILITY MAY BECOME FOCUS OF BBC TRIAL," a banner headline in the *Daily News* trumpeted. That article, like several others, recounted the testimony from BBC members of Joe's oratorical skills and persuasive powers. "It was his ability to speak that made [his ideas] so persuasive," Evan Dicker had told the jury. Al Gore put it more succinctly: "He knew how to brainwash the brains."

The headline on the front page of the next morning's *Los Angeles Times,* though, read, "NEW TACTIC STUNS TRIAL: HUNT WILL NOT TESTIFY." "In a surprise move that caused a packed courtroom to gasp, the defense in the murder trial of Billionaire Boys Club leader Joe Hunt abruptly rested Monday," wrote reporter Lois Timnick, who reminded her readers that only a few months earlier, "Barens told the *Times,* 'Hunt is brilliant, a genius. And he must testify.'"

Citing the gag order imposed by Judge Rittenband, Barens refused comment but pointed to the last lines on a transcript of his opening statement: "Not proven, not guilty." A moment later, however, Joe was in the hallway with Ron Ostroff of the *Daily News,* telling the reporter, "I was completely prepared to testify," and pointing to his bulging briefcase. Rudy Durand, who claimed to have been in on the decision, explained that he, Joe, and the lawyers all had agreed that "leaving the jury with the thought that these two people, who have no reason to lie, saw Ron Levin alive six months ago is stronger than anything anybody else could say, even Joe." "And this way," Rudy added, "he doesn't have to be cross-examined."

The one person in the courtroom who seemed not at all surprised by Barens's announcement was Judge Rittenband. Nodding like a man whose private speculation had been publicly confirmed, the judge announced that the prosecution could present its rebuttal witnesses the following morning.

How seriously Wapner took the Tucson couple the prosecutor demonstrated with a rebuttal case that pointedly ignored the testimony of Brooke and Lynne Roberts. Instead, the prosecutor focused entirely upon impeaching Carmen Canchola. Marty Levin was his main witness. After Lynne Roberts's appearance on the stand, Marty declined to call Brooke's mother a liar, asserting in fact that he believed the woman. It had been his theory all along, Marty explained, that "Brooke was there that night, in the apartment, either during or right after the time Ronnie was killed. She probably called her mother from Ronnie's own phone." That Brooke would walk away from all this ate at his innards worse than Dean Karny's deal, Marty admitted. "I think a lot of them should go to jail, but of all the ones who got off, Brooke's the one I'd really like to see behind bars." Though he said none of this on the stand, Marty's bearing and tone were all Wapner needed to let the jury know that Ron Levin's family—the people who would most like to believe Carmen Canchola and Chino Lopez—weren't buying a word of it. The prosecutor showed Marty the photograph that had brought Carmen to tears in Barens's office a few days earlier. That picture, Marty said, his tone dismissive, was almost ten years old.

The courtroom was filled to capacity again on the morning of April 13. Marty Levin came early to take a seat in the front row of the press section and announced he was not moving for anyone. Brooke Roberts, by contrast, arrived fashionably late and was without a seat until Joe ventured into the spectator section to solicit one. Lynne Roberts and Mrs. Arthur Barens were left standing at the back of the courtroom in linen suits that looked as if they were being soiled by mere proximity to the scruffy soundmen and photographers.

Wapner, whose mother was once again the audience member nearest his chair, had come to court with a new collection of color-coordinated charts, titled "RON LEVIN'S HABITS," "NO PLANS TO LEAVE," "THE MURDER," "HUNT'S CONSCIOUSNESS OF GUILT," and "KARNY'S CORROBORATION." The prosecutor remained true to form, meticulous if predictable, poring over the testimony of each prosecution witness in painstaking detail as he designed the busy package for a fundamentally simple argument: Ron Levin would never have left town of his own free will, so Joe Hunt must have killed him. Did they really believe, Wapner asked the jurors, that a man who could scarcely bear to be gone from Beverly Hills for a week at a time, who thrived on contact with the rich and famous, who loved to see and be seen, who kept his closets filled with the latest and most expensive fashions, was going to walk away with a gray jogging suit and a robe?

On the other side of the ledger, why had Joe Hunt claimed credit for the murder? Why had Pittman flown to New York with Ron Levin's credit cards? And, of course, why were seven pages of lists in Hunt's handwriting found in Ron Levin's apartment? Joe Hunt had promised to answer these questions; had anyone heard him do it?

Wapner did not so much refute the Robertses' testimony as revile it. While he denounced Brooke's testimony as "a bald-faced lie," though, the prosecutor was unwilling to say the same of Lynne's: "I don't know whether Joe Hunt conned Mom into lying and going along with the program or there was a mistake in the dates," the prosecutor conceded, but either way, the alibi was an obvious fabrication.

Wapner became emotional only once, when he showed the jury the seven pages. "This is sickness," he said, standing as close to the panel as he could get. "I shake every time I see these," the prosecutor added, and his hands indeed were trembling as he leafed through the legal pad pages. It became clear that a hung jury—John Vance's prediction—was the best Joe could hope for when juror number eight, Andie Deeg, began to nod her head in agreement as Wapner noted "the ultimate irony of this case," that Hunt had indeed planned the perfect crime, "right down to the 'take holes' notation," then left the list in Levin's apartment. Joe affected indifference, leafing through a copy of Thomas Wolfe's *Look Homeward, Angel* at the defense table.

Wapner's best visual aid was a copy of the one-inch-by-one-inch "sketch" from the September 1986 *Esquire* that he tacked by itself to a large easel, against which Ron Levin's image appeared absurdly tiny. Carmen and Chino weren't liars, Wapner conceded, they were "simply mistaken." He made the obvious points: Carmen was an emotionally unstable young woman from a sheltered background; Chino worked for her father.

At the end of his statement, it was not Joe Hunt of whom the prosecutor spoke but rather Ron Levin. Think of his mother, Wapner urged, who had received at least one phone call from her oldest son every week for the past twenty years, and upon whom Ron had "lavished" cards and gifts for every occasion. In the nearly three years since June of 1984, however, there had been no phone calls, no birthday gifts, no Mother's Day cards, Wapner reminded the women in the jury box. "That's because on the night of June 6, 1984, Ron Levin's life was interrupted," he concluded, "cut short."

The first two rows of spectator seats in the center section were a truly odd tableau on the morning of the final defense argument, April 14: The Levins, Marty and Bob, were right behind the Barenses, mother and daughter, in two seats posted with a RESERVED sign that had been written on, naturally, yellow sheets of legal pad paper. Sitting next to them was the ever-faithful Mrs. Wapner. Beside the Barenses, in the front row, sat the Robertses: Bobby, Lynne, and, lastly, Brooke, who occupied the seat nearest the jury. Joe had assumed an attentive pose, hands folded on the table in front of him. He suggested someone sitting for a photographer who used one of those nineteenth-century cameras that took five hours to consolidate an image.

The jury saw what it was in for when Joe's attorney hoisted to the podium a thick black notebook filled with a text four hundred pages long. Eternally bronzed and immaculately groomed, Barens exuded, as ever, elegance. To those given an opportunity to observe him at close range, however, the attorney's appearance disclosed details that seemed a sort of fleshly metaphor for life in Los Angeles: the pockmarked skin camouflaged but not concealed by the George Hamilton tan he aided with applications of an orange-based makeup; the high heels on the loafers that lifted a short man to middle height; the exquisitely fitted pinstriped suits that molded a stocky build into a sleek one; the bald spot at the crown of his head covered with an uncanny knack for cross-combing.

Barens went into his man-of-the-people mode as he described to jurors the responsibility of counsel under the American system of jurisprudence: modest, sincere, invocatory—you wanted to give him your Visa number. The prologue alone, though, lasted thirty-five minutes, and jurors were slouching in their seats by the time Barens got to the "Let us now turn to this case and its facts" part of his speech. The expressions of relief on the jurors' faces were gone ten minutes later. By four o'clock, they were listing and heavy-lidded, having heard the defense attorney chalk up a total of one point in the past three hours, registering his scorn for the prosecution's theory that Jim Pittman, "a former doorman," had been able to pull off "an antiseptic killing" in which no trace of bloodshed was left behind. "It was the perfect crime because there was no crime," he told the jurors, who by then were barely listening.

The text inside the black notebook had been cut by more than half when Barens returned to finish his argument the next morning. He took on the ghost of Ron Levin first, a man "who had only one business—Deception." "I'll bet he despised jail and the prospect of four more years of it a lot more than he loved Beverly Hills," Joe's attorney told the jurors. This was a man who had run up $49,000 in charges for clothing alone in the last month before he disappeared, Barens noted; the $36,000 he left behind was "small change for a big crook." Furthermore, there was the matter of some $278,000 in "unaccountable funds" that Ron had "amassed" in the months before his "departure." "Where's the money?" Barens demanded. "Find the money and you find Levin."

Far more significant than what he left behind was the successful application for a reduction of his bail that Ron "effected" only two days before his disappearance, Barens pointed out, saving Marty and Carol Levin some seventy-five thousand dollars. As for Ron's failure to phone his mother since June of 1984, "It came down to the nitty-gritty of Levin's life," Barens argued, "and what he characteristically opted for is 'Me first.'"

The prosecution's star witness was an "unbelievable scoundrel" whose testimony had been "a neatly constructed story-line," Barens said, that Dean Karny had "cooked up" to save himself from a certain prison sentence for his own crimes. "Thank God the State Bar is not under the auspices of the Attorney General or the police," Barens told the jurors, "for surely Karny would be here practicing law as he practices perjury."

The attorney readily acknowledged his client's "immaturity." Joe's announcement at the June 24 meeting was the rash boast of an impetuous youth who "wanted to make himself look like a tough guy," Barens contended: "You have Hunt creating an illusion for the BBC, so he could keep it going. Don't convict on the appearance of things."

The appearance the attorney knew he was up against in the worst way, though, was not Joe's announcement on June 24 but rather the August 16 discovery of the seven pages in Ron Levin's apartment. Nowhere in the seven pages was there "a single word on murder or a plan for murder," Barens asserted. There was "no 'Shoot Levin,' no 'Remove Corpse,'" on the seven pages, he reminded the jury. The "AT LEVIN'S, TO DO" list, Barens argued, "speaks most loudly by its silence."

The one bit of "irrefutable and overwhelming" evidence was the testimony of Carmen Canchola and Chino Lopez, Barens said. The Tucson couple, he noted, used many of the same words to describe the man at the gas station that Ron Levin's friends drew upon when they came to court as witnesses for the prosecution: "They saw Levin. Whatever the seven pages may or may not mean, Levin's not dead—plain and simple."

Barens began his summation by describing Joe Hunt as a young man who "for the past two and a half years has struggled to keep his head up in this valley of shame." The attorney approached the jury then, looking each one in the eye, speaking softly and with what seemed genuine emotion: "If [Joe Hunt] can be in this courtroom judged guilty of murder, then it is my fault as his counsel," Barens said. "My limitations would be responsible. If I could be so inept in showing you people the innocence of my client, which is so obvious, then how could I face Lynne and Bobby Roberts, who gave me this case and the proof to save him? How could I tell them that I wasn't enough, even with the proof sent to us by a greater power in the form of Carmen and Chino? If I cannot make this point, if I cannot utter a single truth and be understood, then condemn me rather than this young man. For I would be the one guilty of the crime of murder."

Barens had Mrs. Shelby with him for sure, and three or four other jurors appeared to be leaning. Unfortunately for Joe, however, his attorney was not done. "Fifty years ago, Irving Berlin wrote a song, 'God Bless America,'" Barens continued. "Its words are an anthem for our country and for our generation." The jurors sat stricken; even the gracious Juel Janis experienced some difficulty in containing her amusement. Barens, though, was choked up and swept away: "In the words of that song, I see the same country you do," he continued. "I see a country that is willing to forgive this young man his ambition, to forgive him for being Ron Levin's fool. Forgive him for attempting to exploit Ron Levin's disappearance. This country, long on justice, bars from its gates mere suspicion. Joe Hunt has paid for his immaturity. He paid for his failed dream.

"Do your duty," Barens told the jury. "Set him free. Set Joe Hunt free."

THE PRICE OF EXPERIENCE   533

Wapner, caught off guard when the defense attorney finished half a day ahead of schedule, began his rebuttal without prepared notes. It probably was the best thing that could have happened to him. For once, the prosecutor led with emotion, approaching the jury red-faced, his thin lips a seam of suppressed fury. "Forgive Joe Hunt for his immaturities?" Wapner repeated, barely able to keep his voice down. "We're talking about murder."

Wapner devoted most of his rebuttal to the testimony of Carmen and Chino, achieving his single inspired stroke with a variation on the famous, if fictional, lines attributed to sly old J. Miller Leavy in the L. Ewing Scott case. "Put yourself in Joe Hunt's position," Wapner told the jurors. "You are innocent of a crime you didn't commit. No murder ever happened. And now you are presented with evidence that says that the man you are alleged to have killed is in fact alive and well in Tucson, Arizona. What is the very first thing that you are going to do? You hotfoot it down to Tucson, Arizona, with as much manpower as you can muster. You send people all over the city and you find this guy." Joe, implacable in his composure up to this point, joined Barens and Chier in a pantomime of outrage, which was all they were allowed. "You are going to get to Tucson immediately," Wapner went on. "You are going to put fliers all over the city. You are going to take out ads in the paper. You are going to put things on television." Had the jurors heard or seen any evidence of this? "Nothing," Wapner answered, then sat down to let them think about it.

They would not commence their deliberations until Monday morning, April 20, so that they might "enjoy the weekend," Rittenband told the jurors before dismissing them. A series of hearings ensued after the panel left the courtroom. Barens and Chier had filed for mistrial on the basis of "judicial misconduct" the same morning Wapner commenced his closing argument. "Belittlement" and "banishment" of the defense attorneys were the principal accusations made against the judge by the motion's author, Richard Chier.

Yet Rittenband showed surprising restraint when Wapner moved for a revocation of Joe's bail. "Circumstances have dramatically changed," the prosecutor asserted. "[Hunt] has nothing to lose and everything to gain by not coming back." Barens was indignant, reminding the judge that the Robertses had put up their home to secure Joe's bail and that his client had never once been late for court. Rittenband ruled that Hunt would remain free until the verdict was in.

The judge then summoned the attorneys to his chambers for a discussion of the final jury instructions. The issue was whether Rittenband should inform jurors they had a right to bring in a verdict of second-degree murder, which would mean a prison sentence of perhaps fifteen years. It was a ticklish situation for Hunt's attorneys: On the one hand, a first-degree murder/special-circumstances conviction limited the choice of penalties to life in prison without possibility of parole or execution; on the other hand, it might be possible for the "guilty" voter's to compromise with the "not guilty" voters on a second-degree murder conviction if that was an option. Chier asked if he might have a moment alone with Joe in the judge's cloak-room. "The bathroom," Rittenband replied, "that's an appropriate place for you."

It had been the defendant's decision, Barens and Chier reported to Rittenband five minutes later: No mention of the second-degree murder option should be made. It would be "all or nothing," as Joe himself had put it.

26

THE JURORS STILL WERE SORTING THROUGH THE EXHIBITS ON THE MORNING OF April 21 when Judge Rittenband summoned the panel back to his court-room and advised them to disregard completely any stories in the media concerning the case before them. "We had no idea what that was about," recalled Katherine Keenan, the IRS auditor who had finished second to Juel Janis in the voting for foreperson. "We were more confused than curious."

The judge's admonition was prompted by the revelation earlier in the day that a City News Service staffer named Robbie Robinson had phoned Fred Wapner on Friday afternoon to inform the prosecutor he had seen Ron Levin in the ticket line at a theatre in Westwood during 1986, more than two years after Levin's reported disappearance.

The story broke in all three papers on Wednesday morning, April 22. Forty-four years old, Robinson had worked as a police reporter in Los Angeles for more than fifteen years, the last nine with City News, a down-town wire service that fed breaking stories to daily newspapers and local television stations. Robbie had known Levin, it was agreed, from Ron's Network News days, when the two worked together out of the press room at LAPD headquarters in Parker Center. *Crocodile Dundee* had just opened on the evening in early September of 1986 when Robinson inadvertently stepped into the line for people who already had tickets, as he recalled it. Ron Levin, heading toward the end of that line, stopped to "exchange pleas-antries," Robinson told the Associated Press. "He said, 'Hi Rob! How are you?'" the reporter recalled, adding, "If I knew he was dead, I would have been flabbergasted." It was "a battle of conscience" that compelled his deci-sion to come forward, said Robinson, who professed astonishment at the repercussions of his phone call to the DA's office: "I was just trying to pass on information." The question was why he waited so long.

City News Managing Editor Bob Lauffer told the *Herald,* "It is my understanding—are you sitting down?—that he didn't know the trial was going on." "I'm so loaded up on crime I want to get away from it when I'm off duty," Robbie explained. Due to "a potential conflict of interest," Lauffer told the *Herald,* Robinson had been placed on suspension from his job. "Paid suspension," noted Robbie, who now acknowledged he had "noticed" stories in the newspapers about the Hunt trial but hadn't read them closely: "I thought [Levin] had disappeared after I saw him."

The reporter had contradicted himself already, however, claiming to have learned of the Hunt trial "just this morning" when he phoned Wapner on April 17, then admitting on the following Monday that he had been aware of the proceedings for some time. "I was trying to avoid a problem of lateness in coming to them," Robinson explained. "Obviously I shouldn't have told Wapner I had just read about the thing and had not known about it before. But on the twentieth, I made a clean breast of it and, without prompting, told the truth to the police." Investigators, though, soon spotted a second discrepancy in Robinson's story: *Crocodile Dundee* had not opened in Westwood until September 26, 1986. Robinson was called to the Beverly Hills Police Department on Tuesday morning for a lie detector test and an all-day interrogation. "I knew there was going to be hassles," he told the *Santa Monica Evening Outlook,* "although I didn't know it was going to be this bad."

Judge Rittenband refused Barens's demand that he should halt the jury's deliberations and allow them to hear Robbie Robinson. "I have to wait until we complete this inquiry," the judge said.

The jurors remained oblivious. They were an unusually tight group, perhaps because ten of the twelve survivors were white women or perhaps simply because they had spent so much time together, not just the six months in court but in the lunch groups and car pools they formed. While not one of them would confess any breach of the judge's order to refrain from discussion of the case, the women on the jury freely admitted they had amused one another during the months they spent in Department C by casting the adult parts in the BBC movie, by inventing names for the assorted spectators and reporters they saw day after day in the courtroom, and by humming "Stand by Your Man" in unison whenever they saw Joe and Brooke together. Most entertaining of all was the "Recipe of the Week" submitted each Monday by juror Linda Mickell, better known among her colleagues as "Mrs. Ortho Mattress" (for her marriage to the man who ran the company). The recipe Hunt's attorneys got hold of described "six easy steps":

1. Invert a butterfly in a frying pan.
2. Add some diced porkbellies and Swiss frankfurters.
3. Simmer over low heat for 10 minutes.
4. A little margin *may* be called for to prevent shrinkage.
5. Add 1 can Hunt's tomato sauce and generous amounts of spice.
6. Simmer over low heat for an additional hour.

This dish may be served over rice, over noodles, or over the counter. Best prepared ahead of time (a futures dish). Serves 4–6 financially secure people who wish to gain. Low in calories and nutritional value, it is not advised for people with a faint-of-heart condition.

The panel had completed its review of the exhibits in evidence and was preparing for its first vote as newspaper stories reporting Robinson's phone call to Wapner hit the streets. "We really had no idea what was going on, though, not even with each other," said Carolyn Ghaemmaghami, the mother of seven whose marriage to an Iranian had been the subject of much discussion during voir dire. "I honestly felt I would be alone when I voted guilty on the first ballot. I looked at the rest of them, and they seemed like sweet little girls. So I was stunned when it turned out there was only one vote for not guilty."

Mrs. Ghaemmaghami knew what the others in the room only suspected, that the lone vote for acquittal had been cast by Barens's favorite juror, Mrs. Shelby. "I was sitting right next to Gloria, and I could see what she wrote," Mrs. Ghaemmaghami admitted. "Anyway, I was flabbergasted when the first vote was eleven to one. You know, it was so quiet in there. It didn't seem like anyone was breathing."

The first juror to break the silence was the lone male, a Vietnam veteran named Dean Rutherford: "Dean said, 'Who was the person who did that? Speak up,'" Mrs. Ghaemmaghami recalled. "The dope. We said, 'What's the matter with you?' We had to defend the person's right to privacy, even though we were all pretty sure it was Gloria." Ms. Keenan suggested that those who had voted guilty should give their reasons. Mrs. Ghaemmaghami went first. The seven pages were the strongest piece of evidence, obviously, she said, followed by the testimony of Dean Karny and Joe's announcement at the June 24 meeting.

The jurors agreed that most—"and probably all," Ms. Keenan said—of the BBC Boys who took the stand had lied about one thing or another. Steve Taglianetti ("the most obvious liar") and Tom May ("dim, dim, dim") were not taken seriously by any of them. Evan Dicker had not gone over well, either: "It was like 'I am not a Nazi, I have never been a Nazi, but when I was a Nazi I was a very good Nazi,'" Ms. Keenan said. "I thought he was smart, though, the only one besides Dean who seemed intelligent." Steve Lopez the jurors generally liked. They were divided, though, on Lopez's enemy, Eisenberg: "Of all the BBC people, Eisenberg made the best impression on me," said Ms. Keenan. "He was older, even if he was younger." "Eisenberg was so flat," countered Mrs. Ghaemmaghami. "Some of them, you could see they had a dream, however ridiculous it was. But Eisenberg seemed like he had no dream at all, except money."

Dean Karny inevitably was the witness who generated most discussion in the jury room. "For Dean, I felt pity," said Ms. Keenan. "At the same time, it seemed wrong that he had committed two murders, really, and was walking away. And yet I think he actually felt something about the intrinsic wrongness of it, which I didn't get from any of the others." "It seemed the things Dean left out said as much as the things he left in," observed Mrs. Ghaemmaghami. "He kept trying to give the impression he was just following Joe, when he was really in on it all the way. What I thought was that Dean didn't tell the truth about himself, but he did tell the truth about everyone else."

The attorneys for the defense and prosecution had "reversed their order of regard," as Ms. Keenan put it, during the course of the trial. "Barens made a better impression by far during voir dire," recalled Mrs. Ghaemmaghami. "He was so smooth, but his patina is a lot better than what's underneath. Fred Wapner, on the other hand, made no impression at all, except that he looks like somebody who works hard. And he is. That's about all there is to him, though. Still, we came to respect Wapner. He seemed like he had really put his heart and his soul into this case." All the jurors had been stunned by the brevity of the defense case. "I was kind of worried whether Hunt got an adequate defense, to be honest," Ms. Keenan explained. "The defense never explained anything, they just depended on us to believe Carmen and Chino." "And Carmen just didn't hold it," said Mrs. Ghaemmaghami. "We didn't think she was lying—we thought she was a hysteric," explained Ms. Keenan.

Brooke was the witness most easily dismissed. "She looks as sweet as pie," Ms. Keenan said. "It's when she starts to talk that the image is dispelled. She made me feel young and naïve by comparison." Nearly every one of the jurors believed Brooke had helped plan the murder. "I think Brooke is as guilty as Dean," said Mrs. Ghaemmaghami.

It had been more difficult to discount Lynne Roberts. "I couldn't dislike her. She kept smiling at us during the trial, when she was sitting in the audience," recalled Mrs. Ghaemmaghami. "Mr. Roberts too; he would sit out there in the audience and smile at us like we were his children or something." "I thought Lynne Roberts *believed* she was telling the truth but *knew* she wasn't," said Ms. Keenan. "Personally, I felt like there was a lot more going on in that family than we were ever told," Mrs. Ghaemmaghami added.

Several jurors admitted the urge to interrupt Barens during the attorney's final argument. The jury room had erupted into laughter at each mention of "the 'God Bless America' bit" from the defense attorney, Mrs. Ghaemmaghami recalled.

The jurors were more amused than affected by the animus between Judge Rittenband and Richard Chier. "The judge I liked and respected," said Mrs. Ghaemmaghami. "I could understand how he would find Chier offensive—I know I did." "And the way he treated Chier probably had a counter effect," Ms. Keenan explained, "because you wanted to give Joe every advantage."

Nearly every juror had remarked upon the "parallels" between Joe Hunt and Ron Levin. "They were very alike, but Levin had more of a human touch," Ms. Keenan explained. "He actually had people who had known him for years that loved him, even though they knew the truth about him. Whereas I don't think Joe ever revealed the truth about himself to anybody." It was more complicated for Mrs. Ghaemmaghami, who was reminded by both Joe and Ron of her oldest son, who had been sentenced to sixty years in a federal prison just a few weeks into the Hunt trial. "He's twenty-four, very intelligent, very charming—everything they said about Joe," Mrs. Ghaemmaghami explained. "But he reminded me more of Ron. The whole time I was hearing about Ron Levin, I was thinking about my son. What Ron did with his mother reminds me a lot of my son, who would call me collect three times a day from jail. He never has forgotten my birthday, the only one of my children who hasn't. I couldn't believe my own son, no matter where he was, wouldn't call me. So that was a very compelling argument for me, when they talked about Ron calling his mother."

The case came down to the defendant, of course, and it was for the insolence of his self-assertion that Joe would be judged most harshly. "What struck us all was the way Joe seemed to want everyone to see that he was running the show, that his lawyers were working for him," Mrs. Ghaemmaghami remembered. "So there was a tendency to hold Joe somewhat responsible for how poor his defense was," explained Ms. Keenan.

The jury was "stunned and disappointed when Joe didn't testify," Mrs. Ghaemmaghami said, "but not angry. That was his right." "He had to explain the seven pages," countered Ms. Keenan. "The only version we had was the prosecution's, so naturally we accepted it."

In the end, it was their feeling that Joe did not deserve to take this fall alone that made conviction most difficult, the jurors explained. "I'm not even sure Joe was the worst of the BBC Boys," said Mrs. Ghaemmaghami. "The rest were using him. A lot of them were in on the murder, in my opinion, at least five or six. It seemed like there was an unspoken conspiracy." "We all thought that," agreed Ms. Keenan. "The other Boys all were counting on Joe, and I thought without them, Joe never would have done it."

Less than one hour after the first ballot, Juel Janis called for a second. This time the vote was unanimous. "I would say Joe Hunt's signal error was that he misjudged the general run of humanity," Ms. Keenan said. "He thought they could be manipulated so easily, that he was so much smarter than everybody else. His attitude seemed to be not that 'I'm not guilty,' but that 'You didn't *prove* me guilty.'"

A message that the jury had a verdict was sent to Judge Rittenband at a little past 11 A.M. on April 22. He scheduled its announcement for 1:30 P.M., which gave the camera crews time to assemble. Hunt and Barens arrived together at just past 1 P.M.; while Joe looked nothing less than serene, tension had compressed his attorney's features to a gnomish density.

It was almost two when the verdict was read aloud by Diane Tschekaloff: "We, the jurors . . . find Joseph Hunt guilty of murder in the first degree." It was difficult to distinguish the gasps of surprise from the sighs of relief in the roar of suspiration that echoed through Department C. The first voice that rose above the din was Bob Levin's: "Thank God!" he shouted.

Joe sat without expression for a moment, then turned to embrace Barens and Chier, each of whom had received the verdict with more apparent anguish than their client. Brooke and Lynne Roberts, sitting side by side, raised their hands to their mouths and whispered "Oh my God!" in unison. When Joe turned to them, his eyes were not angry—not even cold; he looked softer, actually, than at any time since the start of the trial. He shrugged at Brooke and extended his open palms.

Joe stared into the jury box then. "I saw him looking at the others, and I knew he'd get to me," Mrs. Ghaemmaghami recalled. "I was tempted to turn my eyes away, but I just looked back. You can't see into Joe Hunt, though. He's one person who can't be penetrated."

A number of spectators stepped to the rail to shake Joe's hand or offer encouragement; several people promised to write letters to the appeals court complaining that he had not received a fair trial. While Barens and Chier conferred with Wapner, Joe slid his chair to the rail, pulled Brooke's hands, then Lynne's, to his lips, removed his striped tie, handed them his watch, wallet, keys, and the quartz crystal Rudy Durand had sent him the day before, then faced the reporters lined up three-deep to question him. "Astonished," Joe answered, when asked how he felt, though he scarcely looked it. "I think [the verdict] is a tragedy because Ron Levin is alive and I'm sure he'll be found in the next couple of years, with the sort of visibility he's had lately," Joe told the assembled media. "And for those who know I'm innocent, it's a compound tragedy." The jury had been "conscientious," Joe added, his voice devoid of rancor, "but for those of us who were there, our memory serves us better than their logic. Ron Levin is alive!" he repeated, vehemently, then added, "At least he did not die by my hand on that night."

"Joe Hunt's never at a loss for words," Marty Levin told the media a moment later. "He's guilty as hell. I hope he gets the death penalty."

Bobby and Lynne Roberts left the courtroom pursued by a pack of reporters. "Get lost!" Bobby snarled. Brooke trailed behind them, still sobbing "Oh my God!" as she stumbled down the courthouse steps.

Barens was funereal as he stepped toward the TV cameras in the hallway: "I'm personally and professionally extremely disappointed," the attorney said, his voice shaking. The verdict would "definitely be appealed," he added. Chier seemed to be gargling bile as he faced the cameras: "It's not over yet. When he gets a fair trial, he'll get a right verdict."

Fred Wapner had a grin for everyone as he emerged from Department C. Enjoying at last the attention of the media, the prosecutor allowed himself to be led under the halo of TV lights. "A just verdict," he said, beaming.

Before he was removed from the courtroom for the trip to county jail, Joe made one last statement, in response to a question about his "future plans": "My only responsibility is to keep my chin up," he said. "And that's what I do best."

Judge Rittenband summoned Barens and Chier to the bench shortly after the reading of the verdict to ask the defense lawyers when they would be ready to begin the penalty trial. "When you pay me," snapped Chier, angry that his fee had been slashed repeatedly by the judge. "You're fired," Rittenband retorted. "Mr. Barens will be better off without you."

The attorney the defendant wished to be rid of, however, was not Chier but Barens. "You're right—Arthur is a joke," Hunt wrote to Rudy Durand from his cell in the "high power" section at county jail. Despite Durand's falling-out with Bobby Roberts (the *Return of Billy Jack* deal had dissolved, and Tom Laughlin was threatening to sue Roberts for fraud), Rudy had become Joe's confidant of last resort, supplying Hunt with reading material saved from that lost year in Houston: *The I Ching, The Tao of Philosophy, Creative Solitude,* and the book that would become Joe's bible during the next few months, *Tales Of Power.*

Joe had spent only two nights at county jail when he sent Rudy the first of more than twenty letters he would write in number two pencil on sheets of yellow legal paper during the spring of 1987. In Greek mythology, Hades was bordered by three rivers, Joe observed in one posted a few days after his conviction—Styx, Acheron, and, finally, Lethe, the river of forgetfulness. "It always struck me as odd that the myth would give one of Hades's rivers that aspect," he wrote. "But here on this bank and shoal of time I can hear that dread river and hear its waters murmur their promise of oblivion. It is death for me to be forgotten. It is death for me to forget. Either would buy me a ride across the river and into hell."

Joe was in no danger of being forgotten in the near future, at least among entertainment executives in Los Angeles. For most of the past year, gossip columnists and trade press reporters had chased every fugitive rumor or idle boast emanating from the apparently bottomless pit of "producers" angling to bring the BBC story to the screen. The first property to make the rounds at the studios and networks was an eighteen-page treatment submitted by Joe and Dean's former Harvard schoolmate, Charley Matthau, son of Walter, coauthored, according to the reader's report at the Creative Artists Agency, by "one of the members of the conspiracy." Matthau's collaborator was widely assumed to be Dave May, conspicuous by his absence from the five-page CAST OF CHARACTERS that transformed Joe Hunt into "Dan Foxx," Paradox Philosophy into "Contradictory Law," and the BBC into the "Associated Millionaires Club."

The John Sack–Jim Pittman–Mike Canale/Rob Lowe–Cary Elwes–Bob Wyman consortium had generated a BBC treatment as well, authored by Sack, but the project failed to obtain financing. According to *American Film,* "Hollywood's attention was focused on" the *Esquire* article, which the *Los Angeles Times* reported had been optioned by producer Adam Fields. This was untrue, but Fields was soon taking calls from the industry's elite screenwriters, among them Robert Towne (*Chinatown*) and Kurt Ludtke (*Absence of Malice*). Tom Cruise wanted to play Joe Hunt, Fields reported, but so, it seemed, did every other young actor in town.

As late as the second week in April, Hunt's agents had been reminding the studios that no BBC film could be made without Joe's consent. "We're asking one million for the theatrical rights—books, movie or miniseries—in one package," Sy Marsh had told the *Daily News* back in March. "I hope we can get into a bidding war after Hunt gets on the stand. The fees on this are going to explode." Joe hadn't gotten on the stand, of course, and no one was offering him even one dollar, let alone a million, after he was found guilty.

While the Rob Lowe project foundered and the Joe Hunt approach failed, the May twins' version of the BBC was moving forward at NBC, whose vice president for TV movies, Susan Baerwald, had phoned ITC on the morning the Hunt jury began its deliberations to announce that her network was prepared to sign a contract. By early May, it had been determined that the BBC script would be written not by Robert Towne or Kurt Ludtke but rather by former sitcom scenarist Guy Waldron, who agreed to turn out the teleplay in seven weeks.

Even as NBC announced its plans to air a *Billionaire Boys Club* miniseries in October of that year, dozens of other BBC projects continued to swirl through Department C during the penalty phase trial, each stewarded by somebody claiming an inside track to this principal or that one. Len Marmor proposed that the BBC movie should be told from the point of view of Ron Levin: "Why the fuck not?" he demanded. "Ron's the most interesting character in the whole thing. And since he's dead, you don't have to pay him a penny."

The tale of Joe Hunt and the Billionaire Boys seemed to have become an abyss to which seekers of fame and fortune found themselves inescapably drawn, even when they had no hope of profit. Poor Robbie Robinson remained the principal case in point. Five days after Joe's conviction, Robinson's "suspension" from City News Service became a "termination." He had failed the lie detector test conducted by the Beverly Hills Police Department, Robbie admitted: "The polygraph said I was lying, but I wasn't," he insisted. "There was a lot of tension and feelings of guilt that I didn't come forward sooner." Still, Robinson recognized he had made "a mistake": "I admit I was wrong in my actions, but I don't think they were so wrong, I deserved termination."

Speculation in the city rooms of all three Los Angeles newspapers was mainly about what might have driven the miserable bastard to do it. He was poorly paid and pitifully obscure, but at least had obtained a sinecure of sorts. Perhaps it was the accumulated ache of seeing his anonymous dispatches rewritten by newspaper hacks who got the bylines. Los Angeles itself was blamed most often, not just for what had befallen Robbie but for the not so temporary insanity that seems to possess so many who come to the city from other places: L.A. does such strange things to people's heads. In New York, an alien struggles, adapting by a process of jarring collisions and stabs of recognition. Lines are flat, edges sharp, seasons distinct. Los Angeles, though, curves, yields, and encloses, preferring seduction to conquest. Visitors may see the danger clearly at first, but the place grows on them—like a fungus, according to those who flee—while those who remain find themselves admitting more and more often to an equivocation that can become a kind of conviction in the aftermath of a subtropical rainfall. As desert winds scour the sky, the spectral light takes on a sparkling translucence; memory begins to seem an unnecessary burden, a way of punishing oneself for sins committed so long ago that they can't possibly matter now, here.

For jurors, the worst was yet to come. "A group of us walked out on the Santa Monica Pier during the break, and Kathy and I were holding each other up, crying on each other's shoulders," Mrs. Ghaemmaghami remembered. "We needed air, but it was hard to breathe . . . then when we came back to court and the judge started telling us we weren't done, I didn't want to hear it." She had no choice. Their duty, Judge Rittenband reminded the jurors, included deciding what punishment fit this crime. There were two choices: life in prison without the possibility of parole or death by lethal injection.

The "penalty phase" of the Hunt trial began on May 11, and by then Joe had eschewed his striped Armani suits for blue jail coveralls. Led into the courtroom with hands cuffed behind his back, he looked as if he had been sleeping in a coffin. The sun had shined every day during the three weeks since his return to custody, but Joe was a whiter shade of pale than the death rockers who haunted Hollywood Boulevard, his black eyes sunken into hollows so deep that the skin seemed bruised by daylight. He no longer pretended to suffer gladly and glowered at the bailiff who moved his manacles from back to front. Taller than anyone in the room, he hunched his shoulders and lowered his head in a way that made him appear to be looking up, an affect that merely amplified the malevolence of his eyes. "Holy shit, the horns are growing," whispered a young studio executive still hoping to make the BBC movie.

Joe seemed slightly more human when he exchanged chagrined smiles with Rudy Durand and the Robertses, then took his seat at the defense table, where Brooke had placed a small white orchid. Still wearing cuffs on both wrists, Joe cradled one hand in the other to scrawl a series of notes, his "high-profile prisoner" jail ID bracelet clicking against the tabletop. Rittenband instructed the bailiff to remove the handcuffs, then informed the jury that Mr. Hunt was wearing jail blues "at his own election and desire." Joe also had combed his hair over geek style, one snide observer noted, "going for the sympathy vote."

Barens wore a black suit to make his opening statement, somber as a minister at graveside. Mentioning only once that he disagreed with their verdict, Barens left aside the case against Joe Hunt and reminded the jury that the United States was the only Western democracy that still imposed capital punishment. "Never in the history of this state has a man been put to death in a case where no body has been found," Barens told the jurors. "I ask you to consider the tragedy of what has already happened in Joe Hunt's life and not to add to that tragedy by state-sanctioned murder."

Barens's dread arose out of what he imagined might be a jury's reaction to a description of Hedayat Eslaminia's death during that drive south on the Golden State Freeway three years earlier. The prosecutor's opening statement, though, was brief, little more than a promise that "the state will introduce evidence of three other criminal acts engaged in by the defendant." Terse, clipped, almost flat, Wapner had never seemed more human; his tone conveyed the sense that it was not in him to pray for anyone's death, even Joe Hunt's.

Jerry Coker of the FCI Laboratory was the first witness called. Coker described the problems with the BMWs sent to him by West Cars, the meeting with BBC members to discuss "reducing costs," and the phone call he received one week later from an employee who told him the lab had been shot to pieces. The jury was impassive up this point but began to lean and whisper when Coker recalled Jim Pittman's suggestion that they kill the culprit and dissolve his body in acid.

An enormous red rose from Brooke and Bertrand Russell's *The Age of Reason* were waiting for Joe at the defense table when he returned to Department C the next morning. After a series of police officers established that the shell casings found at the scene of the FCI shooting were fired out of the same .30 caliber carbine seized from Jim at the warehouse in Gardena two months later, Joe's old adversary Bruce Swartout strode into the courtroom. Listening to Swartout's self-serving account of their business dealings, Joe seemed actually to suffer, squeezing his forehead so tightly that his knuckles whitened.

Steve Taglianetti came back to court to tie the testimony of Coker and Swartout to Hunt and Pittman, but in the end both incidents would be largely discounted by the jury. "The prosecution really didn't prove beyond a reasonable doubt that Joe was responsible for those things," explained Ms. Keenan.

As they listened for the next week to testimony involving the third "criminal act" Wapner had mentioned, however, the number of jurors who wanted Joe dead would increase daily. "The Eslaminia thing was *so* scary," said Ms. Keenan.

Bernice Rappaport brought the first real moment of drama to the penalty-phase proceedings, revealing that on the afternoon Joe and Dean looked at the Beverly Glen house they had been accompanied by "a girl." Did she see the young woman she met that afternoon in the courtroom? Wapner asked. "It was her," the realtor answered, pointing to Brooke, who responded by shaking her head, aghast, as the jurors gazed at her with sheer disgust.

Dean Karny consolidated the case for execution, devoting most of the next three days to a chronicle of Project Sam's design and execution. Dean began to heave and sigh when he arrived at the afternoon of July 30, 1984, gripping the rail of the witness stand with both hands as he took the jury into the back of the U-Haul, then described those "noises" that had come from the trunk.

Several jurors moaned aloud during the next hour of Dean's testimony. "I had a different nightmare every night during the time Karny was on the stand," recalled Ms. Keenan. "How could he and Dosti sit there in the back of that truck? Then he talked about taping the holes. I think there were several people on the jury who would have voted the death penalty for Dean at that point." "It was strange," said Mrs. Ghaemmaghami. "I felt sorrier for Dean but also more repulsed by him."

Several jurors raised open palms to their brows, using them like eyeshades, when Dean described how he and Joe and Ben dined in the living room at the Beverly Glen two or three hours later, discussing "what to do with the body" that reposed only a few feet away.

Evan Dicker and Jerry Eisenberg returned to explain the origins of the forged power of attorney and fraudulent conservatorship. Then Oscar Breiling took the stand to bring the horror home, producing photographs of the Iranian's broken, sun-bleached, coyote-gnawed skeleton, then submitting a large print of the dead man's skull to "verify his identity."

Little more than morbid curiosity attended the procession to the stand of those Roberts family members—Bobby being the sole exception—who had not testified during the guilt phase of the trial. Todd's fiancée Michelle Berenek described her first meeting with Joe at county jail in November of 1984 ("He was so articulate; if you closed your eyes you could imagine him in a business suit") and told the jury how Joe got in touch with his feelings through Lifespring. Todd followed her to the stand and explained what had distinguished Joe from "the others in that crowd" when he first met the BBC Boys back in the fall of 1982: "Joe was much less materialistic than the rest of them, one of the few in that group that didn't have a Rolex watch or drive a BMW or wear the cashmere sweaters and alligator loafers." The jurors tittered as Todd told them Joe had studied closely the careers of Napoléon and Huey Long, using them both to illustrate his "'REAP WHAT YOU SOW' philosophy." The Robertses were paying a huge price for their public support of Joe Hunt, Todd told the jury: "We've been avoided, criticized, ridiculed. We've gone through all this because we put up his bail. People said he'd [run] and we'd lose the house. But he's still here—because he's innocent."

The defense produced another witness who claimed to have seen Ron Levin alive after June of 1984. This was not Robbie Robinson, however, but a legal secretary named Louise Waller. Ms. Waller was a woman with faded good looks and a flattened affect whose age could have been anywhere from thirty to fifty. She knew Ron Levin from the period when she worked for a law firm in a suite adjoining his in the late 1970s, Ms. Waller said. She had heard Levin's name for the first time in years, the woman told the jury, from the office manager at the firm where she was working in January of 1987: "She said, 'You know he's missing and they think he's been murdered.'" Naturally it came as a surprise, Ms. Waller explained, when, one afternoon barely a month later, she saw Ron Levin striding purposefully through the lobby of a building on Little Santa Monica Boulevard. "He looked the same," she recalled, "except he had put on a few pounds."

The woman's persona altered astoundingly during cross-examination: A rapid series of squirms, giggles, and nervous tics were the process of her transformation from glacial placidity to what seemed an eerie replication of Lorelei Lee as played by Marilyn Monroe in *Gentlemen Prefer Blondes*. Wapner looked more confused than pleased by her burbling, seeking only some stray fact that might explain what she was doing here.

"I don't know why she did what she did," said Ms. Keenan, "but I didn't believe her for a minute, and neither did any of the others. Carmen I at least found an honest witness. But that woman scared me."

Steve Solomon came as a relief, after Louise Waller, Ms. Keenan recalled: "He seemed so normal by comparison." Solomon at least seemed to have a unique concept of what it meant to be a witness at a death penalty trial. Smiling sweetly at everyone from the prosecutor to the jury foreperson, beaming at Joe and waving to Brooke, Steverino strode into Department C wearing tight jeans, cowboy boots, and a tapered white shirt, plucking and tugging at his clothes as he took the stand until they were arranged to show off his physique to maximum advantage. He told the jurors about meeting Joe with the Robertses at the Sunshine Health Bar and recalled that his new friend was not put off when Steve confided he was a Jehovah's Witness, expressing interest in the "scientific and historical data that back up the Bible."

When his parents flew to Southern California from Ohio, Joe was the one friend outside the church to whom he had introduced them, Steve said: "I wanted them to meet just the nice people in my life," he explained. "I consider [Joe] very clean and moral and my parents are very clean and moral."

"There's a lot of uncleanliness in Los Angeles," he added, and seemed sincerely surprised when this detonated near-hysterical laughter in the courtroom.

He knew Joe was a person of some notoriety but hadn't inquired about the details, Steve said: "I don't pry. We have a lot of celebrities, TV people mainly, coming into the club, and you learn not to ask a lot of questions." It came as a shock, of course, when Joe revealed that he was on trial for murder, Steve admitted: "I said, 'Sure, guy.' I thought he was joking."

Joe said he couldn't talk about the case, which was fine with him, Solomon explained to Wapner on cross: "My attitude was 'Let's just go on with life and get this thing over with, so we can have more fun.'"

Leslie Eto was Joe's other character witness. Diminutive and demure, the young Japanese woman refuted every allegation that had been made about Hunt's conduct in Chicago. "Joe was fair, even and respectful to me," Eto told the jury, "and more fair—to a fault—than the others on out-trades." Also, for one of such tender age, Hunt was remarkably supportive to those of lesser abilities, Leslie said. "Enormous composure, compassion and empathy," Eto answered, when asked by Barens to characterize the Joe she knew. "A very internalized person who does not ask anything for himself."

Once again, nearly every juror was looking either at the floor or the ceiling. Joe would not be rescued from the death chamber by Leslie Eto or Steve Solomon, and certainly not by Brooke's brothers. Someone the jurors cared about had to beg for his life.

There was not only indignity but exquisite irony in his circumstance: The one person who could save him was not a new friend or a future in-law, but rather the haggard, handsome woman in the second-row seat whom he had studiously ignored since her appearance in Department C earlier that week. Willowy but worn, with a strong jaw and anguished eyes, she sat among the Robertses, though not with them, wearing a cheap dress and no makeup, unidentified but too like Joe in appearance to be anyone other than the mystery woman he claimed had been shut up in a mental institution years ago.

"The defense calls Kathleen Gamsky," Chier announced. The attempted smile of the witness as she took the stand was so pitiful that several jurors began to blink back tears even before she had opened her mouth. "Mrs. Gamsky, you are related to Joe Hunt?" Chier began. "Yes," she answered. "I am his mother."

27

JOE WAS FIVE WHEN THE FAMILY FOUND ITS WAY TO ALBERS STREET. LARRY called one day at noon, Kathy remembered, gave her an address in Van Nuys, and said to meet him there in twenty minutes. Joe and Greg observed their mother's long-suffering look as the old Plymouth pulled into the drive-way. Head-high heaps of trash and tree trimmings hid most of a small stucco house that stood shedding its paint like pink scales. The yard was brown and the windows tiny. There was a pool, Larry said, and led them all out back to look at a concrete teardrop containing a few fetid feet of marinated monkey puzzle tree droppings. The house was a foreclosure, available for no money down on a land-sale contract, he explained. Kathy asked if this was why she had come back to California.

Joe and Greg worked with their father all summer. The cactus was cut back, the house painted, the lawn watered. Twenty trailer loads of trash were hauled away. The three of them spent weeks pumping out the pool, scraping and plastering its walls. By August, when the southern horizon was darkened by smoke from fires set during the Watts riots, the pool was in working order and became the best thing about Albers Street. Joe and Greg and the Chicano kids from next door, the Largys, would while away whole afternoons playing Marco Polo by the pool. Larry built all the furniture for the room the boys shared, slapping together two-by-fours and sheets of ply-wood to make bunk beds and desks. He repaired the water heater and then the swamp cooler—even Kathy had to admit he was handy. The boys also got a dog, a little collie they called Beauty.

By the time they started school in September, though, Larry was driving back across Coldwater to spend all day and most of the evening on Sunset Boulevard at the American Institute of Hypnosis, where he had be-come both patient and protégé to the Institute's famous proprietor, Dr. William Jennings Bryan Jr. The doctor gave Larry a job as office manager but would pay him a salary of only sixty dollars a week to start. Dr. Bryan promised more if Larry could bring in business, but in the meantime his earnings were less than what he paid the doctor for his own therapy. Kathy never was more defeated than on the day she learned Larry had spent the last five thousand dollars in his trust fund to buy a seat in the doctor's Self-Motivation Seminar.

She tried to help, taking a job as a technical illustrator at McDonnell Douglas. After taxes, transportation, and child care, Mrs. Gamsky was clearing $8 a week and decided it was better economy to stay home with Greg and Joe and their new baby sister, Kay. Kathy asked for a car to carry Joe to his kindergarten class at Kester Avenue Elementary, but Larry told her their son was quite capable and should walk. Joe said it was all right, but Joe always said that. Her middle child was never a fussy type like Kay or Greg, Kathy recalled: He would eat any food, wear any clothes, play with any toy. A pile of wooden blocks was all it took to make him happy. "Self-sufficient" was the word Mrs. Gamsky used most often to describe her younger son. Joe, she told neighbors, had toilet-trained himself.

During the spring of 1968, a difficult period for the family, financially, Joe, then eight years old and a third grader, came home from school one day and announced, "I have a great idea." Her younger son then loaded his little sister's red wagon with boxes of candy bars, Kathy recalled, and wheeled it off to the junior high school a few blocks away, where he intended to wait by the buses for the three o'clock bell. "He said, 'When the kids come out, I am going to sell them candy bars for a little more than I paid and I am going to make a lot of money,'" she remembered. Joe returned home half an hour later with both the red wagon and the pockets of his blue jeans empty, crying because a gang of older boys had roughed him up, confiscated his candy, and stolen his money. Kathy tried to comfort him, but Joe wiped away the tears himself, and his mother was more than impressed when the boy lifted his face, looked her in the eye, and vowed, "I will forget it ever happened."

A favorite family legend of William J. Bryan Jr., M.D., J.D., Ph.D, LL.D., was that his more famous fourth cousin, William Jennings Bryan I, had been made mockery of in the "Scopes Monkey Trial" by Clarence Darrow's clever application of hypnotic technique. The story went that just before Bryan began his fulminating final argument, the defense lawyer requested a brief recess and used it to run a piano wire through his Cuban corona from tip to tip. Darrow lit the cigar as Bryan stood to speak and continued smoking throughout the prosecuting attorney's thundering oration. As the ash at the end of the cigar grew, Darrow began to rotate the stogie slowly between his thumb and forefinger. By the time the cylinder of ash was as long as the remaining cigar, every man in the jury box had surreptitiously shifted his gaze from Bryan to Darrow, more deeply engaged by the question of when the ash would spill onto the Chicago lawyer's shirtfront than by the three-time presidential nominee's account of the hellish torments reserved for those who embraced the apostate creed of evolutionist atheism.

Clarence Darrow apparently understood the basic principle of hypnotic suggestion, the prosecuting attorney's descendant observed: "People will imitate what you do rather than follow what you say."

Though a law school graduate, William J. Bryan Jr. never was permitted to stand in the stead of his illustrious ancestor, arguing passionately before a panel of twelve fair-minded peers. Yet the younger Bryan would appear often in court during the 1960s, most often as a paid advisor to some of the nation's top trial attorneys. Among these was Melvin Belli, who authored the first of the two forewords to Bryan's best-known book, *The Chosen Ones*. "The redoubtable academician, doctor, lawyer, hypnotist, lecturer, writer, *bon vivant,* and philosopher" was Belli's description of his associate. F. Lee Bailey, who wrote the book's second foreword, praised Bryan as a man "who can tell more about a human being in a few minutes than many people can ever learn about themselves in a lifetime."

The lesser-known Reno attorneys who had been familiar with Dr. Bryan back in the days when he ran a private medical practice just outside town in East Sparks, Nevada, were less laudatory. This was understandable, considering that the last time they had seen the doctor was on that afternoon in 1959 when he was escorted to the shore of Lake Tahoe by three police cruisers and left off at Stateline with the warning that his return to Nevada would result in arrest on several counts of sexual abuse. The most serious of the accusations against Bryan had been made by a fifteen-year-old girl who claimed she intended to have a cyst removed when she visited the doctor's office, where he anesthetized her with champagne until she passed out and was on top of her when she awoke.

A damnable lie, said Bryan. His campaign for the Nevada state legislature on a reform ticket had so alarmed the incumbents that they resorted to frame-up in a last-ditch effort to stop him. No one cared really in Southern California, where Bryan would spend the next fifteen years successfully reinventing himself out of a series of offices stretching along Sunset Boulevard from Whiskey A Go Go to the Crossroads of the World.

Bryan could contend with no small amount of justification that the career in conventional medicine he abandoned at the border between Nevada and California was a distinguished one. The doctor had earned the first of his college degrees from Duke University at the age of nineteen, worked as an electrical engineer in the U.S. Navy at the end of World War II, was a graduate of the University of Illinois College of Medicine at twenty-four, served as director of medical survival training for the U.S. Air Force during the Korean War, and would be described as the American military's "leading expert on brainwashing" before he turned thirty.

After leaving Reno, Bryan intended to take up practice of the law in Los Angeles and was flabbergasted when the state bar denied his application on grounds of moral turpitude, citing the three cases of sexual misconduct that had resulted in the revocation of his license to practice medicine in Nevada. Not a man to dwell on disppointments, however, Bryan went on to serve as a member of the defense team at the two most sensational murder trials of the 1960s, each involving wealthy M.D.s accused of murdering their wives—first, Dr. Carl Coppolino of New Jersey, and later, Dr. Sam Sheppard of Ohio. It had been Bryan's principal task in each case to rate prospective jurors. When Coppolino and Sheppard were acquitted by the juries Bryan chose—both before and after being convicted by jurors he had not selected—reports of his astounding skills appeared in newspapers and magazines across the country. "Dr. Bryan has an ability to spot reactions that I'd maybe pick up only half the time," F. Lee Bailey, who had defended both men, would tell *Playboy* in 1967.

Bryan's appearances in court beside the likes of Bailey and Belli were hardly his only claims to fame. During the same period the doctor would serve as technical advisor on three feature films, beginning with *The Manchurian Candidate;* be ordained as a Baptist minister; sit in on snare drums at concert performances by Fats Domino; appear at ringside as a "personal counselor" to a pair of heavyweight boxing champions; share a "Supreme Court Day" speakers' podium with Democratic presidential nominee Hubert Humphrey; conduct seminars on human sexuality attended by thousands of M.D.s from all over the United States; obtain a Ph.D. in psychology and a doctor of laws degree during the same year; not only author three books but publish and edit a quarterly academic journal in which most of the articles were bylined "William J. Bryan Jr."

All of Bryan's activities and accomplishments, however, remained subordinate to his primary occupation as director of the American Institute of Hypnosis. Bryan's formal training in the theory of hypnosis had commenced in the early 1950s, when he was assigned by the air force to a team of military doctors charged with rehabilitating American POWs subjected to psychological torture during the Korean War. He had developed his interest in mesmerism even earlier, though, Bryan said, back in the days when he was working his way through college as a drummer with the house band in a burlesque theater. Between strippers, the doctor explained, the theater's stage was occupied by an old carny who used a hypnotist act to extract the sexual fantasies of any ladies in the audience. It was the military, however, that taught Bryan the techniques he packaged on Sunset Boulevard as "Marathon Therapy." The procedure involved around-the-clock counseling by a team of hypnotherapists working in shifts on a patient who was kept awake for at least seventy-two hours. "The goal is to break a person down completely, deprogram them, and then reprogram them," explained Bryan's student, colleague, rival, biographer, and debunker, Gil Boyne, director of the Hypnotism Training Institute, also in Los Angeles.

Boyne recalled vividly the first case in which Bryan and his staff had employed "Marathon Therapy": A retired film actress of some stature showed up at the institute one day to say that her daughter had disappeared after taking LSD at a party in Hollywood and now was living in San Francisco's Haight Ashbury. "The woman told Bryan, 'Bring her back to me the way she was,'" Boyne recalled. "Bryan told her, 'We're talking about brainwashing here.' And she said, 'I don't care what you do, just do it.' And he said, 'This would be extremely expensive.' She said, 'What do you need?'" Two days later, Bryan sent his new office manager Larry Gamsky to San Francisco to retrieve the girl, Boyne remembered. "And Larry got her down here," Boyne recalled, "I don't know how. Bryan hired off-duty L.A. cops to watch her at the motel where they kept her. They worked on her around the clock. It cost the woman a fortune, but she got her daughter back the way she wanted her."

Reports of Bryan's success with patients who proved "impervious to traditional psychotherapy" circulated by word of mouth—often the doctor's own. He was quoted regularly in the Los Angeles press, a result of his decision to hire Bob Hope's former public relations man as the institute's "director of information services." By the late 1960s, Bryan's institute had become a kind of clearinghouse for the emotional ailments of an increasingly confused leisure class. It was a disorienting time for the rich and famous in Southern California. Movie stars wore dungarees, joined cults, and protested against offshore oil wells. L.A.'s first real rock star, Jim Morrison, celebrated the connection between sex and death. Even the Beach Boys resorted to fuzz guitars and psychedelic imagery. The assassination of Bobby Kennedy at the Ambassador Hotel during the summer of 1968 was less disturbing and not nearly so frightening to most Angelenos as the Manson family murders during the summer of 1969.

Dr. Bryan, though, not only became wealthy during this period but seemed to be among the few people left who could enjoy prosperity. Now in his late thirties, Bryan supported a home in the Hollywood Hills, a "party house" in the San Fernando Valley, a ranch outside Palm Springs, and an apartment in Paris. His profits at the institute increased dramatically, Bryan said, when he began to apply "the principle of palatability" to his system for obtaining advance payment from patients. It was his use of the palatable word *sincere* that made this technique work, Bryan explained: Each patient who made an appointment received a stamped envelope with a note reading, "We have found that there are some insincere people who do not keep their appointments because they really do not wish help; and so we have been forced to institute a program to protect those sincere individuals who *do* wish an appointment with the doctor."

Joe was a fourth grader when Larry began to insist that the children should address him by his first name. The whole concept of nuclear family and rigidly defined parental roles was outmoded, he said. Limiting.

Mr. Gamsky lived in another world during the day, far removed from Albers Street. The institute was right in the fluttering heart of West Hollywood, and the people who sought treatment from Dr. Bryan suffered the strange maladies of those who have more money than they can spend and no real idea what they've done to deserve it. There were people who ate themselves into orgasms and others who starved themselves into comas, forty-year-old women on their fifth face-lift and fifty-year-old men addicted to prepubescent prostitutes, writers who had to be put in a trance to finish a sitcom script and actresses who believed beauty was a disguise they put on in the dressing room. There was a wealthy woman who picked up boys in bus stations and paid them to urinate on her face; there was also a middle-aged man who donned a dress every Wednesday and went shopping with his wife as her sister. A studio executive who came to the institute to be treated for his inability to sustain an erection seemed more distressed that the summer's most successful youth movie, *Easy Rider,* had ended with the main characters looking down the barrel of a shotgun.

When Larry was in therapy, he would come home aching with an urge to express that turned the evening meal into an encounter session. He sobbed and laughed uncontrollably, insisted they all had to understand how he felt, what it was like for him, screamed out of his bowels into that void that was the gulf between what he wanted and what he got or swung blindly at his demons, overturning the dining table one time, smashing his chair against the floor another.

He began to make more money, helping the doctor stage such extravaganzas as the "Six-Day Intensive" aboard an ocean liner bound for Mazatlán from San Pedro. Kathy was scandalized when she heard how Dr. Bryan had concluded his last lecture by making love to his wife on deck while the other passengers watched. Larry spent most of those new earnings on himself, complained Greg, transforming the garage into a "private domain" where he hung a collection of expensive power tools that were displayed like objects of art. Larry also bought motorcycles, keeping as many as four at a time, and all sorts of electronic equipment, Greg said, writing *LG* on his possessions with a new engraving pen and forbidding the family to touch them.

The older son could not forgive his father for breaking Beauty's spirit on that afternoon when Larry found a puddle of urine in the garage and responded by heaving the collie into the swimming pool. The day the dog disappeared was one of only two times his mother could remember Joe crying as a child.

Despite this early estrangement from his father, Greg continued to look forward to the week the Gamskys spent each summer camping in Idyllwild Canyon. He and Joe would hike down a winding dirt road to the bottom of the canyon, a place where they felt completely removed from the city: "There were tall trees and a beautiful park," Greg remembered, "and you could see all of the stars." The camping trips ended when Greg was ten or eleven, though, and after that Mr. Gamsky spent very little time with his sons, their mother recalled.

Larry did attempt to instruct both boys in some of the auto-suggestion techniques he was learning at the institute. They would achieve powers of concentration few grown men could match, he promised, and concentration was what the mind used to manufacture success. Joe sat listening for hours as his father explained that you got where you wanted to be by first forming a Clear and Present Image of the Goal, then seeing it Solidify into Reality as you learned to treat Obstacles as Opportunities and Losses as Lessons.

It frightened her sometimes, Kathy admitted, how well her younger son contained himself. Whenever her arguments with Larry escalated into shouting matches, Greg and Kay would retreat to their rooms, crying and fuming, but not Joe. "If my parents got in a fight, he'd take his bike and be gone," Joe's little sister remembered. Most often Joe rode off with the new dog, Blue, running alongside and steered his bicycle north toward the Santa Susanas. He pedaled for miles some days, out past Pacoima up Little Tujunga Road through Antelope and Cougar Canyons, ranging as far north as Soledad, where the light was so harsh that it hurt to look at the sky. Barely a few hundred feet above the suburban tracts of Sylmar and fifteen minutes from the Pacific Ocean, he explored an empire of dry gulches and desiccated ridges, contemplated the Los Angeles that lived like an ancient lizard beneath the sod and asphalt of the Valley floor, then returned home four or five hours later, cool and impervious. "Joe always was easygoing," Kay reflected. "He kept his emotions under control."

At times, though, that unreachable expression on her younger son's face upset Kathy far more than the tears shed by the other two children. "He would always say, 'Everything is okay. It is fine. I can take care of this. Don't worry. I can handle it. It doesn't matter. It is all right,'" Kathy recalled. "That was Joe."

His mother did not discover even that Joe had become a paperboy until he woke her one rainy morning while struggling to load the wet bags onto his bicycle. "I don't know how he drove that bike around," she reflected. "He had two sacks that you can put papers in. One was on the front of the bike and one was on the back of the bike. You had to hold the bike up, and then put the bike down and load one side, and then turn it over to load the other side. Then you had to try to get up on it and go out on the route." Joe needed two bags because he had two routes, Kathy learned, and had been on the streets before dawn every morning for the past month.

She hadn't objected, Mrs. Gamsky explained, because it was clear by then her children would have little beyond what they bought for themselves. His mother was infuriated, though, when she learned that Joe was "loaning" Larry most of the money he made. Her husband promised to repay the boy but never did, Kathy remembered. Her second son, as usual, played the man in the family: "All Joe would say was 'Well, he needed it.'"

The father was supposed to be the provider, Mrs. Gamsky told her husband. What he provided, Larry answered, no amount of money could buy.

Joe was most distinguished at the age of ten by the way he could bring a group of children together, Kathy recalled, and keep them all happy. Joe, his mother said, was the type that people wanted for a leader because he was so subtle. "He would find out what you liked or what you wanted to do," she explained. "Then he would always make time to do that particular thing with you or to learn about it and share it with you."

"You couldn't ask for a better older brother," Kay said. The sweetest memory of her childhood, his little sister recalled, was the birthday when Joe "spent his paycheck on me before my father could get it." He had taken her first to Toys "R" Us and then to Farrell's, Kay recalled, walking five miles at least round-trip, and spent every penny in his pockets.

Kathy knew by now that both her sons were exceptional. The teachers at Kester Elementary told Mrs. Gamsky that Joe and Greg were the brightest students ever to attend the school, suggesting the two take a special state test to see if they might qualify as "gifted" and receive the attention they deserved. Both boys passed the state's exam, and though their mother was inordinately proud, Kathy felt a new sense of responsibility now that she was living in a "House of Presidents," as she put it. Mrs. Gamsky joined the Gifted Children's Association when Joe and Greg were nine and eleven, enrolling the boys in "enrichment" classes taught by professors from UCLA and USC. The association made it a policy to remind parents that gifted children had the same emotional and physical needs as other youngsters, and Kathy's efforts to balance her sons included membership in the Boy Scouts and the Woodcraft Rangers. She sent Joe for one whole summer to the Van Nuys–Sherman Oaks War Memorial Aquatic Park, where he had been the only boy willing to take high-diving lessons. The instructor was a former Olympic competitor who told Mrs. Gamsky that Joe lacked every asset a diver needed except the one that mattered most, an absence of fear, and made Joe the star of that season's Water Carnival.

Kathy and Larry argued often about the boys' education, and it rankled their mother to no end that a man who had been given every advantage during his own childhood would let his sons languish in schools where half the students spoke English as a second language. She wanted better for the boys and enrolled Greg at a private school called Mid-Town, but she could keep him there for only one year before the cost of tuition broke her. The summer after Greg finished the seventh grade at Van Nuys Junior High, Kathy saw a story in the *Valley News* about the Helms Scholarship offered to one student each year at the most exclusive preparatory academy in California, the Harvard School. It took all Kathy's nerve to steer her old rattletrap Rambler up Coldwater past those stone pedestals and Anglican icons to ask if Greg could take the aptitude test Harvard required of scholarship applicants. Greg made the highest mark of anyone who took the test that year and started eighth grade at the school with all expenses paid. In the early autumn afternoons he returned home awestruck and shaken. "There are Mercedes and Rolls-Royces and they drive them in the senior parking lot," he explained. Transferring from Van Nuys to Harvard was "like going from this planet and landing on the moon," Greg said: An A-plus in public school, he told his mother, was a C-minus at Harvard.

Kathy inquired at the school if Joe could take the scholarship test, too, and the administrators asked if he was as bright as Greg. She told them about the afternoon she stopped by Kester Avenue Elementary and found Joe working in the school's office. The principal explained that her son already knew everything they had to teach him, so the staff tried to keep the boy busy by assigning him to raise and lower the flag every morning, clean the chalkboards, and run errands. He also tutored first- and second-

grade students in math and reading. All the teachers marveled at his attention span and his patience, Kathy recalled. Like a little adult, they kept saying, like a little adult.

Joe's score on the scholarship test was even higher than Greg's, and
he started the seventh grade at Harvard in the fall of 1971. When he came
home from his first day on the Coldwater campus, Kathy asked if all the
obvious wealth and extravagant display at the school, the fancy cars and the
important names, bothered him as it did Greg. "Why should it?" Joe asked.

"It is a generally accepted proposition in the United States," Dr. Bryan would
observe in *The Chosen Ones,* "that no one is obtaining sufficient sexual gratification." For better or worse, in sickness and in health, Dr. Bryan had
proven and profited from this proposition to a degree matched by few other
medical men, even in Los Angeles. His seminars in "Sexual Function and
Dysfunction" were attended by more than fourteen thousand M.D.s during the late 1960s. Bryan was a natural raconteur whose integration of formal education, vaudeville instinct, and cold-blooded efficiency riveted his
audiences. "He had it down to a science," recalled one former therapist from
AIH. "His syllabus was like in two-minute bites, and he kept right on it."

By the early seventies, Bryan was organizing tax-deductible ocean
cruises to move his advanced classes beyond the range of small-minded
local authorities. He led one seminar titled "Investigating the Fleshpots of
the World" that began with a communal bath in Tokyo and ended in an
Amsterdam brothel. Bryan's best-known class, though, was "Sex 506." "The
doctors and their wives would walk into the lobby, and he'd have the whole
wall covered with hard-core pornographic photos," recalled Gil Boyne.
"They were in shock before they sat down." Bryan always introduced his
first guest lecturer as "a lovely young lady from Las Vegas, Nevada." She
was a professional prostitute, the doctor would explain, and had come
to Los Angeles to teach them fellatio. "So she'd step out and do a whole
description," Boyne recalled, "miming the motions, I mean with her mouth
open and the hands going, and everyone's looking awestruck." The cunni-
lingus demonstration was presented by a man Bryan described as "probably
the nation's most skilled practitioner"—himself. "Sex 506" always ended
with Bryan's selection of six people from the audience, three men and three
women. The "volunteers" would be summoned to the stage, where Bryan
handed each a package wrapped in foil. "When I say, 'Go,'" the doctor
explained, "I want you to apply what you've learned in this course." Upon
opening the foil, the six volunteers found penises and vaginas made of
molded chocolate. Invariably, his students were unable to "perform," Bryan

noted. "He'd say, 'See what I mean? That's just chocolate, but you can't put your mouth on it,'" Boyne recalled. "And they'd all be ashamed."

He himself was among the few men in America to transcend such neurotic inhibitions, boasted Bryan, who claimed in one interview to have had sex with thirty-five thousand women. "If I don't have at least ten orgasms a day," the doctor said, "I start to climb the walls." Even those who doubted Bryan's math were impressed by the heroic efforts of a man who had transmuted handicap into motivation, overcoming a physical abnormality that would have proved a profound obstacle to sexual adventurism in a lesser man. "He had a micropenis, less than three inches long when erect," according to Boyne. Even before he undressed, though, the doctor was a physical grotesque whose height of six feet one inch could scarcely support a weight that approached three hundred pounds. He was balding, wore horn-rimmed glasses, sported jowls that would have been the pride of a bulldog, and yet "the ladies loved him," recalled the AIH therapist. "It was the bubbling of energy, I think; it just poured off him. He was charismatic and he was brilliant. When he opened his mouth, there was nobody who didn't stop to listen. When he couldn't inform, he'd entertain. You learned a lot about what really attracts women just by being around him."

Bryan permitted hundreds of colleagues, employees, associates, and admirers to watch him in action, purchasing a bungalow out on the Valley floor that served as a sort of annex to the sexual laboratory at Topanga Canyon's Sandstone Institute. "The place was a party house, that's all it was used for," recalled the therapist. "And I mean swing parties, partner swapping, three-way, four-way, you name it. Lots of very well-known people participated, movie stars, politicians—even judges."

Among the lesser-known individuals who appeared occasionally at Bryan's Valley house was Larry Gamsky. "Larry wanted to be a ladies' man, but he never was," recalled the therapist. "He was a good-looking guy, a bodybuilder, but Bryan, who was this big fat man, drew the ladies in droves, while Larry hardly ever could make out."

No one at the institute was either so devoted to or so envious of the doctor as Gamsky. Larry hung on Bryan's every word, and yet the moment the doctor was absent from a room would accuse him of malefactions that ranged from raping young girls to robbing old women. All the employees at the institute knew Gamsky had been Bryan's patient before becoming his henchman. The rumor around the office was that Larry had come in to be treated for impotence, but then everyone at the institute wanted to believe the worst of the man they called "Herr Gamsky." "Larry ran the office like a Gestapo," explained the therapist. "He was into discipline and control. He had a background in accounting and he was into numbers. Larry was the most disliked person at the institute, but Bryan let him run the office because he wanted the dirty work done, but not by himself."

Bryan exploited Larry's mechanical skills to double and then triple the institute's earnings, designing a system of cameras and audio equipment wired through the walls of adjoining cubicles where patients were seated by nurses in reclining chairs, blindfolded, then outfitted with headset and microphones. The doctor himself worked out of a central console room, seated at a bank of closed-circuit televisions and relay switches that allowed him to supplement his personal attention with tapes of his voice as he changed channels from patient to patient. "So he would work with, like, six people at a time and get six times the payment," recalled the therapist. "It was Bryan's idea, but Larry executed it, and when he didn't receive the recognition and payment he felt he had coming, he became very resentful. He kept threatening to leave, then leaving, then coming back. It went on for years."

By their teens, Joe and Greg shared hardly any common feeling for their father. It bored and shamed the older brother that Larry insisted still upon "creating theatres at the dinner table, wanting everyone to talk about his problems." Joe, however, tried to comfort Larry, Greg recalled: "Joe understood my father and tried to be the son my father wanted."

Their little sister, though, remembered best the evening when Joe rebuked Larry for bullying their mother: "Larry wanted us to call her 'Kathy,' but she wouldn't go along with it," Kay explained; when Joe supported his mother, Larry responded by turning the dining room table over on him, then threw a chair against the wall above the boy's head. "My father liked to smash furniture," Greg said.

A majority of the fights between husband and wife, as between father and oldest son, were about money. It had been a mother's lonely struggle to keep Joe and Greg enrolled at Harvard, according to Kathy, especially after the school chose to double the number of scholarships it offered by cutting each one to half the cost of tuition. The Gamskys were behind on Joe's fees almost every semester after this, warned repeatedly that their son would be asked to leave if payment was not forthcoming. Yet even as Larry pleaded poverty, "he continued to buy himself boats, motorcycles, electronic devices—anything to entertain himself," Greg remembered. Kathy took part-time jobs, clipped coupons, hoarded nickels and dimes to pay the boys' tuition. "Our mother was instrumental in keeping us in that school until we graduated," said Greg, "because my father wished to take us out several times . . . he always wanted to move and change things."

Most of Larry's plans for relocation were born of dissatisfaction with his lot at the institute. He had broken with Dr. Bryan for the first time during the same month Joe started at the Harvard School, September of 1972, applying for a position as a broker at the American Standard Real Estate Investment Co. "He had a good appearance and a fine presentation," recalled the company's president, Frank Dana, "but no license." Not a problem, said Larry, who passed the state's licensing exam on his first try. "Taking tests was the one thing Larry did really well," Dana reflected. Larry also needed no time at all to set up his first big deal, locating a developer in Marina del Rey who was behind on loans he had taken to complete construction of a high-rise apartment building. The hard part was assembling the principals—builder and banker, along with their assorted attorneys and accountants—in the same place at the same time. After weeks of appointments and cancellations, the meeting finally came together. "So there we all are, right on the brink of closing this deal," Dana recalled, "when we hear this snoring. We look over, and there's Larry, with his chin on his chest, sleeping away. *This* is how I find out he had narcolepsy; any stressful situation, he nods off. We lost the deal, naturally."

Dana hadn't given up on Gamsky for one reason only, and that was Larry's association with the American Institute of Hypnosis. Dana had been a student of hypnotherapy since what he liked to call "my days as an actor." Those days hadn't been many, really, though the man would nourish his self-image for years with the memory of his big scene in the John Cassavetes TV series *Staccato*. After plummeting from this apogee of his career, Dana clung to the fringes of show business into his early thirties, then went the way of so many aspiring actors around Los Angeles—into real estate, apprenticing himself to syndication genius Dick Firestone, the wheeler-dealer who put more doctors and lawyers into orchards than any man in American history. "Dick taught me how to depreciate a tree," Dana recalled. "You never buy an avocado grove because those trees can produce fruit for two hundred years, while an orange tree's life is only about thirty years; you get big write-offs on oranges." While real estate proved profitable, providing Dana with a spectacular home in the Hollywood Hills, he yearned for that level of engagement he had known on the set of *Staccato*. "So I'm looking through Larry's résumé," Dana recalled, "and I say, 'Hey, I've heard about Dr. Bryan; I'd love to study with him.' He tells me, 'I'll set it up.'"

After American Standard went under in 1973, Dana and Gamsky agreed to form a new company, one they called MDG, the M being for Mingarella, as in Frank Mingarella, Larry's dearest friend. Gamsky and Mingarella were the oddest of couples: Larry was long and lean, with thick tousled dark hair and penetrating pale eyes, anxious but opinionated, disdainful yet desperate. Frank was short and squat, his red hair thin under an ill-fitting toupee. Blunt and businesslike, Mingarella's only talent was for making money, which he did most successfully as operator of one of the earliest health maintenance organizations in California. Despite their obvious differences, the two men appeared devoted to one another. Larry's story was that he had "saved Frank emotionally," Dana recalled, after Mingarella's fiancée died in a car crash. All Dana knew was that Mingarella sold his interest in the HMO before forming MDG, coming in with half a million dollars, "while Larry couldn't put together two nickels."

Dana hadn't realized how marginal Larry was financially until he was invited for the first time to the Gamsky home in Van Nuys. The tiny house on Albers Street was absolutely barren, Dana remembered. Larry, who was in the kitchen repairing a refrigerator from the Salvation Army, explained that his creditors had taken the furniture when he declared bankruptcy. The two of them sat on crates in the living room to talk, Dana recalled, and it was there he had been introduced to Mrs. Gamsky. "Kathy I always liked," he remembered. "Tall, fragile, an artist. A lot of people said she was nuts, but I never saw any sign." Later, Dana could not forgive Larry for bringing Kathy to Dr. Bryan's party house: "She didn't belong in a place like that, and I know it caused some problems for her."

Kathy was the first person he met who offered insight into Larry's abrasive attitude: Her husband's advantaged childhood had produced a profoundly resentful adult, Mrs. Gamsky explained, a man "angry at himself and at everyone else," Dana recalled, "because he didn't have what he thought he should have."

The central focus of Larry's resentment continued to be Dr. Bryan. His office manager retaliated against the doctor's disdain by duplicating the electronic wizardry he had wrought at AIH in the offices of nearly a dozen other M.D.s, and, after his real estate ventures failed, attempted to break away from the institute by returning to pharmaceutical sales. Each time he left, though, Gamsky was drawn back to the offices on Sunset Boulevard within a few months.

She and Larry slipped further apart each year, Kathy recalled: "I was out in the Valley with the children and he was on Sunset Strip. It was two different worlds. I'd ask him, 'What is it exactly you do there?' He'd laugh."

The indignities of poverty never seemed to tear at Joe as they did at Greg. It was the older brother who resented riding his secondhand Schwinn four miles each way to a campus where he saw other students driving Stutz

Bearcats; Joe said he enjoyed the exercise. He remained bitter, Greg admitted, about the shame he had known during those furtive trips to Goodwill and the Salvation Army as a teenager, shopping with Joe in thrift stores for the suits they would wear to that year's debate tournaments. While Greg chafed and grumbled and burned with envy of classmates who had charge accounts at Brooks Brothers, though, his brother refused to utter one word of complaint. Even as a child Joe had taken the position that such matters were trivial. When Greg outgrew his old jeans jacket, his younger brother, who already was taller, wore it for another two years. Joe wore his one good shirt, the yellow oxford cloth, day after day and week after week during his first two years at the Harvard School, until the cuffs were black with grime and ink. "He hated to give that shirt up but finally had to," Kathy recalled. "He liked the yellow."

Joe tried not to show it, but he struggled during the first year after his transfer from Kester, Mrs. Gamsky said: Not only were the standards much higher at Harvard, but the school required scholarship students to maintain a B-plus average, be active in a sport, and participate in at least one extracurricular activity.

While high-diving had been Joe's sport at Harvard, it was the extracurricular activity he chose that consumed most of his free time after freshman year. Soon after he joined the debate squad, Joe began reading the dictionary each evening, learning ten new words every day. "Once he decided to do something," Greg explained, "he did it."

Their debate tournaments were among the few of his son's activities that Larry Gamsky found worthy. Even Kathy was taken aback, though, when, in the fall of 1974, Larry invited an associate from the institute, Frank Dana, out to Albers Street to work with their younger son. "Larry wanted me to teach Joey some of the things I had learned as an actor," Dana explained, "about delivery and gesture and expression." He found the boy an apt pupil, yet remarkably reserved for one so young, Dana recalled: "Joe was taking in every word I said, I could see that, but he wouldn't respond. He just looked at me and maybe nodded his head once or twice. I told him, 'You're too stiff; it comes across as arrogance.' He just nodded again."

In his practice as a hypnotherapist, Dr. Bryan regularly cited the theory of conductivity formulated by the German physicist Georg Simon Ohm, whose "Ohm's law" held that the amount of electrical current that will pass through a point of resistance is dependent upon the amount of voltage behind the current. In his adaptation of Ohm's law, Dr. Bryan substituted for electricity what he called "the Stream of Suggestion," contending that— first through concentrating the mind in a hypnotic state, then by increasing the intensity of suggestion—one might implant beliefs and tendencies so powerful that they would continue to control a person's behavior long after the trance state was broken. "All human behavior, including the decisions we make," the doctor explained, "is based on the strength of the pressure or the voltage behind past suggestions."

In his practice at the American Institute of Hypnosis, Bryan had compiled a number of important corollaries to his version of Ohm's law. Perhaps most important was "Whenever possible, permissive suggestions should be utilized rather than dominative, since the dominative suggestion is far more likely to create resistance in the mind." Also, "smart people," the doctor discovered, "learn to accept suggestions more rapidly than dull ones."

The early 1970s found Bryan at his acme, wealthy, famous, and liberated to a degree critics called licentious. "He went wherever he wanted, however he liked it," recalled Gil Boyne, "always first-class."

Boyne had been present when Dr. Bryan was confronted in public for the first time with his sordid past, by the popular Los Angeles TV talk show host Joe Pyne. "They were a few minutes into their interview," Boyne recalled, "when Pyne asked him, 'Dr. Bryan, have you ever been arrested?' Bryan said, 'No.' Pyne said, 'That's very interesting because I have this police report from East Sparks, Nevada.' And Bryan went berserk, swearing and cursing Pyne. They had to stop the cameras. Then they started taping again, and Bryan told how it had been a politically motivated frame-up."

For years Bryan's associations with well-placed persons had insulated him from legal action in Los Angeles. "Most of the top people in town were his friends," explained Frank Dana (who would spend six years at the institute, three as a client and three more as a therapist), "and Dr. Bryan probably knew more of the secrets of this city than anyone." Bryan's abuse of his position was catching up with him, though, and by the time he moved his offices from atop the Whiskey A Go Go to an abandoned bank building at the corner of Sunset and Fuller, complaints about private therapy sessions had begun to penetrate the doctor's protective veil of friendly judges and sympathetic prosecutors. There were elements of humor in the earliest police reports: One woman told detectives that during a private session with Bryan, the doctor put her into a trance, urged her to "reach out for life, reach out for what you want," then lifted her hand to his crotch.

The complaints that came later were more disturbing: A young woman who had become obsessed with her inability to achieve orgasm first told Boyne, then the district attorney's office, that Bryan devoted their therapy sessions to the proposition that shame and fear were "obstructing" her natural response. "He told her, 'You're so concerned about falling in love and being rejected that you can't allow yourself to have an orgasm,'" recalled Boyne. "'What you need,' he told her, 'is the kind of lover you can't fall in love with.' He said, 'I've figured it out—a professional athlete.' He said, 'I have some friends on a baseball club, and they stay at a certain hotel, and the next time they come in, I'm going to make arrangements for you, and all you'll have to do is go down there and check in.'

"So that's what happened: She checked in, left the door unlocked, took her clothes off, and got into bed. Not long after, a young man came in, undressed, and got in with her. He said nothing and neither did she. About fifteen minutes later, the door again opened and two more ballplayers came in. Not long after that, two more. By the end of that evening she had sex with ten men. And still didn't have an orgasm. I said to her when she told me about it, 'Didn't some part of your mind wonder?' And she answered, 'I trusted him—he's a doctor.'"

Greg had broken with his father forever at sixteen. The falling-out was brought on by Larry's decision to employ his son as an assistant at the vitamin distributorship where Mr. Gamsky had hired on after his most recent resignation from the institute. When he refused to let Larry take his paychecks, Greg recalled, his father fired him. The older son went straight to work as a box boy at a supermarket, supporting himself with his own wages after that. "My father cut me off," Greg explained. "I was in the house, but my father decided I was not worth the effort anymore. I just wasn't going to pan out for him. I wasn't going to be part of the program."

It was right around this time that "Mr. Gamsky seemed to suddenly realize how bright Joe was, and how motivated," Kathy remembered. And all at once, she noticed, "things began to seem kind of secret between he and his father." Joe and Larry would spend hours alone, out in the garage, doing what Kathy could only guess. Mr. Gamsky referred to the boy as his "project," she remembered. At first, Larry spoke of "training" Joe, Kathy recalled, but later he described it as "programming" the boy. Frank Dana recalled Larry boasting that he shopped with Joe at the beginning of each school vacation for the textbooks used in the courses his son would be taking during the next term at Harvard. He should read both the first and last chapters of each volume before classes began, Mr. Gamsky instructed his son. "He wanted Joe to focus on projecting a knowledge of the material, of having this mastery," Dana remembered.

Kathy told herself their son's intense involvement with his father was natural. Entering adolescence, "any young man wants to know what his father knows, and the father becomes a hero, and, suddenly, the mother is kind of in the background and out of the picture," Mrs. Gamsky explained, "especially if she doesn't have a career."

The summer after Joe turned sixteen, he too went to work with Larry, in this case at a pharmaceutical company. They would leave at 7 A.M. and get home around 9 P.M., recalled Kathy, who didn't remember Joe ever getting paid: "His father would say, 'Well, you know, the money will help pay for Harvard next year.'"

It was during this period that Larry began to make what she considered some very odd remarks for a man in his early forties, Kathy reflected: "He would say things like 'Well, I have done all of this for you, and when I get old, you are going to—' He expected [Joe] to support him and take care of him. It was a strange thing to me that he would even be thinking about that."

When she "objected to Joe being pressured so greatly and having such long hours," however, Mrs. Gamsky's second son assured her he was happy to help. Even as their divisions deepened, the family's one article of agreement was a mutual admiration for Joe's exemplary character. Kay, whose dyslexia made school a tribulation, remembered that each night after he finished reading the dictionary, Joe would correct her homework. "Joe was very accepting of everyone the way they were," his sister observed. Kathy, who had taken to jogging at night, recalled that no matter how busy Joe's schedule might be, he insisted upon coming along: "He didn't want me out there by myself."

Despite Joe's attempts to hold them together, lines of separation were clearly drawn among the Gamskys by then. The parents rarely spoke to one another, the silences between them broken only by Larry's fits or Kathy's sullen tears. While he endured the rancor between his parents by brooding in the back bedroom, Greg recalled, "Joe played the peacemaker. He would take the time to talk to each of them separately and try to keep them together, where I took a different attitude because I was so upset with one of the parties." It pained her, Kathy admitted, when Joe defended his father: "He would say, 'You have to make allowances for him. He is trying to do his best.'" Kathy, however, had made all the allowances she could. The parents separated for good during the summer after Joe's junior year at the Harvard School. Greg and Kay went with her to a rented home in Granada Hills, Kathy remembered, but Joe stayed on with Larry at the Albers Street house. "Joe was a very compassionate person, and he felt it would be less of a burden to me [if he remained with his father]," she explained. Her brother, Kay said, "was always a lot less trouble than Greg and I were."

***

The accumulation of complaints and accusations on file against William J. Bryan Jr. eventually reached a point at which the Los Angeles County Medical Association felt compelled to place advertisements in the *Times* and *Herald Examiner* soliciting information from women who believed they had been abused by the doctor while under hypnosis. After the medical association's findings were presented to the district attorney's office, Bryan was charged with twenty-seven counts of sexual assault.

The doctor fled to Paris and taught at the Sorbonne while his attorneys in Los Angeles attempted to negotiate financial settlements with the accusers. Two victims, however, would not be bought off, and in the end the cost of Bryan's return to L.A. included a guilty plea to a pair of second-degree rape charges. He was sentenced to probation, with a promise of restitution.

The doctor came back to California from France immensely obese, recalled Frank Dana, and in declining health. Open-heart surgery complicated an addiction to a diet of amphetamines and barbiturates. Unable to work without the former and to sleep without the latter, the doctor sought desperately to revive his practice at the institute, but "things were never the same," Dana remembered. "The entire profession of hypnotherapy was under a cloud for some time locally because of him," said Gil Boyne, who by then had replaced Dr. Bryan as the highest-profiled practitioner in California.

By the time of Bryan's return from Paris, Larry Gamsky had his own credential as a hypnotherapist, provided by a man who sold degrees out of his home in Orange County, Boyne recalled. Larry still was not permitted by Bryan to work as a therapist at the institute, however, "which frustrated him more than anything," Frank Dana remembered, "except not having money." How deeply embittered Larry had become about his personal finances was clarified for Dana one evening when he invited Gamsky to dinner at his home in the Hollywood Hills: "The envy that Larry felt when he walked through the door, you could see it and feel it. He had brought his girlfriend of the moment with him, and even she could see how it was eating him. Finally she reached over and patted his knee, and said, 'It's all right, Larry, you'll have one of these, too.'"

Larry's chance came in the spring of 1977, just as Joe was preparing to graduate from the Harvard School. Dr. Bryan, in Las Vegas to attend a heavyweight championship fight, would never make it to his ringside seat, collapsing in his suite at Caesar's Palace shortly after arrival and dying in the back of an ambulance on the way to the hospital. "A combined drug overdose—heart attack," Boyne recalled. Before the end of that year, Larry Gamsky had become both vice president and minority owner at the American Institute of Hypnosis, appointed to the former position by the institute's new president and majority owner, Frank Mingarella.

She and Mr. Gamsky had been separated only a few months when Kathy began to hear disquieting reports of the "accelerated program" in which her estranged husband had enrolled their younger son. Larry had Joe taking accounting courses at UCLA while he completed his senior year at the Harvard School, Greg said, in order to hasten the process of making him a CPA.

"This was the beginning of where I was being shut out by the father," Kathy reflected. Nevertheless, she continued to see her younger son every Sunday: "Joe was very busy, but we were never estranged. It was just that Joe didn't have a lot of time to himself." Other than that he seemed always in a hurry, she saw little sign of change in Joe, Kathy said: "I remember when he graduated from Harvard, one of my father's friends gave him a calculator. He was just thrilled. It was the first really nice gift he had ever received."

Still, the feeling persisted that "secret things were going on between Joe and his father," Kathy said. She did not learn even that Joe had become the youngest person ever in the U.S. to pass the CPA exam until she saw his picture in the *Valley News*.

Kathy's divorce from Larry was granted late that summer, and her last really intimate moment with Joe came a few weeks later, shortly after his enrollment in USC, when she drove down to the college for a mother-and-son function. They spent the entire afternoon together, Kathy recalled, and Joe walked her across the campus from one end to the other.

Greg was at USC now as well, having transferred from UCLA after his freshman year. "We didn't talk about our family life," the older brother remembered. "There was too much pain." The brothers saw one another maybe twice a month, usually when Greg visited Joe's fraternity. Greg called his brother's room at the Chi Phi house "Grand Central Station." "People were constantly coming and going," he explained. Halfway through his freshman year, Joe already was something of a legend on the USC campus, Greg remembered, having been elected president by the Chi Phis at the beginning of his second semester at the school. "Unheard of," the older brother said. Even more amazing, that spring Joe started his own campus newspaper. "It really was very, very impressive," Greg recalled, "especially since these things were happening at such a rapid rate."

"The understanding between Frank and Larry, when they took over the institute, was that Larry would run the place because Larry convinced Frank he had done that for Dr. Bryan," Gil Boyne recalled. Explained Frank Dana: "Larry's lies and exaggerations grew out of what was his biggest fault, which was that he had to have everything right now, instant gratification. He was always looking for shortcuts. And as soon as he took over at the institute, he started playing the big shot. When Frank made Larry vice president, Larry went around telling everyone he met what a big position he had. It was the one thing that finally got him over with the ladies."

Boyne discovered how tenuous was Gamsky's newfound status when he drove to AIH from his office in Glendale to discuss purchasing the reprint rights to Dr. Bryan's books and articles. "They had a xerox copy list of all the effects left by Bryan that were available," Boyne recalled, "which basically included everything they had. It turned out they hadn't paid the rent in months and were desperate for cash."

The Gamsky/Mingarella takeover at AIH couldn't have come at a worse time, in Boyne's opinion, since the practice of hypnotherapy was enduring its worst public relations fiasco in fifty years: the controversy surrounding the suicide of young comedian Freddie Prinze. After the death of the *Chico and the Man* star by a self-inflicted gunshot wound, a number of articles had suggested that the blame belonged to Prinze's hypnotherapist, Dr. William Kroger. Once a successful obstetrician in Chicago, Kroger had taken up hypnosis in his early fifties after moving to L.A. and purchasing the magnificent Bel Air estate at 666 Saint Cloud Road. "An extraordinary case," Boyne called Kroger (the UCLA professor who had hailed Ron Levin as "a real genius"): "He got involved with some very high-powered lawyers, and they helped make him a prominent person in Los Angeles. Then he become involved with Freddie Prinze." After the comedian died, there were rumors that he had become an addict because of pills prescribed by Kroger, Boyne recalled: "What was known for sure was that Prinze had a gun and Kroger took the gun. But then Prinze got loaded up and came by Kroger's house and said, 'I want my gun,' and Kroger gave it to him. And that night Prinze blew his brains out. Afterward, Kroger—or his insurance company—paid mucho bucks, to the tune of two point nine million, to settle the malpractice lawsuit. Suddenly the state legislature was deluged with bills to require state licensing of hypnotherapy. So it was not a really good time to get into the business."

Boyne had the advantages of tabloid celebrity (he was about to be anointed "Hypnotist to the Stars" by the *Midnight Globe*'s Hollywood correspondent, Robin Leach) and a private practice that served such clients as Sylvester Stallone, whose movie *Rocky* had just won the Academy Award. Gamsky and Mingarella attempted to cut in on Boyne's burgeoning business by offering a specialized "addiction treatment" in association with a series of medical doctors. "They did it at the building on Sunset," Boyne recalled, "using Bryan's technique of keeping patients in a trance around the clock, for days at a time if necessary, working on them in shifts."

The problem was that Larry had no ability to improvise, Dana said: "He had his formula and if it didn't work, he didn't know what to do."

Mingarella was a more likable person, in Dana's opinion, but even Frank became pretty scary when he and Larry got onto the subject of Hitler and the Third Reich. "It was like 'They really weren't so bad, they had a lot of good ideas,'" Dana remembered. "They used it as sort of an example of what you could do if you got together five good people. 'Three more like us,' they'd say."

The Institute was floundering and expanding at the same time. The staff at AIH now included a licensed marriage, family, and child counselor who specialized in treating phobias and sexual dysfunctions. Not on the institute's staff but in an office just down the hall was a specialist in "cult deprogramming" just arrived from Florida, where he had been working with former Scientologists. "He used them, and they used him, on a referral basis, in one door and out the other," Gil Boyne recalled.

Without the magnet of Dr. Bryan AIH still was struggling to stay alive financially two years after Mingarella and Gamksy took control. "Frank was trying to build the business up, getting on talk shows, doing PR work—he even bought his own radio station to promote the institute," Dana recalled. The only sustaining success the new owners achieved, however, had come through their collection of Medi-Cal payments for treatment approved by licensed physicians. Two M.D.s were the institute's aegis for hypnotherapy billings submitted to the state. One was Dr. Dan Kuska. "Larry had built up Dan's practice in Denver by doing the same electronic setup he did for Bryan," Dana explained, "and they were tight." Kuska obtained his California medical license specifically to serve on the staff at the institute, Dana remembered: "After about a year, though, he became disillusioned and wrote a letter saying he was withdrawing."

He remained close with Gamsky and friendly with Mingarella, Kuska said, but did not give either permission to sign his name on the Medi-Cal insurance claims they continued to submit. According to the institute's new receptionist, Jean Clarke, Medi-Cal provided 60 percent of all monies received at AIH.

Jean, once a moderately successful television actress, had been hired in February of 1979. "Larry's biggest trophy, his prize," said Frank Dana. The breakup of her first marriage to comedian/agent Marty Ingels had been played out as a kind of public psychodrama in Los Angeles. "Marty kept bringing her up, and their divorce, every time he got on a talk show," Dana recalled. "It was talking about her that flipped him out on *The Johnny Carson Show*. People thought he had a nervous breakdown right on the set. He *hated* her. She, meanwhile, wrote a short story about them going to get a divorce and having this wonderful time."

A "writer of romantic fiction" was how Jean identified herself these days, though she retained her Screen Actors Guild card and occasionally worked in television. "This was a lady who really held onto her looks," said Dana. "She was beautiful to begin with and she kept herself absolutely immaculate." She took the job at AIH because, as a writer, she needed the extra income, Jean explained. "What happened next was like right out of a movie," remembered Dana. "See, Larry had a real problem with his masculinity. He lifted weights and he looked good, but he was never that confident. Once he took over at the institute, though, he started taking advantage of the power over women he suddenly had. And Jean was his ultimate conquest. Right after she came to work, she became Larry's patient, and within a session or two, they were involved. Frank Mingarella was pissed off because we had a rule that therapists were not to date the patients, but Larry kept seeing her as a patient even when they had become lovers.

"Larry was so proud of her, he could hardly stand it. Not long after they got involved, he drove her off to Denver on the back of his motorcycle, so he could show her off to Kuska. Larry's problem, though, was that he still didn't have a lot of money, and after he met Jean, it was like he wanted what he wanted even worse than he wanted it before."

The move Joe made at the end of his third semester at USC was his boldest to date, less a leap of faith than an attempt to dictate destiny.

The on-campus representative for the powerful accounting firm of Peat Marwick Mitchell Main & Co., Terry Dibble, was a fast-rising executive in the company who volunteered to supervise recruiting at his alma mater. Postings for interviews went up on the walls of Southern Cal's accounting department each September, and Dibble had interviewed dozens of applicants at the university. None, though, so impressed him as the imposingly tall nineteen-year-old who introduced himself during October of 1979 as Joseph Gamsky, a "fast track" undergraduate who would receive, he said, his bachelor's degree in December.

"Enormous self-confidence," Dibble remembered. "I don't know if I've ever met anyone that young who seemed so sure of himself. There wasn't a slip or a hesitation in him, yet he came across as tremendously composed. He was very good at giving you the impression you'd be lucky to get him."

While he never saw a transcript to verify Gamksy's accelerated course of studies, Dibble *was* presented with a newspaper article identifying Joseph Gamsky as the youngest person ever to pass the CPA exam. *Very* impressive, said Dibble, who knew of no other accountant who had passed the test prior to graduation from college. "Most don't take the CPA test until after graduate school," he explained, "and a lot don't pass it even then."

A young man who knew where he was going and wanted to get there as fast as he could, Dibble described Joe to the other executives at Peat Marwick, where Gamsky went to work less than two weeks later. As an assistant accountant, it was Joe's job to requisition records, test systems, voucher in bank documents—"basically do the manual labor," Dibble explained—as part of a team assigned to prepare the annual financial statements of Peat Marwick clients. Joe proved his remarkable capacity for abstracting data within a few weeks, yet at the same time demonstrated he was unsuited to the job of assistant accountant, Dibble recalled: "Very simply, he was not willing to accept supervision. He always felt his ideas were the better ideas. It wasn't long before we found that our managers were just not taking him onto accounts because he could not get along. So he didn't have much to do; we were forced to find him busy work."

Gamsky's transfer—after less than two months of employment—to the elite Consulting Options E program, raised eyebrows; no other assistant accountant had been permitted to make this jump with less than two years' experience in the trenches with the audit teams. Dibble's argument was that it would be a shame to waste—or lose—so gifted a mind. The Consulting Options E program involved working closely with the CEOs of major corporations to plan investment, pension, insurance, and health programs. Enormous sums of money were involved, and many at the company thought it preposterous that a young man just turned twenty should be given such responsibility. "That was not the real problem, however," Dibble recalled. "The problem was the same as on the audit teams: No one wanted to work with him. So he sat around a lot. It's my understanding that this is when he began to study the stock market and to make some investments. People complained he was on the phone to his broker during office hours."

***

Joe's dissatisfaction with his position at Peat Marwick, according to Greg, was in large part a function of Larry's "notions concerning what his utility might be." "My father found that the accounting job simply wasn't proceeding fast enough, income-wise," Greg explained. Larry wanted "a big kill real fast," his older son said, "so he encouraged Joe to follow the commodities market, where you could make fortunes overnight."

Joe began trading through the Paine Webber office upstairs from Peat Marwick in late 1979. Within a few months, Joe boasted, his success was such that he had been given a power of attorney over the account of his former employer, Dr. Milton Rubini. As Greg understood it, by early 1980 his younger brother was earning more as a commodities trader than as an accountant. Joe showed up at USC one day driving a showroom shiny Buick Le Sabre, Greg recalled, and said he had paid for it with his earnings at Paine Webber.

Greg's own car was a brown Dodge beater provided by Kathy so he could visit her new home in Ventura County. Mrs. Gamsky hadn't seen her other son since he left school.

In February and March of 1980, Joe began to recruit investors for a commodities partnership, beginning with his father's associates at the American Institute of Hypnosis. "We all called Joey 'the Genius,'" Frank Dana remembered. "Larry started it, but then the rest of us took it up. Because it was true; he really had been the youngest person to ever pass the CPA exam."

Larry set up the meetings where Joe unveiled his "breakthrough discovery," Dana recalled: "Joey had this great idea about using computers to trade commodities. He had found this lag, he said, of like thirty seconds, between the time an order is put in by phone and when it's entered into the computer at the exchange. He could move faster than the market, Joey said, and always stay ahead of the game. He and Larry were trying to raise money so he could buy a seat on the Mercantile Exchange in Chicago and take advantage of what he had found."

It was right around this time, Dana remembered, when Larry began to offer elaborate descriptions of his younger son's childhood training: "He started bragging about how he had programmed Joe from a very early age to succeed at all costs, that the kid had a capacity for clearing his head and concentrating his mind that was way out there, beyond the understanding of mere mortals." Recalled an attorney who was offered the opportunity to invest with Joe: "There were stories about Larry planting posthypnotic suggestions administered under sodium pentothal in his son, to create this superintellect that could operate without doubt or hesitation."

When people began phoning to ask what he thought of Joe's trading scheme, Dana told them the son was too much like his father to be trusted. "The thing I saw in both of them is that neither Larry nor Joe can stand to be wrong and will never admit it if they are," Dana explained. "It's like saying they made a mistake is impossible for them. Also, I suspected that Joey, like Larry, lacked common sense. They both came across to me as entirely academic in their awareness, as if they believed more in ideas than in reality." Nevertheless, Dana recalled, "several people who had a lot more money to spend than I did bought the story hook, line, and sinker."

The first and biggest fish the Gamskys landed was Dr. Rubini, whose investment in Joe eventually would exceed one hundred thousand dollars. "Larry had Rubini convinced Joey was a genius—nobody ever bought it bigger," Dana recalled.

Even as Joe's trading fund approached six figures, the financial pressure on Larry was peaking toward a climax in the spring of 1980. The institute continued to fall deeper into debt each month; Gamsky and Mingarella were so desperate for cash that they attempted to peddle a treatment for a television series about hypnotherapists titled "The Mind Explorers." The treatment was rejected at almost the same time a lawsuit was filed against the institute by the mother of a young musician whose "Psychosynthesis Therapy" had done more harm than good, the woman claimed. Several other former patients were threatening to sue as well. Most ominously of all, an investigator from the state had showed up at AIH during the previous summer to ask questions about "medical licensing."

A spooky sense of dangerous experiments and stabs in the dark pervaded the institute when Gamsky and the cult deprogrammer began to team up, remembered Dana, whose apprehensions would be realized one afternoon when he walked in on a marathon therapy session and discovered that the two were using not only sodium pentothal on a patient, but nitrous oxide—laughing gas—as well. "I went straight to Frank Mingarella and he made them stop," Dana recalled, "but after that I was more and more worried about what was going on behind closed doors."

The first of several complaints that "unlicensed physicians" were practicing medicine at the American Institute of Hypnosis, 7188 Sunset Boulevard, Los Angeles, was filed during the spring of 1979, according to Edward Perkins, senior special investigator for the California Board of Medical Quality Assurance (BMQA), whose probe had commenced on April 23 of that year.

"I was there when Perkins came up and wanted to see Frank Mingarella and/or Larry Gamsky," remembered Frank Dana. "He talked to Mingarella first, and I was with Frank when he handed the state guy's card to Larry and said, 'You deal with this.' Larry just ignored it. So the state people decided to get tough about it, really tough."

During his visit, Perkins had noted that the institute continued to display the M.D. license of Dr. Dan Kuska on its walls. "The staff were never told anything about Kuska quitting," said Frank Dana, "so none of us knew we were practicing medicine without a license. What happened was, the state people set the place up, sent in a female agent posing as a patient, waited until the sodium pentothal drip was going, then came storming through the front door, telling us all we were under arrest. What an experience. They handcuffed every one of us—except Jean Clarke—led us out the front door, and drove us to jail. They closed the place down, just like that."

That afternoon was the third and last time he saw Larry Gamsky do his narcoleptic nod-out, Dana recalled: "The state agents are reading Larry his rights, asking if he understands, and suddenly they hear the guy snoring. The weirdest part was, [another therapist at AIH] did the same thing. He had narcolepsy, too, only I didn't know that until I saw him go down, just like Larry." The expressions on the faces of the BMQA agents as they attempted to interrogate a pair of sleeping men made being arrested almost worth it, Dana conceded, "but not quite—the thing cost me a small fortune in attorney's fees."

The AIH was represented at first by a lawyer named Lawrence Levy, referred through the AFL-CIO "Lay Hypnotists" union. The institute people, though, "were of a different order," Levy hastened to explain. "Way out there. They kept referring to Dr. Bryan like he was this ghost that haunted the place. Very private references and in-jokes."

The charges against Dana and other staff members ultimately were dropped, but the state continued to press its criminal claim against Gamsky and Mingarella, deciding that the best case was not for practicing medicine without a license but on a charge of Medi-Cal fraud. Senior Special Investigator Perkins obtained a subpoena for all AIH records, but by then the only documents of real value, Dr. Bryan's case histories, had been removed, recalled Dana: "Right after the arrests, Joey and Larry loaded them all up in a truck and drove off."

The date of the raid on the institute was April 14, 1980. Ten days later, Joe announced he was leaving Peat Marwick. "We were riding together in the elevator," Terry Dibble remembered, "and Joe told me he was resigning. He said he had inherited a substantial sum of money from his grandmother that would require his personal management." Two weeks after that, Joe met Dean Karny and Ben Dosti on the sidewalk in Westwood. "What nobody seems to realize," Dana explained, "is that the BBC was at least as much Larry's idea as it was Joe's."

***

"Your Honor, I wish my father to act in my behalf in regards to changing my name from Joseph H. Gamsky to Joseph Hunt. I am doing this to retain my father's last name," Joe wrote on the sheet of TRUST BONUS PLAN stationery he sent in October of 1980 to Los Angeles Superior Court Judge Richard Amerain, who had accepted petitions for a name change from Lawrence Gamsky, his only daughter, and his younger son one month earlier. All three listed their address as 15701 Index Street, Granada Hills, California. Larry and Kay appeared in person before Judge Amerain to hear his decision on election day, November 4, 1980. Joe, however, was not present in court, sending in his stead a note that read, "I am unable to attend the hearing due to business out of state."

The business was commodities trading and the place was Chicago, where Joe had begun making T-bill calls from the floor of the Mercantile Exchange one day earlier. Joe and Larry were joined in Illinois by Jean Clarke, who helped them find the house on the water in Glencoe.

"The name Hunt was Jean's idea," remembered Frank Dana. "She thought it sounded like money. Jean had this flair for changing her image. She could dye her hair, or just change the style, or even just put on a different set of clothes and seem like an entirely different woman, but still beautiful. She was also into changing her name a lot, and it was from her that Larry got the idea he could do it too. He had always wanted to be Ryan; I guess he thought it sounded less like Auschwitz and more like Malibu."

It was Joe who told her of the move east, recalled Kathy, not suspecting then that it would be the spring of 1987 before she saw her younger son again. "He said he was going to Chicago, and that there were many people that wanted to invest, to buy him a seat on the exchange," Kathy remembered. No matter how her son tried to help his father hide it, though, Kathy was certain her ex-husband had "engineered" the move.

Larry, or rather Ryan, wanted his daughter in Chicago as well and sent Kathy a letter saying that "Kay should come and spend time with him there because he had a five-bedroom house that he said was very beautiful, and the backyard was a forest and he wanted her to come and enjoy these things," Mrs. Gamsky remembered. Kay said she didn't want to see Larry ever again. The last straw for the girl had come during her freshman year in high school, when she made the softball team but had to play bare-handed. "Larry ignored me when I told him, over and over, that I needed a glove," she recalled. "Finally, one day Joe took me to the store—I thought just so I could show him which one I wanted—and he bought it for me."

Kay continued to adore her brother but saw little of him in that last year before he left for Chicago. "I knew there was tremendous pressure on

Joe, and he was very busy, so I didn't think he had time to talk," she explained. She went along with the name change, Kay said, only because she didn't want to lose touch with Joe. Like Greg, she would anyway.

Just before his graduation from USC in December, Greg had mailed a letter to Chicago from the campus post office, addressed to Joseph Gamsky and marked F.Y.I.O. An envelope came back to him from Chicago less than one week later, Greg remembered, but he refused to open it. "The return address was Ryan Hunt," he explained. "I don't read anything from him. I throw it away." He was not really surprised, though, Greg said, when Ryan arrived at his door a few days after the letter. The only one of his children who had kept the Gamksy name was so upset by his father's unannounced appearance that he moved out of his apartment at the end of that month, leaving no forwarding address. Greg's last communication with Joe was passed through the registrar's office at USC early in 1981, when the university's administration sent the older brother a letter of notification that Joe was trying to contact him and asking permission to divulge his address. He refused, Greg said, "only because I was afraid I would find my father on my doorstep soon after if I consented."

Kathy not only accepted but anticipated Joe's calls and letters. She also took the child support checks her ex-husband sent, though not without reservations. Ryan Hunt "was not to my knowledge employed," she explained, and although "the checks were signed by Mr. Hunt," Kathy added, "I think the money was Joe's."

The letters and calls from Joe ceased in 1981. She knew her son was very busy, Kathy said, but when the letters she sent him were returned unopened and stamped MOVED—NO FORWARDING ADDRESS, she became alarmed and phoned her sister in Wisconsin. "I asked her to please go and talk to my ex-in-laws and ask them if they knew where Joe was . . . and they told me they didn't know where he was," Kathy remembered.

While Kathy alone was looking for Joe at that point, the number of people who joined in the search for Larry Gamsky increased every month. Among the most determined was Robert Schlifkin, attorney for the New Jersey woman who had filed the lawsuit on behalf of her son, the musician. He was able to serve Mingarella without a great deal of difficulty, Schlifkin recalled, but could not locate Larry Gamsky: "We had no idea he had become Ryan Hunt."

Kathy knew that Larry was Ryan and that Joe now went by the name Hunt as well, but beyond this she was without a clue as to what had happened to them—until late in 1982 when she heard that Ryan Hunt had returned to L.A. Assuming that Joe would be with his father, Kathy tracked her ex-husband down through the child support collection division of the

Ventura County district attorney's office. "Mr. Hunt talked to them, though," she explained, "and told them he needed more time because he needed to get a lawyer and he had absolutely no money. And they were very, very kind to Mr. Hunt. He is a very charming man, they said." After that, she began to spend her evenings "just driving around the Valley looking for Joe," Kathy said.

The people who said she didn't care had no idea: "I prayed a lot, and I called the sheriff's department at one point and I asked them what I could do."

She and Kathy seemed to be moving every few months after she finished high school, Kay recalled, first east to Granada Hills, then west again to Ventura, from Ventura to Canoga Park, from Canoga Park to Malibu, and then back to the San Fernando Valley, where they took an apartment in Northridge. "Whenever we moved, we left no forwarding address," she said, "because we didn't want any contact with my father."

The case of *People v. Larry Gamsky aka Ryan Hunt and Frank Mingarella* came before Judge Brian Crahan during October of 1983. The charge before the court was grand theft, the victim in this case being Blue Shield of California, which had paid out thousands of dollars on insurance claims for therapy at the American Institute of Hypnosis. Restitution already had been ordered. "That's why the company called Fire Safety existed," explained Frank Dana. "The deal between Gamsky and Mingarella was that, if they got convicted, Frank would take the fall while Larry—or rather Joe—put up the money for their defense and what they owed the state."

Dana had been called to testify for the prosecution, whose principal witness was Dr. Dan Kuska. He last had seen Larry Gamsky during April of 1980, one week after the raid on AIH, Kuska told the court. This was in Las Vegas, where the doctor was treating the reigning heavyweight champion, Muhammad Ali. "Larry showed up at my hotel," recalled Kuska, who found his old friend one of the few remaining vacant rooms in town on the eve of Ali's last title defense. The Denver doctor recalled that he had notified Gamsky and Mingarella of his resignation as an AIH vice president "by letter" more than one year earlier but did not retain a copy. So it was his word against Larry's.

Dr. Kuska was visibly distraught as he listened to the chief witness for the defense, Joseph Hunt. Joe was testifying for his father during the same month in which he, first, informed the May twins that their money had been lost at Cantor Fitzgerald and, later, learned that Ron Levin had played him for a fool at Clayton Brokerage. Before Judge Crahan, though,

Joe presented himself as a young man of accomplishment, testifying that by the age of twenty he had taken his "BA in accounting" at USC, as well as "another degree in finance and economics." A newspaper clipping showing that he had been the youngest person ever to pass the CPA exam was offered into evidence.

Under Dr. William J. Bryan Jr., the American Institute of Hypnosis had been "the leading Institute of its kind in the country," Joe told the court. "It had a great deal of prestige." AIH had fallen in stature during his father's tenure at the helm, Joe allowed, but continued to produce gross revenues of nearly twenty thousand dollars per month. He knew Dan Kuska quite well and in fact considered him a close friend of the family, Joe said. So naturally he was astonished, Joe told the court, when, during 1980 and 1981, Dr. Kuska began to make a series of threatening phone calls to his home in Chicago, insisting that, as Ryan Hunt's son, he should pay off the outstanding loans owed by AIH. Dr. Kuska warned him that, unless those loans were made good, "things would be a lot more uncomfortable for Larry and Frank in these proceedings," Joe advised Judge Crahan. "It was a rather strong and heavy-handed inference."

"Kuska couldn't believe Joey would do that to him," Frank Dana recalled. "He told me, 'I treated him like my own son.'"

By the time a verdict was rendered, Mingarella had informed the court he alone was responsible for the fraudulent Medi-Cal filings. "Frank was in a tough spot financially, so he bit the bullet and took the deal Larry and Joe offered him," Dana remembered. "There were supposed to be some sort of compensations down the line, from the BBC."

Mingarella was pronounced guilty and sentenced to a suspended term in state prison on June 27, 1984, three days after Joe Hunt announced to the BBC that he had "knocked off" Ron Levin.

She and Kay were together still, sharing yet another one-bedroom apartment in the Valley, during the autumn of 1986, Kathy Gamsky told the jury. Six years had passed since his mother and sister last heard from Joe, and neither owned the vaguest idea where he was or what he was doing.

Kathy's prayers were answered on the morning of Sunday, November 2, 1986, when she received a phone call from Greg. "In the Los Angeles Times in his neighborhood there was an article showing that Joe was in prison and this whole thing about the BBC," she remembered. "And it was not in our edition. We had at that point no idea that Joe was in any kind of a situation, and that he had been in prison, and was there all by himself, and nobody visited him from our family. We were never told."

She and her mother drove straight to Malibu to buy the *Times*'s Westside edition, Kay recalled: "We read the story, and it said Mr. Barens's name in it." "Since Greg is more in command of himself at this point," Kathy explained, "he called Mr. Barens's office, and Mr. Barens contacted Joe. Joe called us immediately."

His brother was calm, even soothing, when they spoke, Greg recalled, insisting, as always, that no help was needed. He had wanted to attend this trial from the first day, Greg explained to the jury in Santa Monica, but Joe "said he didn't wish for me to jeopardize my marriage or my job or my friends, or anything." Joe was as "giving" as ever, Greg recalled: "He said he wished to do this by himself, to shoulder the burden himself. That is why he didn't contact us."

It was Kathy and Kay, though, for whom Joe went looking first. "My brother drove to our house, saw my mom, then came to my work," remembered Kay, employed then as a saleswoman in a lighting store. "He was just the same as he always was, very worried that we'd be upset."

Joe told his mother and sister he had hired a private investigator to locate them in 1984 and even drove out to Ventura himself "looking for us," Kay recalled. "I desperately missed Joe," said Kathy, and seeing him again, however it came to pass, was for her a happy moment, she assured the jury: "I told him that I had this feeling like I wanted to put him in my pocket and never let him out of my sight again."

As with Greg, however, Joe had asked his mother and sister to stay away from the trial in Santa Monica. "He said it would upset us," Kay explained. Joe's little sister was the same age as Brooke, twenty-two, but the contrast could scarcely have been more complete: Large and pale, with blond hair that definitely had not been bleached in Beverly Hills, Kay looked hot and uncomfortable as she was sworn in wearing a black sheath dress that bound her thick waist and clung to her heavy thighs. Yet she was ten times the witness that Brooke had been, putting on neither airs nor a happy face as she told the jury, "Joe said he was innocent, to wait until it's over and he'd start up his normal life again."

What angered her most as she followed the proceedings from afar, Kay said, was seeing Joe described in the newspapers as a "high school nerd." "He was never a nerd," she insisted. "He had lots of friends." When she and Kathy attempted to locate people from his past who would speak for Joe in court, however, Kay admitted, none could be found. Jamie Hogan, whom Joe had defended back in Mr. Rock's English class at the Harvard School, had been their best hope, but Jamie was a naval officer now, stationed on a ship at sea. None of the men who had worked with his father would speak for Joe, either. "Kathy asked me to testify as a character witness, but I wouldn't do it," Frank Dana explained. "She seemed sad but not surprised. She told me she had called Dr. Rubini also, and he said, 'I don't want anything to do with that murderer.' The lawyers didn't want to use Mingarella. So she couldn't get anybody."

His mother insisted, however, that she had no doubt of Joe's innocence. "Don't worry, I'm sure your son will show up some day soon," Kathy told Carol Levin during a break in her testimony.

Joe kept the promise he made about calling every day, but they had seen very little of him during the trial, Kay conceded: "Three times since November." She told Joe he was welcome to stay with them in the Valley, Kathy recalled, but her son preferred to remain with the Robertses. Joe never did invite his family to visit him at the Bel Air estate, Kathy and Kay admitted, though Brooke had phoned to ask them to dinner just a few days before Mrs. Gamsky was sworn in as a witness.

Joe did not even look at his mother when she was called to the stand in Santa Monica. He began, in fact, to leaf through the pages of a book, Alice Miller's classic critique of maternal love, *The Drama of the Gifted Child*.

Anyone who knew her son as a boy could understand how the BBC had come to exist, Kathy told the jury: "I think Joe gathered around himself people who needed to be taken care of, who couldn't do it on their own. He always was that way." No matter what was said of him in this courtroom, Kathy said, as far as she was concerned, "Joe is everything I had ever hoped he would be." Joe's forbearance extended even to the twelve people who had convicted him unjustly of Ron Levin's murder, his mother observed: "He said about the jury that they were all good people, that they were doing their very best. They just have not been given sufficient information regarding him."

28

THE JURORS HAD ENOUGH INFORMATION, APPARENTLY, IN THE OPINION OF THE
prosecutor. Wapner called one rebuttal witness, the office manager whom
Louise Waller said had told her of Ron Levin's alleged murder. She was
not working at the law firm where Ms. Waller claimed to first have met her
during the mid-1970s until the early 1980s, the woman told the jury. And
she never had met Ron Levin there or anywhere else. Furthermore, there
had been no conversation with Waller about Levin or Joe Hunt's trial.

Final arguments were May 29. Joe arrived that morning with his
hair blown dry and brushed back, wearing his good gray pinstripe suit for
the first time since the reading of the guilty verdict more than a month earlier. Spectators again were being turned away at the door, the entire middle
section of the front row having filled with deputy district attorneys, there
to hear how Fred Wapner would go about asking the eleven women in the
jury box to kill Joe Hunt.

Colleagues who expected dramaturgy from Wapner, though, didn't
know the man. His case for execution was quite simple, the prosecutor explained as he stepped to the podium: Each of the criteria for "aggravating
factors" Judge Rittenband had instructed jurors to consider was satisfied by
the evidence in connection to the murder of Hedayat Eslaminia. Wapner
asked the panel to remember the family of Ron Levin as they considered
the testimony of Kathy Gamsky, wished them well, then said good-bye.

For Barens, the time had come to truly *plead* his client's case. He
felt it would insult the jury to reiterate Mr. Hunt's claim of innocence, the
attorney began, but when Barens acceded to the guilty verdict, Joe cut him
off, requesting a recess "to discuss with counsel." Rittenband ordered the
defendant to keep quiet and waved his bailiff toward the defense table.

Brooke fumed, shooting expressions of shared outrage Joe's way as
Barens began to ask that "one of you speak for Joe Hunt, and vote for life."
Lynne Roberts stepped into the courtroom just as Rittenband was announc-
ing the adjournment for lunch and was only a step behind her daughter as
Brooke followed Barens into the hallway screaming, "You're shit! You're

shit!" Mrs. Roberts pulled her daughter away, but Barens was visibly shaken, seeking out the TV cameras to explain that his job now was to keep Joe Hunt alive.

At one-thirty, though, the attorney prefaced the resumption of his argument by asking the jury not to "misconstrue" his remarks. "The defendant has never admitted guilt," Barens said. "And I *do not* believe the defendant is guilty." From standing tall, Barens went straight to his knees: "Blessed are the merciful," he reminded the jurors, "for they shall obtain mercy."

Brooke did not come back to court, but Lynne was there, sitting beside Kathy Gamsky in a contrast of wardrobe, grooming, and cosmetic enhancement so striking that one's eyes went out of focus trying to keep them in the same picture. It was Lynne rather than his mother who collected Joe's suit, tie, and tasseled loafers when the arguments were concluded.

That night, Joe wrote a letter to Rudy Durand in which for the first time he described what it was like inside:

> We have 26 cells in a row that is called a "tier." I am in Cell 1. All of the cells face out so no one inmate can see another. At about 10 P.M., however, everyone starts to talk. As each inmate seeks to be heard the voices begin to overlap and then to compete in volume. All these manly baritones trapped beneath tons of cement and steel echoing and overlaying—the total effect is like a troop of howling monkeys upon catching sight of a panther.

And now Joe's best hope seemed to be that it might continue this way forever.

The first vote was six for death, three for life, and three undecided. Those who voted life or undecided admitted surprise that their foreperson, Dr. Janis, had cast her ballot for death and were astonished when she was joined by "little Linda King," the young blonde with the cowed expression who appeared overwhelmed by much of the testimony during the penalty-phase trial. The two most adamant proponents of execution were Mrs. Deeg, the pinch-faced woman who had nodded her approval during Wapner's final argument, and Dean Rutherford, the truck-driving Vietnam veteran who owned a Harley-Davidson motorcycle and a feeling the country was going to hell. "Dean kept bringing up patriotism and how America is declining," Mrs. Ghaemmaghami recalled, "and he felt Joe Hunt should be made an example of. I think he would have liked to line the whole BBC up against a wall somewhere."

Joe's humanity that became the ultimate issue of contention in the jury room. Several times during final argument, Barens had referred to Joe, with intended irony, as "the Monster." Only after his second or third such stab at sarcasm, however, did it dawn on the defense attorney that a solid majority of the jury saw Joe as just that: "A ghoul," "a demon," "a fiend," they called him. "I think without his mother's testimony it would have been ten to two for death the first time we voted," said Ms. Keenan.

By the fourth ballot, the death votes were reduced to three. "Some were still worried about what Joe Hunt might be able to do in prison," remembered Ms. Keenan. "They thought he had that much power, that he might be able to manipulate the other prisoners and build his own little empire inside."

After the fifth vote, it was down to Deeg and Rutherford. The truck driver was turned by Mrs. Ghaemmaghami's argument that, for Joe Hunt, prison would be worse than execution. Mrs. Deeg was the last holdout for death. "She was determined but just sat there and cried and wouldn't respond to anything," recalled Mrs. Ghaemmaghami. On the afternoon of their fourth day in the jury room, though, Mrs. Deeg relented and the vote was unanimous.

"JURY GIVES HUNT LIFE TERM, SAYING DEATH IS 'TOO QUICK'" read the headline on the *Herald*'s June 5 front-page story. Dean Rutherford and Pacific Bell supervisor Pat Robles, who also had voted death on the first ballot, were sent out to face the media. Both spoke most passionately not of Joe's crimes but about his lack of emotion during the reading of their guilty verdict six weeks earlier. "Cold and emotionless," Robles said of the way Joe had taken the news. "If I had been convicted of a crime I didn't commit, I would have been beside myself." She and every other member of the jury had wept at one time or another during their "six months in hell," Robles noted, but the defendant never cried once.

"'Joe Hunt—The Retrial,' coming soon to a courtroom near you," Joe wrote to Rudy Durand five days later. Joe's belief he had a "better than fair chance" for a victory on appeal was not unfounded. Rittenband's imperious conduct created bases for any number of claims that the defense case had been subverted.

Joe already was interviewing some of the biggest names in the legal profession about handling his appeal. First choice was Harvard Law School professor Alan Dershowitz, who once had told *Time* magazine, "The system of justice is only as good as it is to the worst person." "I believe we have established a beach-head with the esteemed Professor Dershowitz," Joe wrote to Rudy Durand after meeting with the appeals specialist at the L.A. County Jail on June 21. The sticking point with Dershowitz, though, as with Joe's second choice, Dennis Fischer, was where the money would come from to pay their enormous fees. No one was going to defend the leader of the Billionaire Boys pro bono, and the well was dry at Rancho Roberts.

While Rittenband's bias from the bench seemed the most obvious basis for appeal, "it'll be incompetence of counsel Joe uses," Oscar Breiling predicted. Barens's broken promise to the jury that Joe Hunt would testify already was being cited as a textbook example of what not to do in a criminal case. "How was he ever going to explain those seven pages?" Barens asked in his own defense.

Barens was back in Department C on June 25 to submit Richard Chier's latest motion for a mistrial in *People v. Hunt*. Chier cited eleven pages of "judicial errors," beginning with Judge Rittenband's decision permitting jurors to hear evidence of Joe's involvement in the death of Hedayat Eslaminia, while at the same time he prohibited the defense from asking Dean Karny about the murder of Richard Mayer. The most grievous errors, of course, involved Rittenband's "abusive remarks to co-counsel (Chier), such as: (a) telling him to 'shut up'; (b) telling him he belongs in a bathroom; (c) telling him to 'shove it.'" Rittenband took it surprisingly well, barely scowling as he scanned Chier's motion, tersely denied it, then granted the defense an additional nine days to prepare for the sentencing hearing.

Joe's probation report was presented to the court on June 25. Other than his claim of innocence, Hunt submitted just one quote to the formal sentencing record: "I wanted to take the stand and explain myself. I had prepared one hundred pages of single-spaced typewritten questions for my attorney to ask me, cross-referenced to over seventy documents. I thought I was taking the stand on Sunday; the defense rested on Monday."

Judge Rittenband sentenced Joe to life in prison without possibility of parole on July 6, 1987. The book Hunt brought to court that day was not one of Castenada's but rather a blue volume that had begun to appear in Westside salons about three years earlier, *A Course in Miracles*. For Joe, it seemed a remarkable choice. In the universe of "the Course," God was a spirit of infinite mercy, devoid of judgment, before whom even the most heinous crimes were forgiven in the instant of their commission. One need only forgive oneself, the narrator explained, to be free forever from "past error." Joe clearly did not expect forgiveness from Judge Rittenband, who told him, "Perhaps, as expressed by several of the jurors, it will be a greater punishment for you to be confined to the state prison for the rest of your life rather than suffer death, which could also have been appropriately imposed."

"So long, Joe Hunt," Bob Levin called out as Joe was led away in handcuffs. "I hope they do to you what you did to my brother." "When your brother shows up, what will you say then?" retorted a teary Lynne Roberts, blowing Joe a kiss as he disappeared from Department C.

Joe wrote his last letter from county jail one week later, having learned only the day before that his request in Northern California for a severance from Ben Dosti and Reza Eslaminia (whose trial was scheduled to begin August 24) had been granted. Joe's satisfaction, however, was dampened by NBC's announcement that Hunt would be played in its *Billionaire Boys Club* miniseries by Brat Packer Judd Nelson. The production was certain to be "trite, plasticized, and studied," he predicted.

The next letter Hunt sent had been mailed from the maximum-security section of the "California Men's Colony" at Chino, where Joe was doing his ninety-day diagnostic. He was permitted just one visit a week, and only by a blood relative, which excluded Brooke. The guards wouldn't even let him have books. He had found that discipline was what it took to survive such a place, Joe wrote, reporting that he scrubbed his cell each day from floor to ceiling with toilet paper:

> If photographed, the picture would be an excellent example of the
> verist school of art, which holds that ugliness is valid so long as it is
> true. I choose to see my cell in that way: as part of a verist's photo
> exhibition hanging in a well-lit hall of one of the more progressive
> modern museums. I am the unseen care-taker who ensures that
> the cleanliness remains as counterpoint to the meanness, austerity
> and sullen functionality of the photo-depicted cage.

Joe ended by imploring Rudy to help him head off NBC and dam the flood of negative publicity. "From the catacombs," he signed off.

Most media coverage of the impending miniseries focused on the pace at which the production was being rushed to the small screen. The proposition of NBC executives was that their alacrity arose from an urge to "timeliness." In truth, the network's race was not with the clock but with rival ABC. The degree to which NBC feared preemption could be inferred from attempts to disguise the *Billionaire Boys Club* script with the title "Tough Boys." In the first draft, dated June 30, 1987, the real names of all the Boys had been used. The title sequence was a "montage of high impact BBC activity" that ended with "three figures—Joe, Tom and Dave in tennis shorts—leaping into space for a Slo-Mo descent, their images slowly dissolving into infinity." The twins would rank right behind Joe as central characters in NBC's version of the Billionaire Boys, rendered sympathetic more by a process of selective omission than of wholesale fabrication.

If Hunt stood alone among defendants in objecting to the miniseries on grounds of inanity, he was joined by the others in protesting that NBC's planned airing of the program during the November sweeps would find them guilty of crimes for which they had yet to be convicted in court. Pittman was back on trial in Santa Monica, facing a prosecution case in the killing of Ron Levin that was exactly as the miniseries script described it. Dosti and Eslaminia were scheduled to begin presenting their defense cases at trial in Redwood City just about the time the miniseries would be broadcast.

Attorneys for every defendant other than Reza threatened NBC with lawsuits, but the network was undeterred. "Our focus is Joe Hunt," explained NBC's vice president for law, Donald Zachary. "And Joe Hunt is now what we lawyers call libel-proof."

This seemed certainly the case at the ten-year reunion for the Harvard School's class of 1977, where those young men who had known him as Joseph Gamsky tried out joke after joke to explain why the "guest of dishonor" was unable to attend. The line that got the biggest laugh, though, was one about Dean Karny showing up undercover, disguised as a waiter. "Everyone agreed it wasn't the school's fault, that Harvard had nothing to do with it," recalled Brad Reifler, who had flown in from New York for the event.

Dollar for dollar and bauble for bauble, no success story from the class of '77 could match Reifler's: Brad lived in a spectacular townhouse in Greenwich Village, tooled about Manhattan in either the Porsche Cabriolet or the Rolls-Royce Silver Shadow he kept in a garage down the street, and only that summer had announced his engagement to a beautiful aerobics instructor named (no kidding) Ashley Ashforth.

The other three leaders of the "wealthy group" had kept pace: Bob Beyer was making almost as much money in the stock market as Brad was earning in commodities; Bob Wyman was not only Rob Lowe's business partner but also a rising star in the Beverly Hills law firm of Rosenfeld, Meyer, and Susmen; Rick Berg (whose brother Jeff now ran the International Creative Management agency) was pursuing a career in politics, leaving the Washington office of California Congressman Mel Levine to attend Stanford Law School.

The biggest disappointment for many at the reunion was not Joe Gamsky but rather their former first prefect, Dan Greenberg. Dan had dropped out of Princeton more than six years earlier and was still adrift. He gave his occupation as "drummer" and showed up for the reunion "wearing ripped jeans and an eye patch, with his hair kind of unkempt," Brad recalled. "He couldn't put two words together without 'man' in between." The eye patch was to cover the vacancy created when Dan, now a born-again Christian, took literally that biblical instruction about plucking out one's right eye if it offended the Lord. There remained a glimmer of the old twinkle in the eye Greenberg had left, however, and he still could "do that sweeter-than-thou number," as Mike Kaplan put it, like nobody else. Dan also remained one of two—Jamie Hogan being the other—graduates from the class of '77 who spoke with sympathy of Joe's plight. "He was mumbling about how at least Joe tried to do something, had pursued some kind of vision," Peter Kleiner remembered. It was Joe's memory for faces that had impressed Mike Kaplan in his last encounter with the former Gamsky, back in February of that year: "I went to his trial on the first day, and he saw me in the hall. I was a lot thinner than in high school, and I had gotten contacts; a lot of people who knew me well don't recognize me. But in the hall after Barens spoke, Joe walked by and sort of looked at me, then muttered, 'Kaplan,' like 'I know who you are.' My blood froze. I fled, literally."

Both the failures and the successes from the class of '77 would be upstaged at the reunion by the late arrival of Tom and Dave May. "They pulled up in a limo with Donald March and Guy Waldron, acting like movie stars," recalled Taglianetti, who had been frozen out at NBC, "then told everyone how they saved the world from Joe Hunt, and a lot of people were eating it up." Not everyone. "I was sickened by the Mays," said Brad Reifler. "Bragging that they were the heroes of the story and there was a big TV movie being made about them. What really offended me was Tom's holier-than thou-attitude. Then he tells me, 'If you need a drink, come out to our limo; it has a bar.'"

Brad and many others from the class agreed that the most disturbing part of the story was the role played by Dean Karny. "I'm still shocked that Dean could be actually involved in murder," Reifler said. "It just doesn't fit. On the other hand, it doesn't surprise me at all that he turned everyone in for his own benefit."

As for Joe, "of him I could believe almost anything," said Brad, who admitted an abiding regard for his ex-classmate's powers of mind and will. "Personally, I think he'll find some way to get out of prison," Reifler predicted, "either by escaping or by doing it on appeal. If he can't escape, I think he'll kill himself. Not out of weakness but out of strength, to prove he can't be beaten. I think winning means more to Joe than living."

Before catching his return flight to New York, Brad had stopped in for lunch at La Scala Boutique in Beverly Hills, where he spotted Ben

Dosti sitting alone at the bar: "He came over and sat with me, had a glass of wine. I said, 'I only know what I read, but it seems like you're pretty popular.' He says, 'They're really after me.' He seemed very depressed and kind of lonely, actually. He told me they were going to get involuntary manslaughter because they didn't mean for [Eslaminia] to die and were only going to scare him into turning over the money."

"Showtime," muttered the man with the earjack who spoke into his shirtsleeve as Dean Karny was called to the stand in Redwood City on the morning of October 6, 1987. After two emotional appearances in Santa Monica, Dean came across flat again in San Mateo County, terse—even hard—as he answered John Vance's preliminary questions. Dean's voice broke, however, whom he identified Ben Dosti, and Karny's composure was brittle after that. Vance and Oscar Breiling had admitted they feared what facing Ben in court might do to their witness.

During the first six months of 1987, Tom Nolan repeatedly had encouraged Ben to consider the only deal offered by the state, a chance to plead guilty to first-degree murder in exchange for a sentence of twenty-five years to life in state prison; he believed he might have negotiated a sentence of as little as fifteen years in Soledad, Nolan explained. Nolan could not say whether his client rejected the state's offer "because he can't confess to his family what he's done," but admitted "sometimes I think that's the case." John Vance had little doubt: "Ben's own denial system and his parents' are now so interlocking that he could never admit to them that he actually went along with this."

The Dostis had followed Ben north to prepare for the Redwood City trial, renting a house in Palo Alto ten minutes from the courthouse. Rose, Ben, and his sister Marya were living there, joined by Luan and their married eldest daughter, Lisa Jeffs. Ben's parents already had signed over a note on their own home in Hancock Park to pay for what would be an extraordinarily expensive defense.

In Tom Nolan, the Dostis again had given their boy the best money could buy. Current president of California Attorneys for Criminal Justice, Nolan had defended Harold Tanner in the state's "Use a Gun, Go to Prison" test case, represented Charles Garry in the San Francisco grand jury's investigation of the Jonestown massacre, and presently was appearing in federal court on behalf of Synanon founder Charles Dederich. Even as he defended Ben Dosti in San Mateo County, Nolan would take time out to represent U2's singer Bono on a charge of defacing public property after the performer spray-painted an overbearing sculpture during a free concert in downtown San Francisco. "Formidable" was the word John Vance kept using to describe Nolan.

For Vance, forty-one, the BBC prosecution was shaping up as "something akin to a life's work." Stolid and straight-arrow, a man excessive only in his deliberation, Vance seemed a person who would be more comfortable teaching the law than practicing it. The son of a West Point graduate, he had taken a master of law degree at the London School of Economics and was among the most widely published prosecutors on the West Coast.

Vance permitted the state's star witness to portray defendant Dosti sympathetically early in his testimony, nodding again and again as Dean described their seduction by Joe Gamsky during the spring and summer of 1980. It was "Ben and I" this, "Ben and I" that.

As in Santa Monica, women were a majority of the Redwood City panel. These, though, were modestly middle-class citizens, by and large, people with technical and trade educations who supported small families and suburban mortgages. They seemed at times to be watching and listening to the BBC story from behind a large and semipermeable television screen. Dean, who had been living among the fly-over people for the past two years, stared back at them a moment, shook his head slightly, then bowed it before continuing with his explanation of the Shadings' role as the BBC's "philosophical interpreters."

Karny recalled the afternoon when Ben volunteered to retrieve a letter to Ron Levin from Lore Leis's desk but was blocked by Nolan from recounting Dosti's participation in the June 24 meeting. Nolan was successful as well in excluding Dean's recollection of his conversations with Ben about Paradox Philosophy. The attorney had used the same "prejudicial effect outweighs probative value" argument to bar the testimony of Julie Marks. Julie had phoned to *ask* if she could testify against Ben, Breiling explained: "She really has it in for him."

By the time Dean came to that July 9 meeting with Joe and Ben on the street corner outside the Third Street office, Nolan had successfully excluded almost every bit of testimony that might implicate his client in the BBC's "dirty deeds." There was no stopping Dean now, though. Karny was five minutes into the meeting the next day at the Manning when Reza leaped to his feet, shouting, "Why don't you tell the truth?" Dean stared at him coolly for a moment, then answered, "I am telling the truth." The jury, whose attention up to now had shifted between Vance, Nolan, Karny, and Eslaminia, began to study Ben Dosti as Dean recalled the events of July 30, 1984. Several jurors reached involuntarily for the person next to them as Dean described the hours he and his friend had spent in the back of the

U-Haul with the man in the trunk. Even Rose Dosti's note-taking ceased when Dean re-created the scene at the Beverly Glen house, where Joe and Ben had carried the dead man to the basement before searching his body.

Reza's attorney Gary Merritt went first on cross-examination. Merritt seemed intent upon presenting himself as the Joe Sixpack of the legal troupe, a former high school basketball star who subjected even the most common Persian names to Okie inflection. What concerned the prosecution in Redwood City, however, was Merritt's pretrial warning that he intended to release "evidence the U.S. government was using Hedayat Eslaminia to smuggle opium to raise money to pay for anti-Khomeini mercenaries" and to time his disclosures with the 1988 presidential election. Merritt threatened also to make public a list of CIA agents who had worked with Hedayat Eslaminia: "I wrote to the Iranian government to tell them I would send a copy of that list to Teheran if they would line all those bastards up against a wall somewhere and shoot them," he said.

The first questions the attorney asked Dean Karny, however, were about the party at Evan Dicker's where most of the Boys met Reza for the first time, establishing that "the BBC were all in tuxedos" as if a significant point had been made. Merritt then demanded a description of Paradox Philosophy, responding with hammy bewilderment to Dean's explanation that "our theoretical goal was that the application of Paradox would be second nature." Reza's attorney repeated the tactic of Doug Young and Arthur Barens, asking Dean to name all the people he had lied to during his BBC period. Your parents? "Yes." Your friends? "Yes." Joe Hunt? "No." Reza Eslaminia? "Yes." Ben Dosti? Dean's smile was strange, smug and shamed at the same time. He exchanged a glance with Ben, then answered, "Maybe." When Merritt asked about the attempt on Bruce Swartout's life, though, Dean replied, "Only Joe and Jim were really in on it," then glanced at Ben, who nodded slightly, in thanks.

Tom Nolan spent the first four hours of his cross-examination going over Dean's decision to seek an immunity agreement, asking the witness what he planned to do with his next "forty-three years of freedom, if you live to age seventy." Nolan approached the climax of his cross-examination on October 19 by demanding that the witness tell the court which of the five conspirators first had uttered the words "kill," "kidnap," and "torture." Dean's distress was visible. When he attempted to evade the question, Nolan, sensing a soft spot, pressed forward. Dean glared at him, then blurted, "It might have been your client."

Evan Dicker was the next BBC Boy called to the stand. Evan was a wealthy orphan now, his mother having passed away the previous spring. He and his brother Layne were living together at the family home in Beverly

Hills, dividing their inheritance and deciding their futures. Evan had finished finally at Whittier Law School and planned to take the bar exam in February.

He and Dean had spoken just before the trial, Evan said, "when he called to offer condolences after my mother died. I had the feeling he was keeping his chin up and weathering it all very well. We talked about 'Joe's been convicted, Joe's going to jail, et cetera,' but we don't go into details or talk about things that could come up in court. We talk mostly about who we—I—have run into lately and what people look like and how they're doing, et cetera. And it feels bad talking about all the fun I'm having when he's obviously not. But he seems to want to hear about it. There's always a sadness in the conversation, the knowledge that we may never see each other again, except a glimpse through a courtroom window."

People he didn't know were constantly approaching him in restaurants and clubs to ask if he was *the* Evan Dicker, and the question he heard most often, Evan said, was how he felt about Dean walking away while Ben went down. "A lot of people are very upset that Dean got off," Evan allowed, "but I still think Dean has to pay really a much higher price than anyone does, because Dean cannot to himself or anyone else protest his innocence—Dean is the only one of the five who has agreed to live with the fact that he murdered a man. I will say that I don't think either Ben or Dean was predisposed to murder. Joe, my feeling is, even before the BBC, wanted to kill somebody to see if he could get away with it. He wanted that kind of power over somebody, and he wanted to see if he was smarter than the police. Yes, he could convince people he was warm and caring, but that was just how good he was at manipulation. I think Joe enjoyed the opportunity to prove he could charm anyone; it was another chance to exercise power . . . It would have been all right with me if both Ben and Dean had gotten deals. Between the two of them, though, there's no doubt in my mind that Dean is the more feeling and caring person, and also the more moral. So just on the basis of poetic justice, I'm glad it was him who was given another chance."

Ben he had avoided until his call to the stand in Redwood City, Evan admitted: "I ran into Marya at City Restaurant when she was hostessing there, but it was just 'How's your family? Hope everyone's well.' She was still cordial when I saw her at the trial up north. Even Ben and I exchanged hellos. Mrs. Dosti, though, obviously wasn't happy to see me."

What made Rose most unhappy was Evan's recollection of her son's attendance at a meeting in the Wilshire Manning on June 24, 1984, and of his participation in later discussions of plans to kill Renee Martin, Jeff Raymond, and the May twins.

Steve Lopez still was trying to be everybody's friend, nodding and smiling as he entered the courtroom, first at Reza and Mina, then at Ben and his parents. He believed even the Dostis understood "I don't want to be damaging to anybody," Steve explained: "I came to this country to do business, which is what America is supposed to be all about."

A series of FBI and U.S. Passport Office agents closed out the prosecution case, which concluded just in time to coincide—"inadvertently, I assure you," said John Vance—with the broadcast of the "much-dreaded miniseries," as the prosecutor called it, on November 8 and 9.

NBC's vindication of *The Billionaire Boys Club* was a Nielsen rating of 21.4 (with a 34 share), making it the most-watched miniseries of the past three seasons. Even NBC president Brandon Tartikoff admitted, however, that his network had "crossed the line" on this one.

Those issues raised by the miniseries prior to its airing were either "legal" or "ethical," depending upon which attorney was speaking at the time. The state's case against Jim Pittman (whose second trial for the murder of Ron Levin had begun in Santa Monica a week before the Dosti/Eslaminia trial started in Redwood City) went to the jury on October 19, but the panel still was deliberating at the time of the program's originally scheduled broadcast dates on November 1 and 2. The network's promotional spots had begun to air more than one week earlier, on October 25, and those alone could influence jurors, Jim's new lawyer Jeff Brodey asserted.

The sole attorney to take direct action, however, was one Jeffrey Melczer, the same innovative legal mind who back in 1983 had posed the "reporter's privilege" defense of Ron Levin's right to remain silent during the Cantor Fitzgerald depositions. In 1987, though, Melczer wasn't representing Levin but rather his convicted killer, Joe Hunt, on whose behalf the attorney had filed a lawsuit in federal court, demanding an injunction barring NBC from airing *The Billionaire Boys Club*. "Disinformation," Melczer called the network's version of the BBC. "It depicts Joe Hunt the myth rather than Joe Hunt the reality. Fact and fiction are merged here. You may ultimately have Joe Hunt becoming a character like John Dillinger or Bonnie and Clyde. Who knows what they did or didn't do?" The Levin family was incensed by Melczer's appearance on Hunt's behalf: "Turning the knife in the wound," Bob Levin called it. The attorney's reply effused from that wicked sense of humor he once had shared with the deceased: Blocking the broadcast, Melczer contended, couldn't possibly harm Ron Levin "unless he contributed to the miniseries in some way or collaborated with NBC—which would mean he is still alive."

NBC answered the lawsuit with case law demonstrating that the First Amendment afforded protection for "fiction in general." Fiction? NBC's own promotions described the miniseries as a "true story." "Although it is a fact-based drama," the network's vice president for law, Donald Zachary, clarified, "it does not purport to be a documentary." The ruling in its favor by District Court Judge Francis C. Whelan was celebrated at NBC with a new commercial for *The Billionaire Boys Club.* "The show Joe Hunt doesn't want you to see," the network called it.

The lone attorney to dent NBC's resolve was Brodey, whose written request for a one-week delay of the broadcast had been granted (so that the jury in Santa Monica might conclude its deliberations before the miniseries aired). NBC also made one other concession to Brodey, changing Jim Pittman's name at the last minute to "Frank Booker."

Three true names *would* be used in the miniseries, however, an NBC spokesman said: Ron Levin's, because he was dead and therefore no longer had any legal rights; Dean Karny's, because, as a friend of Evan Dicker's put it, "Dean's not using it anymore," and, of course, that of the show's libel-proof lead character. "Judd Nelson *is* Joe Hunt," blared the commercials that promoted the program during the weeks prior to its airing.

Nelson handed out "FREE JOE HUNT" T-shirts to those who attended the wrap party for the miniseries at the Hard Rock Café and told the assembled media at a Century City press conference, "He's like someone out of the Iran-contra hearings. Although [Joe] committed crimes, he really believed what he was doing was right." "The things Judd said were absolutely embarrassing," conceded Evan Dicker, who had joined the Mays and Jeff Raymond on the NBC team as a "technical consultant." Nothing Nelson said could be more embarrassing, however, than what issued from the show's "creative team." Director Marvin Chomsky, defending the pace of the NBC production, explained that "your dramatic TV forms are approaching the production speed of newsmagazines. Just edit a bunch of elements together, and *bam,* it's done." Chomsky's statements at least evinced a cynical candor. The remarks of writer Waldron, however, invited outright derision: "What we did here," he explained, "was take a series of events and compress them into fictional scenes to tell the story. We're looking for an essential truth."

By broadcast date, Judd Nelson was attempting more considered statements: Joe Hunt was "symptomatic of an ill in contemporary society," the actor explained. "Joe is a believer in situational ethics, and the end justifies the means. We see that a lot nowadays, and Joe pays a tremendous price because of his way of looking at the law. Hopefully, we can learn from him." Not if Nelson could help it. Despite a remarkable talent for flaring his nostrils, the actor hired to portray Hunt lacked the stature—in every sense of the word—required to capture Joe's combination of imposing physical presence, fervid intellect, incantatory speech, calibrated charm, and static power.

What Nelson, with an assist from Waldron, missed most completely, however, was the process of a soul's possession that had held spellbound those Boys who watched it as members of BBC back in 1984. "Judd Nelson played Joe as a psycho from day one, and that was really wrong," Evan explained after attending an advance screening of the miniseries. "There were a few who said he was a con man, but nobody said he was crazy. It wasn't until around the time of the Renee plan and when he started talking about killing the Mays that Joe really began to look, you know, anything like the way Judd Nelson played him, with the bulging eyes and all that. Joe always had been intense, but not like Nelson, because Joe's intensity was something that drew people to him, while Nelson's was something that would repulse you."

Some of the Boys, of course, were only too pleased with the portraits of themselves they saw at a preview of the four-hour program in Beverly Hills. The characters who had been Dave and Tom May in the "Tough Boys" script now were Chris and Eric Fairmount, a pair of BBC members described as "skeptical" and "impressionable" in the *San Francisco Chronicle*'s review. The Mays had been paid sixty-five thousand dollars for their participation in the production, a pittance next to the millions they stood to inherit, but it was their billing as "modern-day heroes" the twins cherished. Dave was strutting around town in one of Judd Nelson's "FREE JOE HUNT" T-shirts, only with the "FREE" crossed out and replaced by "FRY." Tom no longer chose to lead by introducing himself as an heir to the department-store fortune, but rather as the "the guy who stopped Joe Hunt." Steven Cowan sat directly in front of the twins at the *Billionaire Boys Club* screening and was invited to their home for a party afterward: "Everybody was in black tie," he reported, "just like they were doing it all over again."

Among the many who expressed their displeasure with the Mays' revisionist eminence was Dean Karny. "Just before it ran, I finally told Dean I was cooperating with NBC and getting money," Evan recalled. "I put off telling him as long as I could. He didn't come down on me, but I knew he wasn't pleased. He made it clear, though, that he thought it was pretty sad that the Mays ended up being the heroes of the story."

During the days just prior to the airing of the miniseries, NBC's PR people boasted to the press that, despite the accelerated shooting schedule, no "production values" had been spared: The actors who played the Boys wore Armani or Valentino suits, and those Cole-Haan loafers on Judd

Nelson's feet had been purchased from the very same store where Joe bought his. What resulted from this versimilitude was a program most remarkable for the seamlessness of its transitions from dramatic scenes to the Porsche and BMW commercials dividing them. So smooth were the segues that they seemed like more of the show until the intrusive appearance on-screen of KNBC anchorwoman Sylvia Chase, who urged those watching to "stay tuned for the latest on the *real* Billionaire Boys Club at eleven."

"Fictionalization," however, had proved more legal ploy than aesthetic device. All that could be described as inventive in the NBC program were the new names that had been given to the supporting players: Ben Dosti was "Todd Melbourne," Steve Taglianetti was "Toby Kabak," Jeff Raymond was "Brad Sedgwick,"and Evan Dicker was "Bob Holmby." Evan, the only BBC member other than Tom, Dave, and Jeff to participate in the production, admitted his regret: "Embarrassingly bad," he said of the show, then added, "If I ever talk to Dean again, I'm going to apologize for having anything to do with it."

Los Angeles Times critic Howard Rosenberg devoted much of his review to chastising NBC for its irresponsibility in airing the miniseries before all the court proceedings were concluded: "Trial by TV," he termed it. A more insightful if equally sanctimonious assessment of the miniseries ran in the *L.A. Times* one day later, authored by the reporter who had covered Joe's trial for her paper, Lois Timnick: "Smaller than life," she called the NBC program.

Only the legal consequences of the miniseries, however, still were being debated one week later as the defense prepared to present its case in San Mateo County. Jeff Brodey had cited the NBC program in his decision, one day after *The Billionaire Boys Club* concluding segment aired, to cut a deal with the prosecution. "The whole possibility of Pittman getting a fair trial was severely diminished," said Brodey, who called the miniseries "racially biased and untrue." The unbiased truth was that Pittman's color was about all he had working for him: A jury that deliberated for nearly two weeks had reported itself deadlocked on November 3, with the vote eight to four in favor of acquittal on the charge of first-degree murder. The nonverdict was in large measure an expression of sympathy for the poor black man used by those rich white Boys who were the real BBC.

For Wapner, his reputation secured by the conviction of Joe Hunt (he would be appointed a municipal court judge within the next year), Pittman's trial—virtually unattended by the media—had been a matter of small personal consequence. The DA's post-trial offer permitting Pittman to plead guilty as an accessory to murder after the fact was "really too good to turn down," explained Brodey. No doubt about that: The maximum sentence Pittman now faced for his part in the slaying of Ron Levin was not the death penalty but three years in state prison, less time than he had spent already at the Hall of Justice Jail, and credit for time served was part of the deal. Wapner justified the plea bargain, in part, with the assertion that Jim faced almost certain conviction in San Mateo County.

"Thank God this is over," Pittman told reporters after his sentencing. Over it wasn't, of course. Deputies at the San Mateo County Jail already had reserved a cell in their maximum-security wing for Jim. The BBC's bodyguard would be heading north three years older and thirty pounds lighter than at the time of his arrest in 1984. The only one of the defendants never released on bail, Jim had been ravaged physically by his incarceration, spending most of 1986 in the county hospital's jail ward because of a high blood pressure condition (250 over 200 at one reading) aggravated by stress. His kidneys had failed several times and never would be fully functional again, according to doctors. Pittman's condition seemed unlikely to improve: Jim was the only one of the four defendants seen at the Belmont condominiums on the day of Hedayat Eslaminia's abduction and faced a case in Redwood City that was stronger against him than against Joe Hunt. Already Pittman's attorneys had discussed with prosecutors a plea of guilty plus a promise to testify against Hunt in exchange for a murder conviction that would mean a minimum of seventeen years in state prison.

The bodyguard's strongest card was any information he could offer in connection to the murder of Richard Mayer. Jim's attorneys had hinted they could deliver evidence that would convict Joe Hunt of the Hollywood homicide, but by November that seemed "wishful thinking," said Vance. Tom Nolan reported hearing a rumor that Diaz and Rozzi were close to an arrest in the Mayer case because they had found a makeup artist who said he had done Joe Hunt up to look like Oscar Breiling. That story had been invented by the LAPD detectives themselves, Nolan asserted a short time later "to try to get Pittman to turn."

As Nolan and Merritt prepared to present the defense case(s) when the Redwood City trial resumed on November 19, the attorneys still were arguing the ramifications of the NBC miniseries. "Even if jurors didn't watch it," Nolan said, "their families and friends would probably have watched the show and talked about it in the jurors' presence." That would be the argument on appeal, anyway, if Ben was convicted. Reza's lawyer, though, said he was less concerned about the effect of the miniseries than with how jurors would react to the recent Iranian missile attack on a U.S. oil tanker in the Persian Gulf.

The Iranian connection to the BBC story clearly was what most engaged the media in Northern California. It was not the BBC-as-metaphor for-the-eighties that the Bay Area press chose to play up, but the "international intrigue" angle. This was perhaps less an attempt to widen the scope of the story than to move its center upstate. The menace of that Moloch to the south was an obsession in the Bay Area, where the knowledge that power, money, and influence had shifted irrevocably to L.A. during the past twenty years was a harrowing reminder of what passed for progress these days. "There are seventeen million people in Southern California," *San Francisco Chronicle* TV commercials were reminding the local audience that autumn, "and they want your water." The irony was that Southern Californians were fond of San Francisco, happy to agree it was the prettiest city in America, quaint and lovely, the ideal spot for a romantic weekend (and just an hour away by plane). In San Francisco, however, there was the sense that civic dignity must be asserted at every opportunity, and the choice to treat the BBC trials in Redwood City as if they were a local story with international implications seemed a function of this imperative. "Shadowy secret agents and national security were injected yesterday into the already bizarre Redwood City murder case of two members of the so-called Billionaire Boys Club" read the lead on the *Chronicle*'s coverage of the opening statements.

Tom Nolan had done the injecting. "This is a case of deceivers and believers," Nolan told the jury. "Ben Dosti was a believer."

Nolan's problem was that his client stood trial with Reza Eslaminia, who claimed *he* had been the believer, and that among those who deceived him was Ben Dosti. Reza smiled at the jury as he took his seat in the witness stand and again as he began to tell the sad story of his life, confessing to Merritt that he didn't know if he was twenty-four or twenty-five or twenty-six: his immigration papers, his mother, and his father all gave different dates for his birth. Reza's unctuousness was better concealed than earlier in the trial, and the almost-feminine beauty of his features surfaced through layers of taint. He looked as if he might weep when he recalled the sexual peccadilloes of first one parent, then the other, and described at length the loss of self-respect that in his family's fall from power had led to drug addiction and numerous suicide attempts.

By the summer of 1984 the Eslaminias were at the brink of obscurity, Reza explained: He had known that his father was, "for him, broke," with no more than $350,000 to his name, yet boasted of Hedayat's wealth when he met Ben Dosti in June of 1984, hoping this would help him gain admission to the BBC. Reza recalled how Joe welcomed him to the Wilshire Manning and how grateful he had been when the BBC leader gave him $200 and the use of a BMW upon learning that Reza was planning to celebrate the anniversary of his first date with Debi during the last weekend of July. He had no idea any of the BBC would be in the Bay Area at the same time and was startled when Joe left a message at Debi's office asking if they could meet for lunch that Monday, Reza recalled: Joe said he was in San Francisco on business and that while up north "wanted to see my father and see if he could patch things up." He gave Joe the Belmont address and agreed to meet him there at 3 P.M., Reza said, but the only BBC member he met in Davy Glen that afternoon was Dean Karny, whom he saw wearing a gray suit and walking along the shoulder of the road. He braked the BMW to a stop, and Dean came to the window, Reza recalled, explaining that Joe had tried his best but Mr. Eslaminia still didn't want to see his eldest son. This had not surprised him, Reza said, and he drove away.

He first learned of his father's disappearance when he arrived the next evening in Los Angeles and was informed by his mother of Olga's phone call, Reza said. It was for counsel that he had gone to Joe on Wednesday afternoon. Dean, Jim, and Brooke were with Joe in the larger condo at the Manning when he told them his father was missing and asked if he should get an attorney, Reza recalled: Joe announced then that his father was dead and that the BBC was responsible. When he said he didn't believe it, Reza recalled, Joe told him it wasn't the first time they had done something like this and showed him a photograph of a corpse lying in the middle of a dirt road. The same thing would happen to him and his family, Joe warned, if he failed to understand that the BBC intended to obtain Hedayat Eslaminia's assets and would require his son's full cooperation. Joe told him he had someone watching Debi and could have her kidnapped at any moment, Reza recalled; Jim brandished an Uzi and threatened to blow his head off. They would kill his mother first, then his brothers, Joe said. He accepted the conservatorship of his father's assets and traveled to Europe with Ben, Reza explained, because Joe Hunt "literally had a gun at my family's head."

John Vance, who had expected that "some Svengali interpretation of Joe Hunt" would be the defense, appeared taken aback by the scope of the conspiracy Reza described—Hunt, Karny, Dosti, Graham, Dicker, Eisenberg, Adelman, and Allen all were in on it, he said. The jurors, though, were looking less often at the witness than at each other, checking to see if anyone was swallowing this stuff. They all by then had stopped taking notes, and as Reza described how Ben had ordered him to claim the money in the Geneva account, the jury box became a tableau of fixed expressions and folded arms. One juror, then a second, began to stare at the ceiling.

The same jurors would be in tears by the time Ben Dosti's defense was done. One sensed that the weeping was not for Ben, though, but for his family. While Rose and Marya Dosti were in court daily, the anguish of Luan and Lisa, who commuted from Los Angeles whenever they could, was most evident. Ben's father rolled his eyes and shook his head during Dean

Karny's testimony, but it was the desperate, clutching quality of Luan's expression as he searched the jury box for a sympathetic face that was most affecting. Rose's bearing was restrained, even regal; only the retraction of her eyes into the black circles surrounding them suggested suffering. At the same time Mrs. Dosti watched her son face the prospect of life in prison, she was pointed out in restaurants as the mother of a BBC defendant; whispers circulated even among colleagues. The indignity was not equal to the agony, perhaps, but had become part of it.

Rose remained unflinching, though, even when the cameras turned on her. Filling dozens of steno pads with notes during the testimony of one prosecution witness after another, Ben's mother managed at the same time to keep up her Culinary SOS column for the *Times*. The family needed her salary now more than ever. The Dostis, parents who possessed nothing like the wealth of those among whom their children were educated, had yet contrived an aura of eminence—some synthesis of good taste and discreet snobbery—that lifted them into the upper strata of Los Angeles society. The cost of Ben's defense, however, was mounting at a rate of more than two thousand dollars per day, and a couple who for years had invested their earnings in gracious living found themselves plunged into near-hopeless debt.

In the end, though, Ben's case was Ben. At considerable cost to his parents, the defendant had been elaborately prepared for the witness stand, rehearsing his testimony before an audience of junior associates at Nolan's Palo Alto office. Each recitation was videotaped so that Ben might see for himself what the women, in particular, meant when they described him as "unemotional," "distant," and "aloof."

Nolan might have been better informed by the comments of Ben's Harvard School classmate Allen Myerson, who observed that the only true moment in NBC's "awful" miniseries had been the scene in which the camera lingered upon the "Todd Melbourne" character during the drive to Los Angeles with the Iranian in the trunk. "They depicted Ben as not saying a word, just staring off into space, with these sad eyes," Myerson recalled. "And I'll bet that's exactly how it was. He just shuts up and shuts down when he's in deep shit."

Whatever seethed beneath Ben's placid surface was well hidden when he ascended to the stand wearing a blue Valentino suit and striped silk tie, looking more like thirty-five than twenty-six, no longer compactly muscular but gone soft in the middle, showing jurors the face of a dark moon. Everything he had been warned against at Nolan's office seemed forgotten: Ben slumped in the uncomfortable chair, eyes shifty and shrouded by their lazy lids, his mouth more sullen than sorrowful. If he hadn't looked at himself, though, Ben seemed at least to have listened; his voice was strong and clear as he began to explain that he indeed had been involved in a plan to remove Hedayat Eslaminia from his Belmont condominium on July 30, 1984, but that this was never to his knowledge an "abduction." As he understood it, the BBC was working *for* Mr. Eslaminia that day, Ben said. He had been apprised of the plan during a meeting at the Manning in mid-July when Joe Hunt and Reza explained that Mr. Eslaminia was being watched by agents of the Ayatollah Khomeini. Joe and Reza said Mr. Eslaminia wanted to leave his current situation and enter into a new one without detection, Ben remembered, and also would need help in collecting his assets. For their assistance in this regard, the BBC would be paid a large sum, though how much was never specified.

His first assignment in connection to Project Sam was to find a large secluded house where Mr. Eslaminia might spend the first month after his disappearance from Northern California, Ben said: he looked at homes in Palm Springs but *never* saw the Beverly Glen house.

It was true that he had been sent north to inspect the Hillsborough estate, Ben said, in order to determine if Reza's father possessed the wealth Reza claimed. He used his Chicago driver's license to rent a car at the airport for the same reason he gave a false address when he checked into the Fairmont Hotel, Ben explained: He had been told this was a "semi-clandestine operation."

He returned to San Mateo County in the company of Joe, Jim, and Reza on July 29, Ben recalled, to assist in Mr. Eslaminia's "escape." The four of them traveled north in a West Cars BMW and a yellow pickup truck borrowed from Ryan Hunt: he knew the steamer trunk they brought with them was intended for Hedayat Eslaminia, Ben said, but thought Mr. Eslaminia would be in the trunk only for as long as it took to get him from his apartment to the pickup.

His assigned role in the next day's operation was to act as a lookout, Ben explained. He rented the U-Haul that morning and was waiting with the others at the Villa Hotel when Dean Karny arrived. After they wrapped the trunk in brown paper, Ben said, everyone lay down; he fell fast asleep and was awakened an hour later by Joe. Everyone else was gone then, and the trunk also was gone, he remembered. Joe told him to go back to sleep, that he wasn't needed, Ben recalled, and this he had done. Half an hour later, he remembered, Joe came back to the room alone and said, "Let's go to L.A." They drove directly back to the Wilshire Manning, stopping only for gas, Ben said, and he never saw the U-Haul again.

The plan was that they would all meet with Mr. Eslaminia the next day, Ben explained, but he had been awakened early by a call on the intercom from "a very sullen Joe Hunt," who appeared at his front door a few minutes later. Joe told him then that Mr. Eslaminia had died of a heart attack in transit between San Francisco and Los Angeles, Ben recalled, and that he and Dean had discarded the body between the two cities. Joe said it had all happened because Dean panicked, but he refused to elaborate. He felt terrible, Ben said, and thought about calling the police, but Joe told him there really was nothing they could do at this point. Ben became contrite as he admitted knowing Reza's conservatorship was falsely obtained. He had been persuaded by Joe and Reza that Mr. Eslaminia's assets should be protected from Olga Vasquez, Ben explained.

The most affecting moment in Ben's testimony was his recollection of the arbitrage project upon which he had "embarked" during his stay in Zurich: If the loan had gone through, Ben explained, he intended to pay off the BBC's investors. As he described the five-hundred-million-dollar deal he negotiated in Switzerland, a wistful note broke the monotony of Ben's recitation. Even John Vance admitted feeling something like pity for Dosti in that instant: "It was as if he still believed everything could have been salvaged, even then, if only he had been able to raise enough money."

From the time his parents' phone call pulled him off that People Express plane back in December of 1984 until his arrest in the summer of 1985, he had refused to believe that Reza or Joe or Jim were involved in a deliberate plot to kidnap and kill Mr. Eslaminia, Ben said. All he wanted to do was return to Los Angeles and refute Dean's story by telling the authorities what really happened. He was advised, however, to stay away and to find a false identity, Ben explained to the jurors, who looked not at the witness but at his mother.

It was exhausting to listen to her son for more than a few minutes at a time, and he went on hour after hour. Ben's greatest gift was for being a blank screen, and he seemed to believe that in this case his best hope was to make the story so boring that jurors would lose interest. Instead of emotion he offered an arch of his left eye or a wink of his right. Every detail was omitted that could be, and nine answers out of ten began with one of those phrases Oliver North had used as body armor during his appearance before the Senate Select Committees a few months earlier: "My impression was"; "Most probably I think"; "I believe possibly"; "It was my understanding"; "I have no specific recollection."

On cue—as was apparent to everyone in the courtroom not related to him—Ben produced tears even less convincing than Brooke Roberts's when Vance asked the inevitable question, "Why didn't you call the police when you knew there was a body lying out there?" Ben had dried up, though, by the time he sneaked a glance at the jury and saw that not one of them was crying with him. Tom Nolan admitted being disappointed by Ben's "performance" in court: "I wish he had projected himself better."

Ben was followed to the stand by his father. Luan had returned to court wearing an amused expression that was too obviously forced, looking like a sober W. C. Fields. He had decided not to call Rose Dosti as a witness, Nolan explained, because "with her, the problem would be too much rather than too little emotion." Luan was scarcely a stoic. He managed a cheerful smile as he informed the jurors, "Ben is my son," but his voice began to break in the next breath when he admitted to Nolan that "this situation has been a nightmare for three years."

Unlike the parents of other Boys, he noticed no alienation of Ben from his family during the BBC period, Luan said: "We still saw him every weekend for dinner and sometimes during the week also. We are a very tight unit." Luan admitted being impressed by Joe Hunt when he met him in 1980 but added that he developed "a very low opinion of Hunt" after the Chicago debacle, and he remained skeptical when told of the millions Joe had earned by trading a commodities account for Ron Levin. "I asked [Ben] how much his share was and he said four hundred thousand dollars," Luan recalled. "I said, 'Grab it and run away. Take half, take a quarter.' [Ben] said he couldn't," Luan remembered, his voice breaking again. "I said, 'Get out of there. Get out of the BBC.'"

Mr. Dosti's testimony had been the most difficult part of the entire BBC prosecution for him, Oscar Breiling admitted. "I didn't doubt his suffering for a moment. And he's right to believe that Ben had just as good a chance to come in and cut a deal as Dean did. Both families are close, but Ben couldn't admit to his what he had done, while Dean could, and that's the difference."

He would take the word of his son over Dean Karny's until the day he died, Luan told the jury before stepping down. The defense rested a moment later.

Final Arguments were scheduled for the first week of 1988. As during the penalty-phase trial of Joe Hunt in Santa Monica, the presentation of the state's case against Ben and Reza seemed subsumed by a sense of portent. The first event had surfaced out of the earth itself three months earlier when the biggest earthquake in more than fifteen years struck Los Angeles on the morning of October 1. It was 6.1 on the Richter scale, enough to shatter windows, snap power lines, and burst gas mains from Altadena to Anaheim. More than one hundred people had been injured, and six were killed.

The city shivered for a moment when the *Times* reminded L.A. that the Big One, when it came, would make the previous day's temblor seem a mild jostle. By week's end, though, most people had recovered that "Tell me something I don't know" insouciance that for Southern Californians is the essence of good form. The best story of Olympian detachment in the press was how the earthquake had been handled by Michael Milken. As the Rodeo Drive building where he kept his offices "started quivering, and colleagues began diving under desks," *Fortune* reported, "Milken quickly checked around to make sure all was well—then matter-of-factly returned to his calls. Business as usual in blasé La La land."

Business as usual would be interrupted not only in La La land but in every other American city less than three weeks later, however. Like the dervish-in-disguise of a Sufi story, a bedraggled public defender had stormed into Division 13 on the morning of October 20 to demand of the assembled media why none of them were interested in the murder trial he was handling two floors down, in a courtroom where one homeless man was charged with killing another for his shoes. Tom Nolan had just asked Dean Karny if he put tape over the airholes in the steamer trunk because "you couldn't stand the screams" when a reporter from the *Chronicle* slipped into a front-row seat and whispered to those sitting next to him, "It's 1929 all over again." The crash of the stock market that began that morning and continued until the bell at five, eastern time, would be known as "Black Monday" by the end of the week. And in negative numbers, if not in long-term impact, the debacle far surpassed what had taken place on "Black Tuesday" during the same month fifty-nine years earlier. The official tally at the close of trading on Monday was a drop of 508 points in the Dow-Jones average, more than twice the total of any previous one-day decrease in the market's history, and a plunge in stock values of 22.6 percent (the drop had been 12.8 percent in October of 1929). The day's aggregate loss was estimated at more than five hundred billion dollars, greater than the gross national product of France.

As trading topped six hundred million shares at midafternoon on Monday, nearly double the previous record, New York Stock Exchange Chairman John Phelan described the selling binge as "the nearest thing to financial meltdown I ever want to see." Outside the exchange building on Wall Street, a distraught investor stood on top of a parked car shouting, "Down with Reagan! Down with MBA's! Down with yuppies!"

The compact explanation was that the economy had run out of room: Since the Reagan tax cuts of 1981 the United States had been generating deficits of a size that dwarfed anything before them. The parallels to 1929, however, were most obvious in the concentration of domestic wealth: The richest 1 percent of U.S. citizens now controlled 36 percent of the nation's privately held assets, the highest figure since the Black Tuesday crash. Yet the market had continued to climb for the first nine months of 1987. "You look around sometimes, and it seems like they're doing it all with mirrors," Joe Hunt's former trading partner on the Mercantile Exchange, Richard Duran, observed that summer, "but then you figure, 'As long as they have enough mirrors, why worry?'"

Ronald Reagan insisted the supply was endless. "The underlying economy remains sound," the president assured the nation on the evening of the crash, and the stock market did indeed begin to rally. Wall Street sought help from Madison Avenue to reassure a shaken nation; Merrill Lynch's ad copy read as though it had been written by a flack recruited from a studio lot: "IT'S NOT A SOLUTION, IT'S A PROCESS. IT'S NOT A DESTINATION, IT'S A JOURNEY."

The journey had ended, though, for Reza Eslaminia and Arben Dosti; only their destination remained in doubt. Reza would go down one way or another, that was understood. Even the younger Eslaminia's attorney offered a final argument that struck most who heard it as perfunctory, and Merritt's distaste for those who had been among the accomplices was more persuasive than any assertion he made of his own client's "gullibility." If Reza's future seemed certain, however, "most spectators thought it unlikely," as one reporter put it, that all twelve jurors would agree to convict his codefendant.

Ben owed most of what chance he had for a hung jury to Tom Nolan, whose final argument had moved several members of the panel to tears. What worked best for Nolan was his decision to place a chair on the courtroom floor only a few feet from the jury box so that he might sit at eye-level with those who would judge his client. For Ben Dosti, the BBC was a business opportunity, nothing more, Nolan insisted. Every one of the Boys called to testify in court had agreed that it was Dean rather than Ben who served as Joe Hunt's intellectual consort. None of the Boys recalled Ben even once proselytizing Paradox Philosophy. Prior to his arrest on this charge, Ben had no criminal record at all other than traffic violations. In the end, when all the details of Ben's story were checked against both independent evidence and unbiased testimony, the state's case against Ben came down to Dean Karny, a young man who confessed to participation in at least two murders but was permitted to walk away free and clear. Yet while Karny's parents hired lawyers to help their son avoid "limitations" on his life, Nolan observed, Ben Dosti's mother and father hoped their boy would not spend the rest of his days in a prison cell. This was the question before them, Nolan told the jurors: "Are you willing to walk arm-in-arm with Dean Karny?"

An "admiring" John Vance offered a persuasive reply to Nolan's argument on rebuttal: It was true that Dean admitted his complicity in the murder of Hedayat Eslaminia; Dean indeed had described his own conduct not only as criminal but as cowardly and despicable. No one made Karny look worse than Karny, and that was the point: Dean had nothing to hide and no reason to lie.

The duration of the jury's deliberations alone gave the defense cause for hope. Jurors took their time because they had doubts, and doubts inevitably looked more and more reasonable as time passed. The handwritten questions the panel sent to Judge Miller on January 14, a full week after they had taken the case, were full of good signs for both sides. Nolan was encouraged by the juror whose questions suggested she believed that the reason for the trip to San Mateo County had been withheld from at least one defendant. A shaken Vance found consolation in the questions of the jurors who asked whether confinement in a trunk or suffocation could be considered "infliction of force." (Absolutely, the judge answered.) One juror asked for a reading of Ben Dosti's testimony describing the events of July 30, 1984. This resulted in the trial's best moment of theater, as Nolan and Vance took turns reading aloud to the jury from the transcript of Ben's testimony; what gave it flavor was that while Nolan was assigned by the judge to read Vance's questions, Vance's duty was to read back Ben's answers, right up to "I've never seen a dead body in my life."

The jurors then resumed their deliberations: Vance predicted a verdict by four o'clock that afternoon. When the jurors sent the clerk out with a note at a little past three, however, it was to announce that further deliberations would be "pointless" for the rest of that day. A hung jury seemed likely now.

While she awaited the jury's verdict, Rose Dosti kept busy by preparing a column for the *Times* reporting the suggestions of chefs who ranged from Patrick Terrail of the Hollywood Diner to Mary Sue Milliken of City Restaurant as to how one might suitably feed guests on Super Bowl Sunday.

On Friday, January 21, forty-eight hours before the big game, jurors who had been deliberating for almost two weeks sent out a question that lifted Nolan's mood to hopeful anticipation even as it plunged the prosecutor to near despair: Could a defendant be convicted of murder if it was found that Hedayat Eslaminia had committed suicide? Vance and Breiling were beside themselves: The only suggestion of suicide had been Dean's testimony about hearing the Iranian repeat *"Vi, vi, vi"* while locked in the trunk, which Reza described as an ancient Persian technique for "willing" one's death. The prosecution team regarded the story as so absurd that they did not bother to address it during the trial, and now, apparently, some jurors were prepared to accept it as an alternative to conviction.

The entrance to the San Mateo County Courthouse was blocked by two hundred sign-waving demonstrators from San Francisco who marched in a circle chanting, "Act up! Fight back! Fight AIDS!" on Monday morning, when Judge Miller told the jury that if they decided Mr. Eslaminia had killed himself, Ben and Reza could not be convicted of causing his death. Vance's stomach turned over when the court clerk called less than two hours later to announce that the jury had reached a verdict.

The judge silently studied the jury's decision, then handed it to his clerk, who read aloud: "Guilty," "guilty," "guilty." The vibration in Vance's sigh made it closer to a sob. Ben had been convicted on all counts, while Reza was found guilty of everything but conspiracy to commit murder, including the special-circumstances kidnapping charge that carried a sentence of life in prison.

Debi Lutkenhouse wept, but shock was the Dostis' anesthesia as they kissed Ben good-bye, then watched him led away in handcuffs to a jail cell on the building's fifth floor.

29

SENTENCING FOR BEN AND REZA WAS DELAYED UNTIL MAY OF 1988. EVEN AS the judge, the lawyers, and the jurors debated what to do with young Dosti, however, Joe Hunt continued to commmand center stage. ABC's *20/20* segment on Joe and the Boys had aired shortly after the trial in Santa Monica, but CBS's *60 Minutes* was about to offer an exclusive. He had been interviewed the day before by Ed Bradley, Joe wrote to Rudy Durand during the last week of testimony in Redwood City, and believed it had gone well. All three department of corrections officers detailed to the proceedings had seen the NBC miniseries, Joe noted, and "each took special pains afterward to tell me they hoped I was released, that they thought I had been wronged and each said they would pray for me."

The *60 Minutes* interview was conducted at Folsom State Penitentiary, where its subject had been in residence since the previous August. Joe's new home generally was regarded among state prison inmates as the toughest place to do time in California. Built in the nineteenth century, Folsom's sunken entrance, heavy limestone walls, dungeonlike cells, and spindly legged sniper towers gave it the look of a place where early settlers sent horse thieves and claim jumpers to live on bread, water, and fifty lashes a week. San Quentin might house death row, but at least prisoners there enjoyed the balmy weather of San Francisco Bay. Folsom was an oven in summer, an icebox in winter, set out east of Sacramento on a high, windswept plain surmounted by bluffs to the south and east. Its inmates nearly all were murderers or multiple felons. Gang battles between the Mexican Mafia, Aryan Brotherhood biker gangs, and the Crips/Bloods contingents were the social climate of the prison, where 186 stabbings would be reported during 1987.

"A war zone," Joe described Folson to Durand: Four out of the first five times he went into the main yard, inmates had been fired upon from the sniper towers to break up attempted murders.

Ed Bradley and the *60 Minutes* crew had arrived at Folsom on December 12, but the segment would not be aired until early January, during the Redwood City jury's deliberations. It was obvious from the moment the camera closed on him that Joe had read the reviews of his performance in Santa Monica. His transformation was astonishing: Not only was he pale and haggard, hair combed over to the side again in what Santa Monica jurors called "the computer nerd look," but Joe seemed to have subsided entirely into the feminine side of his nature, speaking in a voice so soft and humid that Oscar Breiling was moved to remark, "It sounds like he decided he'd do better in prison as Josephine than as Joseph."

He knew jurors felt he appeared "detached" during the trial in Santa Monica, Joe said, but that had been nothing more than a psychological defense against the venomous prejudice of Judge Rittenband, whose conduct he considered the main cause of his conviction. Rittenband's handling of the evidence, Joe explained, created "a very ugly mood in the courtroom. [The jury] was absolutely convinced that I had led all these kids astray. It was convinced I had, with malice aforethought, plotted to kill Ron Levin and did so in a cold dispassionate fashion. And that I'm—something you mentioned earlier—I've been known as a person that had some virtues. And it was the juxtaposition of these virtues, versus what I had supposedly done, [that] created this thing [that] I was almost a monster, some sort of special dimension of being able to maintain the dichotomy of being so easygoing, so relaxed, so obviously—or apparently—a caring sort of person, and nonetheless to do that. There was the sense that I had betrayed all these kids. And they kind of began to, I think, feel that I was setting them up for a similar betrayal. That I was going to get on the stand and, through some devices in the rhetoric, change their mind."

When Bradley asked about Paradox Philosophy, Joe began by sucking in the draft of air this subject would require. The key phrase of Paradox—"Black is white, white is black, and all the shadings are in between" —had been presented to the jury in Santa Monica as "banner language for situational ethics," Joe observed, which was grossly misleading. This adage was one that could be found again and again in books on philosophy. In fact, the first time he had encountered it, Joe told Bradley, was in a pamphlet on racial discrimination arguing there should be no color concept between human beings. "But when I read it, it struck me that it was true in a lot of other ways," he explained. "And what it means to me personally is that no matter what terrible thing befalls the human race or a human being, there's always a possiblity of transforming it into something better. Indeed, it's our responsibility to do so. And never to lose hope."

That was his belief still, Joe added, and his reason for granting this interview: "I'm not sure whether I'm ever going to leave this place. Because life without possibility of parole means that. And it's very difficult to get cases overturned, even when you have everything on your side—new evidence like we have—even when the fellow that was accused with you gets time served on the same charges . . . I don't know if I'll ever unravel this, but—like I said—I wanted to talk earlier. And I don't want this to end without me ever having made my say."

He had been "misinterpreted," Joe said when offered the chance to say a few final words. "I recognize I made a series of blunders that perhaps will keep me here for the rest of my life. But I didn't kill anybody. So I don't want to put my head down. There's no shame. When I go up in San Francisco and face the death penalty again, I hope I'll do it with my head up, because I did my absolute best. Which, in retrospect, isn't a lot to be proud of. But the state of my heart is something I remain proud of."

Joe was in transit again by the time *60 Minutes* aired his interview, headed through San Quentin back to the San Mateo County Jail, where he would be held until his trial for the murder of Hedayat Eslaminia. Jim Pittman was waiting in the jail's maximum-security wing when Joe arrived. Reza and Ben were there as well, held in the special-housing section, awaiting their sentencing. "A BBC reunion," Oscar Breiling called it.

Joe granted a second television interview shortly after his arrival in Redwood City, this one with a reporter from the NBC affiliate in Los Angeles. The purpose was to demand that details of the LAPD's investigation into the Richard Mayer murder be made public. (While at San Quentin, Hunt had filed a Freedom of Information Act lawsuit in Los Angeles naming Chief of Police Daryl Gates as defendant.) "The only reason why it would be necessary to keep [the Hollywood homicide] under wraps," Joe advised KNBC's Patrick Healy, "is to protect their star witness."

The struggle for the hearts and minds of the jurors who had rendered judgment in the Dosti/Eslaminia trial continued for months after the reading of their verdict in court. Tom Nolan initiated the conflict, instructing his lead investigator to begin "polling" the jurors during the first week of February 1988. Not only did a majority of the jurors agree to discuss the case, but five sent letters to Judge Miller. "Your Honor, I feel that this young man is a credit to society," wrote the young woman known as juror number ten. "He was young and foolish in the things he was involved in. Yet, he is responsible for his actions. Therefore, I voted guilty. However, life without parole seems to me too harsh for a young man with such great potential as a citizen . . . please grant him leniency." Each of the other jurors who wrote the judge asked for a reduced sentence; one suggested "five years should teach him that you can't get involved in a shady scheme and not pay for it.' "

Her brother's "greatest sin was his trust in other human beings," Marya Dosti advised the judge. Wrote Lisa's sister-in-law Georgia Jeffs, "Ben was whole, unwounded when he joined Joe Hunt in business. The cocoon so carefully spun for him by his doting parents left him totally unprepared to face a world of people who use each other."

Even the San Mateo County probation officer assigned to prepare the sentencing report for Judge Miller credited the Dostis' "devotion" to their son. Indeed, "a study of the defendant's background . . . makes his participation in this heinous offense seem incomprehensible," Ben's probation officer observed. An interview with Luan Dosti was included in the report: "Ben is not at all a criminal," his father said. "Joseph Hunt is just a super con [and] Ben never sees evil. He was known as 'Honest Ben' throughout school. His sole objective in this situation was to sell equipment." Ben himself declined to be interviewed, the officer noted, but submitted a written statement in which he portrayed himself as a victim of "blind trust."

"One last washing of the hands," John Vance called Dosti's continued claim of innocence. Evan Dicker, though, insisted Ben was making the sanest choice available to him: "If he spends the rest of his life in jail, he'll never really be a human being again, at least not on the terms of what Ben thinks a human being is," Evan explained. "So he has to hold on to the idea that he can have a successful appeal and a new trial and get out. He *has* to insist he's innocent. And even if he never gets out, it may be easier for Ben not to admit what he did because what he did was a terrible thing."

Reza stood first to face sentencing on May 10, 1988, wearing that same contradictory expression, incredulous eyes and a smirking mouth, he had displayed again and again during his trial. All Gary Merritt could do was remind Judge Miller that Reza was not from the same background or in the same "posture" as other BBC defendants, then ask the court to hear Mina Hakimi. "I represent the victim's family," Mina, dressed all in white, told the judge, then insisted that her son was "innocent in this political affair."

Sucking on his dentures and watching the clock, scheduled for retirement at the end of that day, Judge Miller faced his last official duties with a huge sigh, then said, "Mr. Eslaminia, your application for probation is denied and you are sentenced to the Department of Corrections for a life sentence without the possibility of parole."

Ben Dosti was ordered to stand a moment later and appeared not to harbor the slightest doubt about what was coming. His mother and sisters still hoped, though, and grasped one another's hands in tortured anticipation. Tom Nolan knew how long a shot this was and, after a few preliminary remarks, asked the court to hear the defendant's mother.

Rose Dosti's aggrieved air suggested umbrage as much as agony. "I have never in my wildest dreams, maybe my most demented dreams, thought that I would be in a court of law pleading for my son's life," she began. "I am a mother blessed with a son who has made my life a joy from the moment he was born," Rose went on, speaking at once to Miller and to the reporters who took the best spectator seats. "How easy he made it for all of us. We were not plagued for one moment with the problems of drugs, alcohol, troubles with the law that affect families of youth today. On the contrary, we were blessed with a boy who was reasonable, who excelled in school, who cared and was generous and thoughtful to his family and friends." His mother looked directly at Ben, then added, "He is a son any parent would be proud to call her own."

Every day of the past three and a half years had been "a living hell without one moment of relief in sleep or waking," Mrs. Dosti said; of course she understood what was at issue this day, yet still found the situation inconceivable: "Punishment? How can a mother of Ben Dosti think of punishment when we sincerely believe that he has been punished enough?" Her son was in no sense a threat to those around him, Rose ended, speaking directly to the judge now, "and society cannot be served by destroying a person of Ben's talents and vitality, sentencing him to know life without parole, without hope. Outside, Ben can become the valued member of society which he dearly wishes and promises to be."

Rose had stirred Tom Nolan, if not Judge Miller. The attorney seemed sincerely at a loss for words in the first few moments after she finished. "I have been practicing [law] seventeen years, and I am not sure that any of us knows what's right," he began. "I don't think any of us here have seen a case like this. I think that it scares us to think that our children could end up where Ben Dosti is today. Any of our children." Nolan lapsed into silence for a moment before continuing: "There are people in the world like Joe Hunt who—and thank God there are very few of them, and I think all of us will agree that he is exceptional—that I would not want my children to get to know at a point in their life when they are vulnerable. Ben was nineteen years old walking down the street when Joe Hunt came up to him. It is that beginning of a set of circumstances that leads Ben to this place here. Is that the end of his life?"

Though he knew it would stab Rose in the heart, Nolan finished by voicing what nearly everyone who knew both his client and the state's prison system believed: Put Ben Dosti in a place like Folsom or San Quentin, and "you have sentenced him to death."

During Nolan's remarks about the possibility of hope for Ben Dosti "ten, twenty, thirty years from now," Oscar Breiling had whispered to John Vance, "Yeah, but in ten or twenty or thirty years, Hedayat Eslaminia will still be dead." Like Breiling, Vance took the long view, but his focus was on the defendant rather than the victim: "In July of 1984, Arben Dosti made a choice, and that choice made him turn his back on his mother, his father, his sisters, his friends . . . it doesn't take all the advantages that Arben Dosti had to understand that. It doesn't take a college education to understand that. What it takes is something that brings people before this court every day."

Miller's sigh wheezed out with his words: "Mr. Dosti, your application for parole is also denied, and on Count III you are sentenced to the Department of Corrections for a life sentence without the possibility of parole."

The AP photographer in court caught Ben and Reza in the moment each turned to face his mother. Reza's curious smirk was absent entirely in that instant, but he did have an expression, and it was chagrin. Ben's countenance was as profound as resignation could be.

The hearing on Joe's Freedom of Information Act claim (based on "public interest" in the murder of Richard Mayer) was held in Los Angeles three weeks after Ben and Reza were sentenced in Redwood City. Unable to appear in person before Judge Robert O'Brien, the plaintiff instead dialed O'Brien's clerk that morning from a pay phone at the San Mateo County Jail to ask if he might make his argument by collect call. "Yet another first," John Vance noted. O'Brien refused Hunt's request, then denied Joe's FOI motion on the basis of "government interest."

Nine days later, Joe answered with a writ requesting an in camera hearing in the San Mateo County Court of Judge Dale Hahn, who would preside at Hunt's Redwood City trial. The same Detective Diaz who swore to the court in Los Angeles that public disclosure of any information regarding the Hollywood homicide would compromise his investigation, Joe noted, had released to KNBC several key documents from the Mayer Murder Book, including the composite of the suspect. "A blatant act of differential treatment," Hunt argued.

Judge Hahn reluctantly agreed and scheduled a hearing in his chambers for late July. Present were Joe; his Redwood City attorney, Parker Kelly; John Vance; and Oscar Breiling, as well as Detectives Diaz and Rozzi. The principal witness was a Salvadoran refugee who spoke no English. Speaking through an interpreter, the maid who had discovered the trunk containing Richard Mayer's body recalled that room 304 at the Hollywood Center Motel had been empty the first time she went in, the only sign of occupancy a dent in the bed, as if someone had sat there. Parker Kelly asked the woman if she ever had seen anyone go into or out of that room. Vance and Breiling were startled when the maid answered, "Yes, there was a man on a motorcycle." The man was wearing a helmet, however, and she couldn't see his face, the maid explained. When Kelly asked if the man's build had resembled Breiling's, the woman shook her head, then pointed at Joe. "It was more like his," she said. Joe just smiled and shook his head, recalled Oscar Breiling: "I keep expecting to see him flinch, but he never does."

While the subject of the senora's scrutiny was setting up a paralegal practice in the maximum-security section of the San Mateo County Jail, Ben and Reza were assigned to share a cell on the same block at Folsom Prison where, a few months earlier, Joe Hunt had reposed. "I don't know who else either of them would be safe with," Breiling observed.

Even as he planned for his 1989 retirement, the state's investigator continued to defend a reputation tarnished by the state's deal with Dean Karny. "I made a prediction," said Gary Merritt. "I said that one day Oscar Breiling will go to the doctor and they'll run some tests and they'll tell him he has six months to live. He'll go home, look at himself in the mirror, then go out and waste Karny."

Dean still was joined to Joe as the only remaining defendants in the case brought by the SEC. Evan Dicker, trimmed from the list of those charged, had been called to testify against Dean that spring: After giving his name, Evan answered each question by pleading the Fifth Amendment. Evan's last pending matter was his application to the state bar. He had been told only that an investigation was in progress. If his application was denied, he would appeal all the way to the U.S. Supreme Court, Evan said, then added a trenchant, if unintended, commentary on his chosen profession: "What else can I do? I have absolutely no other job skills that would pay above minimum wage."

Four years after accepting his grants of immunity from Breiling and Zoeller, Evan was feeling so free from the past that he had become a collector of BBC memorabilia, saving such items as the "Ghost of Wall Street" issue featuring Marvel Comics' ultra-violent hero "Punisher" in his battle with a group of young insider traders called "the Billionaire Boys Club." "I recall Joe telling us, 'We'll all be famous some day,'" he reflected.

Few of the other Boys shared Evan's appetite for self-satire. Jerry Eisenberg, growing wealthier by the week, devoted more time these days to the construction of condominiums than to the practice of law. "For me, it's like the whole BBC thing never happened," he said.

Steve Lopez, though still muttering predictions of Eisenberg's eventual ruin, was a cheerier soul by the late summer of 1988. Arriving for lunch one August afternoon at the Rive Gauche restaurant on Ventura Boulevard, Lopez drove up in a brand-new BMW sedan and announced he had come upon "the last sure thing out there," buying up second mortgages on private homes. "You're guaranteed fifteen percent interest, and you hope they don't pay," Steve explained, "because then you pick up a two-hundred-thousand-dollar house for whatever's left on the bank mortgage." The screenwriter's strike that had dragged on for several months was a tremendous boon to his business, Lopez added: He and his partners had foreclosed on three writers already, "and there are several other houses I expect to get if this thing goes on another month."

"California isn't a place; it's a way of life," Ronald Reagan would explain to Barbara Walters in his first TV interview after giving up the White House to George Bush. The former president was back on the West Coast within a month of leaving office, comfortably ensconced at his new residence, the magnificent hillside manor in Bel Air that appreciative associates and a legion of admirers had purchased as his retirement home from the estate of Ron Levin's former mentor, Dr. William Kroger (after petitioning the city to change the street number from 666 to 668). Evan Dicker still had said it best: "What a small wonderful world it is." Especially in Los Angeles.

If Reagan continued to fascinate the public, the spotlight on Joe Hunt was fading. Hunt's lawsuit against the LAPD went all but unremarked during May of 1988, when the whole city seemed to be following the Earthquake Rumor Hotline, better known as the Nostradamus Hotline. The phone service was a response by the Griffith Observatory staff to a roar of table talk that persuaded thousands of Southern Californians that the ancient seer had forecast the Big One for the last week of the month.

Joe was not entirely forgotten, however. As counterpoint to the Nostradamus Hotline story and a report on the recent rash of Elvis sightings broadcast by rival KABC, the NBC affiliate in Los Angeles had chosen to run its interview with Joe in four parts during sweeps week. The station did its best to envelop the Mayer murder in a fog of mystery, showing side-by-side, look-alike photos of Oscar Breiling and the composite of the suspect that police had created from interviews with the staff at the Hollywood Center Motel. Each of the four segments opened with a shot of Joe in inmate coveralls as he stepped through a set of steel-barred doors that clanged shut behind him. The slight smile that played on the prisoner's lips was perhaps confusing to some but made sense to those who were beginning to comprehend that, while California might have him behind bars, it was Joe Hunt who held the state hostage.

Part Five

THE UNDEAD

Circumstantial evidence is sometimes capable of two radically different interpretations.

—Sherlock Holmes to Dr. Watson in Arthur Conan Doyle's "The Bascombe Valley Mystery," quoted by Joe Hunt during his final argument to the jury in Redwood City

30

JOE'S NEWSWORTHINESS HAD WANED TO THE POINT WHERE HE WAS LITTLE MORE than an entry in the index of the decade by the late summer of 1988, when the *L.A. Times* mentioned his name in print for the last time during the Reagan years. The citation was almost lost among those mordant briefs that ran on page 2 of the paper's Metro section, a one-paragraph item reporting that a listing for BBC Consolidated of North America could be found on page 202 of that year's *Encyclopedia of Associations.* "Just in case would-be investors are unaware that BBC founder Joe Hunt is serving time for murder," the *Times* noted, "an asterisk accompanies the listing. The asterisk means the BBC's out of business."

The newspaper had provided Joe—or rather "Judd Nelson as Joe Hunt"—with more prominent display one month earlier, when an article reporting that NBC planned a repeat showing of its *Billionaire Boys Club* miniseries ran at the top of the Calendar section's front page. Jeff Brodey protested that the NBC program showed Jim Pittman killing Ron Levin after two juries had failed to convict him of that crime but was ignored.

Joe made real news up north in November, though, when he came before Judge Hahn to announce he was firing Parker Kelly and intended to act as his own attorney in Redwood City. No one else in California history had handled his own defense in a special-circumstances murder trial, Joe was reminded: Be careful, Hahn warned, "you may get what you ask for." He understood that self-representation in a murder case was "like trying to hit a major-league home run without ever having picked up a bat," replied Joe, sounding more exhilarated than daunted by the prospect. "I think you're making a terrible mistake," said the judge, who had no choice, however, but to grant the defendant's request.

On January 10, 1989, Joe submitted his first full-scale filing, a "PROJECTED MOTION CALENDAR" listing defense counsel as "Joe Hunt, *In Pro Per,* Maximum Security, San Mateo County Jail, Redwood City, California." It was clear from this document that Hunt still intended to obtain every bit of evidence unearthed by the Los Angeles Police Department in connection with the murder of Richard Mayer.

All the LAPD detectives would reveal—even to Oscar Breiling—was that Hunt remained the focus of their investigation. The case against Joe was entirely circumstantial, but "don't be surprised if we walk into court one day and arrest him," Diaz advised Breiling. It was Oscar who suggested the LAPD detectives obtain a driver's license photo of Bobby Roberts, enlarge it, and use plastic overlays to see if Roberts might have been made up to resemble the composite drawing of "Tim Mill." Diaz and Rozzi went a step further, delivering a copy of the composite to the president of the makeup artist's union in L.A., then asking him to distribute copies to each of the five hundred members. The LAPD detectives also were investigating the possibility that the man behind the gray beard had been Ryan Hunt, they told Breiling, after learning that Joe's father was visiting Jim Pittman at the Hall of Justice Jail. Diaz and Rozzi even ran DNA tests on the envelope in which the "Mean Dean Karny" letter was sent, only to discover that the seal had been moistened not with saliva but with water and a sponge. And whoever mailed the letter, they concluded, wore gloves.

John Vance still seemed confident that Joe never would get the "Mean Dean Karny" or "Honest Cop's Friend" letters before a jury: "What could be more unreliable," the prosecutor sniffed, "than an anonymous letter?" Vance was affirmed when Hunt's demands for discovery were denied by separate judges in Los Angeles. Inexorable, however, had always been Joe's best gear, and he kept at "the Mayer matter" with moving papers that shredded arguments submitted by the combined forces of the Los Angeles city attorney and the California Department of Justice. Detectives Diaz and Rozzi swore to the courts that Dean Karny had an airtight alibi in the Hollywood homicide, Joe observed, yet the L.A. County medical examiner's autopsy report described Mayer's remains as "moderately severely decomposed" and stated that "the place, date and hour of death were unknown." Diaz, infuriated, charged that an investigator working for Joe had fraudulently obtained reports from LAPD's Records and Identification Unit.

Judge Hahn agreed to review the LAPD's Murder Book on Richard Mayer in chambers before ruling. It was May 8, 1989, when Hahn called the parties back to his courtroom. While "it continues to appear to the court that Mr. Karny was framed in this instance," the judge explained, "the question remains whether a jury would come to that conclusion if presented with the information. And I think the only answer is 'Perhaps.'" The Mayer murder book was in Joe's hands one week later.

The magnitude of Dean Karny's implication went far beyond what had been reported in the press. Besides the Mobil credit card slip with Dean's signature on it, police had recovered from the motel room a list of words—apparently from a game of Boggle—written in Dean's hand. There were several scraps of paper covered with jottings—mostly phone numbers and names—that had been made, forensics experts agreed, by Shalom and Danielle Karny. A scrawled note on a fragment of envelope with a Boston postmark read, "Rodney says meat [*sic*] Dean at the Hollywood Center Motel." From the reports filed by Diaz and Rozzi, Joe learned that tins of "La Vosigenne" pastilles had been removed not only from room 304 at the Hollywood Center Motel but also from the residence of Dean Karny when it was searched during the fall of 1986 by LAPD detectives. Perhaps most intriguing was the description of a silver-gray hair recovered from the folds of the plastic bag that had been used to wrap Richard Mayer's body: The follicles were not human but feline. The Karnys' family pet, Joe noted, was a sixteen-year-old Siamese cat.

Joe would not be satisfied to stop there, of course. It was imperative, Hunt argued at his next appearance before Judge Hahn, that he be allowed to examine personally all evidence seized from Room 304 during October of 1986. Another round of court battles ensued. Joe won them all.

It was the afternoon of August 10, 1989, when Detective Rozzi and Los Angeles deputy city attorney Donna Jones carried a steamer trunk containing the physical evidence held by police in the Richard Mayer murder to a small room on the second floor of the Redwood City Hall of Justice, where Joe Hunt was waiting. Also present as observors were John Vance, Parker Kelly, California Department of Justice Agent Verne Piccinotti, a defense criminologist, and two San Mateo County sheriff's deputies. Vance, Piccinotti, Rozzi, Jones, and the two deputies spread themselves about the room so that Hunt could be observed from every angle.

Wearing rubber gloves and using a pair of tweezers, Joe began to sort through the scraps of paper first—the receipts, the Boggle list, the scribbled notes, the envelope with the Boston postmark. He inspected the trunk itself and the green plastic garbage bags in which Richard Mayer's body had been wrapped. Then Joe picked up a piece of evidence that had been subjected to less scrutiny than perhaps any other: a Nike running shoe the detectives had removed from the motel room closet. Turning the shoe this way and that, Joe loosened the laces then stuck his gloved fingers inside and began to probe. When he withdrew his hand, Hunt held a wad of paper. It was a tightly folded ten-page letter, handwritten—forensics experts would agree—by Richard Keith Mayer.

"Dear Dean," the letter began.

I feel cold inside. You and Rodney scared the shit out of me. You don't have to threaten my life. Threaten shit! I thought you were going to kill me then. I didn't mean anything I said. O.K. I will never leave you, and I don't want anymore [*sic*] money from you . . . I never ask [*sic*] you to tell me all that shit anyhow . . . I don't care what shit you've pulled! You mean everything to me.

Rambling and often incoherent, its tone alternating between outrage and adoration—"Dean Karney [*sic*] you are a ratt [*sic*], but I still love you"—the "tennis shoe letter," as it would become known, referred to much of the physical evidence recovered from room 304: the envelope with the Boston postmark ("Couldn't you have taken me to Boston with you? I appreciated the letter that you sent me from there"), the Boggle list ("Remember the crossword puzzle we worked on together? I helped a little. See I am not so dumb") and the cat hairs ("I want to see the familys [*sic*] new kitty").

Eventually the letter got around to describing in greater detail what exactly "the shit you've pulled" might be:

It's amazing the mess you got into. Actually it's not so much the mess that's unreal, it's the way you put it off on those four guys. I know you had to like you say. If you didn't make up that story to set up those guys, the cops never would have given you a deal. I'm glad you did because those guys might have told what they knew and then who knows what would have happened.

It ended with yet another declaration of devotion: "I love you Dean!!!! Know [*sic*] matter what."

All the faces but one were grim as they filed out of the windowless room half an hour later. Diaz and Rozzi went to work at once to defuse the bombshell: Each item of physical evidence that implicated Dean Karny, they noted—the credit card receipt, the Boggle list, the notes written by Danny and Shalom, the envelope with the Boston postmark, even the cat hairs— could have been collected by someone foraging through garbage cans on Outpost Drive. And Richard Mayer's "Dear Dean" letter, the detectives observed, was replete with misspellings and errors of punctuation but generally was correct grammatically—as if it had been dictated. Mayer's friends from his days as a roadie with Whitesnake and Leatherwolf had described a young man so marginal that he stole spare change from their pockets to buy microwave tacos at the 7-Eleven, ran errands for the dregs of a soda or a half-eaten slice of pizza, and would have done virtually anything for a hundred dollars.

What could not be disputed, however, was the rude truth of the headline on the *Los Angeles* magazine article reporting Hunt's "discovery" of the tennis shoe letter: "JOE'S BACK!"

***

"Much like the case in Charles Dickens' *Bleak House,* this case has developed a life and a logic of its own" began the "Points and Authorities in Opposition to Defendant's Motion to Continue the August 28, 1989 Jury Selection Date" that John Vance submitted to Judge Hahn on the morning after Joe's recovery of the tennis shoe letter. "Unlike *Bleak House,* however, where the participants had long ago forgot why the case had been brought, we must never forget the reason why we are here: to determine whether or not the defendant is guilty of murder. So far, we have spent 53 trial days deciding everything but that. Seven jury selection dates have come and like leaves in the wind are gone."

Given the "revelation" of the tennis shoe letter, Joe countered, he obviously needed more time to investigate "links" between Dean Karny and Richard Mayer. It was September 7, 1989, when Joe sent his first subpoena for Dean through the U.S. marshal's office. On November 1, Hunt was informed that the subpoena had been served and Dean intended to ignore it. The defense must have the opportunity to question Karny prior to trial, Joe argued before Judge Hahn a few days later. Dean was more than merely the chief witness against him, Joe explained: "I'll make it very clear: Dean Karny killed Hedayat Eslaminia."

The largest newspaper in San Mateo County, the *Peninsula Times Tribune* of Palo Alto, remained oblivious to these developments but did inform its readers that Joe was making news as a self-defender. In the first nine months after becoming his own attorney, the paper reported, Hunt had filed more than one hundred motions that consumed an estimated sixty days of court time.

Aware that his jury would be selected out of a pool of citizens from the *Times Tribune*'s circulation area, Joe granted the newspaper the first interview he had given in nearly two years. Speaking by telephone from his cell in the maximum-security wing of county jail, the defendant strove to present his court appearances in a sympathetic light. "I like being in court," he explained. "I'm in a suit and . . . I can forget about spending most of my time in a cage . . . it's almost like I walked in off the street." The decision to act as his own counsel, however, Joe added, was motivated solely by a desire to assume personal responsibility: "If I lose this case," he observed, "I have only one person to point my finger at."

Joe's trial had been rescheduled once more, this time for January 23, 1990, but that no longer seemed a firm date. Shortly before his interview with the *Times Tribune,* Joe had filed a motion demanding "Dean Karny's current whereabouts and new identity." Judge Hahn worried the prosecution by taking the matter under advisement, then left Vance profoundly shaken with his ruling that Hunt was entitled to a full accounting of all contacts between Karny and the attorney general's office from the time of his immunity grant in 1984 until he was admitted into the Federal Witness Protection Program in 1987.

The sheaf of papers—mostly memoranda written by Oscar Breiling —delivered to his cell from Sacramento a few weeks later detailed for Joe his betrayer's submersion into a new identity.

It was early in 1985, Breiling's notes revealed, when Dean called to say he had passed the bar exam and reminded Oscar of the state's promise to assist in obtaining his full accreditation as an attorney. During the fall of 1985, Karny phoned almost every day to ask about Joe's bail hearings. On October 28, 1985, Breiling called to tell Dean that Joe had gotten his bail reduced by half in Santa Monica; Karny expressed "alarm," according to Breiling's notes, and requested admission at once into the California Witness Protection Program. On November 6, Oscar phoned to announce that he had arranged through the Arizona AG's office for lodgings near Phoenix. After discussing it with his parents, Dean called back to say he preferred Sacramento. Two days later, Karny was permitted to choose a new "undercover name:" As "Dean Codray" he flew from Burbank to Sacramento to scout for housing. On November 14, 1985, the day Joe was released from the L.A. County Jail, Shalom Karny rented his son an apartment in Sacramento. Shalom also bought Dean a new car that day. Oscar Breiling flew in from San Francisco with a checkbook and driver's license, each bearing the name Dean Codray.

Breiling's memoranda trailed off into the notes of detectives Diaz and Rozzi as Joe followed Dean's paper trail into the fall of 1986, during the days and weeks that surrounded the discovery of Richard Mayer's remains at the Hollywood Center Motel. Dean's "airtight alibi," as Diaz called it, rose off the page of the detective's report and struck Joe with one more blow for the alliance of fate and irony against him. While the deteriorated state of Richard Mayer's remains indeed made it impossible to determine a precise time of death, the coroner who performed the autopsy was able to say with certainty that Mayer had died sometime between the late morning of October 2 and the early afternoon of October 3. It was Joe's bad luck that Dean had flown from Sacramento to San Francisco on the morning of October 2 for a series of interviews with Breiling and Vance that continued into the afternoon of October 3. Breiling's notes were corroborated by the SEC subpoena served on Dean at Oscar's office.

According to Breiling's notes, Karny was moved "from place to place" during late 1986 and early 1987, while awaiting word on his application to the Federal Witness Protection Program. There apparently had been some disagreement within the state attorney general's office about whether to press the reluctant feds. Vance's superior in Sacramento, John Gordnier was not sure he wanted to cash in favors for a witness who carried Dean's "baggage." Breiling had been adamant, however, championing Karny's cause even after learning on February 2, 1987, that Dean was having large sums of money transported through the AG's courier service from his parents' home to the apartment in Sacramento.

The Karnys had steered police toward Steven Cowan, Joe learned: A friend of Shalom's was the landlord at Cowan's apartment building and phoned Dean's father with word that Joe Hunt had been seen about the premises on a number of occasions. Diaz showed Danny Karny the contact lens case Cowan had found in his Datsun when Joe returned it during the summer of 1986; it was exactly like one she had thrown out with her garbage, Dean's mother said.

When Rozzi and Diaz explained that they believed Hunt had been collecting items from the Karnys' trash bins during the time he was driving Steven Cowan's car, the U.S. marshal's office decided Joe might be as dangerous as Breiling said he was. On March 20, 1987, Dean interviewed for the Federal Witness Protection Program in Sacramento. He spent the weekend of March 21 and 22 with Shalom and Danny in San Francisco, then disappeared into his "permanent confidential identity" on March 24.

Joe was back in the news during the spring of 1990. Hunt's defense now had cost the taxpayers of San Mateo County more than half a million dollars, the *Times Tribune* reported, a price that was certain to inflate further after the county's fire inspector toured the Redwood City jail on March 9 and pronounced himself appalled by conditions in Joe's cell. Thirty cartons of legal papers and nearly three dozen law books were crammed into a six-by-eight-foot space, the fire inspector reported. Hunt not only had stacked his documents floor to ceiling along the walls, leaving barely enough room for one person to enter, but had given even his narrow bunk to the files and was sleeping on the floor.

Sheriff Don Horsley ordered Joe to pare his materials to one box of documents and no more than six legal texts. "Can you imagine depriving a lawyer of his files?" Joe, incredulous, asked a *Times Tribune* reporter during a phone conversation the next day. He had made every physical sacrifice to accommodate his files, Joe explained, and still was forced to rotate boxes on a weekly basis, since another thirty-five cartons were stored at Parker Kelly's office.

Sheriff Horsley suggested that perhaps Hunt should be sent to San Quentin to await trial. Joe responded with moving papers that opposed both his transfer to state prison and the removal of his files from county jail. He presently was putting in an average of fifty hours per week on case-related work, Joe advised the court, and would have pushed himself even harder, except that, "whenever I try, I am overtaken by a restless sort of melancholy that I feel has little to do with my prospects at my upcoming trial (I am rather sanguine about those) and everything to do with life in a rather grubby and crowded cage." He understood that the good men working as deputies were overtaxed already, Joe explained, and not wanting to be a nuisance he had forfeited both showers and access to the jail's law library. He was willing even to continue sleeping on the floor but would resist any attempt to remove his files. The failure of the sheriff to offer accommodation, Joe warned, would "occasion significant new delays and a ton of avoidable litigation."

Convinced by now that Mr. Hunt was quite capable of producing two thousand pounds of paperwork on any subject, Judge Hahn suggested that the sheriff arrange some sort of work space within the jail. The next day, Horsley announced he had ordered the conversion of a paint locker into an office for Joe.

This triumph was not nearly so upsetting to the prosecution as Hunt's determination to locate Dean Karny. Frustrated by Judge Hahn, Joe's alternative tactic was to pursue Dean through his parents. He first demanded Shalom's and Danny's bank records for the past seven years, then served them with a subpoena signed by Hahn demanding that the family produce hairs from their Siamese cat. The Karnys sent attorney Brian O'Neill north to join John Vance in a motion to quash the subpoena. As a "note of mockery," O'Neill informed Hahn, "Hunt [had] scotch-taped a hair to the first page of the court order" he sent Dean's parents. "Hunt has repeatedly abused the subpoena process as he has humiliated and harassed Shalom and Danielle Karny," John Vance put in. Though obviously pained, Hahn ruled that the defendant had established a legitimate interest in the records he requested. Joe promptly upped the ante by preparing a new subpoena that demanded hair samples from Dean Karny's head, legs, and pubic area.

Ron Morrow answered this time, seizing the opportunity to make public a fact that had been suppressed by the LAPD for almost five years: "Artfully omitted from Hunt's motion is that he and [Richard] Mayer were in the Los Angeles County Jail at the same time" during 1985. He would not be surprised if Dean's hair *was* found in the plastic bags used to wrap Mayer's body, Morrow added: "It is surmised by this writer that Joe Hunt knows Dean Karny's hair is in the evidence because he put it there."

On the heels of a declaration from Stanford Law School Professor Robert Weisberg in support of his motion to admit the tennis shoe letter as evidence at trial, Joe submitted moving papers that articulated for the first time precisely where he was headed with the Hollywood homicide: "The defense seeks to link Karny to the murder of a bisexual named Richard Mayer. Mr. Mayer was known to be a homosexual prostitute . . . To connect Karny to that murder, the defense wishes to establish Karny's own bisexuality, his tendency to associate with male prostitutes and his use of sexual paraphernalia."

By now Hunt had demonstrated that virtually any accusation he chose to make—if presented as an integral part of his defense—would justify subpoenas that reached into the private lives of his accusers. Joe demanded all records pertaining not only to Dean's state bar application but to Evan Dicker's as well. Dean, Evan, Tom May, Steve Taglianetti, and Jeff Raymond all were compelled to deliver finger and palm prints to Joe's investigators. A lengthy subpoena was served on Carol Levin that required her to surrender all family phone records for the past six years, all financial records and legal documents relating to her son Ronald, every photograph of Ron in her possession, and each card, poem, or letter she had saved. Like the Karnys, the Levins hired a private attorney to object that the purpose of the subpoena was "harassment and intimidation." Like the Karnys, they lost.

ITC Productions and NBC television were served with subpoenas as well, these demanding all documents relating to the *Billionaire Boys Club* miniseries. Joe soon was in possession of the contracts negotiated by Tom and David May, Jeff Raymond, and Evan Dicker. He also received a contract he hadn't known about, signed by Les Zoeller, who—despite claiming to the press that he could not discuss the case until all appeals were exhausted—had sold himself to ITC as a consultant.

Joe now was spending eighteen hours a day, seven days a week, in the converted paint locker at the San Mateo County Jail, and virtually no opening for a discovery demand or a motion to exclude evidence against him was overlooked. By mid-1990, subpoenas had been served on the cities of Los Angeles, Beverly Hills, and San Francisco; on LAPD, the San Mateo County Sheriff's Department, the California Department of Justice, and the Belmont Police Department; on the California attorney general's office, the U.S. marshal's office, and the FBI; on the U.S. Immigration and Naturalization Service, the Internal Revenue Service, the CIA, and the U.S. State Department. When the CIA, IRS, INS, and FBI refused to turn over records pertaining to Hedayat Eslaminia on grounds of national security, Joe filed a Freedom of Information Act lawsuit in San Francisco against all four agencies.

One of Hunt's most inspired motions involved an exhibit from the search of the Roberts residence that the state reported lost. "Or destroyed," insisted Joe, who claimed to know exactly what exhibit 37 had been, a note written to him by Dean Karny that read:

Joe,

As you know, I had the meeting with Hedayat. As Reza said, he feels his life is in imminent danger and he believes he is under constant surveillance. He says "our" plan is a good one, but is still worried. We also talked about biz. I will fill you in later.

Your Buddy,
Dean

P.S.—I have gone shopping.

Even Joe's enemies in law enforcement were not beyond his reach. He led with a declaration from one of his investigators stating that she had contacted Richard Mayer's mother, Verna Verser, at her home in Sun Valley and was met with an obviously rehearsed rebuff. Her son did not know Dean Karny or any of the BBC Boys, Ms. Verser had told the defense investigator, and in her opinion "they were out of his class." Detective Rozzi felt Joe Hunt was responsible for her son's death, the woman added, and her own feeling was that Rich had been "picked out randomly and murdered as a cover-up." She agreed with the police that "if Joe Hunt didn't actually do the murder, he probably paid someone to do it." The motion Joe filed with his investigator's affidavit accused Detective Rozzi of "engaging in 'dirty pool.'" Judge Hahn agreed, humiliating Rozzi with an order that the detective write to Ms. Verser—on LAPD letterhead—informing her that "defense investigators are an important part of our criminal justice system" and she should feel free to speak with them. Rozzi was instructed also to advise Richard Mayer's mother that the investigation was "ongoing," and that police did not know who killed her son, or why.

Joe's motion to exclude "all discussion involving Paradox Philosophy" began with a citation lifted from his favorite reference work, *Webster's II New Riverside Dictionary,* which, he noted, defined *sociopath* rather loosely as "'a person manifesting antisocial behavior patterns or character traits.'" Foremost among his concerns, Joe explained, was that testimony about his philosophical discussions with BBC members might mislead jurors to suspect that he had framed Dean Karny for the Mayer murder. In his adjunct demand for a "Protective Order against Publicity," Joe sought to prohibit police and prosecutors from discussing "inadmissible character evidence concerning character traits and attitudes alleged to be mine." This filing was followed shortly by a pleading entitled "Defense Motion Concerning Tom May's Potential Testimony on Fortune Tellers, Dead Cats and Mexicans."

In September of 1991, after the eleventh postponement of a jury selection date during the past three years, the *Times Tribune* reported that Joe's defense had cost the taxpayers of San Mateo County slightly more than one million dollars, a new record. The number of pretrial motions now numbered nearly four hundred, and the file was so enormous that a walk-in closet had been cleared to store the cartons of documents. When the *Times Tribune* failed to report his side of the matter, Joe offered the newspaper a second telephone interview. In preparing for a murder trial, he explained, "you get the feeling of being caught up in something so much larger than you are." In this case, both the prosecution and the defense had spent a great deal of money preparing for his trial, Joe allowed, and "I've often wondered what's in it for society. I think the value to society is that the trial is really a morality play where important issues are dealt with. It's a way of bringing moral lessons into people's homes."

The public should recognize that it was "enormously difficult to prepare for trial in a jail setting," Joe added. A human body required fresh air and sunlight; years of deprivation were causing him some serious health problems: Among other things, he had developed the respiratory affliction known as Sick Building Syndrome. "Also, the diet is way inadequate," Joe explained. "It's not enough and not the right stuff. I get half of my calories from candy. You get one or two ounces of salad-like material a month— some okra or some swamp-grass-like stuff, which I devour because I know I have to." With his immune system "under siege," Joe said, he had become perhaps the first person in history to request a temporary transfer to Folsom Prison—for six weeks—in order to regain a sense of well-being. To sustain himself, he had taken up the practice of Hatha Yoga: "The only equipment you need is your body," Joe explained. "Being in cages, usually small cages, it's an exercise system that can work . . . also, I meditate. It's become a cornerstone of my daily routine."

He was optimistic about his impending trial, Joe said, but concerned about the effect of the NBC miniseries: "I'm looking for a jury that understands they're prejudiced against me. All I'm asking is that they're willing to struggle with that . . . If I could just get a little receptivity from the jury, I'd be delighted."

He would not have made it this far without "support from the outside," Joe added at the end of the interview. He declined, however, to identify those who stood by him: "I don't think it would help anyone to have their name next to mine in print."

Much of Joe's outside support came still from his mother and sister. Kathy and Kay had made something akin to a career of their reconciliation with Joe, moving to Redwood City not long after his transfer from

Folsom. The two still were roommates, living on the wages from Kay's job as a salesclerk and the regular monthly stipend they received from Greg. Kathy came to see Joe at least once a week, accompanied by her daughter more often than not. A less frequent visitor but still a regular correspondent was Ryan Hunt, who lived less than two hours away on the Monterey Peninsula, where he and Liza Bowman Hunt had purchased a house in Pacific Grove. John Vance, accompanied by Oscar Breiling, had visited Ryan at his home in 1988 and found him "remarkably forthcoming." Joe, however, remained reluctant to discuss the former Larry Gamsky with anyone: "His father is the one subject I've learned to stay away from," explained Peter Brooke, the TV writer (introduced by Sy Marsh) who had become an ardent defender of—and the only interviewer with regular access to—Hunt. "Joe made it clear right off that he didn't want to go into all that. It's a very sensitive area with him."

Brooke Roberts had not seen Joe for several years, but she and her mother still were listed as defense witnesses. Though the entire family had visited Joe at Folsom, the Robertses never came once to the Redwood City jail.

In Brooke's absence, a new woman had entered Joe's life, his paralegal assistant, Tammy Gandolfo. Tammy had appeared on the scene first during the defense case at Hunt's trial in Santa Monica. Dark-haired and pale-skinned, with full lips and hollow eyes, she was one of those young women who look as if they belong to the night, somehow sexy and scary at the same time. She had a story, one knew that at a glance, but wasn't telling it, except to say she had contacted Joe after the Levin trial because of her outrage at Judge Rittenband's conduct. During their first meeting at the L.A. County Jail, Tammy explained, she offered to work for Joe on a volunteer basis to help with his appeal. By the time Joe was transferred from Folsom to the San Mateo County Jail, she had become convinced of his innocence, Tammy said, and moved to Redwood City to work for him full-time, paid out of funds provided by the county's private defender office.

Almost no one outside Joe's circle believed he could beat the case against him in Redwood City, where the prosecution possessed both the remains of the victim and a witness who had been there when he died. What made even the remote possibility of acquittal scary to those who had testified against Hunt, however, was his pending appeal of the Santa Monica conviction. As Oscar Breiling had predicted back in 1987, the principal basis of Joe's attempt to overturn the jury verdict in the Levin case was the inadequacy of Arthur Barens's work as his attorney—"Breakdown of Defense Advocacy" as Joe's massive opening brief had it. The appeal that was accumulating volume by volume in the State of California's new Ronald Reagan Building in downtown Los Angeles focused on the contract for payment of fees Barens had negotiated with the court during jury selection in late 1986. Judge Rittenband's agreement to pay Barens seventy-five dollars per hour for his work as Joe's attorney (compared to thirty-five per hour for Richard Chier) had one condition, Joe charged: that Chier not speak before the jury. His lead attorney's "conflict of interest between cash and client," Joe accused, "crippled" the defense. Barens also "presented an opening statement which had disastrous consequences in the form of nearly a dozen promises [to the jury] which were never fulfilled," Joe charged. "Most devastating were Barens's repeated promises that Joe Hunt would testify himself."

Joe remained locked up with his files in the converted paint locker at the San Mateo County Jail. He had been living under the fluorescent lights on the fifth floor of the courthouse for almost five years now, and it was his daily struggle to face a world where "history is happening without me," as Joe put it to one loyalist. Ronald Reagan had barely passed the midpoint of his second term in the White House when Hunt was convicted of killing Ron Levin. Now George Bush was scrambling to remain on Pennsylvania Avenue for four more years. The "post–cold war" articles that chronicled the dismantling of the Berlin Wall and the collapse of the Soviet Union were swept off the front pages of the *Chronicle* and *Examiner* within a few months by new stories about conflicts between West Germans and East Germans, Azerbaijanis and Armenians, Czechs and Slovaks, Croats and Serbians, Serbians and Bosnians. Almost overnight, Hedayat Eslaminia's former employer Saddam Hussein was transformed from America's ally to an enemy President Bush would compare with Hitler when he announced the largest U.S. military action since Vietnam.

Nobody knew better how quickly things could change than the incumbent president. During early 1990, the Allies' victory in the Persian Gulf War had sent Bush's approval rating in the Gallup poll soaring to the 90 percent mark, eclipsing even the record 88 percent his predecessor had reached during the 1984 Olympics. The most telling aspect of the nation's "feel-good post-war era" as the *L.A. Times* called it, however, was its evanescence. By the summer of 1991 the Savings and Loan debacle had returned to front pages and nightly newscasts, along with a pervasive sense that the 1990s might be one long awakening to a hangover from the previous decade. The country was beset by rising unemployment and a deepening recession.

The percentage of people who believed that "things" in the U.S. had "pretty seriously gotten off on the wrong track" would increase from 31 percent in January of 1991 to 60 percent in October, according to the *New York Times*.

Joe at least was affirmed in his prediction of economic decline at the decade's end. Even he had to be surprised, though, by what the recession was doing to California. Financial growth in Ronald Reagan's home state had been an upward curve that at times approached vertical during his years in Washington. Two years after Reagan's return to Los Angeles, however, everything seemed to be caving in at once. California, now more than one-eighth of the national economy, was the biggest drag by far on George Bush's hopes for a recovery before the 1992 presidential election. More than eight hundred thousand jobs had been lost in the state during the past two and a half years, and officials in Sacramento were discussing seriously a plan to pay public debts with IOUs.

For former members of the BBC, however, the most shocking local development was the plummeting value of Los Angeles real estate. Between 1986 and 1989 home prices in L.A. had increased an average of 60 percent. During 1990, 1991, and 1992, however, real estate in Los Angeles was declining in value at a rate not seen since the late 1920s, tumbling between 30 and 40 percent. The condition of both state and nation seemed to crystallize in a proposal by Compton Mayor Walter R. Tucker III that the apartment house where George and Barbara Bush had lived back in 1949 should be turned into a national landmark: The mayor's plan was aborted when reporters visited the site and discovered the building was a crack house.

Ronald Reagan still was chauffeured each morning by blue Lincoln limo from the former Kroger estate in Bel Air to the corporate tower in Century City where a private elevator carried him to his office on the thirty-fourth floor. There had been barely any outcry when the former president received a million dollars for a single speech to the Fugisankei Communications Group in Tokyo a few months after leaving the White House. Most Americans still liked Reagan, and many admired him; members of the Committee on Monumental Progress wanted to carve the Gipper's face into the stone alongside Abraham Lincoln's at Mount Rushmore. His eightieth birthday party at the Beverly Hilton in February of 1990 was the glitziest social event of the season in Southern California, attended by more than nine hundred notables who contributed twenty-five hundred dollars apiece to finance construction of the forty-million-dollar, 153,009-square-foot Ronald Reagan Presidential Library in Simi Valley.

Joe, however, was less interested in the former president's enshrinement than in the counterposed career arcs of the two great legal minds he had encountered during the previous decade. Judge Lawrence Rittenband had retired, reluctantly, at age eighty-three, acknowledging his 1978 pledge to stay on the bench until Roman Polanski was returned to the U.S. for sentencing. "I can't wait that long," the venerable jurist admitted, and surrendered his gavel. Pleased as he must have been to hear this, Joe was better instructed by the Harvard Law School professor he had hoped would handle the appeal of his conviction in Judge Rittenband's court. Though passing on Joe, who after all was without funds at this point, Alan Dershowitz had gone on to represent something close to a quorum of the era's other megavillains and currently was handling the appeals of not only Jim Bakker, Leona Helmsley, and Mike Tyson but also the eighties wealthiest felon, Michael Milken. As Milken's attorney, Dershowitz had helped make the "Scapegoat Defense" an effective retort to those who wanted to talk accountability: Just about everybody in the country had tried to take advantage of what was happening during the 1980s, this line of reasoning went, and singling out for scrutiny those who had done it most boldly or successfully was sheer hypocrisy.

It was obvious Joe recognized that the Scapegoat Defense might be his best hope in Redwood City. For all that had been revealed about him during past trials, the complicity of other BBC members was barely mentioned. Quietly, carefully, Joe had gone about collecting what he needed to inculpate the Boys. Hunt's reach, though, extended beyond the BBC into the lives of virtually every key prosecution witness. Dean Factor, for example: Back from college in the east, Factor had become best known in Los Angeles for harboring his girlfriend, *Beverly Hills 90210* star Shannen Doherty, after she was evicted from her apartment for failure to pay thirteen thousand dollars in back rent, then filing for a restraining order against the actress, claiming she tried to run him over with a car. From the Beverly Hills Police Department, Joe had obtained a report that implicated Factor as Ron Levin's collaborator in the theft at Garden Photo.

The prosecution could gauge the scope and shape of Joe's defense only by tracking his discovery subpoenas. Vance and Gordnier knew, though, that Joe had obtained plenty of support for his characterization of Hedayat Eslaminia as a man steeped in intrigue, a character so riddled with warps and aberrations that they were indistinguishable from his talents and charms.

The worst news for the prosecution was that Reza's court testimony—his description of how Joe admitted killing the father, then threatened the son—could not be provided to the jury at Joe's Redwood City trial without Reza's presence for purposes of cross-examination. Because of his pending appeal, Reza would refuse to testify, according to an affidavit delivered to Judge Hahn by Gary Merritt, and would answer every question put to him by citing the Fifth Amendment. Ben Dosti would do the same, reported the attorney handling his appeal.

Ben was still with Reza at Folsom, despite more than a dozen motions requesting his transfer to another prison. After evaluation by the department of corrections at Vacaville, his attorney noted, Ben had been recommended for an "out-of-classification placement" that would permit his transfer to Soledad or Chino. (Young Dosti had been "subjected to inmate pressures," as the CDC report so obliquely phrased it, and would not blend easily with a population like Folsom's). Ben's attorney also submitted a "Petition in Support of Release on Bail" that had been signed by several hundred California residents, ranging from *The Los Angeles Times*'s lofty drama critic Sylvie Drake to a large number of Mexican-Americans living in the San Gabriel Valley.

By the time Joe's twelfth trial date was set for November of 1991, the lawyer who had been assisting him since 1986, Parker Kelly, had resigned to take a position as prosecutor of environmental crimes for San Mateo County, replaced by the considerably more loquacious Douglas Gray. Disarmingly blunt and elaborately modest, punctilious in speech yet unpretentious in manner, Gray's personality was a nest of contradictions that belied almost every entry on his résumé. A former special-forces fighter in Vietnam who attended Stanford on the GI bill and worked as a patrolman for the San Mateo Police Department while paying his way through Hastings Law School, Gray had become well known at the Redwood City courthouse as a particularly aggressive prosecutor before becoming a defense attorney. Though combative indeed, he was more effete than macho. His earliest moment of intimacy with Hunt, in fact, had come when Joe, in court arguing a motion before Judge Hahn, used the phrase "struthion-eyed" to describe John Vance, then interrupted himself to remark, "You know, Your Honor, I used that word last week in conversation with Mr. Gray, and *he* knew what it meant." (*Struthious* relates to the category of large, flightless birds that includes the ostrich.)

Though the court had styled him "chief advisory counsel," Gray conceded the case was Joe Hunt's to win or lose. If he sat quietly at Joe's side before Judge Hahn, however, Gray spoke passionately in Hunt's defense outside the courtroom. News stories depicting Joe as the cause of delays in the trial (seven years had passed since his arrest) were "grossly unfair," asserted Gray, who blamed most of the postponements on John Vance.

Vance *had* often appeared overwhelmed by both the scale and the sophistication of the defense case. When Joe filed a twenty-six-hundred-page brief challenging the admissibility of his conviction in Santa Monica, the prosecutor asked for nine months to craft a reply and reeled when Judge Hahn gave him six weeks. Even Doug Gray, however, admitted a measure of sympathy for Vance, who as a professional prosecuting a defendant handling his own case was "in a terrible position; if he loses, it looks very bad."

As he and Hunt prepared for the new trial date—January 7, 1992—Gray reported that the defendant felt his chances were far better than even money. Joe's only significant fear, in fact, Gray said, was "that some informant will come forward claiming Mr. Hunt confided his part in one or more of the murders."

The appearance of just such an individual, a certain Tomeo Augustus Kovisto III, on the prosecution's witness list had caused the latest delay of the trial. Kovisto, currently residing at a prison in upstate New York, had been an inmate at Folsom during Joe's brief stay there in 1987, a period in which, according to Kovisto, Hunt confided his involvement in the murders of Ron Levin, Hedayat Eslaminia, and Richard Mayer. Judge Hahn's gag order, issued in particularly threatening language, precluded discussion of what precisely Kovisto's story might be, though Doug Gray was prepared to say that the most interesting elements of the man's "tale" involved the Mayer murder.

Hahn had issued the gag order as a counterweight to his decision concerning the Hollywood homicide: John Vance might call Kovisto as a witness, the judge ruled, but could not ask questions about the Mayer murder unless Joe Hunt opened the subject to discussion.

The January trial date, like each of the eleven preceding it, would be canceled by Judge Hahn's order. Again the judge forbade the principals from discussing his reasons, which meant they involved the Mayer murder. Under heavy fire now from the local media for the cost of pretrial proceedings, Hahn announced that the new trial date of February 24, 1992, was "firm."

Joe wasn't quite prepared to get on with it, however. His latest filing with the court announced demands for single-cell housing during the trial, for a pay phone to be installed in the former paint locker now known as the "pro per room," and for special provisions to guarantee that the defendant received at least two hours of "outside recreation" each week. In retaliation for alleged inconveniences caused at the jail by his work schedule, Joe charged, he had been moved recently from his maximum-security cell to B-5, a "tank" containing twelve bunk beds. He now returned from his office each evening, Joe wrote, to a communal cell where the head of his bunk lay fourteen feet from a television set that stayed on until at least midnight during the week and as late as 2:30 A.M. on weekends. The defendant was discreet but evocative as he described the social atmosphere in B-5: "A raucous game of cards or dominoes is being played within 10 feet of my bunk on almost every night ... loud conversations are being held until quite late. Those listening to TV must turn it up to be heard over those conversing, and those conversing must speak up to be heard over the TV. The resulting decibel level is the equivalent of that found in a sports bar on game night." Such living conditions "place me at a substantial, unjustifiable and unnecessary disadvantage to the prosecutor," Joe advised Judge Hahn. "I cannot keep pace with [the workload of trial] if my schedule is being controlled by my twelve roommates in the exercise of their various and deafening prerogatives."

Within the week, Joe was moved back to maximum security. A pay phone was installed in his office, and guards at the jail were instructed to see that he was taken outside to exercise for at least two hours each weekend.

Joe's self-defense now had cost San Mateo County two million dollars over the past four years, the *Times Tribune* reported as yet another trial date approached, more than double the previous record. The local paper conceded, however, that "after watching him during the case's many pretrial hearings, veteran courthouse observers say they've never seen a non-lawyer do as well." By his own estimate, Joe had devoted nine thousand hours to pretrial preparation, leafed through at least three hundred law books, studied more than five hundred exhibits, pored over an estimated one thousand investigative reports, read and reread every word of testimony from each of the eight trials that preceded his arrival in Redwood City, and interviewed perhaps two hundred witnesses over the telephone from county jail. "I've tried," Joe explained to the Associated Press in the last interview he granted before beginning jury selection, "to give myself a very good grounding in criminal law."

31

GASPS WERE HEARD FROM EVERY CORNER OF DEPARTMENT 11 WHEN JUDGE HAHN informed the four hundred area residents summoned to the San Mateo County Hall of Justice on the morning of March 18, 1992, that the eighteen of them selected to serve as jurors and alternates in the case of *People v. Hunt* should expect to spend at least the next six months in his courtroom.

Those who survived the first round of disqualifications were equally astounded by the question Joe Hunt asked them only a few minutes later: "Do you feel I got away with something by escaping the death penalty at my trial in Los Angeles?" Observed IBM executive David Saperstein, "He didn't seem afraid to talk about anything."

Joe's voir dire of Saperstein would develop into the central drama of jury selection. A chemist by training, Saperstein, forty-four, had graduated from Johns Hopkins before receiving his Ph.D. from New York University. Joe found it fascinating that IBM had hired a chemist to supervise the team of techno-wizards employed in the Advanced Disc Pathology division at the company's Silicon Valley complex in San Jose. The people who worked for him—engineers all—designed the programs that would be used in IBM computers five and ten years from now, and he found the job quite a challenge, Saperstein admitted. This was the main reason he preferred not to serve on Joe's jury: A trial of six months would last almost half as long as he had been in his present position, explained Saperstein, who expressed concern that he might "lose ground," possibly even be replaced.

The IBM man gave Joe cause to challenge him just moments later, admitting he had seen the *Billionaire Boys Club* miniseries. He couldn't imagine that a network like NBC would risk airing a program not soundly based in fact, said Saperstein. "Joe and I actually argued about the evidence," he recalled. "I said that if Dean Karny testified, I would be inclined to believe the prosecution. I mean, what does Karny have to gain by lying?"

Saperstein expected—hoped for—dismissal; what he received instead was a series of questions about scientific methodology, the testing of hypothesis against empirical evidence. As a man of reason, did he believe—despite his initial bias—that he could weigh the evidence in a fair and objective manner? Joe asked. "Yes, if you put it that way," the IBM executive answered.

He was stunned, Saperstein said, when Hunt left him on the jury: "It seemed so audacious. For days I went around saying to my wife, 'I can't believe it. Did he really see who I was?'"

During Hunt's opening statement on April 14, 1992, "I wasn't listening all that well," Saperstein admitted. "I was thinking of Joe as this arrogant grandstander." Other members of the panel would observe that the defendant, so self-assured during jury selection, appeared overcome by emotion as he stood to introduce the case for acquittal. "I had counted on being a little scared at this moment," he began. "I hadn't counted on being so angry." Wearing his favorite gray Armani suit, Joe was pale as cloudy water and thinner even than at the Harvard School; his dark hair, however, now showed highlights of silver. He was outraged that the case laid out by John Vance was based on the claims of a single witness, Joe explained to the jurors, and only hoped his fury could conquer his fear: "One of the reasons why I'm scared is that I haven't had good luck in the last years in public places," he told the panel. "I've heard what people say about me. I have heard the stage whispers as I am leaving the room. And I have heard people talk about what they read in the newspaper, as if newspaper reporters were eyewitnesses or oracles. And they say that Joe Hunt is a murderer. That he thinks he's so smart. That he's going to represent himself. And 'What right does he have to make pretty speeches? We're wasting our money on him. Why don't we just throw him away?' . . . To all those people, I say there is one voice that will never be stifled. There is one voice that will always be heard. There is one voice that will always be truthful and precious, and that's the voice of an innocent man talking about his innocence."

Joe had found a persona that struck a perfect balance between the disdainful aplomb he projected at his trial in Santa Monica and the fey simper on display during his 60 Minutes interview. The most remarkable aspect of his speech, in fact, was how well he stayed in character, one man alone against the mob, championing his own cause because there was no one else he could trust to do it. The people who printed rumors and lies "didn't realize there was only one person telling all this," Joe went on. "And this story that this man told was told and told again, and retold until people forgot where it came from . . . reprinted in a hundred million newspapers all around the country and shown in a mini-series on TV . . . this reality one-thousandth of an inch thick."

Before mentioning Dean Karny by name, Joe quoted an author cited by three different jurors as their favorite: "A lie can travel halfway around the world," Mark Twain had observed, "while the truth is putting on its shoes."

Worn down by years of unremitting character assassination in the media and the continuing endorsement of Dean Karny by the state, Joe said, even he had begun to believe that this case was "about me not being good enough, not being smart enough, not being honest enough." The sense of inadequacy he denied for so long had been his undoing in Southern California, Joe admitted: "I was afraid, and I let somebody else talk for me down in Los Angeles."

The simple truth of this case was as follows, Joe told the jurors then: "Dean Karny killed a man, Dean Karny has tricked the government, and Dean Karny has betrayed his friends."

He knew it must be difficult to accept the possibility that the State of California, the County of Los Angeles, the NBC television network, and most of the newspapers in the country could have the story wrong, Joe said, but such was the case. And of the many misrepresentations that had been used against him in court and in the media, none was more outrageous than the distortion of Paradox Philosophy. He had begun to develop the ideas behind Paradox as a boy in the San Fernando Valley, Joe recalled, back when he was one of those driven, introverted youths who spend their afternoons in libraries. From his reading, he had come to understand paradoxes as "statements that seem to conflict with common sense, but which under closer examination may nevertheless be true," Joe explained. Some of the paradoxes he had quoted to the BBC Boys were "things on the nature of, 'It's better to give than to receive,'" Joe said. "Or, as Helen Keller [listed in the "most admired person" category by several jurors] said, 'When a door closes, another one opens.'" "When profound human beings are reaching deep," Joe observed, "they seem to talk to us in paradoxes. Whether it's Christ or Gandhi [two more "most admired"], who said, 'I have the greatest imagination imaginable, to make myself zero.'"

Joe described the BBC's inception, beginning with his "whirlwind of experiences" in Chicago and return to Los Angeles in 1982. "In the dictionary of youth, there is no such word as 'fail,'" Joe explained, and somehow, he and Dean and Ben made it happen, brought together a network of friends to form a group they called the BBC. Almost at once, amazing things began to happen; multimillion-dollar contracts seemed to materialize out of thin air. Joe described in detail the Guaranty Savings and Loan bluff he and Dean had run past Michael Dow and the Gold Sun group: "That's what the BBC was about in those days," he explained. "We would tell each other about our hoaxes, our scams, our frauds."

He and the other Boys became less cocky and more desperate, though, Joe recalled, after learning of the losses at Cantor Fitzgerald and of Ron Levin's scam at Clayton Brokerage. By early 1984 "what we were engaged in was a massive war of deception," he explained, "a game of liar's poker." The web of mendacity had become for him a fatal snarl at a meeting of the BBC on June 24, 1984, Joe said. They would hear two very different accounts of that meeting, he advised the jurors, "the Liar's Club version" and the truth. Pay attention to how his accusers had conducted themselves during the weeks that followed, Joe advised the jurors, to determine whether they should be trusted.

The state's case at this trial hinged upon yet another lie, Joe said, an utterly false description of the relationship between Hedayat Eslaminia and his eldest son: "Reza didn't hate his dad," Joe asserted. "He had a frustrated, anguished, tormented love for his father."

Joe's own story would be more in line with Ben's, however, than with Reza's. The BBC *had* removed Hedayat Eslaminia from his condominium on the afternoon of July 30, 1984, he admitted. This was no kidnapping, but rather the implementation of a plan to help Mr. Eslaminia escape surveillance by agents of the Khomeini government in order to rendezvous with other opponents of the ayatollah's regime in Los Angeles. The Iranian's death less than twelve hours later had resulted from the acts of one person, Dean Karny, Joe said, and he would describe this event in detail on the witness stand.

With police closing in because of the Levin matter, Dean became fearful that the Eslaminia murder would be uncovered, Joe explained, and decided to cut a deal: "I describe Mr. Karny as a crooked man. Well, I am going to take you on a walk and point out a few landmarks, a walk with this crooked man, in the last mile—a very crooked mile indeed."

John Vance called as his first witness the most important. The preparations for Dean's appearance alone lent his testimony an air of gravity. Cameras and reporters were all over the courthouse. Each person entering Department 11 was forced to pass through a metal detector. Purses, bags, and briefcases all were searched. U.S. marshals scuttled down the corridors with walkie-talkies, ushering Dean to and from the witness stand.

Almost thirteen years had passed since that meeting on the sidewalk in Westwood. Dean would be thirty-three in five weeks, an age Joe had reached back in October. Even David Saperstein, whose "detached feeling" had lasted through the opening statements, felt himself succumbing to emotional engagement: "When Karny came on I looked at him, and I looked at him looking at Joe, and Joe looking at him, and I realized they probably hadn't seen each other in years. I was thinking how they'd aged."

Dean's direct examination, which lasted one week, was an almost line-by-line recitation of his previous testimony, altered only by the drama of the confrontation. "The animosity between Joe and Dean was so intense," Saperstein explained. "Dean just glared at Joe, the hatred in his eyes . . . and Joe just stared back with this innocent look on his face. But he never lost eye contact, and neither did Dean." The turbid atmosphere was thickened by a bomb threat that led to an evacuation of the courthouse during Dean's second day on the stand. Even more ominous was the power outage two days after that. When the lights went out, the sheriff's deputy serving as bailiff dashed into the center of the courtroom with one hand on his revolver and ordered everyone to remain seated. "The federal marshals all had out *their* revolvers," Saperstein recalled. "And this is spooky. I mean, what are these people so scared of?"

The moment everyone in the courtroom had been waiting for came on the morning of April 21, when Vance turned his witness over to Joe Hunt for cross-examination. "Mr. Karny," Joe began, "have you ever lied under oath before?" "Yes, I have," Dean answered, adding that he had perjured himself during the Cantor Fitzgerald depositions. "Did you make just one lie on that occasion, or were there many?" Joe asked. "I lied throughout the whole deposition," Dean replied. "Based on your experience in 1982 and 1983 and 1984, how is it that you would go about constructing a good lie?" Joe asked. "Is it important to take into account all the known facts, the facts that are available to you and the facts that you are aware of that are available to other people that you are speaking to?" The master interrogating his disciple; even Dean could not restrain a slight smile. "Yes," he answered, "in lying, using truth can sometimes be kind of a cover for the lie."

"Would you describe yourself as an honest man currently?" Joe asked. Yes, Dean answered. "How long have you been an honest man?" Joe asked. "I think I have always been an honest man," Dean answered, "except for a certain period of my life when I became very dishonest and very bad."

Joe produced his first exhibit, Dean's initial application to the California state bar, submitted three weeks before he had led Les Zoeller to the bones of Hedayat Eslaminia. "At that time, November 4, 1984, I wasn't looking over your shoulder and telling you how to answer, was I?" Joe asked. No, agreed Dean, who admitted he had been "evasive" in his application to the bar. Joe nodded, directing the witness's attention to the "Employment History," "Investment History," and the "Residence History" sections of both this document and a second application Karny had submitted five months later. He was attempting to conceal his involvement with the BBC,

Dean admitted. "Were we friends in April of 1985?" Joe asked. "No," Dean said. "Was I influencing you in any fashion at that point?" "You were scaring me," Dean answered. "Was I directing you to respond to questions in a particular fashion?" Joe asked. Dean shook his head. "You are lying on this application, aren't you?" Joe asked. He was "being deceitful and withholding information," Dean allowed. "Would you say you are lying?" Joe pressed. "It depends on what you mean by a lie," Dean answered. "What do *you* mean by lying? Could you define it for me?" Joe asked. "Saying things that aren't true," Dean replied. "Were you saying things that were not true on this application?" Joe asked. "Yes," Dean answered.

"They were just going for each other," Saperstein recalled. "It was riveting."

This exchange, though, was prelude to a cross-examination that disappointed nearly everyone in the courtroom. Dean had taken the stand expecting to be interrogated for days about his "involvement" in the murder of Richard Mayer. After examining the evidence the state would use to prove that Hunt himself was the killer in that case, however, Joe had elected to omit all mention of the Hollywood homicide. Without it, all he had on Dean, it seemed, were a series of petty deceptions. If the waste of Richard Mayer's life troubled Joe, however, he did not show it. The ability to defer gratification still was one of his strengths: Joe in fact did possess evidence that would discredit Dean's testimony but was saving it for the defense case.

The only chance to set this witness up for a fall, though, would come while he was on the stand, and it was for this purpose that Joe abruptly moved the time to July 30, 1984, and the place to the back of the U-Haul as it rolled south on the freeway toward Los Angeles. Dean described once more how he had punched holes in the lid of the trunk, then covered and uncovered them with tape. Had Mr. Eslaminia begun to "scream extremely loudly" when the tape was removed? Joe asked. Dean glared, sighed, then answered, "I don't recall that he screamed really loudly, but he—he started—once I took the tape off again—he started to make more sounds, and more noises, and more gasping." Hadn't Dean testified previously that he was concerned the man's shrieks might be heard by passengers in other vehicles? Joe asked. "I had the sense that there were other cars right nearby, not necessarily zooming past on the freeway," Dean explained. Joe nodded, glancing at the jurors: During these alleged planning sessions, he asked, "was there some sort of provision discussed concerning how Mr. Eslaminia would be able to survive if he was put in a trunk?" They had talked about opening the trunk during the journey, Dean answered, rechloroforming Mr. Eslaminia, and perhaps leaving the trunk open. Had he done these things? Joe inquired. No, Dean admitted. Contempt for the first time showed on the jurors' faces.

Joe's most daring strategy, and what most clearly distinguished his tactics from those of Arthur Barens, was a decision to admit dishonesty in his financial dealings so that their complicity could be used against the other Boys. His next exhibit was Dean's answer to the SEC charges, in which Karny denied knowledge that "investor monies were being diverted into BBC accounts." Again the witness squirmed: He "had an idea" that funds from Financial Futures were being siphoned off, Dean conceded. Joe produced then a Financial Futures Trading Corporation check for eleven thousand dollars dated July 11, 1984, and made out to "Cash." "Your writing?" he asked. It was, Dean admitted.

Karny had been under cross-examination for more than two days before Joe began to focus exclusively on what he called "the Eslaminia escapade," asking a series of questions that forced Dean to calculate the passage of time from his arrival at the Villa Motel on the afternoon of July 30, 1984, until the discovery that Hedayat Eslaminia was dead during the drive south that evening. Joe wanted to know how dark it was when the U-Haul stopped for gas, how long it had taken to punch fifteen holes with a screwdriver in the lid of a steamer trunk, how much time had passed between each round of taping and untaping, and how many rounds had there been, exactly?

Joe allowed none of the pleasure he took in tormenting Dean to show on his face, and Hunt's tone was most amiable as he demanded that Mr. Karny show the jury how Mr. Eslaminia had looked when Dean opened the trunk and found him dead, "just by taking the position on the floor by the witness stand." The witness did not attempt to conceal his anger, however, when Judge Hahn asked if he could "replicate" the position of the Eslaminia corpse. "I don't think a demonstration like that would serve any purpose other than to make me uncomfortable," Dean answered.

Hahn relented but did allow Joe to introduce a mock-up of the bed of his father's pickup truck (built at the County of San Mateo's expense) so that Dean might show the jury the positions of himself, the trunk, and Ben Dosti. Hunt had permission as well to take Karny through every detail of the events after their discovery that Hedayat Eslaminia was dead, from a recollection of what effect heat and enclosure had on the smell of urine to a description of the darkness as they drove into Soledad Canyon to dump the body. Had he become jaded about such matters? Joe asked. "I had become desensitized to those matters because of being in close contact with you, I think," Dean answered.

As at each of the previous trials, Dean's immunity agreement would be the core of his cross-examination. No one before him, though, had gained so much access to the subject as Joe. "Did you believe," he asked the witness, "that the willingness of the government to give you help with things like the SEC and the State Bar, and to give you complete transactional immunity, depended on how much you were offering them in return?" "I didn't really think about it," Dean answered, but no one in the courtroom believed that, so he continued: "I just planned to come forward and tell what I knew. And I tried to—to get the most—the most for it. Everything that I could think of to help me get on with my life, I mentioned. And the fact that that's how it turned out was my good fortune."

Joe seized upon Dean's admission that his "wretching symptoms" had recurred during the weeks before he first spoke to the police. How long had they lasted after November 28, 1984? Joe asked. "I still get them sometimes," Dean answered. Just this once, Joe let his pleasure show. "Any relationship to the fact that you killed Mr. Eslaminia?" he wondered. "Sometimes," Dean answered. "In relation to the role that you played in causing the imprisonment of the one-time friends, Ben Dosti and Joe Hunt?" Joe asked then. "You caused your own imprisonment, Joe," Dean answered, "not me."

Joe struck back by drawing upon his accounting skills as he marched Dean month by month through his enrollment in both state and federal witness programs, making sure jurors understood it was their money that paid the bills. Dean got a chance to counterpunch when Joe asked, "Mr. Karny, did you have a desire to see Mr. Dosti's and my bail revoked [in 1986]?" "Well, yours for sure," the witness answered. "I didn't regard Mr. Dosti as quite the same threat as I regarded you."

Joe needed a hearing out of the jury's presence to argue one last time his right to know Karny's current identity and to probe Dean's present financial condition. He wanted the jurors to consider "the anonymity benefit to Mr. Karny," Joe explained, "the fact that this witness doesn't have to be Dean Karny, the self-confessed murderer, that he gets to be somebody without a past, free to make new relationships, to be involved in business associations, whatever he might want to do. He gets to have the aura of being a normal citizen, and he can have that in his personal relationships, as well as his public relationships. . . . If Mr. Karny was now about to marry a woman that is unaware of his sordid past," Joe observed, "that is a man who is beholden to an extreme degree to the prosecution."

Before ruling, Hahn heard from an assistant U.S. attorney who informed the court that the government would instruct Mr. Karny not to reveal his current identity and location under any circumstances. Hahn gave Joe permission to ask Dean if he was employed but nothing else about his present situation.

Yes, he had a job, Dean said. Was that the reason he no longer received funds from the Federal Witness Protection Program? Joe inquired, and the witness seemed pleased he had asked. "The reason," Dean answered, "is that I am a self-sustaining person."

The decision to call Dean Karny as the first prosecution witness had been a bad one, though this wasn't clear at the time. The only complaints came from the media, less concerned that Vance had given Hunt an advantage than that the climax of a long trial had come and gone within its first two weeks. The mob of reporters who laid siege to Department 11 during Dean's appearance on the stand were gone the day after his dismissal, and with them went most of the spectators. "It was very strange," recalled David Saperstein. "The courtroom was filled to capacity every day at the beginning, and then by summertime it was a few people sitting in the back."

For the jurors, there was a sense of settling in for the long haul ahead, longer even than they had been warned. Joe's shrinking audience had no reason to suspect that his most dramatic scenes were yet to come.

The next important witness—more important than anyone could have imagined—was Carol Levin. Mrs. Levin's affect was more flattened even than during her appearance at Joe's trial in Santa Monica five years earlier. It was as if she had contracted a form of Alzheimer's that worked on the emotions rather than the memory. Yet her suffering was palpable, one more ghost in a room already crowded with them. Gordnier, who conducted her direct examination, gave Mrs. Levin the now-obligatory grieving mother treatment, leading her through another public recitation of her son's disappearance in much the way one imagined Blanche Dubois had been ushered to shock therapy. The witness brought tears to the eyes of several jurors when she revealed that her last living link with Ronnie, that dear loving dog Kosher, had died of cancer six months earlier. The prosecutor saved his most important question for last: "Mrs. Levin, do you have an opinion at the present time whether your son Ron is living or dead? "Oh, he's dead," Carol answered. "He wouldn't be anywhere in this world and not call me."

Just as Barens had in Santa Monica, Joe acknowledged what he was up against with his first few questions. This interrogator, however, was not afraid to make an old woman bleed. Joe's tone was solicitous as he observed what a difficult job the jurors had. "You want them to understand your son, do you not?" he asked. "Of course I do," Mrs. Levin answered. "And you want to help them understand your relationship with your son, is that true?" Yes, Carol replied. Joe nodded as he picked up a sheaf of documents and laid them on the podium in front of him. With "I'd like to ask you some details about the early years you had with your son," he began what Doug Gray would describe as "the most masterful cross-examination I have ever seen."

Joe went way back to the late 1940s, when Carol Levin had been Marjorie Feldman, a young war widow recently moved to Los Angeles from Cleveland with her mother and infant son. Did she and her mother, who was Orthodox Jewish, have any disagreements about how Ron should be raised? Joe inquired. "You know how grandmothers can be," Carol answered. She did recall, did she not, that between the ages of five and eight, Ron Levin went from one boarding school to the next? Joe asked. "Yes," Carol answered. Why had she first sent Ron away? Joe inquired. "Because there was a lot of friction between my mother and myself, and it was not good for Ronnie," Carol replied. Ron was five years old, wasn't he, when she sent him to the Page Military Academy? Joe asked. "Why, yes," Carol answered, clearly taken aback. And after six months there, he had spent almost two years at a place called the Monrovia Health Camp, correct? "Yes," Carol agreed. From there, her son had been sent to the Southern Military Academy in Long Beach? "Yes." So after three years away from home Ron had not yet reached his eighth birthday, was that right? Joe asked. "Yes. But he wasn't living away from me after that," Carol answered. She began to tremble. Didn't she recall sending Ron to the McKinley Home for Boys? Joe asked. "Yes, for a very short time," Carol conceded. "You must remember I had to work and my mother was getting on and couldn't really take care of Ronnie. I had nothing else to do."

Joe was more interested in what Mrs. Levin imagined had been "Ron's state of mind as he was going from one of these places to the next." "He was a very hyperkinetic child," his mother began, speaking to the jury now. "He was constantly moving. I would take him to the doctor and the doctor would say, 'Well, there's nothing I can give you.'" Would she say it was fair to describe Ron as twenty pounds underweight? Joe asked. "Not twenty pounds," Carol answered. "Maybe ten, but not twenty."

Joe paused, allowing Mrs. Levin a moment to contemplate what was coming. Besides the names Marjorie Feldman, Carol Marjorie Feldman, and Marjorie Glick, hadn't she gone for a time by the name Carol Gray? Joe asked. "Yes. Yes," Mrs. Levin answered, with more fear than hatred in her eyes now. Wasn't it true that during the years between Ron's fifth and eighth birthdays, she had lived in an apartment house at 1773 North Sycamore? Joe asked. "Yes." And did that apartment house have rules about children? Joe inquired. "I was not to have my child there," Carol answered. She looked at the judge, who could only nod impassively.

After Ron was expelled from the McKinley Home for Boys, wasn't it true that he was admitted for a time, at about the age of eight, to the Camarillo State Hospital? Mrs. Levin had lapsed into a benumbed state again; it seemed her only hope. "Could you tell the jury why you had him admitted?" Joe asked. A social worker "suggested I take Ronnie there for care," his mother explained, and those were the days when people heeded "experts." She was only eighteen years old, remember, in 1944, the year her husband died and Ronnie was born.

Ron had been at Camarillo for seven months, correct? Joe asked. She couldn't remember, Mrs. Levin answered. And by the way, Joe interjected, hadn't there been a short period of time before Ron went to Camarillo when she had tried to keep him with her at the apartment house on Sycamore? "Yes." During that time, did she recall sending her son to the movies during the day so he wouldn't be seen around the complex? Joe asked. For two or three months one summer, yes, Mrs. Levin answered. And after Camarillo, hadn't Ron gone for seven or eight months to live with his aunt in Cleveland? "Yes."

"Can you tell the jury whether Ron ever showed any signs of being terribly affected by that period of time at Camarillo?" Joe asked. "Was that a trauma for him?" "I'm sure it was," answered Mrs. Levin, who had begun to tremble again. "After that, didn't he show a peculiar interest in dead bodies, cadavers?" Joe asked. "No!" Mrs. Levin answered. "Do you recall an incident where he said to you that he had seen a dead body covered with newspapers?" "No. Never." Joe moved a sheet of paper to the side and laid his palm on it.

She had been working as a dental assistant, supporting herself, her son, and her mother, during those years at the Sycamore apartment house, correct? Joe asked. "Yes." "And I'm sure these health camps were very expensive?" Joe prompted. "They were expensive for me," Carol answered. She spoke to the judge then: "I don't see what all this has to do with Ronnie now." "Mrs. Levin, the way we work is that the attorneys ask the questions," Hahn advised her.

Between the ages of nine and seventeen, had she sent Ron away to any other boarding schools? Joe asked. "Not that I recall," Mrs. Levin answered. Had she forgotten a place called Secret Harbor in Anacortes, Washington? Joe asked. "Oh, yes," Mrs. Levin said. Ron had gone there at age fifteen and stayed for eighteen months, correct? "Yes." Secret Harbor was a "Longterm Residential Treatment Facility for Children with Behavioral Problems," correct? Joe asked. "Right," Mrs. Levin agreed. Did Ron want to go? Joe asked. "No. And we didn't want him to go," his mother answered.

In fact, Ron had begged her not to send him away to another boarding school, hadn't he? Joe asked. "Yes. And we begged the doctor not to send him," Carol said. At Secret Harbor, hadn't Ron written a series of long letters pleading with his mother to bring him home? asked Joe, as he shuffled a stack of yellowing paper. "Yes," Mrs. Levin answered. And hadn't Ron actually tried to run away from Secret Harbor at one point? "Yes." "Did it seem to you, Mrs. Levin," Joe asked, "that Ron had an extreme fear of being locked up?" No more than anyone else, Carol replied.

Gordnier objected when Joe produced a letter Ron's mother had written to a doctor at Secret Harbor almost thirty years earlier: Medical records were confidential, the prosecutor argued. Joe was amused: "If you are finding, Your Honor, that some holder of patient-client privilege is in existence, then you are making a finding that I'm an innocent man." Hahn had no choice: The prosecution had placed "virtually all aspects of the relationship between Mrs. Levin and her son squarely before this jury," he ruled.

Joe read aloud a long passage from Carol's letter to the doctor, written shortly after Ron's attempt to run away from Secret Harbor. She wanted him to know "what fears bother Ronnie most," Mrs. Levin had explained. "I guess being locked up in Camarillo was the start of this fear of loss of freedom."

"Do you feel this incident at Camarillo left a terrible scar on Ron Levin?" Joe asked. "I don't know," Carol answered. Joe read from another of her letters to Secret Harbor, this one involving Ron's story of being forced by an orderly at Camarillo to look at a dead boy whose body was covered by newspapers: "I feel this incident left a terrible scar on Ronnie and is the beginning of his real problems," his mother had written.

Mrs. Levin looked about the courtroom again, as if she could not conceive that there was no person present who would come to her defense. The only offer was from Joe, whose voice softened, became almost gentle as he asked, "Did you have any regrets about how [Ron] was raised between the ages of his birth and eighteen?" "Absolutely," Carol replied, as if grateful for the opportunity to say so. "And did you have some feeling of responsibility, maybe even of guilt, about that?" Joe asked. "Yes. I did and I do," Carol said.

"Do you feel," Joe asked, his voice still soft, "there was any connection between [Ron's being sent away in early childhood] and the fact that Ron started to get into trouble as an older man?" Mrs. Levin couldn't say.

Wasn't it true that she and her husband had supported Ron financially up to the time he moved into the Peck Drive apartment? Joe asked. It was, Carol agreed. And hadn't she continued to give Ron money even after that? asked Joe, picking up a stack of canceled checks, including one for five thousand dollars she had written to her son in 1984, just weeks before his disappearance. Possibly, Carol said.

It was now nearly four o'clock on Friday afternoon, Joe noted, and clearly he would need Mrs. Levin on the stand for another day. Before they adjourned, though, he had one last question: "Do you feel, if you would have stopped giving Ron Levin money, that he still would have been happy to spend as much time around you, Mrs. Levin?" "Yes!" Carol answered.

Mrs. Levin had an entire weekend to think about the resumption of her cross-examination, and began Monday morning, May 4, by attempting once more to explain Ron's commitment to Camarillo: "This was my first child," she said. "I didn't know how to cope with anything, and I had no money." "You know," she continued, "when you are somebody that doesn't see the situation all the way around, you have different decisions that you make." "I made plenty of mistakes," she added a moment later.

Joe listened patiently, then asked Mrs. Levin to read a "Child Development Questionnaire" she had sent to Secret Harbor in 1967. She was concerned about Ron's fascination with the morbid aspects of medical practice, Carol had written: "He was interested for a while in death, cemeteries, after he first left Camarillo," she explained to her son's doctors. "I felt this was due to his experience of seeing a dead person unexpectedly at the morgue. It seems ever since then he . . . has found a certain satisfaction in discussing gory details of people undergoing an autopsy." Carol's face was blank. She stared into space.

Joe let her go moments later. After Mrs. Levin left the courtroom, the defendant asked if he might offer into evidence a letter written by Ron to Carol and Marty a year before his disappearance, an item his mother had described as among her most precious possessions:

> Dear Mom and Dad,
>   The best friends a man has in this world may turn against him and become his enemy. Those who are nearest and dearest to us, those whom we trust with our happiness, they may become traitors. The money a man has he may lose. It flies away from him perhaps when he needs it most. A man's reputation may be sacrificed in a moment of ill-considered action. The one absolute, unselfish friend that a man can have in this selfish world, the one that never proves ungrateful or treacherous, is his mother and father.

When he first read the letter, Joe recalled, he knew Ron Levin hadn't written it. Doug Gray, being Doug Gray, had recognized at once the "very famous speech that Ron plagiarized," explained Joe, as he offered into evidence a copy of George Graham Vest's "Tribute to a Dog." The court would notice, Joe said, that Ron's letter was a verbatim transcription, the only difference being that he had "exchanged 'dog' for 'Mom and Dad.'" "It doesn't take any Ph.D. in psychology to know that this is an extremely vicious thing to do," observed Joe, who wondered aloud, "What sort of laugh did [Ron] have when he gave it to his Carol? And she said, 'It's the most tender, beautiful thing anybody has given me.'"

By the time Carol Levin's cross-examination was concluded, the jurors had been in Department 11 with Joe for almost two months. During a typical presentation of the prosecution's case, 999 out of 1,000 criminal defendants are no more than silent profiles, alternately stoic and seething as witnesses against them are called one after another to the stand. Joe Hunt, however, had established himself not merely as a presence in Department 11 but as the dominant presence, "taking control of the courtroom," as Doug Gray put it, within the first week or two of the trial.

He and Joe were delighted that Dale Hahn seemed to understand that "a judge is supposed to be a referee, nothing more," said Gray, who believed John Vance never could hold his own against Joe Hunt in a fair fight. The prosecutor was a very decent individual, Gray allowed, but also "the quintessential civil servant: He once said that he had no emotional investment in the case. And I think that is true to a greater degree than in just about any trial attorney I've encountered."

Joe, by contrast, seemed anything but detached. "He made defending himself a big advantage," observed juror Curtis Hackworth, a Hillsborough realtor. "It wouldn't be for most people, but when you can do it well, you develop a personal relationship with people." Each day of his trial, Joe "would look at us all when we walked in, make eye contact with each of us," another member of the panel, Joan Dick, explained. "He's eloquent. He smiles. He flirts." "He not only looked you in the eye," recalled Hackworth, "he looked you in the eye and never blinked."

"After a while, you can't help but think about the waste that having Joe Hunt in prison is," said Joan Dick. "A mind like that, the things he could accomplish." "Awed" was how David Saperstein described himself as he watched Joe add long columns of six-digit figures in his head during the testimony of various bank officers and commodities brokers: "It was absolutely amazing," the IBM man said. "I'm around people with Ph.D.'s in math from top universities, and they can't do that, not like Joe, anyway. It's impossible not to think about what he might have been."

What persuaded him Joe Hunt might be a different person from the one portrayed by the prosecution, however, Saperstein explained, "was seeing the human relationships he had, the way people seemed to care for him and believe in him. Tammy Gandolfo, through her body language, you understood that she was not just working for Joe, she adores Joe. His mother is there every day. This is nine years later. There isn't all the press, the big headlines, but Joe still has supporters." Joe's warm relationship with Doug Gray perhaps had helped most to humanize him. "Mr. Gray was eloquent but not all duded up like some attorneys," explained Harriet Kumetat, the elderly social worker Joe seemed to believe was most sympathetic. "He was more the old country lawyer approach. I found him very likable."

Gray expressed satisfaction but not surprise at reports of how attentive jurors had been to the demonstrations of affection between Joe and his entourage. "Believe me, none of that was accidental," the attorney said.

Vance's turgid interrogations and passionless demeanor contrasted not only with Joe's cross-examinations but also with the direct examinations conducted by his coprosecutor, Gordnier, a man whose style jurors compared to that of a hammerhead shark. "Part of what made things so confusing was going back and forth between the two, Vance and Gordnier," explained Saperstein.

Even the jurors most impressed by Joe's ability as an attorney, though, were unaware of all that his legal skills were keeping from them. Joe barred admission of Reza Eslaminia's trial testimony and excluded as well Xavier Suazo's recollection of his conversation with Reza regarding the group of young men whose business was kidnapping and extortion. No evidence at all was offered regarding the shoot-out at FCI or the attempt on Bruce Swartout's life. Much of the testimony concerning Joe's instruction in Paradox Philosophy was ruled inadmissible (Joe won his "Tom May, Fortune Tellers, Cats, and Mexicans" motion), as was every word about the BBC leader's obsessions with *First Blood* and *Scarface*.

It did not help the state's case either that many of the main prosecution witnesses appeared to be testifying by rote. "It's eight or nine years later, and people's memories fade," Saperstein explained. "Even more important, the emotional impact fades. People are matter-of-fact; it's like they're reading it rather than remembering it."

Not one of the state's witnesses was as effective as at previous trials. Steve Lopez's earlier professions of astonishment at Hunt's appearance in London during June of 1984 were diluted to mild surprise by the time of Joe's trial in Redwood City. Olga Vasquez, perhaps the most important prosecution witness after Dean Karny, seemed cowed by Hunt during cross-examination. Lore Leis was called to the stand to demonstrate the discrepancies in Hunt's accounting of investor funds at Financial Futures, and yet, "you felt like she would have hugged Joe if she didn't feel intimidated," Saperstein recalled.

Also unlike jurors at previous trials, the panel in Redwood City observed a cross-examination of the state's witnesses that left many looking far from sympathetic. The slipshod investigation of Ron Levin's disappearance by the Beverly Hills Police Department in particular offended the jury. Joe took full advantage of the opportunity for payback when Les Zoeller was on the stand answering *his* questions. "The Beverly Hills police were totally corrupt," said Sandra Achiro, the youngest juror. "I didn't believe them about anything." Several times after prosecution witnesses left the stand, Saperstein recalled, "I found myself thinking, 'Why isn't that person in jail?'"

Though he had chosen to call Dean Karny first, Vance saved the rest of the BBC for the later stages of his case. Evan Dicker clearly was the most truthful of the Boys, said Curtis Hackworth, "and also the most likable, because you felt he was admitting what he had done."

Evan was changed considerably since his last appearance on the witness stand in 1987. The "two years of hell" that had elapsed between his application to the California state bar in 1988 and his admission in 1990 accounted for most of the difference. After losing at hearings before the committee of bar examiners, the state bar court hearing panel, and the bar's review department, Evan carried his case all the way to the state supreme court. He had spent those two suffering years clerking in a series of personal-injury law firms, phoning home for his messages three or four times a day. By the time the call he was waiting for came, however, Evan no longer wished to work in private practice. The district attorney's office clearly was not an option, but the public defender's office, he hoped, might consider him. During his interview, Evan presented himself as a person who understood how a wrongly accused defendant felt. After he was hired, the heir to Dicker and Dicker went the way of all deputy PDs, handling preliminary hearings downtown, where nearly every client was black or brown. To his amazement, Evan discovered the pitch he had thrown during his interview was curving across the plate. "When you start to do trials," he explained, "you can't help but become aware that the person sitting next to you is a human being. They have the same feelings, the same hopes that you do. I'm not sure I really grasped that before."

Evan had continued to see the May twins socially until early 1991, when, for no particular reason, he stopped calling. "There wasn't a falling-out," he said. "I just faded away. I don't see any of the others either; we haven't been running in the same circles."

Five years had passed since he last saw Joe, who "was staring at me very hard for all the time I testified on direct" in Redwood City, Evan observed. "He was glaring, really. For about a moment it got to me. It kind of makes you want to duck—my concentration was affected. Then I realized there was nothing in the world he could do to hurt me."

What Joe did was make use of Evan's honesty. "You drank heavily during [the BBC] period?" he asked. "Yes, I did," Evan answered. "Did I drink?" Joe asked. "Absolutely not," Evan replied. "Did I take drugs?" Joe asked. "Not to my knowledge," Evan said. "Did I barely tolerate it in others?" Joe asked. "Just barely," Evan answered.

He was most struck, Evan said, by how well Joe still seemed able to control himself in public: "I don't think the jury was looking at his face during my direct, and he was cool and calm on cross; his demeanor [then] was not hostile at all. He just turned it off, which was something he could always do." As a trial attorney himself, Evan was impressed that Joe had avoided the classic new-lawyer mistake: "He knew when to quit; he got the facts he wanted out, then stopped, instead of going the next step and inviting a comment or an explanation." And the level of Joe's preparation, Evan added, was astounding: "He knew everyone's transcripts of testimony at earlier proceedings backward and forward. He knew mine verbatim."

The most disquieting moment of his cross-examination came during a break, Evan recalled, "when Joe condescendingly asked me to run downstairs to get a document he needed, like I was still his errand boy. I blinked and didn't have a good reply. On the plane back to L.A., I thought of all the things I wished I'd said. But then I realized I was sitting in an aisle seat, drinking beer, and heading back to a nice home in Santa Monica, while Joe was on his way to a jail cell with a sink and a cot. That was all the retort I needed."

Tom May's return trip to L.A. would not be so pleasant. The twin's bifocals of stupidity and arrogance not only made him the perfect foil for what Hunt had planned but also prevented him from seeing it coming. Joe would enjoy himself immensely when he described later the twin's arrival in Department 11: "He sailed in here like some galleon under full sail, chest thrown out, master's in film art from USC, got his life together." Tom met Joe's gaze all during direct examination, delivering his answers with a flourish of exclamation. The wind in his sails had died, however, within moments after Joe began cross-examination, and Tom, adrift, looked very soon as if all he could think of in the world was safe harbor. Joe started with the account at Cantor Fitzgerald, where Hunt had lost fifty thousand dollars of his money, according to Tom's testimony on direct. Joe presented the twin with copies of his trading statements from the brokerage house, showing that the total deposited in his account there had been forty-five thousand dollars, then produced a sheaf of canceled checks drawn on BBC accounts, each made out to cash and bearing the signature *"Tom Frank May."* "You did give me fifteen thousand dollars back," Tom allowed. The signatures on the other checks, though, he said, were forgeries. Joe pointed to the back of one of those checks, where Tom's driver's license number had been recorded as identification. Hunt was in possession of his driver's license for a time during the summer of 1984, Tom explained to the court. Joe asked him to look at the next line, showing where the check had been deposited. It was, Tom admitted, the number for his personal bank account.

Tom was only slightly shaken, but Joe barely had begun. Hunt next asked the twin to view a copy of the bankruptcy petition Tom had submitted to the federal court in Los Angeles on March 11, 1987. Why was it, Joe inquired, that the movie deal with ITC had been omitted from his list of assets? Tom wasn't sure he had been paid by the production company at the time he filed bankruptcy. Joe produced copies of the checks from ITC, which indeed had been issued prior to March 11, 1987. By the way, Joe asked, did Tom have a partnership interest in a company called Silver Star Entertainment that he also failed to mention in the bankruptcy petition? He had no partnership interest in Silver Star, which was his brother Dave's company, Tom said. Joe asked Tom then to look at the application for a $345,000 loan the twin had submitted to Great Western Savings on December 1, 1987. Among the assets Tom offered as collateral for that loan, Joe noted, was a $250,000 interest in a business called Silver Star Entertainment. "Didn't you just testify that you did not have a partnership interest in Silver Star Entertainment?" Joe asked. One must understand "the nature of business," Tom explained: Silver Star was a film production business that really wasn't his and really wasn't worth $250,000, either, but loan applications were often exaggerated.

Joe directed his attention to the bottom of that page: "Do you see where it says right above your signature, 'I fully understand' that it is a federal crime punishable by fine or imprisonment or both to knowingly make false statements?" he asked. "Yes," answered Tom, whose tan was looking more and more like sunburn. "So the three hundred forty-five thousand dollars was a false statement of your assets at the time you signed this document?" Joe asked. "I don't know," Tom answered. "Was the two hundred fifty thousand dollars a false statement of your business's worth?" Joe asked. "I don't remember," replied Tom, who requested a recess at this point. "Are you pleading a lack of recollection because you are concerned with the consequences of admitting a false statement that might subject you to imprisonment?" asked Joe. "No," Tom answered, blushing bright red. "Do you recall a moment ago saying that the business, Silver Star, was not worth two hundred fifty thousand dollars, and that people are known to exaggerate on loan applications?" Joe asked. "Yes." "Are you retreating from that statement?" "No." "So two hundred fifty thousand was an exaggeration for the worth of Silver Star?" "Yes." "So the accurate amount would be zero?" "That," Tom answered, "is difficult to say." "Setting aside the difficulty for a moment, Mr. May, would you answer the question?" Joe asked. No, Tom answered, he wouldn't.

"By the time we were at that point in cross-examination," Joe later would recall for the jury, "Tom May was perspiring so badly he needed a headband." And Joe wasn't close to done. He asked the twin to look again at his bankruptcy petition, under the section where he was required to list all brokerage accounts held during the past five years. Joe then handed Tom a copy of a statement on his account at Bear Stearns. "An honest mistake," Tom called his omission. "What about this?" Joe asked, and handed Tom a copy of the statement on his account at Lehman Brothers. Another honest mistake, Tom said.

The jurors were gazing at Tom with naked contempt when Joe finally began to address the substance of the twin's testimony on direct. Where Joe chose to focus first was not on the June 24 meeting, but rather on the disappearance of the Cyclotrons two months later. "Is it your testimony, Mr. May, that I told you to torch the lock at the warehouse and take those attrition mills?" Joe asked. "Absolutely," Tom answered; Hunt had given him this instruction over the telephone. Joe offered the twin an opportunity to change his answer: He was absolutely certain on this point, Tom insisted. Joe then presented the twin with his original sworn statement, the one in which Tom testified that he had called Dean Karny after discovering that some unknown person had torched the lock at the warehouse. Tom began to blink and sweat. "Your action in torching the lock," Joe asked then, "was any part of your motivation, Mr. May, a desire to take into your possession the attrition mills?" Tom's vehement denial was exactly what Joe had hoped for. "You didn't have any personal interest in controlling the technology at that time?" Joe, incredulous, asked. "None whatsoever," Tom insisted.

"At some point in time, did you reach an agreement with Mr. Browning to develop the machine further?" Joe asked. He had, Tom conceded. "This was prior to going to the police on August 9, 1984, isn't that true?" "No!" "You mean, you reached an agreement with him after you went to the police?" "Yes." Joe presented the twin then with the promissory note written by his brother Dave, made out to Gene Browning in the amount of $5,450 and dated July 22, 1984. "Altruism?" Joe wondered. "A loan," Tom insisted, squirming in his seat. Joe had one more document he wanted Tom to see, a "To Do" list Dave had written, recovered from the wastebasket at the Gardena plant in July: "New Browning Agreement" and "Corporation in Las Vegas," Joe noted, were both listed above "See Police."

Joe had him again, and even Tom knew it, subsiding into sullen monosyllables until Joe asked about the threat that anyone who talked would end up "fish bait in the East River," which Tom had recalled during his testimony about the June 24 meeting. That he *was* sure of, Tom said. "And you recall it even to this very day clearly?" Joe asked. "Yes, I do," Tom answered. Dean already had called Tom a liar on this point, but Joe again impeached the twin with his own sworn statement, the one in which Tom recalled that Joe's "fish bait" threat was made days after the June 24 meeting. Was it possible that his recollection of the meeting at the Wilshire Manning had been mistaken? Joe asked. He was "not sure of anything" at this point, Tom said.

While "it was important for me that Evan Dicker didn't hate Joe," David Saperstein observed, this dynamic reversed itself when the May twin was on the stand: "Tom May did hate Joe, but we hated Tom May, so that was good for Joe."

What Joe had given Tom was a pat on the back compared to the beating he was saving for Jerry Eisenberg. Even before he got the chance to cross-examine the attorney, Joe had succeeded in excluding virtually all of the damaging testimony John Vance attempted to put before the jury on direct. Jim Pittman's admissions at the BBC office on August 7, 1984, were barred as hearsay. Joe's warning at the office on the day Eisenberg resigned from the BBC—"We have taken care of others and we will take care of you"—was too vague to constitute a threat, Judge Hahn ruled. And while Hunt's statement during their meeting one month later at the Hard Rock Café—"If I find out you are involved with what's going on, you will be taken care of"—could be characterized as a threat, the judge allowed, because "it is entirely unclear what the motivation for the threat was," he would rule this inadmissible as well. To top it all off, Eisenberg complained, John Vance was a "terribly weak" prosecutor: "A witness is only as good as the questions that are asked, and Vance didn't ask good questions."

Eisenberg's testimony on direct would be forgotten by most jurors anyway, overwhelmed by the drama of his cross-examination. Jerry's demeanor had been toned down even during questioning by Vance; he no longer was the brash young man who threatened to wear a "HUNTBUSTERS" T-shirt on the witness stand in Santa Monica. Eisenberg's burgeoning real estate empire had crumbled during the statewide recession, and by 1992 most of his property had been "given back to the bank," as he put it, with a self-deprecating laugh. "It's tough out here," explained Jerry, who supported himself these days by practicing personal injury law.

His business failures and assorted legal difficulties had, if not humbled him, at least persuaded Eisenberg he was vulnerable. The terse, taking-care-of-business tone was intact, however, when the prosecutor turned the witness over to Mr. Hunt. Again, Joe started small, referring first to Jerry's description of the afternoon when Jim and Nick had fired the pistol with the silencer at the BBC office. As an attorney, hadn't he been aware that possession of a silencer was a federal crime? Joe inquired. "No," Jerry answered, and that was the first time the jury didn't believe him. As to the discussion at the Stanford Park Hotel on August 7, 1984, concerning plans either to burglarize Olga Vasquez or to seduce her, had he reported these to the police? Joe asked. No, Eisenberg said, but he did argue to the others that "those weren't good ideas." Joe moved then into what only he knew would be the main area of his inquiry. "Mr. Pittman ever offer to obtain paperwork from back east, North Carolina . . . in relationship to cars that you possessed?" Joe asked. "I think he made that offer," Jerry answered. After Eisenberg denied ever being in business with Steve Taglianetti, Joe asked if he didn't recall a meeting in April of 1984 "at which Jeff Raymond, Dave May, Tom May, Steve Taglianetti, yourself, myself, Ben and Dean are present, at which we discussed your activities, David May's activities and Steve Taglianetti's activities in relationship to stolen automobiles, and the use of the Gardena facilities to house those cars?" "Absolutely not!" Eisenberg answered.

Jerry had testified on direct about a "secret tape" made by Jim Pittman in April of 1984. Joe asked him to elaborate. "Mr. Taglianetti, myself and Mr. Pittman had been on an errand, and Mr. Pittman was asking how we thought the BBC was being run, or whether we thought there were problems," Eisenberg explained. "We had expressed to him some reservations over how the operations were going, and we got back to the office. And you said that Mr. Pittman was carrying a voice-activated tape recorder, and that you knew verbatim what our conversation was, and that you would forgive us this time, and that if there were any problems we should come to you instead of talking to third parties."

"Do you recall anything on that tape recording about your and Mr. Taglianetti's operation involving stolen automobiles?" Joe asked. "Absolutely not!" Eisenberg replied. "There never was a conversation like that, was there, Mr. Eisenberg?" Joe offered. "No!" Could the witness recall a conversation in which he had said he would prefer to pay four thousand dollars for a car that needed no work than to pay two thousand dollars for a car that came to him with a broken window and no set of keys? Joe asked.

"Absolutely not!" Eisenberg repeated. Did he recall during this taped conversation with Mr. Taglianetti suggesting that they name their stolen-car ring "Theft International?" Joe asked. "There was no stolen-car operation," Eisenberg answered. "And, to repeat, I have no idea what you are talking about." His agitation, though, interested the jurors. Didn't the witness recall telling Mr. Taglianetti that he intended to sell "hot cars" to members of his family? Joe asked. "No such conversation," Eisenberg reiterated, "ever took place." Joe then asked the question he had been saving for this moment: "Did you have a discussion with me about the fact that if I ever mentioned to the police anything to do with you and Steve Taglianetti, Dave May and Jeff Raymond's involvement in hot automobiles, that you would talk to the authorities about matters relating to the pool of interests in Financial Futures Trading Corporation?" "Mr. Hunt, I knew nothing of any stolen cars, and we never had that conversation." Joe nodded, almost as if in encouragement: "It's just as much a conversation that never took place as conversations between you and Taglianetti about stolen cars, sir?" "No such conversations," Eisenberg repeated, "ever took place."

Joe stared at him a moment with just the barest trace of a smile, then turned to Judge Hahn. "Your Honor, at this point the defense will be offering a tape into evidence." Eisenberg could not believe it: "There was no warning at all," he complained afterward. "If I could have been warned or if [Vance] could at least have taken a recess."

There was no recess, however, and Jerry was asked to remain on the stand while the judge heard Hunt's offer of proof. "This is the original microcassette that I listened to," Joe told Hahn. "It involves a conversation between Taglianetti, Eisenberg and Jim Graham." The tape was critical to his case, Joe explained, "compelling evidence that I'm telling the truth, and that Mr. Eisenberg is some arrant thoroughgoing perjurer."

Given its significance, Hahn ruled, he had no choice but to admit the tape into evidence, pending examination by experts.

Before playing the tape, though, Joe had a few more questions. The jurors knew from Eisenberg's answers that his attitude had changed dramatically during the past few minutes; he now addressed Joe not as "Mr. Hunt" but as "sir." "At any time in your testimony in the last three days, Mr. Eisenberg," Joe inquired, "have you altered incidents that would have reflected badly on you, to reflect badly on other people?" "No, sir!" Eisenberg answered. What about the discussion at the Stanford Park Hotel? Joe asked: "Did you alter your recollection of that conversation or give testimony where you changed your role in that conversation into my role?" Eisenberg seemed in no hurry to answer—how many tapes did Joe have? "No, sir," he said, finally.

He had prepared for the jury a forty-two-page transcript of the microcassette tape, Joe explained to Judge Hahn as Tammy Gandolfo passed out copies, then laid the recorder before the microphone at the podium. It was, Doug Gray observed, "a grand moment. I think Mr. Eisenberg, after having testified at a number of proceedings, had satisfied himself that the tape no longer existed. All of a sudden it fell into the middle of the courtroom, and to watch Mr. Eisenberg as all of that was unfolding was worth the price of admission in and of itself." Juror Hackworth agreed: "When Joe played that tape, Eisenberg turned to jelly. The look on his face, I'll never forget."

It was Jim and Steve and Jerry on the tape all right. Eisenberg could be heard making reference to the bowling alley in Inglewood his father owned, while Taglianetti spoke of his girlfriend Kathy several times. The jurors studied their transcripts as they listened to Eisenberg remark, "She has an old Ferrari. I just told her that I get the cars from back east." "I think they believed it," Jim put in. "Yeah, everybody believes this story," Eisenberg said. Moments later Eisenberg answered Taglianetti's concern that a broken window might look suspicious by rejoining, "Hey, that's what happens when you transport it all the way from back east. You broke a window." "Damn hippies," Taglianetti agreed, "breaking windows." When the chuckling subsided, jurors heard Eisenberg say, "I'd rather pay four thousand for a car I don't have to do anything with than to pay two thousand for a car that . . . comes with a broken window and no set of keys." Asked who would purchase the vehicles under discussion, Eisenberg replied, "I'll sell them to my family. I'll sell them to friends. I'll sell them to the relatives. They don't care. Once we get it registered in North Carolina, we are set." The jurors exchanged glances as they heard Eisenberg and Taglianetti propose names for their company: "AFB—Anything for a Buck," "FLOM—For the Love of Money," and "Theft International."

Hunt described for the jury the witness he confronted when the tape was finished: "See how his shoulders break, and he hunches over on the stand. How his face colors red." Joe still was as good at concealing pleasure, however, as at suppressing pain. "Mr. Eisenberg," he asked first, "did you know anybody else named Jerry, or who was referred to as Jerry, in the BBC?" "No, sir." "Did you recognize Steve Taglianetti's voice in that series?" "I believe so," Jerry answered, betraying not only Tag but himself in that moment. "Did you, yourself, recognize your voice saying [to Jim], 'You'd look good in a Rolls'?" Joe asked. "I don't believe so," Eisenberg replied. This was going to be better than Joe dared hope. "Mr. Eisenberg, did you hear yourself on that tape say, 'My dad's bowling alley?'" Joe wondered. "It's possible," Jerry allowed. "I mean, I heard the term. I believe it probably would be me saying it, yes." "So you are beginning to have a recollection of this conversation?" Joe asked. Eisenberg caught himself: "No, sir."

Joe made Jerry read aloud his statement from the tape transcript about preferring to pay four thousand dollars "for a car I don't have to do anything with" than two thousand dollars for a car that had to "sit in somebody's yard." "Did you recognize your voice as projecting those sounds?" Joe asked. "Not specifically, sir," Eisenberg answered. "It's possible, but I do not specifically recognize my voice on that day."

The jurors, however, *had* recognized Jerry's voice. "There was no question," Saperstein said. "Yet he denied everything, even when it was obvious." "We all agreed Eisenberg was the number one scumbag of the group," added Hackworth, "the type of person you wouldn't want to believe about anything."

Joe, however, wanted to keep Jerry on the stand a while longer. "I don't even know if this tape—when you made this tape, or what compilation of conversations that this tape is comprised of," Eisenberg was explaining now. "Is it your feeling, Mr. Eisenberg, that your voice is there, but that the only way those words would be in that order is if someone altered conversations of yours and spliced them together?" Jerry had heard the judge rule that tests would be run. "No," he said, "I don't want—I don't want you to put words in my mouth. I may—I do not recognize my voice. This may be what I said, but I don't know the context."

Could the witness tell the jury of "any context of legitimate transaction" in which he would say, "'How did they open it? How did they start my car? Hot-wire it?'" Joe asked. "It is possible that Mr. Taglianetti was talking about buying salvage cars, used cars, but I don't have any specific recollection," Jerry answered. The jury laughed, literally, in his face.

The impact of "the Eisenberg tape," as it would be referred to for the remainder of the trial, was felt immediately: The next BBC Boy listed as a witness, Taglianetti (now working as controller at the prestigious downtown L.A. law firm of Gibson, Dunn and Crutcher), was never called, and the prosecution rested its case on the defensive. "The BBC Boys, they just seemed slimier and slimier as they came and went," explained Saperstein. Though only Tom and Jerry were profoundly impeached on cross-examination, taint had spread by association to the others. "The total effect was that they weren't believable witnesses," Hackworth explained. "They'd tell you about hearing all this stuff, that he killed Levin, was going to kill Raymond's girlfriend, was going to kill this one and that one, and they never did anything about it. The big joke in the jury room later was 'Gee, I just killed somebody, let's go get a pizza.'"

Joe's successes during the state's case, though, extended far beyond the former members of the BBC. He had made better use than Vance and Gordnier of several other key prosecution witnesses: Len Marmor underscored the job Joe had done on Carol Levin by describing Ron's relationship with his mother as "very shallow"; James Foulk supported Joe's description of Levin as "a shape changer"; the entire jury despised Clayton broker Jack Friedman by the time Joe was finished with him.

Discrediting a handful of prosecution witnesses and using others to raise doubts wasn't enough, of course; Joe had to offer alternative explanations for the disappearance of one man and the discovery of another's corpse. "How Joe would tie it all together," as Saperstein put it, had become the main suspense of the trial. What "it all" meant, though, Saperstein could not have imagined. Vance and Gordnier needed five weeks to present the state's case; Joe's defense would require almost five months.

The accused understood better than anyone that he was on trial for two murders in Redwood City, Ron Levin's as well as Hedayat Eslaminia's. Joe's rebuttal of the Levin case consumed weeks of court time and was fiftyfold the defense he had offered in Santa Monica. Yet the main alibi witness at the 1987 trial was not among those who testified in Redwood City. Brooke was unable to attend this trial because "she's too depressed, extremely so, and we're not allowed to talk about you, or this case, or anything connected to it," Lynne Roberts explained to Joe when he called her to the stand. His ex-girlfriend's absence, though, only amplified the presence of her mother in court. What made Mrs. Roberts so effective, Saperstein explained, was "my surprise that she would be on Joe's side, clearly on Joe's side, that somewhere she made a decision that Joe's not guilty. So, another person for Joe, and one who had come over from anti-Joe to pro-Joe."

Carmen Canchola and Chino Lopez returned to testify for Joe as well but were no more convincing than in Santa Monica. The couple had broken up not long after the first Hunt trial; Chino had moved to Seattle, and in Redwood City his discomfort was obvious. "You felt he was just backing [Carmen] up," Hackworth said. "He had told this story and now was stuck with it."

Robbie Robinson also was stuck with his story and came to San Mateo County with little left to lose. After his dismissal from City News, Robinson had caught on for a while with *Daily Variety,* but that job lasted less than three months. Now approaching retirement age, Robbie had been unable to find another newspaper job and was employed currently as a security guard at a medical center in Sylmar. He had been given more than five years to organize the facts of his story, however, and was able to account for each of the discrepancies police and prosecutors had pointed out in 1987. The former police reporter now admitted he had learned within days of their encounter in Westwood that Levin was an alleged murder victim and at that time had described his conversation with Ron in a statement that was recorded on videotape. The real reason for his failure to contact the police in 1986 had been "journalistic ethics," Robbie explained: "As a reporter, I didn't want to project myself into the story . . . I had been told repeatedly that you don't get yourself into a story, you just follow the story." Going to the police, he added, "would have compromised me as a journalist," and the proof of this, said Robbie, near tears, was that his decision to come forward six months later "basically ruined my career."

Nadia Ghaleb had known Ron Levin in the late 1970s and early 1980s, when she ran the front desk at Mr. Chow's, which was one of the two or three hippest restaurants in Los Angeles at the time, she explained to the upstate provincials, "kind of like what Spago is today." At Mr. Chow's, she naturally met a number of Beverly Hills characters, Nadia explained, but Ron Levin "was probably the most memorable." Yet she had been unaware that Levin was the purported victim in the notorious Billionaire Boys Club murder case, Nadia claimed: "I never watch TV." Her encounter with the alleged deceased had taken place in February of 1987, Nadia explained, during the morning commute to her job as director of public relations for the Roosevelt Hotel. Her BMW was in the right lane on San Vincente Boulevard as it branched south into Beverly Hills, somewhere close to Camden Drive, Nadia recalled, when she saw Ron Levin climbing into a beige Mercedes parked on the street: "I thought to myself, 'That's funny, I haven't seen him for a long time.'" Ron "evoked a period for me," Nadia explained. "I had definite recognition." It was more than one month later when she made a rare exception to her abhorrence of television, Nadia explained, to watch news coverage of the plane crash that had taken the life of her dear friend Dean Paul Martin, the entertainer's son. That story had been interrupted, however, by an update on the Billionaire Boys Club case and the appearance on-screen of Ron Levin's photograph. Yet she spoke of her Levin sighting to no one other than her assistant, Nadia said, until the afternoon several months later when she attended a baby shower where one of the guests mentioned that she worked for an attorney (Jeff Brodey) involved in the Billionaire Boys Club case. "I said, 'Boy, I have a strange story to tell you,'" Nadia recalled.

The fifth witness who claimed to have seen Ron Levin alive in the years since his murder had known him better than either Ghaleb or Robinson. She had met Ron, Connie Gerrard recalled, through her son-in-law Bob Tur, employed then by Los Angeles's all-news radio station, KFWB (Tur would become better known as the TV "sky reporter" who from his helicopter had been the first to spot that white Bronco during O. J. Simpson's freeway flight in 1994). Ron sort of attached himself to Bob, explained Connie, who had turned into a bit of a news buff herself during those years, trailing along when Tur covered "interesting events." It was, Mrs. Gerrard said, the most exciting period of her life. Ron Levin was "just kind of always around," she recalled, peppering other reporters on the scene with various "projects" in which he was involved, and eventually became a family friend who sent beautiful gifts and arranged spectacular dinner parties. She continued to socialize with Ron right up until the time of his disappearance from Beverly Hills, Connie explained.

Her last encounter with Mr. Levin, however, was not in 1984, but on Christmas Day in 1987, when she spotted him in a restaurant in the middle of the Aegean Sea on the island of Mykonos. She and her husband were the only diners in the restaurant, Mrs. Gerrard remembered, when a pair of English-speaking tourists strolled in, one a silver-haired man in a turtleneck sweater whom she identified at once as Ron Levin. She heard the man in the turtleneck sweater speak, Connie said, and recognized Ron's piping voice. Later she and the man in the turtleneck passed within inches of one another going to and from the restrooms, Mrs. Gerrard recalled, and she *knew* then it was Ron. Yet she never said a word to him.

Unlike Nadia Ghaleb and Robbie Robinson, Connie Gerrard did not plead ignorance of the BBC story. "I follow interesting cases," she explained. Like Carmen Canchola, however, the first person to whom Connie confided her encounter with the alleged murder victim was not a police officer but a journalist, a producer at ABC News in Los Angeles. The producer, though, not only declined to pursue her lead, Connie recalled, but advised her she would be sorry if she got involved. She kept silent about her sighting until May of 1990, Mrs. Gerrard recalled, when her daughter-in-law met a relative of a defense attorney involved in the BBC case at a party.

Joe had discovered a number of other important witnesses not called to testify at his trial in Santa Monica. Oliver Wendell Holmes III remembered that not long before he disappeared, Levin had phoned to ask questions about Brazil's extradition treaty with the United States. John Riley, a former *Newsweek* correspondent who had worked with Ron in early 1984, said he had met Jim Pittman at the Peck Drive duplex. Justine Jagoda, who had been living above Ron's apartment in 1984, remembered that she was home on the evening of June 6, had stayed up late reading in bed with her window open, and heard nothing that sounded suspicious or unusual that night.

Joe presented volumes of evidence to establish that during the last year he lived in Beverly Hills Ron Levin had amassed more than $1.2 million in cash and merchandise from assorted swindles (not counting what he claimed to have scammed up with the Clayton Brokerage statements). Joe also called witnesses who testified that, in addition to the felony charges pending in Beverly Hills, Ron faced criminal exposure at the IRS, which was after him for taxes on unreported earnings, and that on the same day Levin was reported as a missing person, an investigator from Fidelity Savings showed up at the Beverly Hills Police Department to file a charge of grand theft against him.

Among Joe's most effective witnesses was a hairdresser named John Duron, who had cut Ron Levin's hair for thirteen years. Joe warmed up by asking if, during the last year or so before he disappeared, Ron had mentioned moving to South Africa. Oh yes, Duron said: Ron thought "it would be a good place for a person of his standard to live fairly well, and privately." Joe asked then about Mr. Levin's grooming habits. Ron was most attentive to his appearance, said Duron, and believed his outstanding features were his silver hair and beard. So naturally it came as a shock when, one afternoon in the late spring of 1984, Ron said he wanted to dye his hair ash brown. This conversation was especially memorable, the hairdresser said, because Ron didn't want his hair treated at the shop, instead asking for instructions on how to mix the formula himself at home. He attempted to persuade Mr. Levin that a do-it-yourself dye job was a bad idea, Duron recalled, but Ron insisted he would proceed.

There was little Vance could do on cross, other than to establish that Duron also had spoken to a journalist—in his case a producer from *60 Minutes*—before he went to the police and that it was yet another chance meeting with a young woman who worked for a defense attorney that led to the hairdresser's appearance in Redwood City.

By the time the prosecutor was finished, though, Joe had recognized a missed opportunity. How long, Hunt asked, must a person leave Clairol dye on his hair in order for it to set? Forty-five minutes at least, Duron told him. Joe asked the witness to examine a blowup of Ron Levin's bedroom. "Take a good look at that bed for a moment," he suggested. "If you put your head down on a white pillow while this stuff was in your hair . . . would it stain that pillow?" "Oh, tremendously," Duron answered. "Would it be difficult to get that stain out of the pillow, or the comforter?" Joe inquired. "Absolutely. You have to get—you got to get rid of it, probably."

Joe even had found an individual who would help him nullify what always had been the most damning piece of evidence against him. This key witness was Len Marmor's wife, Karen Sue. During the late 1970s and early '80s, when they were next-door neighbors, she got to know Ron Levin well, Mrs. Marmor explained and had noticed some significant changes in the man's demeanor during the months before his disappearance. "His attitude before was very cocky, very sure of himself, very arrogant, careless," she remembered. "And then he became like he was looking over his shoulder, nervous, easily excited." She knew it had to do with his fear of serving another jail sentence, Mrs. Marmor explained: "He was very upset one day and he called me in. He was saying something about, 'They must have something, they must have something.' I asked him who had something. He said, 'The Beverly Hills Police' . . . he said, "I'm not going back to jail, Karen. You have no idea what kind of things they do to you in there.'"

The encounter with Ron that was the main point of Mrs. Marmor's testimony, however, had taken place shortly before his disappearance in 1984. She was leaving the apartment at 148 South Peck that morning when Levin "stuck his head out the door and yelled for me to come in," Karen Sue remembered. Ron was quite emotional that day, she recalled, and rambled on again about not going back to jail until he was interrupted by a ringing telephone. While Ron answered his call, she glanced at his desktop, Karen Sue said, and noticed a yellow pad upon which someone had written "a 'TO DO' list." "What caught my eye," she explained, "was 'Kill the Dog,'" Ron said the list was part of a film treatment that lay on the desk next to it, Mrs. Marmor remembered, a story "concerning New York, video equipment, a man by the name of Edward, some kind of scam, something to do with somebody disappearing." She told Ron she wondered if it really was a script outline, Karen Sue recalled, and "he just laughed." Ron did say something, though, about not returning from his trip to New York, which surprised her. How would he ever give up Beverly Hills? she asked. And what about his mother? Again, "he just laughed."

For the prosecutor, of course, the big question was why this woman did not testify at Joe Hunt's trial in 1987. She had ignored the Billionaire Boys Club murder case entirely, Mrs. Marmor explained, until after that trial, when her husband visited Joe Hunt in jail. Len came home and told her he might have been mistaken, that perhaps Ronnie was still alive, Karen Sue recalled, and that night "I started having flashbacks and started dreaming, started remembering things."

Did she know the police had interviewed her husband back in 1984 about Ron's disappearance? Vance asked. She was not aware of that, said Mrs. Marmor, and though she knew her husband had testified at Joe Hunt's trial (of which earlier she had claimed to be unaware), they never discussed the subject. It got better. Had she asked Ron Levin on that day in 1984 why he wanted to kill his own dog? Vance inquired. "I didn't ask him that question because he was talking in script form," Mrs. Marmor explained. "So that would be a dog in a movie that gets killed, rather than his own dog?" Vance asked. "Yes. That's how he often kept you confused," Karen Sue explained.

As was the case with Connie Gerrard, there were a number of discrepancies between Mrs. Marmor's testimony in court and the sworn statement she had signed for Les Zoeller. As Vance pressed for explanations, the witness remembered something she had failed to mention on direct examination. "Maybe this will help," Karen Sue said: Ron, she explained, had told her, "'I am going to plan something. I'm planning my own disappearance.'" Mrs. Marmor seemed to be experiencing flashbacks at this point, recalling new details every few seconds: "This is getting confusing," she admitted. "When I started remembering these things—I [said] that I was starting to remember them—I had dismissed them. It's been years. They are starting to come back."

Joe attempted rehabilitation on re-direct, asking if it had been difficult to recall every detail of her conversation with Ron. "I have tried Mr. Hunt," Karen Sue said, "but I fell and broke my arm, and I'm still recovering from pneumonia." She would not be here at all, Mrs. Marmor continued, except for a sense of moral obligation: "Maybe it's a problem with my upbringing. My father always told me what you did today, you slept with tonight."

Before turning the jury's attention from Ron Levin to Hedayat Eslaminia, Joe interrupted his Redwood City trial to press the civil lawsuit he had filed in San Francisco against the CIA, the FBI, the Customs Department, and the State Department, demanding they surrender documents that related to the Iranian. The federal government, again pleading national security, at first attempted to "gloamerize" the documents, refusing either to confirm or deny their existence. "The *Alice in Wonderland* approach" Judge Marilyn Hall Petel called it. State and Customs eventually turned over a sheaf of documents. The CIA, though, would provide the Hunt defense with just one of the hundreds of pages of papers seized from the Belmont condominium, and even on that, all but four words—"Reza called to say . . . " —were blacked out.

The irony was that the intelligence agency's insistence upon withholding documents was the best result Joe could have hoped for. The issue was laid before the jury in Redwood City when Hunt compelled the appearance in court of a U.S. attorney to explain the government's position. "Watching as [the government's lawyer] sat there on the witness stand," remembered Doug Gray, "and said in a very clear voice, 'I was instructed by the Central Intelligence Agency and the Federal Bureau of Investigation to inform this court that turning over this information would do grievous damage to the national security of the United States,' and then watching the jury was not unlike watching a brick drop through a sheet of plate glass."

When the jurors reviewed what they *were* allowed to see—plans for an invasion of Iran spearheaded by a joint force of U.S. mercenaries and Iranian expatriates trained in "advanced weaponry, communications, insurgency/infiltration, hit-and-run tactics, combat intelligence, map reading and psychological warfare," in particular—their speculations about what might have been kept from them were unbounded. "For a while I actually thought the prosecution and government were working together to cover up because of the CIA thing," said Joan Dick, "that maybe the whole [prosecution case] was a setup."

John Vance had offered only a stick-figure sketch of Hedayat Eslaminia's background, but Joe's witnesses described it in detail, chronicling Eslaminia's rise during the shah's reign, offering profuse descriptions of the man's splendorous villa and vast citrus gardens. Hedayat's activities following his relocation to the United States were no less dazzling, though far more confusing. Jurors heard Ofick Aghakhani tell of her arrest for smuggling nearly nine ounces of opium sewn into the picture frames Hedayat had given her, heard an old friend say Hedayat smoked at least two pipes of opium per day, and listened as another friend's daughter described Eslaminia's plans for a one-million-dollar insurance swindle that involved faking his death.

Jurors heard also of secret meetings with U.S. government officials and of Hedayat's employment by Saddam Hussein; of visits from "Mel," the American who spoke Farsi fluently; of Eslaminia's trips to Baghdad, Istanbul, Paris, and Cologne, and of the reimbursement checks from Washington, D.C., that Hedayat received for his trips and phone calls overseas. They heard of business deals in which Hedayat's share would have been forty-three million dollars, then of his arrest during the same period for attempting to shoplift chicken patties.

Especially compelling on the witness stand was George Beaudoux, proprietor of Continental Security Services, who described numerous dealings with Mr. Eslaminia: The most fascinating involved a middle-of-the-night phone call that led to Beaudoux's predawn rendezvous at San Francisco International Airport with Eslaminia and a Farsi translator carrying a suitcase containing stacks of American Express traveler's checks in one-hundred-dollar denominations. He and Hedayat flew together that morning to Dulles Airport in Washington, D.C., Beaudoux recalled, where they met officials of Saddam's Iraqi government at the Sheraton Hotel to discuss the assassination of the Ayatollah Khomeini.

Joe found a former neighbor of Eslaminia's at the Davy Glen Apartments who recalled seeing Reza Eslaminia strolling in snakeskin boots through the complex at his father's side. Debi Lutkenhouse Eslaminia (she had married Reza in 1988 at Folsom Prison) told the jury that Reza often swam in the pool at his father's condominium complex.

The most persuasive aspect of the defense in Redwood City, however, would be neither the international-intrigue evidence nor Hunt's appearance as a witness but rather that part of his case to which Joe had referred only fleetingly during his opening statement, and which he had skirted scrupulously during pretrial hearings. This was the testimony of those "qualified personnel" who conducted the tests Joe had mentioned in one of his last requests for a postponement late in 1991. They were well-known scientists, most of them, it turned out, people with international reputations in some cases, intended in each instance to impeach the testimony of the government's first witness, Dean L. Karny. There was a photographer from NASA who provided hour-by-hour satellite images of California during July 30, 1984, shot from twenty-three thousand miles away, an astronomer from the Marston Planetarium who testified about the night sky on July 30, followed by an administrator from the California Academy of Sciences who had shot a videotape of Soledad Canyon after midnight. There even was a professor from Berkeley who had run a DMAC test—for traces of urea—on the underwear collected from Indian Canyon with Hedayat Eslaminia's remains.

Dr. William Krause, a Ph.D. in audio forensics, had been hired to examine Dean Karny's claim he heard "a scream or a shriek" from the Belmont condominium complex during the afternoon of the abduction. To assist him, Krause had retained the services of two rare individuals. One was a man who made a living from his phenomenal hearing, an ability to understand whispered words through two sets of locked doors. He conducted his test, Dr. Krause explained, by seating this man in a car stationed approximately where, according to Dean Karny, the pickup truck in which he sat had been parked on the afternoon of July 30, 1984. Standing just inside the open door of what had been Hedayat Eslaminia's apartment was a woman who made a career of her phenomenal voice, an ability to hit 121 decibels, equivalent to a one-hundred-piece orchestra. When she screamed three times at the top of her lungs, neither the man with the extraordinary ears nor a shotgun microphone wired to state-of-the-art recording equipment had picked up the sound, Dr. Krause reported.

The key scientific witnesses, however, were the group of five men asked to determine how long Hedayat Eslaminia might have stayed alive inside a thirty-nine-by-thirteen-by-twenty-two-inch box. The first surprise was that it wasn't suffocation that would kill someone locked in a trunk but rather heatstroke. How long exactly a man might survive in such confined quarters depended upon both his own physical condition and outside factors, the defense experts explained, such as air temperature and even the speed at which the U-Haul truck was traveling. Gordnier made mockery of the first scientist who testified about heat exchange, and by the time cross-examination was concluded, about all the jurors could recall was that this guy had been paid thirty-one thousand dollars out of county funds.

The scientist whose testimony the prosecution could not dent, however, a man described later by a majority of jurors as the most important witness of the trial, was someone whose existence Vance and Gordnier had discovered only a few weeks earlier. Dr. Ralph Goldman commanded not only the jury's attention but its awe by the time he was halfway through his résumé. Though presently employed as a one-man corporation called Comfort Technology, Dr. Goldman had spent most of his career with the U.S. Army, serving as commander of a research division in which all of the officers and most of the enlisted personnel held Ph.D.s from major universities. Congress also had appointed him to serve as the military's principal consultant on environmental physiology, a position in which he was accorded a rank equivalent to three-star general. He had been loaned out at various times to NATO, Dr. Goldman recalled, and also to the Department of Labor, where he helped establish a national standard for exposure of workers to noise, heat, cold, and chemicals. He had written most of the National Heat Standard and currently was redrafting it for the Environmental Protection Agency. He was perhaps proudest, though, of his successful campaign to persuade the army to change its hydration doctrine and had been "instrumental," the doctor admitted, in convincing the military to air-condition the M-1 tank deployed so successfully in Operation Desert Storm. He presently was an adjunct professor at Boston University and a visiting lecturer at both MIT and Harvard. Perhaps his favorite position was that of consultant to the National Football League. By the time Goldman admitted he was a recent recipient of the Silver Beaver Award, the highest honor bestowed by the Boy Scouts of America—he had been a scoutmaster for thirty years—the jurors were hanging on his every word.

Goldman had been called to the stand to explain heat transfer in the human body, and many of the jurors could recall his description verbatim months later: "Basically the heart is pumping heat," he began. "The blood acts as a radiator fluid of a car, if you will. The heart pumps blood from the deep body center where the heat is produced, out to the skin." Each quart of blood transferred about four calories of heat, which had to escape through the epidermis, Dr. Goldman explained; if this heat was not released, the results were dire indeed.

According to Joe Hunt's calculations, Dean Karny's story described a passage of more than seven hours between the time Hedayat Eslaminia had been stuffed in that steamer trunk and his discovery that the man was dead. Even if Joe had been off by an hour, or two, or three, or four, or five, according to Dr. Goldman, Karny's story was implausible. The maximum rate at which a human heart could function, the doctor explained, would have been achieved under the conditions described by Mr. Karny within one hour and fifteen minutes. The temperature of Hedayat Eslaminia's body would have reached about 109 degrees if he had managed to stay alive four hours, and the doctor doubted that a man fifty-six years old could have stayed alive for an hour and a half under such conditions, whether holes had been punched in the trunk lid or not.

Joe had hired an entire team of scientists to test Dr. Goldman's theories. They used both a replica 1984 steamer trunk and a new model from 1992. They hired a U-Haul truck the same year and make as the one Ben Dosti had rented back in 1984. They created atmospheric conditions that matched those on July 30, 1984. They tested the trunk with airholes and without airholes. What they could not do, of course, was ask a human being to stuff himself into the trunk in order to see how long he would stay alive. The scientists substituted a one-hundred-watt light bulb at first, since the heat it put out was almost exactly that of a human body, but eventually discovered that four large water bottles would work better, since that took into account mass as well as temperature. The results indicated that a human being would have lost the capacity to produce speech within forty-five minutes after being locked in the trunk and would have been dead in less than ninety.

These tests made less impact on the jury, however, than the computer model generated by Dr. Edwin X. Berry. He first had taken up computer modeling in 1965, Dr. Berry told the jurors, while preparing his Ph.D. thesis, "Cloud Droplet Collection by Coalescence." This was the first time he had worked with "physiological concepts." To achieve precision, he had factored in weather conditions along three separate routes between Belmont and Los Angeles, Dr. Berry explained, using latitude and longitude information provided by tactical pilotage maps and weather station reports that allowed him to calculate air temperature minute by minute. His model even charted the reaction of each panel of the U-Haul's van to different solar and outside air conditions, Dr. Berry continued, by calculations based on the sun's azimuth and altitude angles. When his computer's calculations were tested in Sacramento on September 2, 1992, an air temperature of 92 degrees had baked the atmosphere inside the van to the highest temperature the thermometer used could measure, 122 degrees, in less than two hours. What the temperature of the air in a trunk containing a human body inside the van would have been at that point not only was impossible to measure but terrifying to contemplate.

Joe wouldn't make the same mistake he had in Santa Monica. His assumption there that unraveling the prosecution case was all the defense he needed proved disastrous. It would be necessary to take the stand this time and tell the jury how all those frayed edges fit together.

That meant going all the way back to 1972, when he had entered Harvard School as a seventh grader. He found it difficult to make friends on the Coldwater campus, Joe explained, yet he remained generally oblivious to the "disparity" between his family's circumstances and those of other students until he ran for class representative as a junior and received a total of two votes. It was his dismissal from the debate squad, though, that changed him, said Joe, who betrayed bitterness only when he explained, "The debate squad captain in those days was a guy named *Ricky* Berg. And Mr. Berg wasn't really a debater." What made his presentation so compelling was Joe's singular capacity for fusing genuine introspection with self-serving distortion. His removal from the debate squad, Joe acknowledged, was a pivotal event—perhaps *the* event—that altered the course of his young life. "I had planned and had thought I was preparing myself to go to [Harvard or Yale] with what I perceived to be most of the rest of my class," he explained. "[But] as a result of how [school officials] handled that matter, and some other things that occurred, I decided that I was going to change my plans, and I wasn't going to go back east with this same crowd of people . . . I had decided that I didn't really want to get a position in the system. Especially, you know, the IBM, MBA, JD type of thing that I had thought about before. And that I would just try and strike off and do something a little bit less conventional that would keep me away from the hierarchies."

Joe said not one word about his upbringing, did not mention his father at all, and omitted from his story entirely the American Institute of Hypnosis. He did not tell the jury, either, of his experiences at the Chi Phi fraternity; all he said of USC was that, although an accounting major, he had taken mostly literature courses. Joe recalled being hired as a junior accountant at Peat Marwick but mentioned neither his first interview with Terry Dibble nor their last conversation in the elevator. He acknowledged, though, spending "more time than I should have" trading commodities while with the firm. "Basically," Joe said, "I made the wrong choice."

Joe conceded one error after another. Yet at every turn these admissions formed an ellipse that served to omit all that was willful or calculated in his decisions. Confession as cover-up, it was brilliant strategy.

Joe was careful, though not entirely truthful, in describing his rise and fall on the floor of the Mercantile Exchange, claiming he had earned $750,000 before putting on a butterfly trade that "went against me in a huge way." He didn't have the heart, Joe said, to tell his investors their money had been lost. "Devastating," he called the experience.

He *had* been suspended by the Merc's compliance department, Joe acknowledged, "because of this pooling issue," and, as Dean had testified, arrived back in L.A. with four dollars to his name.

What were his plans then? Doug Gray asked. Joe demonstrated by his reply how well he had learned to play humble: "Well, I might have been pretty thick, but it seemed to me that there was nothing to do except to go back to accounting. Because my certainty that I knew how to trade commodities had pretty much vanished by that point. It was just a very punishing two years in Chicago. And even I can take a hint . . . But at the same time, I had given my word, and said I was going to restore these people's losses. And the two positions were incompatible." He would go so far as to say, in fact, that the main attraction of the BBC at the beginning was an opportunity to generate the money he needed to pay off his debts, Joe told the jury.

His first sense of what the BBC might achieve had come during his dealings with Michael Dow and the Gold Sun group, recalled Joe. Catastrophe intervened only a month or so later, though, when the May and Karny accounts were liquidated at Cantor Fitzgerald. He wanted people to recognize, however, Joe added, that this fiasco was purely a result of the scam Ron Levin had run on him with the Clayton account.

Interestingly, Joe did not deny his ill will toward Levin and testified as well that in 1984 he had believed Ron was worth as much as one hundred million dollars. Levin had played him beautifully, Joe acknowledged, with references to the portfolio managers and the merchant bankers who handled his family's finances, the cashier's checks from Swiss banks, long printouts of his stock holdings, and the delivery man with the Ticor badge who brought him a check for twelve million dollars. "I still don't know where that came from, or how he arranged it," Joe said, genuinely marveling for a moment at Ron's attention to detail.

He hadn't been as concerned as he might have been with the losses at Cantor Fitzgerald during August of 1983, Joe explained, because these were insignificant next to his share of the profits from the trading on the Levin account at Clayton. By the end of that year, though, the BBC was counting on the Levin money to cover the illegal diversion of funds at Financial Futures. "It wasn't just Dean that knew about this diversion and encouraged it," Joe explained. "It was really everybody at the BBC at that time that was in the inner circle." Dave May and Jerry Eisenberg not only knew about the diversion but attempted to use it as leverage when they disagreed with his decisions, Joe said.

He remained intent on collecting from Levin, however, and, just as Dean had said, Joe explained, he began to take advantage of his personal relationship with Ron: "His guard was not up. I would be over at his house and he would be going off someplace and I'd say, 'Well, I've got to make some phone calls. Can I use the phone?' He'd leave. It was times like that when I would have fairly lengthy access to his files." The copy of the trading statements from Clayton he found in Ron's office convinced him "this man had that money," Joe said.

By that point in time, Joe explained to the jury, he already had commenced the negotiations with William Kilpatrick that were the springboard of his future plans for the BBC. And there were other contracts either signed or pending, for instance the $2.4 million agreement with William Morton. It was keeping these deals alive and his investors happy that drove him to pursue the money owed by Ron Levin.

Two events during the early spring of 1984, however, had threatened the BBC with collapse. First was the appearance of evidence that Eisenberg and Taglianetti, with help from Jeff Raymond and Dave May, were storing stolen automobiles at the Gardena plant. Second, and more momentous, was a $750,000 loss in the IMF account at Shearson. By May, his struggle to hold the BBC together until the Kilpatrick negotiations were completed consumed virtually every bit of his energy, Joe said. As both a point of pride and an essential setup for the climax of his story, Joe insisted that the jury understand how near the BBC had been to sums of money that dwarfed the trifling amounts lost in the commodity accounts: The Boys would have earned at least $20 million from their share of the UFOI-Saturn-Microgenesis merger; the Morton contracts were nearly due; and Steve Lopez was developing deals through his Asian contacts that might have been the richest deals of all.

So it wasn't just moral indignation but concern for the BBC's survival that fueled his outrage when he heard the Eisenberg tape, Joe explained:

"I was just blown away. I couldn't believe . . . I had let things get so sloppy around there." Eisenberg was by then his biggest problem, Joe told the jurors: "He came to realize that I wasn't in any position just to get rid of him. He began to go around and recruit people under his banner, people that had similar points of view." It was the "Eisenberg group" that had forced him to split Microgenesis into two companies, Joe said, and the BBC attorney himself had drawn up the document that placed operational control of the larger corporation in his own hands.

The BBC's overhead made him desperate for income by late May, Joe explained, and when Ron Levin proposed paying off his debt on the trading in the Clayton account by brokering a deal that involved the silica rights to the Cyclotron machine, there was little choice but to accept. Also, "I thought it was fairly reasonable that [Ron] would fork over half of what he owed me anyhow—and that I made for him—to make me go away."

Unfortunately, the straits he was in forced him to make one concession after another in his negotiations with Levin, Joe recalled. When Ron threatened to make his own deal with unnamed "principals," Joe said, "I didn't doubt for a moment he could do it . . . I just felt kind of emotionally beaten down."

Almost everyone in the BBC expressed disgust that he was involved again with Levin, Joe said, "so I just spilled everything" at a meeting on June 4, 1984, attended by most of the BBC's inner circle. Besides himself, Dean Karny and Ben Dosti, Joe said, Tom May, Steve Taglianetti, Evan Dicker, and Jeff Raymond were present at this "conference," during which the "AT LEVIN'S, TO DO" list had been concocted. The idea to extort Levin was based upon the Boys' belief that Ron had no credibility with law enforcement, Joe explained, and could not turn to the police. Everyone present contributed to the "TO DO" list, Joe said. It was Tom May who had come up with the *"Kill dog"* part of the plan: Tom made a joke about taking Ron Levin's dog hostage that evolved into the idea that one of them should lead the little Sheltie into another room and twist its ear until the dog yelped so that Ron would think something drastic was happening. Tom eventually suggested they actually should kill the dog, Joe said, which was where *"Pack Suitcase"* and *"Jim digs pit"* came in. *"Handcuff"* and *"Put answering service on 668"* were Dean's ideas, said Joe, who took full credit for only one entry on the "TO DO" list: *"Make a file of letters (take holes with you)."*

When he arrived at the BBC office the next morning, Joe recalled, his own feelings had "set into a grim resolve," but there was a noticeable lack of enthusiasm from Dean and the other Boys. "'Ron Levin's got your number,'" Joe remembered Tom May telling him. "'You no more are going to go through with this than the rest of us, so why don't you just admit it?'"

Tom then proposed one of his famous dollar-bill bets, Joe recalled, pulling a single out of his wallet, signing both sides, and tearing it in two. The witness then introduced into evidence an item he had been holding for eight years, half a dollar bill bearing the signature *"Tom Frank May."*

Despite the discouraging words he heard at the BBC office that day, Joe explained, he had decided to use the "TO DO" list—not as a plan, however, but as a "prop." Attempting to draw on lessons he had learned at "Ron Levin's School of Fraud and Con," he arrived at the Peck Drive duplex shortly after noon on June 5, Joe said, and told Ron a story of some "heavy players" who had been backing the BBC since Chicago. Either Levin paid what he owed, Joe remembered warning, or "'they're going to come down on you like a ton of bricks.'" Ron, though, scoffed: "He said, 'You and that [the seven pages] get out of here' . . . So I said, 'Well, you better look at them, and I just dropped them on the table, and spun and left."

Later that same afternoon, Levin stopped by the BBC office to review the Microgenesis contract, Joe recalled, and they scheduled a "late dinner" for the next evening. When he arrived at the Peck Drive duplex on June 6, Joe said, Ron's attitude was very different from the day before: Levin suddenly was quite cooperative, signing the contract and writing out a check on his Swiss account without the slightest haggling. After their business was concluded, however, Joe recalled, Ron acted "like he wanted me off his hands. I got the message and decided to leave pretty quick."

Joe's account of Pittman's trip to New York and arrest at the Plaza Hotel reiterated Jim's own claim that he had been assigned to act as Levin's bodyguard (and as Hunt's spy) during Ron's negotiations with his "principals." The trip to London he had been planning for weeks, Joe said. The only surprise was Dean's announcement that Levin's Swiss check had not been honored. Dean told him the evening he returned to L.A. that the check not only had been returned NSF, but by a wide margin, said Joe, which was what made Karny's story about the four of them checking Ron's post office box so absurd.

There was trouble again, Joe explained, when the rest of the BBC learned the Levin check had bounced: "David May, Mr. Eisenberg again, Jeff Raymond, Steve Taglianetti, that little war party started talking around the office. And I heard about it immediately, about the fact that I was simply unfit to be running things." He and Dean and Jim paid a surprise visit one evening to the Gardena plant, Joe recalled, where they discovered another "To Do" list—torn into small pieces—in one of the wastebaskets. Dean and he pieced the paper together with Scotch tape, Joe said, and recognized the choppy grammar as Dave May's. The two items at the top of the list were "Talk to SEC" and "New Browning Agreement."

The three Shadings had decided the only answer was to counter one threat with another, Joe explained, and began with a "hoax" aimed at Tom May: "I told him I had knocked off Ron Levin in New York. Here they were trying to muscle in on the machines by behaving basically like minor hoods. And we were going to try and talk to them like minor hoods. Scare them."

Later, as Dean had said, Tom was included in discussions of plans for the June 24 meeting and helped pick Evan as the next person who would be told of the Levin murder. The whole idea was premised on his certainty, and Dean's, that word would get around very quickly, Joe explained: "I believed Taglianetti would tell Eisenberg in a hot minute, and that Jeff Raymond, if not his own brother, would tell David May immediately."

It was not easy now to explain his actions, Joe conceded: "This thing gets pretty convoluted, but the situation was, here we had a ploy or a hoax that we wanted to put over on a target audience. We were telling our friends, and using them, basically, to demonstrate our sincerity. The people that we liked, like Jon Allen and Evan Dicker, the fact that they weren't let in on it, and the fact that they responded like real people would in real time . . . was part of our staging." Essential to their plan as well, Joe added, was that no one in the Eisenberg group could go to the police because of the stolen car operation.

He had believed then he needed only another month, Joe recalled, to conclude negotiations with Kilpatrick and collect the six-million-dollar payment due when the Microgenesis/UFOI/Saturn merger went through. Also, Steve Lopez's people were supposed to be arriving from Singapore in August. "I had a short period of time to go," Joe explained, "and didn't need Browning defecting."

An absolutely devastating blow to his hopes, however, had been delivered on July 27. He called Kilpatrick that afternoon to ask if the revised contracts had been signed, Joe remembered, and the Colorado man explained he had become convinced of Bruce Swartout's prior claim on the Cyclotron: A deal might still be possible, Kilpatrick said, but the six-million-dollar payment was out of the question. All at once, everything seemed to be crashing down around him, Joe recalled. He invited Dean for a midnight drive up the Pacific Coast Highway, out past Zuma to Point Mugu and told his old friend it was time to face the facts, which were as follows: "That we had obviously overestimated ourselves. That we weren't as talented as we thought. That we didn't have as much insight into people as we thought. That the small lies that we had started with had become bigger and bigger lies. And that we were beginning to look suspiciously like Jerry Eisenberg— which I thought was just the worst . . . I said, 'All the people that we have been surrounded with from the beginning, probably because we are like this ourselves, have been scammers.' Ron Levin, Mr. Dow, Bruce Swartout, and now Kilpatrick . . . I said, 'Like basically attracts like. It's time we looked in the mirror. This is us.'"

Before going further, Joe wanted the jury to possess a deeper understanding both of his own relationship with Dean and of Dean's place in the BBC. Prior to the appearance of Lisa Marie Sobel, Joe explained, he and Dean had discussed almost daily the subject of Karny's sexual insecurity. Because he had elected not to mention the Hollywood homicide, Joe's plans to play up Dean's "personal problems" were largely abandoned, but he attempted to slip them in edgewise, explaining to the jury that after his rejection by Claudia Stillman, Dean had confided some incidents from his childhood that he feared might have "marked" him. He convinced his friend that what Claudia had done "wasn't necessarily a demonstration of some terrible inadequacy in him," Joe explained, but this success only resulted in Dean's obsession with the messenger rather than the message. He made the situation worse, Joe admitted, by tailoring Dean's position in the BBC to Karny's ego structure: "Dean loved—*loved*—the idea of the BBC [and] his role in it, which was sort of like the roving minstrel philosopher." Dean, in turn, helped him recover when he lost confidence in his ability to lead the BBC, Joe said. This happened for the first time when he returned from Chicago in 1982 and for the last time during that drive up PCH in 1984.

As he prepared to broach the subject of Hedayat Eslaminia, Joe exploited his two tremendous advantages: One, Reza's testimony could not be used to impeach him, and two, the jury was not going to believe a word Eisenberg said about anything. He had met the younger Eslaminia along with the rest of the BBC on July 7, 1984, at Evan Dicker's birthday party, Joe said. When he and Reza got a chance to talk privately a few days later, Hedayat's son boasted that his father, while no longer wealthy, remained a very influential man among expatriate Persians, many of whom *had* been able to transfer their wealth to this country. Reza said he could offer the BBC an immediate opportunity to meet some of these wealthy Iranians, Joe recalled, explaining that his father had asked him to locate a safe meeting place for his anti-Khomeini political group "Gamma" in Southern California. Ben Dosti apparently had proposed that the BBC "play hosts" to this gathering. He regarded the idea as "dubious," Joe said, but Ben's enthusiasm had been infectious. Dean joined in by "pointing out that I had a very good track record of closing people on investments," Joe explained: He agreed to go along, but only if Ben took charge of the project.

Jim Pittman was assigned to handle security for the meeting and went north to consult with Mr. Eslaminia. After returning to L.A., Jim said he had swept Hedayat's home for bugs and discovered that the phone line was tapped, Joe recalled, which impressed the Iranian tremendously. In fact, meeting Pittman was what convinced Hedayat that the BBC could handle the logistics of the Gamma meeting.

He had flown north to consult with Mr. Eslaminia personally on July 26, Joe recalled, in the Sky Room at the Belmont condominium complex. It had been an awkward meeting, however: Mr. Eslaminia didn't speak English, and Joe knew just enough Farsi to say, "Salaame Agha-Ye Eslaminia."

Dean returned to Los Angeles from *his* meeting with Mr. Eslaminia the next day carrying ten thousand dollars in cash and spent much of it during his shopping trip in Hollywood. Joe denied, however, that any hand-cuffs or mouthgags had been purchased and explained that Dean bought the straitjacket (for which there was a receipt) as a challenge to Jim, who boasted he could wriggle out of one, just like Harry Houdini.

The idea for removing Hedayat from his home in a trunk, Joe explained, was Pittman's idea. Jim said it was a technique he had used back east, when he was working for a concert promoter, smuggling musicians into their hotels hidden in speaker cases.

They left Los Angeles for Belmont on the evening of July 29. By the next morning, though, Ben had become ill, Joe recalled, so it was Dean who helped carry the loaded trunk from the condo to the pickup that after-noon. Hedayat was out of the trunk within minutes after they left Belmont, Joe said, and rode the first leg of the drive to Los Angeles in the back of the U-Haul with Dean. He drove the pickup, Joe added, but lost the U-Haul, which was driven by Jim, because Ben had needed to make a number of rest room stops.

After dropping Ben off at the Manning between 10 and 11 P.M, he drove to the Beverly Glen house, where Dean and Hedayat were waiting. Because they both spoke French, it had been decided Karny would stay with Mr. Eslaminia, Joe explained. When he and Dean were alone, however, they spoke briefly about the second trunk Hedayat had asked them to carry in the U-Haul: Both of them had noticed a smell, Joe said, and he suggested that Dean take a look inside the trunk if he got a chance.

He went home and got into bed with Brooke, Joe said, but was awakened at about 4 A.M. by a phone call. It was Dean, who "told me to get over there fast" and "said he would explain when I got there." Just as he pulled into the driveway at the Beverly Glen house, Joe recalled, Dean came dashing out the front door and jumped into the Jeep's passenger seat: "He seemed real happy, though in a weird sort of way. Like, feverish happy, you know. And he said, 'We're millionaires.'" The second trunk had been full of money, Dean explained: "'Millions,' he said. 'And drugs. And Hedayat took a dive down the stairs, and he's dead.'" When he realized Dean was serious, Joe said, he jumped out of the Jeep and ran toward the house. Just inside the front door, on the tile of the foyer, he found Hedayat Eslaminia, "looking very dead." He checked for a pulse, Joe said, but couldn't find one and attempted mouth-to-mouth resuscitation. It was then he noticed the strip of cloth wound around Hedayat's neck: "I turned to Dean and I said, 'What the fuck happened here?'"

He waited until Hedayat went to take a shower, Dean said, then opened the trunk, which had been left at the top of the stairs. Inside were several paper bags; he looked in one and found not only several thick packets of U.S. currency in large-denomination bills but also a pistol, a pair of handcuffs, and a sheaf of papers written in Farsi. He closed the lid then and waited until Hedayat went to bed and began to snore, Dean said, before returning to examine the contents of the trunk more thoroughly. "All of a sudden, though, he felt something was wrong, because the sound, the snoring, had changed," Joe explained. "And so he turned around and looked down the hallway towards the master bedroom. And there was Hedayat standing in the hall, making a snoring sound, looking straight at him." According to Dean, Hedayat charged at him then, caught him by one arm, slapped his face several times, and somehow managed to close one side of the handcuffs from the trunk around Dean's right wrist. Panicked, Dean said, he began to fight back and in the ensuing scuffle sent Hedayat tumbling head first to the foot of the stairs, where he lay unconscious. He decided to get the hell out of there at that point, Dean said, but Hedayat came to and grabbed his leg as he headed for the door. "Dean got into this kind of fight with Hedayat where he was trying to get him off his leg, and was dragging him along," Joe explained. "And he was hitting him with his hands that had this handcuff on it . . . Dean started kicking him, trying to get him off of him, because the guy was screaming, just crazy, mad, and Dean was panicked. And one of these kicks, or something that Dean did to him, knocked him out again." Dean believed he had killed the man this time, Joe explained, and ran to his car, drove to a pay phone, then called the Manning. When Dean returned to the Beverly Glen house, however, Eslaminia once again had recovered consciousness and began screaming at the top of his lungs for the police. "So Hedayat—well, Dean said he hit him on the head with this tennis racket," Joe recalled, "and that Hedayat went down, and then he started kicking him again like he had before, to knock him out, and that at that point, he decided that Hedayat was better off dead. And he took the cord off some pajamas—not some pajamas, this robe—and strangled Hedayat with it. He said it was about that point that I showed up."

Joe's command of the courtroom had deteriorated steadily during this day of his testimony. His voice grew fainter and fainter; at least three jurors wore expressions of incredulity.

The witness did not look at the panel, though, as he pressed forward with his story. Dean wanted to talk about what to do with the money and how to get rid of Eslaminia's body, Joe explained, but "I said, 'Look, forget about the money. Forget about the drugs. Don't even think about that. That's not our problem. Our problem is survival . . . you murdered this guy. This place is just lousy with evidence. I'd hate to see what the police could do to this place the way it stands now. We have got to think of some explanation, some way of playing this off.'" They sat on couches just feet from Hedayat's corpse, Joe recalled; that part of Karny's story was true: "I was trying to be logical. I was trying to get my mind back. I was trying to think. And so I said, 'Let's just brainstorm. What are the options?' And the ones I saw were: Call the police on it right as it is, that was one; number two was, change the evidence, so the police saw a different situation . . . but [Dean] was criticizing every option that I came up with. And it was getting real acrimonious." Each of his suggestions, Dean pointed out, involved bringing in the police, meaning he would be charged with manslaughter at the very least. Dean told him the entire situation was his fault, Joe recalled, "that I had strolled into his life, got involved in all this high-tone trading and multi-million-dollar deals, and created all this pressure. That I had asked him to look in the trunk."

The two of them went back and forth for the next hour and a half, Joe recalled, until "I grabbed him by the neck and pushed him up against the wall, and said, 'Listen, you little idiot, the BBC is not worth it. None of this is worth it. This is over. This is where it ends for me . . . I'm not going a single step further in this nightmare . . . I have had enough of thinking that I was responsible, and thinking that I could handle things. This is just too much for me. And I'm out of here.'"

Dean, in tears, begged him not to leave, Joe said, but he walked out anyway and got all the way to the door of 1505 before realizing "it was a hell of a time to bug out on a friend. Whether drunk, sober, right, wrong, indifferent, Dean Karny had been my best buddy up to that time. When he returned to the Beverly Glen house, however, Dean was gone, the only sign of his departure two lines scraped into the tiles of the foyer. "I thought Dean had dragged this trunk out," Joe explained, "and the truck was gone. So I went back home."

Dean arrived at the Third Street suites at about noon on June 7, Joe recalled: "I apologized to him, because I had basically been torturing myself over the last six or so hours, about having left Dean in the lurch, and not having gone with him to Soledad, or wherever he was planning on going." He had decided he *was* responsible, at least in part, for his friend's state of mind, Joe explained: "I mean, Dean killed the guy, but he was not a homicidal maniac." Dean at first claimed he had buried Eslaminia's body in the Mojave Desert, Joe recalled, but admitted finally that he had simply rolled the corpse down a hillside in Soledad Canyon. When he went back to the Beverly Glen house to empty the trunk, Dean said, what he found wasn't the millions he imagined, but only about four hundred thousand dollars, as well as eight packages of opium, which explained the smell.

Joe's story unfolded from there without much deviation from the testimony offered by other witnesses: Jim and Ben were told that Hedayat had died of a heart attack in transit; the search for Mr. Eslaminia's assets that ensued was Reza's idea; the Shadings had no choice but to play along.

The disintegration of the BBC was nearly complete after the Mays and Jeff Raymond absconded with the Cyclotrons, Joe recalled. "I was numb in this period of time," he explained. "It was just resignation . . . I just had to keep doing everything I could until I couldn't do anything more." It was true that he and Evan Dicker had entered the Mays' apartment after they disappeared, Joe said, and true also that he had heard the message left by a "Les Zoeller" on the twins' answering machine. He phoned Zoeller's number the next day, Joe said, and was answered by a person who said, "Robbery-Homicide." "It sent shivers down me," he recalled.

Easily the most disturbing result of his arrest by the Beverly Hills Police in September of 1984, Joe told the jury, was how his best friend took the news. "Lauren Raab told me that Dean Karny had got the shakes, and an extremely violent emotional reaction to hearing I had been arrested," Joe explained. He and Dean met for dinner at the Old World, after Karny conceived the idea that his friends had talked to the police. "I tried to assure him that I hadn't," Joe recalled. "He just said, 'It doesn't fit. It doesn't fit with the facts, and you know it, Joe. And now you are lying to me. I can't get anything straight out of Ben . . . I know what's going on here; you are all separating from me, cutting away.' I said, 'No, Dean. The opposite is going on. You are the one that's withdrawing.'"

He still did not imagine that Dean himself might go to the police, Joe said, but became concerned after the second arrest in October, when Brooke reported that the cache of cash in 1206—more than one hundred thousand dollars—was missing. By phone, he confronted Dean, whose response was that "he was going to need all the resources he could gather to deal with his problem," Joe recalled.

He and Dean spoke over the phone several times while he was in jail, Joe said, mostly about Karny's concern that the police would connect the disappearance of Ron Levin to the disappearance of Hedayat Eslaminia. "[Dean] said, 'Don't you recall that the last person with the elder Sam was Jim?'" Joe recalled. "And, you know, I kind of paused and thought about it for a while, and said, 'That's not the way I recall it at all, Dean.' And there was a pause on his side. Then he said, 'Well—how about Ben?' And I said, 'Dean, you know, I'm just going to tell them what I recall.'"

And "that," Joe added, "was the last conversation I had with Dean Karny."

By the time Vance concluded his cross-examination, six weeks had passed since Joe took the stand. It seemed like six years to the jury. "Oh, my God, Vance is asking the same question for the tenth time," David Saperstein wrote in his spiral notebook. "It was excruciating," the IBM man explained, "going over Joe's story point by point, with no apparent purpose. It made you really dislike Vance, even though he's a very nice person. And that played into Joe's abilities. Because Joe only hit those points he wanted you to know."

On October 14, 1992, the day the defense rested its case, Joe would agree with the prosecution on just one key point: "Credibility," he affirmed, "is the key issue."

Vance and Gordnier were offered one last chance to prove the defendant a liar in the rebuttal phase of the trial. On the witness stand, Hunt had provided the prosecution with at least a dozen opportunities for impeachment of his testimony. Joe admitted lying during the Cantor Fitzgerald depositions but swore he had told the truth under oath on all other occasions. The transcript of his testimony during October of 1983 at the trial of Ryan Hunt and Frank Mingarella in Los Angeles Municipal Court, however, was replete with perjury. Vance and Gordnier, though, had no idea such a trial had taken place. John Troelstrup, Ed Donlan, and Tom Utrata all could have testified to Joe's dishonesty during proceedings before the Chicago Mercantile Exchange, but none of these three were contacted by the attorney general's office. Joe's story of his hiring at and departure from Peat Marwick might have been used against him to devastating effect had Terry Dibble been called to the stand, but Vance and Gordnier never spoke to Dibble. Joe's account of the "TO DO" list's preparation was not the same one he had planned to tell in 1987; according to Rudy Durand, Hunt's story then was going to be that the list was part of a movie treatment on which he and Ron Levin had collaborated. Arthur Barens, in fact, had tested this version on reporters only a few months before the Santa Monica trial. The state offered not a single scientific witness to refute the testimony of Joe's experts. "And they should have brought Dean back at the end of the trial," Joan Dick observed. "We really needed to hear from him again."

The attorney general's office, though, which had been prosecuting this case for eight years, at a cost that was well into the millions of dollars, concluded that the best rebuttal witness they could bring to court in Redwood City was Hunt's former debate coach, Ted Woods. For Joe, it was a delicious moment.

After more than two decades at the Harvard School, Woods had retired the previous June, his departure coincident with Harvard's decision to merge with the leading private girls' school in Los Angeles, Westlake. The old coach was perfectly clear and entirely inaccurate on direct examination: He had "terminated" Joseph Gamsky from the Harvard School debate squad, Woods testified, because "in one of the debate tournaments, he falsified some evidence and was challenged." This had occurred, Coach Woods added, during Gamsky's junior year at Harvard.

Joe could scarcely contain his delight when the witness was turned over to the defense. "It's not often," he noted, smiling, "that you get an opportunity to cross-examine your debate teacher." He then took the witness back to August of 1974 and the Western Forensics Institute at USC: Didn't Mr. Woods recall that the accusation of falsifying evidence had been lodged that summer, after Joe's freshman year at the Harvard School? Woods denied this. "Sir, isn't it true that it wasn't until two years later, when I was having a dispute with you about who should be debate squad captain, that [an assistant coach] told you I had been involved in that falsification?" Joe asked. There were rumors of cheating earlier, but it was Joe's junior year of high school, Woods insisted, when Hunt had been caught falsifying evidence; he remembered it very well because no such thing had happened before at the Harvard School.

Didn't Coach Woods recall his participation in the district tournament at the end of his junior year? Joe asked. He did not, Woods answered. Joe described the scene: It was in the amphitheater at Pepperdine University, "with a raised platform, a number of seats; the judges were sitting up in back—there were four of them." Woods blinked: "It could be," he said, then shook his head and insisted again that Joe did not debate after being dismissed from the debate squad early in his junior year. Joe had not enjoyed himself so completely since Eisenberg was on the stand. "Who was the debate squad captain in the year that I was dismissed from the debate program?" he asked. "Student by the name of Rick Berg," Woods recalled. "How is it that you recall *Ricky* Berg's name?" asked Joe. "Did there arise a controversy at the school about how the debate squad captain should be chosen?" "Yes, at your instigation," Woods answered, and the old antipathy flashed. "Because you were very unhappy that you weren't chosen . . . among other things you circulated a thirteen-page petition . . . the petition, to my knowledge, came after you were dismissed from the squad." It was getting better by the minute. As Coach Woods had taught him almost twenty years earlier, Joe essayed a consolidation of the evidence: "So it's your recollection, Mr. Woods, that I was kicked off the debate squad for falsification, and then I wrote up a petition?" "That's my recollection," Woods answered.

John Vance had served Joe a chance to end the trial with one last smashing victory. The defense's own rebuttal case was presented by former Harvard School debaters who recalled that Joe, indeed, had admitted falsifying evidence at the USC Debate Institute in the summer after his high school freshman year: None of the other boys on the squad had considered this much of a scandal, though, since virtually everyone falsified evidence. They remembered that Joe Gamsky had debated all during his junior year at Harvard and that Joe was still on the debate squad at the beginning of his senior year. They recalled the petition Joe had written that fall, demanding not that he be chosen to replace Rick Berg as captain but that the debaters be allowed to elect a five-man board. They described the peculiar animus Coach Woods seemed to bear toward Gamsky and the shock waves it sent when the coach—acting purely out of personal malice, most of those who signed the petition thought—dismissed Joe from the squad.

By the time Joe finished, the jurors were seething with contempt for the prosecution. "What a mistake to put the old debate coach on," said Harriet Kumetat. "Joe made a complete fool of him."

John Vance made a fool of himself with the prosecution's final argument. After a prologue that went on for eighteen pages in the trial transcript and ended with most of the jurors stifling yawns, Vance acknowledged that his case hung on Dean Karny. It was Karny who established the *corpus delicti* of Joe Hunt's crimes, Vance explained, and "once you find that Mr. Karny's testimony is corroborated, the People have carried their burden of proof." When Vance then proceeded to "corroborate" Karny repeatedly with the testimony of Jerry Eisenberg, however, the jurors were horrified. "You had to ask yourself, 'Was he in the room when the tape was played?'" Saperstein said.

The prosecutor at least seemed to realize the weight jurors would give the "expert testimony" they had heard. "Mr. Hunt has enlisted science in the aid of escape from the consequences of his actions," Vance said. "The old adage goes, 'Figures don't lie, but liars figure.'" "We have to judge science," Vance went on, then answered the computer model with another old adage: "'Garbage in, garbage out.' If what's going into the computer isn't correct, then it doesn't have any meaning." Saperstein took umbrage: "Berry had his model right there, and they just accepted it," explained the jury's own scientific expert. "They never asked him to vary the conditions, to use different data. And it would have been easy."

Vance did propose in his final argument some plausible factors that might have modulated the computer's calculations: What if the trunk lid had been damaged when Hedayat Eslaminia was being shoved inside? There might have been holes in the panels of the U-Haul van the BBC Boys rented on that day in 1984; even a worn set of shock absorbers could have affected air flow. Good science, Vance observed, required "peer review" and "there's been no such work on the model that Dr. Berry has produced." The jurors looked at one another: Wasn't it the prosecution's job to produce such "work"?

Vance would have a second chance with the jury in his rebuttal argument, but for Joe there was just one shot, and he made the most of it, talking nonstop for almost two days. He began with the absurdity of Vance's statement, "In all the evidence you have heard, there's very little controversy." Hearing this, he felt trapped in a Kafka novel, Joe said: "You are accused of killing a man who's seen at various places around the world [and] the prosecutor doesn't even mention [those who made the sightings] in closing argument."

Despite what Vance and Gordnier were attempting, however, never before had he so appreciated what it meant to be an American, Joe said. In the USA, "we don't spend all this money for one individual," he explained. "We spend all this money on a principle"—the search for truth. John Vance by his own admission had based the prosecution case on Dean Karny, Joe observed, and argued that if Dean Karny was corroborated, a guilty verdict should result. By the same token, though, "if reasonable doubt has been left in your mind about this man's credibility, then the appropriate thing is an acquittal, not only for Joe Hunt, but for the community."

Before he addressed the subject of Karny, Joe asked the jury to consider the testimony they had heard from the rest of the BBC. He wrote on a blackboard the names of each Boy who appeared on the prosecution's list of witnesses. He had bunched them because "the gentlemen are sticking together," Joe explained: Back in 1984, "they were getting together while the world was falling down around their ears, and they were shaping how they were going to cope with it."

Joe made his defense explicit when he quoted Leviticus: "And the goat shall bear upon him all their iniquities."

Hadn't it been fascinating, Joe asked the jurors, to watch how Tom May, who testified with such self-assurance on direct, "crumbled" during cross? As he itemized Tom's false statements, Joe again and again offered the twin as a paradigm for the rest of the BBC: "It's amazing how these gentlemen are able to get away with this sort of outright sleazy behavior on the witness stand," he observed, "and nobody just gets ahold of some chain and yanks them off." Several jurors nodded as Joe reminded them how Tom tried to "wriggle away" from one direct question after another. "I pity those guys in the BBC," Joe said, and looked each of the jurors in the eye. "I paid a pretty price for getting straightened out, but it was absolutely worth paying. And I don't care what the circumstances were. I was never a guy that wanted to be wrong or far off. And I'm comfortable with one thing: That is, I got rewarranted. I got it right. This guy is obviously living in a world where everybody gives in. He never backs off." More nodding. Tom even had been able to sell his hero-for-the-eighties story to NBC, Joe reminded the jurors. He put the twins' ITC contract on an overhead projector, then pointed to the paragraph that promised to portray the Mays as innocent victims of Joe Hunt, their bravery resulting in the villain's downfall. Tom had been "able to project the fantasy onto the big screen through the mini-series," Joe observed, "and he was going to do so in court. And the fellow is so unthinking and so shallow, ultimately, that he never considered that he was going to have to face cross-examination."

Joe had saved the best for last, of course: "Let's talk about Eisenberg. You know, it's easy to talk about these guys. It's not hard work. Eisenberg. This man [Vance] had the presumption to mention Jerry Eisenberg's name in his closing argument, as if he was somebody solid who has testimony of substantial value." Joe read aloud a series of excerpts from the transcript of the "Eisenberg tape," then drew lines through each name on the blackboard. "My reasonable doubt number one," Joe called the BBC Boys. "They are properly crossed off, properly eliminated from your consideration."

The characters of the two men he was accused of murdering were equally corrupt, if considerably more complex, Joe observed. In *The Screwtape Letters,* "C. S. Lewis says nothing helped towards a man's damnation so much as the discovery that almost anything he wants to do can be done not only without disapproval, but with the admiration of his fellows, if it can only get itself treated as a joke," Joe told the jurors, and Ron Levin understood this better than anyone he had ever met. He reminded the jurors of Ron's good reasons for disappearing, then scoffed at the state's claim that Ron would never abscond without contacting his mother. He bore Mrs. Levin no malice, Joe assured the jury: "Willfully false? No. She's a person in this condition, where we backfill and justify the wrongs that we have done, because we can't stand to look at it straight."

His strongest defense of all against the charge that he had murdered Ron Levin, of course, was that the alleged victim "has been seen alive by sensible, non-partisan witnesses." Mr. Vance had asked them to distinguish between possible doubt and reasonable doubt, Joe reminded the jurors: "If I was saying Ron Levin might be out there, well, that's an illusory statement. That's the area of possible or imaginary. But if I bring in five credible witnesses that say they saw him . . . then I'm not talking about a possible or imaginary doubt, am I? I'm talking about a doubt for which there is a reason."

Joe began his consideration of the chief witness against him by quoting Coleridge ("Experience tells us that the first offense of a coward is to point the finger at another"), then Seneca ("All cruelty springs from weakness"). Dean Karny himself had testified that in a good lie "the plot line derives from the circumstance," Joe noted, and the jury should bear in mind that Dean was a person who "can think under pressure. I mean, he managed to pass the bar exam and to complete law school during the midst of this tumult." Karny's story probably had seemed perfectly plausible, Joe allowed, until they heard Dr. Ralph Goldman, speaking "from the Olympia light of his experience," denounce it as preposterous.

He hadn't always been completely truthful himself, of course, Joe admitted: "I lied to my investors . . . I take personal responsibility for that, and I agree and believe that it is a disastrous reflection upon my character . . . but understand one thing, that at the point those investors got lied to—and there's never been any other proof in this case—their money had been lost legitimately at Cantor Fitzgerald. So they were not being lied to because somebody had stolen from them, but because I couldn't stand to face them with [the truth]."

His own story was no less fantastic than Karny's, Joe conceded, but "remember, Hedayat Eslaminia is no simple guy." He recalled the testimony of George Beaudoux, which revealed Hedayat as "a man you have to place in the context of a le Carré novel." Add up all that was known of Eslaminia, from the dazzling to the disgusting, and the aggregate effect was mind-numbing: "How do you understand it and appreciate this man?" Joe asked. "He comes from an entirely different world."

Joe again met each juror's gaze, then quoted a Chinese philosopher translated by Thomas Merton: "'The hanged man cannot cut himself down. God cuts the thread.' That's also true in this situation. I am powerless to remove myself." Still, Joe said, he couldn't help but feel "that the clouds have lifted and the circumstance is less extreme." He thought perhaps it was the way the trial had ended, with Coach Woods's appearance on the witness stand and the sense that somehow Joseph Gamsky had come full circle. "That's where it all started for me," he recalled. "The point where I went from a young man on the way to an Ivy League college with the rest of my classmates, to a person who was troubled and somehow ended up founding something like the BBC . . . so it's interesting that that energy returns to me so late in this trial through an unexpected witness, Coach Woods. And that even that little kink in my life is straightened out and the truth gets known."

As he faced their judgment, Joe told the jury, he felt no self-pity. "How much punishment is appropriate for the sort of lying I did to my investors back then?" he asked. "I don't know. I can't say five years is enough, or ten, or twenty. But I find extremely strange one thing: No one's ever charged me with a crime I committed."

As for the crime with which he *had* been charged, Joe finished, "I am innocent . . . I did not kill Hedayat Eslaminia. I ask that you acquit me."

32

BY THE END OF FINAL ARGUMENTS ON OCTOBER 29, 1992, THE JURORS HAD BEEN on duty for more than seven months. The Hunt trial, as the *Times Tribune* reported the next morning, was "the longest-running and most expensive in San Mateo County history."

During its thirty-one weeks of service thus far, the jury had followed the rise of Bill Clinton as if in dispatches from a neighboring country. At that distance, the Arkansan's most amazing gift seemed to be a knack for turning one incipient scandal after another on its head. By the time it dawned on his opponent that a past that included pot smoking and extramarital sex no longer disqualified a person for the presidency, George Bush was reduced to calling the Democratic nominee a "bozo," and his own defeat was a fait accompli. The signal moments of the campaign—Clinton facing down the infidelity charges on *60 Minutes* with his wife at his side and blowing sax on *Arsenio Hall*—announced, if nothing else, that baby boomers were no longer just the target audience of prime-time television but of presidential politics as well.

Any sense among the Hunt trial jurors that they had missed a changing of the guard was mitigated between April and October by an exceptional spirit of camaraderie. Curtis Hackworth had sat on two other juries in San Mateo County and said none was as compatible as this one. "Before deliberations, we were a friendly little group," agreed Harriet Kumetat. "We had birthday parties, picnics in the park." He had gone into the jury room "looking to get this thing over pretty quick," said Hackworth, a feeling that was intact after an informal discussion of the final arguments. The jurors were unanimous in their opinion that John Vance had been a poor prosecutor and expressed considerable criticism also of Judge Hahn. "So weak," said Joan Dick. "He and Vance let Joe run the courtroom."

Yet Hackworth and Kumetat each anticipated that there would be only one "not guilty" voter on the first ballot, Sandra Achiro. Her problems with Curtis and Harriet were due mostly to the age difference, said Sandra, a slim, blond, twenty-eight-year-old dental assistant. "Everything I would say, they would either shun me down or get annoyed at what I said," she explained. "Or they would think that I'm so immature that I just don't understand what I'm saying."

That first morning, an exchange of words between Hackworth and Achiro grew so heated that the realtor traded seats with another juror. The next morning, the panel decided to take a straw vote—"not official, but just how you feel," Hackworth explained—that came out ten to two for guilty. The woman with whom the realtor had traded seats, Helen SoRelle, was the other "not guilty" voter. Since these were two of the three "least intellectual" members of the panel, as one juror put it, the "guilty" voters believed they might be worn down. When the floor was opened to discussion, however, "I was stunned by what I was hearing," Hackworth recalled. "David Saperstein in particular was saying that he was having problems voting guilty officially because he didn't feel the prosecution had proved its case."

The jury's foreman, high school algebra teacher Harry Morrow, suggested they discuss everything about the case *but* Joe Hunt. "So we spent the next two and a half weeks talking about the witnesses and their credibility," Hackworth recalled. Dean Karny was once again the most crucial prosecution witness, and again even those jurors who believed him admitted that Karny's culpability created a moral dilemma. "We all felt he was the person most responsible for Eslaminia's death," said Hackworth. "Knowing he had gotten off with immunity made us very angry."

Joan Dick dismissed the scientific testimony offered to discredit Dean as "a smoke screen," but the other jurors—even those who voted guilty—conceded to Joe's experts. She didn't dispute any of the testimony by Dr. Goldman and Dr. Berry, Harriet Kumetat said, yet saw no reason to change her vote: "I thought Dean Karny was confused, in a state, freaked out, and lost all concept of time. I explained that to the other jurors and I got back, 'He's lying. He's willfully lying.' Sandra kept saying it."

"Dean's stories didn't connect," Achiro explained. "Saying he didn't know about any money coming in and out of the company. Well, there were checks with his signature on them." Karny's credibility was hardly enhanced by the witnesses called to corroborate him. "The other BBC Boys were jokes," said Achiro. "When we went in the jury room, we put their names down, and then we just threw them out the window. We didn't even consider them."

The NBC miniseries, which Joe had feared would prejudice the jury against him, turned out to be an enormous boon to his defense. Once jurors decided that the agreement to tell the Mays' version of the BBC story had thoroughly corrupted the network's program, they became both deeply offended by and profoundly suspicious of any witness who had participated in the production. Joe's purported statement when he was handed the seven pages during the interrogation after his first arrest—"I don't know anything about these," according to Les Zoeller—could not be reconciled with the account Joe gave on the witness stand. The jurors were inclined to take a police officer's word over that of a convicted murderer, but "when you learned that Zoeller had been involved in the miniseries," Saperstein explained, "it tended to make you not like him very much. Or trust him either."

Though the jury's duty was to deliver a verdict on the charges involving the death of Hedayat Eslaminia, "Ron Levin became the crux of the matter," Saperstein recalled. "Because if Joe didn't kill Levin, then it doesn't come over that he killed Hedayat." Hackworth put it differently: "There were people who voted not guilty on Eslaminia because they felt [Joe] had been wrongly convicted in the Levin case."

Saperstein was especially critical of the prosecution's failure to present Levin as a character they knew and understood: "We were told by Gordnier and Vance about how Ron Levin never would have left Beverly Hills, was known by all, would have been seen by thousands if he was back in town, but they never brought in real people to establish that." Joe Hunt, on the other hand, delivered five witnesses who claimed to have seen Levin alive. "All these people say they saw Ron Levin alive," Saperstein explained. "If it was one or two, it would be easier to dismiss." Harriet Kumetat compared the testimony of these witnesses to "Elvis sightings." Hackworth tried hardest to explain why he did not believe the people who claimed they had seen Levin alive: "Robbie Robertson thought he'd become a somebody in the news business. Nadia Ghaleb saw him driving down the street; how many times have you thought somebody was somebody else? The story from Greece, I just didn't believe that woman. The Arizona couple, they made a mistake." It was to no avail. "The jury just could not get the Ron Levin case out of their minds," Hackworth recalled.

The testimony of Carol Levin that her son would have contacted her if alive was dismissed by nearly all the jurors. Sandra Achiro put it most unkindly: "Mrs. Levin was a joke. It was a love-hate relationship: She loved him, he hated her."

Hackworth was astonished that a number of jurors said they believed Karen Sue Marmor: "That woman, I just looked at her and knew she wasn't telling the truth." Joe's own description of how the TO DO list had been prepared, however, made even most of those who were leaning toward acquittal uncomfortable. "Not high on my credibility list," admitted Saperstein. Joan Dick, though, was troubled by how the police had come into possession of the TO DO list: "Joe, being as brilliant as he is, why would he leave that behind? Did he leave it behind? Or was it planted there?"

Joe's description of the BBC's deal with Hedayat Eslaminia was even more difficult to swallow than his version of the TO DO list. The absurdity of Hunt's testimony in this regard was what had turned Hackworth into a "guilty" voter: "I started out being very sympathetic toward [Joe]," the realtor explained. "His appearance, his opening statements, were very attractive and persuasive. He really projected being innocent and put upon . . . I remember when Karny came in, I was writing in my notes, 'This doesn't sound right.' But when I heard Hunt's own story, I said, 'This is bullshit.' I don't think that any of us believed it." Even Sandra Achiro admitted doubt, yet insisted Joe's version of Eslaminia's death was "a possibility." Saperstein agreed: "Joe's story was incredible, but so was Hedayat's life."

The IBM man argued that there were elements of fact and fiction in both Hunt's story and Karny's: "Joe tells his story that he hears from Dean in such vivid detail that you think, 'He had to be there,'" Saperstein explained. "Definitely this is a weird story. On the other hand, there are lots of things in Dean's story that are equally weird. Both stories, though, get Hedayat back to the house. Something about the house rings true. You have the feeling something happened there, but we never heard what. It comes down to 'Do you believe Joe's story?' No. 'Do you believe Dean's story?' No. So you have to disregard both stories and just look at the facts."

The jurors became increasingly emotional after their first formal vote, which came out nine to three for acquittal. "Astounded," Kumetat pronounced herself. Joan Dick, who had cast her initial ballot for not guilty, said Saperstein had swayed her and a number of others: "David monopolized the discussion. He kept arguing that [the prosecution case] didn't prove guilt beyond a reasonable doubt. I think he liked having all these people looking up to him." "If the standard had not been reasonable doubt, but just what do you believe, then I would have voted guilty," Saperstein responded. "But to Joe Hunt's credit in picking the jury and to John Vance's discredit in letting Joe pick the jury, we were people who scrupulously applied the letter of the law." The jury's true vote, the IBM man added, "was three for guilty, three for innocent, and six for reasonable doubt."

"I knew there was no hope," said Harriet Kumetat, "when, during our discussion of the 'TO DO' list, David said, 'You know, I'd feel a lot better about voting for conviction if he'd written, "Kill Ron Levin" on it.' David's a well-meaning person, but incredibly naïve and dense in some way."

Saperstein, though, would prove a particularly effective advocate for the scientific testimony offered by the defense. "Dave's a doctor himself, remember," noted Sandra Achiro.

Tensions among the jurors after the first vote ruptured the affinities they had nurtured between April and October. The vote moved from nine–three to eight–four three weeks into deliberations when Joan Dick switched her vote to guilty, but after this both sides became intractable. "The 'not guilty' voters, my big problem was that I just couldn't understand them," Hackworth explained. "I knew Sandra had become infatuated with Joe and that Helen SoRelle had some sort of maternal reaction, but it was awfully hard to get an idea what the others were thinking." Finally the realtor suggested that the jurors discuss how they felt about Joe Hunt. "Everyone but Sandra agreed," he recalled. "We went around the table, and they were saying, 'Well, he's a young guy, his life is wrecked, he's already been in jail for eight years' . . . they just didn't want to vote against this guy. It was a personal thing. He's a nice-looking young guy. He speaks well, he plays to the girls. He's got that cute little smile. They'd come in every morning, and he'd look at each one of them like he was so glad to see them, and they loved it. When I'd ask them to tell me specifically why they didn't think he was guilty, they kept being vague. It was if he had mesmerized these people."

The grand theft charge against Joe seemed the easiest to decide. "We had the evidence, and it was irrefutable," Hackworth explained. "I mean, there was the forged power of attorney and Joe admitted forging it." Yet Achiro and one other juror, Diane Farrar, refused to vote guilty. "Sandra wouldn't say anything, though—she never did when confronted with hard facts. But this was the most pressure applied to her, and it was at that point she broke and ran out of the room: 'I don't want any more to do with this jury.'" Sandra had locked herself in the ladies' room, Harriet Kumetat reported. "But after she thought about it awhile, she came back," Hackworth recalled. "She had to be there to make sure there was no chance for a guilty verdict."

After this, Sandra let Diane Farrar do her talking. Educated and articulate, Farrar's arguments for acquittal frustrated the "guilty" voters almost as completely as Saperstein's. "Diane was telling all these stories about people who were convicted and it was found out twenty years later they weren't guilty," recalled Joan Dick. "It was like she was researching a book."

As exhaustion set in and civility wore away, exchanges between jurors grew increasingly nasty. Conflicts were exacerbated by obvious distinctions of age, class, and education. All three jurors who voted guilty on the first ballot were over the age of sixty and residents of San Mateo County's most affluent community, Hillsborough.

The fractions multiplied when "guilty" voters began to discuss their suspicion that Achiro had been in communication with the defense. "Mostly it was things she said that weren't characteristic of her," explained Kumetat. "During the first week Sandra read this famous proverb about 'It's better to free a hundred guilty men than to convict an innocent one,' or however it goes. And I was startled. It was totally uncharacteristic of her. I mean, this isn't someone who reads. And I wondered where that came from. Because Joe had been using proverbs all through the trial." After the first formal vote, Sandra would take notes on everything the "guilty" voters said, then come back the next day with answers, recalled Joan Dick: "And you knew they weren't hers."

"By the end, it was more the jurors against the jurors than the defense against the prosecution," Hackworth reflected. "The people who were for guilty became very frustrated, so we finally stopped talking. At one point Harriet picked up a newspaper and started reading. Then Sandra sent a note to the judge: 'There's people in here who don't care.'"

The "guilty" voters received stern admonitions on their "duty to deliberate" from Judge Hahn, who sent the panel back into the jury room to try again.

Another note was sent to Hahn on December 8, almost six weeks after the jury had taken the case, informing the judge that Kumetat and Hackworth were meeting privately each morning in the courthouse's law library. She indeed did go to the law library each morning when she arrived at the courthouse, Kumetat told Judge Hahn—to read back issues of the *New Yorker*. Hackworth explained he was using the library to research harbor commission statutes for his business. The scene in the hallway outside while the judge questioned Hackworth and Kumetat convinced Joan Dick that the jury was being tampered with. "It was so obvious," she explained. "The two alternates came up and Sandra told them, 'Don't go away. We might need you.' They wanted to get Harriet and Curt off the jury."

When Hackworth and Kumetat returned to the jury room, the panel agreed to take one last ballot. On December 10, 1992, a front-page story in the *Times Tribune* announced the result: "The longest and costliest trial in San Mateo County history ended Wednesday, after the jury said it was hopelessly deadlocked 8 to 4 in favor of murder defendant Joe Hunt's acquittal."

"SHOCKING" and "STUNNING" read headlines that greeted news of the jury's vote in Los Angeles, where the outcome of Joe's Redwood City trial had been treated as a foregone conclusion. In San Francisco, the *Chronicle*'s headline was "JURORS PLEDGE SUPPORT FOR BILLIONAIRE BOYS DEFENDANT."

After the jury vote was announced, Joe's two staunchest defenders on the panel had headed straight from Judge Hahn's court to the press room on the first floor of the building. "Joe Hunt has good in him," Sandra Achiro told the *Chronicle,* then added, "He should have his wings again and be able to fly." "There were qualities that I saw in him during the trial," Helen SoRelle explained, "an honesty and kindness."

Joe granted a telephone interview to the *Chronicle* in order to thank the "not guilty" voters personally. "Heartwarming" and "rejuvenating" he said of offers to help with his appeal extended by several jurors. "These people are now experts on my case," he explained, "and they have been very helpful with their insights." The suggestion that he had put jurors into some sort of trance Joe dismissed as ridiculous. "There was nothing slick or charismatic about it," he said, "no mask or magnetic emanations coming from me that led to the decision. It was just a very difficult struggle and I was hanging on by my fingernails."

While John Vance was telling reporters outside Judge Hahn's courtroom that he would recommend the state file for a new trial as soon as possible, his boss Ron Bass "paid tribute" to Hunt, as the *Chronicle* put it: "You couldn't help but be impressed by his intelligence and the presentation of the case," Bass said.

In San Mateo County, the expense of the proceedings still was bigger news than the outcome, and Joe's first public statement took this into account: His next trial, should there be one, Joe warned the *Times Tribune,* would be even longer and costlier, since he expected to call thirty or forty new witnesses in addition to those who had testified before this jury. Local taxpayers would "pay for the fact that the state doesn't care about this county's budget," he advised the Palo Alto paper.

The first public official to hit the bait was Bill Schumacher, president of the San Mateo County Board of Supervisors, who informed the *San Mateo Times* that the county had asked the state to send its case south or drop the charges. "They have had their bite of the apple here," explained Schumacher, describing the case against Hunt as "weak." San Mateo County DA Jim Fox, though, admitted moral quandary: "Do lives here," he wondered, "count any less than lives in Los Angeles?"

Joe responded with one more public statement: "You have to ask," he told the same reporter, "whether it's morally correct to continue seeking a conviction when the jury is 8 to 4 for the defendant. They put a tremendous burden on the county."

Judge Hahn had given the attorney general's office until the second week of January to decide whether it would ask for a retrial in Redwood County. Ron Bass did not need that long, announcing on January 5, 1993, that the State of California was dismissing the charges against Hunt related to the abduction and death of Hedayat Eslaminia. The case remained open, pending a "re-investigation," John Vance advised the media, and there was no statute of limitations on murder.

No investigation would change what Joe Hunt had done to the state's case, Doug Gray retorted. The BBC Boys "all were liars," Gray said, and "Dean Karny is profoundly damaged goods."

Vance had until February 12 to inform the court whether the state would continue its prosecution of Jim Pittman in San Mateo County. By the end of January, the prosecutor's confidence in his case was so shaky that he conceded the possibility Joe Hunt had testified truthfully: "We're always open to that," Vance said. The prosecutor would not accept that he had failed in the Hunt trial: the process of justice unfolded according to time-tested logic, Vance insisted, and "the system works every time a jury deliberates."

Doug Gray, though, asserted that incompetent attorneys had been the story at *both* Hunt trials. "As inept as the prosecution was here," he said, "the defense of Joe Hunt in Los Angeles was even more inept." The lawyers were not the only difference between the Santa Monica and Redwood City proceedings, however, added Gray, who offered his highest praise— and Joe Hunt's—for a man who "admitted his bias, then voted his conscience." "David Saperstein is my hero," the attorney said. "He is the kind of person we need to make society function as it should."

Saperstein was feeling more perplexed than proud, however, after an investigator from the state provided him with a partial list of the evidence jurors had not seen during the trial. "You spend eight months of your life on this," the IBM man complained, "and at the end there's so much that's been kept from you." By this time, though, Saperstein already had given further aid and comfort to Joe Hunt. "Joe called me after the trial to say thank you and to ask if I'd be willing to just write down my comments," Saperstein explained. "We talked about how I felt, he wrote it down, in the form of a declaration, which I edited and sent back." All of the other "not guilty" voters had signed declarations as well, submitted as supporting documents for the habeas corpus petition attached to Joe's appeal of his conviction in the Levin case. Each of the eight wrote that they did not believe the state's evidence was sufficient to convict Joe of murdering Ron Levin.

"Oh my God, no!" Harriet Kumetat moaned when she learned of the declarations. "Do they really want to let him out of prison?" Kumetat's perception of Joe had grown ever more dire since the trial's end. "People are always saying that this murderer or that murderer is 'capable of anything,'" she observed, "but Joe Hunt really is." Kumetat's ally Curtis Hackworth admitted he had walked out of Judge Hahn's courtroom a bitter man: "I came into this feeling pretty patriotic about it all, thinking this was my duty, but the longer I sat there, the more I felt like a chump." On the day the jury announced its nonverdict, Hackworth barely could contain his animosity toward the "not guilty" voters. "You wonder how much perspective people have these days," he said, "and how much they care about coming to a correct decision."

Both jurors had been able to unwind a little after the Guiltys party. "That's what we called ourselves, 'the Guiltys,'" Kumetat explained. "We felt like a persecuted minority by the end. We never had an opportunity to talk after the trial and we all just wanted out of there by then, anyway. But about two weeks later we had a party at this Mexican restaurant, and it really helped us all, I think." Over margaritas, the Guiltys read Joe Hunt's letter to Joan Dick.

She was the only "guilty" voter Joe wrote to, Dick explained: "I got it December 18. He starts out, 'You and I have shared many smiles, many thoughts, many feelings.' Like we were intimate. He goes on, 'I feel that in friendship and in life, first impressions are nearly always right. I know you liked me from very early on.' He blames me changing my vote on 'the length of the deliberations,' then writes, 'As I said, I go by first impressions and I will stay with my first impression of you. I liked you then and I like you now.' Like he's forgiving me. He said he knew if we spent one hour in simple conversation outside court that I would have held on to my original impression of him: 'There are so many opportunities in life to misunderstand people.' He said we should have had a chance to get to know each other without 'all the big egos and loud voices.' This is how he ended it: 'May a dawn of joy break across the new morning of the rest of your life.' The guy should write for Hallmark."

While Sandra Achiro denied speaking to Joe during the trial, she readily admitted visiting him on the evening the jury's final vote was reported to Judge Hahn. "My conversation with Joe was wonderful," Sandra said. "You know, he's a boy in a man's body, trapped. I just talked about what I had to go through, and he thanked me for the long hard haul."

When news of the Redwood City jury's vote reached them in Los Angeles, the BBC Boys sounded echoes of the awe he had inspired in them ten years earlier: "A remarkable victory," said Evan Dicker. "I don't know if I was surprised, however. Joe is more than just very smart—he's very brilliant. I always saw him as the most exceptional person I'd ever encountered, and in a lot of ways I still think he is. The most interesting thing to me now is imagining all that he could have been."

Shortly after his transfer back to Folsom Prison in January of 1993, Joe granted an extended interview to Peter Brooke. It was published a month later in *Los Angeles* magazine. Why had the result of the Redwood City trial been treated by the local media as "such a shocking surprise"? Brooke asked first. His previous conviction in the Levin case and the attendant publicity were the main reasons, Joe supposed: the "prejudicial attitudes toward me" were so overwhelming, Joe said, that he had devoted most of his energy during the past few years to "keeping a clear sense of myself." "The government, the media and the environment itself—these cell bars surrounding me—constantly present me with the false accusation that I am a killer," he explained. "That stigma continues to plague me in the press, even now that an eight-to-four jury declared that label to be wrong. The real struggle is not to let one's heart die in the face of such complete rejection."

When he learned that the state had dismissed the charges against him involving Hedayat Eslaminia, Joe went on, "my hands began to shake, so I wrapped them in the waistchain my hands were shackled to. I was emotionally prepared for something else . . . I figured the prosecutors would not be able to accept the loss. These guys have such an investment in declaring me guilty."

His exultation had been constrained, Joe said, by a refocusing of his energies on the appeal in Los Angeles: under his present sentence, he would not even see a parole board until the year 2020. He asked the public to recognize that eight jurors in Redwood City "thought there was no proof that Levin was dead, let alone that I had killed him," Joe explained.

The NBC miniseries that Joe insisted was the main source of the "prejudicial attitudes" toward him had once more become the center of a controversy: The psychiatrist for Lyle and Erik Menendez told police that they were inspired to kill their parents after watching a re-airing of *The Billionaire Boys Club* in July of 1989.

He felt like a real-life character trapped in a work of fiction, Joe said: "I am in jail for a story that was told about Ron Levin being dead. Being a perfect Hollywood cultural commentary of the '80s, the story caught fire, with no one caring what *really* happened. The concept of the Billionaire Boys Club and a yuppie madman—à la Judd Nelson—sold with a tawdry, easy-to-believe sizzle. The reality, up until just recently, got no press."

If granted a retrial on the Levin charges, Brooke asked, would Hunt handle his own defense in Southern California? "You bet I will," Joe said. "If I'd known nine years ago what I know now, I could have proved my innocence then and been a free man today."

His one hesitation about voting not guilty in Redwood City, David Saperstein admitted, had been that "gut level, I was worried he might beat the whole thing, however long it takes. One thing I know about Joe Hunt is that he's gonna stay with this to the end. He isn't a person who gives up."

That inability to turn back or even aside, the insistence that whatever he started must be carried to its logical conclusion, always had been what made Joe so dangerous. Never had he abandoned his belief that a man at large must consider all possibilities, and those who feared his freedom were being forced to recognize that the number of possibilities available to Joe might multiply dramatically during the coming months.

His appeal before the Second District Court now was fully briefed, awaiting a scheduled date for oral arguments. Already there had been discussions between the attorney general's office in Sacramento and the DA's office in Los Angeles about who would handle the "reprosecution," as John Vance termed it, should Joe's arguments prevail. It was not outside the bounds of possibility, of course, that the Los Angeles authorities also would dismiss the murder charges against Joe. The prosecution of Hunt to this point had cost city, state, and county governments more than ten million dollars, and California's present financial crisis was so severe that convicted felons were being released from prison years before their earliest parole dates.

In San Mateo County, the price for Hunt's defense remained a hotter issue than the pending criminal charges against Jim Pittman. The most recent story in the local papers announced that a retired judge had been appointed to review billings submitted by Joe to the private defender's office, with particular emphasis on claims by Tammy Gandolfo. Tammy was not around to answer her accusers in person, having evacuated Redwood City for Folsom, where she rented a house close to the penitentiary and made plans with Joe for the marriage that would permit conjugal visits.

In Los Angeles those who had been tracking Joe longest responded to the rumor that he would be back out on the streets before the end of 1993 with predictions of his future—and theirs—that managed to be at once sunny and chilling. "Joe won't need to kill anymore if they let him out," opined an editor at the *Daily News*. "He's learned he can get what he wants without resorting to murder." Evan Dicker sounded only slightly wishful when he said, "If you released Joe from jail tomorrow, I don't think the first thing he'd do is come after me. I never bought the 'Levin for revenge' motive; I think Joe killed Ron for money—that's what motivated Joe, money and power. So if it was all over and he was out, I don't think he'd want to kill me. Maybe I just hope he wouldn't want to kill me."

On February 10, the State of California announced it was dropping all charges against James Pittman, now thirty-nine, in connection to the death of Hedayat Eslaminia. Jeff Brodey and John Gordnier were "working out the details" of Pittman's release from the San Mateo County Jail, explained John Vance. The state's last leverage was the ten-year-old warrant from Virginia on a charge of receiving stolen property, and Brodey advised the

San Francisco Chronicle it was "very unlikely" that Virginia authorities would extradite his client on an outdated warrant involving such a minor charge. The attorney's prediction proved in this instance, however, a poor one: Though officially released on his own recognizance at a February 12 hearing, Jim was arrested on the Virginia warrant before he left the courtroom and flown cross-country the next day.

Four-way phone negotiations between the California attorney general, the L.A. County district attorney, prosecutors in Virginia, and Brodey's office in Century City continued for the next few weeks. That some sort of bargain had resulted was revealed on May 20, 1993, when *A Current Affair* ran a taped interview with Pittman that had been filmed in and around Los Angeles. The segment opened with Jim riding in the backseat of a limousine as he confided to Steve Dunleavy, "Yes, I did kill Ron Levin, but I can't be tried for it twice . . . it would be like double jeopardy." Jim's eyes were cold and his voice matter-of-fact as he recalled the fatal moment at the Peck Drive duplex: "Joe nodded, and that was my signal to do what I had to do. And that was to shoot him—not shoot him, but to kill him. I shot him one time in the back of the head and he died immediately. The first thing I did was pick up the casing so they couldn't find it. I put the casing in my pocket. Then we wrapped up Ron Levin real quick in a comforter." Pittman was standing on a knoll just above the ridge where the Indian Canyon Truck Trail veered off from Soledad Canyon Road as he described the disposal of Ron's remains in a ravine nearby. "We had shovels, a pick and water to soften the dirt up," he remembered. "We had lime, because Joe was told that if you spread lime over a body, that the lime would deteriorate the body and people wouldn't find anything . . . we had two shotguns to shoot up the body and disfigure it in case anybody found it. We put maybe seventy rounds in there."

Video of Jim praying with the congregation of the South Central Los Angeles church he had joined one week earlier ran over Pittman's voice as he insisted he was "basically a good person" who had been "brainwashed" by Joe Hunt. "I wasn't functioning," Jim explained. "I was doing what Joe wanted me to do. Joe had charisma. You could feel the power around him. He made you feel powerful too."

It was a betrayal that rivaled Dean's: The one BBC member Joe believed was in lockstep with him to the end had sold him out to avoid a few months of jail time and for whatever compensation could be offered by a tabloid television show.

Doug Gray called the prosecution "desperate" and insisted Pittman's claims cut both ways: Jim was "just one more witness who sold himself to the state," the attorney said, and Joe Hunt had proved in San Mateo

County how one might turn the "slimy tactics of law enforcement" to his own advantage.

Gray was saying just about whatever he wanted these days. The attorney's absorption in Hunt's cause and the "nonjudgmentalism" that in Joe's presence became an atmosphere had triggered Doug's ultimate assertion of identity: Late in the defense case, Gray mailed everyone he knew invitations to a "Coming Out Party" at which the father of two, ex–Green Beret, former street cop, and tough-guy prosecutor announced he was gay. Shortly after August 9, 1993, when the Second District Court heard oral arguments on Hunt's appeal, Gray suspended the chemotherapy treatments he was receiving for throat cancer, and by November 23, when the appeals court judges issued their decision, Doug was dead.

The ruling of the Second District Court ran to 188 pages (the average length of the court's decisions in criminal cases is three pages) and affirmed Joe's conviction. Judge Rittenband had "walked a very fine line between partisan advocacy and impartial intervention," the justices allowed, but the legal standard was whether a judge's conduct had caused a miscarriage of justice, and it was clear to them, the Second District judges explained, that the evidence of Hunt's guilt presented to the jury in Santa Monica had been "overwhelming."

Before news of his defeat could reach Joe at Folsom, however, the same court had awarded him a victory nearly as significant, issuing that same afternoon a sweeping order to show cause on Hunt's habeas corpus petition. "Newly discovered evidence that Ron Levin is still alive" as well as "additional impeachment evidence," the Second District judges agreed, "casts a fundamental doubt on the accuracy and reliability of the jury's verdict that defendant murdered Levin."

In addition to the testimony of Robbie Robertson, Nadia Ghaleb, and Connie Gerrard, the appeals court emphasized Karen Sue Marmor's claim she had seen the "AT LEVIN'S, TO DO" list on the desk in Ron's apartment as well as "evidence contained in a 'Dear Dean letter'" that the chief witness for the prosecution had committed perjury.

While the court exonerated Arthur Barens on the charge he had sold out Richard Chier to appease Judge Rittenband, the justices ruled that Hunt's claims of incompetence against the attorney merited consideration. Cited were Barens's failure to discover and use: the "terms of Tom May's movie contract, which would have required May to falsely portray himself as an innocent victim"; evidence that Ron Levin's relationship with his mother was not the one portrayed by the prosecution; the testimony of Oliver Wendell Holmes III that Ron Levin was considering fleeing to Brazil; documents possessed by the conservator of Levin's estate showing that the missing man had amassed $1.2 million to finance his disappearance; evidence that Jim Pittman and Ron Levin had met; and the testimony of the woman who lived upstairs from Levin at the Peck Drive duplex that she neither saw nor heard anything unusual on the night of June 6, 1984.

The conduct of Fred Wapner should be scrutinized as well, the justices ruled: Public examination was warranted because of evidence the prosecutor failed to disclose that Dean Karny was given immunity or leniency in connection to the murder of Richard Mayer; that Karny had lied in saying he did not know Mayer; that Karny had confided to Mayer his testimony against Hunt was perjured; and that law enforcement officials committed perjury in suppressing evidence of Karny's connection to the Mayer murder.

The district attorney's office in Los Angeles reeled under the weight, literally, of Joe's habeas petition. It was the largest he'd ever seen, admitted the head of the DA's appellate division, more than five hundred pages of text, plus fifteen hundred pages of exhibits. What it had won for Joe was the right to a hearing that resembled a superior court trial. The difference was that the burden this time would be on the defendant—Joe was presumed guilty rather than innocent. The standard, however, would not be proof beyond a reasonable doubt, as in a criminal trial, but merely the "preponderance of evidence" required in a civil proceeding. If Hunt proved it was *likely* he had not killed Ron Levin, explained Andy McMullen, one of two deputy DAs assigned to oppose Hunt in court, then "we're back to square one."

Those windblown wildfires that surrounded Los Angeles—literally a ring of fire in the displays broadcast by local TV stations—on his thirty-fourth birthday had seemed a good omen for Joe. Back in 1987, when he was sent away to spend the rest of his life in Folsom Prison, Southern California had been what its self-image required, the most prosperous region of the nation. Even that superannuated organ of eastern elitism, the *Atlantic Monthly,* was about to publish an article describing L.A. as "the city of the future," predicting it might become the most important metropolis on the planet before the turn of the century. So secure was L.A. with its position at the end of the 1980s that idealism had become the city's hottest trend: All at once, just about every resident of the Westside was an environmentalist. By 1993, however, decline and disparagement were the Southland's new themes. For the first time in its history, more people were leaving L.A. than arriving, and profiles of the city in the national press focused unrelentingly on what those who had taken flight were escaping: crime, crowding, unemployment, and pollution. The failure of momentum was so sudden and stunning that poll after poll predicted things would get worse before they got better.

How could Joe fail to observe that the rebound of his fortunes up north had coincided with a steady slippage in the south? His defense against all charges was based upon a demolition of façades that would expose his accusers for the corrupt and complacent liars they were. He had demonstrated to the satisfaction of jurors in Redwood City the dishonesty not only of the Billionaire Boys but of institutions that ranged from the National Broadcasting Company to the Central Intelligence Agency. His indictment of the sham and cant from the forces arrayed against him had been so persuasive that even a jury that believed by a margin of ten to two in his guilt had voted eight to four the other way.

It hardly hurt Joe's cause that nearly every key witness for the prosecution came from Los Angeles. The adage that most succinctly expressed the ethos of the city—variously attributed to individuals as diverse as Errol Flynn and Timothy Leary—was one anybody who enjoyed the attention of the entertainment industry was bound to hear within a few weeks of inclusion. "YOU CAN'T BEAT SINCERITY" newcomers were advised. "When you can fake that, you've got it made."

To live in Los Angeles for any length of time was to understand that its forces majeures served the function of religious rites, being all that kept the city's inhabitants even slightly honest. A convergence of disasters had become both the Southland's deepest fear and its only hope, so it seemed auspicious at least when, two months after the fires in the hills were extinguished, Joe's transfer from Folsom Prison to the Los Angeles County Jail was delayed by the biggest earthquake to hit Southern California since 1971. Apartment buildings all over the San Fernando Valley were destroyed and the Santa Monica Freeway lost whole pieces of itself, but the January 6 quake's impact was more psychological than geological. Aftershocks that went on for weeks made relaxation seem like asking for it, and a case of nerves became a chronic disorder among people for whom fatuousness had been etiquette one month earlier. Other Angelenos, though—and maybe they were the people who really belonged there—tingled with an inexplicable euphoria in the days following the earthquake, shaken out of routines that had begun to make one week seem very like another. Cinder-block walls separating backyards collapsed all across Canoga Park; some neighbors exchanged words for the first time ever as they sifted through the rubble. Thousands of people, mostly Mexican immigrants, swarmed to the parks to sleep in tents, singing to one another around bonfires until well after midnight.

What frightened the circumspect was how many people in Los Angeles insisted they had survived the Big One, utterly deaf to those Cal Tech scientists who warned that at 6.7 on the Richter scale the January temblor had relieved only slightly those stresses that were moving the entire Santa Ynez Mountain Range south at the rate of an inch every forty-eight months, that there was, in fact, a continuing "slip deficit" that made a truly large-magnitude earthquake far more likely than not within the next ten years.

The quake cleanup was still underway when Joe returned to Los Angeles in March of 1994 to begin preparing for a habeas hearing assigned to the same Santa Monica courthouse where Judge Rittenband had sentenced him almost seven years earlier. He was followed by his new bride, Tammy Gandolfo (the two had been married in the Folsom Prison chapel). Though he declined interviews, Joe did issue a "news release" shortly before his first court appearance in May. "The authors and screenwriters who have repackaged the prosecution case in books, films and articles have, unwittingly, misled the public," Joe wrote, then announced that he expected to call as many as 130 witnesses to a hearing that would last at least six months. All that the other Boys had attempted to obscure, Hunt vowed, he would bring to light, revealing the BBC as "a knot of lies . . . honeycombed with fraud." He not only would link Dean Karny to the murder of Richard Mayer, Joe warned, but demonstrate as well "how the misconduct and perjury of prosecutors and detectives assigned to the case distorted the outcome of my first trial." "There are going to be," he promised, "a lot of red faces."

That summer, Joe kept up a steady correspondence with supporters, sending out copies of what he said had become his favorite book, Paramahansa Yogananda's epic *Autobiography of a Yogi*. It would have been instructive to know how Joe had negotiated Yogananda's admonition, "He who is unwilling to observe the universal moral precepts is not seriously determined to pursue truth," though possibly more compelling to hear what Larry Gamsky's son made of "A hypnotic state is harmful to those often subjected to it; a negative psychological effect ensues that in time damages the brain cells." Perhaps what consoled Joe was the swami's reconciliation to the phenomenological world: "Creation is light and shadow, else no picture is possible. The good and evil of *maya* must ever alternate in supremacy."

The dark side was in ascendance at this point, without question. Joe had been delighted when the DA's office announced in July that, with the assistance of Jim Pittman, it was again searching for Ron Levin's remains in Soledad Canyon. The failure to recover Levin's bones (and the prosecution search, led by Les Zoeller, *did* fail) would only support his claims that Ron was alive, Joe noted. "I told everyone," he advised a public defender on an August afternoon when they were sharing an attorney's room at the Men's

Central Jail with Erik Menendez and O. J. Simpson, "that I'd be back in L.A. by 'ninety-four and out by 'ninety-five."

This was perhaps optimistic only in terms of timing. The district attorney's office wanted a minimum of six months to "come up to speed on the case," as Andy McMullen put it, and at least another year to investigate before filing its return to Hunt's habeas pleading. Though Joe did manage to make himself the first habeas petitioner in Los Angeles County history to gain a bail hearing (release was denied), his case would spend most of 1994 adrift in the court system after Judge Jacqueline Weissberg (whose husband Stanley was handling the Menendez brothers' trial) removed herself. Another judge in Santa Monica had been challenged for cause by the prosecution, and the case was transferred to Malibu, but the judge who took it there had heard Jim Pittman's second trial, so the *People v. Hunt* file was moved again, this time to the Criminal Courts building in downtown Los Angeles, and assigned to Judge J. Steven Czulagher, a jurist considered smart and tough even by those who disliked him, one savvy enough, at least to recognize that Joe Hunt was, as he put it, "more qualified than ninety-nine percent of the lawyers in the country."

The downtown courthouse was under the heaviest media siege in world history on the day of Joe's first appearance before Judge Czulagher, not because of the Hunt hearing, however, but for the defense opening statement in the double-murder trial of O. J. Simpson. After a long article in the *New York Times* about his victory in Redwood City, Joe had been relegated once again to intermediate local coverage: "The graying 35-year-old," he was described by a *Daily News* reporter who added four months to his age.

He might be thirty-six or thirty-seven or even thirty-eight when it came, but Joe *was* within sight of a time when he once again could face his accusers. Until then, perhaps it was enough to know that those who had betrayed him would approach the end of the twentieth century waiting in turn to face yet another cross-examination, that somewhere out there in America, living in another state and under a different name, the now not so young man whose testimony remained the key to the prosecution's case could only anticipate the dreaded call summoning him back to Los Angeles, to the courtroom where once again the two of them might discuss those things they had done so long ago—that other Dean Karny and the real Joe Hunt.

This was a case, after all, in which familiarity bred not contempt but ever-darkening realization. What they owed would be paid out on an installment plan lasting a lifetime by those who understood—and nobody did better than Dean—that for them there was just one guarantee: As long as Joe Hunt lived, it would not be over.

ACKNOWLEDGMENTS

I'M INDEBTED TO A NUMBER OF REPORTERS AND WRITERS, AT LEAST SEVERAL OF whom merit mention by name. Of all those books I read on the rise and fall of the Pahlevi regime in Iran, both most informative and most engaging was William Shawcross's *The Shah's Last Ride*. With regard to the history of Southern California, of greatest service was Kevin Starr's *Inventing the Dream*. I owe special gratitude to David Talbot, who was kind enough to share material from his first-person account of enrollment at the Harvard School (eventually published in *LA Weekly*) even as it was being written. And Steve Oney's *California* magazine article "Adventures in Paradise" (itself drawn in part from articles in the *Orange County Register*) helped inform the Newport Beach section of this book. Also, the interview with Don Johnson quoted in chapter 5 was conducted by Pat Hackett for *Interview* magazine.

Joe Hunt, the Robertses, the Karnys, the Dostis, the May twins, Jeff Raymond, and Jon Allen all declined to be interviewed. Joe Hunt and I had a number of short conversations, but these were more in the nature of repartee than interrogation. Of those BBC Boys I did interview at length (Evan Dicker, Steve Taglianetti, Jerry Eisenberg, Steve Lopez, Alan Lieban, and a couple of early members who demanded confidentiality) by far the most helpful was Evan, who not only gave me more than twenty-five hours of taped interviews, but access to his diaries, calendars, photo albums, and assorted memorabilia. He also was the only one I could trust to tell the truth even about himself. A lengthy interview with Jim Pittman was conducted by John Sack.

I've done my best to avoid anonymous quotes; a few sources insisted that their names not appear in print, and I've tried to use them principally to provide background. "Bill Smith" is a pseudonym.

For personal support, my gratitude goes to Kathy Robbins, Ron and Deborah Kaye, Steve and Kathleen High, and Joy Candace Welp.